Footprint

Indian Himalaya Handbook

The travel guide

Robert & Roma Bradnock

For the greater part of its length only the Himalayan eagle can trace it. It lies amidst the eternal silence of vast snow fields and icebound peaks..... never was such a God-given boundary set to such vast impressive and stupendous frontier.

Sir Thomas Holdich, former Surveyor General of India

Indian Himalaya Handbook
First edition
© Footprint Handbooks Ltd 2000

Published by Footprint Handbooks
6 Riverside Court
Lower Bristol Road
Bath BA2 3DZ. England
T +44 (0)1225 469141
F +44 (0)1225 469461
Email discover@footprintbooks.com
Web www.footprintbooks.com

ISBN 1 900949 79 2
CIP DATA: A catalogue record for this
book is available from the British Library

In USA, published by
NTC/Contemporary Publishing Group
4255 West Touhy Avenue, Lincolnwood
(Chicago), Illinois 60712-1975, USA
T 847 679 5500 F 847 679 2494
Email NTCPUB2@AOL.COM

ISBN 0-658-01456-0
Library of Congress Catalog Card
Number 00-135726

Credits

Series editors
Patrick Dawson and Rachel Fielding

Editorial
Editors: Claire Boobbyer and Stephanie
Lambe
Maps: Sarah Sorensen

Production
Typesetting: Patrick Dawson and
Leona Bailey
Maps: Robert Lunn, Claire Benison and
Alasdair Dawson
Colour maps: Kevin Feeney
Cover: Camilla Ford

Design
Mytton Williams

Photography
Front cover: Images Colour Library
Back cover: Impact
Inside colour section: Jaideep Mukerji;
Jamie Marshall; Ffotograff; Impact
Photos; Robert Harding Picture Library;
BBC Natural History Unit

Print
Manufactured in Italy by LEGOPRINT

Every effort has been made to ensure
that the facts in this Handbook are
accurate. However, travellers should still
obtain advice from consulates, airlines
etc about current travel and visa
requirements before travelling. The
authors and publishers cannot accept
responsibility for any loss, injury or
inconvenience however caused.

Indian Himalayas

AFGHANISTAN

XINJIANG

PAKISTAN

1 JAMMU &
KASHMIR

TIBET

HIMACHAL
PRADESH

PUNJAB

UTTARANCHAL

HARYANA

□ DELHI

2

RAJASTHAN

UTTAR
PRADESH

NEPAL

3

SIKKIM

ARUNACHAL
PRADESH

BHUTAN

ASSAM

NAGALAND

MEGHALAYA

MANIPUR

4

BANGLA-
DESH

BIHAR

GUJARAT

MADHYA
PRADESH

WEST
BENGAL

□ **KOLKATA**

MYANMAR
(BURMA)

ORISSA

MAHARASHTRA

□ **MUMBAI**

GOA

ANDHRA
PRADESH

*Arabian
Sea*

KARNATAKA

*Bay of
Bengal*

*Andaman
Islands*

□ **CHENNAI**

KERALA

TAMIL
NADU

SRI
LANKA

*Nicobar
Islands*

Indian Ocean

See back of book for colour maps 1-4

▬▬▬	Highway
▬▬▬	Road
───	Minor road
NH1	Highway number
───	Railway
◆	National Park
─·─·─	State border
▬··▬··▬	International border

Altitude in metres
3000
2000
1500
1000
500
200
100
0

Neighbouring
Country

N

0 km   200

0 miles   200

The Government of India state that
"the external boundaries of India
are neither correct nor authenticated"

Contents

1

3 A foot in the door

2

9 **Essentials**
11 **Planning your trip**
11 Where to go
14 When to go
15 Tours and tour operators
17 Finding out more
18 Language
18 **Before you travel**
18 Getting in
19 What to take
20 Money
22 **Getting there**
22 Air
24 Road
24 **Touching down**
24 Airport information
26 Tourist information
27 Rules, customs and
   etiquette
29 Safety
31 **Where to stay**
34 **Getting around**
44 **Keeping in touch**
46 **Food and drink**
47 **Shopping**
49 **Holidays and festivals**
51 **Entertainment**
51 **Sport and special
   interest travel**
53 **Trekking**
53 Types of trek
54 Local and foreign agents
55 Trekking seasons and
   areas
56 Trekking practicalities
59 **Health**
67 **Further reading**
70 Maps
70 India on the web
71 Embassies and
   consulates

Western Himalaya

76 **Access from Delhi**

3

91 **Garhwal and Kumaon**
96 Dehra Dun and
   Uttaranchal

4

145 **Himachal Pradesh**
150 Shimla and Southern
   Himachal
159 Kinnaur and Spiti
176 Kullu Valley
191 Lahul
198 Dharamshala and
   Northern Himachal
213 Trekking in Himachal
   Pradesh

5

221 **Jammu and Kashmir**
227 Srinagar
235 Ladakh
258 Zanskar

Eastern Himalaya

264 **Access from Kolkata**

6

273 **Darjeeling and North
   Bengal**

7

293 **Sikkim**

8

313 **Assam, Meghalaya &
   Arunachal Pradesh**
316 Assam
332 Meghalaya
339 Arunachal Pradesh

9

343 **Background**
345 History
353 Modern India
358 Religion
377 Culture
384 Land and environment

10

397 **Footnotes**
399 Glossary
405 Useful words and
   phrases
411 Index
417 Advertisers
418 Shorts
419 Maps
426 Colour maps

Inside front cover
Hotel and restaurant price
   guide
Dialling codes
Useful numbers and websites

Endpapers
Acknowledgements
About the authors

Inside back cover
Map symbols
Weights and measures

Opposite page: 550 steps lead to the top of the Japanese Shanti stupa which overlooks Leh

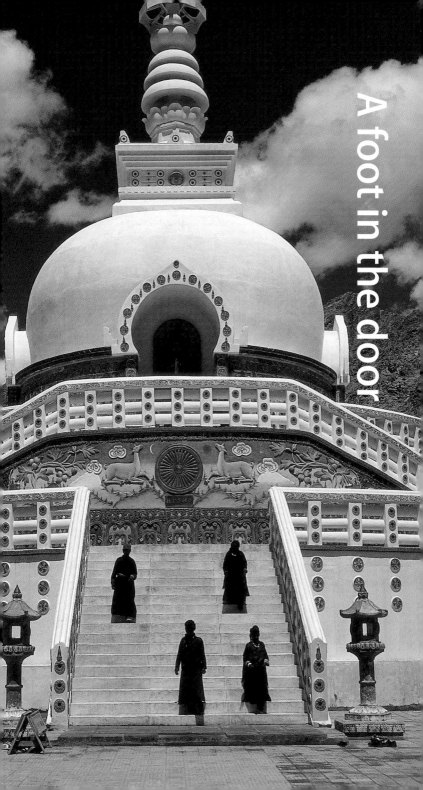

A foot in the door

River deep, mountain high

By far the greatest mountain range in the world, the Himalaya have captured the imagination of philosophers, mystics, mountaineers and empire builders from the earliest ancestors of contemporary Hindus and Buddhists to the present day. Mount Kailash, home of the greatest of the gods, and Meru, centre of the Hindu and Buddhist universe, rise from their surrounding ridges of the central Himalaya. From the high slopes to the foothills people have carved out an often meagre existence in the harshest of environments with determination, subtlety and imagination enriched by powerful cultural identities. Tribal peoples living often at high altitudes have made their living from their tough environment through trade over the highest passes in the world and from semi-nomadic pastoralism, while farmers have developed agriculture on the man-made terraces of the warmer, lower-lying valleys and hills of the southern ranges. Although the mountain environment gives a common character to the whole region, each hamlet has its own identity. The villages of the arid high altitude plateau of Ladakh could scarcely be more different from the homesteads of the monsoon forests of Arunachal Pradesh.

Beauty &
the beast
Animal life is rich, varying sharply with the different habitats associated with different altitudes. National parks have been developed to provide a protected home to such rare species as the great one-horned Indian rhinoceros, tiger and panther, still found in the eastern reserves such as Kaziranga. The wild yak and its domesticated relative are common at higher altitudes, where the snow leopard still prowls, and the blue sheep, or bharal, is found on the open slopes of Ladakh. Their backdrop is equally as varied. Rhododendrons give spectacular swathes of colour to the hillsides of the eastern Himalaya, especially during April and May, while in the lower and wetter regions of the far east, unique bamboo forests dominate huge areas. In the western Himalaya deodar and chir pine forests cover much of the slopes along with with a huge range of valuable medicinal and commercial plants. The most famous, the saffron crocus, covers meadows in Kashmir.

Hill stations &
train stations
Eastern and western Himalaya have their share of hill stations. Darjeeling, approached by the world famous narrow gauge mountain railway, offers the fresh air and dramatic views of the Kangchendzonga range which draw holidaymakers from the plains. The smaller and more remote small town of Kalimpong, picturesquely surrounded by hills and mountains, is famous for its orchid nurseries. The Western Himalaya have their own hill stations. Shimla, the hill capital of British India for over half a century, has become a summer holiday capital for thousands of Indians from the plains, but retains something of its colonial architectural charm. Nainital, Almora, Mussoorie and many other small hill towns still enjoy the bracing fresh and pine-scented air and the high ridge-positions, while Dharamsala has the added distinctiveness of the Dalai Lama's presence while in exile from Tibet.

Cultural
crossroads
At first glance the dusty brown hills of Ladakh may seem an unspectacular landscape, yet for many Ladakh has an almost magical quality. Large enough and sufficiently isolated to have developed its own distinctive culture, it is none the less home to a variety of different groups. Its name - meaning 'many passes' - suggests its role as a crossroads, so it is not surprising that in addition to the powerful influence of Buddhist culture other influences are also evident. Occupied by Mongols from the north and subsequently by Mughal India from the south, Islam too has a long history, and Shi'a

5

Left*: A Himalayan funeral - chanting at a solemn service of farewell*
Below*: Majestic mountain peaks near the source of the Ganga in the Garhwal Himalaya*

Above*: Tea fields where the best Darjeeling brew comes from*
Left*: A masked dance by a monk to ward off evil spirits during a festival*

imambaras, strongly influenced by Persian architecture, illustrate the Muslim heritage both in Leh and along the banks of the Indus towards Kargil. Yet it is the Buddhist influence which is both the most obvious and the most pervasive. Although most Buddhist festivals take place in the winter when the region is cut off from the outside world, many of the famous gompas, or monasteries, are accessible through the summer. But Ladakh also has some astonishing scenery. The barren and stony surface is punctuated by ribbons of cultivation along the winding river courses, clinging to the highest peaks are the remnants of the last great Himalayan ice sheet and beautiful high-altitude lakes such as the Pangong Tso can be found.

Pilgrims' progress The Himalayan region is a land of pilgrimage. Reverence for the great rivers of India, symbols of divine power and goodness, source of fertility and life, draws thousands every year up the often dangerous tracks to their remote sources. The arduous climb from Rishikesh where the Ganga leaves the mountains for the plains, to Badrinath and on to the glacial source of the great river is over 300 kilometres long. The source of the Yamuna is almost equally revered and difficult to access, while further west the shrines to Vaishno Devi in Jammu and Amarnath in Kashmir continue to draw people in their thousands. Join pilgrims at the Kumbh Mela, held at Haridwar once in twelve years, and you can experience with millions of others the special significance of bathing in India's holiest river.

The Buddhist heritage Since the Dalai Lama was forced to flee from Tibet, Dharamsala has been the home in exile of Tibetan Buddhism. Yet Tibet's influence has been a powerful cultural force throughout the Himalaya for generations. From the thousand year old monasteries of Kaza and Tabo, high in the Spiti region of Himachal Pradesh, or Hemis, Alchi and Thikse around Leh, to the monasteries at Rumtek in Sikkim, Kalimpong in West Bengal, or the remote and beautiful Tawang in Arunachal Pradesh, the visitor can see and feel the pervading Buddhist and Tibetan influence on tribal culture. Chortens, prayer flags and prayer wheels, the cultural landmarks of Buddhist faith, are scattered across the landscape, markers to pilgrims, traders and residents. Whether you go to the high passes of Ladakh or the green wooded hills of Sikkim, the landmarks of Buddhism are inescapable. The images, thangkas and wall paintings all tell a story which the sensitive outsider is welcomed to as a participant in the ongoing drama. At festival time, the air is thick with the sound of horns, drums and cymbals as masked dancers play out powerful tales of the victory of Good over Evil.

The wettest place in the world The eastern Himalaya are among the wettest regions in the world. Arunachal Pradesh, Sikkim and the North Bengal Himalayan margins all receive torrential rainfall through the monsoon, causing landslides, washing away roads and bringing floods to the plains. Even in the western Himalaya, especially in the Dauladhar Ranges around Dharamshala, the monsoons bring regular downpours. But, if you really want to experience rain, you should go just to the south of the eastern Himalaya to Meghalaya - the abode of the clouds. Here the small towns of Cherrapunji and Mawsynram have broken all world records, each having received over 20 metres of rain in a year, most of it in just six months.

Left: The large 15th century Thikse monastery atop a craggy ridge
Below: Three generations in distant Ladakh where a traditional way of life is still the norm

Above: The beautiful and elusive snow leopard with its handsome speckled coat and long bushy tale resting on a carpet of snow
Left: A Gelugpa monk in typical maroon robes worn in the Himalaya looks out from his monastery quarters
Next page: Mother and son visit isolated Lamayuru in Ladakh

Essentials

2

Essentials

11 Planning your trip

11 Where to go

14 When to go

15 Tours and tour operators

17 Finding out more

18 Language

18 Before you travel

18 Getting in

19 What to take

20 Money

22 Getting there

22 Air

23 Overland

24 Road

24 Touching down

24 Airport information

25 Public transport to and from airport

26 Tourist information

27 Rules, customs and etiquette

29 Safety

31 Where to stay

34 Getting around

34 Air

35 Road

39 Train

44 Keeping in touch

44 Internet

44 Post

44 Telephone

45 Media

46 Food and drink

47 Shopping

49 Holidays and festivals

51 Entertainment

51 Sport and special interest travel

59 Health

67 Further reading

70 Maps

70 India on the web

71 Indian embassies and consulates

Planning your trip

Where to go

First time visitors are often at a loss when faced with the vast possibilities for travel in the Indian Himalaya. We have made a few suggestions here for two to three week trips on the basis that some journeys will be flown and that air or rail tickets have been booked in advance. Reliable travel agencies are listed through the book, who can make the necessary arrangements for a relatively small fee saving you time and bother. Air tickets can be difficult to get at short notice for some trips, eg Delhi-Leh-Delhi, but it is now possible to book them in advance with the internet. (See page. 22.) Figures in brackets are number of nights we suggest you spend.

Access For visiting the Western Himalaya, the most convenient access from abroad is by flying into Delhi and for the Eastern Himalaya, by flying into Kolkata.

Arrive in **Delhi** (3) and visit Agra by train to see the splendour of the Taj. Travel by road or train to **Dehra Dun** (1) and onward to the place of the sages, **Rishikesh** (2) by the Ganga which gives access to some of Hinduism's holiest places of pilgrimage. Next stop is at **Corbett** National Park (3), rich in both flora and fauna (tigers are occasionally seen) before heading for **Almora** (2) surrounded by wonderful scenery and with several old temples nearby. **Nainital** (2) around its lake gives you the experience of a hill station "discovered" by the British, before returning to **Delhi** (1).

1 The Foothills (14 days)

The Pilgrim route and treks in Garhwal and Kumaon You need to allow extra time for these. The Yatra (Pilgrimage) route is best attempted from Rishikesh in May or between mid-September to early November. You will need to show a certificate of immunization against cholera and typhoid.

Extension (7 - 10 days)

Trekking routes are open from end-April to November but avoid the rainy season from July to mid-September. With at least a week in hand you can attempt a trek from Rishikesh, Almora or Nainital, but you will need to contact a trekking agent.

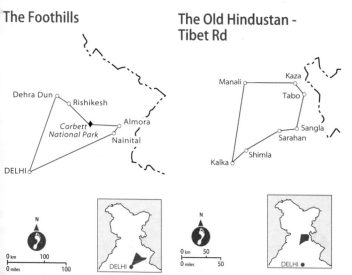

The Foothills

The Old Hindustan - Tibet Rd

2 The Old Hindustan-Tibet Road (18 days) Start in **Delhi** (3) as above and take the 'Himalayan Queen' which connects with the narrow gauge Shivalik train from Kalka to **Shimla** (3). Travel by road along the old Hindustan Tibet Road eastwards stopping at **Sarahan** (2) with its Bhimakali temple, **Sangla** (1) and **Kalpa** (1) before continuing into Spiti and the remote Buddhist settlements of **Tabo** (2) and **Kaza** (1). The road through the wide Spiti Valley and over the Kunzum La and the Rohtang Pass in Upper Lahul brings you down to **Manali** (3). From there you return to **Delhi** (2). The route through Spiti and Lahul may not be open during the monsoon and in winter.

Extensions (7-14 days) **Treks** There are several opportunities to trek in Lahul, Spiti and Kinnaur. Some routes also lead into Zanskar and Leh but all these are only possible from mid-June (sometimes mid-July) until mid-October and you need to join a group organized by an approved agent.

3 Ladakh - Little Tibet (16 days) Arrive in **Delhi** (2) and travel up by road to **Manali** (3) via perhaps **Mandi** or **Nalagarh** (1). (Alternatively, from Delhi you can fly to Bhuntar, just south of Manali and spend a couple of days there, thus shortening your tour by 2 days). From July to September the Manali-Leh road is usually open so you can travel by 4-wheel drive or bus to **Sarchu** camp (1) through the spectacular high-altitude desert (about a 10 hour journey). Then a 12-hour drive through Taglang La (the second highest motorable pass in the world) takes you to **Leh** (6). While in Leh visit some monasteries and Pangong Tso or Nubra. Fly back to **Delhi** (3) and visit Agra for the Taj Mahal by train. If you wish to get to Leh before July and after September you can fly out from Delhi but you will need to allow 2 days to acclimatize.

4 The Valley of the Gods (12-14 days) Arrive in **Delhi** (2) and travel via Pathankot on the Kangra Valley mountain railway to **Kangra** (2) and visit **Palampur** (1) and Andretta. Experience the Tibetan Buddhist presence in **McLeodganj** (Upper Dharamshala) (3) then travel to **Kullu** or **Naggar** (4) with rewarding walks and unspoilt Pahari villages and temples in the surroundings. Return by road via Mandi (1), Pragpur or Nalagarh to **Delhi** (1) or fly back from Bhuntar near Kullu.

Ladakh - Little Tibet   The Valley of the Gods

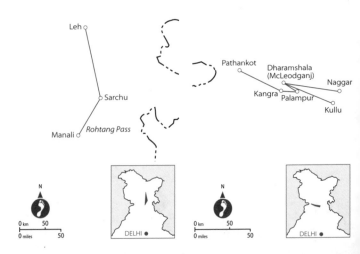

Essentials

Manali, just to the north of Kullu and Naggar, is the gateway to Leh as well as to Lahul and Spiti, and a complete circuit through Kinnaur brings you to Shimla.

Extensions (10-14 days)

Arrive in Delhi or **Kolkata** (2). Fly to Bagdogra, the airport for the hill station of **Darjeeling** (3), which you can reach by the steam Himalayan Railway (when it is running) or by road. Drive through tea gardens and along the Tista valley on the way to **Kalimpong** (3). Continue your journey into Sikkim **Gangtok** (3) which is a good base to visit the important Buddhist monastery at Rumtek and, via a precipitous road, the beautiful Changu Lake. You can then go west to the small town of **Pelling** (3), a base from which to see the awe inspiring Pemayangtse monastery and the Khechopari 'Wishing' Lake. Return to Bagdogra for the flight back to Kolkata or **Delhi** (2).

5 North Bengal and Sikkim (16 days)

Trekking in the Darjeeling area or in Sikkim is best between October and December and in April-May, avoiding the monsoon.

Extensions (7- 10 days)

Kolkata (2) or Delhi. Fly (or take the train) to **Guwahati** (2). Take to the hill road (or catch a helicopter) to **Shillong** (3) in the 'Abode of the clouds'. From there visit Cherrapunji, in perpetual mist or rain, high waterfalls, caves and tribal villages. Stop at **Kaziranga** National Park (2), and see rhinos from elephant back. Then on to **Tezpur** (1) and **Bomdila** (1) via Tipi with its orchids. Continue to the rarely visited **Tawang** (3) for its ancient Buddhist monastery and the high altitude lakes nearby. Return via **Bhoreli** Eco Camp (1) to **Tezpur** (1) for a flight back to **Kolkata** (2).

6 The north-eastern hills (18 days)

Trekking in Megalaya and Arunachal Pradesh is best between October and February.

Extensions (7-10 days)

If you have **4 to 6 weeks**, you can take it more leisurely. **Tours 2** and **3** can be added to **Tour 4** quite easily and the flight between Bagdogra and Guwahati allows you to combine **Tours 5** and **6**.

Longer visits

For an extended stay of **2 to 3 months** it is possible to combine tours in the west with those in the east but take care to check the best times to visit the different areas.

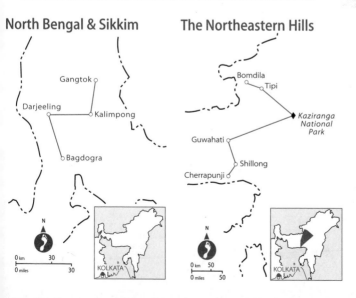

North Bengal & Sikkim

Gangtok
Darjeeling
Kalimpong
Bagdogra

0 km 30
0 miles 30

KOLKATA

The Northeastern Hills

Bomdila
Tipi
Kaziranga National Park
Guwahati
Shillong
Cherrapunji

0 km 50
0 miles 50

KOLKATA

Essentials

When to go

In most of India, by far the most pleasant time to visit is from the end of the monsoon in November to the end of March. However, there are important exceptions. The hill stations in the Himalaya are beautiful in the hot weather months of April to early June. Parts of the western Himalaya can be excellent through to September though it can be very cold and sometimes very wet in spring.

The chart below gives an idea of which states can be visited comfortably during any particular month. Because local variations are important, the handbook gives temperatures and rainfall details for all regions and many cities, indicating the most comfortable times to visit.

Peak season difers across the Himalayan region depending on monsoon (low season) and mid-winter (low season). Hill stations have peaks during the summer holiday months (May-June) and the Pujas (September-October). The Leh peak season is July-September. Peak seasons in the trekking areas are mentioned under Essen. Jumping off points (Almora, Nainital, Darj Gangtok etc) will raise prices during these times.

Some of the county's great festivals such as *Dasara* and *Diwali* are celebrated in the autumn and winter.

	Uttaranchal	Himachal Pradesh	Ladakh	Jammu & Kashmir	North Bengal	Arunachal Pradesh	Sikkim
January	✔	✔			✔	✔	
	Cold, snow & ice in hills	Cold, snow & ice in hills. Skiiing	Bitterly cold, only access by plane	Vale under snow	Cold, clear & dry	Cold, clear & dry	Cold, clear & dry
February		✔			✔	✔	✔
	Cold, snow & ice in hills	Cold, snow & ice in hills. Skiing	Bitterly cold, only access by plane	Vale under snow	Cold clear & dry	Cold, clear & dry	Cold, clear & dry
March	✔				✔	✔	✔
	Still cold but clear & bright	Still cold but clear & bright	Bitterly cold, only access by plane	Vale under snow	Warming up in daytime, generally dry & clear skies	Warming, still mainly dry, excellent views	Warming, still mainly dry, excellent views
April	✔	✔	✔	✔	✔	✔	✔
	Excellent weather in lower hills	Excellent in lower hills, high passes opening	Still very cold, only access by plane	Clearing, still cold	Heavy showers possible, generally good weather	Very warm in lower valleys	Very warm in lower valleys
May	✔	✔	✔	✔	✔		
	Best month for treks	Excellent weather, passes mainly open	Rapid warming, trek in or fly	Clear, beautiful weather	One of the best months, though heavy showers common	Heavy showers, very warm	Heavy showers, very warm
June	✔	✔	✔	✔			
	Start of monsoon	Start of monsoon, excellent in Spiti & Lahaul	Warm days Road may open	Some rain at end of month	Rains very heavy, views obscured	Rains almost continuous	Rains almost continuous

Tours and tour operators

You may choose to try an inclusive package holiday or let a specialist operator quote for a tailor-made tour. Out of season these can be worth exploring. The lowest prices quoted for 2001 from the UK vary from about US$550 for a week (flights, hotel and breakfast) in the low season, to over US$3,000 for three weeks during the peak season. Most will chalk out individual itineraries and cover the major sights with small groups. Tour companies are listed here who arrange anything from general tours to mountain biking, trekking or visiting wildlife sanctuaries.

See page 54 for a list of trekking operators and page 23 for ticketing agents

Adventures Abroad, T0114-2473400 (USA & Canada, T800 665 3998, Australia T800 890 790), info@adventures-abroad.org Outward bound; **Asian Journeys**, T01604 234401, F234866, www.asianjourneys.com Fairs, festivals, culture, religion, **Banyan Tours**, T01672-564090, BanyanUK@compuserve.com www.india-traveldirect.com Tailored tours, local contact. **Andrew Brock** (*Coromandel*), T01572-821330, abrock@aol.com Special interest (crafts, textiles, botany etc). **Cox & Kings** (Taj Group), T020-78735001, F6306038. Palaces, forts, tourist high spots. **Discovery Initiatives**, T020-79786341, www.discoveryinitiatives.com Wildlife safaris, **Dragoman**, T01728-86113, www.dragoman.co.uk Overland, adventure, camping. **Encounter Overland**, London, T020 7370 6845, www.encounter-overland.com **Exodus Travels**, London, T020 8772 3822, sales@exodustravels.co.uk **Gateway to India**, T044 870-4423204, F044 870-4423205, specialist-travel@gateway-to-india.co.uk Tailor-made, off-the-beaten-track, local reps.

Essentials

Uttaranchal	Himachal Pradesh	Ladakh	Jammu & Kashmir	North Bengal	Arunachal Pradesh	Sikkim	
✔	✔	✔	✔				**July**
Often heavy rain, & slides high up, main pilgrimage season	Often heavy rain, & slides high up, but good in drier areas	Warm days. Road open trekking	Hot, heavy downpours, but clear spells	Rains very heavy, views obscured	Rains almost continuous	Rains almost continuous	
✔			✔				**August**
Very wet	Generally very wet, high passes still open	Hot in the sun. Road open trekking	Still hot & humid, showers	Rains very heavy, views obscured	Rains almost continuous	Rains almost continuous	
✔	✔		✔		✔	✔	**September**
Very clear skies at end of month	Clearing, excellent mountain views in later period	Cool nights Road open trekking	Clearing, a bit cooler, pleasant season	Rains very heavy, views obscured	Rains more broken	Rains more broken	
✔	✔		✔		✔	✔	**October**
Clear, excellent days but getting cold at night	Cooling fast but clear and fresh	Road closes Cold	Cooler and drier, clear skies	Drying, excellent views and clear skies	Clear and dry, cooling and very pleasant	Clear and dry, cooling and very pleasant	
			✔	✔	✔	✔	**November**
Cold at altitude	Cold at altitude	Very cold	Clear and bright, cold at night	Dry, clear, cooling	Cooler, dry, excellent views	Cooler, dry, excellent views	
							December
Very cold	Very cold, some skiing	Sub-zero temps	Cold, sometimes damp and overcast	Cold at night, snow in hills	Cold at night, snow in hills	Cold at night, snow in hills	

Greaves Tours, T020-74879111, F74860722, sbriggs@greavesuk.com Railways, cities, heritage. *Guerba Expeditions*, T01373-826611, info@guerba.co.uk Adventure, treks. *Indian Magic*, T020-84274848, sales@indiamagic. co.uk Homestays, small-scale, pulse of India. *Myths and Mountains*, USA T800-6706984, www.mythsandmountains.com Culture, crafts, religion. *Paradise Holidays*, 20-B, Basant Lak, Community Centre, Vasant Vihar, New Delhi - 110057, T6145116, F6145112, www.paradiseholidays.com.in *Pettitts*, T01892- 515966, F521500, www.pettitts.co.uk Unusual locations, activities, wildlife. *Royal Expeditions*, R-184, Greater Kailash-1, New Delhi - 110048, T91 (11) 623 8545, F647 5954, www.royalexpeditions.com *Snow Lion Expeditions*, USA, T800-525-8735, www.snowlion.com *Spirit of India*, USA T888-3676147, inquire@spirit-of-india.com Focussed, local experts. *Trans Indus*, T020-85662729, F8405327, www.transindus.co.uk Activities, wildlife. *Western & Oriental*, T020-73136611, F73136601, enquiries@westernoriental.com Upmarket, unique heritage hotels.

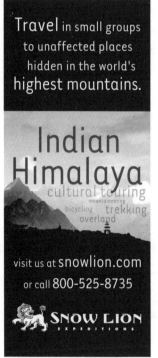

Finding out more

There are Government of India Tourist offices in Delhi and the state capitals, as well as State Tourist Offices (sometimes Tourism Development Corporations) in the major cities and a few important sites. In addition, some regions eg Kumaon (KMVN) and Garhwal (GMVN) in Uttaranchal, Darjeeling (DGHC) in West Bengal have their own offices. They produce their own tourist literature, either free or sold at a nominal price, and some also have lists of city hotels and paying guest options. The quality of material is improving though maps handed out are often inadequate. Many offer tours of the city, neighbouring sights and overnight and regional packages. Some run modest hotels and mid-way motels with restaurants, and may also arrange car hire and guides. The staff in the regional and local offices are usually helpful.

Don't take advice from unofficial 'Tourist Offices' at airports or railway stations

Essentials

India Tourist Offices Overseas

Australia Level 1, 2 Picadilly, 210 Pitt St, Sydney, NSW 2000, T612-292644855, F92644860.

Canada 60 Bloor St, West Suite No 1003, Toronto, Ontario, T416-9623787, F9626279.

France 11-13 Bis Boulevard Hausmann, F75009, Paris T45233045, F45233345.

Germany Baserler St 48, 60329, Frankfurt AM-Main 1, T069-2429490, F24294977.

Italy Via Albricci 9, Milan 20122, T8053506, F72021681.

Japan Pearl Building, 9-18 Chome Ginza, Chuo Ku, Tokyo 104, T33-5715062, F5715235.

The Netherlands Rokin 9-15, 1012 Amsterdam, T020-6208891, F6383059.

Singapore 20 Kramat Lane, 01-01A United House, Singapore 0922. T2353800, F2358677.

Sweden Sveavagen 9-11 1st Flr, S-lll 57 Stockholm 11157, T468-101187, F210186.

Switzerland 1-3 rue de Chantepoulet, 1201 Geneva, T41-227321813, F7315660.

Thailand 3rd Flr, KFC Bldg, 62/5 Thaniya Rd, Bangkok 10500, T662-2352585, F2368411.

UK 7 Cork St, London W1X 2AB, T020-74373677, F74941048.

USA 3550 Wilshire Blvd, Room 204, Los Angeles, California 90010. T213-3808855, F3806111; Suite 1808, 1270 Avenue of Americas, New York, NY 10020, T212-5864901, F5823274.

Language

It is possible to study a number of Indian languages at language centres eg Mussoorie. Some are listed on page 377

Hindi, spoken as a mother tongue by over 400 million people, is India's official language. The use of English is also enshrined in the Constitution for a wide range of official purposes, notably communication between Hindi and non-Hindi speaking states. The most widely spoken Indo-Aryan languages are: Bengali (8.3%), Marathi (8%), Urdu (5.7%), Gujarati (5.4%), Oriya (3.7%) and Punjabi (3.2%). Most of these languages have their own scripts. In all there are 15 major and several hundred minor languages and dialects. In this edition of the Handbook many town names are written in the relevant regional language, as many place names on sign boards, buses and stations are only given in a regional script.

Before you travel

Getting in

Documents
For details of overseas embassies & consulates, see page 71

Virtually all foreign nationals require a visa to enter India. Nationals of Bhutan and Nepal only require a suitable means of identification. The rules regarding visas change frequently and arrangements for application and collection also vary from town to town so it is essential to check details and costs with the relevant office. These remain closed on Indian national holidays. In London, applications are processed in a couple of hours (0800-1200). Visitors from countries which do not have an Indian representation may apply to the resident British representative, or enquire at the *Air India* office. An application on the prescribed form should be accompanied by three passport photographs and your passport which should be valid three months beyond the period of the visit.

Visa fees vary according to nationality. In mid-2000 the following visa rules applied: **Visas**
   Transit For passengers en route to another country. **Tourist** One month visa (entry must be within a month of issue), or six month visa, from the date of issue with multiple entry. Same fee. **Business** Up to one year from the date of issue. A letter from the company giving the nature of business is required. **Five year** For those of Indian origin only, who have held Indian passports. **Student** Valid up to one year from the date of issue. Attach a letter of acceptance from the Indian institution, and an AIDS test certificate. Allow up to three months for approval. **Visa extensions** Applications should be made to the Foreigners' Regional Registration Offices at New Delhi, Mumbai, Kolkata or Chennai, or an office of the Superintendent of Police in the District Headquarters. After 6 months, you must leave India and apply for a new visa – the Nepal office is known to be difficult.

Some areas are politically sensitive. The border regions, tribal areas and Himalayan **Restricted &** zones are subject to restrictions and special permits may be needed to visit them **protected areas** though the government is relaxing its regulations.

Currently the following require special permits: **Arunachal Pradesh**. Apply to the Under Secretary, Ministry of Home Affairs, Foreigners Division, Lok Nayak Bhavan, Khan Market, New Delhi 110003 at least four weeks in advance. Special permission is no longer needed to visit Assam, Meghalaya and **Himachal Pradesh**. Parts of Spiti (Poo, Khabo, Sumdo, Dhankar, Tabo, Kaza). **Jammu and Kashmir** Areas in Ladakh (Khaltsse, Nubra and Nyona). **Sikkim** Permits for 15 days are issued by a large number of government offices.

No foreigner needs to **register** within the 180 day period of their tourist visa. All foreign visitors who stay in India for more than 180 days are required to get an **income tax clearance** exemption certificate from the Foreign Section of the Income Tax Dept in Delhi, Mumbai, Kolkata or Chennai.

Foreigners should apply to the Indian representative in their country of origin for the **Work permits** latest information about work permits.

Periodically some Indian states have tried to enforce prohibition. States which have **Liquor permits** some degree of prohibition in force are Gujarat, Mizoram and Manipur. If you plan to extend your trip to visite these states, when applying for your visa you can ask for an All India Liquor Permit. You can also get the permit from any Govt of India Tourist Office in Delhi or the state capitals.

What to take

Travel light. Most essentials are available in the larger cities, items are cheap and laundry services are generally speedy. Here are some items you might find particularly helpful in India:
   The clothing you need in the Himalaya varies greatly with both the season and the altitude. There are great contrasts in snow and rainfall, the eastern Himalaya being among the wettest regions on earth, while extensive parts of the western Himalaya are high altitude desert. In the dry summer months - generally April to early June - it can get warm even at quite high altitude, up to around 3,000 metres, so layers of cotton clothes in the daytime can give comfortable protection from sunshine, and warmth for when it cools off. If you spend any time at altitude, especially nights, warmer clothing is essential . During the monsoon you have to be ready for heavy, and at times prolonged rain, especially in the east and areas like southern Himachal Pradesh, between July and September. An umbrella can be very handy.

Essentials

 Money matters

It can be difficult to use torn or very worn currency notes. Check notes carefully when you are given them and refuse any that are damaged.

A good supply of small denomination notes always comes in handy for bus tickets, cheap meals and tipping.

Remember that if offered a large note, the recipient will never have any change!

It can be worth carrying a few clean, new sterling or dollar notes for use where travellers' cheques and credit cards are not accepted.

It is best to take a sufficient supply of personal **medicines** from home, including inhalers and anti-malarial drugs (Proguanil is not available from pharmacists). For protection against mosquitoes, take *Mosiguard* repellent which is recommended by MASTA. Most **toiletries**, contact lens cleaners, tampons and barrier contraceptives are available in the larger cities.

Photocopies of essential **documents**, passport identification and visa pages, and spare photos are useful when applying for permits or in case of loss or theft. Contact lens wearers can be affected by pollution in some large cities. Carry spectacles.

Budget travellers Nets are not always provided in cheap hotels so try to take an impregnated mosquito net. Earplugs come in handy when a hotel room is particularly noisy, especially during festivals when loudspeakers playing Hindi film music tend to work overtime. On overnight journeys, blocking out the perpetual light is effective with eyeshades (given away by the airlines). Take a good padlock to secure your budget room too. A cotton, sheet sleeping bag which can cover a pillow, makes all the difference when you can't be sure of clean linen. Toilet paper, soap, towel and the washbasin plug may all be missing so be prepared.

Money

Prices in the handbook are quoted in Rupees, although top hotels often quote rates in US$. Very few people are familiar with international currencies apart from currency touts on city street corners. Visitors do best to think in Rupee terms.

Currency Indian currency is the Indian Rupee (Re/Rs). It is **not** possible to purchase these before you leave. If you want cash on arrival it is best to get it at the airport bank. Rupee notes are printed in denominations of Rs 500, 100, 50, 20, 10. The Rupee is divided into 100 Paise. Coins are minted in denominations of Rs 5, 2, 1, and 50, 25, 20, 10 and 5 Paise, though coins below 50 paise are rarely seen. **NB** Carry money, mostly as TCs, in a money belt worn under clothing. Have a small amount in an easily accessible place.

Travellers' Travellers' cheques issued by reputable companies (eg Thomas Cook, American cheques Express) are accepted without difficulty. Travellers' cheques nearly always have to be exchanged in banks or hotels, and can only very rarely be used directly for payment. Identification documents – usually a passport – need to be shown. Except in hotels, encashing travellers' cheques nearly always takes up to 30 minutes or longer, so it is worth taking larger denomination travellers' cheques and changing enough money to last for some days. Most banks, but not all, will accept US$ travellers' cheques. Many will also accept sterling so it is a good idea to carry some of each. Other major currency travellers' cheques are also accepted in some larger cities. A traveller warns that replacement of lost AmEx travellers' cheques may take weeks. If you are travelling to remote areas it can be worth buying Indian Rupee travellers' cheques from a major bank, as these are more widely accepted than foreign currency ones.

Exchange rates

	Rs		Rs
Aus $	26.62	Japanese Yen	0.42
Dutch G	18.85	NZ $	20.71
Euro	41.57	Swiss Fr	26.85
French Fr	6.34	UK $	68.48
German DM	21.25	US $	45.77

Essentials

Credit cards Major credit cards are increasingly acceptable in the main centres, though in smaller cities and towns it is still rare to be able to pay by credit card. Payment by credit card can sometimes be more expensive than payment by cash. **Visa** have a growing number of ATMs in major cities (see below), but many ATMs only deal with local account holders. It is however straightforward to obtain a cash advance against a credit card. Railway Reservation centres in 17 major cities are now taking payment for train tickets by Visa card which can be very quick as the queue is very short.

Changing money The *State Bank of India* and several others in major towns are authorized to deal in foreign exchange. Some give cash against **Visa/Master cards** (eg *Standard Chartered Grindlays*, *Bank of Baroda* who print a list of their participating branches, *Andhra Bank*). **American Express** cardholders can use their cards to get either cash or travellers' cheques in the four major cities. The larger cities have **licensed money changers** with offices usually in the commercial sector. Changing money through unauthorized dealers is illegal. Premiums on the currency black market are very small and highly risky. Large **hotels** change money 24 hours a day for guests, but banks often give a substantially better rate of exchange than hotels.

Request some Rs 100 & 50 notes. If you cash sterling, always make certain that you have been given Rupees at the sterling & not at the dollar rate

It is best to get exchange on arrival at the airport bank. Thomas Cook has a high reputation. Many international flights arrive during the night, and it is generally far easier and less time consuming to change money at the airport than in the city.

You should be given a foreign currency **encashment certificate** when you change money through a bank or authorized dealer, ask for one if it is not automatically given. It allows you to change Indian Rupees back to your own currency on departure. It also enables you to use Rupees to pay hotel bills or buy air tickets for which payment in foreign exchange may be required. The certificates are only valid for three months.

Transferring money to India *HKSB*, *Barclays* and *ANZ Grindlays* and others can make 'instant' transfers to their offices in India but charge a high fee (about US$30). *Standard Chartered Bank* issues US$ travellers' cheques. Sending a bank draft (up to US$1,000) by post (four to seven days by Speedpost) is the cheapest option.

Cost of living The cost of living in India remains well below that in the West. The average wage is about Rs 10,000 per month (US$220) for government employees according to government statistics – manual workers, unskilled labourers (women are often paid less than men), farmers and others in rural areas earn considerably less.

Cost of travelling Most food, accommodation and public transport, especially rail and bus, are exceptionally cheap. There is a widening range of moderately priced but clean hotels and restaurants outside the big cities, making it possible to get a great deal for your money. Budget travellers sharing a room, eating in local restaurants, and using the cheapest means of travel can expect to spend around Rs 420-500 (about US$10-12) a day, though you can each get by on less in the south. Those looking for the comfort of the occasional night in a simple a/c room, and using reserved seats on trains and luxury buses, should budget for about US$25-30 a day. However, if you travel alone and are looking for reasonably comfortable a/c rooms, use taxis and second class a/c train berths, expect to spend US$60-70 a day. When shopping or hiring an unmetered vehicle, bargaining is expected, and essential.

Getting there

Air

India is accessible by air from virtually every continent. International flights arrive in Delhi and Kolkata to give access to the Himalaya area. Some carriers permit 'open-jaw' travel, arriving in, and departing from, different cities in India. Some (eg *Air India*, *British Airways*) have convenient non-stop flights from Europe, from London to Delhi taking only nine hours.

Stop-overs & Round-the-World tickets
You can arrange several stop-overs in India on Round-the-World and long distance tickets. RTW tickets allow you to fly in to one and out from another international aiport. You may be able to arrange some internal flights using international carriers eg *Air India*, www.airindia.com sometimes allows stop-overs within India for a small extra charge.

Discounts
The cheapest fares from Europe tend to be with Eastern European, Central Asian or Middle Eastern airlines. You can also get good discounts from Australasia, Southeast Asia and Japan.

If you plan to visit two or more South Asian countries within three weeks, you may

qualify for a 30% discount on your international tickets. Ask your National Tourist office. International air tickets can be bought in India though payment must be made in foreign exchange.

Companies dealing in volume and taking reduced commissions for ticket sales can offer better deals than the airlines themselves. The national press carry their advertisements. *Usit Campus*, T0870-2401010, www.usitcampus.co.uk, is good for students and have offices in several university cities. *Trailfinders* of London, T020-79383939, worldwide agencies; *STA*, in London, T020-79379962, T0870-1606070, www.statravel.co.uk with over 100 offices worldwide, offers special deals for under-26s; *Travelbag*, T01420-541007, www.travelbag. adventures.co.uk quotes competitive fares. **General Sales Agents** (GSAs) for specific airlines can sometimes offer attractive deals: *Jet Airways*, 188 Hammersmith Rd, London W6 7DJ, T020-89701500, for *Gulf Air, Kuwait Airways* etc; *Welcome Travels*, 58 Wells St, London W1P 3RA, T020-74363011, for *Air India*. *Orient International (Travels) Ltd*, 91 Charlotte Street, London W1P 1LB, T020-76371330, 76370037, F73239755, offer good discounts.

Ticket agents

Essentials

International airlines vary in their arrangements and requirements for security, in particular the carrying of equipment like radios, tape-recorders, lap-top computers and batteries. It is advisable to ring the airline in advance to confirm what their current regulations are. **Internal airlines often have different rules from the international carriers**. You are strongly advised not to pack valuables in your luggage. Avoid repacking at the airport.

Airline security

The best deals are offered from the UK. You can pick up attractive deals on *Air India* which flies direct to Delhi and Mumbai throughout the year. A few European airlines (eg *Lufthansa, KLM*) and several from the Middle East (eg *Emirates, Gulf Air, Kuwait Airways, Royal Jordanian*) offer good discounts to Delhi from London, but fly via their hub cities, so adding to the journey time. Good deals can be offered by **General Sales Agents** (GSAs), see above. Consolidators in UK quote competetive fares: *Bridge the world*, T020-79110900, www.b-t-w.co.uk *Flightbookers*, T020-77573000, www.ebook ers.com *North South Travel*, T01245-492882 (profits to charity).

From the UK, Continental Europe & the Middle East

Qantas, Singapore Airlines, Thai Airways, Malaysian Airlines, Cathay Pacific and *Indian Airlines* are the principal airlines connecting the continents. They fly to one of the Indian regional capitals. *STA* and *Flight Centres* offer discounted tickets from their branches in major cities in Australia and New Zealand. *Abercrombie & Kent, Adventure World, Peregrine*, and *Travel Corporation of India*, organize tours.

From Australasia via the Far East

From the east coast, it is best to fly direct to India from New York via London by *Air India* (18 hours). Discounted tickets on *British Airways, KLM, Lufthansa, Gulf Air* and *Kuwait Airways* are sold through agents although they will invariably fly via their country's capital cities. From the west coast, it is best to fly via Hong Kong, Singapore or Bangkok to Mumbai using one of those countries' national carriers. *Hari World Travels*, www.hariworld.com and *STA*, www.sta-travel.co.uk have offices in New York, T627311, Toronto and Ontario. Student fares are also available from *Council Travel*, www.counciltravel.com, with several offices in the USA and *Travel Cuts*, Toronto T9792406, www.travelcuts.com, in Canada.

From North America

Overland

Crossings between India and its neighbours are affected by the political relations between them. Note also that you are not allowed to take any Indian currency from India into Pakistan. Indian Rupees can be changed on a 1:1 basis a t the border.

Get your Indian visa in advance, before arriving at the border

Road Several road border crossings between India and its neighbours are open periodically, but permission to cross cannot be guaranteed. Those listed below are the main crossings which may be useful for visiting the Indian Himalaya are normally open throughout the year to tourists. 'Friendship' **buses** have been introduced between Dhaka and Kolkata.

From Bangladesh To Kolkata from Dhaka and Jessore. The Bangaon-Benapol crossing is the most reliable. On the Bangladesh side rickshaws are available from Benapol, while buses and minibuses go to Bangaon railway station from the border. Regulations are subject to change so find out in advance. In London, Bangladesh High Commission, T020-7584 0081, F7225 2130.

From Bhutan To Bagdogra The nearest airport is 3-4 hours' drive from Jaigaon, the rather untidy and unkempt Indian border town. The Indian Immigration checkpost is on the main street, about a kilometre from the 'Bhutan Gate' at the border town of Phuntsholing where it is possible to spend a night. Accommodation ranges from the simple Central Hotel to the moderate government run Druk Hotel. To enter Bhutan you need an Entry Permit and a Visa.

Touching down

Airport information

Duty free allowance
Some airports have duty free shops though the range of goods is very limited
Tourists are allowed to bring in all personal effects 'which may reasonably be required', without charge. The official customs allowance includes 200 cigarettes or 50 cigars, 0.95 litres of alcohol, a camera with five rolls of film and a pair of binoculars. Valuable personal effects or professional equipment must be registered on a Tourist Baggage Re-Export Form (TBRE), including jewellery, special camera equipment and lenses, lap-top computers, sound and video recorders. These forms require the serial numbers of such equipment. It saves considerable frustration if you know the numbers in advance and are ready to show the serial numbers on the equipment. In addition to the forms, details of imported equipment may be entered into your passport. Save time by completing the formalities while waiting for your baggage. **It is essential to keep these forms** for showing to the customs when leaving India, otherwise considerable delays are very likely at the time of departure.

Currency regulations There are no restrictions on the amount of foreign currency or travellers' cheques a tourist may bring into India. If you were carrying more than US$10,000 or its equivalent in cash or travellers' cheques you need to fill in a currency declaration form. This could change with a relaxation in the currency regulations. You may not take out Rs 500 notes into Nepal.

Prohibited items The import of dangerous drugs, live plants, gold coins, gold and silver bullion and silver coins not in current use are either banned or subject to strict regulation. It is illegal to import firearms into India without special permission. Enquire at consular offices abroad for details.

Export restrictions Export of gold jewellery purchased in India is allowed up to a value of Rs 2,000 and other jewellery (including settings with precious stones) up to a value of Rs 10,000. Export of antiquities and art objects over 100 years old is restricted. Ivory, skins of all animals, *toosh* and *pashmina* wool, snake skin and articles made from them are banned, unless you get permission for export. For further information enquire at the

- -

Touching down

Electricity 220-240 volts AC. Some top hotels have transformers. There may be pronounced variations in the voltage, and power cuts are common. Socket sizes vary so you are advised to take a universal adaptor (available at most airports).

Many hotels even in the higher categories don't have electric razor sockets. During power cuts, diesel generators are often used in the medium and higher category hotels to provide power for essential equipment but this may not always cover air-conditioning.

Hours of business Banks: 1030-1430, Monday-Friday; 1030-1230, Saturday. Top hotels sometimes have a 24-hour service. **Post offices:** Usually 1000-1700,

Monday-Friday; Saturday mornings. **Government offices:** 0930-1700, Monday- Friday; 0930-1300, Saturday (some open on alternate Saturday only). **Shops:** 0930-1800, Monday-Saturday. Bazars keep longer hours. **NB** There are regional variations.

IDD 91. A double ring repeated regularly means it is ringing. Equal tones with equal pauses means engaged.

Official time GMT +5½ hours throughout the year (USA, EST +10½ hours).

Weights and measures The metric system has come into universal use in the cities. In remote rural areas local measures are sometimes used.

Essentials

- -

Indian High Commission or consulate, or access the Government of India at www.indiagov.org or the customs at konark.ncst.ernet.in/customs/

The formalities on arrival in India have been increasingly streamlined during the last five years and the facilities at the major international airports greatly improved. However, arrival can still be a slow process. Disembarkation cards, with an attached customs declaration, are handed out to passengers during the inward flight. The immigration form should be handed in at the immigration counter on arrival. The customs slip will be returned, for handing over to the customs on leaving the baggage collection hall. The immigration formalities can be very slow. You may well find that there are delays of over an hour in processing passengers passing through immigration who need help with filling forms. | **Documentation & tax**

Rs 500 is payable for all international departures other than those to neighbouring SAARC countries, when the tax is Rs 250. This must be paid in Rupees in India unless it is included in your international ticket; check when buying. (To save time 'Security Check' your baggage before checking-in at Departure.) | **Departure tax**

Public transport to and from airport

Delhi airport has special bus services into the town centre from early morning to around midnight. | **Bus**

Pre-paid taxis to the city are available at all major airports. Some airports have up to three categories, 'limousine', 'luxury' and ordinary. The first two usually have prominent counters, so you may have to insist if you want to use the standard service. Insist on being taken to your chosen destination even if the driver claims the city is unsafe or the hotel has closed down. | **Pre-paid taxis** *See detailed advice under international airports*

Essentials

First impressions

On arrival at any of India's major cities the first impressions can take you aback. The exciting images of an ancient and richly diverse culture which draw many visitors to India can be completely overwhelmed by the immediate sensations which first greet you. You need to be prepared for:

Pollution All the cities suffer from bad air pollution, especially from traffic fumes.

Noise Many people also find India incredibly noisy, as radios, videos and loudspeakers seem to blare in unlikely places at all times of day and night.

Smells An almost baffling mixture of smells, from the richly pungent and unpleasant to the delicately subtle assaults the nose.

Pressure From stepping out of the airport or hotel everybody seems to clamour to sell you their services. Taxi and rickshaw drivers are always there when you don't want them, much less often when you do. There often seems to be no sense of personal space or privacy. Young women are often stared at and sometimes touched.

Public hygiene – or lack of it. It is common to see people urinating in public places (eg roadside), and defecating in the open countryside. These can all be daunting and make early adjustment difficult. Even on a short visit you need to give yourself time and space to adjust!

Tourist information

India is not geared up specially for making provisions for the physically handicapped or wheelchair bound traveller. Access to buildings, toilets (sometimes 'squat' type), pavements, kerbs and public transport can prove frustrating, but it is easy to find people to give a hand with lifting and carrying. Provided there is an able-bodied companion to scout around and arrange help, and so long as you are prepared to pay for at least mid-price hotels or guest houses, private car-hire and taxis, India should be perfectly rewarding, even if in a somewhat limited way.

Some travel companies are beginning to specialize in exciting holidays, tailor-made for individuals depending on their level of disability. For those with access to the internet, a Global Access – Disabled Travel Network Site is www.geocities.com/Paris/1502 It is dedicated to providing travel information for 'disabled adventurers' and includes a number of reviews and tips from members of the public. You might also want to read *Nothing Ventured*, edited by Alison Walsh (Harper Collins), which gives personal accounts of worldwide journeys by disabled travellers, plus advice and listings.

Gay & lesbian travellers Indian law forbids homosexual acts for men 'but not women' and carries a maximum sentence of life imprisonment. Although it is common to see young males holding hands in public, it doesn't necessarily indicate a gay relationship and is usually an expression of friendship.

Student travellers Full time students qualify for an ISIC (International Student Identity Card) which is issued by student travel and specialist agencies (eg *Usit, Campus, STA*) at home. A card allows certain travel benefits (eg reduced prices) and acts as proof of student status within India allowing ticket concessions into a few sites. For details contact *STIC* in Imperial Hotel, Janpath, New Delhi, T3327582. Those intending to study in India may get a one year student visa (see above).

Children of all ages are widely welcomed, being greeted with a warmth in their own right which is often then extended to those accompanying them. However, care should be taken when travelling to remote areas where health services are primitive since children can become more rapidly ill than adults. It is best to visit India in the cooler months since you need to protect children from the sun, heat, dehydration and mosquito bites. Cool showers or baths help, and avoid being out during the hottest part of the day. Diarrhoea and vomiting are the most common problems, so take the usual precautions, but more intensively. Breastfeeding is best and most convenient for babies. In the big cities you can get safe baby foods and formula milk. It doesn't harm a baby to eat an unvaried and limited diet of familiar food carried in packets for a few weeks if the local dishes are not acceptable, but it may be an idea to give vitamin and mineral supplements. Wet wipes, always useful, are sometimes difficult to find in India as are disposable nappies. The biggest hotels provide babysitting.

Travelling with children
See also the health section, page 60

Essentials

It is best to arrange voluntary work well in advance with organisations in India (addresses are given in some towns, eg Darjeeling, Dharamshala, Leh); alternatively, contact an organisation abroad. In the UK: *International Voluntary Service*, St John's Centre, Edinburgh EH2 4BJ, or *VSO*, 317 Putney Bridge Rd, London SW15 2PN, www.sci.lvs.org. Alternatively, students may spend part of their 'year off' helping in a school through 'GAP' or teach English or help with a conservation project through 'i to I', 1 Cottage Rd, Headingley, Leeds, L36 4DD, T0870 3332332, www.i-to-i.com In the USA: *Council for International Programs* 1101 Wilson Blvd Ste 1708, Arlington, VA 22209. www.voluntarywork.org is an international directory of organizations.

Volunteering

Although it is relatively safe for women to travel around much of the Indian Himalaya, most people find it an advantage to travel with a companion. Even so, privacy is rarely respected and there can be a lot of hassle, pressure and intrusion on your personal space, as well as outright harassment. If you are blonde, you are quite naturally likely to attract more attention. Some seasoned travellers find that dying their hair dark helps. See also below.

Women travellers

Rules, customs and etiquette

Most travellers experience great warmth and hospitality in India. You may however, be surprised that with the warm welcome comes an open curiosity about personal matters. Total strangers on a train, for example, may ask for details about your job, income and family circumstances, or discuss politics and religion.

Respect for the foreign visitor should be reciprocated by a sensitivity towards local customs and culture. How you dress is mostly how people judge you. Clean, modest clothes and a smile go a long way. Scanty, tight clothing draws unwanted attention. Nudity is not permitted on beaches in India and although there are some places where this ban is ignored, it causes widespread offence. Displays of intimacy are not considered suitable in public.

Conduct

You may at times be justifiably frustrated by delays, bureaucracy and inefficiency, but displays of anger and rudeness will not achieve anything positive, and may in fact make things worse. We suggest you remain patient and polite. The concept of time and punctuality is also rather vague so be prepared to be kept waiting.

It takes little effort to learn and use common gestures of courtesy but they are greatly appreciated by Indians. The **greeting** when meeting or parting, used universally among the Hindus across India, is the palms joined together as in prayer, sometimes accompanied with the word *namaste* (North and West), *namoshkar* (East). Muslims use the greeting *assalām aleikum*, with the response *waleikum assalām*, meaning

Courtesy

'peace be with you'; **"please"** is **mehrbani-se**; **"thank you"** is often expressed by a smile, or with the somewhat formal **dhannyabad**, **shukriya** (Urdu).

Hands & eating Traditionally, Indians use the right hand for eating, cutlery being alien at the table except for serving spoons. In rural India, don't expect table knives and forks though you might find small spoons. Use your right hand for giving, receiving, eating or shaking hands as the left is considered to be unclean since it is associated with washing after using the toilet.

Women Indian women in urban and rural areas differ in their social interactions with men. Certainly, to the westerner, Indian women may seem to remain in the background and appear shy when approached, often hiding their face and avoiding eye contact. Yet you will see them working in public, often in jobs traditionally associated with men in the West, in the fields, in construction sites or in the market place. Even from a distance, men should not photograph women without their consent.

Women do not, in general, shake hands with men since physical contact is not traditionally acceptable between acquaintances of the opposite sex. A westernized city woman, however, may feel free to shake hands with a foreign visitor. In traditional rural circles, it is still the custom for men to be offered food first, separately, so don't be surprised if you, as foreign guest (man or woman), are awarded this special status when invited to an Indian home, and never set eyes on your hostess.

Visiting religious sites Visitors to all religious places should be dressed in clean, modest clothes; shorts and vests are inappropriate. Always remove shoes before entering. Take thick socks for protection when walking on sun-baked stone floors. Menstruating women are considered 'unclean' and should not enter places of worship.

Non-Hindus are sometimes excluded from the inner sanctum of **Hindu** temples and occasionally even from the temple itself. Look for signs or ask. In certain temples, and on special occasions, you may only enter if you wear unstitched clothing such as a *dhoti*.

In **Buddhist** shrines, walk clockwise around shrines and stupas (keeping them to your right), and turn Buddhist prayer wheels in a clockwise direction.

In **Sikh** gurudwaras, everyone should cover their head, even if it is with a handkerchief.

In **Muslim** mosques, visitors should only have their face, hands and feet exposed; women should also cover their heads. Mosques may be closed to non-Muslims shortly before formal prayers.

Some temples have a register or a receipt book for **donations** which works like an obligatory entry fee. The money is normally used for the upkeep and services of the temple or monastery. In some pilgrimage centres, priests can become unpleasantly persistent. In general, if you wish to leave a donation, put money in the donation box; priests and Buddhist monks often do not handle money. It is also not customary to shake hands with a priest or monk. **Alms** *Sanyasis* (holy men), and some pilgrims, depend on gifts of money.

Begging Beggars are often found in busy street corners in large Indian cities, as well as at bus and train stations where they often target foreigners for special attention. Visitors usually find this very distressing, especially the sight of severely undernourished children or those displaying physical deformity. You may be particularly affected when some persist on making physical contact. Say a firm *"Jaao"* (go away). In the larger cities, beggars are often exploited by syndicates which cream off most of their takings. Yet those seeking alms near religious sites are another matter, and you may see Indian worshippers giving freely to those less fortunate than themselves, since this is tied up with gaining 'merit'. How you deal with begging is a matter of personal choice but it is perhaps better to give to a recognized charity than to make largely ineffectual handouts to individuals.

Young children sometimes offer to do 'jobs' such as call a taxi, carry shopping or pose for a photo. You may want to give a coin in exchange. However, it is not helpful to hand out sweets, 'school pens' (which are often sold) and money indiscriminately to open-palmed children who tag on to any foreigner. Some visitors prefer to give fruit.

A pledge to donate a part of one's holiday budget to a local charity would be an effective formula for 'giving'. Some visitors like to support self-help co-operatives, orphanages, refugee centres, disabled or disadvantaged groups, or international charities like *Oxfam*, *Save the Children* or *Christian Aid* which work with local partners, by either making a donation or by buying their products. Some of these are listed under the appropriate towns. A few (which also welcome volunteers) are listed here. www//Indiacharitynet.com is useful. *Novartis*, T0044-616977200, novartis.foundations@group.novartis.com (sustainable development, leprosy). *Oxfam*, Sushil Bhawan, 210 Shahpur Jat, New Delhi 110049, T011-6491774; 274 Banbury Rd, Oxford OX2 7D2, UK, oxindia@giasdl01.vsnl.net.in (400 grassroots projects). *SOS Children's Villages*, A-7 Nizamuddin (W), New Delhi 110013, T011-4647835, www//pw2.netcom/sanjayd/sos.html (over 30 poor and orphaned children's projects in India eg opposite Pital Factory, Jhotwara Rd, Jaipur 302016, T0141-322393). *Trek-Aid*, 2 Somerset Cottages, Stoke Villages, Plymouth, Devon, PL3 4AZ, T0510-7975601 (health, education etc through self-help schemes for displaced Tibetan refugees).

Charitable giving

A tip of Rs 10 to a bell-boy carrying luggage in a modest **hotel** (Rs 20 in a higher category) would be appropriate. In up-market **restaurants**, a 10% tip is acceptable when 'Service' is not already included, while in places serving very cheap meals, round off the bill with small change. Indians don't normally tip **taxi drivers** but a small extra amount over the fare is welcomed. **Porters** at airports and railway stations often have a fixed rate displayed but will usually press for more. Ask fellow passengers what the fair rate is – they will nearly always advise.

Tipping

Given the dusty conditions, a UV filter is best left on the lens permanently and a polarising filter can often give you stronger colours, better contrast and a bluer sky. Although good quality films are available in all major cities and tourist centres, it is best to take rolls of films from home and certainly any specialist camera batteries. In India, only buy films from a reputable shop since hawkers and roadside stalls may not be reliable; check the carton carefully as well as the expiry date.

Many monuments now charge a camera fee ranging from Rs 20 to Rs 50 for still cameras, and as much as Rs 500 for video cameras (more for professionals). Special permits are needed from the Archaeological Survey of India, New Delhi for using tripods and artificial lights. When photographing people, it is polite to first ask – they will usually respond warmly with smiles. Visitors often promise to send copies of the photos – don't, unless you really mean to do so. Photography of airports, military installations, bridges and in tribal and 'sensitive border areas', is not permitted.

Photography

Safety

In general the threats to personal security for travellers in India are remarkably small. In most areas it is possible to travel either individually or in groups without any risk of personal violence. However, care is necessary in some places, and basic common sense needs to be used with respect to looking after valuables.

Personal security

Some parts of India are subject to political violence. The Vale of Kashmir and Jammu remains under tight military control. Even when the border area is relatively quiet, very few hotels are open in Srinagar and the army is massively deployed and on constant alert. Despite the promises of travel touts that Kashmir is completely safe, tourists who visit, do so at considerable risk. Some areas have long been noted for banditry. However in the great majority of places visited by tourists, violent crime and personal attacks are extremely rare.

Theft Theft is not uncommon. It is best to keep travellers' cheques, passports and valuables with you at all times since you can't regard hotel rooms as automatically safe; even hotel safes don't guarantee secure storage. Avoid leaving valuables near open windows even when you are in the room. Use your own padlock in a budget hotel when you go out. Pickpockets and other thieves operate in the big cities. Crowded areas are particularly high risk. Take special care of your belongings when getting on or off public transport. Never accept food or drink from casual acquaintances. Travellers have reported being drugged and then robbed.

Confidence tricksters These are particularly common where people are on the move, notably around railway stations or places where budget tourists gather. A common plea is some sudden and desperate calamity; sometimes a letter will be produced in English to back up the claim. The demands are likely to increase sharply if sympathy is shown. See also page 47, shopping.

Security on trains It can be difficult to keep an eye on your belongings when travelling. Nothing of value should be left close to open train windows. First class a/c compartments are self-contained and normally completely secure. Second class a/c compartments, which have much to recommend them especially in the summer, are larger, allowing more movement of passengers but are not so secure. Attendants may take little notice of what is going on, so luggage should be chained to a seat for security overnight. Locks and chains are easily available at main stations and bazars.

Police
Some states have introduced special Tourist Police to help the foreign traveller If you have items stolen, they should be reported to the police as soon as possible. Keep a separate record of vital documents, including passport details and travellers' cheques numbers. Larger hotels will be able to assist in contacting and dealing with the police.

Dealings with the police can be very difficult and in the worst regions such as Bihar even dangerous. The paperwork involved in reporting losses can be time consuming and irritating, and your own documentation (eg passport and visas) may be demanded. In some states the police themselves sometimes demand bribes, though tourists should not assume, however, that if procedures move slowly they are automatically being expected to offer a bribe. If you have to go to a police station, try to take someone with you. If you face really serious problems, for example in connection with a driving accident, you should contact your consular office as quickly as possible. You should ensure you always have your International driving licence and motorbike or car documentation with you.

Drugs Certain areas have become associated with foreigners taking drugs such as Dharamshala, Manali and Manikaran (Himachal). These are likely to attract local and foreign drug dealers but be aware that the government takes the misuse of drugs very seriously. Anyone charged with the illegal posession of drugs risks facing a fine of Rs 100,000 and a minimum 10 years imprisonment. Several foreigners have been imprisoned for drugs related offences in the last decade.

Women travelling alone There are some problems to watch out for and some simple precautions to take, to avoid both personal harassment and giving offence. Modest dress is always advisable: loose-fitting non-see-through clothes, covering the shoulders, and skirts, dresses or shorts of a decent length. Many find the *shalwar-kameez*-scarf ideal. In mosques women should be covered from head to ankle. In Sikh temples everyone should cover their heads. Unaccompanied women are most vulnerable in major cities, crowded bazars, beach resorts and tourist centres where men may follow them and touch them. "Eve teasing" is the euphemism for physical harassment; some buses have seats reserved for women. If you are harassed, it can be effective to make a scene. As one woman traveller wrote, "they should not get away with it, and in many public places other people will quickly take your side". Be firm and clear if you don't wish to speak to someone. Most railway booking offices have separate women's ticket queues or ask women to go to the head of the general queue. It is best to be accompanied at night, especially when travelling by rickshaw or taxi in towns. Be prepared to raise an alarm if anything unpleasant threatens. Women have reported that they have been molested while being measured for clothing in tailors' shops, especially in North India. If possible, take a friend with you.

Advice It is better to seek advice on security from your own consulate than from travel agencies. Before you travel you can contact: British Foreign & Commonwealth Office, Travel Advice Unit, Consular Division, 1 Palace Street, London SW1E 5HE, UK, T020-72384503 (Pakistan desk T020-72702385), F020-72384545, www.fco.gov.uk/. US State Department's Bureau of Consular Affairs, Overseas Citizens Services, Room 4800, Department of State, Washington, DC 20520-4818, USA, T202-6474225, F-6473000, http://travel.state.gov/travel_warnings. html Austrailian Department of Foreign Affairs, Canberra, Austrailia, T06-62613305, www.dfat.gov.au/consular/advice.html Canadian official advice is on www.dfait-maeci.gc.ca/travelreport/menu_e.htm

Where to stay

India has an enormously wide range of accommodation. You can stay safely and very cheaply by western standards right across the country. In all the major cities there are also high quality hotels, offering a full range of personal and business facilities. In small centres even the best hotels are far more variable. In the peak season bookings can be extremely heavy in popular destinations. It is sometimes possible to book in advance by phone, fax or email either from abroad or in India itself. However, double check your reservation, and always try to arrive as early as possible in the day.

Hotels

Hotels in hill-stations, because of their location and special appeal, often deviate from the description of our different categories.

Price categories The categories are based on prices of double rooms excluding taxes. They are **not** star ratings, and individual facilities vary considerably. Modest hotels may not have their own restaurant but will often offer 'room service', bringing in food from outside. Many hotels operate a '24 hour check-out' system. Make sure that this means that you can stay 24 hours from the time of check-in.

Regional variation Expect to pay more in Delhi, and to a lesser extent in Kolkata for all categories. Prices away from large cities tend to be lower for comparable hotels.

Off-season rates Large reductions are made by hotels in all categories out-of-season in many resort centres. Always ask if any is available. You may also request the 10% agent's commission to be deducted from your bill if you book direct. Clarify whether the agreed figure includes all taxes.

Taxes In general most hotel rooms rated at Rs 1,200 or above are subject to an expenditure tax of 10%. Many states levy an additional luxury tax of between 10 and 25%, and some hotels add a service charge of 10%. Taxes are not necessarily payable on meals, so it is worth settling the meals bill separately from the room bill. Most hotels in the **C** category and above accept payment by credit card. Check your final bill carefully. Visitors have complained of **incorrect bills**, even in the most expensive hotels. The problem particularly afflicts groups, when last-minute extras appear mysteriously on some guests' bills. Check the evening before departure, and keep all receipts.

Hotel facilities You have to be prepared for difficulties which are uncommon in the West. It is best to inspect the room and check that all equipment (a/c, TV, water heater, flush) works before checking in at a modest hotel.

Power supply In some states power cuts are common, or hot water may be restricted to certain times of day. The largest hotels have their own generators but it is best to carry a good torch.

Air-conditioning (a/c) Usually, only category **C** and above have central a/c. Elsewhere a/c rooms are cooled by individual units and occasionally by large 'air-coolers' which can be noisy and unreliable. When they fail to operate tell the management as it is often possible to get a rapid repair done, or to transfer to a room where the unit is working. During power cuts generators may not be able to cope with providing air-conditioning. Fans are provided in all but the cheapest of hotels.

Heating Hotels in hill stations often supply wood fires in rooms. Usually there is plenty of ventilation, but ensure that there is always good air circulation, especially when charcoal fires are provided in a basket.

Toilets Apart from those in the **A** category and above, 'attached bath' does not necessarily refer to a bathroom with a bathtub. Most will provide a bathroom with a toilet, basin and a shower. In the lower priced hotels and outside large towns, a bucket and tap may replace the shower, and an Indian 'squat' toilet instead of a Western WC (squat toilets are very often the cleaner). Even mid-price hotels, which are clean and pleasant, don't always provide towels, soap and toilet paper.

Water supply In some regions water supply is rationed periodically. Keep a bucket filled to use for flushing the toilet during water cuts. Occasionally, tap water may be discoloured due to rusty tanks. During the cold weather and in hill stations, **hot water** will be available at certain times of the day, sometimes in buckets, but is usually very restricted in quantity. Electric water heaters may provide enough for a shower but not enough to fill a bath tub! For details on drinking water see page 47.

Laundry can be arranged very cheaply (eg a shirt washed and pressed for Rs 10-20 in **C-D** category; Rs 50 in luxury hotels) and quickly in 12-24 hours. It is best not to risk delicate fibres, though luxury hotels can usually handle these and also dry-clean items.

Insects At some times of the year and in some places mosquitoes can be a real problem, and not all hotels have mosquito-proof rooms or mosquito nets. If you have any doubts check before confirming your room booking. In cheap hotels you need to be prepared for a wider range of insect life, including flies, cockroaches, spiders, ants and geckos (harmless house lizards). Poisonous insects, including scorpions, are extremely rare in towns. Hotel managements are nearly always prepared with insecticide sprays. Many small hotels in mosquito-prone areas supply nets. Remember to shut windows and doors at dusk. Electrical mat and pellets are now widely available, as are mosquito coils which burn slowly. Dusk and early evening are the worst times

Hotel categories

LL and **L** (US$150+)   These are exceptional hotels. They are in the metropolitan cities or in exclusive locations such as a commanding coastal promontory, a lake island or a scenic hilltop, with virtually nothing to fault them. They have high class business facilities, specialist restaurants and well-stocked bars, several pools, sports.

AL (US$100-150) and **A** (US$50-100)   Most major towns have at least some in these categories which too reach high international standards but are less exclusive. Many quote an inflated 'dollar price' to foreigners.

B (US$25-50)   Comfortable but not plush, choice of restaurants, pool, some have a gym. These are often aimed at the business client.

C (US$15-25) and **D**   In many small towns the best hotel is in the **C** category, but they are not necessarily the best value. Some charge higher prices for a flash reception area, usually central a/c, restaurant, satellite TV, foreign exchange and travel desk. **D** (Rs 400-750) hotels often offer very good value though quality and cleanliness can vary widely. Most have some a/c rooms with bath, satellite TV, restaurants. **D** hotels may have some rooms in the **E** price range, so if you are looking for good but cheap accommodation, start here!

E (Rs 200-400)   Simple room with fan (occasionally air-cooler or a/c), often shared toilet and shower. May not have a restaurant or provide bed linen, towel etc. **F** (Under Rs 200)   Very basic, shared toilet (often 'squat'), bucket and tap, variable cleanliness and hygiene. **E** and **F** category hotels are often in busy parts of town. They may have some rooms for under Rs 100, and dormitory beds for under Rs 50. (Some only have four or six beds.)

Prices appear on the inside front cover

Essentials

for mosquitoes so trousers and long-sleeved shirts are advisable, especially out of doors. At night, fans can be very effective in keeping mosquitoes off. A traveller recommends Dettol soap to discourage mosquitoes.

Service   Where staff training is lacking, the person who brings up your cases may proceed to show you light switches, room facilities, TV tuning, and hang around waiting for a tip. Room boys may enter your room without knocking or without waiting for a response to a knock. Both for security and privacy, it is a good idea to lock your door when you are in the room. It is worth noting these failings in the comments book when leaving as the management may take action.

Noise   Hotels close to temples can be very noisy, especially during festivals. Music blares from loudspeakers late at night and from very early in the morning, often making sleep impossible. Mosques call the faithful to prayers at dawn. Some find earplugs helpful.

The different State Tourism Development Corporations run their own hotels and hostels which are often located in places of special interest. These are very reasonably priced, though they may be rather dated, restaurant menus may be limited and service is often slow. Upkeep varies and in some states it is sadly well below standard.

Tourist 'Bungalows'

Railway stations often have 'Retiring Rooms' or 'Rest Rooms' which may be hired for periods of between one and 24 hours by anyone holding an onward train ticket. They are cheap and simple though some stations have a couple of a/c rooms, which are often heavily booked. They are convenient for short stops, though some can be very noisy. Delhi airport has similar facilities.

Railway & airport retiring rooms

Indian style hotels These, catering for Indian businessmen, are springing up fast in or on the outskirts of many small and medium sized towns. Most have some air-conditioned rooms and attached showers. They are variable in quality but it is increasingly possible to find excellent value accommodation even in remote areas.

Youth hostels The Department of Tourism runs 16 youth hostels, each with about 50 beds, usually organized into dormitory accommodation. The YHA also have a few sites all over India. Travellers may also stay in religious hostels (*dharamshalas*) for up to three days. These are primarily intended for pilgrims, and are sometimes free of charge though voluntary offerings are always welcome. Usually only vegetarian food is permitted; smoking and alcohol are not.

Camping Mid-price hotels with large grounds are sometimes willing to allow camping. Regional tourist offices have details of new developments. For information on YMCA camping facilities contact: *YMCA*, The National General Secretary, National Council of YMCAs of India, PB No 14, Massey Hall, Jai Singh Rd, New Delhi 1.

Getting around

Air

India has a comprehensive network linking the major cities of the different states. In addition to *Indian Airlines* (the nationalized carrier) www.nic.in/indianairlines and its subsidiary *Alliance Air*, there are several private airlines such as *Jet Airways* www.jetairways.com and *Sahara*, www.saharaairline.com which provide supplementary flights on several routes as well as filling gaps in a particular area, as with *Jagson*. Competition from the efficiently run private sector has, in general, improved the quality of services provided by the nationalized airlines. The Airports Authorities too have made efforts to improve handling on the ground.

Although flying is expensive, for covering vast distances or awkward links on a route, it is an option worth considering, although delays and re-routing can be irritating. However, for short distances, and on some routes it makes more sense to travel by train.

Air tickets All the major airlines are connected to the central reservation system and there are local travel agents who will book your tickets for a fee if you don't want to spend precious time waiting in a queue. Remember that tickets are in great demand in the peak season on some sectors (eg Delhi-Leh-Delhi) so it is essential to get them

Indian Airlines: approximate economy fares on popular routes

Sector	US$	Sector	US$	Sector	US$
From Agra to:		From Kolkata[1] to:		From Delhi to:	
Delhi	55	Delhi	185	Leh	110
From Bagdogra for Darjeeling to:		Guwahati	80	From Jammu to:	
		From Chandigarh to:		Leh	70
Kolkata[1]	85	Delhi	65		
Delhi	185	Leh	75	**Alternative names:**	
Guwahati	55			[1] Kolkata (Calcutta)	

Essentials

months ahead. If you are able to pre-plan your trip, it is even possible to ask if the internal flights can be booked at the time you buy your international air ticket at home through an agent (eg *Trailfinders, SD Enterprises*, London) or direct (eg *Jet Airways*). You can also book internal flights on the internet - www.welcometravel.com and collect and pay for them on your arrival in India.

Payment Foreign passport holders buying air tickets in India must pay the 'US dollar rate' and pay in foreign exchange (major credit cards, travellers' cheques accepted), or in rupees against an encashment certificate which will be endorsed accordingly. There is very little difference in prices quoted by competing airlines.

Special fares *Indian Airlines*, www.nic.in/indian-airlines and *Jet Airways*, www.jetairways.com offer special 7, 15 and 21 day unlimited travel, deals from around US$300 to US$750 (some are limited to one sector) which represent good savings. **Youth fares** 25% discount is given on US$ fares for anyone between 12 and 30 years. **Night savers** 25% discount fares are being introduced on late night flights between some metropolitan cities.

Delays Be prepared for delays during the winter. Nearly all northern routes originate in New Delhi, where from early December through to February, smog has become an increasingly common morning hazard, sometimes delaying departures by several hours. These delays then affect the whole northern system for the rest of that day.

Air travel tips **Security** Domestic airlines don't permit batteries in cabin baggage, and once confiscated, you may never see your batteries again. You may need to identify your baggage after they have been checked in and just before they are loaded onto the plane.
Telephone There is a free telephone service at major airports (occasionally through the tourist office counter), to contact any hotel of your choice.
Wait-lists If you don't have a confirmed booking and are 'wait-listed' it pays to arrive early at the airport and be persistent in enquiring about your position.

Road

Road travel is often the only choice for reaching many of the places of outstanding interest in which the Indian Himalaya is so rich. For the uninitiated, travel by road can also be a worrying experience because of the apparent absence of conventional traffic regulations and also in the mountains, especially during the rainy season when landslides are possible. Vehicles drive on the left – in theory. Routes around the major cities are usually crowded with lorry traffic, and the main roads are often poor and slow. There are no motorways, and many main roads are single track. Some district roads are quiet, and although they are not fast they can be a good way of seeing the country and village life if you have the time.

☛ *The hazards of road travel*

On most routes it is impossible to average more than 50-60 kph in a car. Journeys are often very long, and can seem an endless succession of horn blowing, unexpected dangers, and unforeseen delays. Villages are often congested – beware of the concealed spine-breaking speed bumps – and cattle, sheep and goats may wander at will across the road. Directions can also be difficult to find. Drivers frequently don't know the way,

maps are often hopelessly inaccurate and map reading is an almost entirely unknown skill. Training in driving is negligible and the test often a farce. You will note a characteristic side-saddle posture, one hand constantly on the horn, but there can be real dangers from poor judgement, irresponsible overtaking and a general philosophy of 'might is right'.

Bus Buses offer a cheap, if often uncomfortable means of reaching your destination. Services are run by the State Corporation (from the State Bus Stand) (and private companies. The latter allow advance reservation and though tickets prices are a little higher, they have fewer stops and are a bit more comfortable.

There are three categories. **A/c luxury coaches**: though comfortable for sight-seeing trips, even these can be very uncomfortable and tiring for really long journeys. **Express buses**: run over long distances (frequently overnight). These are often called 'video coaches' and can be an appalling experience unless you appreciate loud film music blasting through the night. Ear plugs and eye masks may ease the pain. They rarely average more than 45 km per hour. **Local buses**: these are often very crowded, quite bumpy and slow and usually poorly maintained. However, over short distances, they can be a very cheap, friendly and easy way of getting about. Even where signboards are not in English someone will usually give you directions.

Bus travel tips Some towns have different bus stations for different destinations. Booking on major long-distance routes is now computerized. Book in advance where possible and avoid the back of the bus where it can be very bumpy. If your destination is only served by a local bus you may do better to take the Express bus and 'persuade' the driver, with a tip in advance, to stop where you want to get off. You will have to pay the full fare to the first stop beyond your destination but you will get there faster and more comfortably.

Car Several routes into the Himalaya have now been opened up to car or 4 wheel drive travel. However, if driving in India generally poses unusual problems for western drivers, the difficulties are increased dramatically on the mountain roads. In many parts of the Indian Himalaya it is normally only possible to drive during the summer. However, roads are severely disrupted by monsoon rains and associated landslides. Delays are common and the quality of road surfaces is often very poor. In Kashmir military traffic dominates the roads and convoys grind slowly through the high passes. Higher roads are narrow and winding, and often the mountain side plunges hundreds of metres to a river below. For most people hiring a car with a driver familiar with the conditions is the best way to take advantage of the skeletal road network. A variety of suitable vehicles (Jeep, Maruti Gypsy, Tata Sumo) is available for hire in several Himalayan towns, and car hire arrangements can also be made by some tour operators in Delhi, Kolkata and abroad.

Car hire, with a driver, is often cheaper than in the West. A car shared by three or four can be very good value and "Hill" driving also give excellent opportunities for sightseeing off the beaten track in reasonable comfort. Local drivers often know their way much better than drivers from other states, so where possible it is a good idea to get a local driver who speaks the state language, in addition to being able to communicate with you. Drivers may sleep in the car overnight, though hotels sometimes provide a bed for them. They are responsible for all their expenses, including their meals. A tip at the end of the tour of Rs 100 per day in addition to their daily allowance is perfectly acceptable. Check beforehand if fuel and inter-state taxes are included in the hire charge.

Cars can be hired through private companies. International companies such as *Hertz*, *Europcar* and *Budget* operate in some major cities and offer reliable cars; their rates are generally higher than those of local firms. The price of an imported car can be three times that of the Ambassador.

Car hire rates

Car with driver	Economy Maruti 800 Ambassador	Regular A/C Maruti 800 Ambassador	Premium A/C Maruti 1000 Contessa	Luxury A/C Esteem Opel etc
8 hrs/80 km	Rs 800	Rs 1,000	Rs 1,400	Rs 1,800+
Extra km	Rs 7	Rs 9	Rs 13	Rs 18
Extra hour	Rs 40	Rs 50	Rs 70	Rs 100
Out of town				
Per km	Rs 7	Rs 9	Rs 13	Rs 18
Night halt	Rs 160	Rs 200	Rs 250	Rs 250

Importing a car Tourists may import their own vehicles into India with a Carnet de Passage (Triptyques) issued by any recognized automobile association or club affiliated to the Alliance Internationale de Tourisme in Geneva.

Self-drive car hire is still in its infancy and many visitors may find the road conditions difficult and sometimes dangerous. If you drive yourself it is essential to take great care especially in the hills, where roads are often narrow, winding and precipitous and prone to being blocked by land slips during and after the monsoon. Pedestrians, cattle and a wide range of other animals roam at will. This can be particularly dangerous when driving after dark especially as even other vehicles often carry no lights.

Car travel tips Fuel: on main roads petrol stations are reasonably frequent, but some areas are poorly served. Some service stations only have diesel pumps though they may have small reserves of petrol. Always carry a spare can. Diesel is widely available and normally much cheaper than petrol. Petrol is rarely above 92 octane. **Insurance**: drivers must have third party insurance. This may have to be with an Indian insurer, or with a foreign insurer who has a national guarantor. **Asking the way**: can be very frustrating as you are likely to get widely conflicting advice each time you stop to ask. On the main roads, 'mile' posts periodically appear in English and can help. Elsewhere, it is best to ask directions often. **Provisions**: ensure that you have adequate food and drink, and a basic tool set in the car.

When booking emphasize the importance of good tyres & general roadworthiness

The **Automobile Association** offers a range of services to members. **New Delhi**: AA of Upper India, Lilaram Bldg, 14F Connaught Place; **Kolkata**: AA of Eastern India, 13 Promothesh Barua Sarani.

The larger cities (Delhi, Kolkata) have metered "yellow-top" taxis. Increased rates are shown on a fare conversion chart. When a taxi doesn't have a meter, you will need to fix the fare before starting the journey. Ask at the hotel desk for a guide price.

Taxis

Taxi tips At stations and airports it is often possible to share taxis to a central point. It is worth looking for fellow passengers who may be travelling in your direction and get a *pre-paid taxi*. At night, always have a clear idea of where you want to go and insist on being taken there. Taxi drivers may try to convince you that the hotel you have chosen 'closed three years ago', is 'completely full' or is an 'unsafe den'. You may have to say that you have an advance reservation. See under Delhi for more details.

Rickshaws
It is best to walk a short distance away from a hotel gate before picking up an auto to avoid paying an inflated rate

Auto-rickshaws ('autos') are almost universally available in towns across India and are the cheapest convenient way of getting about. In addition to using them for short journeys it is often possible to hire them by the hour, or for a half or full day's sight-seeing. In some areas younger drivers who speak some English and know their local area well, may want to show you around. However, rickshaw drivers are often paid a commission by hotels, restaurants and gift shops, so advice is not always impartial. Drivers sometimes refuse to use a meter, quote a ridiculous price or attempt to stop short of your destination. If you have real problems it can help to threaten to go to the police.

Cycling It is easy to hire bikes in most small towns for about Rs 15-20 per day. Indian bikes are heavy and without gears, but on the flat they offer a good way of exploring comparatively short distances outside towns. It is also quite possible to tour parts of the Himalaya on a mountain bike. You can join an organized tour (see page 15 for some operators). For expert information contact *Cyclists' Touring Club*, Cotterel House, 69 Meadowgrow, Godalming, Surrey, UK. T01483 417217.

A week's cycling trip could cover about 250 km in the Garhwal foothills, starting in Rishikesh, passing through the Corbett and Rajaji National Parks over easy gradients, to finish in Ramnagar. Expert guides, cycles and support vehicle, accommodation in simple resthouses or tents, are included.

Imported bikes have the advantage of lighter weight and gears, but are more difficult to get repaired, and carry the much greater risk of being stolen or damaged. If you wish to take your own, it is quite easy if you dismantle it and pack it in its original shipping carton; be sure to take all essential spares including a pump. All cyclists should take bungy cords (to strap down a backpack) and good lights from home; take care not to leave your machine parked anywhere with your belongings though. Bike repair shops are universal and charges are nominal.

Motorcycling
See under Car & Cycling above for general advice

Motorcycling in India is particularly attractive for bike enthusiasts. It is easy to buy new Indian-made motorcycles including the Enfield Bullet and several 100cc Japanese models, including Suzukis and Hondas made in collaboration with Indian firms. Buying new ensures greater reliability and fixed price – (Indian Rajdoots are less expensive but have a poor reputation for reliability). Buying second hand in Rupees takes more time but is quite possible; expect to get a 30-40% discount. You can get a broker to help with the paper-work involved (certificate of ownership, insurance etc) for a fee. They charge about Rs 5,000 for a 'No Objection Certificate' (NOC) which is essential for reselling; it is easier to have the bike in your name.

When selling, don't be in a hurry, and only negotiate with "ready cash" buyers. A black bike is easier to sell than a coloured one! Repairs are usually easy to arrange and quite cheap. Bring your own helmet and an International Driving Permit.

Peter and Friends Classic Adventures, an Indo-German company based in Goa at Casa Tres Amigos, Socol Vado 425, Assagao, T0832-273351, F276124, runs organized motorbike tours in Himachal Pradesh. They also hire out Enfield motorbikes (US$120-US$165/week). Tours with full back up are also offered by *Royal Enfield Motors*, Chennai, T044-543300, F543253. Himachal/Ladakh about US$1,200-1,600 for 14 days. *Chandertal Tours & Himalayan Folkways*, based in the UK, organizes *Royal Enfield* tours of the high Himalaya (Himachal and Ladakh). Contact 20 The Fridays, East Dean,

On the road on a motorbike

An experienced motorbiker writes: unless you bring your own bike (Carnet de passage, huge deposit) the only acceptable machine is the legendary Enfield Bullet 350 or 500 cc. Humming along the Indian roads or tracks this lovely four stroke classic machine is a must. Also available in diesel version (1.5 litres per 100 km and much cheaper fuel) the 500 cc is much better for travelling with luggage and easier to take home as brakes and 12v lights conform with EC regulations.

Expect a cruising speed of around 60 kph. Riding above 80 gets very tiring due to the lack of silent blocks and the nerve-wracking Indian roads. A good average distance is 200 km per day. Riding at night furthers the excitement – practise at home on a death race video first, but bear in mind that accidents can turn into a first-hand lynching experience! If you stop, prepare to settle quickly in cash, but while third party insurance is cheap (Rs 53 per year!) refunds are less than guaranteed.

Buying In Delhi, Karol Bagh is the biker's den, where you can have your second hand bike assembled to order. It's also good for arranging shipping (Rs 13,000 to Europe), and for spares and gear. You can now find good helmets at a fraction of the European price (Studds Rs 300-Rs 2,000 for a full face type), also goggles, sturdy panniers and extras. A Bullet will cost from Rs 25,000 to Rs 40,000 second hand, or Rs 50,000-Rs 60,000 new.

Allow plenty of time to shop around. Before buying, negotiate the essential extras: mirrors, luggage carriers, better saddle, battery.

Papers Many Indians and tourists don't bother changing the name on the ownership papers. If you are driving through more than one state this is rash, as it is essential to have the papers in your name, plus the NOC (No Objection Certificate) from the Motor Vehicles Department if you intend to export the vehicle home. Regardless of the dealer's assertions to the contrary, demand the NOC as otherwise you will have to apply for it in the state of origin. You have to allow 15 days.

Spares Spares are cheap and readily available for the 350cc model. Take along a spare throttle and clutch cable, a handful of nuts and bolts, an import quality inner tube, puncture repair kit and a sturdy foot or hand pump or emergency canister and a head torch so you don't have to leave the bike unattended while hitching a lift to the nearest puncture wallah – and of course a full set of tools. For the mountains, take strong sunglasses, good warm clothing, gloves, and rain and wind jammer. Check the oil level daily.

Finally, remember that for long distances you can load your bike on a night train (Rs 100 per 100 km). Just turn up at the parcel office with an empty petrol tank at least two hours before departure.

Essentials

Eastbourne, East Sussex, BN20 0DH, UK, T00-44 1323422213, www.steali.co.uk/india Two other operators recommended are asia bike_tours@hotmail.com (North India) and motoraid@yahoo.com (North India including Ladakh).

Hitchhiking is uncommon in India, partly because public transport is so cheap. If you try, you are likely to spend a very long time on the roadside. However, getting a lift on motorbikes/scooters and on trucks in areas with little public transport can be worthwhile. It is not recommended for women on their own.

Hitchhiking

Train

Train services are very restricted in the Indian Himalaya, though they offer an attractive way to get to key hill towns to the hills such as Shimla and the Kangra Valley in the west or Darjeeling in the east. They can still be a cheap and comfortable means of travelling. They can still be a cheap and comfortable means of travelling long distance saving you hotel expenses on overnight journeys. It gives access to booking station Retiring Rooms, which can be useful from time to time. Above all, you have an ideal opportunity to meet local travellers and catch a glimpse of life on the ground.

High-speed trains There are over 170 air-conditioned 'high-speed' *Shatabdi* (or 'Century') for day travel across India, and *Rajdhani Express* ('Capital City') for overnight journeys. These are in high demand you need to book them well in advance - up to 60 days ahead. Meals and drinks are usually included.

Steam For rail enthusiasts, the steam-hauled narrow-gauge train between Siliguri and Darjeeling in North Bengal (which is now a World Heritage Site). There are also narrow gauge mountain railways from Kalka to Shimla and from Palthanket to Jogindernagar.

Classes *A/c First Class*, available only on main routes and cheaper than flying, is very comfortable (bedding provided). It will also be possible for tourists to reserve special coaches (some a/c) which are normally allocated to senior railway officials only. *A/c Sleeper* two and three-tier, are clean and comfortable and good value. *A/c Executive Class*, with wide reclining seats are available on many *Shatabdi* trains at double the price of the ordinary *a/c Chair Car* which are equally comfortable. *2nd Class* (non-a/c) two and three-tier, provides exceptionally cheap travel but can be crowded and uncomfortable, and toilet facilities can be unpleasant. It is nearly always better to use the Indian style toilets as they are better maintained.

Indrail passes These allow travel across the network without having to pay extra reservation fees and sleeper charges but you have to spend a high proportion of your time on the train to make it worthwhile (see boxes). However, the advantages of pre-arranged reservations and automatic access to 'Tourist Quotas' can tip the balance in their favour for some travellers.

Tourists (foreigners and Indians resident abroad) may buy these passes for periods

Main Railways

Note: Indications about
gauges are approximate

——— Broad Gauge

——— Metre Gauge

▪▪▪▪▪▪ Mountain Railway

ranging from seven to 90 days from the tourist sections of principal railway booking offices, and pay in foreign currency, major credit cards, travellers' cheques or rupees with encashment certificates.

Indrail passes can also conveniently be bought abroad from special agents. For most people contemplating a single long journey soon after arriving in India, the Half or One day Pass with a confirmed reservation is worth the peace of mind; 2 or 4 Day Passes are also sold. The **UK** agent is *SD Enterprises Ltd*, 103, Wembley Park Drive, Wembley, Middx HA9 8HG, England, T020-89033411, F89030392, dandpani@dircon.co.uk They make all necessary reservations and offer excellent advice. They can also book *Indian Airlines* and *Jet Airways* internal flights.

Other **international agents** are: Australia: *Adventure World*, PO Box 480, North Sydney NSW 2060, T9587766, F9567707. **Bangladesh**: *Omnitrans International*, National Scouts Bhavan, 4th Flr, 70/1 Inner Circular Rd, Kakrail Dhaka, T9121053057,

Essentials

Shatabadi Expresses

No	From	To	Days	Dep	Arr	One-way Fare (Rs)	
						Chair	Exec
2005	ND	Kalka	Daily	1715	2115	470	945
2006	Kalka	ND	Daily	0600	1000	"	"
2011	ND	Chandigarh	Daily	0735	1045	435	865
2012	Chandigarh	ND	Daily	1220	1530	"	"
2017	ND	Dehradun	Daily (ex Th)	0710	1240	495	985
2018	Dehradun	ND	Daily (ex Th)	1705	2230	"	"

Th = Thursday;   **ND**= New Delhi

Rajdhani Trains

No	From	To	Days	Dep	Arr	Fare (Rs)[1]	
						2-Tier	3-Tier
2425	ND	Jammu Tawi	F	2050	0545*	1,380	950
2426	Jammu Tawi	ND	Sa	2030	0515*	"	"
2424	ND	Guwahati	Tu, W (Sa†)	1700	0945**	3,175	1,875
2423	Guwahati	ND	M, F (W†)	1615	1000**	"	"
2436	ND	Guwahati	M, F	1245	2030	3,175	1,875
2435	Guwahati	ND	W, Su	0600	1430	"	"

Tu = Tuesday; **W** = Wednesday; **F** = Friday; **Sa** = Saturday; **Su** = Sunday;
ND = New Delhi Station

Sa† = 2424 terminates in Dibrugarh at 2030

W† = 2423 originates in Dibrugarh

[1] = First class fares are about 70-80% higher than 2-Tier

* Next day ** Third day

Canada: *Hari World Travels*, 1 Financial Place, 1 Adelaide St East, Concou Level, Toronto, T3662000, F3666020. Denmark: *Danish State Railways*, DSW Travel Agency Div, Reventlowsgade – 10, DK 1651 Kobenhaven V. Finland: *Intia-Keskus*, Yrjonkatu 8-10, 00120 Helsinki, Finland, T46856-266000, F100946. **France**: *Le Monde de L'Inde et de L'Asie*, 15 Rue Des Ecoles, Paris 75005. Germany: *Asra-Orient*, Kaiserstrasse 50, D-6000 Frankfurt/M, T069253098, F69232045, asra-orient@t-online-d Hong Kong: *Cheung Hung*, B1&2 Carnarvon Mansion, 12 Carnarvon Rd, Tisimshatsui, Kowloon, Hong Kong, T852-2369-5333, F2739-9899. Israel: *Teshet*, 32 Ben Yehuda St, Tel Aviv 63805, T6290972, F6295126. Japan: *Japan Travel Bureau*, Overseas Travel Div, 1-6-4 Marunouchi, Chiyoda-ku, Tokyo-100, T031-284739. Malaysia: *City East West Travels*, 23 Jalan Yapah Shak, 50300, Kuala Lumpur, T2930569, F2989214. Oman: *National Travel & Tourism* , PO Box 962, Muttrah, Muscat, T968566046, T968566125. South Africa: *MK Bobby Naidoo*, PO Box 2878, Durban, T3094710. Thailand: *SS Travel*, 10/12-13 Convent Rd, SS Building, Bangkok, T2367188, F2367186. UAE: *Sharjah National Travels*, PO Box 17, Sharjah, T/F97165- 374968. USA: *Hari World Travels*, 25W 45th St, 1003, New York, NY 10036, T9573000, F9973320.

A White Pass allows first class a/c travel; a Green, a/c two-tier Sleepers and Chair Cars; and the Yellow, only second class travel. Special half and one day passes are only sold abroad.

Cost A/c first class costs about double the rate for two-tier shown below, and non a/c second class about half. Children (five to 12) travel at half the adult fare. The young (12-30) and senior citizens (65+) are allowed a 30% discount on journeys over 500 km (just show passport).

Period	A/c 2-tier US$	Period	A/c 2-tier US$
½ day	26	21 days	198
1 day	43	30 days	248
7 days	135	60 days	400
15 days	185	90 days	530

Fares for individual journeys are based on distance covered and reflect both the class and the type of train. Higher rates apply on the Mail and Express trains and the air conditioned *Shatabdi* and *Rajdhani Expresses*.

Rail travel tips **Food and drink**: it is best to carry some though tea and snacks are sold on the platforms (through the windows). On long distance trains, the restaurant car is often near the upper class carriages (bogies).
Timetables: regional timetables are available cheaply from station bookstalls; the monthly 'Indian Bradshaw' is sold in principal stations, while the handy 'Trains at a Glance' (Rs 25) lists popular trains likely to be used by most foreign travellers.
Delays: always allow time for booking and for making connections. Delays are common on all types of transport.
Tickets: you can save a lot of time and effort by asking a travel agent to get yours for a small fee. Non-Indrail Pass tickets can be bought over the counter. It is always best to book as far in advance as possible (usually up to 60 days). Avoid touts at the station offering tickets, hotels or money changing.
Ladies' queues: separate (much shorter) ticket queues may be available for women.
Credit cards: some main stations now have separate credit card booking queues – even shorter than women's queues!
Quotas: a large number of seats are technically reserved as 'quotas' for various groups of travellers (civil servants, military personnel, foreign tourists etc). In addition, many stations have their own quota for particular trains so that a train may be 'fully booked'

Train touts

Many railway stations – and some bus stations and major tourist sites – are heavily populated with touts. Self-styled 'agents' will board trains before they enter the station and seek out tourists, often picking up their luggage and setting off with words such as "Madam!/Sir! Come with me madam/sir! You need top class hotel ..." They will even select porters to take your luggage without giving you any say. If you have succeeded in getting off the train or even in obtaining a trolley you will find hands eager to push it for you. For a first time visitor such touts can be more than a nuisance. You need to keep calm and firm. Decide in advance where you want to stay. If you need a porter on trains, select one yourself and agree a price **before** the porter sets off with your baggage. If travelling with a companion one can stay guarding the luggage while the other gets hold of a taxi and negotiates the price to the hotel. It sounds complicated, and sometimes it feels it. The most important thing is to behave as if you know what you are doing!

when there are still some tickets available from the special quota of other stations. These are only sold on the day of departure so wait-listed passengers are often able to travel at the last minute. Ask the Superintendent on duty to try the 'Special' or 'VIP Quota'.

Reservations: ask for the separate Tourist Quota counter at main stations, and while queuing fill up the Reservation Form which requires the number, name, departure time of the train, and the passenger's name, age and sex; you can use one form for up to four passengers. If you don't have a reservation for a particular train but carry an Indrail Pass, you may get one by arriving about three hours early.

Porters: carry prodigious amounts of luggage. Rates vary from station to station but are usually around Rs 5 per item of luggage (board on the station platform). They can be quite aggressive particularly on the main tourist routes: be firm but polite and re-member that they will always leave the train when it pulls out of the station!

Getting a seat: it is usually impossible to make seat reservations at small 'intermedi-ate' stations as they don't have an allocation. You can sometimes use a porter to get you a seat in a 2nd class carriage. For about Rs 20 he will take the luggage and ensure that you get a seat!

Berths: it is worth asking for upper berths, especially in second class three-tier sleep-ers, as they can also be used during the day time when the lower berths are used as seats, and which may only be used for lying down after 2100.

Overbooking: passengers with valid tickets but no berth reservations are sometimes permitted to travel overnight, causing great discomfort to travellers occupying lower berths.

Bedding: travelling at night in the winter can be very cold in North India and in a/c coaches. Bedding is provided on second class a/c sleepers. On others it can be hired for Rs 30 from the Station Baggage Office for second class.

Ladies' compartments: a woman travelling alone, overnight, on an unreserved sec-ond class train can ask if there is one of these.

Security: keep valuables close to you, securely locked, and away from windows. For security, carry a good lock and chain to attach your luggage.

Left-luggage: bags left in station cloakrooms must be lockable. Don't leave any food in them.

Pre-paid taxis: many main stations have a pre-paid taxi (or auto-rickshaw) service which offers a reliable, fair-price service.

Keeping in touch

Internet Access is becoming increasingly available in major cities as cyber cafés mushroom and PCOs (Public Call Office) are beginning to offer the service, but in small towns the machines can be woefully slow. Alternatively, you can ask a large hotel or a travel agent if they will allow you to use their system.

Post The post is frequently unreliable, and delays are common. It is advisable to use a post office where it is possible to hand over mail for franking across the counter, or a top hotel post box. Valuable items should only be sent by **Registered Mail**. Government Emporia or shops in the larger hotels will send purchases home if the items are difficult to carry. **Airmail** service to Europe, Africa and Australia takes at least a week and a little longer for the Americas. **Speed post** (which takes about four days to the UK) is available from major towns. Specialist shippers deal with larger items, normally approximately US$150 per cubic metre. **Courier services** (eg *DHL*) are available in the larger towns. At some main post offices you can send small packages under 2 kg as Letter Post (rather than parcel post) which is much cheaper at Rs 220. 'Book Post' (for printed paper) is cheaper still, approximately Rs 170 for 5 kg. Book parcels must be sewn in cloth (best over see-through plastic) with a small open 'window' slit for contents to be seen.

Parcels The process can take up to two hours. Check that the post office holds necessary customs declaration forms (two/three copies needed). Write 'No commercial value' if returning used clothes, books etc. Air mail is expensive; sea mail slow but reasonable (10 kg, Rs 800). 'Packers' outside post offices will do all necessary cloth covering, sealing etc for Rs 20-50; you address the parcel, obtain stamps from a separate counter; stick stamps and one customs form to the parcel with glue available (the other form/s must be partially sewn on). Post at the Parcels Counter and obtain a Registration slip. **Maximum dimensions**: height 1 m, width 0.8 m, circumference 1.8 m. Cost: sea mail about Rs 775 for first kilogram, Rs 70 each extra kilogram. Air mail also Rs 775 first kilogram, Rs 200 each subsequent kilogram.

Warning Many people complain that private shops offering a postal service actually send cheap substitutes. It is usually too late to complain when the buyer finds out. It is best to buy your item and then get it packed and posted yourself.

Poste restante facilities are widely available in even quite small towns at the GPO where mail is held for one month. Ask for mail to be addressed to you with your surname in capitals and underlined. When asking for mail at Poste Restante check under surname as well as Christian name. Any special issue foreign stamps are likely to be stolen from envelopes in the Indian postal service and letters may be thrown away. Advise people who are sending you mail to India to use only definitive stamps (without pictures).

Telephone
International code: 00 91. Phone codes for towns are printed after the town name

International Direct Dialling is now widely available in privately run call 'booths', usually labelled on yellow boards with the letters 'PCO-STD-ISD'. You dial the call yourself, and the time and cost are displayed on a computer screen. They are by far the best places from which to telephone abroad. Cheap rate (2100-0600) means long queues may form outside booths. Telephone calls from hotels are usually much more expensive (check price before calling).

Ringing tone: double ring, repeated regularly; **Engaged**: equal length, on and off. Both are similar to UK ringing and engaged tones.

One disadvantage of the tremendous pace of the telecommunications revolution

The email explosion

As the internet shrinks the world, travellers are increasingly using emails to keep in touch with home. Their free accounts are invariably with **hotmail.com**, **yahoo.com**, **email.com** or **backpackers.com**; usually the less common the provider, the quicker the access.

India has its own set of problems which can be frustrating: very few machines which may also be out-dated; untrained staff and poor technical support; the server may be unreliable; the system may be clogged with users, especially during day; there may be frequent power cuts ... there are exceptions, of course.

New offices are opening weekly and new towns are getting connected. To track down the most reliable and best value internet service, ask other travellers. The length of the queue can be a good indicator. On the web, you can get a list from **www.netcafeguide.com** Don't always head for the cheapest since they may also have the oldest and slowest equipment. Rates vary, but in 2000, it cost around Rs 50 for 30 minutes.

Hot Tips

■ Use the folder facility to save mail
■ Keep your in-box clear to reduce loading time
■ Avoid junk mail by not giving your address to on-line companies
■ Avoid downloading and using scanned pictures and documents
■ Save files and back up regularly

The system can be efficient and satisfying but it can also become an expensive habit with more than its fair share of frustrations. As one sending an email to us mused, "many a hard-up traveller will wax lyrical about 'getting away from it all' and escaping 'the pressure of western society'. They will then spend hours and several hundred rupees a week slaving over a computer keyboard in some hot and sticky back street office".

Essentials

is the fact that millions of telephone numbers go out of date every year. Current telephone directories themselves are often out of date and some of the numbers given in the Handbook will have been changed even as we go to press. Directory enquiries, **197**, can be helpful but works only for the local area code.

Fax services are available from many PCOs and larger hotels, who charge either by the minute or per page.

Newspapers International newspapers (mainly English language) are sold in the bookshops of top hotels in major cities, and occasionally by booksellers elsewhere. India has a large English language press. They all have extensive analysis of contemporary Indian and some international issues. The major papers now have internet sites which are excellent for keeping daily track on events, news and weather. The best known are *The Hindu,* www.hinduonline.com/today/ *The Hindustan Times* www.hindustantimes.com *The Independent, The Times of India* www.timesofindia.com/, and *The Statesman* www.thestates man.org/ *The Economic Times* is possibly the best for independent reporting and world coverage. *The Telegraph* published in Kolkata, www.telegraphindia.com/, has good foreign coverage. The *Indian Express* www.expressindia.com/ has stood out as being consistently critical of the Congress Party and Government. *The Asian Age* is now published in the UK and India simultaneously and gives good coverage of Indian and international affairs. Of the fortnightly magazines, some of the most widely read are *Sunday, India Today* and *Frontline,* all of which are current affairs journals on the model of *Time* or *Newsweek.* To check weather conditions, try www.wunderground.com

Media

Television and radio India's national radio and television network, *Doordarshan,* broadcasts in national and regional languages but things have moved on. The advent

Essentials

 Best short-wave frequencies

BBC World service: *Signal strength varies throughout the day, with lower frequencies better during the night. The nightly "South Asia Report" offers up to the minute reports covering the sub-continent. Try 15310, 17790 or 1413, 5975, 11955, 17630, 17705. More information on www.bbc.uk/ worldservice/sasia*

Voice of America: *1400-1800 GMT; 1575, 6110, 7125, 9645, 9700, 9760, 15255,15395 Mhz. www.voa.gov/sasia*

Deutsche Welle: *0600-1800 GMT; 6075, 9545, 17845; other frequencies include 17560, 12000 and 21640.*

of satellite TV has hit even remote rural areas. The 'Dish' can help travellers keep in touch through Star TV from Hong Kong (accessing BBC World, CNN etc), VTV (music) and Sport, now available even in some modest hotels in the smallest of towns.

Food and drink

Food
See page 407 for a food glossary
In many of the towns of the Indian Himalaya it is now possible to get a wide range of standard Indian and Chinese dishes, as well as western food. However, Tibetan influence is strong in all the higher regions from Ladakh to Sikkim and Arunachal Pradesh. Distinctive Tibetan dishes include *thukpa* (soup), *momos*, a variety of stuffed dumpling, and *tsampa*, a roasted barley which is a basic ingredient. Two drinks are universal, *chhang*, a sour fermented millet, barley or rice drink, and *gurgur*, Tibetan tea made with tea leaves, soda-bicarbonate, salt and butter.

It is essential to be very careful since food hygiene may be poor, flies abound and refrigeration in the hot weather may be inadequate and intermittent because of power cuts. It is best to eat only freshly prepared food by ordering from the menu (especially meat and fish dishes); avoid salads and cut fruit.

If you are unused to spicy food, go slow! Stick to Western or mild Chinese meals in good restaurants, and try the odd Indian dish to test your reaction. Those used to Indian spices may choose to be more adventurous. Popular local restaurants are obvious from the number of people eating in them. Try a traditional *thali*, which is a complete meal served on a large stainless steel plate (or very occasionally on a banana leaf). Several preparations, placed in small bowls, surround the central serving of wholewheat *chapati* and rice. A vegetarian *thali* would include *daal* (lentils), two or three curries (which can be quite hot), and crisp poppadums, although there are regional variations. A variety of pickles are offered – mango and lime are two of the most popular. These can be exceptionally hot, and are designed to be taken in minute quantities alongside the main dishes. Plain *dahi* (yoghurt), or *raita*, usually acts as a bland 'cooler'.

Western food Many city restaurants offer some so-called European options such as toasted sandwiches, stuffed pancakes, apple pies, crumbles and cheese cakes. Italian favourites (pizzas, pastas) can be very different from what you are used to. Western confectionery, in general, is disappointing. Ice creams, on the other hand, can be exceptionally good (there are excellent Indian ones as well as international brands such as *Cadbury's* and *Walls*).

Fruit India has many delicious tropical fruits. In season some of these reach Himalayan markets (eg mangoes, pineapples and lychees), while others (eg bananas, grapes, oranges) are available throughout the year. It is safe to eat the ones you can wash and peel.

Drinking water used to be regarded as one of India's biggest hazards. It is still true that water from the tap or a well should never be considered safe to drink since public water supplies are often polluted. Bottled water is now widely available although not all bottled water is mineral water; some is simply purified water from an urban supply. Buy from a shop or stall, check the seal carefully (some companies now add a second clear plastic seal around the bottle top) and avoid street hawkers; when disposing bottles puncture the neck which prevents misuse but allows recycling for storage. There is growing concern over the mountains of plastic bottles that are collecting and the waste of resources to produce them, so travellers are encouraged to use alternative methods of getting safe drinking water. In some towns (eg Dharamshala, Leh) purified water is now sold for refilling your own container. Travellers may wish to purify water themselves (see above). A portable water filter is a good option, carrying the drinking water in a plastic bottle in an insulated carrier. Always carry enough drinking water with you when travelling. It is important to use pure water for cleaning teeth.

Hot drinks Tea and coffee are safe and widely available. Both are normally served sweet, and with milk. If you wish, say 'no sugar' (*chini nahin*), 'no milk' (*dudh nahin*) when ordering. Most city restaurants will usually serve instant coffee but even in aspiring smart cafés in Delhi or Kolkata, *Espresso* or *Capuccino* may not turn out quite as one would expect in the West.

Soft drinks Bottled carbonated drinks such as 'Coke', 'Pepsi', 'Teem' and 'Gold Spot' are universally available but always check the seal when you buy from a street stall. There are now also several brands of fruit juice sold in cartons, including mango, pineapple and apple. Don't add ice cubes as the water source may be contaminated.

Alcohol Indians rarely drink alcohol with a meal, water being on hand. In the past wines and spirits were generally either imported and extremely expensive, or local and of poor quality. Now, the best Indian whisky, rum and brandy (IMFL or 'Indian Made Foreign Liquor') are widely accepted, as are good Champagnoise and other wines from Maharashtra. If you hanker after a bottle of imported wine, you will only find it in the top restaurants and have to pay Rs 800-1,000 at least.

For the urban elite, cooling Indian beers are popular when eating out and so are widely available, though you may need to check the 'chill' value. The 'English Pub' has appeared in the major cities, where the foreign traveller too would feel comfortable. Elsewhere, seedy, all male drinking dens in the larger cities are best avoided. Head for the better hotel bar instead. In rural India, local rice, palm, cashew or date juice *toddy* and *arak* should be treated with great caution. However, the Sikkimese *chhang* makes a pleasant change drunk out of a wooden tankard through a bamboo straw!

Most states have alcohol free 'dry' days, or enforce degrees of Prohibition. For 'dry' states and Liquor Permits, see page 19. Some up-market restaurants may serve beer even if it's not listed so it's worth asking.

Shopping

India excels in producing fine crafts at affordable prices through the tradition of passing down of ancestral skills. You can get handicrafts of different states from the government emporia in the major cities which guarantee quality at fixed prices (no bargaining), but many are poorly displayed, not helped by reluctant and unenthusiastic staff. Private upmarket shops and top hotel arcades offer better quality, choice and service but at a price. Vibrant and colourful local bazars (markets) are often a great experience but you must be prepared to bargain.

Export of certain items is controlled or banned (see page 24)

Drink

Essentials

Bargaining Bargaining can be fun and quite satisfying. It is best to get an idea of prices being asked by different stalls for items you are interested in, before taking the plunge. Some shopkeepers will happily quote twice the actual price to a foreigner showing interest, so you might well start by halving the asking price. On the other hand it would be inappropriate to do the same in an established shop with price-tags, though a plea for the "best price" or a "special discount" might reap results even here. Remain good humoured throughout. Walking away slowly might be the test to ascertain whether your custom is sought and you are called back!

Carpets & dhurries
Flat woven cotton dhurries in subtle colours are best seen in Rajasthan

The superb hand-knotted carpets of Kashmir, using old Persian designs woven in wool or silk or both, are hard to beat for their beauty and quality. Kashmiri traders can now be found throughout India, wherever there is hint of foreign tourism. Tibetan refugees in Darjeeling and Gangtok produce excellent carpets which are less expensive but of very high quality. They will make carpets to order and parcel post them safely.

Jewellery Whether it is chunky tribal necklaces, heavy 'silver' bangles, settings of semi precious stones the visitor is drawn to the arcade shop window as much as the way-side stall. It is best to buy from reputable shops as street stalls often pass off fake ivory, silver, gems, stones and coral as real.

Metal work The choice is vast – from brass, copper and white-metal plates and bowls with ornate patterns or plain polished surfaces, exquisite enamelled silver pill boxes, to Nawabi silver-on-gun metal Bidri pieces.

Paintings Coveted contemporary Indian art is exhibited in modern galleries in the state capitals often at a fraction of London or New York prices. Traditional Buddhist `thangka`s are painstakingly painted on silk in the high mountains while 'Mughal' miniatures, sometimes using natural pigments on old paper (don't be fooled) and new silk, are mass produced levels in Rajasthan's back alleys. Fine examples can still be found in good crafts shops.

Stoneware Artisans in Agra inspired by the Taj Mahal continue the tradition of inlaying tiny pieces of gem stones on fine white marble, to produce something for every pocket, from a small coaster to a large table top. Softer soap stone is cheaper.

Textiles Handlooms produce rich shot silk, skillful *ikat*, brocades, golden *muga* from Assam, printed silks and batiks from Bengal. *Sober* handspun *khadi*, colourful block-printed cottons using vegetable dyes and tribal weaving from remote Himalayan villages, are easier on the pocket. Kashmiri embroidery on wool is world renowned.

Wood craft Each region has its special wood – walnut in Kashmir, sandalwood in Mysore, rosewood in the South, sheesham in the North. Carving, inlay and lacquer work are specialities.

Pitfalls Taxi/rickshaw drivers and tour guides sometimes insist on recommending certain shops where they expect a commission, but prices there are invariably inflated. Some shops offer to pack and post your purchases but small private shops can't always be trusted. Unless you have a specific recommendation from a person you know, only make such arrangements in government emporia or a large store. Don't enter into any arrangement to help 'export' marble items, jewellery etc which a shopkeeper may propose by making tempting promises of passing on some of the profits to you. Several have been cheated through misuse of their credit card accounts, and being left with unwanted purchases. Make sure that credit cards are not run off more than once when making a purchase.

Holidays and festivals

In common with the whole of India, the Indian Himalya has an extraordinary wealth of festivals. Many festivals fall on different dates each year depending on the Hindu lunar calendar so check with the tourist office.

Hindus follow two distinct eras: The *Vikrama Samvat* which began in 57 BC and the *Salivahan Saka* which dates from 78 AD and has been the official Indian calendar since 1957. The *Saka* new year starts on 22 March and has the same length as the Gregorian calendar. Across North India, the New Year is celebrated in the second month of *Vaishakh*. The 29½ day lunar month with its 'dark' and 'bright' halves based on the new and full moons, are named after 12 constellations, and total a 354 day year. The calendar cleverly has an extra month (*adhik maas*) every two and a half to three years, to bring it in line with the solar year of 365 days coinciding with the Gregorian calendar of the West. The year is divided into six seasons: *Vasant* (spring), *Grishha* (summer), *Varsha* (rains), *Sharat* (early autumn), *Hemanta* (late autumn) and *Shishir* (winter).

The Hindu Calendar *For the Hindu & the corresponding Gregorian calendar months, see page 371*

Some major national and regional festivals are listed below; details of these and others appear under the particular state or town. A few count as national holidays: **26 January**: *Republic Day*; **15 August**: *Independence Day*; **2 October**: *Mahatma Gandhi's Birthday*; **25 December**: *Christmas Day*.

January 1 *New Year's Day* is accepted officially when following the Gregorian calendar but there are regional variations which fall on different dates, often coinciding with spring/harvest time in March and April: *Losar* in Ladakh, *Naba Barsha* in Bengal (14 April), *Goru* in Assam, **14** *Makar Sankranti* marks the end of winter and is celebrated with kite flying. **26** *Republic Day Parade* in New Delhi.

Major festivals & fairs

February *Vasant Panchami*, the Spring (Vasant) festival when people wear bright yellow clothes to mark the advent of the season with singing, dancing and feasting. In Bengal it is also *Saraswati Puja* when the goddess of learning is worshipped in schools, colleges, homes and community marquees. *International Yoga Festival* – Rishikesh, UP.

February-March *Maha sivaratri* marks the night when Siva danced his celestial dance of destruction (*Tandava*) celebrated with feasting and fairs at Siva temples, but preceded by a night of devotional readings and hymn singing. Orthodox Saivites fast during the day and offer prayers every three hours; devotees who remain awake through the night believe they will win the Puranic promise of prosperity and salvation.

March *Holi*, the festival of colours, marks the climax of spring. The previous night bonfires are lit in parts of North India symbolizing the end of winter (and conquering of evil). People have fun throwing coloured powder and water at each other and in the evening some gamble with friends. If you don't mind getting covered in colours, you can risk going out but celebrations can sometimes get rowdy. Some link the festival to worship of Kama the god of pleasure; some worship Krishna who defeated the demon Putana.

April *Mahavir Jayanti*. *Baisakhi* – North India.

April/May *Buddha Jayanti*, the first full moon night in April/May marks the birth of the Buddha. Celebrations are held in several parts of the country. *Sikkim Flower Festival* – Gangtok, Sikkim. *Bihu* – Assam.

Essentials

● ●

 Purnima (Full Moon)

June/July *Hemis Festival* – Leh, Ladakh.

Many religious festivals depend on the phases of the moon. Full moon days are particularly significant and can mean extra crowding and merrymaking in temple towns throughout India, and are sometimes public holidays.

July/August *Raksha (or Rakhi) Bandhan* (literally 'protection bond') commemorates the wars between *Indra* (the King of the Heavens) and the demons, when his wife tied a silk amulet around his wrist to protect him from harm. The festival symbolizes the bond between brother and sister, celebrated

● ●

mainly in North India at full-moon. A sister says special prayers for her brother and ties coloured (silk) threads around his wrist to remind him of the special bond. He in turn gives a gift and promises to protect and care for her. **15 August** *Independence Day*, a national secular holiday. In cities it is marked by special events, and in Delhi there is an impressive flag hoisting ceremony at the Red Fort. *Ganesh Chaturthi.* The elephant-headed God of good omen is shown special reverence. On the last of the five-day festival after harvest, clay images of Ganesh (Ganpati) are taken in procession with dancers and musicians, and are immersed in the sea, river or pond.

August/September *Janmashtami*, the birth of Krishna is celebrated at midnight at Krishna temples.

September/October *Dasara* has many local variations. In North India, celebrations for the nine nights *(navaratri)* are marked with *Ramlila*, various episodes of the Ramayana story (see section on Hinduism, page 211) are enacted and recited, with particular reference to the battle between the forces of good and evil. In some parts of India it celebrates *Rama*'s victory over the Demon king *Ravana* of Lanka with the help of loyal *Hanuman* (Monkey). Huge effigies of *Ravana* made of bamboo and paper are burnt on the 10th day (*Vijaya dasami*) of *Dasara* in public open spaces. In other regions the focus is on Durga's victory over the demon *Mahishasura*. Bengal celebrates *Durga* puja. An oil lamp is kept alight for the nine days and nights. On each night Durga takes a new form, armed with a different weapon for her battle with the demon *Mahisasura* who threatened all the gods. She finally succeeds in slaying the demon on the 10th day.

October/November 2 October *Gandhi Jayanti*, Mahatma Gandhi's birthday is remembered with prayer meetings and devotional singing. Diwali/Deepavali (the Sanskrit Di-pa lamp), the festival of lights, is celebrated particularly in North India. Some Hindus celebrate Krishna's victory over the demon Narakasura, some Rama's return after his 14 years' exile in the forest when citizens lit his way with earthen oil lamps. It falls on the dark *chaturdasi* (14th) night (the one preceding the new moon), when rows of lamps or candles are lit in remembrance, and *rangolis* are painted on the floor as a sign of welcome. Fireworks have become an integral part of the celebration which are often set off days before Diwali. Equally, Lakshmi, the Goddess of Wealth (as well as Ganesh) is worshipped by merchants and the business community, who open the new year's account on the day. Most people wear new clothes; some play games of chance. In Bengal *Kali Puja* is celebrated the day before Diwali but is a wholly distinct festival.

25 December *Christmas Day*, Indian Christians celebrate the birth of Christ in much the same way as in the West; many churches hold services/mass at midnight. **31 December** *New Year's Eve* Each year hotel prices peak during this period and large supplements are added for meals in the upper category hotels. Some churches mark the night with a *Midnight Mass*.

These are fixed according to the lunar calendar, see page 373. According to the Gregorian calendar, they tend to fall 11 days earlier each year, dependent on the sighting of the new moon.

Ramadan . Start of the month of fasting when all Muslims (except young children, the very elderly, the sick, pregnant women and travellers) must abstain from food and drink, from sunrise to sunset.

Id ul Fitr. The three-day festival marks the end of Ramadan.

Id-ul-Zuha/Bakr-Id. Muslims commemorate Ibrahim's sacrifice of his son according to God's commandment; the main time of pilgrimage to Mecca (the Hajj). It is marked by the sacrifice of a goat, feasting and alms giving.

Muharram when the killing of the Prophet's grandson, Hussain, is commemorated by Shi'a Muslims. Decorated *tazias* (replicas of the martyr's tomb) are carried in procession by devout wailing followers who beat their chests to express their grief. Shi'as fast for the 10 days.

Entertainment

Despite an economic boom in cities like Delhi and the rapid growth of a young business class, India's night life remains meagre, focused on club discos in the biggest hotels. More traditional, popular entertainment is widespread across Indian villages in the form of folk drama, dance and music, each region having its own styles, and open air village performance being common. The hugely popular Hindi film industry comes largely out of this tradition. It's always easy to find a cinema, but prepare for a long sitting with a standard story line and set of characters and lots of action. See also pages 52 for spectator sports and 382.

Sport and special interest travel

The Himalaya have perhaps the greatest potential for sport and adventure travel in the world, yet the opportunities are as yet still little developed. Mountaineering itself has been by far the most important single sporting activity during the last century, and trekking has now become popular in several areas of the Indian Himalaya. Today specialist operators offer activities ranging from skiing - near Manali or Kufri, for example - to hang-gliding, white water rafting and mountain biking. With the exception of a few trekking routes it is essential to seek advice and to go as part of a group or organised tour (see below).

The snow-fed rivers which flow through Kashmir, Himachal, Uttar Pradesh and Sikkim offer excellent white water rafting. The options range from a half-day trip to one lasting several days, and again allows a chance to see scenery, places and people off the beaten track. The trips are organized and managed by professional teams who have trained abroad. The Ganga and its tributaries offer the most developed white water rafting in the Indian Himalaya. Between October and April from a base camp at Beasi-Shivpuri just 70 km from Rishikesh is a set of Grade III and IV rapids. Further into the mountains near Deoprayag there are Grade IV and V rapids on the Alaknanda and Bhagirathi, tributaries of the Ganga itself. Much further north in the arid regions of Ladakh and Zanskar you have to wait until the monsoon season from July to September for the Indus and Zanskar rivers to become accessible, and further west the Chenab has nearly 230 km of superb Grade IV and V rafting, open through November to March. In the east, the Tista and Rangit also have excellent stretches open after the monsoon, between October and April.

White water rafting
The rivers can sometimes be dangerous except when low in Aug & Sep

Fishing Fishing is popular in both the western and the eastern Himalaya, the famous mahseer being found all the way from the Indus system to the Brahmaputra. The Rivers Beas and Jhelum in Himachal, and Jammu and Kashmir respectively, the Ganga above Tehri in Uttaranchal, and the Bhoreli in Arunachal and Manas in Assam all offer excellent fishing opportunities for trout and mahseer.

Bird watching The country's diverse and rich natural habitats harbour over 1,200 species of birds of which around 150 are endemic. Visitors to the Himalayan region can enjoy spotting Oriental species whether it is in towns and cities, in the country side or more abundantly in the national parks and sanctuaries. The highlands are ideal between May and June and again after the monsoons when visibility improves in October and November. Water bodies large and small draw visiting water fowl from other continents during the winter.

A Birdwatcher's Guide to India by Krys Kazmierczak and Raj Singh, published by Prion Ltd, Sandy, Bedfordshire, UK, 1998, is well researched and comprehensive with helpful practical information and maps.

Yoga & mediatation There has been a growing Western interest in the ancient life-disciplines in search of physical and spiritual wellbeing, as practised in ancient India. Yoga is supposed to regulate the nervous system and aims to attain perfect equilibrium through the practice of *asanas* (body postures), breath control, discipline, cleansing, contemplation and awareness. It seeks to achieve moral purification through abstinence and restraint (dietary and sexual). Meditation which complements yoga to relieve stress, increase awareness and bring inner peace prescribes *dhyana* (purposeful concentration) by withdrawing oneself from external distractions and focusing ones attention to consciousness itself, which leads ultimately to *samadhi* (release from worldly bonds). At the practical level *Hatha Yoga* has captured the Western imagination as it promises good health through postural exercises, while the search for inner peace and calm drive others to learn meditation techniques.

Centres across the country offer courses for beginners and practitioners. Some are at special resort hotels which offer all inclusive packages in idyllic locations, some advocate simple communal living in an ashram while others may require rigorous discipline in austere monastic surroundings. Whether you wish to embark on a serious study of yoga or sample an hour's introductory meditation session, India offers opportunities for all though you may need to apply in advance for some popular courses. Popular centres in places frequented by travellers are listed thoughout the book. The *International Yoga Festival* is held in Rishikesh in the Himalayan foothills, each February.

Biking For those keen on moving faster along the road, discover the joys of travelling on the two wheels of a motorbike (preferably a 'Bullet'). See page 38.

Spectator sports

Cricket Sport has become one of India's greatest popular entertainments. Cricket has almost a fanatical following across India. Reinforced by satellite TV and radio, and a national side that enjoys high world rankings and much outstanding individual talent, cricket has become a national obsession. Stars have cult status, and you can see children trying to model themselves on their game on any and every open space.

Soccer Soccer is played from professional level to kickabout in any open space. Professional matches are played in large stadia attracting vast crowds; the latter holds 40,000 spectators. The season is from October to March and details of matches are published in the local papers. The top class game tickets are Rs 25, but they are sold for much more on the black market. The crowds generate tremendous fervour for the big matches, and standards are improving. African players are now featuring more frequently with Indian teams and monthly salaries have risen to over Rs 40,000 per month, a very good wage by Indian standards.

Trekking

The Himalaya offers unlimited opportunities to view not only the natural beauty of mountains and the unique flora and fauna, but also the diverse groups of people who live in the ranges and valleys, many of whom have retained unique cultural identities because of their isolation. The treks described in this Handbook are only for guidance. They try to give you a flavour of an area or a destination. Some trails fall within the 'Inner Line' for which special **permits** are required. Other parts of India offer attractive options for hikers.

Independent trekking There are some outstandingly beautiful treks, though they are often not through the 'wilderness' sometimes conjured up. However, trekking alone is not recommended as you will be in unfamiliar territory where you may not be able to communicate with the local people and if injured you may not have help at hand. Independent trekkers should get a specialist publication with detailed route descriptions and a good map. Remember, mountain topography is subject to constant change, and tracks and crossings can be affected very rapidly. Speak to those who know the area well and have been trekking to the places you intend visiting.

Types of trekking

Backpacking camping Hundreds of people arrive each year with a pack and some personal equipment, buy some food and set off trekking, carrying their own gear and choosing their own campsites or places to stay. Serious trekkers will need a framed backpack. Supplies of fuel wood are scarce and flat ground suitable for camping rare. It is not always easy to find isolated and 'private' campsites.

Trekking without a tent Although common in Nepal, only a few trails in India offer the ease and comfort of this option. Exceptions are the Singalila Ridge trail in the Darjeeling area, the Sikkim Kanchenjunga trek, the Markha Valley trek in Ladakh and some lower elevation trails around Shimla and Manali. On these, it is often possible to stay in 'trekking huts' or in simple village homes. You carry clothes and bedding, as with youth hostelling, and for a few rupees a night you get a space on the floor, a wooden pallet or a camp bed, or in the more luxurious inns, a room and shower. The food is simple, usually vegetable curry, rice and *daal* which although repetitive, is healthy and can be tasty. This approach brings you into more contact with the local population, the limiting factor being the routes where accommodation is available.

Locally organized treks Porters can usually be hired through an agent in the town or village at the start of a trek. They will help carry your baggage, sometimes cook for you, and communicate with the local people. A good porter will know the area and some can tell you about local customs and point out interesting details en route. Away from roads, the footpath is the principal line of communication between villages. Tracks tend to be very good, well graded and in good condition. In remoter areas away from all habitation, tracks may be indistinct and a local guide is recommended. Although some porters speak a little English (or another foreign language) you may have communication problems and misunderstandings. Remember, you may be expected to provide your porter's warm clothing and protective wear including shoes, gloves and goggles on high altitude treks.

Porters hired in the bazar may be cheaper than agency porters but may be unreliable. Make sure they are experienced in carrying loads over distances at high altitude

Hiring a *sardar* and crew is more expensive but well worthwhile since he will speak some English, act as a guide, take care of engaging porters and cooks, arrange for provisions and sort out all logistical problems. A *sardar* will cost more and although he may be prepared to carry a load, his principal function will be as a guide and overseer for the porters. Make sure your *sardar* is experienced in the area you will be travelling in and can show good references which are his own and not borrowed. An older, experienced man is often more reliable.

Using a trekking agent Trekking agents based in Delhi or at hill stations (eg Dehradun, Shimla, Manali, Dharamshala, Leh, Darjeeling, Gangtok) will organize treks for a fee and provide a *sardar*, porters, cooks, food and equipment, but it requires effort and careful thought on your part. This method can be excellent and is recommended for a group, preferably with some experience, that wants to follow a specific itinerary.

You have to follow a pre-arranged itinerary in some areas, as required by the government, and also as porters expect to arrive at certain points on schedule.

You can make arrangements from abroad in advance; often a protracted business with faxes and emails. Alternatively, wait until you get to India but allow at least a week to make arrangements.

Fully organized and escorted trek A company or individual with local knowledge and expertise organizes a trip and sells it. Some or all camp equipment, food, cooking, planning the stages, decision-making based on progress and weather conditions, liaison with porters, shopkeepers etc are all taken care of. When operating abroad, the agency may take care of all travel arrangements, ticketing, visas and permits. Make sure that both you and the trekking company understand exactly who is to provide what equipment. This has the advantage of being a good, safe introduction to the country. You will be able to travel with limited knowledge of the region and its culture and get to places more easily which as an individual you might not reach, without the expense of completely kitting yourself out. You should read and follow any advice in the preparatory material you are sent, as your enjoyment greatly depends on it. This applies particularly to recommendations concerning physical fitness.

An escorted trek involves going with a group; you will camp together but not necessarily all walk together. If you are willing to trade some of your independence for careful, efficient organization and make the effort to ensure the group works well together, the experience can be very rewarding. Ideally there should be no more than 20 trekkers (preferably around 12). Companies have reputations to maintain and try to comply with western concepts of hygiene. Before booking, check the itinerary (is it too demanding, or not adventurous enough?), whether the leader is qualified and is familiar with the route, and what exactly is provided by way of equipment.

Local agents Tourist offices and government approved trekking agents in **New Delhi** and the hill stations will organize fairly inexpensive treks (on some routes, it is compulsory to trek in this way). Tour operators and travel agents are listed in each town. The following are recommended: *Ibex Expeditions*, G-66 East of Kailash, T6912641, F6846403, www.ibexpeditions.com; *Mercury Himalayan Explorations*, Jeevan Tara Bldg, Parliament St, T3732866; *Peak Adventure Tours*, T-305 DAV Bldg, DDA Shopping Complex, Magur Vihar Phase-1, T2711284, F2711292, peakadv@nde.vsnl.net.in (also mountain biking, see page 38); *Wanderlust*, M 51-52 Palika Bhawan, opposite Hyatt Regency, T6875200, T6885188, travel.wanter@axcess.net.in In **Dehra Dun**, *Garhwal Tours & Trekking*, 151 Araghar, T/F627769.

The following government organizations can advise and organize treks: *Garhwal Mandal Vikas Nigam*, Kailash Gate, By Pass Rd, Rishikesh, T431793, F430372; *Kumaon Mandal Vikas Nigam*, Secretariat, Mallital, Nainital, T/F36209. *Himalayan Mountaineering Institutes* in hill stations in UP and Himachal and Darjeeling, West Bengal.

• •

Himalayan environment trust code of practice

Campsite Leave it cleaner than you found it.

Deforestation Make no open fires and discourage others making one for you. Limit use of firewood and heated water and use only permitted dead wood. Choose accommodation where kerosene or fuel-efficient wood burning stoves are used.

Litter Remove it. Burn or bury paper and carry away non-degradable litter. If you find other people's litter, remove their's too! Pack food in biodegradable containers. Carry away all batteries/cells.

Water Keep local water clean. Do not use detergents and pollutants in streams and springs. Where there are no toilets be sure you are at least 30 m away from water source and bury or cover. Do not allow cooks or porters to throw rubbish in nearby streams and rivers.

Plants Do not take cuttings, seeds and roots – it is illegal in all parts of the Himalaya.

Begging Giving to children encourages begging.

Donations to a project, health centre or school are more constructive.

Be aware of **local traditions and cultures**; respect their **privacy**, and ask permission before taking photographs; respect their **holy places**, never touching or removing religious objects, and removing shoes before entering temples; be aware of local **etiquette**, dressing modestly particularly when visiting temples and shrines and while walking through villages avoiding shorts, skimpy tops and tight-fitting outfits. Do not hold hands and kiss in public.

Essentials

• •

These, having contacts with agents in India, offer relatively expensive trips to include food, porters, cooks, *sardar* (guide), mess and toilet tents.

Foreign operators

Australia *Adventures Abroad*, T01-800-890790, info@adventures-abroad.com *Adventure World*, 73 Walker St, N Sydney, PO Box 480, T9567766. *Travel Corp of India*, 7 Bridge St, Balmain 2041, Sydney, NSW, T5551079. *World Expeditions*, 441 Kent St, T264336 (also mountain biking.) **Canada** *Adventures Abroad*, 2148-20800 Westminster Highway, Richmond, BC, V6V 2W3, T1-800 6653998. *Canadian Himalayan Expeditions*, 2 Toronto St, Suite 302, Toronto, Ontario, M5C 2B6, T3604300. *Trek Holidays*, 8412-109 St, Edmonton, Alberta, T6G 13Z, T4390024. **Denmark** *Everest Travels*, Vesterbrogade 11 A, 2 van. DK-1620, Copenhagen V, T33-212160, F35-212125. *Inter-Travel*, Fredriksholms Kanal 2, DK 1220, Copenhagen K, T33-150077.**France** *Nouvelle Frontières*, 87 Blvd de Grenelle, 75015 Paris, T730568. *Peuple du Mode*, 10 rue de Montmorency, 75003, Paris, T725036. *Voyageurs en Inde*, 45 rue St-Anne, 75001 Paris, T617708. **Germany** *Fargo Tours*, Frauenlob Str 26, München 80337, T532080. *Mercury Himalayan Explorations*, 6 Kurhessenstrasse, 6000 Frankfurt/Main 50, T512620. **Netherlands** *Ganesh Reizen*, Lijsterstraat 27, 3514 TA Utrecht, T719239. *Snow Leopard Reizen*, Calandplein 3, 2521 AB, Den Haag, T070-3882867. **Ireland** *Club Travel*, 30 Lower Abbey St, Dublin 1, T729922. *Maxwells*, D'Olier Chambers, 1 Hawkins St, Dublin 2, T6779479.**Japan** *Mercury Himalayan Explorations*, 204 Villa Hirose, 2-30-2 Yoyogi Shibuya-Ku-Tokyo, T3757908. **New Zealand** *Adventure World*, 101 Gt South Rd, Remuera, Auckland, DX69501, T5245118. *Himalayan Travellers*, PO Box 2618, Wellington, T863325. **Sweden** *Himalayaresor*, Box 17, 123 21 Farsta, Stockholm, T6055760. **Switzerland** *Nouvelle Frontières*, Chantepoulet 10, 1201 Genève. Suntrek, Birmensdorferstr 187, CH-8003, Zurich, T01 -4626161. **UK** *Adventures Abroad,* T0114 2473400, www.adventures_abroad.com *Exodus*, T020-8675 5550, T020-87723822, www.exodus.co.uk, sales@exodustravels.co.uk (also mountain biking). *Explore*

Worldwide, T01252-760100, info@explore.co.uk *High Places*, T0114-2757500, highp@globalnet.co.uk *Himalayan Kingdoms*, T0117-9237163, 10146.2022@compu serve.com *KE Adventures*, T01768-773966, keadventure@enterprise.net *Sherpa Expedition*, T020-85772717, sherpasales@dialpipex.com **USA** *Mercury Himalayan Explorations*, NY, T6610380, F9835692. *Sita World Travel*, 8127 San Fernando Rd, Sun Valley Ca 91352, and 9001 Airport Blvd No 202, Houston TX 77061, T6260134. SnowLion Expeditions, Oquirrh Pl, 350 South 400 East, Salt Lake City, T801-3556555. *Tiger Tops International*, 2627 Lombard St, San Francisco, CA 94123, T3463402.

Trekking seasons

These vary with the area you plan to visit and the elevation. Autumn is best in most parts of the Himalaya though March to May can be pleasant. The monsoons (mid-June to end-September) can obviously be very wet and localized thunderstorms can occur at any time, particularly in the spring and summer. Start your trek early in the morning as the monsoon approaches. It often continues to rain heavily up to mid-October in the eastern Himalaya. The Kullu valley is unsuitable for trekking during the monsoons but areas beyond the central Himalayan range, eg Ladakh, Zanskar, Lahul and Spiti are largely unaffected. Be prepared for extremes in temperatures in all seasons so come prepared with light clothing as well as enough waterproof protection. Winters can be exceptionally cold; high passes can be closed and you need more equipment. Winter treks on all but a few low-altitude ones (up to 3,200 m) are only recommended for the experienced trekker accompanied by a knowledgeable local guide.

Western Himalaya

Garhwal & Kumaon Himalaya Uttar Pradesh (pages 120-123) This area is an all-season trekking destination because of its variety of climate and terrain. It is perhaps best in May-June when days are cool and clear. Even with the onset of the monsoons when mist covers the mountains you may get breaks in the rain of three or four days. Clouds can lift to give you some good mountain views but equipment may feel a little damp. The mountains are best for flowers in July-August. Late September to mid-November is again good for trekking.

Himachal (pages 213-219) The best times are as in Garhwal and Kumaon. The monsoon (mid-July to mid-September) is generally very wet and offer no mountain views. Trekking is usually possible from May to October when most passes are open (the Parvati Pass may be blocked until early July). In July-September high altitude flowers are in bloom including summer rhododendrons.

Kashmir (Kashmir, currently risky because of the political situation, Ladakh, page 255 and Zanskar, page 259) Trekking is ideal between April-November. In Ladakh (the area open to trekkers), the motorable road from Manali to Leh is normally open from mid-June to October though flights to Leh from Delhi operate all year round. Most treks cross passes above 4,500 m and are passable from early July to September.

Eastern Himalaya

Darjeeling area (pages 279-286) April-May has a chance of occasional showers but the rhododendrons and magnolias are in full bloom; October-November is usually dry with excellent visibility. Early December is possible but very cold.

Sikkim (pages 309-312) Mid-February to late May and again October-early December are possible; April-May, October-November are best.

Arunachal October to February is best for trekking in this remote wilderness.

Leeches

When trekking in the monsoon, beware of leeches. They usually stay on the ground waiting for a passerby and get in boots when you are walking. Then when they are gorged with blood they drop off.

Don't try pulling one off as the head will be left behind and cause infection. Put some salt (or hold a lighted cigarette to it)

which will make it quickly fall off. It helps to spray socks and bootlaces with an insect repellent before starting off in the morning.

Leeches are generally absent in Kashmir, Ladakh, Lahul and Himachal as the trekking areas there are too cool for them.

The Sierra Club motto is worth remembering: 'Leave only footprints, take only photographs'. Burn or bury litter and insist that guides and porters do the same. Don't use firewood and discourage others. Carry away all that is not biodegradable. When trekking, don't give money, cigarettes, sweets etc indiscriminately, but do give alms to pilgrims and holy men. Don't swim or bathe nude in rivers or hot springs. See also box.

Ecology, conservation & etiquette

Health You will probably experience mountain sickness in its mildest form if you go much over 3,000 m (very occasionally at lower altitudes). It is best to move at a slow pace and take plenty of rest and fluids. See page 64 for details.

Being prepared

Security Thefts and muggings are very rare but on the increase. Guard your money at the point of departure. Keep your valuables with you at all times, make sure the tent 'doors' are closed when you are going for meals, and lock your room door in lodges. Be particularly careful with rucksacks carried atop buses on long journeys – always keep a watch on them when other passengers are loading/unloading their belongings. Be particularly careful of pickpockets at the start of a trek. Thieves sometimes hang around groups of trekkers knowing that many will be carrying all their money for the trek in cash.

Trekking is permitted in all areas other than those described as Restricted or Protected and within the '**Inner Line**', so that you may not go close to the international boundary in many places. Often, destinations falling within these 'sensitive' zones which have recently been opened for trekking, require treks to be organized by a recognized Indian Travel Agent for groups of at least four, travelling on a specified route, accompanied by a representative/liaison officer. Sometimes there are restrictions on the maximum number of days, season and type of transport used. The 'Inner Line' runs parallel and 40 km inside the international boundary; Kaza (Himachal Pradesh), however, is now open to group trekkers though overnight stay is not allowed at Puh, Khabo or Sumdo. Other areas now open to tourists include Kalindi Khal (Garhwal), Milam Glacier (Kumaon), Khardung La, Tso Moriri and Pangong (Ladakh), Tsangu Lake, Lachung and Yumthang (Sikkim) and Kameng Valley (Arunachal Pradesh).

Trekking permits
Always carry your passport. Without one you can be turned back or, if in a restricted area, be deported at one of the regular trekking permit inspection points

On arrival in India, Government approved trekking agencies can obtain permits relatively easily, usually within three or four days. It can be much slower applying for trekking permits from abroad and may also slow down your visa application.

Some restricted areas are still totally closed to foreigners. For other restricted areas, permits are issued at the Foreigners' Regional Registration Offices in Delhi, Mumbai, Kolkata and Chennai (and sometimes at a local FRRO), from Immigration officers at some points of entry, and sometimes at the District Magistrate's.

There are also entrance fees for the various national parks and conservation areas which can be as much as Rs 350.

Mountaineering courses Information on mountaineering is available from *Indian Mountaineering Federation*, Benito Juarez Marg, New Delhi. Courses in mountaineering, skiing, high altitude trekking and mountain-rescue are offered by: *Mountaineering Institute and Allied Sports Complex*, 1.5 km out of Manali; *Garhwal Mandal Vikas Nigam* (GMVN), Muni-ki-Reti, Rishikesh; *Himalayan Mountaineering Institute*, Nehru Hill, Darjeeling; *The Nehru Institute of Mountaineering*, Uttarkashi.

Equipment & clothing If you have good equipment, it is worth taking it, especially your own boots. Mountaineering and trekking equipment can sometimes be hired from various hill stations. Ask the *Institutes of Mountaineering* and tourist offices there. Guard against cold, wet, sudden changes of temperature, strong sun and wind! Waterproof jacket with hood and over-trousers (windproof, waterproof and 'breather' type); warm sweater; 'fleece' jacket; tracksuit; hiking trousers or shorts (knee length but not cycling); cotton T shirts; cotton underwear; thermal underwear (vests, longjohns); gloves; balaclava or ski toque; sun hat; swimwear. Try to carry lightweight, quick-drying fabrics that can be easily washed in cold water streams. (After the trek, you might consider offering clothes you can part with to your porter.) Good lightweight walking boots with ankle support should be comfortable and well worn in, as blisters can ruin a trek; spare laces, good trainers (for resting the feet; also suitable for many low-level treks except in snow and off-the-trails); polypropylene undersocks, heavy walking socks. Sunglasses (with UV filter), snow glasses if you are planning to go above the snow line, high-factor sun block (15+), lip cream, a good sleeping bag (cheap ones from a local market are unsuitable above 4,000 m) plus cotton liner, a Thermarest pad or a double thickness foam sleeping mat, two metres square plastic sheet (sold locally), torch (flashlight) with replacement batteries or a Petzl headtorch, a compass, binoculars, insulated bag water-bottle (to also take to bed!), a day pack, a tent (in certain areas). Those expecting to climb high, cross glaciers etc may need to hire crampons, ice axes, snow gaiters, ropes etc as well as a silver survival blanket and a reinforced plastic 'bivouac bag'. A kerosene stove and strong fuel container suitable for high altitudes (kerosene is widely available); water filter and containers; nesting cooking pots (at least two); enamel mug and spoon and bags for provisions. Be sure to eat a balanced diet. Local foods will be available along the trail, and in fact the porters' meal of *chapati* or rice, vegetables, daal and sweet milky tea is quite nutritious. Some shops stock limited amounts of dry goods for trekkers (noodles, chocolate bars, canned foods, fruit, nuts, porridge etc). You might prefer to take some freeze-dried packs of favourites from home. Remember to thoroughly boil the fresh (unpasteurized) local milk.

Books **Chris Bonnington** *Annapurna South Face*, London, Cassell, 1971; *Everest the hard way*, London, Hodder & Stoughton, 1979 and **Edmund Hillary** *High Adventure*, New York, Dutton, 1955. Both classic accounts of Himalayan climbs. **P Chabloz and N Cremieu** *Hiking in Zanskar and Ladakh*, Geneva, Olizane, and Artou, 1986. **G Chand and M Puri** *Explore Himachal*, New Delhi, International Publishers, 1991. Descriptions of 110 routes and 27 detailed trekking maps. **Charles Genoud** *Ladakh, Zanskar*, Artou, Leh. **T Iozawa** *Trekking in the Himalayas*, Delhi, Allied Publishers, 1980. **GD Khosla** *Himalayan circuit*, OUP, 1989. *Nest & Wings*, Post Box 4531, New Delhi 110016, T6442245: 'Trekking', 'Holiday & Trekking' and 'Trekking Map' titles (Rs 40-140) cover most trekking destinations in the Indian Himalaya; trekking itineraries are listed in brief but some booklets give additional insight into the history and culture of the area. **Charlie Loram** *Leh & trekking in Ladakh*. Trailblazer, Hindhead, Surrey, UK. 1996. **Audrey Salkeld** *The History of Great Climbs*, The Royal Geographical Society, 1995. A magnificently illustrated and written account of historic climbs.

Hugh Swift *Trekking in Pakistan and India*, London, Hodder & Stoughton, 1990. Detailed practical guide, based on extensive first hand experience. Also useful are **Himalayan Club's** *Himalayan Journal* (annual) from PO Box 1905, Mumbai 400001, and

Indian Mountaineering Foundation's *Indian Mountaineer* (six-monthly) from Benito Juarez Rd, New Delhi 110021. Also see Further reading page 67.

Maps

Survey of India has started producing trekking maps, Scale 1:250,000; a few only are available covering the Himachal and UP areas. For details see page 70. **Leomann** Indian Himalaya maps (1:200,000) cover UP, Himachal Pradesh and Jammu and Kashmir in eight sheets (1987-1994), and give descriptive itineraries of trekking routes. The **US Army Series (AMS)** U502 at the scale of 1:250,000 are available from selected booksellers in the United States and Europe. Showing contours at 250 or 500 ft, the series was completed before 1960, so some features, notably roads, are out of date. However, they provide good topographic information. For sources outside India please see Maps page 70.

Essentials

Photography
See also page 29

The wealth of photographic opportunity justifies good equipment. The following are recommended: a single reflex camera with interchangeable lenses; wide angle (28-35mm), tele-photo (70-200), macro lens (for good close-ups); ultra-violet and a polarising filter for high altitudes; plenty of film (a roll a day!) and extra batteries (they are affected by very low temperatures); waterproof covering for all equipment. Take advice on taking pictures of snow so as not to produce over exposed pictures.

Health

Travellers to Himalayan India are exposed to health risks not encountered in Western Europe or North America. Because much of the area is economically underdeveloped, serious infectious diseases are common, as they were in the West some decades ago. Obviously, business travellers staying in international hotels and tourists on organized tours face different health risks to travellers backpacking through rural areas. There are no absolute rules to follow; you will often have to make your own judgement on the healthiness of your surroundings. With suitable precautions you should stay healthy.

There are many well qualified doctors in India, most of whom speak English, but the quality and range of medical care diminishes rapidly as you leave the major cities. If you are in a major city, your embassy may be able to recommend a list of doctors. If you are a long way from medical help, some self-treatment may be needed. You are more than likely to find many drugs with familiar names on sale. Always buy from a reputable source, and check date stamping. Vaccines in particular have a much reduced shelf-life if not stored properly. Locally produced drugs may be unreliable because of poor quality control and the substitution of inert ingredients for active drugs.

Before you go

Take out good medical insurance. Check exactly what the level of cover is for specific eventualities, in particular whether a flight home is covered in case of an emergency, whether the insurance company will pay any medical expenses directly or whether you have to pay and then claim them back, and whether specific activities such as trekking or climbing are covered. If visiting for a while have a dental check up. Take spare glasses (or at least a glasses prescription) and/or lenses, if you wear them. If you have a long-standing medical problem such as diabetes, heart trouble, chest trouble or high blood pressure, get advice from your doctor, and carry sufficient medication to last the full duration of your trip. You may want to ask your doctor for a letter explaining your condition.

Self-medication may be forced on you by circumstances so the following text contains the names of drugs and medicines which you may find useful in an emergency or in out-of-the-way places. You may like to take some of the following items with you from home: **anti-infective ointment** eg cetrimide; **dusting powder** for feet, containing fungicide; **antacid tablets; antibiotics** (ask your GP); **anti-malarial tablets**; **painkillers** (paracetamol or aspirin); **rehydration salts** packets plus anti-diarrhoea preparations; **travel sickness tablets; first aid kit** including a couple of sterile syringes and needles and disposable gloves (available from camping shops) in case of an emergency.

Travelling with children Children get dehydrated very quickly in hot countries and can become drowsy and uncooperative unless cajoled to drink water or juice plus salts. The treatment of diarrhoea is the same for adults, except that it should start earlier for children and be continued with more persistence. Colds, catarrh and ear infections are also common so take suitable antibiotics. To help young children to take anti-malarial tablets, one suggestion is to crush them between spoons and mix with a teaspoon of dessert chocolate (for cake-making) bought in a tube.

Vaccination & immunization If you require travel vaccinations see your doctor well in advance of your travel. Most courses must be completed in a minimum of four weeks. Travel clinics may provide rapid courses of vaccination, but are likely to be more expensive. The following vaccinations are recommended:

Typhoid This disease is spread by the insanitary preparation of food. A single dose injection is now available (*Typhim Vi*) that provides protection for up to three years. A vaccine taken by mouth in three doses is also available, but the timing of doses can be a problem and protection only lasts for one year.

Polio Protection is by a live vaccine generally given orally, and a full course consists of three doses with a booster every five years.

Tetanus If you have not been vaccinated before, one dose of vaccine should be given with a booster at six weeks and another at six months. Ten yearly boosters are strongly recommended. Children should, in addition, be properly protected against diphtheria, mumps and measles.

Infectious Hepatitis If you are not immune to hepatitis A already, the best protection is vaccination with *Havrix*. A single dose gives protection for at least a year, while a booster taken six months after the initial injection extends immunity to at least 10 years. If you are not immune to hepatitis B, the vaccine Energix is highly effective. It consists of three injections over six months before travelling. A combined hepatitis A & B vaccine is now licensed and available.

Malaria For details of malaria prevention, see below.

The following vaccinations may also be considered:

Tuberculosis The disease is still common in the region. Consult your doctor for advice on BCG inoculation.

Meningococcal Meningitis and Diphtheria If you are staying in the country for a long time, vaccination should be considered.

Japanese B Encephalitis (JBE) Immunization (effective in 10 days) gives protection for around three years. There is an extremely small risk in India, though it varies seasonally and from region to region. Consult a travel clinic or your family doctor.

Rabies Vaccination before travel gives anyone bitten more time to get treatment (so particularly helpful for those visiting remote areas), and also prepares the body to produce antibodies quickly. The cost of the vaccine can be shared by three persons receiving vaccination together.

Smallpox, **Cholera** and **Yellow Fever** Vaccinations are not required, although you may be asked to show a vaccination certificate if you have been in a country affected by yellow fever immediately prior to travelling to India.

You can get all your injections done at your local surgery for a fee but you will need to give them some notice. If you are in London, you have a choice. *Nomad*, c/o STA, 40 Bernard St, Russell Square, London WC1, T020-78334114, and 3-4 Wellington Terrace, Turnpike Lane, London N8, T020-88897014, operates a small clinic with a visiting pharmacist twice a week, free advice on preventative treatment; medicines and vaccinations are available at the Dispensary. *British Airways Travel Clinic*, Harrow, Middx, offers a similar service on weekdays. All this is cheaper at the *Hospital for Tropical Diseases*, 4 St Pancras Way, London, N1 0PE, T020-72889600, 0900-1630 (call for an appointment).

On the road

Intestinal upsets are due, most of the time, to the insanitary preparation of food. Do not eat uncooked fish, vegetables or meat (especially pork, though this is highly unlikely in India), fruit with the skin on (always peel fruit yourself), or food that is exposed to flies (particularly salads).

Intestinal upsets

   Shellfish eaten raw are risky and at certain times of the year some fish and shellfish concentrate toxins from their environment and cause various kinds of food poisoning.

   Tap water should be assumed to be unsafe, especially in the monsoon; the same goes for stream or well water. Bottled mineral water is now widely available, although not all bottled water is mineral water; some is simply purified water from an urban supply. If your hotel has a central hot water supply, this is generally safe to drink after cooling. Ice for drinks should be made from boiled water but rarely is, so stand your drink on the ice cubes rather than putting them in your drink. For details on water purification, see box.

   Heat treated **milk** is widely available, as is ice cream produced by the same methods. Unpasteurized milk products, including cheese, are sources of tuberculosis, brucellosis, listeria and other food poisoning germs. You can render fresh milk safe by heating it to 62°C for 30 minutes, followed by rapid cooling or by boiling. Matured or processed cheeses are safer than fresh varieties.

   Diarrhoea is usually the result of food poisoning, occasionally from contaminated water. There are various causes: viruses, bacteria or protozoa (like amoeba and giardia). It may take one of several forms, coming on suddenly, or rather slowly. It may be accompanied by vomiting or by severe abdominal pain and the passage of blood or mucus with stools. How do you know which type you have and how do you treat them?

   All kinds of diarrhoea, whether or not accompanied by vomiting, respond favourably to the replacement of water and salts taken as frequent small sips of some kind of rehydration solution. Proprietary preparations, consisting of sachets of powder which you dissolve in water (ORS, or Oral Rehydration Solution) are widely available in India, although it is recommended that you bring some of your own. They can also be made by adding half a teaspoonful of salt (3½ g) and four tablespoonfuls of sugar (40 g) to a litre of safe drinking water.

   If you can time the onset of diarrhoea to the minute, then it is probably viral or bacterial, and/or the onset of dysentery. The treatment, in addition to rehydration, is Ciprofloxacin (500 mg every 12 hours). The drug is now widely available. If the diarrhoea has come on slowly or intermittently, then it is more likely to be protozoal (ie caused by amoeba or giardia). These cases are best treated by a doctor, as should any diarrhoea continuing for more than three days. If medical facilities are remote a short course of high dose Metronidazole (*Flagyl*) may provide relief. This drug is widely available in India, although it is best to bring a course with you after discussion with your family doctor. If there are severe stomach cramps, the following drugs may sometimes help: *Loperamide* (*Imodium*, *Arret*) and *Diphenoxylate* with *Atropine* (*Lomotil*).

Essentials

Essentials

 Water purification

There are various ways of purifying water in order to make it safe to drink. Dirty water should first be strained through a filter bag, and then boiled or treated.

Bringing water to a rolling **boil** at sea level is sufficient to make water safe for drinking, but at higher altitudes you have to boil the water for longer to ensure that all the microbes are killed.

Various sterilizing methods can be used and there are propriety preparations containing **chlorine** (eg 'Puritabs') or **iodine** (eg 'Pota Aqua') compounds. Chlorine compounds generally do not kill protozoa (eg giardia). Prolonged usage of iodine compounds may lead to thyroid problems, although this is rare if used for less than a year.

There are a number of **water filters** now on the market, available both in personal and expedition size. There are two types of water filter, **mechanical** and **chemical**. Mechanical filters are usually a combination of carbon, ceramic and paper, although they can be difficult to

use. Ceramic filters tend to last longer in terms of volume of water purified. The best brand is possibly the Swiss made Katadyn. Although cheaper, the disadvantage of mechanical filters is that they do not always remove viruses or protozoa. Thus, if you are in an area where the presence of these is suspected, the water will have to be treated with iodine before being passed through the filter. When new, the filter will remove the taste, although this may not continue for long. However, ceramic filters will remove bacteria, and their manufacturers claim that since most viruses live on bacteria, the chances are that the viruses will be removed as well. This claim should be treated with scepticism.

Chemical filters usually use a combination of an iodine resin filter and a mechanical filter. The advantage of this system is that according to the manufacturers' claims, everything in the water will be killed. Their disadvantage is that the filters need replacing, adding a

Thus, the lynch pins of treatment for diarrhoea are rest, fluid and salt replacement, antibiotics such as Ciprofloxacin for bacterial types and special diagnostic tests and medical treatment for amoeba and giardia infections.

Salmonella infections and **cholera** can be devastating diseases and it would be wise to get to a hospital as soon as possible if these were suspected. Fasting, peculiar diets and the consumption of large quantities of yoghurt have not been found to be useful in calming travellers' diarrhoea or in rehabilitating inflamed bowels. As there is some evidence that alcohol and milk might prolong diarrhoea, they should probably be avoided during and immediately after an attack. Antibiotics to prevent diarrhoea are ineffective and some, such as Entero-vioform, can have serious side effects if taken for long periods.

Heat & cold
Full acclimatization to high temperatures takes about two weeks. During this period it is normal to feel relatively apathetic, especially if the relative humidity is high. Drink plenty of water and avoid extreme exertion. When you are acclimatized you will feel more comfortable, but your need for plenty of water will continue. Tepid showers are more cooling than hot or cold ones. Remember that especially in the mountains, deserts and the highlands, there can be a large and sudden drop between temperatures in the sun and shade, and between night and day. Large hats do not cool you down, but do prevent sunburn. Warm jackets or woollens are essential after dark at high altitude. Loose cotton is still the best material when the weather is hot.

The burning power of the sun is phenomenal, especially at altitude. Always wear a wide brimmed hat and use some form of sun cream or lotion. Normal temperate sun tan lotions (up to factor seven) are not much good. You will need to use the types designed specifically for the tropics or for mountaineers/skiers, with a protection factor between seven and 25 (dependent on skin type). Glare from the sun can cause conjunctivitis, so wear good quality UV protection sunglasses on beaches and snowy areas. There are several variations of 'heat stroke'. The most common cause is severe dehydration, so drink plenty of non-alcoholic fluid. Sun-block and cream is not widely available in India, so you should bring adequate supplies with you.

Insects

These can be a great nuisance. Some of course are carriers of serious disease. The best way to keep mosquitoes away at night is to sleep off the ground with a mosquito net, and to burn mosquito coils containing Pyrethrum (available in India). Aerosol sprays or a 'flit' gun may be effective, as are insecticidal tablets which are heated on a mat which is plugged into a wall socket. These devices, and the refills, are not widely available in India, so if you are taking your own make sure it is of suitable voltage with the right adaptor plug. Bear in mind also that there are regular power cuts in many parts of India.

A better option is to use a personal insect repellent of which the best contain a high concentration of Diethyltoluamide (DEET). Liquid is best for arms, ankles and face (take care around eyes and make sure you do not dissolve the plastic of your spectacles). These are available in India (eg *Mospel, Repel*), although it is recommended that you bring your own supply. Aerosol spray on clothes and ankles deter mites and ticks. Liquid DEET suspended in water can be used to impregnate cotton clothes and mosquito nets. MASTA recommends *Mosiguard* which does not contain DEET as an insect repellent.

If you are bitten, itching may be relieved by cool baths and anti-histamine tablets (care with alcohol or driving), corticosteroid creams (great care and never use if hint of infection or on the face) or by judicious scratching. Calamine lotion and cream are of no real use, and anti-histamine creams may sometimes cause skin allergies so use with caution.

Bites which do become infected (common in India) should be treated with a local antiseptic or antibiotic cream such as Cetrimide, as should infected scratches. Skin infestations with body lice, crabs and scabies are unfortunately easy to pick up, particularly by those travelling cheaply or trekking to mountain grazing pastures. Use Gamma benzene hexachloride for lice and Benzylbenzoate for scabies. Crotamiton cream alleviates itching and also kills a number of skin parasites. Malathion five percent is good for lice, but avoid the highly toxic full strength Malathion used as an agricultural insecticide.

Malaria

In India malaria was once theoretically confined to coastal and jungle zones, but is now on the increase again. It remains a serious disease and you are strongly advised to protect yourself against mosquito bites and to take prophylactic (preventive) drugs. Certain areas are badly affected particularly by the highly dangerous falciparum strain. Mosquitos do not thrive above 2,500 m, so you are safe at altitude. However, to get to altitude you will be passing through low-lying areas where mosquitoes thrive and protection must be taken. Recommendations on prevention change, so consult your family doctor or see the further information at the end of this section. However, the current combination of anti-malarial drugs for use in India requires a daily dosage of *Proguanil* (brands such as *Paludrine*) and a weekly dosage of *Chloroquine* (various brands). Start taking the tablets one week before exposure and continue to take them for four weeks after leaving the malarial zone. For those unable to use these particular drugs, your doctor may suggest *Mefloquine*, although this tends to be more expensive, less well tried, and may cause more serious side effects so it is best to try two doses before leaving.

The subject of malaria prevention is becoming more complex as the malaria parasite becomes immune to some of the older drugs. In particular, there has been an increase in the proportion of cases of falciparum malaria which is particularly dangerous. Some of the preventive drugs can cause side effects, especially if taken for long periods of time, so before you travel you must check with a reputable agency the likelihood and type of malaria in the areas you intend to visit. Take their advice on prophylaxis, but be prepared to receive conflicting advice. Do not use the possibility of side effects as an excuse not to take the drugs.

You can catch malaria even when taking prophylactic drugs, although it is unlikely. If you do develop symptoms (high fever, shivering, severe headache, sometimes diarrhoea) seek medical advice immediately. The risk of disease is obviously greater the further you move from the cities into rural areas with primitive facilities and standing water.

Infectious hepatitis (jaundice) Medically speaking there are two types. The less serious but more common is **hepatitis A**, a disease frequently caught by travellers, and common in India. The main symptoms are yellowness of eyes and skin, lack of appetite, nausea, tiredness and stomach pains. The best protection is careful preparation of food, the avoidance of contaminated drinking water and scrupulous attention to toilet hygiene.

The other, more serious version is **hepatitis B**, which is acquired as a sexually transmitted disease, from blood transfusions or injection with an unclean needle, or possibly by insect bites. The symptoms are the same as hepatitis A, but the incubation period is much longer.

You may have had jaundice before or you may have had hepatitis of either type without becoming jaundiced, in which case it is possible that you could be immune to either form. This immunity can be tested for before you travel. There are various other kinds of viral hepatitis (C, E etc) which are fairly similar to A and B, but currently vaccines do not exist for these.

Altitude sickness Acute mountain sickness (AMS) can strike from about 3,000 m upwards. It is more likely to affect those who ascend rapidly (eg by plane, or by not allowing sufficient acclimatization time whilst trekking), and those who over-exert themselves. Teenagers seem to be particularly prone. It can affect you even if you have not had problems at altitude before.

On reaching heights above 3,000 m, heart pounding and shortness of breath, especially on exertion, are almost universal responses to the lack of oxygen in the air. Acute mountain sickness takes a few hours or days to come on and may present with headache, fatigue, dizziness, loss of appetite, nausea and vomiting. Insomnia is common and often associated with a suffocating feeling when lying down in bed. Keen observers may note that their breathing tends to wax and wane at night and their faces tend to be puffy in the morning – this is all part of the syndrome. If the symptoms are mild, the treatment is rest, painkillers for headaches (preferably not Aspirin based), and anti-sickness pills for vomiting. Oxygen may help at very high altitudes but is unlikely to be available.

The best way of preventing acute mountain sickness is a relatively slow ascent and, when trekking to high altitudes, some time spent in the foothills getting fit and adapting to moderate altitude is beneficial. On arrival at places over 3,000 m, a few hours rest and avoidance of cigarettes, alcohol and heavy food will help prevent the problem. **Should the symptoms be severe or prolonged, it is best to descend to a lower altitude and to re-ascend slowly or in stages.** Symptoms disappear very quickly even with a few hundred metres of descent. If a staged ascent is impossible because of shortage of time, the drug Acetazolamide is proven to prevent minor symptoms, but some people experience funny side effects, and it may mask more serious symptoms. The usual dose is 500 mg of the slow release preparation each night, starting the night before ascending above 3,000 m. The drug will not prevent severe altitude sickness.

There is a further, albeit rare, hazard due to rapid ascent to high altitude; a kind of complicated mountain sickness presenting as acute pulmonary oedema or acute cerebral oedema. Both conditions are more common the higher you go. Pulmonary oedema comes on quite rapidly, with breathlessness, noisy breathing, cough, blueness of the lips and possibly frothing at the mouth. Cerebral oedema usually presents with confusion, going on to unconsciousness at later stages. Anyone developing these symptoms should be evacuated from the mountain as a medical emergency.

Other problems experienced at high altitude are sunburn, excessively dry air causing skin cracking, sore eyes (it may be wise to leave your contact lenses out) and stuffy noses. It is unwise to ascend to high altitude if you are pregnant (especially in the first three months), or if you have a history of heart, lung or blood disease, including sickle cell anaemia. Do not ascend to high altitude in the 24 hours following scuba-diving (though the opportunity is unlikely). Rapid descent from high altitude may aggravate sinus and middle ear infections and cause toothache. The same problems are sometimes experienced during descent at the end of a plane flight.

Remember that the Himalaya are very high, very cold, very remote and potentially very dangerous. Do not travel in them alone, if you are ill, or if you are poorly equipped. Telephone communication can be extremely difficult, mountain rescue all but non existent, and medical services extremely basic. Despite these various hazards (mostly preventable) of high altitude travel, many people find the environment healthier and more invigorating than at sea level.

AIDS

In India, AIDS is increasing in prevalence with a pattern typical of developing societies. Thus, it is not wholly confined to the well known high risk sections of the population ie homosexual men, intravenous drug abusers, prostitutes and the children of infected mothers. Heterosexual transmission of HIV which leads to AIDS is now the dominant mode and so the main risk to travellers is from casual unprotected sex. The same precautions should be taken as when encountering any sexually transmitted disease.

HIV can be passed via unsterile needles which have previously been used to inject a HIV positive patient, but the risk of this is very small. It would, however, be sensible to check that needles have been properly sterilized, or better still, disposable needles used. The chance of picking up hepatitis B in this way is much more of a danger. If disposable needles are carried as part of a proper medical kit, customs officials in India are not generally suspicious.

The risk of receiving a blood transfusion with blood infected with HIV is greater than from dirty needles because of the amount of fluid exchanged. Supplies of blood for transfusion are now usually screened for HIV in reputable hospitals, so the risk may be small. Catching HIV does not necessarily produce an illness in itself; the only way to be sure if you feel you have been at risk is to have a blood test for HIV antibodies on your return to a place where there are reliable laboratory facilities. The test does not become positive for many weeks and you are advised to be re-tested after 6 months.

Bites & stings

The best precaution against a snake bite is not to walk in snake territory with bare feet, sandals or shorts & not to touch snakes even if assured they are harmless

If you are unlucky enough to be bitten by a venomous snake, spider, scorpion, centipede or sea creature, try (within limits) to catch the animal for identification. Failing this, an accurate description will aid treatment. See the information on rabies (below) for other animal bites.

The reactions to be expected are fright, swelling, pain and bruising around the bite, soreness of the regional lymph glands (eg armpits for bites to hands and arms), nausea, vomiting and fever. If, in addition, any of the following symptoms supervene get the victim to a doctor without delay: numbness, tingling of face, muscular spasm, convulsions, shortness of breath or haemorrhage. Commercial snake bile or scorpion sting kits may be available but are only useful for the specific type of snake or scorpion for which they are designed. The serum has to be given by injection into a vein, so it is not much good unless you have some practice in making and giving such injections. If the bite is on a limb, immobilize the limb and apply a tight bandage (not a tourniquet) between the bite and the body. Be sure to release it for 90 seconds every 15 minutes.

Essentials

Do not try to slash the bite and suck out the poison because this will do more harm than good. Reassurance of the bitten person is important. Death from snake-bite is extremely rare. Hospitals usually hold stocks of snake-bite serum, though it is important to have a good description of the snake, or where possible, the creature itself.

If swimming in an area where there are poisonous fish such as stone or scorpion fish (also called by a variety of local names) or sea urchins on rocky coasts, tread carefully or wear footwear. The sting of such fish is intensely painful but can be helped by immersing the stung part in water as hot as you can bear for as long as it remains painful. This is not always very practical and you must take care not to scald yourself. At certain times of the year, coincidental with the best surfing season, stinging jelly-fish can be a problem.

Avoid spiders and scorpions by keeping your bed away from the wall, look under lavatory seats and inside your shoes in the morning. Dark dusty rooms are popular with scorpions. In the event of being bitten, consult a doctor quickly.

Other afflictions **Rabies** is endemic in India. If you are bitten by a domestic or wild animal, do not leave things to chance. Scrub the wound immediately with soap and water/disinfectant. Try to capture the animal (within limits). Treatment depends on whether you have already been vaccinated against rabies. If you have (and this is worthwhile if you are spending lengths of time in developing countries) then some further doses of vaccine are all that is needed. Human diploid cell vaccine is best, but expensive; other, older types of vaccine such as that made of duck embyos may be the only type available. These are effective, much cheaper and interchangeable generally with the human derived types. If not already vaccinated then anti-rabies serum (immunoglobulin) may be required in addition. It is wise to finish the course of treatment whether the animal survives or not.

Dengue fever is present in India. It is a viral disease, transmitted by mosquito bites, presenting severe headache, fevers and body pains. Complicated types of dengue known as haemorrhagic fevers occur throughout Asia, but usually in persons who have caught the disease a second time. Thus, although it is a very serious type, it is rarely caught by visitors. There is no treatment; you must just avoid mosquito bites as much as possible.

Athlete's foot and other fungal infections are best treated by sunshine and a proprietary preparation such as Canesten or Ecostatin.

Influenza and respiratory diseases are common, perhaps made worse by polluted cities and rapid temperature and climatic changes.

Intestinal worms are common, and the more serious ones such as hook worm can be contracted by walking barefoot on infested earth.

Leishmaniasis can be a serious disease taking several forms. It is transmitted by the bite of a sandfly. Visceral leishmaniasis is a severe disease characterised by prolonged high fever found in the Himalayan foothills and in the Ganges-Brahmaputra plains of North Eastern India. Cutaneous leishmaniasis, causing a persistent crusty sore or ulcer, occurs in North West India. Protect against sandfly bites by wearing impregnated long trousers and long sleeved shirt, and DEET on exposed skin. Sleep under an impregnated bed net.

Prickly heat is a very common itchy rash, and can be avoided by frequent washing and wearing loose clothing. It is helped by the use of talcum powder to allow the skin to dry thoroughly after washing.

Returning home

It is important to take your anti-malaria tablets for four weeks after you return. Malaria can develop up to one year after leaving a malaria area. If you do become ill with fever or the other symptoms listed above, make sure your doctor knows about your travel. If you have had attacks of diarrhoea, it may be worth having a stool specimen tested in case you have picked up amoebic dysentery, giardiasis or other protozoal infections. If you have been living rough, a blood test may be worthwhile to detect worms and other parasites.

Further information

The following organizations give information regarding well trained English speaking physicians throughout the world: *International Association for Medical Assistance to Travellers*, 745, 5th Avenue, New York, 10022; *Intermedic*, 777, Third Avenue, New York, 10017. Information regarding country by country malaria risk can be obtained from: *Malaria Reference Laboratory*, UK, T0891-600350; *Liverpool School of Tropical Medicine*, UK, T0891-172111 (both have recorded messages, premium rate); and *Centre for Disease Control*, Atlanta, USA, T404-3324555. The organization MASTA (Medical Advisory Service to Travellers Abroad), T020-78375540, F0113-2387575, www.masta.org and Travax (Glasgow, T0141-9467120 ext 247) will provide up to date country by country information on health risks.

Further information on medical problems abroad can be obtained from: *"Travellers' Health: How To Stay Healthy Abroad"*, edited by Richard Dawood (Oxford University Press), recently updated. A new edition of the HMSO publication "Health Information for Overseas Travel" is available. The London School of Hygiene and Tropical Medicine, Keppel Street, London, WC1E 7HT, UK, publishes a strongly recommended book titled *"The Preservation of Personal Health in Warm Climates"*.

This information has been compiled by Dr David Snashall, Senior Lecturer in Occupational Health, United Medical Schools of Guy's and St Thomas' Hospitals and Chief Medical Advisor, Foreign and Commonwealth Office, London. Added comments and recommendations specific to India are from Dr Martin Taylor, Kensington Street Health Centre, Bradford, West Yorkshire and Dr Anthony Bryceson, Emeritus Professor of Tropical Medicine at the London School of Hygiene and Tropical Medicine.

Further reading

The literature on India is as huge and varied as the subcontinent itself. Below are a few suggestions which throw light on the Himalayan region followed by some on India in general. *See page 58 for books on trekking*

India is a good place to buy English language books as foreign books are often much cheaper than the published price. There are also cheap Indian editions and occasionally reprints of out-of-print books. There are excellent bookshops in all the major Indian cities.

Ian Cameron *Mountains of the Gods.* About the people of the Himalaya. *Ladakh* by **H Harres**, Innsbruck, 1980; *A Journey in Ladakh* by **Andrew Harvey**, Cape, London, 1983; The **Dalai Lama** *My land and my people* and *Freedom in Exile.* **John Keay**, *When Men and Mountains meet.* Tales of early explorers of the Western Himalaya. **John Murray**, London, 1977. **JS Lall**, Ed. *The Himalaya: Aspects of Change.* New Delhi, Oxford **General** India

Paperbacks, 1996. A selection of essays by world renowned experts covering a range of aspects from flora/fauna, to geology, economy and development and people and society. **SS Negi** *Himachal Pradesh: the land and people.* Indus, New Delhi, 1993. A wide, thorough coverage of diverse topics. *Ancient Futures: Learning from Ladakh* by **Helena Norberg-Hodge**, Rider, London, 1992; **J Rizvi** *Ladakh, Crossroads of High Asia.* OUP, Delhi, 1983. **NK Rustomji and Charles Ramble**, eds *Himalayan Environment and Culture.* Indu, New Delhi. **Eric Shipton** *That Untravelled World.* Hodder and Stoughton, London, 1969. Personal experiences of climbing in the Western and Central Himalaya. **Madanjeet Singh** *Himalayan Art.* Macmillan, 1968. Covers sculpture and art from Ladakh to Bhutan. Dhanu **Swadi and Deepak Sanan** *Exploring Kinnaur and Spiti in the Trans-Himalaya* 1998, Indus, New Delhi. **Graeme D Westlake** *An Introduction to the Hill Stations of India.* Indus, New Delhi, 1993. Part deals with the Himalayan hill resorts, tracing their development from the Raj period to the mid-1900s. **Francis Younghusband.** *The Heart of the Continent.* OUP, 1984.

Natural History   **S Ali.** *Birds of Sikkim.* 1962, OUP, Bombay, *Field Guide to the birds of the Eastern Himalayas.* 1997, OUP, Delhi. *Indian Hill birds.* 1979, OUP, Bombay.
GB Corbett and JE Hill *The Mammals of the Indomalayan Region.* 1992, OUP, Oxford. **Frank Kingdon-Ward** *Himalayan Enchantment: an anthology.* Serindian London, 1990. A celebration of the writings of a plant hunter in the Eastern Himalaya. **Polunin, Oleg and Stainton** *Flowers of the Himalaya,* OUP, New Delhi, 1984.

Art &   **T Richard Burton** *Hindu Art* British Museum P. A well illustrated paperback; a broad
architecture   view of art and religion. **Ilay Cooper and Barry Dawson** *Traditional Buildings of India,* Thames & Hudson. **George Michell** *The Hindu Temple,* Univ of Chicago Press, 1988. An authoritative account of Hindu architectural development. *Monasteries of Ladakh* by **Paldang.** *Himalayan art* by M Singh, UNESCO, 1971. *The Cultural Heritage of Ladakh* by **DL Snellgrove and T Skorupski**, Aris & Phillips, Delhi, 1977, 1980; **Giles Tillotson** *Mughal architecture,* London, Viking, 1990; *The tradition of Indian architecture,* Yale 1989. Superbly clear writing on development of Indian architecture under Rajputs, Mughals and the British.

Current affairs &   **Patrick French** *Liberty or Death.* Harper Collins, 1997. Well researched and serious yet
politics   reads like a story. **Sunil Khilnani** *The idea of India,* Penguin, 1997. Excellent introduction to contemporary India, described by the Nobel prize winner Amartya Sen as "spirited, combative and insight-filled, a rich synthesis of contemporary India". **James Manor (ed)** *Nehru to the Nineties: the changing office of Prime Minister in India,* Hurst, 1994. An excellent collection of essays giving an insider's view of the functioning of Indian democracy. **Mark Tully** *No full stops in India,* Viking, 1991. An often superbly observed but controversially interpreted view of contemporary India.

History: **Bridget and Raymond Allchin** *Origins of a civilisation,* Viking, Penguin Books, 1997.
pre-history &   The most authoritative up to date survey on the origins of Indian civilizations. **AL**
early history   **Basham** *The Wonder that was India,* London, Sidgwick & Jackson, 1985. Still one of the most comprehensive and readable accounts of the development of India's culture.

History: **Mohandas K Gandhi** *An Autobiography,* London, 1982. **Jawaharlal Nehru** *The*
medieval &   *discovery of India,* New Delhi, ICCR, 1976. **John Keay** *India: a History,* Harper Collins. A
modern   major new popular history of the subcontinent. **Francis Robinson (ed)** *Cambridge Encyclopaedia of India,* Cambridge, 1989. An introduction to many aspects of South Asian society. **Percival Spear & Romila Thapar** *A history of India,* 2 vols, Penguin, 1978. **Stanley Wolpert** *A new history of India,* OUP, 1990.

Language   **Helena Norberg-Hodge & GT Paldan** Ladakhi-English, English-Ladakhi Dictionary.

Rebecca Norman *Getting started in Ladakhi*, Melong, SECMOL Leh, Ladakh. **Rupert Snell and Simon Weightman** *Teach Yourself Hindi* and **William Radice** *Teach Yourself Bengali*, Hodder and Stoughton. Two excellent, accessible, authoritative and up to date teaching guides with cassette tapes. **H Yule and AC Burnell** (eds), *Hobson-Jobson*, 1886. Paperback edition, 1986. A delightful insight into Anglo-Indian words and phrases.

Nirad Chaudhuri Four books give vivid, witty and often sharply critical accounts of India across the 20th century. *The autobiography of an unknown Indian*, Macmillan, London; *Thy Hand, Great Anarch!*, London, Chatto & Windus, 1987. **EM Forster** *A Passage to India*. **Rudyard Kipling** *Plain Tales from the Hills*, Penguin, London, (1991. Original 1888). **VS Naipaul** *A million mutinies now*, Penguin, 1992. Naipaul's 'revisionist' account of India turns away from the despondency of his earlier two India books (*An Area of darkness* and *India: a wounded civilisation*) to see grounds for optimism at India's capacity for regeneration. **Salman Rushdie** *Midnight's children*, London, Picador, 1981. A novel of India since Independence. At the same time funny and bitterly sharp critiques of South Asian life in the 1980s. **Salman Rushdie** and **Elizabeth West** *The Vintage book of Indian writing*, Random House, 1997. **Paul Scott** *The Raj Quartet*, London, Panther, 1973; *Staying on*, Longmans, 1985. Outstandingly perceptive novels of the end of the Raj. **Vikram Seth** *A Suitable Boy*, Phoenix House London 1993. Prize winning novel of modern Indian life. **Simon Weightman** (ed) *Travellers Literary Companion: the Indian Sub-continent*. An invaluable introduction to the diversity of Indian writing. — **Literature**

Raghava R Menon *Penguin Dictionary of Indian Classical Music*, Penguin New Delhi 1995. — **Music**

Elizabeth Bomiller *May you be the mother of 100 sons*, Penguin, 1991. An American woman journalists' account of coming to understand the issues that face India's women today. **Lakshmi Holmstrom** *The Inner Courtyard*, a series of short stories by Indian women, translated into English, Rupa, 1992. — **People & places**

W Theodore de Bary (ed) *Sources of Indian Tradition: Vol 1*. Columbia U.P. Traces the origins of India's major religions through illustrative texts. **Wendy Doniger O'Flaherty** *Hindu Myths*, London, Penguin, 1974. A sourcebook translated from the Sanskrit. **IH Qureshi** *The Muslim Community of the Indo-Pakistan Sub-Continent 610-1947*, OUP, 1977, Karachi. **David Snellgrove** *Indo-Tibetan Buddhism*. Serindia, 1987. **Paul Williams** *Mahayana Buddhism: the doctrinal foundations*. Routledge, 1989. **RC Zaehner** *Hinduism*, OUP. — **Religion**

Alexander Frater *Chasing the monsoon*, London, Viking, 1990. An attractive and prize winning account of the human impact of the monsoon's sweep across India. **William Dalrymple** *The Age of Kali*, published in edited form in India as *In the court of the fish-eyed Goddess*, is his second anecdotal but insightful account. **John Hatt** *The tropical traveller: the essential guide to travel in hot countries*, Penguin, 3rd ed 1992. Excellent, wide ranging and clearly written common sense, based on extensive experience and research. **John Keay** *Into India*. London, John Murray, 1999. A seasoned traveller's introduction to understanding and enjoying India; with a new foreword. — **Travel**

Salim Ali *Indian hill birds*, OUP. **DV Cowen** *Flowering Trees and Shrubs in India*. **RE Hawkins** *Encyclopaedia of Indian Natural History*, Bombay Natural History Soc/OUP. **Krys Kazmierczak & Raj Singh** *A birdwatcher's guide to India*. Prion, 1998, Sandy, Beds, UK. Well researched and carrying lots of practical information for all birders. **SM Nair** *Endangered animals of India*, New Delhi, NBT, 1992. **O Polunin & A Stainton** *Flowers of the Himalaya*, OUP, 1984. **SH Prater** *The Book of Indian Animals*. **Martin Woodcock** *Handguide to Birds of the Indian Sub-Continent*, Collins. — **Wildlife & vegetation**

Essentials

Essentials

Maps

The export of large scale maps from India is prohibited

For anyone interested in the geography of India, or even simply getting around, trying to buy good maps is a depressing experience. For security reasons it is illegal to sell large scale maps of any areas within 80 km of the coast or national borders.

The **Bartholomew** 1:4 m map sheet of India is the most authoritative, detailed and easy to use map available. It can be bought worldwide. *GeoCenter* World Map 1:2 m, covers India in three regional sections and are clearly printed.

For trekking maps, see page 59

Sources of maps outside India: **Australia:** *The Map Shop*, 16a Peel St, Adelaide, SA 5000, T08-82312033. **Canada:** *Worldwide Books*, 552 Seymore St. Vancouver, BC. **Germany:** *Geo Buch Verlag*, Rosenthal 6, D-8000 München 2; *GeoCenter GmbH*, Honigwiessenstrasse 25, Postfach 800830, D-7000 Stuttgart 80; *Zumsteins Landkartenhaus*, Leibkerrstrasse 5, 8 München 22. **Italy:** *Libreria Alpina*, Via C Coroned-Berti, 4 40137 Bologna, Zona 370-5. **Switzerland:** *Travel Bookshop*, Rindermarkt, 8001 Zurich. **UK:** *Blackwell's*, 53 Broad St, Oxford, T01865-792792, www.bookshop.blackwell.co.uk *Stanfords*, 12-14 Long Acre, London WC2E 9LP, T020-78361321, www.stanfords.co.uk **USA:** *Michael Chessler*, PO Box 2436, Evergreen, CO 80439, T800-6548502, 303-6700093; *Ulysses*, 4176 St Denis Montreal, T0524-8439447.

The Survey of India publishes large scale 1:10,000 town plans of approximately 70 cities. These detailed plans are the only surveyed town maps in India, and some are over 20 years old. The Survey also has topographic maps at the scale of 1:25,000 and 1:50,000 in addition to its 1:250,000 scale coverage, some of which are as recent as the late 1980s. However, maps are regarded as highly sensitive and it is only possible to buy these from main agents of the Survey of India.

India on the web

General sites
www.tourindia.com The official government promotional site with useful information but no objective evaluation of problems and difficulties. Has separate state entries within it. 'India Travel Online' is informative and issued fortnightly.

www.indiacurrentaffairs.com/ Regularly updated cuttings from Indian national dailies.

www.fco.gov Advice from the Foreign Office, London.

www.travel.indiamart.com Commercial site Details of online bookings for selected hotels.

www.india.org The sites on India section contains excellent information on the structure of Indian government. Tourism Information is less useful.

www.123india.com Wide ranging current affairs and general India site.

www.tourismindia.com Yellow pages for major cities.

www.wunderground.com An excellent weather site, world wide, city specific and fast.

State tourism sites
Search by state under www.indiatouristoffice.co.uk Also under separate states, eg www.himachaltourism.nic.in and www.hptdc.com, assamtourism.com, meghalaya.nic.in

Natural history sites
ENVIS@BNHS for the Bombay Natural History Society. centre@sacon.ernet.in The government's Salim Ali Centre for Ornithology and Natural History (SACON) in Coimbatore. www.orientalbirdclub.org, biks@giasdl01.vsnl.net.in for Bird Link, concerned with conservation of birds and their habitat.

Indian embassies & consulates

Australia, 3-5 Moonah Place, Yarralumla, Canberra T6273-3999; Level 2, 210 Pitt St, Sydney T9264-4855; Melbourne T9386-7399. **Austria**, Kärntner Ring 2, A-1015 Vienna, T50-58666669, F50-59219. **Bangladesh**, 2 Chanmodi RA, House 129, Dhaka-2, T503606, Chittagong T507670. **Belgium**, 217-Chaussée de Vleurgat, 1050 Brussels, T6409802, F6489638. Consulates: Ghent T091-263423, Antwerp T03-2341122. **Bhutan**, India House Estate, Thimpu, T2162. **Canada**, 10 Springfield Rd, Ottawa, Ontario K1M 1C9, T613-7443751. Consulates: Toronto T416-9600751, Vancouver T9266080. **Denmark**, Vangehusvej 15, 2100 Copenhagen, T3918-2888, F3927-0218. **Finland**, Satamakatu 2 A8, 00160 Helsinki-16, T608927. **France**, 15 Rue Alfred Dehodencq, Paris, T45203930. **Germany**, Adenauerallee, 262/264, 5300 Bonn-1, T0228-54050. Consulates: Berlin T8817068, Frankfurt T069-271040, Hamburg T338036, Munich T089-92562067, Stuttgart T0711-297078. **Ireland**, 6 Lesson Park, Dublin 6, T01-4970843. **Israel**, 4 Kaufmann St, Sharbat, Tel Aviv 68012, T0368-580585, F510143. **Italy**, Via XX Settembre 5, 00187 Rome, T4884642. Consulates: Milan T02-8690314, Genoa T54891. **Japan**, 2-11, Kudan Minami 2-Chome, Chiyoda-ku, Tokyo 102, T03-2622391. Consulate: Kobe T078-2418116. **Korea**, 37-3, Hannam-dong, Yongsan-Ku, Seoul, T7984257, F7969534. **Malaysia**, 19 Malacca St, Kuala Lumpur, T221766. **Maldives**, Mafabbu Aage 37, Orchid Magu, Male 20-02, T323015. **Nepal**, Lainchour, PO Box No 292, Kathmandu, T211300. **Netherlands**, Buitenrustweg 2, The Hague (2517KD), T070-3469771. **New Zealand**, 10th Flr, Princess Tower, 180 Molesworth St (PO Box 4045), Wellington, T4736390. **Norway**, 30 Niels Jules Gate, 0272 Oslo-2, T443194. **Pakistan**, G5 Diplomatic Enclave, Islamabad, T050-8144731, Karachi T021-814371. **Singapore**, India House, 31 Grange Rd, Singapore 0923, T7376777. **Spain**, Avda Pio XII 30-32, 28016 Madrid, T457-0209. Consulate: Barcelona T93-2120422. **Sri Lanka**, 36-38 Galle Rd, Colombo 3, T421605 Kandy, T446430. **Sweden**, Adolf Fredriks Kyrkogata 12, Box 1340, 11183 Stockholm, T08-107008, F08-248505. **Switzerland**, Kirchenfeldstrasse 28 CH - 3005 Bern, T031-351 1110. **Thailand**, 46, Soi 23 (Prasarn Mitr) Sukhumvit 23, Bangkok 10110, T2580300. Also in Chiang Mai. **UK**, India House, Aldwych, London WC2B 4NA, T020-78368484 (0930-1300, 1400-1730; visas 0800-1200), www.Hcilondon.org Consulates: The Spencers, 19 Augusta St, Hockley, Birmingham, B18 6DS, T0121-2122782; 6th Flr, 134 Renfrew St, Glasgow 3 7ST, T0141-3310777, F331-0666. (Send SAE for postal applications.) **USA**, 2107 Massachusetts Ave, Washington DC 20008, T202-9397000. Consulates: New Orleans T504-5828105, New York T212-8797800, San Francisco T415-6680662, Chicago T312-781680, Cleveland T216/696.

Essentials

Western Himalaya

74

Western Himalaya

76 Access from Delhi

91 Garhwal & Kumaon, Uttaranchal

145 Himachal Pradesh

221 Jammu and Kashmir

From the high altitude deserts of Ladakh and Spiti to the lush foothills of Kangra, the western Himalaya embrace as wide a range of cultures as they do of landscapes.

These mountains are home to the sources of India's greatest rivers. From the snowy heights fast flowing mountain rivers tumble down towards the plains while the deeply shaded valleys still have the feel of some of the remotest spots on earth.

Once known only to nomadic pastoralists and traders, the most accessible of the hills of Uttaranchal are attracting increasing numbers of mountaineers, trekkers, and white water rafters. They join the annual stream of summer pilgrims to the holy shrines, and stay en route in the long popular hill stations of Nainital, Almora and Ranikhet. Further west Shimla, once the summer capital of British India, Dharamsala, the residence of the exiled Dalai Lama, and Leh in Ladakh, are magnets to visitors from around the world.

The Western Himalaya are still relatively sparsely populated, but agriculture has pushed up the mountain sides, using sophisticated terracing and irrigation on the steepest of slopes. A network of roads has gradually extended into some of the remotest areas, making access possible to even some of the highest regions for at least part of the year. The area's overwhelming beauty and unique culture offer great rewards for any who wish to get to know 'mountain India'.

Access from Delhi

Delhi is the most convenient access point for foreign travellers to the Western Himalaya. A much more detailed description of the city and its surroundings appears in the current edition of the India Handbook.

Ins and outs

Getting there

Phone code: 011
Colour map 2, grid C1
Area: 434 sq km
Altitude: 216 m

Be on your guard around New Delhi station, confidence tricksters frequent the area

Air Delhi is served by the **Indira Gandhi (IGI) Airport** to the southwest of the city. The Domestic **Terminal 1** is 15 km from Connaught Circus, the central hub of activity and the main hotel area in New Delhi. It handles flights from 2 separate sections: 'A' (exclusively for *Indian Airlines*) and 'B' (for others). The International **Terminal 2** is 23 km from the centre. During the day, the journey to Connaught Circus, can take from 30 to 45 mins from the Domestic Terminal and 45 mins to 1 hr from the International Terminal. A free shuttle runs between the terminals. To get to town take a pre-paid taxi or an airport coach unless your hotel sends its own bus.

Bus The principal **Inter State Bus Terminus (ISBT)** is at Kashmir Gate (near the Red Fort) about 30 mins by bus from Connaught Place, which can appear totally bewildering. Services connect it to the other Delhi ISBTs.

Rail Travellers are likely to use the 2 main stations. The busy **New Delhi** station, a 20 min walk north of Connaught Place, can be maddeningly chaotic; you need to have all your wits about you. The overpoweringly crowded **Old Delhi (Main) Station** (2 km north of Connaught Place) has some important trains.

Getting around Auto-rickshaws and taxis are widely available, though few are prepared to use their meters, especially for foreigners. They offer the only realistic choice for getting about the city, which is much too spread out to walk, as city buses are usually packed and have long queues. The **City Guide** published by Eicher Goodearth, New Delhi, 1998 (Rs 345), is well illustrated and the best available.

First impressions The drive from the airport along the broad tree-lined streets of New Delhi, is in marked contrast to Old Delhi where your senses are bombarded by noise, bustle, smells and apparent chaos. Outside the railway stations taxi drivers, rickshaw wallahs and hotel touts jostle for attention.

History

The cities of Delhi Modern Delhi spreads over the remains of nearly a dozen earlier centres which once occupied this vital strategic site.

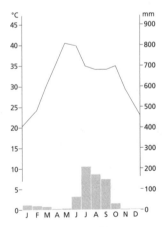

Climate: Delhi
Oct-Mar are the best months, but Dec & Jan can get quite cold at night. Pollution can affect asthma sufferers. Monsoon lasts from mid-June to mid-Sept. May and Jun are very hot & dry

Old Delhi or **Shah Jahanabad** (the '7th City'), was built by Shah Jahan in the 17th century. Focusing on his great Red Fort and Jama Masjid, this old city is still a dense network of narrow alleys and tightly packed markets and houses.

Immediately to the south is the British-built capital of **New Delhi**. Post-Independence Delhi has dramatically accelerated its suburban expansion.

Sights

The sites of interest are grouped in three main areas. In the centre is the British built capital of **New Delhi**, with its government buildings and wide avenues. **Old Delhi** is about 7 km north of Connaught Circus. Ten kilometres to the south is the **Qutb Minar** complex, with the old fortress city of **Tughluqabad** 8 km to its east.

Central New Delhi

A tour of New Delhi will usually start with a visit to India Gate. This war memorial is situated at the eastern end of **Rajpath**. Designed by Sir Edward Lutyens, it commemorates more than 70,000 Indian soldiers who died in the First World War.

India Gate

Rajpath leads west from India Gate towards **Janpath**. To the north are the **National Archives**, formerly the Imperial Record Office. To the south is the **National Museum**.

Standing on either side of Raisina Hill, **North Block** houses the Home and Finance Ministries, **South Block** the Ministry of Foreign Affairs. These long classical buildings, topped by Baroque domes, were designed by Baker.

★ **The Secretariats**

In the **Great Court** between the Secretariats are the four **Dominion Columns**, donated by the governments of Australia, Canada, New Zealand and South Africa – ironically, as it turned out. In the centre of the court is the Jaipur column of red sandstone topped with a white egg, bronze lotus and six-pointed glass star of India. Across the entrance to the Great Court is a 205 m wrought iron screen.

At the Secretariat and Rashtrapati Bhavan gates, mounted and unmounted troops parade in full uniform. ■ *Sat 1030, worth attending.*

Once the Viceroy's House, Rashtrapati Bhavan is the official residence of the President of India. Designed by **Sir Edward Lutyens**, it combines western and eastern styles.

★ **Rashtrapati Bhavan**

To the south is Flagstaff House in 1948 it became the Prime Minister's residence. Re-named **Teen Murti Bhawan** it now houses the Nehru Memorial Museum (see page 83). The **Martyr's Memorial**, at the junction of Sardar Patel Marg and Willingdon Crescent, has 11 statues of national heroes headed by Mahatma Gandhi.

Northeast of the Viceroy's House is the **Council House**, now **Sansad Bhavan**. Inside is the library and chambers for the Council of State, Chamber of Princes and Legislative Assembly – the **Lok Sabha**.

Parliament House

Connaught Place and its outer ring, **Connaught Circus**, comprise two-storeyed arcaded buildings, arranged radially. In 1995 they were re-named **Rajiv Chowk** and **Indira Chowk** respectively, but are still widely known by their original names. They have become the main commercial

Connaught area

Access from Delhi

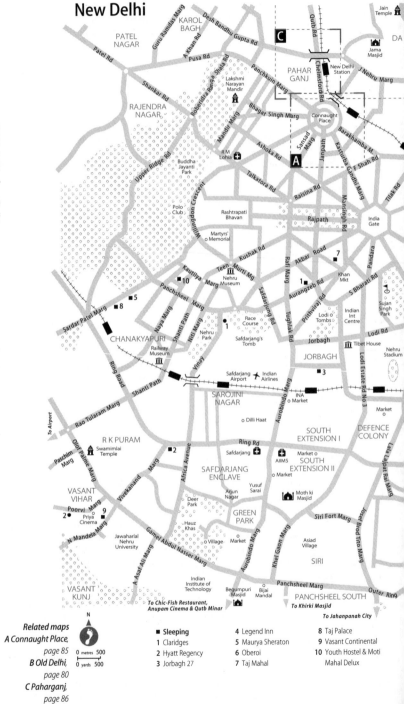

New Delhi

PATEL NAGAR

KAROL BAGH

Jain Temple

DA

Jama Masjid

Desh Bandhu Gupta Rd

Qutb Rd

Patel Rd

A Khan Rd

Guru Ramdas Marg

Pusa Rd

Panchkuin Marg

PAHAR GANJ

New Delhi Station

J Nehru Marg

Shankar Rd

Mandir Marg

Rajendra Bhawan Shala Rd

Lakshmi Narayan Mandir

Bhagat Singh Marg

Chelmsford Rd

Connaught Place

Barakhamba M

Kasturba Gandhi Marg

F Shah Rd

RAJENDRA NAGAR

Ashoka Rd

Sansad Marg

A

Janpath

RM Lohia

Talkatora Rd

Tilak Rd

Upper Ridge Rd

Buddha Jayanti Park

Willingdon Crescent

Raisina Rd

Polo Club

Rashtrapati Bhavan

Rajpath

Maningh Rd

India Gate

Martyrs' Memorial

Kushak Rd

Akbar Road

7

Pandara

Kautliya

Teen Murti Mg

Nehru Museum

Rafi Marg

Aurangzeb Rd

1

Khan Mkt

S Bharati Rd

Panchsheel Marg

10

Safdarjung Rd

Prithviraj Rd

Lodi Tombs

Indian Int Centre

Sujan Singh Park

Sardar Patel Marg

8

5

Naya Marg

Shanti Path

Niti Marg

Nehru Park

Race Course

Tughlak Rd

Jorbagh

Lodi Rd

Tibet House

Nehru Stadium

CHANAKYAPURI

Vinay

Safdarjang's Tomb

JORBAGH

3

Lodi Estate Rd No 3

Ring Road

Railway Museum

Shanti Path

Safdarjang Airport

Indian Airlines

INA Market

Market

To Airport

Rao Tularam Marg

SAROJINI NAGAR

Aurobindo Marg

SOUTH EXTENSION I

DEFENCE COLONY

Dilli Haat

Paschim Marg

Olof Palme Marg

R K PURAM

Swamimlai Temple

Africa Avenue

2

Ring Rd

Safdarjang

AIIMS

SOUTH EXTENSION II

Market

Lala Lajpat Rai Marg

VASANT VIHAR

Vivekanand Marg

SAFDARJANG ENCLAVE

Yusuf Sarai

Market

Arjun Nagar

Moth ki Masjid

Poorvi Marg

2

9

Priya Cinema

Deer Park

GREEN PARK

Siri Fort Marg

Jaisor Bhod Tito Marg

N Mandela Marg

Jawaharlal Nehru University

Hauz Khas

Village

Market

Khel Gaon Marg

Asiad Village

SIRI

Outer Ring

VASANT KUNJ

A Asaf Ali Marg

Camel Abdul Nasser Marg

Indian Institute of Technology

Begumpuri Masjid

Bijai Mandal

Panchsheel Marg

PANCHSHEEL SOUTH

To Chic-Fish Restaurant, Anupam Cinema & Qutb Minar

To Khirki Masjid

To Jahanpanah City

Related maps
A Connaught Place,
page 85
B Old Delhi,
page 80
C Paharganj,
page 86

N

0 metres 500
0 yards 500

■ **Sleeping**
1 Claridges
2 Hyatt Regency
3 Jorbagh 27

4 Legend Inn
5 Maurya Sheraton
6 Oberoi
7 Taj Mahal

8 Taj Palace
9 Vasant Continental
10 Youth Hostel & Moti
   Mahal Delux

Access from Delhi

centre of Delhi. Vendors of all sorts gather in the area as well as aggressive touts ready to take advantage of the unwary traveller by getting them into spurious 'official' or 'government' shops and travel agencies.

To the south in **Janpath** (the People's Way), with the east and west Courts with their long colonnaded verandahs.

The Mughal Emperor Muhammad Shah (ruled 1719-48) entrusted the astronomer **Maharaja Jai Singh II** with the task of revising the calendar and correcting the astronomical tables used by contemporary priests. Daily astral observations were made for years before it was built in 1725. Plastered brick structures were favoured for the site instead of brass instruments.

★ **Jantar Mantar**

Beyond Delhi Gate the bank of the **Yamuna**, marked by a series of memorials to India's leaders. The most prominent memorial, is that of **Mahatma Gandhi** at ★ **Raj Ghat**. To its north is **Shanti Vana** ('forest of peace'), landscaped gardens where Prime Minister Jawaharlal Nehru was cremated in 1964, and subsequently his grandson Sanjay Gandhi in 1980, daughter **Indira Gandhi** in 1984 and elder grandson, Rajiv, in 1991.

The Memorial Ghats

The Purana Qila, now an attractive and quiet park, witnessed the crucial struggle between the Mughal **Emperor Humayun** and his formidable Afghan rival **Sher Shah Suri**. The massive gateways and walls were probably built by Humayun around 1534.

Purana Qila (Old Fort)
Though the fort is in ruins, the mosque is in good condition

The **Qila-i-Kuhna Masjid** (mosque of the Old Fort) is considered one of the finest examples of Indo-Afghan architecture with arches, tessellations and rich ornamentation in black and white marble against red sandstone.

A small museum near the Humayun Darwaza houses finds from the excavations. ■ *0800-1830. Entrance by west gate. Guide books and postcards. Clean toilets.*

● **Eating**
1 Basil & Thyme, Santushti Complex

2 McDonalds, TGI Friday & Baskin Robbins

Old Delhi

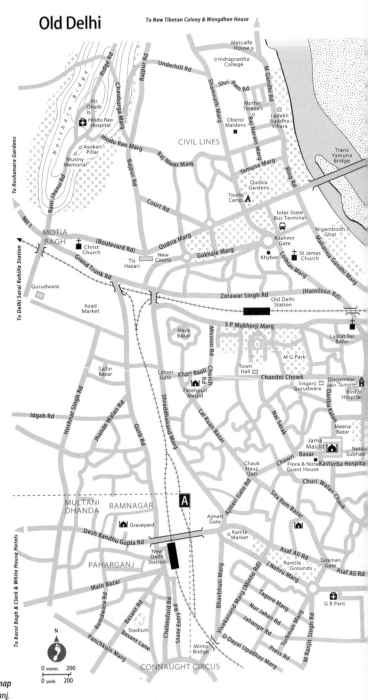

To New Tibetan Colony & Wongdhen House

Metcalfe House

Indraprastha College

Shri Ram Rd

M Gandhi Rd

Underhill Rd

Shamnath Marg

Raj Narain Marg

Mother Teresa's

Oberoi Maidens

Ladakh Buddha Vihara

CIVIL LINES

Ridge Rd

Rajpur Rd

Chauburja Marg

Northern Ridge

Pir Ghaib

Hindu Rao Hospital

Asokan Pillar

Mutiny Memorial

Hindu Rao Marg

Raj Niwas Marg

Rajpur Rd

Yamuna Marg

Trans Yamuna Bridge

Ring Rd

Rani Jhansi Rd

To Roshanara Gardens

Court Rd

Qudsia Gardens

Tourist Camp

Inter State Bus Terminal

Nigambodh Ghat

NH 1

MOTIA BAGH

Christ Church

(Boulevard Rd)

Qudsia Marg

Gokhale Marg

Kashmir Gate

St James Church

Mahatma Gandhi Marg

To Delhi Sarai Rohilla Station

Grand Trunk Rd

Tis Hazari

New Courts

Khyber

Lothian Marg

Gurudwara

Azad Market

Zorawar Singh Rd

(Hamilton Rd)

Old Delhi Station

Lajpat Rai Bazar

Naya Bazar

S P Mukherji Marg

Sadar Bazar

Hoshiar Singh Rd

Jhande Walan Rd

Qutb Rd

Shraddhanand Marg

Mission Rd

Lahori Gate

Kharl Baoli

Church Rd

Fatehpuri Masjid

M G Park

Town Hall

Chandni Chowk

Sisganj Gurudwara

Digambar Jain Temple

Bird Hospital

Dariba Kalan

Idgah Rd

Lal Kuan Bazar

Nai Sarak

Meena Bazar

Jama Masjid

Netaji Subhash

Chauk Hauz Qazi

Chawri Bazar

Flora & Nora Guest House

Kasturba Hospital

Churi Walan Chauk

MULTANI DHANDA

RAMNAGAR

A

Sita Ram Bazar

Ajmeri Gate Rd

Graveyard

Ajmeri Gate

Kamla Market

Asaf Ali Rd

Turkman Gate

To Karol Bagh & Clark & White House Hotels

Desh Bandhu Gupta Rd

New Delhi Station

Ramila Grounds

J Nehru Marg

Asaf Ali Rd

PAHARGANJ

Main Bazar

Bhavbhuti Marg

Vivekanand Marg (Minto Rd)

Tagore Marg

Nur Jahan Rd

G B Pant

Ramdwara Rd

Basant Rd

Basant Lane

Chelmsford Rd

State Entry Rd

Jahangir Rd

D Dayal Upadhay Marg

Press Rd

Turkman Marg

M Ranjit Singh Rd

N

Stadium

Panchkuin Marg

Minto Bridge

CONNAUGHT CIRCUS

0 metres 200
0 yards 200

Related map
A Paharganj,
page 86

Access from Delhi

South New Delhi

The spacious layout of New Delhi has been preserved despite the modern building boom.

The Lodi Gardens The beautiful gardens, with mellow stone tombs of the 15th- and 16th-century Lodi rulers are 1 km to the south of the Purana Qila.

★ Hazrat Nizamuddin At the west end of the Lodi Road is the shrine of Sheikh Nizamuddin Aulia (1236-1325), a Chishti saint. It is visited by pilgrims of all faiths and is particularly stirring when *Qawwalis* are sung at sunset after *namaaz* (prayers). ■ *Dress ultra-modestly if you don't want to feel uncomfortable.*

★ Humayun's tomb Eclipsed later by the Taj Mahal and the Jama Masjid, Humayun's tomb is the best example in Delhi of the early Mughal style of tomb. The tomb has an octagonal plan, lofty arches, pillared kiosks and the double dome of Central Asian origin. Here also is the first standard example of the garden tomb concept: the **char bagh** (garden divided into quadrants), water channels and fountains. The red sandstone dome has white marble to highlight the lines of the building and there is attractive inlay work, and some *jalis*. ■ *Open daily, sunrise to sunset. Entry Rs 5, Fri free. Video cameras Rs 25. 15 mins by taxi from Connaught Circus.*

★ Hauz Khas Ala-ud-din Khalji (ruled 1296-1313) created a large tank here for the inhabitants of **Siri**, the second capital city of Delhi. Fifty years later **Firoz Shah Tughluq** cleaned up the tank and raised several buildings on its banks. Firoz Shah's austere tomb, a *madrasa* (college) and some octagonal and square *chhattris*.

Classical music concerts, dance performances and a son et lumière show are held in the evenings. ■ *1 hr cultural show, 1845, Rs 100 (check with Delhi Tourism). Upmarket restaurants and shops have opened.*

Access from Delhi

★ The Qutb Minar Complex

The Qutb Minar, built to proclaim the victory of Islam over the infidel (unbeliever), dominates the countryside for miles around. Visit the Minar first.

Qutb Minar In 1199 work began on what was intended to be the most glorious tower of victory in the worldland which was also to serve as the minaret attached to the Might of Islam Mosque. From here the muezzin could call the faithful to prayer. Later every mosque would incorporate its minaret.It is 73 m high and consists of five storeys. The calligraphy bands are verses from the Koran and praises to its patron builder. The staircase inside the tower to the balconies are closed.

Quwwat-ul -Islam Mosque The Quwwat-ul-Islam Mosque (The Might of Islam Mosque), is the earliest surviving mosque in India. It was completed in 1198 using the remains of local Hindu and Jain temples. The screen (4) formed the façade of the mosque and, facing in the direction of Mecca, became the focal point. The sandstone screen is carved in the Indo-Islamic style, lotuses mingling with Koranic calligraphy.

Ala'i Minar To the north of the Qutb complex is the **Ala'i Minar**, intended to surpass the tower of the Qutb, but not completed beyond the first storey.

Iltutmish's Tomb Built in 1235, it is the first surviving tomb of a Muslim ruler in India. The idea of a tomb was quite alien to Hindus, who had been practising cremation since around 400 BC. ■ *Open from sunrise to sunset. Rs 5. Bus 505 from New Delhi Rly station (Ajmeri Gate), Super Bazar (east of Connaught Circus) and Cottage Industries Emporium, Janpath.*

★ Tughluqabad
From the walls you get a magnificent impression of the strategic advantages of the site. 7½ km east from Qutb Minar
Tughluqabad's ruins still convey a sense of the power and energy of the newly arrived Muslims in India. **Ghiyas'ud-Din Tughluq** (ruled 1321-25) built this massive fort around his capital city which stands high on a rocky outcrop of the Delhi Ridge. ■ *Sunrise-1700; free. Allow 1 hr. Very deserted so don't go alone. Take plenty of water. For return rickshaws, turn right at entrance and walk 200 m.*

★ Baha'i Temple (Lotus Temple) Architecturally the temple is remarkably striking. Built out of white marble, it is in the characteristic Baha'i temple shape of a lotus flower surrounded by nine pools. The **Baha'i faith** was founded by a Persian, **Baha'u'llah** whose teachings were directed towards the unification of the human race. ■ *1 Apr-30 Sep 0900-1900, 1 Oct-31 Mar 0930-1730. Closed Mon. Visitors are welcome to servicesAudio visual presentations in English, 1100, 1200, 1400, 1530. Getting there: Taxi or auto-rickshaw though Bus 433 from the centre (Jantar Mantar) goes to Nehru Place, within walking distance (1½ km) of the temple.*

Old Delhi

Shah Jahan (ruled 1628-58) decided to move back from Agra to Delhi in 1638. Within 10 years the huge city of **Shah Jahanabad**, now known as Old Delhi, was built. Chandni Chowk, its principle street, retains some of its former magic, though now it is a bustling jumble of shops, labyrinthine alleys running off a main thoroughfare with craftsmen's workshops, hotels, mosques and temples. Here goldsmiths, silversmiths, silk traders and embroiderers can all be found.

★ The Red Fort (Lal Qila) The plan of Shah Jahan's new city symbolized the link between religious authority enshrined in the Jama Masjid to the west, and political authority represented by the Diwan-i-Am in the Fort, joined by Chandni Chowk, the route used by the Emperor.

Chatta Chowk Inside is the 'Covered Bazar', quite exceptional in the 17th century. Originally they catered for the Imperial household and carried stocks of silks, brocades, velvets, gold and silverware, jewellery and gems.

Swatantra Sangrama Sangrahalaya The museum tracing India's history from the colonial period and focuses on the struggle for independence is interesting, educative and well organized. ■ *1000-1700, closed Fri.*

Diwan-i-Am Between the first inner court and the royal palaces at the heart of the fort, stood the Diwan-i-Am (Hall of Public Audience), a showpiece intended to hint at the opulence of the palace itself.

Life-Bestowing Gardens (Hayat Baksh Bagh) The original gardens were landscaped according to the Islamic principles of the Persian *char bagh*, with pavilions, fountains and water courses dividing the garden into various but regular beds.

Diwan-i-Khas Beyond is the single-storeyed 'Hall of Private Audience', topped by four Hindu-style *chhattris* and built completely of white marble. The *dado* (lower part of the wall) on the interior was richly decorated with inlaid precious and semi-precious stones. ■ *Open daily sunrise to sunset. Small entry fee, free on Fri when it is packed.* **NB** *The palaces within the fort may not open to visitors.*

The magnificent Jama Masjid, 1 km to the west of the Red Fort, is the largest mosque in India and the last great architectural work of Shah Jahan. The mosque is much simpler in its ornamentation than Shah Jahan's secular buildings – a judicious blend of red sandstone and white marble, which are interspersed in the domes, minarets and cusped arches. The minarets have great views from the top; well worth the climb for Rs 10. ■ *Visitors welcome from 30 mins after sunrise until 1200; and from 1345 until 30 mins before sunset*

★ **Jama Masjid (The Friday Mosque)**
Remove shoes & cover your head

Museums

This is a rich collection of the artistic treasure of Central Asia and India including ethnological objects from prehistoric archaeological finds to the late Medieval period. There is a research library. ■ *1000-1700, closed Mon. Janpath, T3019272. Entry: foreigners Rs 150, students Rs 1, Indians Rs 10, camera Rs 300; free guided tours 1030, 1130, 1200, 1400. Films, 1430.*

★ **The National Museum**

The official residence of India's first Prime Minister, Jawaharlal Nehru, converted into a national memorial. Films and *son et lumière*. Very informative and vivid history of the Independence Movement. ■ *Museum 0930-1645, closed Mon. Library 0900-1900, closed Sun, free. Teen Murti Bhavan, T3014504.*

★ **Nehru Memorial Museum & Library**

The large 'Village Complex' has over 20,000 pieces of traditional crafts from all over India –including terracottas, bronzes, enamel work, wood painting and carving, brocades and jewellery. Good crafts for sale. Interesting, evocative and highly recommended. ■ *1000-1700, closed Mon. Bhairon Rd, T3317641.*

★ **Craft Museum**

The museum preserves a memorable account of 144 years of the history of Indian Railways with 26 vintage locomotives. ■ *Apr-Sep 0930-1230, 1330-1930; Oct-Mar 0930-1230, 1330-1730, closed Mon and public holidays. Entry Rs 5; camera Rs 10. Good booklet. Auto from centre Rs 40. T/F6880804. Chanakyapuri, southwest of Connaught Place.*

★ **Rail Transport Museum**

Access from Delhi

Essentials

Sleeping

Hotels are grouped by area.

See page 33 for hotel classification.

Pre-paid taxis at aiport may pretend not to know the location so give full details. Cheaper **E**, **F** accommodation is concentrated around Janpath, Paharganj and Chandni Chowk. Some have dormitory beds for under Rs 100. **Tax** 10% Luxury Tax, 10% Service Charge, 20% Expenditure Tax (where rooms are over Rs 1,200 per night).

Airport **LL** *Radisson*, Mahipalpur, next to International Airport, T6129191, F6129090, raddel@del2.vsnl.net.in

Central New Delhi

Airport about 20 km
Railway about 2-3 km

LL-L *Inter-Continental*, Barakhamba Rd, Connaught Place, T3320101, F3325335, newdelhi@interconti.com **LL-L** *Le Meridien*, Windsor Place, Janpath, T3710101, F3714545. **C-D** *Andraprastha* (ITDC), 19 Ashoka Rd, T3344511, F3368153. Excellent a/c *Coconut Grove* south Indian restaurant, (full tariff plus a day's refundable deposit in advance), good value.

See map, page 85
Airport about 20 km
Railway about 2 km

Connaught Place **LL-L** *Park*, 15 Sansad Marg, T373247, F3732025, resv.del@park. sprintrpg.ems.vsnl.net.in **L-AL** *Imperial*, Janpath, T3341234, F3342255. 200 rooms, colonial feel, well tended gardens, good pool. **AL-A** *Hans Plaza*, 15 Barakhamba Rd (on 16th-20th floor), T3316868, F3314830. 'boutique hotel', quiet, superb views.

B *Alka*, P-16 Connaught Circus, T3344328, F3732796. 23 rooms (small but modern) good Indian restaurant, friendly, avoid annexe. **B** *Centrepoint*, 13 Kasturba Gandhi Marg, T3324805. Well located, though front rooms can be noisy. **B** *Marina*, G-59 Connaught Circus, T3324658, F3328609. 93 rooms, some cramped but refurbished, good coffee shop. **B** *Nirula's*, L-Block, Connaught Circus, T3322419, F3353957. good restaurant clean, comfortable, friendly, efficient.

C *York*, K-10, Connaught Circus, T3323769, F3352419. 28 simple rooms on upper floor, restaurant (good snacks), quiet. **C-D** *YWCA International Guest House*, Sansad Marg (near Jantar Mantar), T3361561. 24 a/c rooms, centre 1 km, open to both sexes. **C-D** *YMCA Tourist Hostel*, Jai Singh Rd, T3746031, F3746032. Some a/c rooms with bath (B-Block, non a/c, shared bath), good pool (Rs 100 extra), luggage stored (Rs 5 per day), unhelpful reception, pay in advance but check bill, reserve ahead.

E-F *Jain's Guest House*, 7 Pratap Singh Building, Janpath Lane. Rooms without bath, quiet, clean. **E-F** *Palace Heights*, D-Block Connaught Circus, 3rd Floor, T3321369. 18 simple rooms, 8 a/c, some with bath, breakfast only. Off **Kasturba Gandhi Marg**: **E-F** *Ringo Guest House*, 17 Scindia House, T3310605. Tiny rooms (some window-less) crowded dorm or beds on rooftop, no hot showers, basic toilets, lockers, good restaurant friendly.

New Delhi

See map, page 78

Airport 12-18 km
Railway 5-9 km
Centre 5 km

LL *Taj Mahal*, 1 Mansingh Rd, T3016162, F3017299. Excellent restaurants and service lavishly finished. **LL** *Taj Palace*, 2 Sardar Patel Marg, T6110202, F6110808. pur-pose-built for business travellers). **LL-L** *Maurya Sheraton Hotel and Towers*, Sardar Patel Marg, T6112233, F6113333. splendid pool, avoid rooms near disco,good restau-rants **LL-L** *Oberoi*, Dr Zakir Hussain Marg, T4363030, F4364084. immaculate, quietly efficient **L-AL** *Claridges*, 12 Aurangzeb Rd, T3010211, F3010625. Colonial atmo-sphere, grand but frayed around the edges.

A-B *Orchid*, G4 S Extn 1, T4643529, F4626924. 18 a/c rooms, crowded area, restaurants nearby, pleasant, helpful.

B *Nirula's*, C-135 Sector 2, NOIDA, T85-526512, F85-551069 (also in Connaught Circus). Free transfer to town centre, pleasant atmosphere. **B** *Rajdoot*, Mathura Rd, T4699583, F4647442. 55 rooms, near Nizammuddin Rly, pool. **D-E** *Master Paying Guest*, R-500 New Rajendra Nagar (near Shankar & GR Hospital Rds), T5850914. Clean rooms, shared facilities, rooftop for breakfast, secure.

Youth hostels **F** *Youth Hostel*, 5 Naya Marg, Chanakyapuri, T3016285. Basic dorm (Rs 30), breakfast, prefer International YHA members, popular, recommended.

Connaught Place

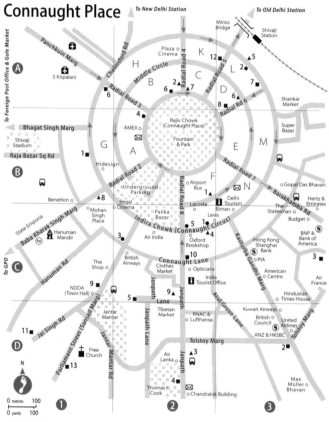

■ **Sleeping**
1 Alka *B1*
2 Centrepoint *D3*
3 Hans Plaza *C3*
4 Imperial *D2*
5 Jain's Guest House *C2*
6 Marina & Chemists *A1*
7 Nirula's, Ice Creams & Potpouri Restaurant *A3*
8 Palace Heights *A3*
9 Park *C1*
10 Ringo Guest House & Don't Pass Me By Restaurant *C2*
11 YMCA Tourist Hostel *D1*
12 York *A3*
13 YWCA International Guest House *D1*

● **Eating**
1 Amber *C2*
2 Delhi Darbar *A3*
3 Kwality *C2*
4 Wengers & Rodeo *B2*
5 Wimpy & Pizza King *C2*
6 Zen *A2*

▲ **Other**
1 Automobile Association *B2*
2 Bookworm *A2*
3 Central Cottage Industries Emporium *D2*
4 Delhi Transport Corp (DTC) *C2*
5 First Class Railway Reservations *A3*
6 ITDC Transport *A3*
7 Jains Bookshop *A2*
8 Khadi Gramodyog *B1*
9 Map Sales Office *C2*

Old Delhi

See map, page 80
Airport about 30 km
Railway about 10 km
Old Delhi Rly 2 km

AL-A *Oberoi Maidens*, 7 Sham Nath Marg, T2914864, F2915134. Colonial style in quiet area, spacious gardens with excellent pool. Personal attention. **A** *Broadway*, 4/15A Asaf Ali Rd, T3273821, F3269966. Indian business hotel, 32 clean rooms, friendly, efficient, unique *Chor Bizarre* restaurant. **E** *Noor*, 421 Matia Mahal, Jama Masjid (first left after Flora's Restaurant, then 3rd left), T3267791. 34 clean, quiet rooms, shared facilities (Indian WC), fans. **E** *Wongdhen House*, 15A New Tibetan Colony, Manju-ka-Tilla, by the Yamuna, T2916689, F2945962. Very clean rooms safe, homely, good breakfast and Tibetan meals.

Camping F *New Delhi Tourist Camp*, Nehru Marg, opposite JP Narayan Hospital, T3272898, F3263693. 130 tiny rooms (deluxe **E** rooms, cooler/TV Rs 35 extra) plus cheaper dorm beds, hot water, restaurant, exchange, pleasant gardens, EATS bus to airport (Rs 50), friendly atmosphere, secure. **F** *Tourist Camp*, Qudsia Gardens, opposite ISBT-, T2523121. Camping and huts, food available.

Paharganj Area

See map, page 86
There are several fairly
cheap, noisy, basic
hotels, often with shared
baths. Inspect before
deciding. Avoid
street-side rooms

D *Gold Regency*, 4350 Main Bazar, T3540101, F3540202, goldregency@hotmail.com Good, clean a/c rooms, restaurants, disco, Cyber Club. **D** *Tourist Delux*, Qutb Rd, T7770985, F7777446. Comfortable a/c rooms, few **C** suites with bath tubs, vegetarian restaurant. **D-E** *Major Den's*, Lakshmi Narain St, off Rajguru Rd, T7529599. Clean, good value. **D-E** *Saina International*, 2324 Chuna Mandi, near Imperial Cinema, T3529144, F7520879. Clean rooms, some a/c, hot water, open-air restaurant serves beer. **E** *Anoop*, 1566 Main Bazar, T735219. Rooms with bath, some air-cooled, very clean though basic, noisy at times, safe, good 24-hr rooftop restaurant. **E** *Hare Krishna*, 1572 Main Bazar, T7533017. Very clean rooms with bath (some windowless, stuffy), friendly, travel, restaurant (good selection of cheap pizzas). **E** *Metropolis*, 1634 Main Bazar, T7535766,

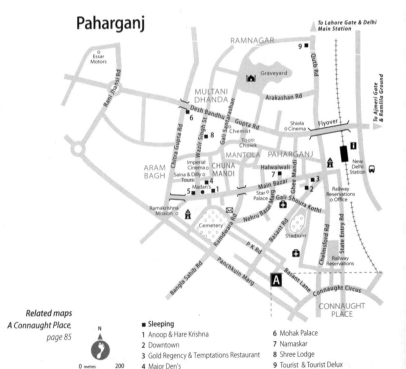

Paharganj

Related maps
A Connaught Place,
page 85

0 metres 200
0 yards 200

■ **Sleeping**
1 Anoop & Hare Krishna
2 Downtown
3 Gold Regency & Temptations Restaurant
4 Major Den's
5 Metropolis & Restaurant

6 Mohak Palace
7 Namaskar
8 Shree Lodge
9 Tourist & Tourist Delux

F7525600. 13 rooms, some air cooled, good 4-bed dorm, clean, restaurant with wide choice but pricey. **E-F** *Downtown*, 4583 Dal Mandi, T3555815. Clean and quiet rooms, some with bath. **F** *Mohak Palace*, Multani Dhanda. Clean, friendly, safe to leave luggage. **F** *Namaskar*, 917 Chandiwalan, Main Bazar, T7521234, F7522233. Small rooms (2-4 beds) with bath and bucket hot water, clean but some windowless, newer **E** a/c rooms in extension (no generator), safe, quiet at night, stores luggage, 'poste restante'. **F** *Shree Lodge*, 2012-2015 Chuna Mandi, T3526864. Clean rooms, quiet.

LL *Hyatt Regency*, Bhikaiji Cama Place, Ring Rd, T6181234, F6186833. Rooms tiny for price. **A** *Vasant Continental*, Vasant Vihar, T6148800, F6873842. 110 rooms, convenient for airports (free transfer). **B-C** *Jorbagh '27'*, 27 Jorbagh, T4698647, F4698475. 20 a/c rooms, not plush but very quiet. **C** *Legend Inn*, E-4 east of Kailash, T6216111, F6483353. Comfortable a/c rooms, no restaurant, homely. **C-D** *Naari*, Vasant Kunj (easy access from airport), guest house for women in pleasant residential area, simple rooms with shower, some air-cooled, (reserve ahead T6138316, F6187401, naari@del3.vsnl.net.in

South Delhi
Airport about 18 km
Railway 12 km
Centre 10 km

Several are 20 mins'
drive from the airport
(see map, page 78)

Eating

The larger **hotel restaurants** are often the best for cuisine, décor and ambience. **Buffets** (lunch or dinner) cost Rs 500 or more. **Alcohol** is served in most top hotels, but only in some non-hotel restaurants.

● *on maps*
Price codes:
see inside front cover

Expensive *Amber*, N-Block, T3312092. Lightly spiced Indian. *Zen*, T3724458. enerous portions for Chinese.

Connaught Place Area
See map, page 85

Mid-range *Berco's*, L-Block, T3318134. Chinese, Japanese. Generous helpings, fast service. *Kwality*, Parliament St. International. Try spicy Punjabi dishes with various breads. *Mughal Hans*, at Hans Plaza, Karol Bagh. Indian. Smart, beautifully presented, delicious Mughal. *Potpourri*, Nirula's, L-Block. Indian and continental. Bright, clean and very popular –light meals, salad bar (safe!) beers, Defence Colony Flyover. *Rodeo*, A-12. Excellent Mexican and Italian.

Cheap *Delhi Darbar*, 49 Connaught Circus. North Indian. Good mutton dishes, bar. *Don't Pass Me By*, by *Ringos*, 17 Scindia House. Chinese. Bit dingy, but good basic food and plenty of it. *Nathu's*, Bengali Market (east of Connaught Place). Indian. Mainly vegetarian. Good *dosa idli*, *uthapam* and North Indian *chana bathura*, clean, functional canteen style.

Expensive *Bukhara*, *Maurya Sheraton*, T6112233. Stylish Northwest Frontier cuisine. Amidst rugged walls draped with rich rugs. *Corbett's*, Claridge's Hotel, T3010211. Authentic North Indian. Animal park theme outdoor, jungle soundtrack, hidden animals delight children, good value. *Chinese*, does great soups. *Dum Phukt*, Maurya Sheraton, T6112233. North Indian. Slowly steam cooked to produce melt-in-the-mouth Nawabi dishes. *Las Meninas*, Park Hotel, 15 Sansad Marg, T3733737. Good Spanish dishes, pricey but generous *tapas* Rs 100-475. *Orient Express*, Taj Palace Hotel, T6110202. Continental. Recreated luxury of the famous train carriages. *Spice Route*, Imperial Hotel. Excellent Kerala, Thai, Vietnamese cuisines, spectacular decor.

Central New Delhi

Mid-range *Basil and Thyme*, Santushti Complex, Chanakyapuri, T4673322. Continental. Pleasant setting, simple décor, a/c, modestly priced Western snacks at lunch.

Cheap *Nathu's*, 2 Sunder Nagar Market. Indian. Mainly vegetarian. Good *dosa idli*, *uthapam* and North Indian *chana bathura*, clean.

Access from Delhi

Old Delhi & **Mid-range** *Khyber*, Rajendra Place, T5762501. Peshawari dishes.
the North
See map, page 80

Cheap *Flora*, Daryaganj. North Indian. Optional floor cushions, excellent *kalmi* chicken kebab, *biryani* and breads, dark and gloomy but good food. *Peshawari*, 3707 Subhash Marg, Daryaganj. Northwest Frontier. Tiny, with tiled walls, serves delicious chicken, closed Tue.

Paharganj Rooftop restaurants tend to be pricier. *Madan's*, 1601 Main Bazar. International. Egg and chips to *thalis*, not special but friendly, popular, good value. *Temptation*, at *Chanakya*, 4350 Main Bazaar. Pleasant. Good western (veg burgers, cakes), internet, disco and bar.

Transport: local

Auto-rickshaw Widely available at about half the cost of taxis (Rs 4 per km); agree fare in advance. Add 25 % for a night charge (2300-0500). **Cycle-rickshaws** are available in the Old City but are not allowed into Connaught Place.

Bus The city bus service run by the Delhi Transport Corp connects all important points in the city. Buses are often hopelessly overcrowded so only use at off-peak.

Car hire **Private taxi** : full day local use with driver (non a/c) is about Rs 700-850, 80 km/8 hrs, driver overnight *bata* Rs 150 per day. Companies include: *Metropole Tourist Service*, 244 Defence Flyover Market, T4312212, F4311819, metropole@vsnl.com, car/jeep; *Mohindra Tourist Taxis*, corner of Poorvi/Paschimi Margs, Vasant Vihar, T6143188; *Western Court Tourist Taxis*, 36 Janpath, outside *Hotel Imperial* T3321236; *Nature Tour*, 2591 Mandir Wali Gali, W Patel Nagar, T5709584, nature_tour_travels@yahoo.com
Budget, 78/3 Janpath, T3715657, F3739182; 82 Nehru Place, T6452634; *Europcar*, 14 Basant Lok, Vasant Vihar, T6140373, F6145383; M3 Connaught Circus, T6862248; *Hertz*, Barakhamba Rd, T3318695; Bhikaji Cama Place, T6197188, F6197206.

Motorcycle Karol Bagh shops: *Chawla Motorcycles*, 1770, Shri Kissan Dass Marg, Naiwali Gali; *Inder Motors*, 1744 Hari Singh Nalwa Gali, Abdul Aziz Rd, T5725879; *Nanna Motors*, 112 Press Rd (east of Connaught Circus), T3351769; *Ess Aar Motors*, Jhandewalan Extn, west of Paharganj.

Taxi **Yellow-top taxis** Meters are often not updated so ask for the conversion card. Add 25% night charge (2300-0500).

Transport: long distance

Air **Air** International flights arrive at the **Indira Gandhi International Terminal (II)**, 23 km southwest from Connaught Circus. Enquiries T5622011; pre-recorded arrivals and departures, T144/5; reservations, T146. Money changing; Thomas Cook accepts only their own TCs. The **Palam Domestic Terminal (I)** is 15 km from Connaught Circus. Enquiries T3295121; pre-recorded arrivals and departures, T142/3, private airlines, T149, reservations, T141.

Delhi has flights to: **Bagdogra** (for Darjeeling). **Dibrugarh, Guwahati, Kolkata Kullu; Shimla, Srinagar**

Some hotel buses leave **Transport to and from the airport** **Bus**: run by Ex-Servicemen's Airlink Trans-
from the Domestic port Service (EATS), F Block Connaught Pl, T3316530, **Delhi Transport Corp (DTC)**
terminal and **Airports Authority of India (AAI)** from the 2 terminals go to Connaught Place,

New Delhi Railway Station and ISBT (Kashmir Gate) via some hotels. One leaves from IA office, Connaught Place, goes to the Domestic and then the International terminal, 0400, 0530, 0730, 1000, 1400, 1530, 1800, 1900, 2200, 2330; Rs 50; Rs 10 luggage. There is a booth just outside 'Arrivals' at the International and Domestic terminals. A bus is a safe, economical option, particularly for the first-time visitor on a budget. At night, take a pre-paid taxi. **Free shuttle** between the 2 terminals every 30 mins during the day. **Bus 780** runs between the **airport** and **New Delhi Rly station**.

Taxi: The International and Domestic terminals have **pre-paid taxi** counters outside the baggage hall which ensure that you pay the right amount (give your name, exact destination and number of all items of luggage). Most expensive are white 'DLZ' **limousines** and then white 'DLY' **luxury taxis**. Cheapest are 'DLT' **ordinary Delhi taxis** (black with yellow top Ambassador/Fiat cars, often very old). (see page 25). Take your receipt to the ticket counter outside to find your taxi and give it to the driver when you reach the destination; you don't need to tip. From the International terminal **DLT taxis** Rs 200 for town-centre (Connaught Place area); night charges, double, 2300-0500.

The Government **Tourist Information** desk will book a hotel but not in the 'budget' category. **Indian Railways Counter**. Helpful computerized booking; easier and quicker than at a station.

Bus Inter-State Bus Termini (ISBT); these have bus services between them. Allow at least 30 mins for buying a ticket and finding the right bus. **Kashmir Gate**, T2968709, has a restaurant, left luggage (Rs 5 per day). **Delhi TC**, T2968836. For Manali: Himachal Roadways. **Ajmeri Gate**: **UP Roadways**, T2968709; to Almora (5 hrs), Dehradun, Haridwar, Mussoorie. **Rajpur Rd**: **Himachal Roadways**, T2966725; Dharamshala (12 hrs), Manali (15 hrs), Shimla (10 hrs). **Jammu and Kashmir RTC**, *Hotel Kanishka*, T3324511; to Jammu; *Yatri Niwas Hotel* to Srinagar. **Anand Vihar**, Yamuna Bundh Rd, T2152431: **UP Roadways**, T2149089, to Dehradun (259 km, 6 hrs via Roorkee); Haridwar (5 hrs) etc.

Road
All road journeys in India are slow. Main roads out of Delhi are very heavily congested. Best time to leave is very early morning

New Delhi Rly Station and **Hazrat Nizamuddin Station** (just north, and 5 km southeast of Connaught Place, respectively) connect Delhi with most major destinations. The latter has many important south-bound trains. **Old Delhi (Main) Station**, 6 km north of the centre, has broad and metre gauge trains. **Enquiries** T131, T3366177. **Waiting Rooms**, and **Rest Rooms**, are for those 'in transit'. Authorized **porters** (*coolies*), wear red shirts and white *dhotis;* the number on the brass badge identifies each so it is best to make a note of it, and agree the charge, before engaging one. For **left luggage**, you need a secure lock and chain.

Train

    Reservations T3348686, Old Delhi T3975357. Allow time (1-2 hrs) and be prepared to be very patient as it can be a nightmare but don't be tempted to go to an unauthorized agents (see below). The Central Booking Office has counters for paying by credit cards. **Computerized reservation offices** (in separate building in Connaught Circus); 0745-2100, Sun 0745-1400; fee Rs 20. The Sarojini Nagar office is quick, hassle free (especially the credit card counter). Alternatively, you can use a recommended travel agent for tickets/reservations and pay Rs 30-50 fee. At **New Delhi Station**: **International Tourist Bureau (ITB)**, 1st Floor, Main Building, T3734164, for foreigners, Mon-Fri 0930-1630; Sat 0930-1430. You need your passport and visa; pay in US$, or rupees (with an encashment certificate). Those with **Indrail passes**, should look for sign to confirm bookings. The *Airport* counter here is quick and efficient for tickets and reservations. **Exchange**: Thomas Cook, near Platform 12, by VIP Parking, Ajmeri Gate, open 24 hrs. The **pre-paid taxi** and **auto-rickshaw** kiosks are next to the taxi rank as you come out of the station. See under airport taxis above. An auto to Connaught Place costs Rs 12, Old Delhi Station Rs 25.

NB Rickshaw drivers/touts may say the ITB is closed/ has moved and suggest alternatives. Ignore them.

NB Stations from which trains originate are given codes: **OD** – Old Delhi, **ND** – New Delhi, **HN** – Hazrat Nizamuddin.

Agra: *Shatabdi Exp*, *2002*, ND 0615, 2 hrs; *Taj Exp*, *2180*, HN, 0705, 2¾ hrs. **Dehradun**: *Shatabdi*, ND daily except Wed 0710, 5¼ hrs. **Guwahati**: *Rajdhani*, *2424*, ND, Tue, Thu, Sat, 28 hrs. **Haridwar**: *Shatabdi Exp*, 2017, daily except Wed, ND, 0655, 4¼ hrs; *Mussoorie Exp*, *4041*, OD, 2225, 7¾ hrs. **Jammu** (for Kashmir): *Malwa Exp*, *4667*, HN, 1213, 11 hrs. *Rajdhani Exp*, *1425*, ND, Fri, 2020, 9½ hrs. **Kalka**: *Shatabdi Exp*, ND 1715, 4¾ hrs. . **New Jalpaiguri** (for Darjeeling): *Rajdhani Exp*, ND, 1700, 21½ hrs. **Shimla**: *Haora-Kalka Mail*, *2311* DSR, 2245 (change at **Kalka** to *101 railcar*), total 11 hrs (book sleeper; ahead). From ND: *Himalayan Queen*, *4095*, 0600 to Kalka, 5 hrs, change to narrow gauge *255*, 1140, total 11¼ hrs (see Shimla & Kalka, pages 156 & 159).

Directory

Airline offices

Abbreviations used:
A = Airport phone no.
KG Marg = Kasturba Gandhi Marg

Domestic: check in for all *Indian Airlines* flights at terminal 1-A. Check in for all other domestic airlines Terminal 1-B. Arrivals for all domestic flights Terminal 1-C. *Indian Airlines*, Safdarjang Airport, Aurobindo Marg, 24-hr daily (to avoid delays be there at 0830), T141, T4620566, 4624332 (2100-0700), closed Sun; pre-recorded flight information (English) T142; Reservations also 1000-1700, Mon-Sat, at PTI Building, Sansad Marg, T3719168; at *Ashok Hotel*, T6110101; A 5665121. *Alliance Air* is a subsidiary, Safdarjang Airport, T4621267, A 5665854. **Private**: *Jagson Airways*, 12 E Vandana Building, 11 Tolstoy Marg, T3721594, A 5665545. *Jet Airways*, 13 Community Centre, Yusuf Sarai, T6517443; G-12 Connaught Place, T3320961, A 5665404. *Sahara*, 7th Flr, 14 KG Marg, T3326851, A 5665234. *Trans Bharat Aviation* (see Kullu). *UP Air*, A2 Defence Colony, T4638201, A 5665126.

Tourist offices

Information offices: *Govt of India Tourist Office*, 88 Janpath, T3320008 (0900-1800, closed Sun). *Delhi Tourism*, N-36 Connaught Place, T3315322, F3313637. For hotel, transport and tours: 18, DDA SCO Complex, Defence Colony, T4623782, Coffee Home Annexe, Baba Kharak Singh Marg, T3365358.. *ITDC*, L-Block Connaught Place, T3320331. Counters at ITDC hotels (Ashok). **State tourist offices**: open 1000-1800, Mon-Fri. On Baba Kharak Singh Marg: *Assam*, T.3345897.*West Bengal*, A-2, T3732640. In the Chandralok Building (opposite *Imperial Hotel*), 36 Janpath Rd*Himachal Pradesh*, T3324764; *Uttaranchal*, T3322251. In the Kanishka Shopping Plaza, 19 Ashoka Rd:. *Jammu and Kashmir*, T3345373. T3323055. **Others**: *Arunachal Pradesh*, Kautiliya Marg, Chanakyapuri, T3017909. *Meghalaya* 9 Aurangzeb Rd, T3014417. *Sikkim*, 14 Panchsheel Marg, T6883026.

Travel agents

We list a few. Some will get air and rail tickets/reservations for about Rs 50 *American Express*, A-Block, Connaught Place, T3324119. *Bholenath*, near *Ajay's*, Main Bazar, Paharganj, T3558975, F7515102. *Cozy Travel*, opposite 'Out' gate of New Delhi Rly Station, T7774768, F7534446, cozy@ndf.vsnl.net.in *Creative Travel*, 27-30 Creative Plaza, Nanak Pura, Moti Bagh, T4679192, F6889764. *Highland*, N-29 Middle Circle, Connaught Pl, opp DSIDC, T3318236, F3329121, highlandtravel@usa.net *Ibex*, G66 East of Kailash T6912641, F6846403, www.ibexexpeditions.com Adventure tours, treks. *Outbound*, 216A/11 Gautam Nagar, T6521308, F6522617, outbound@vsnl.com *Paradise Holidays*, 20-B Basant Lok, Community centre, Vasant Vihar, T6145116, F6145112, www.paradiseholidays.com.in *Peak Adventure*, T-305, DAV Complex, DDA Shopping Complex, Mayur Vihar Phase-1, T2711284, F2711292, peakadv@nde.vsnl.net.in *Royal Expeditions*, R-184, Greater Kailash-1, New Delhi - 110048, T91 (11) 623 8545, F647 5954, www.royalexpeditions.com *STIC*, *Hotel Imperial*, Janpath, T3327582. Student specialists. *Thomas Cook*, *Hotel Imperial*, Janpath, T3342171; 85A Panchkuin Marg, T3747404; International Trade Towers, Nehru Place, T6423035. *Trans Indus*, T020-85662729, F8405327, www.transindus.co.uk Activities, wildlife. *Wanderlust*, M51/52 Palika Bhawan, opposite *Hyatt Regency*, T4102180, F6885188, www.wan derlustindia.com *Y's*, YMCA Tourist Hostel, Jaisingh Rd, T3361915. Discounted tickets. See also page 23.

Emmergencies **Ambulance** (24 hrs): T102. **Fire**: T101. **Police**: T100.

Garhwal & Kumaon Himalaya

3

Garhwal & Kumaon Himalaya

**96 Dehra Dun and Uttaranchal
    Himalaya**

 99 Mussoorie

103 Haridwar, (Uttar Pradesh)

106 Rishikesh

110 Garhwal and the Pilgrimage

118 Trekking in the Garhwal and the
     Kumaon Himalaya

128 Nainital

133 Almora

138 Corbett National Park

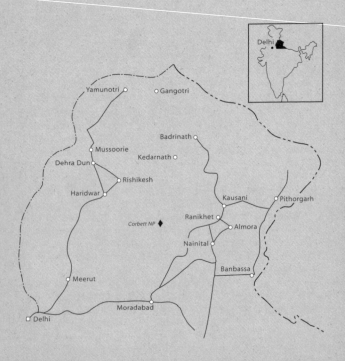

Among the high peaks of the Uttar Pradesh ('Northern Province') Himalaya, now the new state of Uttaranchal, springs the source of the sacred river Ganga (Ganges), regarded by Hindus as the physical and spiritual life source of the country. It has been the heart of much of India's religious and cultural life, the cradle of Hinduism

The Garhwal and Kumaon (Kumaun) Himalaya, have been a proving ground for some of the world's greatest mountaineers. The 'holy abodes' of the Gods in this area of Central Himalaya attract Yatra pilgrims to the mountain shrines. The region contains such treasures as the Valley of the Flowers and offers some of the country's greatest trekking and whitewater rafting.

Background

The newly created state of Uttaranchal, which comprises thirteen districts from the densely populated foothills up to the heights of the Nanda Devi range, has some of India's most magnificent mountain scenery and outstanding, yet relatively little known, trekking.

The land The extraordinarily contorted geology of the Garhwal and Kumaon Himalaya reflects the fierce uplifting and the complex movements which have taken place since the Himalaya began to be formed. The outer ranges of the Siwaliks, generally less than 2500 metres high, are a jumble of deeply dissected sediments. In places these are separated from the Lesser Himalayan ranges by great longitudinal valleys, or *duns*, such as Dehra Dun, while in the Lesser Himalaya immediately to their north, towns such as Mussoorie, Almora and Nainital offered coolness in the summer from the overpowering heat of the plains. Immediately to their north again the high peaks are surrounded by deep valleys, at their heads still some of the world's largest glaciers. Some meteorologists predict that the Himalaya will be glacier-free within thirty years or so. This is not the result of recent global warming, but the latest phase in the ten thousand year retreat of the latest northern hemisphere Ice Age. Glaciers such as the Milam, still several kilometres long, are covered in boulders, and float over the masses of material which have been dropped by glaciers too shrunk to move it any further. Forming a massive barrier to their north are the permanent snows and high peaks such as **Nanda Devi** (7,816 metres), **Badrinath**, **Shivling** and other peaks over 6,000 metres.

Climate The climate of Uttaranchal is dominated by the monsoon, with over three quarters of the rainfall coming between June and September, but temperature is controlled both by height and by season. In the lower valleys, such as Dehra Dun, summers are hot and sticky and maximum temperatures can go up to 45 C. Towns on the ridges up to 2000 metres high such as Almora and Ranikhet experience maximum temperatures in the summer of up to 34 C. Yet in winter these same towns experience snow fall, and temperatures even in the outer valleys are as low as 3 C or 4 C. Despite a drop of temperature between June and September humidity increases, making it a very uncomfortable season in the foothills. The high peaks are under permanent snow. In the higher hills the air is always fresh but can be very cold, making late April to early June and September-October generally the best times for trekking.

Culture Ethnically, on the plains the inhabitants have Aryan features, northwards giving way to strong Mongoloid features on the border with Tibet. Most people speak Hindi, but Urdu is still quite widely used among Muslims. There are numerous local dialects. A broad division can be made between those on the plains and the *Pahari* (hill) dialects, one of the reasons given by the residents for the creation of a separate state of Uttaranchal in the Himalayan region of Uttar Pradesh which became a reality on 9th November 2000.

History Up until the 14th century Garhwal (Land of the Forts) comprised a number of petty principalities. Ajai Pal (1358-70) consolidated these and became the Raja of Garhwal. The region was a popular plundering ground for Sikh brigands – see Rampur (page 160). The **Gurkhas** overran it in 1803, taking men, women and children into slavery and conscripting males into their army. Gurkha encroachments on the territory around Gorakhpur led the British to expel them from Garhwal and Kumaon in 1814. They took the eastern part of Garhwal as British Garhwal and returned the western part, Tehri Garhwal, to the deposed Raja.

Economy

Scattered farming villages among picturesque terraces present the skill with which Uttaranchal's mountain people have adapted to their hill environment. Agriculture is still by far the most important economic activity throughout the hills, often carried out with apparent simplicity but considerable sophistication, both of engineering and of cropping types. On many of the cultivated hillsides terracing is essential and wonderfully intricate, and a wide variety of crops - paddy, wheat, barley and lentils on the low lying irrigated terraces, sugar cane, chillies, buckwheat and millets higher up, are just some of the major crops. Market gardening and potato cultivation have spread around all the townships. Rotation of crops is widely practised and intensive use of animal manure helps to fertilise the soil. The terraces themselves, sometimes as high as 6 metres, may have as many as 500 flights, and some villages have as many as 6000 individual terraces. Given that it takes one man a day to build a wall a metre high and two metres long, it is easy to see what vast amounts of labour have gone into their construction, and how much care is lavished on their maintenance, for they are the peoples' security.

The forests also supply vital wealth. Apart from the timber itself resin is often a valuable export, and wood carving is a widely practised skill. Today tourism is an increasingly important source of income, both of Indian visitors from the plains and of foreigners seeking to experience something of the high Himalayan ranges.

Dehra Dun देहरादून and Uttaranchal

Phone code: 0135
Colour map 2, grid B1
Population: 370,000
Altitude: 695 m

Dehra Dun (dera – camp; dun – valley, pronounced 'doon'), lies in a wooded valley in the Shiwalik Hills. In Hindu legend the Dun Valley was part of Siva's stamping ground. Rama and his brother are said to have done penance for killing Ravana, and the five Pandavas stopped here on their way to the mountains. It makes a pleasant and relaxing stop on the way to the hills, and its mild climate has made it a popular retirement town. The cantonment, across the seasonal Bindal Rao river, is spacious and well wooded, while the Mussoorie road is lined with very attractive houses.

Ins & outs
See page 98 for further details

Getting there The railway station, off Haridwar Road to the south of town, has trains from Delhi, Varanasi and Kolkata. Buses heading for the hills use the Mussoorie Bus Stand outside the station, while those bound for the plains use the Delhi Bus Stand near *Hotel Drona*, 500 m away. Share taxis operate services to the hills from the stand outside the railway station. **Getting around** The City Bus Stand, also used by private buses, is just north of the Clock Tower in the busy town centre, about 10 mins on foot from the railway station. Although the town centre is compact it is best to get a taxi, an auto-rickshaw for visiting the various institutions which are between 4-8 km (10-20 mins ride) away.

History A third century BC Asoka rock inscription found near Kalsi suggests that the area was ruled by the Emperor. During the 17th-18th century Dehra Dun changed hands several times. The Gurkhas overran it on the westward expansion from Kumaon to Kangra, finally ceding it to the British in 1815 who developed it as a centre of education and research. It is still a major centre for Government institutions like the Survey of India and for the Indian Army.

Sights The **Survey of India** (founded 1767) has its headquarters on Rajpur Road, about 4 km from the Clock Tower. The **Doon School**, off Kaulagarh Road, India's first public school, is still one of its most prestigious. Further along, the highly regarded **Forest Research Institute** (1914), an impressive red-brick building which was designed by Sir Edward Lutyens is surrounded by fine lawns of the Botanical Gardens and forests. It has excellent museums; 0900-1730 weekdays, but unfriendly staff. The **Royal Indian Military College** (1922), in quaint mock Tudor style and the Indian Military Academy (1932), which opened with 40 cadets now takes 1,200.

The **Tapkesvar Cave Temple**, 5 km northwest, is in a pleasant setting with cool sulphur springs for bathing. Open sunrise to sunset. There is a simple Indian café nearby. Buses stop 500 m from the temple

Robber's Cave (8 km), **Lakshman Sidh** (12 km), the snows at **Chakrata** (9 km) and sulphur springs at **Shahasradhara** (14 km) are also within easy reach. The springs were threatened by limestone quarrying on the hills around until the High Court forced their closure. Replanting of the deforested hills has been allowing the water table and the springs to recover.

Forest Research Institute's six museums and the Wadia Institute of Himalayan Geology, west of town, are open 1000-1700.

The cheaper hotels are near the station and the Clock Tower; the upmarket ones are north, along Rajpur Rd. Good discounts out-of-season (Aug-Feb). **B** *Madhuban*, 97 Rajpur Rd, T749990, F746496, madhuban@nde.vsnl.net.in 42 rooms, good restaurants, pleasant garden, comfortable though rather characterless, but friendly staff, excellent views. **B** *Great Value Dehradun* (Clarks), 74C Rajpur Rd, 4 km rly station, T744086, F746058. 53 pleasant a/c rooms, restaurant (Indian classical singing, evenings), business centre, modern, clean, good service, lives up to its name. Recommended. **B-C** *Ajanta Continental*, 101 Rajpur Rd, T749595, F747722. 30 rooms, good restaurant and bar, pool, pleasant ambience. **B-C** *Inderlok*, 29 Rajpur Rd, T658113, F652111. 50 rooms, some a/c, good restaurant. **C** *President*, 6 Astley Hall, Rajpur Rd, T657386, F658883. 18 a/c rooms, good restaurant, bar, coffee shop, exchange, travel, golf and riding arranged, pleasant, good service, good value. **C-D** *Meedo's Grand*, 28 Rajpur Rd, T647171, F645722. 35 rooms, restaurant, bar, exchange, modern, attractive, pleasant atmosphere, friendly service. **D** *Deepshikha*, Rajpur Rd, T659888. 22

Garhwal & Kumaon Himalaya

Dehra Dun

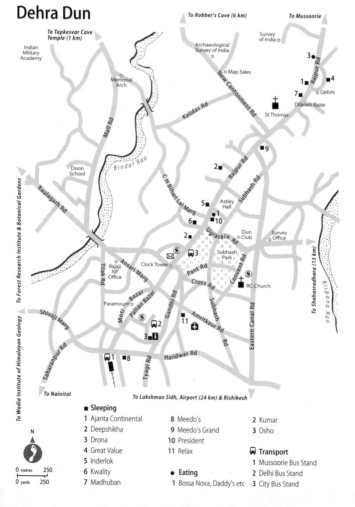

To Robber's Cave (6 km)
To Mussoorie
To Tapkesvar Cave Temple (1 km)
Survey of India
Indian Military Academy
Archaeological Survey of India
Map Sales
Memorial Arch
St Thomas
Dilaram Bazar
GMVN
New Cantonment Rd
Kalidas Rd
Rajpur Rd
Mall Rd
Bindal Rao
Doon School
C H Bihari Lal Marg
Rajpur Rd
Subhash Rd
Kaulagarh Rd
Astley Hall
Ugrasain Rd
Dun Club
Survey Office
Ansari Marg
Clock Tower
Subhash Park
Rajaji NP Office
Tilak Rd
Pant Rd
Convent Rd
RC Church
Cross Rd
Bazar
Paramount
Patan Bazar
Gandhi Rd
Amritkaur Rd
Subhash Rd
Eastern Canal Rd
Rispana Rao
Shivaji Marg
Saharanpur Rd
Tyagi Rd
Haridwar Rd
To Nainital
To Lakshman Sidh, Airport (24 km) & Rishikesh
To Forest Research Institute & Botanical Gardens
To Wadia Institute of Himalayan Geology
To Shahasradhara (13 km)

N
0 metres 250
0 yards 250

■ **Sleeping**
1 Ajanta Continental
2 Deepshikha
3 Drona
4 Great Value
5 Inderlok
6 Kwality
7 Madhuban
8 Meedo's
9 Meedo's Grand
10 President
11 Relax

● **Eating**
1 Bossa Nova, Daddy's etc

2 Kumar
3 Osho

🚌 **Transport**
1 Mussoorie Bus Stand
2 Delhi Bus Stand
3 City Bus Stand

rooms (some a/c), pleasant, modern. **D** *Drona* (GMVN), 45 Gandhi Rd, T654371, F654408. 68 rooms, some a/c, dorm (Rs 70, men only), restaurants (good Indian), bar, large, busy and good value, tourist office in compound. **D** *Kwality*, 19 Rajpur Rd, T657001. 20 clean rooms, some a/c, reasonable restaurant, bar. **D** *Relax*, 7 Court Rd, T657776, F651116. 32 clean a/c or air-cooled rooms, restaurant, bar. **E** *Meedo's*, 71 Gandhi Rd, T657088. Quieter rooms at back, some with bath, noisy bar.

Eating
● *on map*
Price codes:
see inside front cover

Cheap Outside hotels, small Indian eateries serve good food. Simple *Vegetarian*, 3 Astley Plaza, Rajpur Rd; non-veg *Daddy's* above, serves travellers' favourites. *Kumar*, 15B Rajpur Rd (towards Kwality). Tasty Punjabi vegetarian dishes. *Bossa Nova* Astley Hall. Ice creams and western snacks. *Osho*, 111 Rajpur Rd. Good snacks in 'Rajneesh' atmosphere. **Bakeries** Several in Paltan Bazar: *Grand* and *Ellora* sell fresh bread, biscuits and local sticky coffee toffee!

Festivals Feb/Mar: *Jhanda Festival*, in honour of Guru Ram Rai, 5 days after Holi and a large fair at Tapkesvar Temple on Sivaratri.

Shopping Shops around the Clock Tower, in Rajpur Rd, Paltan Bazar and Astley Hall, sell handwoven woollens, brassware and jewellery. For trekking equipment, try *Paramount*, 16 Moti Bazar (west of Paltan Bazar). **Books** for natural history and related topics: *The Green Bookshop*, Rajpur Rd.

Transport **Local Bus**: from Rajpur Rd, near clocktower. **Car hire**: from *Drona Travels* (GMVN), T656894, or *Ventures*, BMS Business Centre, 87 Rajpur Rd, T652724. **Taxi** (T627877) and **auto-rickshaw**: the cheaper crowded Vikrants are easily available. **Long distance Air**: Jolly Grant air strip (24 km) is closed. **Road Bus**: Delhi Bus Stand, Gandhi Rd, T653797, for most hill destinations; Mussoorie Bus Stand, outside rly station, T623435. Private buses from City Bus Stand, Parade Ground. Regular services to **Mussoorie**, 1½ hrs; **Nainital**, 12 hrs; **Kulu, Haridwar**, 1½ hrs. **From Shimla**: HP Roadways to Dehra Dun; deluxe buses, dep 0700, 0900, Rs 90; ordinary, last dep 1030 (10 hrs), Rs 70. **Train**: Rly Station, T622131. Reservations opposite; book early for Haridwar. **New Delhi**: *Shatabdi Exp, 2018*, daily except Wed, 1700, 5½ hrs; *Mussoorie Exp, 4042*; *Doon Exp, 3010*, 1945, which continues to **Lucknow** and **Kolkata**, 12½ hrs; *Dehra Dun-Varanasi Exp, 4266*, 1830.

Directory **Banks** *Bank of Baroda*, changes TCs. Exchange is generally difficult to get. **Hospitals** *Doon Hospital*, Amrit Kaur Rd, T623578. **Tour companies & trekking agents** *GMVN*, Old Survey Chowk, 74/1 Rajpur Rd, T656817, F654408. For tours to Chandrapuri Tent Camp and Auli Ski Resort, see page 113; *Garhwal Tours & Trekking*, 151 Araghar, T/F627769, gtt.nde.vsnl.net.in For trekking in Garhwal and Kumaon, experienced and knowledgeable. *President Travel*, T625111. Specialize in ticketing. **Tourist offices** *GMVN*, 74/1 Rajpur Rd, T654408; *Hill Tourism*, 3/3 Industrial Area, Patel Nagar, T623585. *UP*, 45 Gandhi Rd, T653217. **Useful addresses** *Rajaji National Park* office, 5/1 Ansari Marg, T621669. For permits. *Wildlife Institute of India*, PO Box 18, Chandrabani, T620912, wii@giasdlo1.vsnl.net.in

Around Dehra Dun

Roorkee
Phone code: 01332
Colour map 2, grid B1
Population: 90,000

India's first 'canal town', Roorkee is near the headworks of North India's first great experiment with really large scale river diversion. Reputed for its rural development training programme, the Thomason **Engineering College** (1847) was transformed into a university. **Sleeping C** *Motel Polaris*, on NH24, near Central Bus Stand, T2648, 14 decent a/c rooms, restaurant, bar, exchange, pleasant lawns. Recommended.

Saharanpur, 67 km south of Dehra Dun, is famous for woodcarving. It was founded in 1340 as a summer retreat for the Mughals. During the British period it became an important military base but the Government also set out **Botanical Gardens** in 1817. The **Eastern Yamuna Canal**, one of the first great 19th-century canals to irrigate the Ganga-Yamuna doab, transformed the landscape of what had been a heavily overpopulated region. It has become a particularly important source of fruit trees for the whole of India. The *Mango Festival* is held in June/July when hundreds of varieties are displayed. The trigonometrical survey of the Himalaya was extended in 1835 from **Nolji** nearby. **Sleeping and eating D** *Swagat*, near Clock Tower Chowk. Modest business hotel. *Sheetal Restaurant*, west of town, on canal bank in attractive setting.

Saharanpur
Phone code: 0132
Colour map 2, grid B1
Population: 375,000

Mussoorie

Mussoorie, named after the Himalayan shrub mansoor, has commanding views over the Doon Valley to the south and towards the High Himalaya to the north. It is spread out over 16 km along a horseshoe-shaped ridge up to which run a series of buttress-like subsidiaries. Being the nearest hill station to Delhi, it is very popular with Indian tourists though no longer as clean as it was once. Landour, another 300 m higher and away from the crowds, by contrast has fresh, clean, pine scented air.

Phone code: 0135
Colour map 2, grid B2
Population: 30,000
Altitude: 1,970 m

Getting there The road from Dehra Dun, just under 2 hrs away by bus, is the only way to the town, arriving at the library (west end of the long Mall) or the Masonic Lodge bus stand (east end), short of trekking in. Buses from Delhi take 6-7 hrs. **Getting around** Taxis are available for longer journeys, including the steep climb up to Landour but for local trips cycle rickshaws are available or you can hire a bike. **Climate** Summer: maximum 32°C, minimum 7°C. Winter: maximum 7°C, minimum 1°C. Monsoons end Jun/end Jul to Sep. Winter showers and snowfalls in Dec/Jan.

Ins & outs

Captain Young 'discovered' Mussoorie in 1826 and it developed as an escape from the heat of the plains for the British troops. **Landour** (2,270 m) to the east has the

Sights

Mussoorie centre

Garhwal & Kumaon Himalaya

N

0 metres 100
0 yards 100

■ **Sleeping**
1 Broadway
2 Connaught Castle
3 Filigree
4 Garhwal Terrace
5 Great Value Nanda Villa
6 Holiday Inn
7 Meedo's Palace
8 Valley View
9 YMCA Holiday Home

Related map
Mussoorie, page
100

old barracks area. The first British residence was built here which was followed by The Mall, Club, Christ Church (1837) and the library. It makes a really nice walk up through the woods and away from the pressing crowds of The Mall. There are good views, though the weather changes very quickly. Woodstock School and an International Language School are in a magnificent location, and some of the guest houses have stunning views. To the west are Convent Hill, **Happy Valley** where Tibetan refugees have settled (its school may welcome volunteers to teach English), and the pleasant **Municipal Garden**. Mall Road connects Kulri and Library Bazars. Camel's Back and Cart Roads also connect the two, but more circuitously.

Walks From the tourist office, **Lal Tibba** and nearby Childe's Lodge on the highest hill, are 5 km away. **Gun Hill** (where before Independence, a midday gun fire enabled residents to set their watches!) with a 400 m ropeway, can be reached by a bridle path in 20 mins from the Kutchery on The Mall; the view of the snow-capped peaks is stunning and best at sunrise. The **Camel's Back Rd**, from Kulri to the library, is a very pleasant 3 km walk.

Excursions **Kempty Falls**, 15 km on the Chakrata road, is pretty and a popular picnic spot. A taxi is about Rs 250 with a one hour stop. **Dhanolti**, 35 km (3,030m), has the **Surkhanda Devi Temple** nearby. There are superb views of several high peaks over 6,500 m. A taxi is Rs 600 with a two to three hour stop. Buses between Mussoorie and Chamba take you within 2 km of the hill top. **Sleeping C** *Dhanolti Breeze*, comfortable rooms. At **Rauslikhal**, Kanatal, 5 km from the temple, **C-D** *The Hermitage*, on a ridge, 16 comfortable rooms, pleasant lawns and restaurant, nightly bonfire with music, half-price July to April, contact T01-6414307, F6463593.

Mussoorie

Related map
A Mussoorie centre,
page 99

Not to scale

■ **Sleeping**
1 Carlton's Plaisance
2 Dunsvirk Court
3 Kasamanda Lodge
4 Padmini Nivas
5 Savoy
6 Shining Star
7 Sterling Resorts

● **Eating**
1 Coffee House
2 Tavern
3 Whispering Windows & Swiss Café

Operated by **GMVN**. Half day (1100 and 1400), Rs 20; Kempty Falls, Yamuna Valley and Lakhamandal: Sunday, full day (0730), Rs 75, run only when coach is full; Dhanolti-Surkhanda Devi Temple: full day (0900), Rs 40.

Tours

Some are old-fashioned but full of character. The Mall is closed to cars & buses in the high season. You may have to walk to your hotel; porters are available at the bus stands. Prices are based on high-season tariff; some offer big off-season discounts. **L-AL** *Residency Manor* (Jaypee), Barlow Ganj (4 km southeast of town, a long walk), T631800, F631022, jaypee.residency@smt.spritrpg.ems.vsnl.net.in 90 rooms, smart, large and impressive (US$145-240 includes meals). **AL-A** *Nabha Resort* (Claridge's), Airfield, Barlow Ganj Rd, 2 km town centre, T632525, F631425. 22 rooms with verandah arranged around attractive garden in converted hill 'palace', superb views, excellent management, single storey, Raj style but with all modern comforts. Highly recommended. **A** *Dunsvirk Court*, Vincent Hill, Upper Rd, Baroda Estate, T631043 F631669, ashwanik@ndb.vsnl.net.in 43 rooms, pool, very smart but very steep access with many 'hairpins'. **A-B** *Great Value Nanda Villa* (Clarks), Camel's Back Rd, Kulri, T/F631442. Modern comfortable rooms, good value. **A** *Padmini Nivas*, Library, The Mall, T631093. 24 rooms in former palace with character, some with good views, also cottages, not grand but pleasant ambience, restaurant (pure veg Gujarati). **A-B** *Savoy* (Heritage), The Mall, Library, T632120. 121 rooms, upstairs with breezy balcony best, good restaurant (open to non-residents), attractive hotel, opened in 1902 it retains character, old library, superb mountain views, mixed reports ("living off its name", "suffers from being in town").

Sleeping
■ *on map*
Price codes:
see inside front cover

B *Kasamanda Lodge* (Heritage), near The Mall, T632424, F630007, kasmanda@vsnl.net.in 14 comfortable rooms, once Basset Hall of the Christ Church complex (built 1836), a British sanatorium, then royal guest house from 1915, interesting furnishings (hunting trophies, bric-a-brac), 2 dining rooms, peaceful, spacious grounds. **B** *Shining Star*, opposite Vasu Theatre, The Mall, T632468. 25 comfortable rooms, restaurant, exchange. **B** *Sterling Resorts*, New Circular Rd. Quiet, in extensive grounds away from centre, T Delhi 011-6446531. **B-C** *Connaught Castle* (Claridge's), The Mall, T632210, F632538. 27 comfortable rooms. **B-C** *Solitaire Plaza*, Picture Palace, Kincraig Rd, T632937, F643913. 30 comfortable rooms, 24-hr restaurant. **C** *Carlton's Plaisance*, Charleville Rd, T632800. 10 rooms, good restaurant (includes Tibetan), very Victorian with period furniture, lacks views but peaceful orchard, spacious, charming and attentive service. **C** *Filigree*, Camel's Back Rd, Kulri, T632380. 18 rooms, some well equipped, good restaurant, terrace with views. Uninspiring exterior but recommended. **C-D** *Garhwal Terrace* (GMVN), The Mall near Ropeway, T632682. 24 basic but clean rooms, dorm (Rs 100), restaurant, reasonable maintenance,

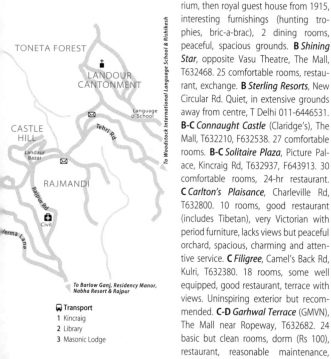

To Woodstock International Language School & Rishikesh

TONETA FOREST

LANDOUR
CANTONMENT

Language
o School

CASTLE
HILL

Tehri Rd

Landaur
Bazar

RAJMANDI

Rajpur Rd

Civil

Verma Lane

To Barlow Ganj, Residency Manor,
Nabha Resort & Rajpur

🚉 **Transport**
1 Kincraig
2 Library
3 Masonic Lodge

Garhwal & Kumaon Himalaya

excellent views. **C** *Holiday Inn*, The Mall, T632794. 20 rooms, no restaurant, modern, clean, excellent views. **C** *Meedo's Palace*, The Mall. Modern clean rooms, restaurant. **D** *Valley View*, The Mall (Kulri) near Ropeway, T632324. 14 rooms (some with kitchenette), restaurant, bakery, garden. **E** *Shalimar*, Charleville Rd, T632410. Pleasant atmosphere. **E** *YWCA Holiday Home*, The Mall, T632513. Meals to order. **E-F** *Broadway*, Camel's Back Rd (next to rink), T632243. 12 rooms (no linen) with bath (bucket hot water), some with views, Indian meals, old hotel.

Eating
● *on maps*
Price codes:
see inside cover

Expensive Hotels *Carlton's Plaisance, Roselynn, Savoy* and *Valley View* have good restaurants. Some have a **bar**. *Prakash*, Landour (above Woodstock School). Snacks. Really good sandwiches, omlettes etc. *Coffee House*, Library, towards Happy Valley. Chinese. *Garhwal Terrace*, between Library and Ropeway. **Fast foods** Bhelpuri, chaat, kababs, ice cream, also chicken curry with pulao, kulchas, dosas. *Kwality*, Kulri. International. Dependable quality. *Tavern*, Kulri. Dancing some nights in season. *Whispering Windows*, Library. International. With a popular bar. **Mid-range** *Char Dukan*, Lasee inside front cover. Restaurants may be closed out-of-season, and to non-residents. **Cheap** *Madras Café*, Kulri. Very good South Indian, friendly staff. Highly recommended. *Shakahari Kutir*, Kulri. Mainly South Indian. **Cafés** *Laxmi Mishtaan Bhandar*. Indian sweets, samosas and snacks. *Swiss Café*, Gandhi Chowk. Reasonable fast food. *Prakash*, Landour. Sells beer and cheese but at a silly price.

Sports

Fishing: in the Aglar and Yamuna rivers for mahseer and hill trout. Permit from Div Forest Officer, Yamuna Division, T632535, is required.

Shopping

The main areas are Library, Kulri and Landour Bazars and Shawfield Rd near Padmini Niwas. **Crafts** *Banaras House*, The Mall. Silks. *Baru Mal Janki Dass* for tribal silver jewellery. *Inder Singh, Nirankari Cottage Industries, Star Walking Sticks*, The Mall, for handcrafted sticks. **Photography** *Computerised Colour Lab* and *Mela Ram*, The Mall. **Woollens** *Anand Gift Emporium, Garwhal Wool House*, near GPO. *Natraj*, Picture Palace. *Tibetan outdoor market* near Padmini Nivas.

Transport

Local Bike hire: near Picture Palace. **Car**: pay Rs 60 to drive on The Mall. **Cycle-rickshaw**: for the Mall, fixed fare chart at tourist office. **Taxi**: Stand at Library, T630587; *Kulwant Travels*, Masonic Lodge Bus Stand, T632717. To Dehra Dun, Rs 300, Delhi Rs 1,500. **Long distance Air** Jolly Grant air strip, 60 km, is closed at present. *Out Agency*, Kulri, 1000-1600, Mon-Sat. **Road Bus** stands: Kincraig T632691; Library (Gandhi Chowk), T632258, Picture Palace (Kulri), T632259. Frequent service from **Dehra Dun** through Ghat roads (1¾ hrs). From **Delhi** ISBT, dep 0515, 2230, 6-7 hrs, about Rs 90; stop for snacks at *Cheetal Grand*. Also buses from **Saharanpur Rly** and **Tehri**. **Train**, T632846. See above for trains from Dehra Dun.

Directory

Banks Exchange can be difficult. *Bank of Baroda*, Kulri; or try Dehradun. **Hospitals & medical services** *Civil Hospital* at Landour, T632053. *Community*, South Rd, T632891. *St Mary's*, Gun Hill Rd, T632845. **GPO**: Kulri. **Language schools** T631487, F631917. Arranges accommodation; have their own textbooks. You choose how many hours per day you want and for how long. Individual lessons, Rs 70 per hr (less if sharing). Standard of teachers varies dramatically so try a few till you are happy. **Library** Gandhi Chowk, small fee. **Tour companies & travel agents** *Kulwant Travels*, Masonic Lodge Bus Stand, T632717. Also recommended for tours. *Garhwal Alpine Tours*, Masonic Lodge, T632507. **Tourist offices** GMVN, Library Bus Stand and *Tourist Bungalow*, The Mall, T632948. *UP Tourism*, The Mall, T632863. **Useful addresses** Ambulance: T632829. **Fire**: T632100. **Police**: Kotwali, T632003. **Foreigners' Registration**: Kotwali, next to Courts, opposite Hakmans, T632205.

Haridwar

Haridwar lies at the base of the Shiwalik Hills where the river Ganga passes through its last gorge and begins a 2,000 km journey across the plains. Legend has sanctified it by placing Vishnu's footprint on the river bank, making Haridwar ('Vishnu's gate') one of the seven holy cities of Hinduism – see Hindu Holy Sites, page 361. From sunrise, pilgrims come to bathe at the ghat to cleanse themselves of their sins. You will notice holy men in their huts dispensing wisdom to the willing, and wandering sadhus who have made make-shift shelters under trees. Here too, you can watch priests performing spectacular Ganga arati at sunset.

Phone code: 01334
Colour map 2, grid B2
Population: 190,000

History Various episodes from the *Mahabharata* are set in this ancient town which was mentioned by the Chinese traveller Hiuen Tsang. It attracted the attention of **Timur** who sacked it in 1399 (see page 347). The town, on the west bank of the river, centres on **Hari-ki-Pairi**, where **Vishnu** is believed to have left his footprint. At this point part of the Ganga has been diverted as irrigation water is drawn off for the Upper Ganga Canal system and for a hydro-electric power station.

Sights Near the steps at Hari-ki-Pairi is a modern clocktower and some temples, none particularly old. Further down, foodstalls and shrines line alleyways leading off into the bazar. There are five bridges to take you across the river, where it is quieter. Although the religious focus is Hari-ki-Pairi ghat, which is

Garhwal & Kumaon Himalaya

Haridwar

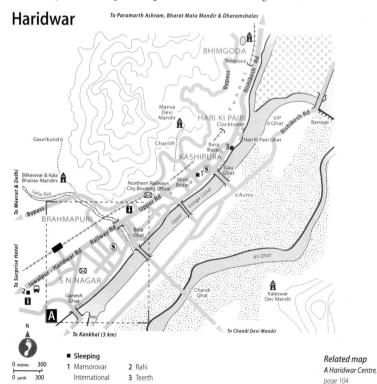

To Paramarth Ashram, Bharat Mata Mandir & Dharamshalas

BHIMGODA

Temposo

Mansa Devi Mandir

HARI KI PAIRI
Clocktower

VIP Ghat

Hari Ki Pairi Ghat

Barrage

Gaurikund

Chairlift

Bara Bazar

KASHIPURA

Gau Ghat

Bilkeswar & Kala Bhairav Mandirs

Lalta Rao

Northern Railways City Booking Office

Moti Bazar

Autos

Bypass

BRAHMAPURI

Upper Rd

Birla Ghat

Nil Dhar

To Meerut & Delhi

To Surprise Hotel

Jawalpur-Haridwar Rd

Railway Rd

S N NAGAR

Ganesh Ghat

Chandi Ghat

Kaleswar Dev Mandir

A

N

To Kankhal (3 km)

To Chandi Devi Mandir

0 metres 300
0 yards 300

■ **Sleeping**
1 Mansorovar International
2 Rahi
3 Teerth

Related map
A Haridwar Centre,
page 104

worth visiting at dusk, the main centre of town is nearer the railway station and bus stand.

Moti bazar along the Jawalapur-Haridwar Road is interesting, colourful, invariably crowded and surprisingly clean and tidy. Stalls sell coloured powder piled high in carefully made cones (for tikas). Others sell saris, jewellery, brass and aluminium pots, sweets and snacks.

Mansa Devi Temple is worth visiting for the view. Set on the southernmost hill of the Shiwaliks, it is accessible on foot or by a chair-lift (about Rs 10 return). Towards Rishikesh, 5 km from Haridwar, are the newer temples: **Pawan Dham** with a Hanuman temple, its spectacular glittering glass interior and the seven-storey **Bharat Mata Mandir** to Mother India.

Kankhal, 3 km downstream, with the **Temple of Dakseshwara** is where Siva's wife, Sati, is believed to have burnt herself to death. Prof Wendy Doniger vividly summarizes the story as told in the *Puranas*: "**Daksa**, a son of Brahma, gave his daughter Sati in marriage to Siva, but he did not invite Siva to his grand sacrifice. Sati, in anger, burnt herself to death. Siva destroyed the sacrifice and beheaded Daksa, but when the gods praised Siva he restored the sacrifice and gave Daksa the head of a goat. When Siva learned that Sati had killed herself, he took up her body and danced in grief, troubling the world with his dance and his tears until the gods cut the corpse into pieces. When the *yoni* fell, Siva took the form of a *linga*, and peace was re-established in the universe".

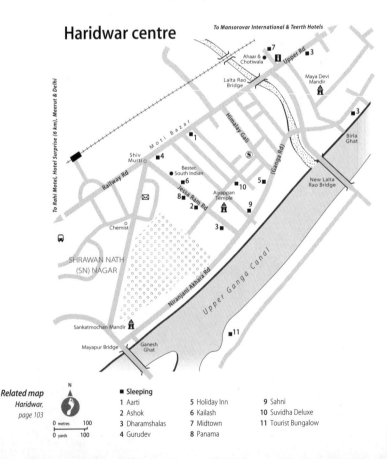

Haridwar centre

Related map
Haridwar,
page 103

N

0 metres 100
0 yards 100

■ **Sleeping**

1 Aarti	5 Holiday Inn	9 Sahni
2 Ashok	6 Kailash	10 Suvidha Deluxe
3 Dharamshalas	7 Midtown	11 Tourist Bungalow
4 Gurudev	8 Panama	

Essentials

C *Suvidha Deluxe*, SN Nagar, T427423. 29 good rooms, some a/c, restaurant (residents'), modern, very clean, central but quiet. **C-D** *Surprise*, Haridwar-Delhi Rd, Jawalapur, 6 km south of town, T427780. 45 rooms, some a/c, restaurants ('surprise' is the non-veg continental!), Indian on rooftop, pool, modern. **C-D** *Tourist Bungalow* (UP Tourism), Belwala (east bank), By-pass Rd, T426379. 29 rooms, best a/c with bath, dorm, restaurant (simple veg), quiet; **C-D** *Aarti*, Rly Rd (1st floor, above shops), T427456. 33 rooms, some a/c, adequate if unexciting. **D** *Mansarovar International*, Upper Rd, towards Hari-ki-Pairi, T426501. 56 clean comfortable rooms, restaurant. **D** *Midtown*, Rly Rd, T427507, F426001. 23 rooms, some a/c, modern, reasonably clean, fairly quiet. **D** *Rahi* (UP Tourism), opposite rly station, T426430. 19 rooms (some a/c), dorm beds (Rs 40), restaurant, tourist information. **D** *Teerth*, Subhash Ghat, Hari-ki-Pairi, T427111. 36 rooms, some air-cooled, restaurant, good river view.

E *Ashok*, Jessa Ram Rd, T427328. 29 rooms, some air-cooled with bath, very basic, rather dark, 'walking distance of Holly Gangas'! **E** *Gurudev*, opposite rly station, T427101. 30 rooms, 7 a/c, some with bath and balcony overlooking courtyard, veg food, adequate. **E** *Kailash*, Shiv Murti near rly station, T427789. 70 rooms with bath, best air-cooled with TV and phone, restaurant, bus/train tickets. **E** *Sahni*, Niranjani Akhara Rd, SN Nagar, T427906. Fairly clean rooms, some with bath, some air-cooled (extra charge), hot water in buckets, helpful service. Some **F** around the bazar and station.

Only vegetarian food is available in town; no alcohol. **Mid-range** *Aahar*, Railway Rd. Punjabi. Chinese and continental. Excellent meals. *Bestec*, Railway Rd. Mughlai and South Indian. "Excellent stuffed *parathas*". *Chotiwala*, Railway Rd, opposite Tourist Office. Indian. Atmospheric. Highly recommended.

Thousands of pilgrims visit the city, especially when the birth of the river (*Dikhanti*) is celebrated in spring. *Kumbh Mela*, held here every 12th year (next in Apr 2010), and *Ardha Kumbh* every 6 years, attract millions of devotees who come to bathe in the confined area near Hari-ki-Pairi.

Local Rickshaw and taxi: Stands near rly station, fares negotiable. *Taxi Union*, T427738. **Long distance Road Bus**: Roadways Bus Stand, Rly Station, T427037; *Garhwal Motor Owners Union*, T426886, also has buses. **Rishikesh** share taxis and buses (45 mins) from bus stand. Share tempos from Bhimgoda tank; autos from across the river. Buses to/from **Delhi**, ½ hourly (4-5 hrs); **Dehra Dun** (1¼ hrs); **Jaipur** (good overnight deluxe dep 1800, Rs 220); **Mathura** and **Vrindavan**, 10 hrs. **Taxi** Rates for visiting the mountains are competitive; 4 day round trip, about Rs 4000. **Train**: Rly Station, T131. **Delhi (OD)**: *Dehra Dun Exp, 9020*, 1325, 7 hrs; **Delhi (ND)**: *Shatabdi Exp, 2018*, except Wed, 1806, 4½ hrs; *Mussoorie Exp, 4042*, 2315, 8 hrs. **Dehra Dun**: *Mussoorie Exp, 4041*, 0615, 1½ hrs; *Shatabdi Exp, 2017*, daily except Wed, 1121, 1¾ hrs; *Dehra Dun Exp, 9019*, 1445, 1¾ hrs. For **Shimla**, travel via Ambala and Kalka (trains better than bus).

Banks *State Bank of India*, Station Rd, 1030-1430. *Bank of Baroda*, Upper Rd. **Communications Post office**: Railway Rd. 1000-1630. **Hospitals & medical services** *District*, Upper Rd, T426060. *RK Mission*, Kankhal, T427141. **Chemists**: on Rly and Upper Rd. **Tourist offices** *UP*, Motel Rahi, T426430. 1000-1700. Lalta Rao Bridge, T424240 (1000-1700). Counter at rly station, T427817 (0500-1200). Ganga Sabha, near Hari-ki Pairi, T427925. **Useful addresses Police**: T426666.

Sleeping
■ *on maps*
Price codes:
see inside front cover

There are over a 100 places. Many offer off-season discounts outside Jun/Jul

Eating
● *on maps*
Price codes:
see inside front cover

Festivals

Transport

Directory

Garhwal & Kumaon Himalaya

Rishikesh

Phone code: 0136
Colour map 2, grid B2
Population: 72,000
Altitude: 356m

The Ganga, at this point still an astonishingly clear water stream, links all the holy places of one of Hinduism's most sacred regions. Rishikesh stands tight-packed on the banks of the river as it runs swiftly through the southernmost ranges of the Shiwaliks on its way to the Plains. At Rishikesh the river begins to cut through the low foothills, which were once more densely forested than today. Those forests offered the prospect of quiet retreat, the original basis of the ashram ideal, but today the whole town has become heavily commercialized, full of ashrams, sadhus and visitors attending courses in yoga and meditation. The dirty and crowded main street is often flooded when it rains and some find it disappointing and lacking in atmosphere. It is however surrounded by wonderful birdwatching territory.

Ins & outs

Getting there Road From Haridwar, buses are both quicker and far more frequent than trains. Buses from Delhi and Dehra Dun arrive at the main bus stand in the town centre and also stop south of Ram Jhula. **Getting around** The centre near the bus stands and station is compact and is an easy walk to the river, less than a kilometre away. The ashrams are to the north. You can take a cycle-rickshaw or shared tempo from the Bazar to the two suspension bridges and then walk across to the east side. You can also cross the river on a boat near Ram Jhula. **Climate** Summer: maximum 41°C, minimum 37°C. Winter: maximum 32°C, minimum 18°C. Average annual rainfall: 1,524 mm, mostly Jun to Sep.

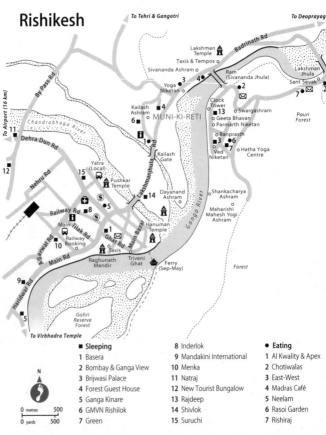

Rishikesh

Sleeping
1 Basera
2 Bombay & Ganga View
3 Brijwasi Palace
4 Forest Guest House
5 Ganga Kinare
6 GMVN Rishilok
7 Green
8 Inderlok
9 Mandakini International
10 Menka
11 Natraj
12 New Tourist Bungalow
13 Rajdeep
14 Shivlok
15 Suruchi

Eating
1 Al Kwality & Apex
2 Chotiwalas
3 East-West
4 Madras Café
5 Neelam
6 Rasoi Garden
7 Rishiraj

Garhwal & Kumaon Himalaya

The Ganga has two suspension bridges – **Ram** (**Sivananda**) **Jhula** (between **Sights** Sivananda Ashram and Swargashram) and **Lakshman Jhula**. The Lakshman Jhula area is very picturesque with the best views though you may be troubled by rhesus monkeys.

Rishikesh ('Hair of Sages') has a large number of ashrams, but beware, not all in saffron/orange clothing are *sadhus*; some are con-men! It is worth walking down to the river bank where pilgrims purify themselves by bathing in the Ganga at **Triveni Ghat**, offering milk and feeding the fish at dawn, and floating lamps after sunset for evening *aarati*. Many ashrams which offer the seeker a spiritual haven are on the east bank of the river at **Swargashram**. Some of them are bizarrely colourful, architectural curiosities leading Geoffrey Moorhouse to describe it as a cross between Blackpool and Lourdes. **Maharishi Mahesh Yogi** had his ashram here and captured the imagination and attention of the Beatles in the early 1960s. Several ashrams are seats of spiritual learning and meditation and offer courses (see below). **Muni-ki-Reti** is the area along the Chandrabhaga River which also has some temples. Walk northeast along the river for secluded **beaches**. This is the base for several pilgrimages and treks, including the **Char Dham Pilgrimage**, see box on page 115 (May-November), or going to the Garhwal hills and Hemkund Sahib.

Essentials

B *Ganga Kinare*, 16 Virbhadra Rd, on quiet riverside 2 km from centre, T431658, **Sleeping** F435243. 36 rooms (best face river), central a/c (heating inadequate in winter), pleasant restaurant, exchange, meditation, yoga (1-3 week courses), treks, boating (Sep-Mar), rafting. **B** *Natraj*, Dehra Dun Rd, T431099, F433355. 50 a/c rooms, restaurant (veg), large gardens, pool, modern, free airport transfer. **C-D** *Basera*, 1 Ghat Rd, T430720, F433106. 39 rooms, some a/c, restaurant (veg), roof top terrace garden. **C-D** *Inderlok*, Railway Rd, T430555, F432855. 32 clean rooms, some a/c, with balconies, restaurant (veg), terrace lawn, older hotel but well kept and with pleasant ambience and mountain views. **D** *Shipra*, Dehra Dun Rd, T430533. 24 rooms in modern hotel, restaurant. **D** *Suruchi*, near Yatra Bus Stand, T432269. Comfortable rooms (some air-cooled) and recommended restaurant. **D-E** *New Tourist Bungalow*, By Pass Rd, T433002. **D-E** *Shivlok*, Main Haridwar Rd, T431055. Fairly modern and reasonably clean, some a/c rooms, good restaurant with fast service. **D-E** *Rishilok* (GMVN), Badrinath Rd, Muni-ki-Reti, T430373, F430372. 46 rooms, some with bath in new cottages and 2-storey blocks, dorm (Rs 80), restaurant, pleasant garden, efficient service, above and away from Main Rd, peaceful.

Across the river: **E-F** *Green* in a lane near Swargashram, T431242. Simple rooms with bath, some air-cooled, clean, quiet, morning yoga classes. Recommended. **E-F** *Rajdeep*, uphill from Chotiwalas, near Geeta Bhavan taxi stand, Swargashram, T432826. Decent rooms with shower (Rs 150+), noisy area but river views. **D-F** *Sudesh*, left before Rajdeep, 6 rooms (Rs 100-450 for deluxe 'sweets', negotiable) , use of kitchen, very peaceful, roof terrace, small garden, English and German spoken. **F** *Brijwasi Palace*, 1st right after Ram Jhula, 2nd left before Ved Niketan, T435181, F433208. Standard doubles (Rs 200) with shower (bucket hot water) despite posh exterior, clean, peaceful garden restaurant, yoga in basement.

Lakshman Jhula: **F** *Bombay Guest House*, with rooms around a courtyard, and **F** *Ganga View*, (Pauri side) are also very popular. **F** *Shikar*. Good clean rooms, some with bath (order hot water), very good restaurant and superb views from rooftop. **E** *Phool Shati*, 6 km on Neelkanth Rd (north of Lakshman Jhula, T433174. Pleasant, quiet retreat, by the Ganga. **In town**: **F** *Tourist*, off Dehra Dun Rd, opposite *Padam*

■ on map
Price codes:
see inside front cover

Some find the peace across the river preferable to the noisy, polluted atmosphere in town

Garhwal & Kumaon Himalaya

Confectioners. Relaxed, very friendly, family run. Recommended. Several **F** hotels near Main Bus Stand include *Menka*, Agarwal Rd, T430285. Simple rooms, room service.

Shivpuri 18 km upstream, has a GMVN Rafting Beach Camp: double tent, Rs 400; meals Rs 80-100. **B** *Ganga Banks*, a 'green' resort by the river with 28 comfortable, eco-friendly cottages with bath, built with local raw materials, restaurant, pool, health spa, in natural surroundings employing recycling techniques, (no plastics), solar heating, well placed for trekking, rafting, birdwatching etc. Also **C** Camp with 35 Swiss tents with beds facing the 'private' riverside beach. Contact *Wanderlust*, T11-4102180, F6885188, www.wanderlustindia.com

Some can be filthy; inspect first **Ashrams** are mostly on the east bank of the *jhulas*. Catering mainly for pilgrims; foreigners may need special permission. Rooms are simple **E-F**, hot water comes in buckets. **Ram (Sivananda) Jhula: E** *Hatha Yoga Centre*, 2 lanes beyond *Green Hotel*, very clean, tranquil and excellent value, occasional evening concert with local musicians on roof, yoga optional! *Banprasth*, next door, has clean rooms with bath in pleasant surroundings. **Lakshman Jhula:** *Sant Sevak*, near Lakshman Jhula, has fairly modern rooms. *Adanyanda*, is very clean, with marble floors, tiled bathrooms.

Eating
● *on map*
Price codes:
see inside front cover

A vegetarian temple town: meat & alcohol are prohibited; eggs are only eaten in private

Mid-range *A1 Kwality*, near GMVN *Rishilok*. Varied menu. Hotels *Shikar*, Lakshman Jhula and *Shivlok*, Main Rd. Recommended. An escape: *Midway*, 'resort' towards Haridwar (Rs 10 by tempo). For those desperate to replenish their protein intake, good tandoori and curries, washed down with chilled beer. **Cheap** Near Ram Jhula: *Chotiwalas* Swargashram, east bank. Crowded, plenty of atmosphere, inexpensive; one closer to the river is a bit cleaner, more spacious, nicer rooftop. On the west bank: *East-West*. Italian. Good breads and olive 'pizzas'. *Madras Café* by boat jetty. Mainly South Indian. Excellent service, cheese on brown toast to masala dosas. Recommended. *Neelam* near Yatra Bus Stand. Indian, Continental. Very good value, attracts backpackers. *Rishiraj*, near Lakshman Jhula. Excellent Italian. *Rasoi Garden*, Swargashram, behind Green Hotel (2 mins walk). Excellent coffee, pizzas, pittas and hummus, peaceful. *Vaishal* Indian. Preferred by local people. Highly recommended.

Sports **Boat rides** On the Ganga from Swargashram Ghat. Fix rates with local boatmen. **Rafting** Several whitewater rafting outfits on the Ganga, north of town. *Himalayan River Runners*. Highly recommended, operate from Mar-May, Sep-Oct, www.hrr.india.com; with an office in Delhi (188A Jorbagh). *Apex* and *Garhwal Himalayan Exploration* (see below) offer rafting from Shivpuri: Rs 580 including lunch. *Apex*'s 5-day Ganga Expedition includes whitewater, Rs 1,200 per day covers food and camping (off-season trips may not be as promised). *Ganga Banks* and *Rafting Beach Camp* also offer rafting (see Sleeping for details). *Kaudiyala*, 38 km away, has tents at Rs 100, beds at Rs 65, meals Rs 150. Rafting Rs 350 per day. Contact *GMVN*, Yatra Office, T431793. **Swimming** *Hotel Natraj* pool (non-residents, about Rs 150). **Trekking** With guides, transport, camping; meals cost about Rs 1,500 per day through local agents. **Yoga, meditation courses** and instruction in Vedanta. Most hotels can put you in touch. *Sivananda Ashram* (Divine Life Society), T430040: short to 3 month courses (apply 1 month ahead); holds music classes and produces herbal medicines. *Onkarananda Ashram* (Durga Mandir) above Yoga Niketan, T430883, good Iyengar yoga courses, also offers music and classical dance. *Parmarth Niketan and Swargashram*, T430252, are vast, and can be impersonal. *Ved Niketan* Flexible programme of yoga; also Hindi, Sanskrit, music and dance classes.

Festivals Feb: *International Yoga week*, 2-7 Feb, an opportunity to learn yoga on the banks of the Ganga.

Dehra Dun Rd, Haridwar Rd, Ghat Rd and Railway Rd have markets and curio shops. **Shopping**
The latter are limited for choice and are overpriced. *Gandhi Ashram Khadi Bhandar,*
Haridwar Rd. *Garhwal Wool and Craft* (opposite Yatra Office), Muni-ki-Reti. *UP*
Handlooms, Dehra Dun Rd. Excellent book shop by Lakshman Jhula at the head of the
bridge, especially spiritual texts, café attached – read, relax and sip a cool drink! *Photo*
Centre, Dehra Dun Rd.

Distances Pilgrim centres of Badrinath (301 km); Gangotri (258 km); Kedarnath **Transport**
(228 km); **Uttarkashi** (154 km); **Yamunotri** (288 km). **Local Tempo**: mostly fixed
routes. From Ram Jhula shared, to Rishikesh Bazar Rs 2; to Haridwar Rs 15, 50 mins.
Cycle-rickshaw: rates negotiable. Constant shuttle between town centre and
Lakshman Jhula. **Ferry boat**: from near Ram Jhula for river crossing, Rs 4; Rs 6 return.
Taxi: (unmetered) from *Garhwal Mandal TCS*, Haridwar Rd or tour operators. **Long**
distance Road Bus: Roadways or **Main Bus Stand**, Haridwar Rd, T430066. Buses
from Delhi finally stop by the Govind-Radha Mandir south of Ram Jhula, 15 min walk
from the bridge. Reserve tickets at the Local (Yatra) Bus Stand from around 1600, the
day before (especially during Yatra season, May-Nov); open 0400-1900. Various State
Govt bus services (DTC, Haryana Roadways, Himachal RTC, UP Roadways). **Major des-**
tinations: Chandigarh (252 km), **Dehra Dun** (42 km), **Delhi** (238 km, 6 hrs, taxi 5 hrs).
Haridwar (24 km); also share taxis from bus stand or auto rickshaws from Ram Jhula.
Mussoorie (77 km), Patiala, Saharanpur. For **Shimla**: best to go to Dehra Dun and stay
overnight and catch 0600 bus; or get a bus from Haridwar (0600, 1000, 1600, 2200)
but it's a long hot journey (see 'Train' under Haridwar). From **Yatra (Local) Bus Stand**,
Dehra Dun Rd, during the Yatra season, to **Char Dhams: buses** leave early for the very
long routes to Hanuman Chatti (for Yamunotri), **Badrinath, Gangotri, Gaurikund** (for
Kedarnath); best to take a 'Luxury' bus, and break your journey. For **Badrinath** and
Hemkund stop overnight at Joshimath (after 1630 road to Govindghat is southbound
only). **NB** Although the **Yatra season** ends in late Oct (Yamunotri, Gangotri,
Kedarnath) to mid-Nov (Badrinath), bus frequency drops drastically during Oct. Even
light rains can cause severe road blocks, mainly due to landslides. From **Delhi**, best to
get a **train** (2nd class sleeper recommended) to Rishikesh: *Mussoorie Exp* dep OD,
2220, 8 hrs; bus for Badrinath dep from Private Bus Stand (100 m right from station), Rs
180, but noisy, crowded and uncomfortable. *Garhwal Motor Owners Union,*
T430076; *Tehri Garhwal MOU, Triveni*, Haridwar Rd, T430989. For travelling north,
cheapest are '**Newspaper taxis**', eg Joshimath, Rs 140 per person; ask at *Sanjay*
News Agency, Main Rd (before turn-off to Ghat Rd) or travel agent. **Jeep** hire for
Badrinath (1-way), Rs 1500-2000, is the best option. **NB** Book the evening before, for
all. **Motorbike (Bullet) Mechanic**: *Bila*, opposite Ganga view Hotel, Lakshman Jhula.
Train There is a branch line from Haridwar to Rishikesh but the bus is quicker.

Banks *Bank of Baroda*, Dehra Dun Rd, T430653. Accepts Visa and Master Card. *State Bank of* **Directory**
India, Railway Rd. *Punjab Bank*. Poor rate. *Marhamaya Tours*, 102 Urvashi Complex, Dehra
Dun Rd, near Bank of Baroda, exchanges any currency. **Communications** GPO: at Harilal Marg,
Lakshman Jhula and Muni-ki-Reti. Ghat Rd. Swargashram GPO by *Chotiwalas*. **Post offices**: open
0700-2200. **Internet**: Near Ram Jhula, next to *Madras Café* Rs 2 per min; also, near Lakshman Jhula
(Pauri side). **Hospitals & medical services** *Govt Hospital*, Dehra Dun Rd, T430402. *Nirmal*
Ashram, T432215. *Sivananda*, Muni-ki-Reti, T430040. **Tour companies & trekking agents**
Apex, Kailash Gate, Muni-ki-Reti, T431503, F431501. *Garhwal Himalayan Exploration*, PO Box 29,
T431654, F431501 and *GMVN* (see below) and *Triveni*, Haridwar Rd, T430989. Recommended for
rafting and trekking (see Sports and activities). **Tourist offices** *Garhwal Mandal Vikas Nigam*
(GMVN) & Yatra Office, Kailash Gate, By Pass Rd, T430372, F431783. Organizes trekking,
mountaineering, rafting and Char Dham tour (12 days). *UP*, 162 Rly Rd, T430209. Helpful. During
Yatra season, only at Yatra Bus Stand. **Useful addresses** Ambulance: T102. Fire: T101. **Police:**
T100. **Rajaji National Park office:** Bilkeshwar, T425193.

Garhwal & Kumaon Himalaya

Rajaji National Park

Colour map 2, grid B1
Altitude: 302-1,000 m

Uttar Pradesh's largest park (named after **C Rajagopalachari**, the only Indian to hold the post of Governor General). The **Shiwaliks** present rugged and precipitous south facing slopes. The vegetation ranges from broad-leaf mixed forest to *Chir* pine forests interspersed with areas of scrub and pasture which support a wide variety of fauna including over 23 mammal and 180 bird species. For entry permit and reservation contact Rajaji National Park, 5/1 Ansari Marg, Dehra Dun, T621669, or Chief Conservator, 17 Rana Pratap Marg, Lucknow, T226140.

Ins & outs The park is accessible from Haridwar, Rishikesh and Dehra Dun. Open 15 Nov-15 Jun, daily, between sunrise and sunset.

Wildlife
Many visitors are disappointed at the lack of wildlife sightings

A large number of elephants, together with the rarely seen tiger, are at the north-west limit of their distribution in India; elephants move up into the hills when the water holes are dry. Other mammals include leopards, spotted deer, sambar, muntjac, nilgai and ghoral. Along the tracks, you may spot wild boar, langur and macaque; the Himalayan yellow-throated marten and civet are rare. Birdlife includes peacocks, jungle fowls and kaleej pheasants in the drier areas; cuckoos, hornbills, woodpeckers, warblers, finches, rollers, orioles, bee-eaters, minivets and nuthatches, while waterbirds attracted by the Ganga and the Song rivers include many kinds of geese, ducks, cormorant, teal and spoonbill among others.

Viewing Entry first three days Rs 100 (foreigners), Rs 15 (Indians). Additional day; Rs 50 and Rs 10. On foot, you are likely to see very little. Even by car (permit Rs 100) or jeep (Rs 500, three hours), many are disappointed as few animals are spotted. Elephants are often 'ill' so no rides ("better tomorrow"!). Chilla, 18 km from Rishikesh, is the best here for viewing.

Sleeping **D-E** *Forest Rest Houses* near all the gates. Those at Motichur, Ranipur and Kunnao have at least 2 suites with electricity and water supply, very basic, self-catering, not good value, 'concrete boxes'. **D-E** *Tourist Bungalow*, Chilla. With rooms, dorm (Rs 100) and tents.

Transport
The park has 8 entry gates

Haridwar is 9 km by road from 4 gates (Motichur, Ranipur, Chilla and Satyanarain), Rishikesh is 6 km from Kunnao Gate, by private bus along the Rishikesh-Pashulok road; tongas, auto-rickshaws and taxis also available. Dehra Dun is 14 km from Ramgarh Gate (Delhi Highway via Clement Town). Mohand Gate is a 5-hr drive from Delhi.

Garhwal and the Pilgrimage (Yatra)

The shrines of Kedarnath, Yamunotri, Gangotri and Badrinath are visited by hundreds of thousands of Hindu pilgrims each summer. They come from all corners of the subcontinent to engage in, what Dalrymple calls, a modern-day Indian Canterbury Tales.

Best season May, mid-Sep to mid-Oct. Jun is very crowded; Jul to mid-Sep being the rainy season which may trigger landslips. Temples and trekking routes open from end of Apr to Oct (mid-Nov for Badrinath).

See page 118 for trekking in the area

Garhwal in the western section of the Uttaranchal Himalaya had its capital in Srinagar on the Alakananda river. Up until the 14th century Garhwal (Land of the Forts) comprised a number of petty principalities. Ajai Pal (1358-70) consolidated these and became the Raja of Garhwal. The region was a popular plundering ground for Sikh brigands, see Rampur. The **Gurkhas** overran it in 1803, taking men, women and children into slavery and conscripting males into their army. Gurkha encroachments on the territory around Gorakhpur led the British to expel them from Garhwal and Kumaon in 1814. They took the eastern part of Garhwal as British Garhwal and returned the western part, Tehri Garhwal to the deposed Raja.

Garhwal's fragmented political history gives no clue as to the region's religious significance. The sources of the Yamuna and the Ganga and some of Hinduism's holiest mountains lie in the heart of the region. Since the seventh century Tamil saint **Sankaracharya** travelled north on his mission to reinvigorate Hinduism's northern heartland, some have been watched over permanently by South Indian priests. The most famous is the Rawal – head priest – at the Badrinath temple, who to this day comes from Kerala. Badrinath is one of the four *dhams* '**holiest abodes**' of the gods. Along with **Dwarka**, **Puri** and **Ramesvaram**, they mark the cardinal points of Hinduism's cultural geography.

After a ritual purificatory bathe in the Ganga at Haridwar and, preferably, Rishikesh, the pilgrim begins the 301 km journey from Haridwar to Badrinath. The purpose is to worship, purify and acquire merit. Roads go all the way to Gangotri and Badrinath, and to within 14 km of Yamunotri and Kedarnath. The correct order for pilgrims is to visit the holy places from west to east: Yamunotri, Gangotri, Kedarnath and Badrinath.

Recommended reading *Peaks and passes of the Garhwal Himalaya* published by Alpinists Club, 1990.

NB *Yatra* tourists on a public bus are required to register with the Yatra Office at the Yatra (Local) Bus Stand, Rishikesh (open 0600-2200). You also need a current certificate covering immunization against cholera and typhoid. In practice, 'Registration' is often waived, but the immunization certificate is checked. Accommodation prices are relatively higher in this area. GMVN **D-E** *Rest Houses* have some 'deluxe' rooms which are still basic, with toilet and hot water, dorm (Rs 60-100). Also simple guest houses in places. Reserve ahead; during Yatra season, GMVN places may only be available if you book their organized tour. Carry some bottled water and take a good torch.

Yamunotri and Gangotri

Yamunotri (3,291 m) can be reached from Rishikesh or from Dehra Dun via Yamuna Bridge and Barkot. The former is the more popular. Yamunotri is 83 km to Tehri (165 km via Deoprayag). **Tehri**, northeast of Rishikesh, the capital of the former princely state, will eventually be submerged by the waters behind the controversial and still unfinished Tehri Dam.

Dominated by **Banderpunch** (6,316 m), Yamunotri, the source of the **Yamunotri**
Yamuna, is believed to be the daughter of Surya, the sun, and the twin sister of *Colour map 2, grid A2*
Yama, the Lord of Death. Anyone who bathes in her waters will be spared an
agonizing death.

To reach the temple you must walk from **Hanuman Chatti** (13 km, five to six hours), the roadhead, usually with an overnight stay halfway along the trail at **Janki Chatti** (three hours) which is pleasanter and where you can leave luggage.

The trek along the riverbank is exhilarating with the mountains rising up on each side, the last 5 km somewhat steeper. The source itself is a difficult 1 km climb from the 19th-century **Yamunotri Temple**, with a black marble deity; open 0600-1200, 1400-2100. The modern temple was rebuilt this century after floods

Garhwal & Kumaon Himalaya

and snow destroyed it. There are hot springs nearby (the most sacred being Surya Kund) in which pilgrims cook potatoes and rice tied in a piece of cloth. The meal, which takes only a few mins to cook is first offered to the deity and then distributed as *prasad*. On the return to Hanuman Chatti, you can visit the **Someshwar Temple** at **Kharsali**, 1 km across the river from Janki Chatti. The temple is one of the oldest and finest in the region and there are excellent views of the mountains.

Sleeping Hanuman Chatti: GMVN **E** *Tourist Rest House*, by the river. Clean, simple rooms, dorm (Rs 100), hot water in buckets, the only decent place. **Janki Chatti**: similar GMVN *Rest House*, and other lodges and places to eat. At Yamunotri, the GMVN *Rest House*, is on a hill. Also dharamshalas and basic lodges.

Transport Early **bus** (0600) best from Rishikesh to Hanuman Chatti (210 km, 9 hrs).

Uttarkashi
240 km from Rishikesh
Colour map 2, grid A2
Altitude: 3,140 m

The busy town en route to Gangotri has several places to stay but are full during the season. The *Nehru Institute of Mountaineering* here offers courses and from here you can trek to **Dodital** (see 'Trekking' below); porters can be hired locally. The bazaar near the bus stand sells provisions. **Sleeping D-E** *Akash Ganga* and **D-E** *Shivam*, T2525, have some a/c rooms. **E** GMVN *Tourist Bungalow*, near bridge, T2236. 33 rooms with bath, few a/c, veg meals. Small **E-F** hotels are clustered near the bus stand. **E** *Ceeway* short walk from bazar. Decent. **Eating** In the bazar serve vegetarian *thalis*. **Festivals** 14 January: *Makar Sankranti*; *Garhwal festival* of music and dance (5-7 October 2000). **Road** Frequent buses to Rishikesh (140 km) and Gangotri (100 km) during the *yatra* season. **Taxi**: return trip to Gangotri, Rs 1,300. **Tour companies & travel agents** Trekking agents: *Crystal Adventure, Hotel Tapovan*, near Tourist Bungalow, T2566. *Mount Support*, Nautial Bhawan, Bhatwari Rd, near bus stand. **Useful addresses** *GMVN Tourist office*, T2290. *District Magistrate*, T2101.

Gangotri
Altitude: 3,140m
240 km from Rishikesh
Colour map 2, grid A2

Gangotri is the second of the major shrines in the Garhwal Himalaya. A high bridge now takes the road across the Jad Ganga River joining the Bhagirathi which rushes through narrow gorges, so buses travel all the way. The 18th-century granite **temple** is dedicated to the Goddess **Ganga**, where she is believed to have descended to earth. It was built by a Gurkha commander, Amar Singh Thapa, in the early 18th century and later rebuilt by the Maharaja of Jaipur.

Hindus believe that Ganga (here **Bhagirathi**) came down from heaven after **King Bhagirath**'s centuries-long penance. He wanted to ensure his dead relatives' ascent to heaven by having their ashes washed by the sacred waters of the Ganga. When the tempestuous river arrived on earth, the force of her flow had to be checked by **Siva** who received her in the coils of his hair, lest she sweep all away. A submerged lingam is visible in the winter months. **Rishikund** (55 km from Uttarkashi) has hot sulphur springs near **Gangnani** suitable for bathing and a 15th-century temple above. The **Gaurikund waterfall** here (another is south of Kedarnath) is one of the most beautiful in the Himalaya. **Bhojbasa** (14 km; 3,500 m) and **Gaumukh** (Cow's Mouth; a further 4 km; 3,970 m) are on a gradual but nevertheless scenically stunning trek – see page 120.

Sleeping & eating C *Shikhar Nature Resort*, 5 km out of town, by the Bhagirathi River, T011-331244, F3323660, www.shikhar.com Luxury tents with mod cons in a scenic setting. **E** *Tourist Rest House*, across footbridge. 20 rooms and dorm, meals. **E** *Ganga Niketan*, across road bridge. Decent rooms and a simple terrace restaurant. The cheaper **E** *Birla Niketan*, nearby, has rooms with bath. Other lodges have rooms without bath and electricity for under Rs 100. Numerous tea and food stalls near the temple. **E** *Monal* is on the road to Gangotri.

Kedarnath and Badrinath

From Rishikesh the road follows the west bank of the Ganga and quickly enters forest. At the 23rd milestone, at **Gular-dogi** village (*phone code*: 013548), is the old orchard and garden of the Maharaja of Tehri Garhwal which is close to a white sand and rock beach. **Sleeping B** *The Glasshouse on the Ganges* (Neemrana Hotels), in idyllic setting, T9218 (sales@neemrana.com). Rooms with views in three cottages, very helpful and willing staff, good food, ideal for total relaxation. The section up to **Deoprayag** (68 km) is astonishingly beautiful. The folding and erosion of the hills can be clearly seen on the mainly uninhabited steep scarps on the opposite bank. Luxuriant forest runs down to the water's edge which in many places is fringed with silver sand beaches. In places the river rushes over gentle rapids. About 5 km after **Byasi** the road makes a gradual ascent to round an important bluff. At the top, there are fine views down to the river. Villages now become more common. The way that small pocket handkerchief-sized fields have been created by terracing is marvellous.

It is an offence to photograph sensitive installations, troop movements & bridges on most routes. Offenders can be treated very severely

The most important of the hill *prayags* because it is at the junction of the **Bhagirathi** and **Alaknanda** rivers, Gangotri is the source of the Bhagirathi and Badrinath is near the source of the Alaknanda. Below Deoprayag, the river becomes the **Ganga** proper. The town tumbles down the precipitous hillside in the deeply cut 'V' between the junction of the two rivers, with houses almost on top of one another. Where the rivers meet is a pilgrims' bathing ghat, artificially made into the shape of India. Jeep hire is easy, to Badrinath or Rishikesh. **Sleeping** On a hillside, **E** *Tourist Bungalow*, 1½ km from main bazar and bus stand, 16 rooms, some with bath, meals. Other tea-stalls near bridge. From Deoprayag, the road is relatively flat as far as Srinagar (35 km) and for much of the way you pass through well cultivated land.

Deoprayag
Colour map 2, grid B2

The old capital of Tehri Garhwal, Srinagar was devastated when the Gohna Lake dam was destroyed by an earthquake in the mid-19th century. The most attractive part of Srinagar, which is a university town, runs from the square down towards the river. There are some typical hill houses with elaborately carved door jambs. **Sleeping D-E** *Tourist Rest House*, near bus stop in central square, T2110, 90 rooms, deluxe with bath, cheaper cabins and dorm, restaurant, tourist office, clean and quiet. Recommended. Opposite are the **E** *Alka* and *Menka* among others in town.

Srinagar
Colour map 2, grid B2
Population: 18,000

The route from Srinagar to Rudraprayag (35 km; 700 m) at the confluence of the Mandakini and Alaknanda is again mostly through cultivated areas. Roughly half way an enormous landslip indicates the fragility of the mountains. Approximately 5 km before reaching Rudrapayag, in a grove of trees by a village, is a tablet marking the spot where the 'man-eating leopard of Rudraprayag' was finally killed by Jim Corbett, see page 138. Rudraprayag is strung out along a fairly narrow part of the Alaknanda Valley. **Sleeping** On a hill, **D** *New Tourist Bungalow*, 25 rooms, deluxe with bath and dorm; **E** *Chandrapuri Camp*, north of town, by the river, has 10 safari type tents for four.

Rudraprayag

Kedarnath

For Kedarnath, leave the Pilgrim road at Rudraprayag, cross the Alaknanda River, and go through a tunnel before following the Mandakini Valley (the tributary) through terraced cultivation and green fields. The road goes past the first town Tilwara (9 km), then Kund, to **Guptakashi** where Siva proposed to

Colour map 2, grid A2

Garhwal & Kumaon Himalaya

Parvati. If time permits stop at **Sonprayag** (26 km) a small village at the confluence of the Mandakini and Son Ganga rivers, to visit the Triyuginarayan Temple (where the gods were married). Find the viewpoint here before continuing to **Gaurikund** (4 km) where the motorable road ends. **Sleeping** at Gaurikund, T2, with 10 rooms; at Guptakashi, T21, with six rooms. Hundreds of pilgrims bathe in the hot sulphur springs in season (not cleaned daily).

From here you either trek (early start recommended) or ride a mule to Kedarnath (14 km). The ascent (fairly steep at first) is through forests and green valleys to Jungle Ghatti and Rambara (over 1,500 m); the latter part goes through dense vegetation, ravines and passes beautiful waterfalls. Beyond Rambara the path is steep again. At intervals tea stalls sell refreshments.

Kedarnath Temple
77 km from Rudraparyag
Altitude: 3,584 m

The area around Kedarnath is known as **Kedarkhand**, the *Abode of Siva*. Kedarnath has one of the 12 *jyotirlingas* – see page 367. In the *Mahabharata*, the **Pandavas** built the temple to atone for their sins after the battle at Kurukshetra.

The **Kedarnath Temple** is older (some claim, originally over 800 years old) and more impressive than Badrinath. Built of stone, unpainted but carved outside, it comprises a simple, squat, curved tower and a wooden roofed *mandapa*. Set against an impressive backdrop of snow-capped peaks, the principal one being the Kedarnath peak (6,970 m), the view from the forecourt is ruined by ugly 'tube' lights. At the entrance to the temple is a large Nandi statue. Pujas held at 0600 and 1800. **Sleeping E** *Tourist Rest House*, 16 rooms, some with bath, and dorm.

Vasuki Tal
A guide is necessary

Vasuki Tal (5,200 m) about 2 km across, the source of Son Ganga, is to the west up along a goat track, with superb views of the Chaukhamba peak (7,164 m). A short distance northwest is the beautiful Painya Tal where through the clear water you can see the rectangular rocks which form the lake bottom.

The Panch Kedars

There are five temples visited by pilgrims: Kedarnath, Madhmaheswar, Tungnath, Rudranath and Kalpeshwar. These vary in altitude from 1,500-3,680 m in the Rudra Himalaya and is an arduous circuit so now the majority only visit Kedarnath. Kedarnath and Badrinath are only 41 km apart with a tiring *yatra* (pilgrim route) between the two; most pilgrims take the longer but easier way round by bus or car.

The myth of the 'five Sivas' relates how parts of the shattered Nandi Bull fell in the five places – the humped back at Kedarnath, the stomach at Madhmaheswar, the arms at Tungnath, the face at Rudranath and the hair at Kalpeshwar. Since all but Kalpeshwar and Tungnath are inaccessible in the winter, each deity has a winter seat in a temple at Ukhimath where the images are brought down in the autumn. They are returned to their principal temples in the spring.

Panch Kedar trek If you wish to undertake the 170 km, 14-day trek, start at Rishikesh, visiting Kedarnath first (see above). Return to Guptakashi and proceed to Kalimath to start the 24 km trek to **Madhmaheswar** from Mansuna village. You can stop overnight at Ransi, 1 km southwest of Madhmaheswar, and continue following the Ganga through the Kedarnath Musk Deer Sanctuary (see below). From near the temple at 3,030 m which has three streams flowing by it, you can see Chaukhamba peak (7,164 m).

Tungnath (3,680 m), the highest temple, is surrounded by picturesque mountains (Nanda Devi, Neelkanth, Kedarnath). You reach it by a 3 km trek from Chopta (on a driving route from Ukhimath to Gopeshwar), passing through

• •

Pilgrimage: purification and piety

Bad karma (see page 359), the impurity caused by bad actions in previous births, and death itself are the focus of some of Hinduism's most important rituals. Rivers are believed to have great purifying power, stronger at the source, at their confluence, and at the mouth. There are five 'Prayags' (confluences) in the Himalayan section of the Ganga – Deoprayag, Rudraprayag, Karnaprayag, Nandaprayag and Vishnuprayag, called Trayagraj (King of Prayags). On the plains, Allahabad is the most important confluence of all, where the Yamuna, the Ganga and the mythical underground river, the Sarasvati, all meet.

Piety Hardship enhances the rewards of the yatra pilgrims. The really devout prostrate themselves either for the whole distance or around the temple, lying face down, stretching the arms forwards, standing up, moving up to where their fingertips reached and then repeating the exercise, each one accompanied by a chant. Most pilgrims today prefer to make the journey by bus or by car.

• •

villages, fields and wooded hills before reaching meadows with rhododendrons. The two-hour climb of 3 km, though steep, is not difficult since it is along a good rocky path with occasional benches. Garhwal University has a high-altitude botanical field station here.

For **Rudranath** (3,030 m) you can get to Gopeshwar by road and then on to Sagar (5 km) for the 24 km trek covering stony, slippery ground through tall grass, thick oak and rhododendron forests. Landslides are quite common. The grey stone Rudranth temple has the Rudraganga flowing by it. The views of the Nandadevi, Trisul and Hathi Parbat peaks and down to the small lakes glistening in the surroundings are fantastic. **Kalpeshwar** (2,100 m) near Joshimath, is the only one of the Panch Kedars accessible throughout the year. (Trekking across the Mandakini starts from Tangni.) Its position overlooking the Urgam valley offers beautiful views of the Garhwal's most fertile region with its terraced cultivation of rice, wheat and vegetables.

The area bounded by the Mandal-Ukhimath road and the high peaks to the north (Kedarnath Temple is just outside) was set aside in 1972 principally to protect the endangered Himalayan musk deer (*Moschus moschiferus*) – the male carries the prized musk pod. There is a breeding centre at Khanchula Kharak about 10 km from Chopta. The diversity of the park's flora and fauna are particular attractions. Dense forested hills of chir pine, oak, birch and rhododendron and alpine meadows with the presence of numerous Himalayan flowering plants, reflect the diverse climate and topography of the area while 40% of the rocky heights remain under permanent snow. Wildlife includes jackal, black bear, leopard, snow leopard, sambar, *bharal* and Himalayan tarh, as well as 146 species of bird. **Kedarnath Musk Deer Sanctuary**

Along the Pilgrim Road, about midway between Rudraprayag and Karnaprayag you pass **Gauchar**, famous locally for its annual cattle fair. The valley is wider here providing the local population with very good agricultural land. The beautiful Pindar River joins the Alaknanda at **Karnaprayag** (17 km; 788 m), while **Nandaprayag** is the confluence with the Mandakini River. All these places have GMVN accommodation. **Chamoli** (40 km; 960 m) is the principal market for the Chamoli district though the HQ is Gopeshwar on the hillside opposite. The valley walls are now much higher and steeper and the road twists and turns **Rudraprayag to Badrinath**

Garhwal & Kumaon Himalaya

more. Troop movements up to the border with Tibet/China are common and military establishments are a frequent sight on the Pilgrim road. From Chamoli onwards the road is an impressive feat of engineering.

Joshimath
243 km
Altitude: 1,875m
Phone code: 01389
Colour map 2, grid B3
Niti Valley is partially open to group tourists; permits required

Joshimath is at the junction of two formerly important trans-Himalayan trading routes. Travellers to Govindghat and beyond may be forced to spend a night here as the road closes to northbound traffic at 1630. Beyond Badrinath is the Mana Pass. To the east along the valley of the **Dhauliganga** is the **Niti Pass** (5,067 m); the route into West Tibet leads to **Mount Kailas** (6,890 m), sacred to Hindus and Buddhists, and **Lake Mansarovar**.

Joshimath is now the base for India's longest and highest cable car route to Auli Ski Resort, with beautiful views of Nanda Devi, Hathi and Ghori peaks; Rs 200 return per person on modern four-seaters. There is a restaurant in the meadow. **Sleeping** Prices rise in high season. Cheap guest houses and hotels including: GMVN's newer **D-E** *Neelkantha Motel*, Upper Mall, by bus stand, T22226. 15 comfortable rooms, some deluxe with bath, dorm, restaurant (acceptable though limited menu), helpful staff (arrange jeep, porter), often full. Older *Dronagiri*, near Ropeway, is dark and less pleasant. **E** *Kamet*, by Ropeway, Lower Mall. Rooms not great value but cheaper rooms in annexe facing main road. **F** *Nanda Devi* between Upper and Lower Mall, in the bazar, T22170. Basic, cheap, porter agents. **Eating** Several serve veg meals. *Pindari*, serves delicious *thalis*, "light years ahead of the competition". *Paradise*, nearby. **Road Bus**: frequent to Badrinath, 4 hrs, via Govindghat, 1 hr, Rs 7; to Kedarprayag, 1300, 4 hrs; Rishikesh, 0400, 0600, 10 hrs; Rudraprayag, 1100, 5 hrs. **Tourist office** In annexe above *Neekantha Motel*, T22181, helpful. **Useful addresses** Trekking agents at *Nanda Devi hotel*: *Great Himalayan Expeditions*. Highly recommended for "local knowledge, good humour, high spirits and reliability". *Garhwal Mountain Services*, T22288. For porters.

Vishnuprayag is at the bottom of the gorge at the confluence of the Alaknanda and Dhauliganga rivers. 12 km and a steep downhill stretch brings the road from Joshimath to the winter headquarters of the Rawal of Badrinath.

Buses for Badrinath, along the narrow hair-raising route start around 0600, the one-way flow regulated by police. You travel through precipitous gorges, past another Hanuman Chatti with a temple and climb above the treeline to reach the most colourful of the *Char Dhams*, in the valley.

The Bhotias (Bhutias), a border people with Mongoloid features and strong ties with Tibet live along these passes – see page 297 –. The women wear distinctive Arab-like headdress. Like their counterparts in the eastern Himalaya, they used to combine high altitude cultivation with animal husbandry and trading, taking manufactured goods from India to Tibet and returning with salt and borax. When the border closed following the 1962 Indo-Chinese War, they were forced to seek alternative income and some were resettled by the government.

Auli
16 km from Joshimath, and a 5 km trek
Altitude: 2,519m
Colour map 2, grid B3

The extensive meadows at Auli on the way to the Kauri Pass had been used for cattle grazing by the local herders. After the Indo-Chinese War (1962), a road was built from Joshimath to Auli and a Winter Craft Centre set up for the Border Police in the 1970s. With panoramic views of mountains (particularly Nanda Devi and others in the sanctuary, and Mana and Kamet on the Indo-Tibet border) and good slopes, Auli has been developed as a **ski** resort by GMVN and UP Tourism from January to early March. There is a 500 m ski lift and 800 m chair lift. **Sleeping** *Tourist Rest House*, T85208. Restaurant. **Transport** A **cable car** carries people from Joshimath, Rs 200 return. **Jeeps/taxis**:

between Joshimath and Auli. Also regular **buses** from Rishkesh (253 km), Haridwar (276 km) up to Joshimath.

According to Hindu *Shastras*, no pilgrimage is complete without a visit to Badrinath, the abode of Vishnu. Along with Ramesvaram, Dwarka and Puri, it is one of the four holiest places in India – see page 361. Guarding it are the Nar and Narayan ranges and in the distance towers the magnificent pyramid-shaped peak of **Neelkanth** (6,558 m); a hike to its base takes two hours. *Badri* is derived from a wild fruit that Vishnu was said to have lived on when he did penance at Badrivan, the area which covers all five important temples including Kedarnath. Shankaracharya, the monist philosopher from South India, is credited with establishing the four great pilgrimage centres in the early ninth century AD - see page 360.

Badrinath
Phone code: 01389
Colour map 2, grid A3
301 km from Haridwar
Altitude: 3,150 m

The main **Badrinath Temple** is small and brightly painted in green, blue, pink, yellow, white, silver and red. The shrine is usually crowded with worshippers. The *Rawal* (Head Priest) always comes from a Namboodri village in Kerala, the birthplace of Shankaracharya. Badrinath is snowbound over winter (when the images are transferred to Pandukeshwar), and open from late April to October. Along with worshipping in the temple and dispensing alms to the official (sometimes wealthy) temple beggars outside, it is customary to bathe in **Tapt Kund**, a hot pool nearby below the temple. This is fed by a hot sulphurous spring in which **Agni** (the god of fire) resides by kind permission of Vishnu. The temperature is around 45°C. *Badrinath Festival*, 3-10 June. **Sleeping** E *Devlok* (GMVN), near Bus Stand, T85212. Thirty large rooms, restaurant, best in the trekking area. For pilgrims: *dharamshalas* and *chattis* (resthouses). **Transport** See under Rishikesh.

Govindghat (1,828 m), 20 km from Joshimath, is on the road to Badrinath. A bridle track leads to Ghangharia, for the Valley of Flowers (19 km) and Hemkund Sahib. This trailhead is very crowded in the peak season (May-June). You can trek or hire mules for the two-day journey; there are several **tea-stalls** along the route. **Sleeping** Among others E *Bharat Lodge*, at the far end of town. Bucket hot water. *Forest Rest House. Govind Singh Gurudwara*, free accommodation and food to all (donations accepted) and reliable cloakroom service for trekkers.

Hemkund & the Valley of Flowers
Colour map 2, grid A3

Ghangharia (3,048 m) is a 14 km walk from Govindghat. **Sleeping** May-June are very busy; those arriving late without a reservation may only find floor space in the Gurudwara or must sleep in a field. **D-F** *Tourist Lodge*, overpriced rooms, dorm (Rs 100), tent (Rs 60). E *Merry Lodge*, rooms with bath. F *Krishna*, cheap rooms with bath. Free *Gurudwara*.

Hemkund (6 km; 4,329 m) After 1 km from Ghangharia leave the main Valley of Flowers track, up a path to the right. **Guru Gobind Singh**, see page 376, is believed to have sat here in meditation during a previous incarnation. It is an important Sikh pilgrimage site. On the shore of the lake (4,340 m) where pilgrims bathe in the icy cold waters, is a modern *gurudwara*; well worth the long trek though some may suffer from the high altitude. Hemkund is also a Hindu pilgrimage site, referred to as **Lokpal**. Lakshman, the younger brother of Rama, meditated by the lake and regained his health after being severely wounded by Ravana's son, Meghnath. A small Lakshman temple stands near the gurudwara. Despite its ancient connections, Hemkund/Lokpal was 'discovered' by a Sikh *Havildar*, Solan Singh, and only became a major pilgrimage centre after 1930.

Best season: Jul–Aug

Valley of Flowers National Park (4 km from Ghangharia; 3,000-3,600 m). The 14 km long trail from Govindghat to Ghangharia runs along a narrow forested valley past the villages of Pulna and Bhiyundar. The Valley of Flowers is a further 5 km. **Hathi Parbat** (Elephant Peak, 6,700 m) rises dramatically at the head of the narrow side valley. Close views of mountains can be seen from Bhiyundar. The trek has beautifully varied scenery. After crossing the Alaknanda River by suspension bridge the winding path follows the Laxman Ganga as its constant companion, passing dense forests and commanding panoramic views of the lovely Kak Bhusundi Valley on its way to the hamlet of Ghangaria (Govind Dham), the base for the Valley of Flowers, nestling amidst giant deodars. As the path from Ghangaria gradually climbs to the Valley of Flowers, glaciers, snow bridges, alpine flowers and wildlife appear at intervals. The 6 km long and 2 km wide 'U' shaped valley is laced by waterfalls. The river Pushpati and many other small streams wind across it, and its floor, carpeted with alpine flowers during the monsoons, is particularly beautiful. It is especially popular because of its accessibility. The Valley was popularized by **Frank Smythe**, the well known mountaineer, in 1931. Local people had always kept clear of the Valley because of the belief that it was haunted, and any who entered it would be spirited away. A memorial stone to Margaret Legge, an Edinburgh botanist, who slipped and fell to her death in 1939 reads, "I will lift up mine eyes unto the hills from whence cometh my strength".

Camping overnight in the valley (or taking pack animals) is prohibited

Permits to enter the national park are issued at the small police post at the road head of Govindghat, Rs 350 (foreigners), plus camera fee, Rs 50; may be negotiable in the off-season, eg Rs 100 for one day.

Satopanth
25 km from Badrinath

Satopanth, a glacial lake, takes a day to reach. You follow the track along the Alaknanda Valley, a gentle climb up to **Mana** village (6 km north) near the border, inhabited by Bhotias. Foreigners need to register here and sometimes deposit their cameras since they are not permitted to take photographs. Nearby is the cave where **Vyasa** is said to have written the epic *Mahabharata*. The track disappears and you cross a snowbridge, trek across flower-filled meadows before catching sight of the impressive 144 m **Vasudhara Falls**. The ascent becomes more difficult as you approach the source of the Alaknanda near where the Satopanth and Bhagirathi Kharak glaciers meet. The remaining trek takes you across the **Chakra Tirth** meadow and over the steep ridge of the glacier till you see the striking green Satopanth Lake. According to legend its three corners mark the seats of Brahma, Vishnu and Siva. The peaks of **Satopanth** (7,084 m) from which the glacier flows, **Neelkanth** (6,558 m) and **Chaukhamba** (7,164 m) make a spectacular sight.

Trekking in the Garhwal and the Kumaon Himalaya

This region contains some of the finest mountains in the Himalaya and is highly accessible and yet surprisingly very few westerners visit it, many preferring to go to Nepal. Of the many treks available, eight routes are included here which offer some of the most spectacular walking and scenery.

Exploration in Garhwal and Kumaon

This region had been open since the British took over in 1815 but it was closed in 1960 due to political troubles with China, and during this period Nepal became popular with climbers and trekkers. Garhwal and Kumaon Himalaya have gradually been opened to explorers since 1975, though parts bordering Tibet remain closed.

Much of the early Himalayan exploration was undertaken here. **Trisul** (7,120 m), after it had been climbed by Dr Tom Longstaff in 1906, remained the highest mountain climbed for the next 30 years. Famous mountaineers of the 1930s like Bill Tilman, Eric Shipton and Frank Smythe all marvelled at the beauty of the region and Edmund Hillary's first Himalayan peak was Mukut Parbat in Garhwal. Later climbers like Chris Bonington, Peter Boardman, Joe Tasker and Dick Renshaw used alpine techniques to conquer Changabang and Dunagiri.

The scenic splendour of these mountains lies partly in the fact that the forests around the big peaks are still in marvellous condition and the local population are unaffected by the ravages of mass tourism. Also in Garhwal and Kumaon there are ranges that you can easily get among, enabling a greater feeling of intimacy with the alpine giants. The mountains have been described as "a series of rugged ranges tossed about in the most intricate confusion" (Walton, 1910).

Trekking

Trekking in this region is not highly organized so you need to be well prepared. On most treks you need a tent (though not The Pindari Glacier trek, for example). Very few villagers speak English, but the rewards for the well-equipped trekker who has planned carefully are great, especially the feeling of being far from the madding crowd. If you are travelling in small groups of three to four persons it is often possible to get overnight accommodation in villagers' houses but despite their hospitality, this is uncomfortable. GMVN and KMVN lodges where available, provide rustic but clean rooms (some have deluxe rooms with bath), and caretakers cook simple meals. If you would like to leave logistics to someone else, hire a government recognized specialist tour operator (see page 54).

Trekking agents
Reliable local agents who will make all arrangements including accommodation and porters, are in Dehradun and Rishikesh (see pages 98 and 54). Porter agents in Uttarkashi, Joshimath, Munsiyari etc who act as trekking agents may not be as reliable; negotiate rates for specific services and insist on reliable porters.

Best season
February and March: at lower altitudes for the spectacular rhododendrons. **April and May**: at higher altitudes, though it can get very hot and views can be restricted due to large scale burning. **July and August**: the **monsoon** is good for alpine flowers but wet, humid and cloudy for much, though not all, of the time. If the monsoon is heavy roads and tracks can become impassable. **September**: the air is beautifully rainwashed, but early morning clear skies can give way by 1000 to cloud, and the views may completely disappear. **October and November**: when temperatures are lower, the skies clearer and the vegetation greener following the monsoon.

Trekking areas
You will not be allowed to go beyond Badrinath
Around **Gangotri** and **Yamunotri** in Garhwal there are a number of very good treks, some suitable for the independent or 'go-it-alone' trekker. **Nanda Devi** is the other area and this forms a ring that includes both Garhwal and Kumaon. There are many more treks than those indicated here. The lower part of the Niti Valley, and the Darma Valley, are open to groups of four with requisite permits.

Gangotri and Yamunotri area

Gangotri to Gaumukh The best known trek here is to Gaumukh (The Cow's Mouth) and, if desired, beyond onto the Gangotri Glacier. Gaumukh can easily be managed in three days with minimal equipment (carry provisions).

From Gangotri (3,046 m) follow the well-defined, gradually ascending path to **Bhojbasa** (14 km; 3,800 m; five hours), see page 112. **Sleeping A** *Tourist Rest House* has four rooms and a dorm (bring sleeping bags). This, however, is often full. You may hire two-person tents for Rs 160 per night (good value). There is an *ashram* where trekkers and pilgrims can stay. **Chirbasa**, 5 km before Bhojbasa has tented accommodation.

The 4 km to **Gaumukh** (the last kilometres across boulder scree and moraine) takes about one hour so it is quite feasible to go from Bhojbasa to Gaumukh, spend some time there then return the same day. There are plenty of tea houses en route. Gaumukh, the present source of the Bhagirathi (Ganga) River, is at the mouth of the Gangotri Glacier where blocks of glacier ice fall into the river and pilgrims cleanse themselves in freezing water. There are breathtaking views. There is basic *tent* accommodation.

Beyond Gaumukh (3,969 m) more care and camping equipment is required. The **Gangotri Glacier** is situated in an amphitheatre of 6,500-7,000 m peaks which include Satopanth (7,084 m), Vasuki (6,792 m), Bhagirathi (6,556 m), Kedar Dome and the prominent trio of Bhagirathi I, II and III;

Garhwal & Kumaon treks

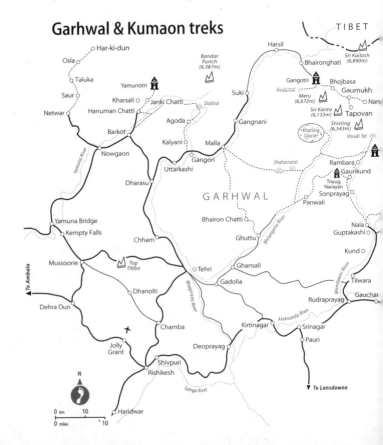

Shivling (6,543 m), standing alone, is one of the most spectacular peaks in the entire Himalaya.

Tapovan
Altitude: 4,463m

In a breathtaking setting in a grassy meadow on the east bank of the Gangotri Glacier, this is the base camp for climbing expeditions to the stunningly beautiful **Shivling** (6,543 m), Siva's lingam and the 'Matterhorn of the Himalaya'. You can either return the same way or make a round trip by crossing over the glacier to **Nandanvan** (3 km; 4,400 m) and going up to Vasuki Tal (6 km) beneath **Vasuki** peak (6,792 m); since the glacier crossing is fairly risky, it is recommended only for the experienced trekker. The return is via Nandanvan, the west bank of the Gangotri Glacier crossing the Raktvarn Glacier to Gaumukh-Raktvarn, so called because of the rust coloured boulders in its moraine.

Gangotri to Kedartal

This is an excellent short trek with scenic variety and spectacular views but you must be aware of the problems associated with altitude and allow time for acclimatization (see page 64). It requires a tent, stove and food. It is 17 km to Kedartal (5,000 m), a small glacial lake surrounded by **Meru** (6,672 m), Pithwara (6,904 m) and Bhrigupanth (6,772 m).

Leaving Gangotri you proceed up the gorge of the Kedar Ganga (Siva's contribution to the Bhagirathi River). It is 8 km to Bhoj Kharak and then a further 4 km to Kedar Kharak, passing through some beautiful Himalayan birch forest (*Betula utilis*) en route. The bark from the trees (*bhoj* in Garhwali) was used by sages and hermits for manuscripts. From Kedar Kharak, where you can camp, it is a laborious 5 km ascent to Kedartal. Besides the peaks surrounding the lake you can also see the Gangotri range.

You return to Gangotri the same way. **Rudugaira Kharak** is the base camp for the peaks at the head of the Rudugaira valley. Coming down towards Gangotri you must cross to the opposite bank near Patangnidhar to avoid the cliffs on the west bank. Nearer Gangotri cross back to the west bank.

Gangori to Yamunotri via Dodital

This is a beautiful trek between Kalyani and Hanuman Chatti, a distance of 49 km. You can do a round trip from either end, allowing five days.

From **Uttarkashi** take a local bus to Kalyani via **Gangori** (3 km) or walk it. At **Kalyani** (1,829 m) with its fish hatchery, the recognized starting point of the trek, you take a track to the right. From here it gets steeper as the path climbs through forest to **Agoda** (5 km; 2,280 m). There is a suitable camping or halting place 2 km beyond Agoda . The next day carry on to **Dodital** (16 km; 3,024 m), picturesquely set in a forest of pine (*Pinus wallichiana*), deodar (*Cedrus*

Garhwal & Kumaon Himalaya

deodara) and oak (*Quercus dilatata* and *Q semecarpifolia*). This is the source of the Asi Ganga and is stocked with trout. There is a dilapidated *Forest Rest House* and several cheap lodges. Above the lake there are fine views of Bandar Punch (6,387 m, Monkey's Tail). To reach **Hanuman Chatti** (2,400 m) walk up to the Aineha Pass (6 km; 3,667 m) which also has splendid views. Then it is a 22 km walk down to Hanuman Chatti, the roadhead for Yamunotri.

Har-ki-Dun Trek Har-ki-Dun (God's Valley) nestles in the northwest corner of Garhwal near the Sutlej-Yamuna watershed. The people of the area have the distinction of worshipping **Duryodhana**, head of the crafty royal family in the *Mahabharata*, rather than siding with the pious Pandavas (see page 378). The valley is dominated by Swargarohini (6,096 m) and Kalanag. From **Nowgaon**, 9 km south of Barkot, take a bus to the roadhead of **Sankri**. From here it is a gradual ascent over 12 km to **Taluka**, and **Osla** (2,559 m), 11 km further. Another 8 km and 1,000 m higher is **Har-ki-Dun** (3,565 m), an ideal base for exploring the valley. Allow three days to Har-ki-Dun. There are Forest and Tourist Rest Houses at all these places.

You can return to Nowgaon or, if properly equipped and provisioned, trek on to **Yamunotri** (29 km) via the Yamunotri Pass (5,172 m). You will need to allow time for acclimatization. The views from the pass are well worth the effort.

Nanda Devi area

Nanda Devi (7,816 m), named after the all-encompassing form of the female deity, dominates the Garhwal and Kumaon Himalaya. With its two peaks separated by a 4 km long ridge, the second highest mountain in India is incredibly beautiful. The Nanda Devi Sanctuary is a World Biosphere Reserve. She is the most important of Garhwal's deities, protected by a ring of mountains, 112 km in circumference, containing 12 peaks over 6,400 m high. In only one place is this defensive ring lower than 5,500 m, at the **Rishi Gorge**, one of the deepest in the world. It is the place of ascetic sages (*rishis*).

Early exploration For half a century the problems which engaged the attention of many experienced explorers and mountaineers was not so much how to climb the mountain but how to get to it. Various attempts were made from a number of places to gain entry into what became known as the Nanda Devi Sanctuary . The riddle was finally solved by the 'Terrible Twins', Bill Tillman and Eric Shipton in a characteristically lightweight expedition (these two great mountaineers would agonize over whether to take one shirt or two on an expeditioon lasting a few months!). The way they discovered was up the Rishiganga and through the difficult Rishi Gorge. They made two trips into the Sanctuary during their five month expedition in the Garhwal Himalaya in 1934. Bill Tillman returned in 1936 (Shipton was on Hugh Rutledge's Everest Expedition) with a small climbing party and climbed the mountain with little real difficulty.**Further reading**: Bill Aitken. *The Nandi Devi Affair*. Penguin; 1994. William Sax. *Mountain Goddess*. OUP; 1991.

Pindari This trek along the southern edge of the Sanctuary is an 'out and back' trek, ie
Glacier Trek you return by the same route. **Sleeping** KMVN *Tourist Lodges* (some with only four beds) are dotted along the route so this trek can be done with little equipment, although a sleeping bag is essential. Book accommodation early or take your own tent. The trek is 66 km from Song, which has the last bus terminus.

From **Bageshwar** – page 137, get a local bus to **Bharari** (1,524 m) which has a PWD *Rest House* and a cheap hotel. From here you can walk 16 km along the Sarju Valley to **Song** or take another bus. It is just over 1½ km further to

Loharkhet (1,829 m) which also has a PWD *Bungalow* in the village and a basic KMVN *Tourist Rest House* overlooking it. Good views of the hillside opposite and the head of the Sarju Valley. It is 11 km from Loharkhet to **Dhakuri** via the Dhakuri Pass (2,835 m) which has a wonderful view of the south of the Nanda Devi Sanctuary including Panwali Dhar (6,683 m) and Maiktoli (6,803 m). The walk to the pass is mostly through forest on a well graded path. About 100 m below the pass on the north side is a clearing with a PWD *Bungalow* and a KMVN *Tourist Rest House*. Great views, especially at sunrise and sunset.

In the Pindar Valley you descend to **Khati** (8 km; 2,194 m), first through rhododendron, then mixed forests dominated by stunted oak. Khati is a village with over 50 households situated on a spur that runs down to the river, some 200 m below. There is a PWD *Bungalow*, KMVN *Tourist Rest House* and a village hotel. You can buy biscuits, eggs and chocolate, brought in by mule from Bharari.

From Khati follow the Pindar to **Dwali** (8 km; 2,580 m) which is at the confluence of the Pindar and the Kaphini rivers. Here there is a KMVN *Travellers' Lodge* and a run down PWD *Bungalow*. If you have a tent, camp in front. The next halt is **Phurkiya** (6 km; 3,260 m) which also has a KMVN *Travellers' Lodge*. This can be used as a base for going up to Zero Point (4,000 m) a view point from where the steep falling glacier can be seen (it is difficult for trekkers to go up to the snout of the glacier itself). On either side there are impressive peaks, including Panwali Dwar (6,683 m) and Nanda Kot (6,876 m). Return to Bharari the same way.

From Dwali, however, a side trip to the **Kaphini Glacier** is worthwhile. Alternatively, you could trek up to **Sundar Dhunga Glacier** from Khati. Including either of these, the trek can be accomplished in a week but for comfort allow nine days.

Roopkund (4,800 m; *kund*; lake in Garhwali). A legend relates Nanda Devi, the wife of Siva, to this small lake. When her sister Balpa, accompanied her husband King Jasidhwal of the medieval Kingdom of Kanauj on a pilgrimage to Kailash (Mt Trisul), she delivered a child at Balpa de Sulera (adjoining Bhagwabasa, thus polluting the entire mountain. Nanda Devi's herald, Latu (who has a temple at Wan), at the command of the Goddess hurled the royal pilgrimage into the small tarn called Roopkund. Hence the remains of the 300 bodies found in the lake. 30 years ago the Indian anthropologist DN Majumdar discovered frozen bodies around this small mountain tarn, the remains of a party of pilgrims on a *yatra* who died when bad weather closed in. Carbon-dating suggests the bones are 600 years old.

This is a highly varied and scenic trek which can be undertaken by a suitably equipped party. A week is sufficient – nine days if you want to take it more comfortably with a rest day for acclimatization. The trek can start in Debal where you can pick up provisions, or at Bagrigadh (see below). You can usually get porters at Gwaldam or Debal.

Roopkund Trek

Gwaldam is a small market strung out along a ridge surrounded by orchards. The British established tea plantations which have since been abandoned. **Sleeping** GMVN *Tourist Bungalow*, splendid views from the garden, especially at dawn and dusk, of Trisul (7,120 m) and Nanda Ghunti (6,310 m). Gwaldam, one of the starting points for the trek to Roopkund (see page 123), overlooks the beautiful Pindar River which the road follows down to its confluence with the Alaknanda River at **Karnaprayag**.

The road joins the pilgrim road which runs from **Rishikesh** and **Haridwar**

Gwaldam
Altitude: 1,950m
Colour map 2, grid B3

to **Badrinath**, see page 113.

From Gwaldam (1,950 m) walk down through attractive pine forest, cross the river Pindar and continue to **Debal** (8 km; 1,350 m) where there is a KMVN *Tourist Rest House*, a *Forest Rest House* and *dharamshalas*. From here you can either walk 12 km along a dirt road through villages with views of Trishul (6,855 m), or go by cramped jeep-taxi to **Bagrigad** which is 500 m below the **Lohajung Pass** (2,350 m) where there is an attractive GMVN *Travellers' Lodge* and two cheap lodges, right on the ridge beside a pretty shrine. Good views here of Nanda Ghunti. If time is at a premium, you can save a day by going by bus from Gwaldam to Tharali, taking another bus to Debal, catching the jeep-taxi to Bagrigadh and walking up to Lohajung in one long day.

From **Lohajung** walk down through stunted oak forest and along the *Wan Gad* (river) to the village of **Wan** (12 km; 2,400 m) which has a *Forest Rest*

Nanda Devi area treks

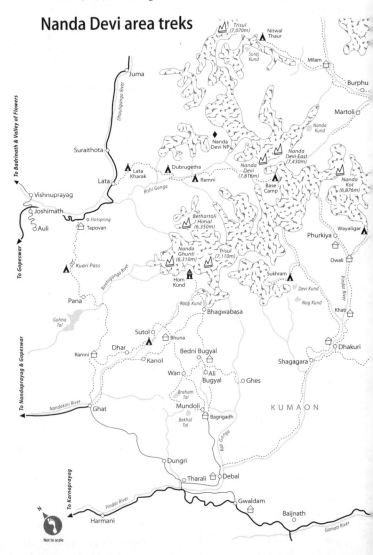

House and GMVN *Travellers' Lodge*. From Wan it is essentially wilderness travel as you make the ascent to Roopkund, first walking through thick forest to **Bedni Bugyal** (*bugyal* – meadow) which is used as summer pasture. This is at 3,550 m and has good views of Trisul, Nandaghunti and the Badrinath range to the north. There are some shepherds' stone huts which you may be able to use but it is better to take a tent.

From Bedni it is a gradual seven kms climb along a well defined path over the 4,500 m **Kalwa Vinayak** to more shepherds' huts at **Bhagwabasa**, the base for the final walk up to Roopkund. A stove is necessary for cooking and it can be very cold at night, but water is available about 150 m northeast and up the slope from the campsite. From here, it is two to three hours up to **Roopkund**. Immediately after the monsoon the views can disappear in cloud by 1000, so it is best to leave early. In the final steep part the ground can be icy. Roopkund Lake itself is small and unimpressive, but from the 4,900 m ridge approximately 50 m above Roopkund there is a magnificent view of the west face of Trisul rising over 3,500 m from the floor of the intervening hanging valley to the summit. Return to Gwaldam by the same route or via **Ali Bugyal** and village Didina which by-passes Wan.

The Curzon Trail is an incomparably beautiful trek. However, rapid ascent follows equally steep descent from one valley to the next, and at no point does the trek get close to the high snow-covered peaks. It was the route followed by Tilman and Shipton on their way to the Rishi Gorge, and by other mountaineers en route to the peaks on the Indo-Tibetan border. The crossing of the Kuari Pass is a fitting conclusion to a trek that takes in three lesser passes and five major rivers – the Pindar, Kaliganga, Nandakini, Birehiganga and Dhauliganga. The trail was named after Lord Curzon, a keen trekker, and the path may have been specially improved for him. After 1947 it was officially renamed the 'Nehru Trail'.

This trek begins at **Gwaldam** and ends at **Tapovan** in the Dhauliganga Valley on the Joshimath-Niti Pass road, after crossing the **Kuari Pass** (4,268 m), one of the finest vantage points in the Himalaya.

From Gwaldam proceed to **Wan** as in the previous itinerary. Then, go over the Kokinkhal Pass to **Kanol** (2,900 m) through thick mixed forest to **Sutol** (10 km; 2,100 m) in the

Curzon Trail
Camping equipment is strongly recommended as some of the halting places have no suitable accommodation

Garhwal & Kumaon Himalaya

Conquering Nanda Devi on apricot brandy

For half a century, the problem facing many experienced explorers and mountaineers was not so much how to climb the mountain but how to get to what became known as the Nanda Devi Sanctuary. The riddle was finally solved by Bill Tilman and Eric Shipton in a characteristically lightweight expedition. They discovered the way up the Rishiganga and through the difficult Rishi Gorge and made two trips into the sanctuary during their five month expedition in 1934. Bill Tilman returned in 1936 with a small party and climbed the mountain with little real difficulty.

Tilman, a purist, wrote "mountaineering is in danger of becoming mechanized. It is therefore pleasing to record that in

climbing Nanda Devi no climbing aids were used, apart, that is, from the apricot brandy we took. Our solitary oxygen apparatus was fortunately drowned, pitons were forgotten at base camp and crampons were solemnly carried up only to be abandoned" (The Ascent of Nanda Devi). The pack goat carrying the entire expeditions' crampons fell into the gorge!

In 1936 the monsoon was particularly heavy. The Pindar River rose dramatically. In the village of Tharali 40 lives were lost on 29 August, the day that Tilman's party reached the summit. Some say the anger of the Goddess was provoked by the violation of her sanctuary.

Nandakini Valley. There is a good campsite by the river. The next two stages follow the Nandakini downstream to Padergaon (10 km; 2,500 m) via Ala. The trail to Tapovan leads up over the rhododendron forest clad **Ramni Pass** (3,100 m) with a good view of the Kuari Pass. The trail southwest of Ramni goes to the nearby road head at **Ghat**, from where you can also start the trek. To reach Tapovan from Ramni is a good three days' walk, down through lush forest to cross the Birehiganga River by an impressive suspension bridge, up around the horseshoe-shaped hanging valley around Pana village, over an intervening spur and into the forested tributary valley of the Kuari nallah. There is no settlement in this area; *bharal* (mountain goats) and the rarely seen Himalayan black bear inhabit the rich forest. Waterfalls tumble down over steep crags. There is a camp and a cave (about one hour) before the Kuari pass at **Dhakwani** (3,200 m).

Leave early to get the full effect of sunrise over the peaks on the Indo-Tibetan border. Some of the peaks seen are Kamet, Badrinath (7,040 m), Dunagiri (7,066 m) and Changabang (6,863 m). There is a wonderful wooded campsite with marvellous views about 300 m below the pass. From here the trail drops down over 2,000 m to **Tapovan** and the Joshimath-Niti road. There is a hot spring here and a bus service to **Joshimath**. Allow 10 days for the trek. A shorter trail leads from the campsite along a scenic ridge to Auli and a further 4 km down to Joshimath.

Nanda Devi & Milam Glacier Trek Much of this area was only reopened to trekkers in 1993 after more than 30 years of seclusion. The Milam Valley, incised by the 36 km long Gori Ganga gorge, was part of the old trade route between Kumaon and Tibet, only interrupted by the Indian-Chinese War of 1962. Milam, which once had 500 households, many occupied by wealthy traders and surrounded by barley and potato fields, has been reduced to a handful of occupied cottages. The trek is moderate, with some sustained steady walking but no really steep gradients or altitude problems. The route is through some of the remotest regions of the Himalaya with spectacular scenery and rich wildlife.

Day 1 From **Munsiari** (10 hours' drive from Almora) a 10 km drive takes you down to Selapani where the trail up the Milam Valley begins. **Lilam** (1,800

m) is an easy 7 km walk (two and a half hours) where the tiny *Rest House* offers a convenient halt or camping ground for the first night.

Day 2 (14 km; seven hours) From Lilam the trail enters the spectacular 25 km long gorge. Etched into the cliff face above the Gori Ganga the hillsides above are covered in dense bamboo thickets and mixed rain forest. After the junction of the Ralam and Gori Ganga rivers the track climbs to a tea shop at Radgari, then goes on to a small *Rest House* at **Bugdiar** (2,700 m). A memorial commemorates villagers and army personnel lost in the avalanche of 1989. Only a few houses remain on the edge of a wasteland.

Day 3 (16 km; six hours) The valley opens up after climbing quite steeply to a huge overhanging cliff, which shelters a local deity. The route enters progressively drier terrain, but there are two waterfalls of about 100 m, one opposite a tea shop at Mapang. The track climbs to **Rilkote** (3,200 m).

Day 4 (13 km; six hours) Passing deserted villages in the now almost arid landscape the track goes through the large village of **Burphu**, backed by the Burphu Peak (6,300 m). Nanda Devi East comes into view before reaching **Ganghar** village (3,300 m) where only three of the former 60 families remain. Some of the houses have beautiful carved wooden door and window frames; the carefully walled fields below are deserted.

Day 5 (7 km; three hours) A steep narrow track leads into the **Pachhu** Valley, dominated by the northeast face of Nanda Devi East 3,800 m above the Pachhu Glacier. Dwarf rhododendron and birch, with anemones and primulas below, line the first section of the track before it emerges into alpine meadows below the debris of the glacier itself. **Tom Longstaff** came through this valley in his unsuccessful attempt to climb Nanda Devi East in 1905 before trying the parallel valley to the south of Pachhu via what is now known as Longstaff's Col. There is a campsite (3,900 m) 3 km from the base of Nanda Devi East with both the col and the summit clearly visible in good weather.

Day 6 Side treks are possible up to the Pachhu Glacier and along its edge to the glacial lake **Nanda Kund**.

Day 7 (17 km; six hours) Returning via Ghanghar at Burfu, the track crosses the Gori Ganga on a wooden bridge then climbs to the former staging post of **Milam** (3,300 m).

Day 8 Another 'excursion' (10 km; eight hours) is possible from Milam to the **Milam Glacier** (4,100 m). There are superb views of the clean ice uncovered by debris from the track which runs along the left bank of the Milam Glacier. Three tributary glaciers join the main Milam Glacier.

Day 9 (13 km; five hours) The track runs along the left bank of the river via Tola village to the base of the 4,750 m Brijganga Pass, outside **Sumdu** village (3,400 m).

Day 10 (12 km; seven hours) Superb views characterize this steady climb to the top of the pass. The razor sharp Panchulis dominate the south while the twin peaks of Nanda Devi are straight ahead. **Ralam** village is a steep drop below the pass (3,700 m).

Day 11 (10 km; six hours) This can be a rest day or a day trek up to the Shankalpa Glacier along the watershed between the rarely visited Ralam and Darma valleys.

Day 12-14 The trek runs steadily down through the thickly forested Ralam valley, generally used only by local people.

Day 15 (11 km; four hours) Return from Lilam to Munsiari via a number of villages.

The easternmost of the Kumaon valleys, the Darma Valley is now also open to trekkers but you need permission. Separated from western Nepal by the

Darma Valley Trek

Garhwal & Kumaon Himalaya

Kaliganga River and with Tibet to the north the valley is one of the least explored in the Himalaya.

From the roadhead at **Dharchula** (on the India/Nepal border) it is possible to trek for four or five days up to Sipu and also to spend time exploring the numerous side valleys.

Buses are available from Pithorgarh and Almora up to Dharchula from where it is often possible to get local transport for a further 32 km up to **Sobala**. Then it is a three to four days' trek up to Sipu, the northernmost point allowed under present regulations.

It is possible to trek east from Sobala over two reasonably easy, low altitude passes to Munsiari and to return from there having completed a circuit (three to four days). For this trek you need a Restricted Area Permit from the District Magistrate, Dharchula or Jauljibi, provided there are four trekkers plus a recognized Indian travel agent in the group.

Nainital नैनीताल

Phone code: 05942
Colour map 2, grid B3
Population: 31,000
Altitude: 1,938 m

Set around a small lake, the charming hill station of Nainital has many villas, bungalows and fine houses with their well kept lawns on the fairly steep tree covered hillsides. Overcrowded in summer, the resort is more pleasant out of season, with some attractive walks and only a few foreign tourists.

Ins & outs **Getting there** The nearest railway station is 1¾ hrs away at Kathgodam, linked to Nainital by frequent buses. The climb from Kathgodam to Nainital is dramatic, rising 1,300 m over 30 km. The road follows the valley of the Balaya stream then winds up the hillsides through forests and small villages. After the long drive the town around the *tal* (lake) appears suddenly; the land south and on the plains-side fall away quite steeply so you only see the lake when you are at its edge. Buses from Delhi and the surrounding hill stations use the Tallital bus stand at the southern end of the lake, while some buses from Ramnagar (and Corbett National Park) use the Mallital bus stand at the northern end. **Getting around** The Mall, pedestrianized at peak times, is the hub of Nainital's life. You can hire a cycle-rickshaw if the walk feels too much, or take a taxi for travelling further afield.

Background In 1841 the small hamlet of Nainital was 'discovered' by a Mr P Barron, a sugar manufacturer from Saharanpur. He was impressed by the 1½ km long and 500 m wide lake that he returned with a sailing boat a year later, carried up in sections from the plains. In due course Nainital became the summer capital of the then United Provinces. An old legend of Siva and Sati (see page 104) associates the place as where Sati's eyes fell (hence *naina*). The *tal* (lake) is surrounded by seven hills, the *Sapta-Shring*.

On 18 September 1880 disaster struck the township. At the north end of the lake, known now as Mallital (the southern part is Tallital) stood the *Victoria Hotel*. In two days nearly 1,000 mm of rain fell leading to a landslip which crushed some

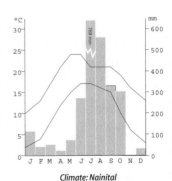

Climate: Nainital
Season: Apr-May (May & Jun are very busy) & Oct-Nov

outhouses, burying several people. The cliff overhanging the hotel collapsed, burying the soldiers and civilians engaged in rescue work and making it impossible to save the 150 buried. Later the area was levelled, became known as The Flats, and was used for public meetings and impromptu games of football and cricket. Today it is more a bus park in the tourist season.

Nainital is popular as an Indian family holiday centre, especially in the summer season, when hotels are full, prices soar and there is little peace and quiet. Congestion and pollution is taking its toll; the *tal*, now much reduced in size, is unable to cope with the increased tourist traffic which has seen a building boom around it. The pony riders, curio-sellers and snack stalls increase in number while the lake water becomes dirty and unable to support fish. It can be very cold in winter, and depressions sometimes bring cloud and rain which obscures the views of the mountains.

Sights
Walking is the major attraction of this town

There is little of architectural interest other than the colonial style villas overlooking the lake. The **Church of St John in the Wilderness** (1846), one of the earliest buildings, is beyond Mallital, below the Nainital Club. The most distinctive building is **Government House** (1899, now the Secretariat) which was designed in stone by FW Stephens who was also responsible for VT and Churchgate Stations in Mumbai (Bombay). Early in the season it is pleasant to walk round (the Lower Mall is pedestrianized) or take a boat across the **lake**; remember it can still be very cold in March. **Sanjay Park** (Manora Manoram) is a botanical garden.

Naina (Cheena) **Peak** (2,610 m) is a 5 km walk from the lake. From the top, there are stunning views of the Himalaya including **Nanda Devi** (7,816 m) and the mountains on the Tibetan border. In season there is a gondola (Ropeway) which runs from the Mallital end of the lake to **Snow View** (2,270 m), another good vantage point for viewing the snow-capped peaks. It is also possible to make the 2 km steep climb up to the viewpoint from the north end of the lake, passing the small Tibetan gompa which has fluttering prayer flags marking it. **Hanumangarh** with a small temple off Haldwani Rd, and the **Observatory** (open evenings) further along the path (3 km from the lake), have lookouts for watching the sun set over the plains. The opposite side has only a few cottages and much higher up near the ridge are two private boys' schools – Sherwood College and St Joseph's. The atmospheric **British Cemetery** with its crumbling graves is about 3 km southeast of town. Take the minor road at the south end of the lake (not the Rampur Rd); on the right side, the remains of the entrance gate are just visible behind some trees.

Essentials

Sleeping
■ *on map, page 130*
Price codes: see inside front cover

Peak rates (given here) can be high. Good off-season discounts are usual but may mean inadequate heating. **AL-A** *Manu Maharani Royal Garden* (Holiday Inn), Grasmere, near Display Garden, T35531, F37350, manumaharani@fhraindia.com 66 modern rooms with good views, good food, bar. **A** *Naini Retreat* (Claridges), Ayarpattha Slopes, 2 km from Mallital Bazar, T35105, F35103. 34 rooms, good restaurant, "excellent quality, service and location". **A-B** *Balarampur House*, Mallital, T36236, travcon.holidays@rsnl.com A royal summer retreat now converted to a luxury hotel. **A-B** *Vikram Vintage Inn*, near ATI, Mallital, T36179, F36117 (or New Delhi T6436451). 34 comfortable rooms, quiet wooded area but not all facilities (no pool). **B** *Arif Castle*, Mallital, T35801, F36231, arif.luc@sprintrpg.ems.vsnl.net.in 66 comfortable rooms, jeep transfers to centre, a mixture of ancient and modern! **B** *Krishna*, The Mall, T36150, F37550. Rooms vary, best have lake view. **B** *Shervani Hilltop Inn*, Waverly Rd, T36304. 21 rooms in old royal home, some in cottages, peaceful, lovely

Garhwal & Kumaon Himalaya

garden, free jeep to centre. **C** *Armadale*, Waverly Rd, T36855. 20 rooms, peaceful.
C *Belvedere*, above Bank of Baroda, Mallital, T37434, F35082. 22 comfortable rooms
(good value family suite) with good lake views, in former Raja's summer palace – a
colonial building with pleasant garden, restaurant, well located, quiet, friendly owners, helpful staff. Highly recommended. **C** *Alka*, The Mall, Tallital, T35220, F36629, and
separate *Annexe* nearby. 72 lake facing rooms, floating restaurant (good Indian).
C *Grand*, The Mall, near Flatties Rock, T35406. 31 basic but clean rooms, colonial style
but faded, good food served on lake-facing verandah (order 3 hrs in advance), family
run, friendly, good service. Recommended **C-D** *Empire*, Tallital, T35325. Clean,
friendly. Recommended. **D** *Silverton*, Sher-ka-Danda, 2.5 km centre, T35249. 27
rooms in 'chalets', some with good views, peaceful, veg restaurant.

Nainital

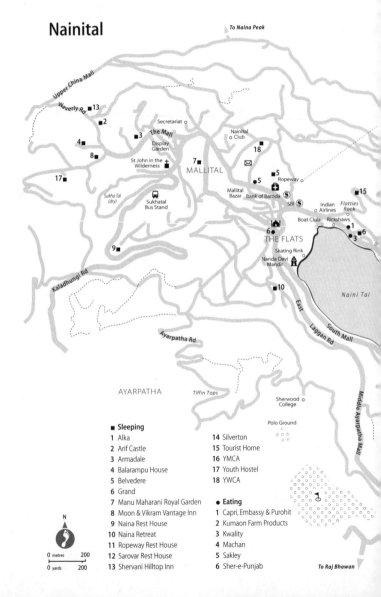

Sleeping
1 Alka
2 Arif Castle
3 Armadale
4 Balarampu House
5 Belvedere
6 Grand
7 Manu Maharani Royal Garden
8 Moon & Vikram Vantage Inn
9 Naina Rest House
10 Naina Retreat
11 Ropeway Rest House
12 Sarovar Rest House
13 Shervani Hilltop Inn
14 Silverton
15 Tourist Home
16 YMCA
17 Youth Hostel
18 YWCA

● Eating
1 Capri, Embassy & Purohit
2 Kumaon Farm Products
3 Kwality
4 Machan
5 Sakley
6 Sher-e-Punjab

KMVN **D-E** *Rest Houses* are good value outside May to mid-Jul: *Naina* near Sukhatal Bus Stand, T35400. 20 rooms with bath, some with TV, restaurant, gardens, good value. *Sarovar*, near Tallital Bus Stand, T35570. 8-bed dorms, hot water, good value. *Ropeway Rest House*, Snow View, T35772. Rooms with bath. **F** *Moon* is before the YH. Good value rooms, some with bath, veg restaurant, only drawback – 30 mins walk from lake. **F** *Youth Hostel*, west of Mallital Bazar, T35353. 2 rooms, 5 and 8-bed dorms, open to non-members (Rs 25), cheap meals, pleasant, quiet, book 15 days ahead. KMVN *Tourist Rest House*s nearby, offer **E/F** accommodation, including dorm: *Kumaon Dwar*, Kathgodam, T05946-22245. *Giri Sarovar*, Giri Lake, Kashipur, T05948-86392. *Sharda*, Tanakpur, T53108. All have restaurants or room service.

Eating

Most are at the N of the lake, on the Mall. Some have a limited off-season menu

Mid-range *Kwality*, on the lake. Western and good Indian. Ideally located. *Machan*, The Mall. Good Indian/Chinese. English spoken. Recommended. *New Capri* and *Embassy* are opposite Kwality on the lake. *Sakley*, The Mall, near GPO. Western dishes and confectionery. **Cheap** *Sher-e-Punjab*, Mallital Bazar. Tasty, North Indian. Another half way to Tallital, with one serving very good local Kumaon dishes. **Vegetarian** *Ahar Vihar* and *Purohit*, The Mall, opposite Kwality. Recommended for *thalis*. **Café** *Kumaon Farm Products*, towards Ropeway, is good for snacks; *Nanak* serves Western fast food.

Sports

Fishing: permits for Nainital Lake from Executive Officer, Nagar Palika. For other lakes Fisheries Officer, Bhimtal. Boat hire from Boat Club, Mallital. **Pony hire** (return): Snow View, Rs 40; Tiffin Top Rs 60; Naina (Chinna) Peak, Rs 80; Naina Devi, Rs 200 (2½-3 hrs; can leave at 0500 to see sunrise from the top, but dress warmly); horses are generally fit and well cared for. Horse Stand in Mallital, opposite *State Bank of India*. **Mountaineering & trekking**: equipment can be hired from *Nainital Mountaineering Club*, T2051, and *KMVN*, Tourist Office, Mallital. The Club organizes rock climbing at Barapathar, 3 km away.

Festivals

Kumaon festival of performing arts and crafts in Nov.

Shopping

Bazars sell local woollens and candles at Tallital and Mallital. Also souvenir shops on the Mall, Mallital, including *UP Handlooms*, *Gandhi Ashram*. Along the far edges of the Flats, Tibetan refugees sell wool and acrylic shawls; you can try

Garhwal & Kumaon Himalaya

■11

Snow View
(2,270m)

Upper Chinna Mall

Tibetan
Monastery

ookshop

14■

●4

SHER-KA-DANDA

The Mall

Library

●6

16

■1

St Francis

Pashan
Devi
Mandir

■12

Tallital
Bus Stand

Haldwani Rd

Bhowali Rd

Ramsay Rd

St Joseph's
College

To Hanumoungarh & Observatory

steaming *momos* at a stall! *Kumaon Woollens*, Mallital Bazar has locally made tweed – see also Almora, below. *Bookshop*, The Mall (below Grand Hotel). A good selection.

Tours *Parvat Tours*, T35656, charges about Rs 80 per day; Bhimtal, half day. Day tours: Sat tal; Ranikhet; Mukteshwar (with the Veterinary Research Centre); Kaladhungi. Two-day trips: Kausani; Ranikhet/Almora; Corbett.

Transport **Local Mall Road**: access Toll Rs 50. Access barred, May, Jun, Oct: heavy vehicles, 0800-1130, 1430-2230; light vehicles, 1800-2200; Nov-Apr: all vehicles, 1800-2000. **Cycle-rickshaw** and **dandi**: about Rs 5-10 along The Mall. **Taxi**: from *Parvat Tours*, Tallital, T35656. Full day Rs 650 (120 km). **Boat hire**: paddle or sail on the lake, Rs 80 per hr; up and down Rs 50; pedal boat Rs 40. **Ropeway**: cable-car/gondola, T35772, from 'Poplars', Mallital (near GB Pant Statue) to Snow View, summer 0800-1700, but usually opens at 1000, winter 1000-1600, return fare Rs 35, advance booking recommended. **NB** Some claim its anchorage is weak.

The hill roads can be dangerous. Flat, straight stretches are rare, road lighting does not exist & villagers frequently drive their animals along them or graze them at the kerbside. Wherever possible, avoid night driving

Long distance Air The nearest airport is Pantnagar (71 km) on the plains. *Parvat Tours* transfer coaches to Nainital (2 hrs). Open 1000-1600. **Train** The nearest railhead is **Kathgodam**, taxi, Rs 350 (peak season). **Delhi (OD)**: *Delhi Exp, 5203 and 5014*, 2245, 6 hrs. *Raxaul-Delhi Exp, 4015*, 0120, 3 hrs. **Kolkata (H) via Lucknow**, *Howrah Exp, 3020*, 1930, Reservations: UP Roadways, Tallital, T35518. For **Lucknow** (*Nainital Exp, 5307*, 2045, 9 hrs) the nearest station is at **Lalkuan**, south of Kathgodam, though some trains go on to Kathgodam. **Road** During the monsoon (Jun-Sep) landslips are fairly common. Usually these are cleared promptly but in the case of severe slips requiring days to clear, bus passengers are transferred. **Bus**: UP Roadways, Tallital, for major inter-city services, T35518, 0930-1200, 1230-1700; DTC, *Hotel Ashok*, Tallital, T35180. **Kumaon Motor Owners' Union** (KMOU), bus stand near Tourist Office, Sukhatal, Mallital, T35451; used by private operators. Regular services to **Almora** (66 km, 3 hrs); **Dehra Dun** (390 km), **Delhi** (322 km), a/c night coach, 2100 (Rs 250, 8-9 hrs), or via Haldwani. **Haridwar** (390 km, 8 hrs), **Kausani** (120 km, 5 hrs), **Ranikhet** (60 km, 3 hrs), and **Ramnagar** for Corbett (66 km, 3½ hrs plus 3½ hrs).

Directory **Banks** In Mallital: *Bank of Baroda*, below Belvedere Hotel. For cash against Visa card. *State Bank of India* for exchange. **Communications** Head Post Office: Mallital. Branch at Tallital. **Hospitals & medical services** *BD Pande Govt Hospital*, Mallital, T35022. **Library** The Library, The Mall, by the lake. Open weekdays (closed mid-morning to mid-afternoon). Pleasant for dropping in. **Tour companies & travel agents** KMVN's *Parvat Tours & Information*, Dandi House, Tallital, near Rickshaw Stand, T35656, among others on the Mall. *Vibgyor*, 56 Tallital Bazar, T/F35806. **Tourist offices** KMVN: *Information Centre*, at *Parvat Tours*; at Secretariat, Mallital, T/F36209. *UP*, Mall Rd, Mallital, T35337. *Tourist Bungalow*, T35400. **Useful addresses** Ambulance: T35022. Fire: T35626. Police: T35424.

Excursions around Nainital **Sat Tal** (21 km) has seven lakes including the jade green Garud Tal, the olive green Rama Tal and Sita Tal. **Sleeping C** *Sat Tal Camp* (KMVN), pyramid tents, kayaking, mountain biking, rock climbing, T/F011-626292, **E** *Damayanti* (KMVN), Sita Tal, T47047, four rooms.

Bhim Tal (23 km) is a large lake in an amphitheatre of hills with a wooded island which is a popular picnic spot. Restaurant, boating and fishing. **D** *Pandava* (KMVN), T47005.

Naukuchiyatal (26 km) is a lake with nine corners, hence the name. It is beautifully unspoilt, and quiet paddling round the lake allows you to see lots of birds; boats for hire. Tour buses stop around 1630. **Sleeping B** *Lake Side* (KMVN), T47138, well maintained and attractive.

Kilbury in oak, pine and rhododendron forest has the **C** *Mountain Quail Camp*, with pyramid tents, T47061.

Pangot, 15 km from Nainital via Kilbury, is in ideal birding territory where over 580 species have been recorded. The **B-C** *Jungle Lore Lodge* has a cottage and hut, with bath and two tents with shared facilities, meals included (home grown produce), library. Contact *Asian Adventures*, T0120-4524874, F011-9394878, www.pangot.com

Jeolikote, a small hamlet on the main road up from Ranpur, 18 km south of Nainital, offers a peaceful weekend retreat. Mrs Bhuvan Kumari's Swiss chalet-style **B** *Cottage*, nestled on the hillside, T44413 (or Vijay Baig, Delhi T6967618), has three beautiful spacious rooms with good valley views, meals included. Highly recommended.

To Almora

From Nainital it is an attractive 66 km drive to Almora passing through Bhowali. As the road winds through forests it has good views down towards Kathgodam and the plains. Bhowali, surrounded by attractive oak and mixed forest, provides a quieter alternative to Nainital. Known in the past for its sanatorium and apple orchards, it is a large centre for fruit cultivation having a bazar with apples, pears, pomelos and apricots available cheaply from August onwards. **Sleeping E** *Pathik* (KMVN), T8362, eight rooms, clean, friendly staff. **Eating** Restaurants and cafés are clustered around the bus stand in the town centre.

Bhowali
12 km E of Nainital
Phone code: 05942

In Ramgarh, within a productive orchard, stands two old bungalows which have been converted to take guests. **Sleeping B** *Ramgarh Bungalows* (Neemrana Hotels), T81156 (sales@neemrana.com). Simply fitted out rooms in *Writers'* and *Old* bungalows, built about 150 years ago, very willing but poorly trained staff, menu inadequate.

Ramgarh
12 km N of Bhowali
Phone code: 05942

The direct road from Haldwani to Bhowali bypasses Nainital, convenient for travellers bound for Almora. Below Bhowali in the valley of the Kosi River is **Garampani**, a popular refreshment stop. The road then runs along the Kosi passing refreshing rock pools, riverside terraced fields and small meadows, before beginning the long gradual climb to Almora. About 5 km before you reach the town proper there is a toll barrier and just beyond is the Almora bypass forking off to the left. Take this to avoid the town's congested main street.

Route

Almora अलमोड़ा

Like many hill towns, Almora occupies a picturesque horseshoe-shaped ridge. The Mall runs about 100 m below the ridge line, while the pedestrianized bazar below is jostling and colourful. Almora is an important market town and administrative centre with an agricultural research station and is also regarded as the cultural capital of the area.

Phone code: 05962
Colour map 2, grid B3
Population: 27,000
Altitude: 1,646 m

Getting there Buses from neighbouring hill towns use the bus stands on the Mall. There are also daily buses to Kathgodam the rail head, and also to Nepal. **Getting around** The Mall and the bazar are within walking distance of several hotels. Almora also has a few viewpoints which call for a pleasant stroll. For others further afield, you can get a taxi near the Mall bus stand.

Ins & outs

Almora was founded in 1560 by the Chand Dynasty who ruled over most of Kumaon, which comprises the present districts of Nainital, Almora and Pithoragarh. Overrun by the Gurkhas in 1798, it was heavily bombed by the

The city

British as they tried to expel them in the Gurkha Wars of 1814-15. Traces of an old Chand fort, stone-paved roads, wooded houses with beautifully carved façades and homes decorated with traditional murals, reflect its heritage.

Sights Swami Vivekenanda came to Almora and gained enlightenment in a small cave at **Kasar Devi** on Kalimatiya Hill, 7 km northeast of town. This makes a pleasant walk and there are good views from the hill. Another vantage point for sunrise and sunset is Bright End Corner, 2½ km southwest of the Mall. The stone **Udyotchandesvar Temple**, above the Mall, houses Kumaon's presiding deity, Nanda Devi, whose festival is in August/September.

Almora's *Tamta* artisans still use traditional methods to work with copper. Copper metallurgy was known to the people here as early as the second century BC and is associated with the Kuninda Dynasty who traded in copper articles. The handbeaten copper pots are 'silver plated' in the traditional way (*kalhai*). **Government Museum** Contains archaeological pieces from 11th century Katyuri and the Chand era. ■ *1030-1630, closed Mon. Near Bus Stand.*

Excursions **Katarmal**, 17 km from Almora, Katarmal has a Katyuri sun temple dating

Nainital - Almora area

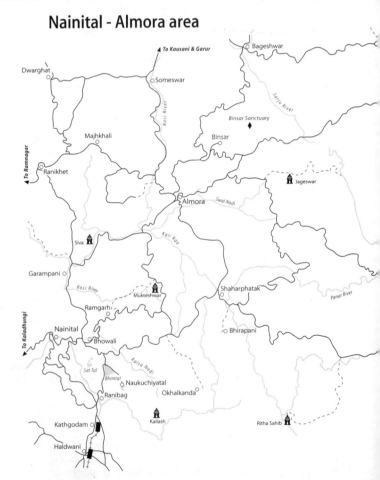

from the 12th century, with sculpture typical of its period.

Jageswar, 34 km, in a serene wooded gorge famous for the 164 ornamented temples built by the Chand rajas, has one of the 12 *jyotirlingas*. The temples here and in nearby Gandeswar are very fine examples of early medieval hill temple architecture but are rarely visited by outsiders. The one dedicated to Jogeswar with finely carved pillars has a small museum; 6 km before Jageswar, a roadside sign points to stoneage cave paintings (about 50 m off the road). These are in red, white and black, depicting human figures, trees, animals and possibly water courses. Though several paintings were damaged by storage of cement bags during bridge building work nearby, many can be seen and are worth the short stop. **Sleeping E** *Jagnath* (KMVN) at Jageswar, has rooms and a restaurant.

Binsar (28 km) Once the capital of the Chand rajas, Binsar has a bird sanctuary sited at 2,410 m; it has superb views of valleys around and panoramic views from Nanda Devi to Api and Saipal in Nepal. **Sleeping B-C** *Binsar Valley Resort*, just outside the sanctuary, nine rooms in cottages, pleasant, clean, in spacious grounds, good food, bakery, dairy, exceptional service, good riding, river fishing, ideal trekking country, family run, contact T011-6152294, manipur@nda.vsnl.net.in; **E** *Nanda Devi* (KMVN) in the heart of the sanctuary, T8219, only filtered rainwater, electricity from solar recharged batteries for few hours each evening. On a thickly wooded spur nearby is a 1920s *Forest Rest House* with 1930s cutlery and table linen lists still hanging on the walls! The furniture and décor are evocative of the Raj, and the caretaker may occasionally be persuaded to open the house for a few hours or for viewing. On a clear day the views are superb.

Sleeping
Some give off-season discounts

C-D *Shikhar*, The Mall, near bus stand, T30253. 40 rooms (vary widely), some with bath, hot water, good restaurant, fairly clean. Recommended. **D** *Savoy*, above the GPO, T30329. Good sized rooms, good restaurant (reserve ahead), quiet garden. **D** *Snow View*. 15 rooms, some in cottages. **E** *Holiday Home, Golu Deva* (KMVN), 2 km southwest of bus stand, near Kumaon Woollens, T22250. 7 basic cottages and 18 rooms with bath, dorm (Rs 50), restaurant, garden, good mountain views. **F** *Forest Rest House*, T30065. **F** *Kailash*, up path opposite GPO, The Mall, T30624. "Weird and wonderful décor" of Mr Shah, *thalis* (disappointing and overpriced) and herbal teas, relaxed atmosphere, friendly family. Recommended.

Eating

Plenty of choice along the busy Mall: **Mid-range** *Glory*. Good North Indian, but a bit pricey. **Cheap** *Madras Café*, beyond the bus stand. Good Indian meals and snacks.

Garhwal & Kumaon Himalaya

Festivals *Dasara* is celebrated with colourful Ramlila pageants. *Kumaon Festival of arts*.

Shopping *Ashok Traders*, LR Shah Rd, sells local copper articles. *Kumaon Woollens*, just above the KMVN *Golu Deva* Holiday Home. Produces and sells 'Harris' type tweed. Locally knitted jumpers and the traditional Panchmarhi shawls ('five weave') in soft wool are popular.

Transport **Road Buses** connect Almora with **Kathgodam** (90 km, 3 hrs) for **rail** links, and with Nainital (3 hrs) and Ranikhet (2½ hrs). Hourly buses to **Kausani** (3 hrs). Direct buses go to **Banbassa** and the Nepal border, dep 0730 (6 hrs).

Tour operators *High Adventure*, Mall Rd opposite Post Office, T31445. Organizes treks, cave tours, bus/train tickets.

Directory **Banks** *State Bank of India*, The Mall. May change foreign currency. **Communications** GPO on The Mall; **Internet** *Joshi*, opposite, joshi@nde.vsnl.net.in, slow connection; RS 2.50 per min. **Medical services** *District Hospital*, Chowk Bazar, T30322. **Tourist offices** *KMVN*, at *Golu Deva* Holiday Home, and *UP*, opposite GPO, T30180. **Useful addresses Foreigners' Registration Office:** Police Station near Almora Inter-College, T30007.

Route Leaving Almora, the road descends to cross the Kosi River where there is a left turn for Ranikhet. The road to the north follows the river, crosses the broad fertile valley at **Someswar** with its fine Siva temple in the Katyur style, then climbs to Kausani.

Kausani
Phone code: 05964
Colour map 2, grid B3
Population: 22,000
Altitude: 1,650m

Kausani sits on a narrow ridge among pine forests with wonderfully wide views of the **Nanda Devi** group of mountains stretching over 300 km along the horizon. The view is particularly stunning at sunrise. You may trek from here to Bageswar, Gwaldam and the Pindari Glacier. **Mahatma Gandhi** spent 12 days here in 1929 during which time he wrote the preface to his commentary on the Gita-Anashakti Yoga. The guesthouse where he stayed is now the **Anashakti Ashram**. **Sleeping B** *Sarovar Hotel*. Sixty rooms. **B-D** *Krishna Mountview*, near Gandhi Ashram, T45008. thirty rooms, some with good views, fine location, credit cards accepted. **E** *Trishul* (KMVN), T45006, 2 km from town. six cottages and dorm, restaurant, compass on the lawn to spot the peaks. **F** *Anashakti Ashram*, own very basic room (Rs 50). Noisy but friendly, stunning views of Nanda Devi from terrace, library. **F** *Uttarkhand Tourist Lodge* (View Point), near bus stand, T263639. Excellent value. Highly recommended. The *Hill Queen* above it serves reasonably priced meals. ■ *Getting there: Buses may be difficult to get. Joshimath is a tough but spectacular 10-hr journey.*

Baijnath & Garur
Colour map 2, grid B3

From Kausani, the road descends to **Garur** and **Baijnath** (17 km). The small town of Baijnath on the banks of the Gomti River has distinctively carved 12th- and 13th- century Katyuri temples. They are now mostly ruined, but its houses have intricately carved wooden doors and windows – see also Kullu Valley (page 176). The main 10th century temple houses a beautiful image of **Parvati**. Siva and Parvati are believed to have married at the confluence of the Gomti and Garur Ganga. The Katyur Dynasty, which ruled the valley for 500 years, took their name from Siva and Parvati's mythical son, **Karttikeya**. **Sleeping** KMVN **E** *Tourist Bungalow*, and *Inspection House*. **Garur** has plenty of buses/taxis northwards.

Route Just north of Garur a road runs northwest to Gwaldam (see Roopkund trek above) and another east to Bageshwar.

Bageshwar, meaning Siva as 'Lord of Eloquent Speech', stands at the conflu- **Bageshwar**
ence of the Gomti and Sarayu rivers. It is Kumaon's most important pilgrimage centre and has several temples and two sacred pools. *Uttarayani Fair*
(January) draws crowds from local villages who bring their handicrafts to sell.
Sleeping E *Bagnath* (KMVN), T2234, 20 rooms, where you can hire trekking
equipment, restaurant.

From Bageshwar the tarmac road northeast runs 7 km along the forested ridge, **Routes**
to **Chaukori**. **Sleeping E** *Panch-chuli* (KMVN) with very good views of the
Nanda Devi range, the Panchuli group of peaks, Nanda Kot and several peaks
that lie in Nepal. **NB** There are no shops or cafés in Chaukori so you must rely
on the caretaker to cook simple meals. From Chaukori, retrace 3 km to rejoin
the main road. **Berinag**, a small market town on a ridge, is a few kilometres
further, but before the Berinag turning the main road turns left past Kande to
Thal and to the roadhead at Munsiari.

This is a quiet hill town overlooked by the majestic five peaks of **Panchuli** **Munsiari**
which, in legend, served as the five *chulis* (stoves) used to cook the last meal of *Altitude: 2,300m*
the five Pandava brothers before they ascended to heaven. Munsiari is a base
for treks into the Milam, Ralam and Namik glaciers, and towards Panchuli. It
is also the start of an easy trek (three to four days) via Namik to Dwali in the
Pindar Valley. **Sleeping C** *Wayfarers' Resort*, 1 km beyond town. Comfortable Swiss tents, toilets, electricity, phone, Rs 1,200 including meals, forest
walks, treks, trout fishing, jeeps, professionally run, March to June, September
to October, contact *Asian Adventures*, B-9, Sector-27, Noida, New Delhi,
T11-8524874, F9394878, info@indianwildlife.com **E** *Tourist Rest House*
(KMVN). Main road just before the town. Comfortable, welcome hot show-
ers, good value; also two other cheap lodges. **Mountaineering and trekking**:
Nanda Devi Mountaineering Institution, SBI Building. In the main bazar:
Panchuli Trekking and *Nanda Devi Trekking*, the former run by an elderly
Milam tribal villager who has vast and accurate knowledge of the area. ■
Getting there: buses from Almora, change at Thal; from Haldwani or Nainital,
take bus to Pithorgarh and change. Buses to Almora and Pithorgarh, 0500 and
another for Pithorgarh in the afternoon.

Pithorgarh sits in a small valley with some fine temples built by the Chands. It **Pithorgarh**
is overlooked by a hill fort, 7 km away, dating from times when the town was at
the crossroads of trade routes. The district, separated from Almora in 1962,
borders Nepal and Tibet and has a number of high peaks such as Nanda Devi
East (7,434 m) and West (7,816 m), and offers trekking to many glaciers
including **Milam**, **Namik**, **Ralam** and **Panchuli**. See page 122 (no permit
needed). There are good views from Chandak Hill (7 km; 1,890 m). It is also on
the pilgrim road to **Mount Kailash** and **Mansarovar Lake**. The Mount
Kailash trek (Indian nationals only) starts from Askot. *Saur Adventure Club* is
in Simalgher Bazar. The place is known for its fine gold and silver jewellery and
bowls carved out of salwood. **Sleeping C** *Rhythm Camp*, spacious tents with
baths, meals included, views of valleys and peaks, T/F011-626292. **D-E** *Ulka*
Devi (UP Tourism), T22434. Restaurant. Others near the bus station are very
basic. Tourist office, T22527.

Garhwal & Kumaon Himalaya

★ Corbett National Park

Colour map 2, grid B2
Phone code: 05945
Altitude: 400-1,200m

The journey from Delhi to one of the finest wildlife parks in India offers excellent views of the almost flat, fertile and densely populated Ganga-Yamuna doab, one of the most prosperous agricultural regions of North India. Corbett is India's first national park and one of its finest. It is notable not only for its rich and varied wildlife and birdlife but also for its scenic charm and magnificent sub-montane and riverain views.

Ins & outs
See transport, page 142, for details

Foreigners Rs 350 per day, Indians Rs 30. Car, jeep Rs 100; foreigners in cars must have a guide, Rs 200 per day. Camera fee Rs 50, video Rs 500. Prior reservation is highly desirable for day visits. The main gate at Dhangarhi is approximately 16 km north of Ramnagar on the Ranikhet road. There is no entry to the park from the Kalagarh side. From 1 Mar until the monsoon all roads around Dhikala, except the main approach road, are closed between 1100-1500 when visitors are not allowed to move about the forest. Only visitors who are staying overnight may enter Dhikala. 100 visitors per day may enter Bijrani and Dhela (permits from Ramnagar before 1100); you may be refused entry when the quota is filled. A reservation at the Bijrani or Dhela *Forest Rest Houses* does not entitle visitors to enter by the Dhangari gate.

Best season
Jan to mid-Jun; for birdwatching, Dec-Feb. Summer is the best time for seeing the larger mammals which are bolder in leaving the forest cover to come to the river and water holes; early summer for scenic charm and floral interest. Closed 15 Jun-15 Nov.

Set up in 1936, in large part due to the efforts of Jim Corbett, this wildlife reserve was named Hailey National Park after the Governor of United Provinces. On Independence it was renamed the Ramganga National Park and later still the Corbett National Park. The park comprises the broad valley of the **Ramganga River** backing onto the forest covered slopes of the Himalayan foothills which rise to 1,210 m at Kanda Peak. Longitudinal ridges separate ravines and uplands. A dam at Kalagarh has created a large reservoir at the western end of the park. The Ramganga itself runs through high and narrow banks in places. The only perennial source of water, and popular for mahseer fishing, it meanders to the northwest, creating a beautiful scene from Dhikala. Another attraction of this park is the extensive areas of grass land.

Flora
There is an immensely rich flora – 110 species of trees, 51 species of shrubs, three species of bamboos and 27 species of climbers. The valley floor is covered with tall elephant grass (*Nall* in the local terminology), lantana bushes and patches of *sal* and *sheesham* (*Dalbergia sissoo*) forest, whilst the enclosing hills on both sides are completely forest covered, with *sal*, *bakli* (*Anogeissus latifolia*), *khair* (*Acacia catechu*), *jhingan* (*Lannea coromandelica*), *tendu* (*Diospyros tomentosa*), *pula* (*Kydia calycina*) and *sain* (*Terminalia tomentosa*). *Charas* (cannabis) grows wild in the fields. Nullahs and ravines running deep into the forests are dry for much of the year, but there are swift torrents during the monsoon. These hold brakes of bamboo and thick scrub growth. Rainfall is heavier in the higher hills, on average the valley receives 1,550mm, the bulk from July to mid-September. Summer days are hot but the nights quite pleasant. Winter nights can get very cold and there is often a frost and freezing fog in the low lying tracts.

Wildlife
The park has always been noted for its **tigers**; there are around 50 but they are

Tiger, tiger, burning bright ...

Jim Corbett *was born in 1875 into the large family of the postmaster at Nainital. From childhood he was fascinated by the jungles around Nainital. This developed into a considerable knowledge of the ecosystem's workings. He became a superb shot, killing his first leopard when he was eight. Tigers were his most sought after prey, followed by leopards which were difficult to sight, let alone shoot.*

He continued to hunt during his working life in the Bengal Northeast Railway and later as an advisor to the army. But from the mid-1920s he turned to photography, tracking and killing only the man-eating leopards and tigers that terrorized the Kumaon hills from *time to time. Later in life he recounted his exploits in a series of books about man-eaters and the jungle:* The Man-Eating Leopard of Rudrapayag, The Man-eaters of Kumaon *and* Jungle Lore. *For a biography of Corbett see* Carpet Sahib: The life of Jim Corbett *by Martin Booth.*

Project Tiger *Jim Corbett has always been an inspiration to India's conservationists. On 1 April 1973 Project Tiger was inaugurated in nine parks, the aim being to preserve the rapidly dwindling population of tigers in India. The scheme was later extended to over 18 reserves.*

Garhwal & Kumaon Himalaya

not easily spotted. About 10% of visitors see one – usually entering at the Bijrani gate. There are leopards too but they are seldom seen. Sambar, chital, para (hog deer) and muntjac (barking deer) are the main prey of the big cats and their population fluctuates around 20,000. Some like the chital are highly gregarious whilst the large sambar, visually very impressive with its antlers, is usually solitary. The two commonly seen monkeys of North India are the rhesus (a macaque – reddish face and brownish body) and the common langur (black face and silvery coat). Elephants are now permanent inhabitants since the Ramganga Dam has flooded their old trekking routes. There are now a few hundred and they are seen quite often. Other animals include porcupine, wild pigs (often seen around Dhikala), - some can be quite dangerous and attack unsuspecting visitors who have food with them. In total there are over 50 species of mammal alone, though the dam appears to have caused significant losses. The last Swamp deer was seen in March 1978, and the loss of habitat has been keenly felt by the cheetal, hog deer and porcupine, all of which appear to be declining.

In certain stretches of the river and in the Ramganga Lake are the common mugger crocodile (*Crocodylus palustris*, notice prohibits swimming – "Survivors will be prosecuted"!), the fish eating gharial (*Gavialis gangeticus*), soft shelled tortoises in the streams, otters and river fish. The python is quite common.

The birdlife is especially impressive with over 600 species and this includes a wide range of water birds, birds of prey such as the crested serpent eagle, harriers, Pallas' fishing eagle, osprey, buzzards, vultures (the solitary King, Cinereous and Himalayan long-billed). Woodland birds include: Indian and Great Pied hornbills, parakeets, woodpeckers, drongos, pies, flycatchers, laughing thrushes, babblers and cuckoos. Doves, bee-eaters, rollers, bulbuls, warblers, finches, robins and chats are to be seen in the open scrub from the viewing towers.

Elephant rides are available from Dhikala where there are about nine, and three at Bijrani. Each elephant can cary 4 people. This is the best way to see the jungle and the wildlife. Morning and evening, two hours, Rs 120 per person (foreigners), Rs 20 (Indians); book at Dhikala Reception. **Cars and jeeps** may

Viewing
Night driving is not allowed in the park

drive round part of the park. Check with Reception. Jeep safari (for 6 persons), two hours, Rs 500; day hire Rs 800 from Ramnagar. Apart from the immediate area around Dhikala, **don't go walking in the park**. Tiger and elephant attacks are not unknown. The two watch towers are good vantage points for spotting wildlife.

Ramnagar
Colour map 2, grid B3

Ramnagar, 134 km from Moradabad, is 18 km from the Park boundary and 50 km from **Dhikala**. It is a noisy and hot town with the Project Tiger for Corbett reservations, and provides a night halt. They will receive faxes and hold them. If you are travelling to the park without reserved accommodation, you **must** call here first to make a booking. **Sleeping D-E** *KMVN Lodge* by Reception Centre south of bus station, T853225. Some a/c rooms with bath, dorm, good restaurant, warm rooms and hot showers in winter. **E** *Govind*, 100 m down the road. Helpful management, excellent restaurant with varied menu, pleasant atmosphere, adequate rooms.

Park information

Dhikala is the park centre and has accommodation. You can also use a good **library** on payment of a deposit. Wildlife films are also shown. There is a very good restaurant. The shop also sells food (cheaper). **NB** During the rainy season the park is closed; the 32 km road to Dhikala from the gate at Dhangarhi is almost impassable.

Corbett National Park

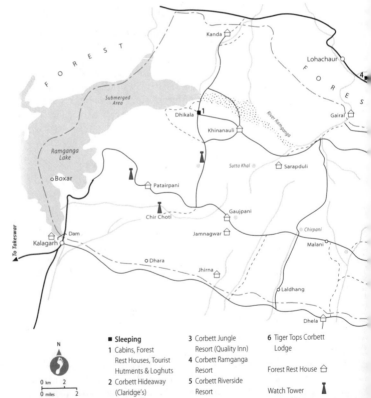

N

0 km 2
0 miles 2

■ **Sleeping**
1 Cabins, Forest Rest Houses, Tourist Hutments & Loghuts
2 Corbett Hideaway (Claridge's)
3 Corbett Jungle Resort (Quality Inn)
4 Corbett Ramganga Resort
5 Corbett Riverside Resort
6 Tiger Tops Corbett Lodge

Forest Rest House ⌂

Watch Tower ▮

GMVN run three-day tours from Delhi departing every Friday in season. Reservations: Uttar Pradesh Tourist Office, Chandralok Building, 36 Janpath, New Delhi, T3322251.

AL *Tiger Tops Corbett Lodge*, T05946-85279, F85280, 8 km north of Ramnagar. 24 rooms, pool, lawns, mango orchards, good food, "unreconstructed, old world feel", charming staff. **A** *Corbett Hideaway* (Claridges), Garija, above the river (10 mins drive from gate), T85959, F85636. Upmarket lodges in orchard on riverside, jeep transfer to park, adequate food, very good naturalist in Imran Khan, well run, friendly management, own elephant for viewing, new pool. **A** *Corbett Jungle Resort* (Quality Inn), Kumeria Reserve Forest, Mohan, T/F05946-85219, about 10 km from the Dhangarhi entrance, among mango and sal trees. 18 small cottages, imaginatively designed and built of natural materials, rooftop restaurant, 2-hr elephant rides (about Rs 250) are very pleasant but expensive, jeeps 5 hrs, Rs 500, jungle walks, swimming in the cool, clear Kosi River, eco-friendly resort. **A-B** *Corbett Riverside Resort*, Garjia, a few mins' drive from the park, T85961, F85960, by the Kosi River. Comfortable rooms and suites, some a/c, meals included, TV in lounge, pleasant garden, jeep and elephant safaris, mahseer fishing, swimming and some watersports. **B** *Corbett Ramganga Resort*, Jhamaria, 17 km from Dhangarhi, T011-4620981, F4640325, on the river. 10 well-appointed rooms in cottages, 8 Swiss cottage tents, electricity for limited hours, safe spring water, river rafting, riding, rockclimbing and gliding, fishing (fighting fish in the river pools below), excellent pool and ground, friendly service, very picturesque position on the river edge – "wonderful for a winter stay". **B-C** *Sterling Resorts*, northwest of Ramnagar, T011-6446531. **B-C** *Tiger Camp*, Dhikala. 5 clean cottages in Kumaoni Village style but modern interiors, rooms with fan and bath (Rs 2,500), tents (shared bath), electricity (plus generator), good food, lovely garden, jeep, hiking, friendly owner, recommended, contact *Asian Adventures*, New Delhi, T011-91524878, F91524878, tigercamp@ indianwildlife.com

Sleeping & eating
In top resorts, meals & guided visits to park are included in price. See Ramnagar, page 140

■ *on map*
Price codes: see inside front cover

Within the park Best to use an agent to reserve. Foreigners pay more than Indians. Get a pass (Rs 300) at the gate on entry and collect Clearance Card from camp reception before leaving.

Dhikala It is often difficult to get rooms even when they are empty. Huts can be dirty and have no net, suites are about Rs 900, log cabins Rs 150 per bed, and huts Rs 500 for 3 beds and bath. *Annexe*, 7 suites and *Cabin 3* with 2 suites, reservations, UP Tourist Office, New Delhi, T3322251. **D** *New Forest Resthouse*, 4 suites; **D** *Old Rest House*, 5 suites, reservations, Chief Conservator of Forests, 17 Rana Pratap Marg, Lucknow, T0522-226140. *Cabin 1 and 4*, 3 suites

Ramnagar detail

▲ To Corbett

■ KMVN Lodge
○ Reception Centre

Govind ⓢ

STD/Fax ⓢ

To Ranikhet ▶

KUMERIA

■3

Mohan

Main
Park
☐ Sultan Entrance
Café ○ Dhangarhi

Garjia ○
■5

2■

River Kosi

Bijrani
■6

Amdanda
Gate

Ramnagar ○
see
detail

▼ To Moradabad   To Haldwani

Garhwal & Kumaon Himalaya

each; **E** *Tourist Hutment*, 5 suites; **F** *Green Hut*, 1 4-bedsuite and **F** *Loghuts*, 24 bunks, reservations, Field Director, Project Tiger, Ramnagar, T05946-853189. There is an extra charge for blankets. The restaurant is good with wonderful views, is reasonably priced but has limited choice.

Khinanauli D *Forest Rest House*, 3 suites, reservations, Chief Conservator, Lucknow, T0522-226140.

Bijrani, Sarapduli, Sultan, Gairal   There are good **F** *Forest Rest Houses* but some have no catering. Bring sleeping bag and food. All accessible by afternoon bus except Gairal. **Bijrani** involves a 6 km walk but the double rooms have bath and the staff are very friendly and helpful, catering available, free blankets, though you pay for electricity, so bring candles if you want to economize. **Sarapduli** Bring your own provisions, stove, water, generator (if you want light) – but well worth it for the offers, kingfishers and a resident crocodile in the river! Reserve early with Chief Wildlife Warden, 17 Rana Pratap Marg, Lucknow, T0522-226140. Enquiries: Field Director, Project Tiger, Ramnagar, T05946-853189, or UP Tourism, New Delhi. Contact an agent.

Transport   **Air** **Phoolbagh airport** at Pantnagar (130 km) has services to Delhi but transport to Corbett is difficult and lengthy. **Avoid this route. Road** The Delhi-Dhikala road (260 km) passes through Moradabad (turn left after Moradabad, towards Kashipur and Ramnagar), 5½-6 hrs – strewn with bus/lorry/car crashes. **Bus**: to **Ramnagar**, 1000 from Dhikala; several from Kumeria, Rs 12; also one afternoon bus to Moradabad and Ranikhet by metalled road. Also buses to Delhi (6½-7 hrs), and Lucknow. Contact KMOU or UP Roadways Bus Stands at Ramnagar. **Jeep**: from near Ramnagar Park office; to Dhikala (return), Rs 500-600. **Train** Nearest station is at Ramnagar (50 km), for connections with Moradabad and Lucknow and Delhi. Train from Old Delhi rly station, 0850, arrives Ramnagar 1530 (travel agents can get tickets); then taxi to Kumeria, Rs 300.

Directory   **Tour operator** Mohit Agarwal, T11-91524874, F91524878, wildindiatours@vsnl.com   Arranges jeep transfer, accommodation etc. Forest officer, Ramnagar, T 244715.

Corbett to Nainital and Ranikhet

It is possible to reach **Nainital** from Corbett via **Ramnagar** and Kaladhungi on a picturesque road. The road crosses the river which has a barrage and skirts along the edge of the hills. At **Kaladhungi** visit **Jim Corbett's house**, now a small museum. The area is an extension of the Tiger Reserve with equally good wildlife but minus the restrictions, and is also excellent for bird watching. **Sleeping B** *Camp Corbett*, 25 km east of Corbett, T42277, F35493. Cottages and tents, wonderful meals, an outstanding resort run by the hospitable Anand family, relaxing and totally hassle free, pick-up from Haldwani station arranged. Highly recommended. Turn up the road opposite and continue up into the hills, travelling along a delightful and well engineered metalled road that winds its way up the hillsides through *chir* pine (*Pinus longifolia*) forest and the occasional village. There are impressive views of the plains. You enter Nainital at the north (Mallital) end of the lake.

For **Ranikhet**, go from Dhikala to Dhangarhi and turn left. Buses will pick up passengers for Ranikhet and intermediate points without you having to return to Ramnagar. This drive is very attractive as the road gradually climbs up to the first ridges of the Himalaya. The forest jungle looks drier and more open here than nearer Nainital but is just as impressive.

Ranikhet

No one knows the name of the queen whose field gave Ranikhet (The Queen's Field) its title. In 1869 the land was bought from local villagers and the British established a summer rest and recreation settlement for their troops, made it a cantonment town governed by the military authorities and developed it as a quiet hill station. Set along a 1,800 m high ridge, Ranikhet sprawls out through the surrounding forest without having a proper centre. This is one of its attractions and there are many enjoyable walks.

At one time, Lord Mayo, Viceroy of India, was so enchanted with the place that he wanted to move the army's Summer Headquarters away from Shimla. That did not happen but Ranikhet became, and still is, the Regimental Centre for the Kumaon Regiment. The views from the ridge are magnificent and the twin peaks of Nanda Devi (7,816 m and 7,434 m) can be clearly seen. At **Upat** (6 km) there is a beautifully located nine-hole golf course, and **Chaubatia** (10 km) has a Govt Fruit Garden and Research Station. **Dwarahat** (18 km) has 55 architecturally interesting temples.

Phone code: 05966
Colour map 2, grid B3
Altitude: 1,800m

Sleeping & eating

B *Chevron Rosemount* (Heritage), The Mall (2 km centre), T3191. Refurbished old colonial building, stylish, croquet lawn, tennis. **C-D** *West View*, MG Rd (5 km centre), T61196. 19 rooms in old fashioned hotel, restaurant, exchange, large grounds, golf club nearby. **D-E** *Kalika* (KMVN), T2297. Pleasant rooms with bath, some 'super deluxe', restaurant (mostly Indian), attractive location in the upper cantonment with good views. **D-E** *Himadri* (KMVN), Chilia naula, 7 km west, T2588. New unit next to the temple complex, rooms, dorm (Rs 50), restaurant. **E** *Norton*, The Mall, T2377. Shabby rooms but welcoming.

Transport

Road Bus: regular buses to Ramnagar, Almora and Nainital operated by KMOU, T2214, and UP Roadways, T2516, with bus stands at each end of the Mall.

Directory

Banks On The Mall, have exchange facilities. **Communications** General Post Office: on The Mall. **Hospital & medical services** *Civil Hospital*, near Bus Stand, T2422. **Tourist office** *UP*, The Mall, T2227.

Garhwal & Kumaon Himalaya

Himachal Pradesh

4

Himachal Pradesh

148	Background
150	**Shimla and Southern Himachal**
157	Around Shimla
159	Shimla to Kinnaur and Spiti
159	Old Hindustan Tibet Road
162	Sarahan
159	**Kinnaur and Spiti**
163	Kinnaur
218	Spiti
176	**Kullu Valley**
176	Kullu
179	Parvati Valley
182	Manali
191	**Lahul**
191	Manali to Leh
193	Pattan Valley
194	Keylong
198	**Dharamshala and Northern Himachal**
198	Dharamshala
	Around Dharamshala
206	Kangra Valley
209	Chamba Valley
209	Dalhousie
211	Chamba
213	**Trekking in Himachal Pradesh**
213	Trekking from Shimla
213	Trekking from Chamba
215	Trekking in Lahul, Kinnaur and Spiti
218	Trekking in the Kullu and Parvati Valley
219	Trekking in Kangra

Himachal Pradesh (Himalayan Province) is dominated by successive ridges of snow covered peaks, the outer ranges of the Himalaya themselves. Known across India for its pleasant early summer climate, its deliciously cool mountain streams and its seemingly endless supplies of temperate fruit, Himachal also has excellent trekking. Shimla, famous as a British Hill Station, Dharamshala, the Indian home of the Dalai Lama, and Kullu and Manali have been favourite destinations for over a decade. Today however it is possible to visit the far more remote and until recently closed regions. Himachal has become the main access route to Ladakh. The road to Leh crosses the Rohtang Pass just north of Manali and has opened up the side routes for trekking. Sarahan's Bhimakali temple, the moraine-filled Baspa Valley, and Spiti's spectacular Tabo monastery more than justify the journey along the dangerously precipitous and landslide-ridden Hindustan-Tibet Road. The beautiful landscape is also the setting for a rich interweaving of Hindu and Buddhist traditions, while in the foothills of Kangra the Mughal miniature artistic heritage was subtly modified to develop a distinctive regional art form.

Background

The land Himachal is wholly mountainous, with peaks rising to over 6,700 m. The
Population: 5,100,000 **Dhaula Dhar** range runs from the northwest to the Kullu Valley. The **Pir**
Area: 55,673 sq km **Panjal** is farther north and parallel to it. High, remote, arid and starkly beautiful, Lahul and Spiti are sparsely populated. They contrast strongly with the well
wooded lushness of those areas to the south of the Himalayan axis.

Climate At lower altitudes the summers can be very hot and humid whereas
the higher mountains are permanently under snow. In Shimla, the Kangra
Valley, Chamba and the Kullu Valley, the monsoon arrives in mid-June and
lasts until mid-September, giving periods of very heavy rain; in the Kullu Valley there can be sudden downpours in March and early April. As in many hill
stations there are often sharp contrasts between sun and shade temperatures,
particularly noticeable in spring and autumn when the average temperatures
are lower, but the sun can be very warm. To the north Lahul and Spiti are
beyond the influence of the monsoon. Consequently they share the high altitude desert climatic characteristics of Ladakh.

History Originally the region was inhabited by a tribe called the Dasas who were later
assimilated by the Aryans. From the 10th-century parts were occupied by the
Muslims. Kangra, for example, submitted to Mahmud of Ghazni and later
became a Mughal Province. The Gurkhas of Nepal invaded Himachal in the
early 19th century and incorporated it into their kingdom as did the Sikhs
some years later. The British finally took over the princely states in the middle
of the 19th century.

Culture **Religion** Although the statistics suggest that Himachal is one of the most
Hindu states in India its culture reflects the strong influence of Buddhism,
notably in the border regions with Tibet and in the hill stations where many
Tibetan refugees have made their homes. In the villages many of the festivals
are shared by Hindus and Buddhists alike. There are also small minorities of
Sikhs, Muslims and Christians.

People Hill tribes such as the Gaddis, Gujars, Kinnaurs, Lahaulis and
Pangwalas have all been assimilated into the dominant Hindu culture though
the caste system is simpler and less rigid than elsewhere. The tribal peoples in
Lahul and Spiti (locally known as Pitians), follow a form of Buddhism while
Kinnauris mix Buddhism with Hinduism in their rituals. Their folklore has the
common theme of heroism and legends of love and Natti, the attractive folk
dance of the high hills, is widely performed.

Language The dominant local language is Pahari, a Hindi dialect derived
from Sanskrit and Prakrit but largely unintelligible to plains dwellers. Hindi is
the medium for instruction in schools and is widely spoken.

Handicrafts Handicrafts include wood carving, spinning wool, leather tan-
ning, pottery and bamboo crafts. Wool products (blankets and clothing), are
the most abundant and it is a common sight in the hills to see men spinning
wool by hand as they watch over their flocks or as they are walking along. Good
quality shawls made from the fine hair from pashmina goats, particularly in
Kullu, are highly sought after. Fleecy soft blankets called *gudmas*, heavier
namdas (rugs) and rich pile carpets in Tibetan designs are also produced.

Chappals (leather sandals) are made in Chamba, and Chamba *rumals* ('hand-kerchiefs'), small finely embroidered cloth squares imitating the famous minia-ture paintings of the region. Now, Buddhist *thangkas*, silverware and chunky tribal silver jewellery are popular with tourists and are sold in bazars.

Himachal Pradesh was granted full statehood in 1970. There are 68 seats in the State Assembly, but as one of India's smallest states Himachal Pradesh elects four members of the Lok Sabha and three representatives to the Rajya Sabha. Since 1966 Shimla has been the state capital. Dharamshala has been the home of the Dalai Lama since 1959, following the Chinese takeover of Tibet.

Modern Himachal Pradesh

Current political developments Even though Himachal; is quite close to Delhi it still has the feel of a political backwater. News from the state rarely makes the national newspapers, and while the contest for representation in the Lok Sabha and in the Assembly is intense, the two-horse race between Con-gress and the BJP rarely attracts much attention. The Congress Party took power in the last State Assembly elections under the leadership of Virbhadra Singh, serving his third term as Chief Minister, but in the 1998 Lok Sabha Elec-tions the Congress and the BJP shared four Lok Sabha seats between them.

Migration to the plains With little employment outside agriculture many men migrate, especially to Delhi. Boys get priority for secondary education which enables them to get better jobs outside the village, for example in the army and government service. Many villages are remittance economies sup-ported by subsistence agriculture.

Tourism Trekking, rock climbing and mountaineering are being strongly pro-moted. Tourists are also being attracted to exciting river rafting, though skiing near Manali and Narkanda does not compare with Western resorts. The only rail-ways, the picturesque narrow gauge lines from Kalka in Punjab to the state capital of Shimla, and from Pathankot to Jogindernagar, are both delightful, if slow.

Himachal Pradesh

★ Shimla शिमला and Southern Himachal

Phone code: 0177
Colour map 2, grid A1
Population: 110,000
approx
Altitude: 2,213 m

Himachal Pradesh

Once a charming hill station and the summer capital of the British, an air of decay hangs over many of Shimla's Raj buildings, strung out along the ridgeline. Below them a maze of narrow streets, bazars and shabby 'local' houses with corrugated iron roofs cling to the hillside. Some visitors find it delightfully quaint and less spoilt than other Uttar Pradesh hill stations. There are still some lovely walks, lined with magnificent pines and cedars giving a beautifully fresh scent to the air.

Ins & outs

Getting there Despite the romance of the narrow gauge railway from Kalka most people get to Shimla by bus or taxi as it is so much quicker. The bus stand and the station are on Cart Road, all arrivals are greeted by hordes of porters jostling to take your luggage up the steep hill to a hotel. If you are staying on the western side of town it is worth getting off the bus at the railway station for a much easier walk. Buses from the east, including Rampur and Kinnaur, stop at the Rivoli bus stand. Jabbarhatti airport has a coach (Rs 50) in season, and taxis (Rs 350) for transfer. **Getting around** The Mall can only be seen on foot, it takes about half an hour to walk from the Viceroy's Lodge to Christ Church. The main traffic artery is Cart Road which continues past the station to the Main Bus Stand, taxi rank and the two-stage lift which goes to the Mall above (Rs 5). The Victory Tunnel cuts through from the Cart Road to the north side of the hill. As in colonial times, vehicles are generally not allowed on the Mall and The Ridge. **Climate** Oct and Nov are very pleasant, with warm days and cool nights. Dec-Feb is cold and there are snowfalls. Mar and Apr are refreshing months but changeable, storms are not infrequent and the air can feel very chilly. Avoid May-Jun, the height of the Indian tourist season prior to the monsoon, prices are high and accommodation hard to find.

History

For the British, the only way of beating the hot weather on the plains in May and June was to move to hill stations which they endowed with the mock Tudor houses, churches, clubs, parks with bandstands of English county towns, and a main street invariably called the Mall.

Sights

Shimla is strung out on a long crescent-shaped ridge which connects a number of hilltops from which there are good views of the snow-capped peaks to the north: Jakhu (2,453 m), Prospect Hill (2,176 m), Observatory Hill (2,148 m), Elysium Hill (2,255 m) and Summer Hill (2,103 m).

Christ Church (1844), on the open area of The Ridge, dominates the eastern end of town. Consecrated in 1857 a clock and porch were added later. The original chancel window designed by Lockwood Kipling, Rudyards father, is no longer there. The mock tudor **library** building (circa 1910) is next door.

The Mall joins The Ridge at Kipling's **Scandal Point**, where today groups

Himachal Pradesh

The seasonal move of government

So beneficial were the effects of the cooler mountain air that Shimla, 'discovered' by the British in 1819, became the summer seat of government from 1865 to 1939. The capital was shifted there from Calcutta and later from Delhi (1912 onwards) and all business was transacted from this cool mountain retreat.

Huge baggage trains were needed to transport the mountains of files and the whole operation cost thousands of rupees. At the end of the season back they would all leave.

Women heavily outnumbered men, as wives of many British men who ran the empire escaped to the hills for long periods. Army officers spent their leave there. Social life in hill stations became a round of parties, balls, formal promenades along the Mall and brief flirtations.

gather to exchange gossip. Originally the name referred to the stir caused by the supposed 'elopement' of a lady from the Viceregal Lodge and a dashing Patiala prince after they arranged a rendezvous here.

The **Gaiety Theatre** (1887) and the **Town Hall** (circa 1910) are reminiscent of the 'Arts and Crafts' style, as well as the timbered **General Post Office** (1886). Beyond, to the west, is the *Grand Hotel*. Further down you pass the sinister looking **Gorton Castle**, designed by **Sir Samuel Swinton Jacob**, which was once the Civil Secretariat. A road to the left leads to the railway station, while one to the right goes to Annandale, the racecourse and cricket ground.

The Mall leads to the rebuilt *Cecil Hotel* (1877). On Observatory Hill (the watershed), the **Viceregal Lodge** (1888) was built for Lord Dufferin in the Elizabethan style but with an indoor tennis court. Now the **Rashtrapati Niwas**, it houses the **Indian Institute of Advanced Study** (IIAS) and stands in large grounds with good views of the mountains. Reminders of its British origins include a gatehouse, a chapel and the meticulously polished brass fire hydrants imported from Manchester. Inside, you may only visit the main reception rooms and the library which are lined from floor to ceiling with impressive teak panelling. It is a long uphill walk from the gate. ■ *1000-1630. A small entry fee to the house includes a very brief guided tour.*

Further reading Paul Scott's Booker Prize winning novel *Staying On* was set in post Independence Shimla. JG Farrell's last unfinished novel *The Hill Station* describes colonial Shimla of 1871, as does Pamela Kanwar's *Imperial Simla: the political culture of the Raj.* OUP, New Delhi, 1990.

There are several pleasant walks in and around Shimla. **Jakhu Temple** on a hill with excellent views (2,455 m), dedicated to Hanuman the monkey god, is 2 km from Christ Church. Walking sticks (handy for warding off monkeys) are available at *chai* shops at the start of the ascent.

The **Glen** (1,830 m), to the northwest, is a 4 km walk from the centre past the *Cecil Hotel*. **Summer Hill** (1,983 m), a pleasant 'suburb' 5 km from town, is a stop on the Shimla-Kalka railway. **Chadwick Falls** (1,586 m), 3 km further, drops 67 m during the monsoons.

Prospect Hill (2,175 m), is 5 km from The Ridge, and a 20 minutes' walk from Boileauganj to the west.

Walks
The monkeys here can be vicious – keep your distance & all food out of sight & reach

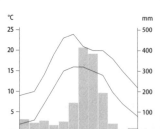

°C   mm

25   500

20   400

15   300

10   200

5   100

0   0
J F M A M J J A S O N D

Climate: Shimla
Best time to visit:
Apr-Jun & Oct-Nov

Tara Devi (1,851 m), with a hilltop temple, 11 km southwest from the railway station, can also be reached by car or train.

Museums **The State Museum**, near Chaura Maidan. A 30-minute walk west from the GPO along the Mall; then a short climb from the *Harsha Hotel*. Small, with a good sculpture collection and miniatures from the Kangra School; also costumes, jewellery and textiles. ■ *1000-1330, 1400-1700, closed Mon.*

Tours Himachal Tourism's various tours during the season are well run, usually 1000-1700 (Rs 110). Some start from Rivoli, pick-up at Lift, visiting Kufri, Chini Bungalow, Fagu, Mashobra, Naldera, Theog, Matiana, Narkanda, Tattapani. Others start from Rivoli, pick-up at Victory Tunnel: Chail, Kufri, Indira Holiday Home, Kiarighat Bungalow. Tour companies charge Rs 600-700 per car for five, Rs 65, luxury coach. For longer tours (Rs 2-8,000) contact Ritz Annexe.

Essentials

Sleeping Prices soar in May and Jun when modest accommodation can be difficult to find espe-
■ *on maps, pages* cially if you arrive after midday, so book ahead. Some close off-season. Some do not
152 & 154 accept credit cards. Most hotels down to **C** category have a car park. **NB** From the rail-
Price codes: way or bus station it is a stiff climb up to hotels on or near the Ridge. Porters available,
see inside front cover but fix a price in advance (about Rs 20 per heavy bag from the bus stand to YWCA, the highest accommodation in town). Also, ask for porter's metal token (to ensure safe

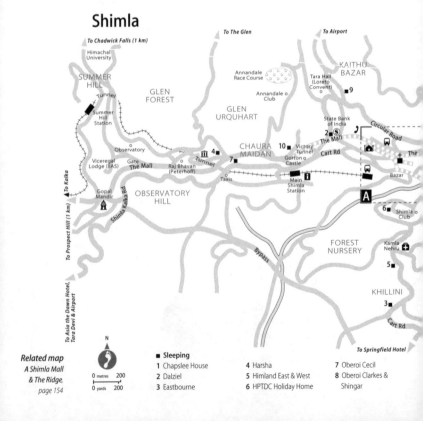

Shimla

To Chadwick Falls (1 km) *To The Glen* *To Airport*

Himachal University

SUMMER HILL

KAITHU BAZAR

Annandale Race Course

Tara Hall (Loreto Convent)

■ 9

GLEN FOREST

Annandale ○ Club

Summer Hill Station

GLEN URQUHART

State Bank of India

2 ■ ⑤

Circular Road

Observatory

CHAURA MAIDAN

10 ■ Victory Tunnel

The Mall

Vicereal Lodge (IIAS)

Gate The Mall

🏛 4 ■

Tunnel

7 ■

Gorton ○ Castle

Cart Rd

The

Raj Bhavan (Peterhoff)

Taxis

Main Shimla Station

Bazar

Gopal Mandir

OBSERVATORY HILL

A

6 ■ Shimla ○ Club

FOREST NURSERY

Kamla Nehru

5 ■

KHILLINI

3 ■

Cart Rd

To Asia the Dawn Hotel, Tara Devi & Airport

To Prospect Hill (1 km)

To Kalka

To Springfield Hotel

Related map
A Shimla Mall & The Ridge,
page 154

N

0 metres 200
0 yards 200

■ **Sleeping**
1 Chapslee House
2 Dalziel
3 Eastbourne

4 Harsha
5 Himland East & West
6 HPTDC Holiday Home

7 Oberoi Cecil
8 Oberoi Clarkes & Shingar

delivery) and return it on reaching your destination! Porters often get a large commission to take you to selected hotels and will insist that all others are full or closed.

AL *Oberoi Cecil*, Chaura Maidan (quiet east end of the Mall), T204848, F211024, cecil@nde.vsnl.net.in 79 rooms, colonial grandeur on the edge of town, with superb views, beautifully renovated, stylishly furnished, special ultramodern pool. **A** *Chapslee House* (Heritage), Lakkar Bazar, T/F258633, chapslee@nde.vsnl.net.in 6 suites only, charming, full of character, large grounds, exquisite interior, good views, excellent meals and excellent service, if you can get in. **A** *Oberoi Clarkes*, The Mall, near Lift, T251010, F211321. 39 large, comfortable rooms, with mountain views at rear may suffer from traffic noise at night, front rooms with town views quieter, impressive dining room (good buffets), pleasant bar, has character, well run but lacks some **A** facilities, no pool, front has had a facelift but rear is falling apart. **A-B** *Springfields* (Quality Inn), opposite Tibetan School, Chhota Shimla, T221297, F221298. 11 "shabby genteel suites still decorated in 1920s style", some with views, in old Maharaja's bungalow "where staff refused to be tipped"! Recommended.

B *Asia The Dawn*, Tara Devi, Kachi Ghati (7 km on bus route), T231162, F231007. 37 rooms, restaurant recommended, terrace barbecue, bar, exchange, modern, well managed, peaceful setting. **B** *Combermere*, The Mall, next to Lift and taxis, T205080, F252251, hot_comb@hotmail.com 37 excellent rooms on 9 levels (partly served by lift), well located, friendly, efficient, very helpful. Recommended. **B** *Woodville Palace* (Heritage), Raj Bhavan Rd, The Mall, T223919, F223098, 14 rooms (variable), some good **A** suites with period furniture (cold in winter), dining hall (worth visiting for eclectic mixture of portraits, weapons and stuffed tigers!), guest individually catered for, owned by Raja of Jubbal's family, good views, spacious, in large grounds, one of the quietest but inefficient Reception. **B** *Eastbourne*, Khillini, near Bishop Cotton School, 5 km from bus stand, T223665, F223890, eastbourne@vacationvalue.com 24 rooms (noisy near reception), good restaurant, flower-filled gardens in wooded setting, well furnished, friendly. **B** *Peterhoff* (Himachal Tourism), T212236. 19 rooms in old mansion. **B-C** *Holiday Home* (Himachal Tourism), Circular Rd, below High Court, near Lift, T212890, F201705. 65 rooms, some with views, rooms vary, some musty, restaurants, exchange, indifferent service.

C *Himland East*, Circular Rd, 3 km bus stand, T222901, F224241. 16 rooms, modest but clean, good views from balconies. **C** *Himland West*, alongside and similar, T2577312, F213298. 11 rooms, restaurant. **C-D** *Harsha*, The Mall, Chaura Maidan, next to State Museum, T258441, F212868. 20 rooms, restaurant, dim, rather uninspired but friendly service, pleasant and quiet location. **C-D** *Mehman*, above Christ Church. Very modern, very clean, great views from the

Stirling Castle

ELYSIUM HILL

1

LAKKAR BAZAR
Circular Rd
Snowdon

Indira Gandhi

To Sanjauli Kufri (Hindustan–Tibet Rd)

Ridge

Tourist Lift
3
United Services Club

Hanuman Temple

JAKHU HILL

The Mall

11

CHHOTA SHIMLA
Himachal Bhavan

To Kasumpti

9 Pineview
10 Tashkent
11 Woodville Palace

Himachal Pradesh

front, can bargain down. **C-D** *Pineview*, Mythe Estate, Circular Rd, T257045,F257834. 35 rooms (**B** suites), Indian restaurant, exchange. **C-D** *Shingar*, The Mall, T2578191, F203382. 32 clean rooms, restaurant.

There are numerous less expensive hotels on The Mall & on Circular Rd, Lakkar Bazar

D *Dalziel*, The Mall, above Station, T2572691. 24 clean rooms with bath (hot water), Indian meals. **D** *Diplomat*, The Ridge, T257754. 23 rooms with bath, some good, restaurant. **D** *Lord St John*, Cart Rd (near *Capital Hotel*), clean rooms, friendly staff. Recommended. If arriving late knock loudly to be heard! **D** *Mayur*, above Christ Church, T72392. 32 rooms, some with mountain views, good restaurant but check bill, modern and clean, helpful staff. **D** *Samrat*, Cambermere Bridge, The Mall, T2578572. 20 small rooms, restaurant (Indian, Chinese). **D** *Surya*, Circular Rd, T2578191. 41 rooms, restaurant, modern. **D** *White*, Lakkar Bazar, T255276. 27 clean rooms with bath, some with good views. Recommended. **D-E** *Woodland*, T211002, The Ridge, behind *Mehman*. 11 rooms, best **C** wood-panelled, downstairs with views, some with bath (even tubs), quiet, nice view, off-season bargain (Rs 850 to 300). Recommended. **D-E** *Dreamland*, The Ridge, 500 m east and above Christchurch, T206897, F204919. 30 large, fairly clean rooms with bath, constant hot water, good views, friendly, but some find it damp and dreary and a bit overpriced.

E *YMCA*, The Ridge, above Christ Church, T252375. Rooms in annexe best with bath (hot water), avoid west side near cinema (can be noisy, last show 2200) mediocre meals (breakfast included), TV (after 1900 only!), very clean, quiet location, relaxed, popular but very institutionalized, gym and billiards, membership Rs 40 per week. **E** *YWCA*, Constantia, behind Telegraph Office, T203081. 20 clean rooms for both sexes, heavily booked May-Jun, off-season discounts (but can be very cold and dark

Shimla Mall & The Ridge

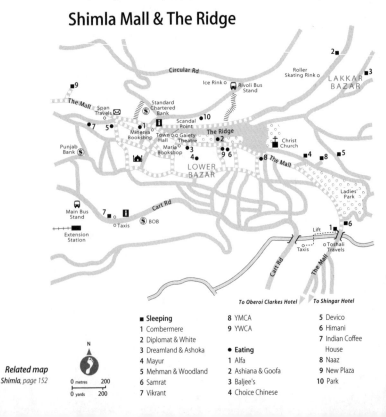

Related map
Shimla, page 152

0 metres 200
0 yards 200

■ Sleeping		
1 Combermere	8 YMCA	5 Devico
2 Diplomat & White	9 YWCA	6 Himani
3 Dreamland & Ashoka		7 Indian Coffee
4 Mayur	● Eating	House
5 Mehman & Woodland	1 Alfa	8 Naaz
6 Samrat	2 Ashiana & Goofa	9 New Plaza
7 Vikrant	3 Baljee's	10 Park
	4 Choice Chinese	

★ By narrow gauge to Shimla

The delightful narrow gauge train journey is very enjoyable (see page 158). The **Kalka-Shimla** (0.76 m) line, completed in 1903, runs 97 km from Kalka in the foothills to Shimla at over 2,000 m; the magnificent journey takes just over five hours. The steepest gradient is one in 33; there are 107 tunnels covering 8 km and bridges over 3 km. Order a meal in advance at Kalka or Shimla station.

with only occasional running water), superb position, safe and very good value. **E-F** *Tashkent*, lane down off Mall, above Victory Tunnel, very basic, rooms vary, some with bath and TV (possible to bargain down), views from balcony overhanging precipitous drop. **E-F** *Vikrant*, near the bus terminal, T255334. Clean rooms, shared bath (bucket hot water), TV, friendly and efficient, handy location. **F** *Ashoka*, The Ridge, above Christchurch. Rooms with bath (24 hr hot water), TV, great views, good value but several items in room broken or unserviceable.

Take special care with food hygiene. Press reports suggest that drinking water sources in parts of the state have been polluted by indiscriminate dumping of hospital waste, in rivers.

Eating

● on maps, pages 152 & 154
Price codes:
see inside front cover

Expensive Top hotels with international menus, specially recommended are: plush, modernized *Cecil*, atmospheric *Chapslee*, old-fashioned *Clarke's* which does a good set lunch but plays painful classical music at dinner, and the more intimate *Woodville Palace*.

Mid-range *Ashiana*, The Ridge. Uninspired food, dismal surroundings (dark tinted glass), in old circular bandstand. *Fascination*, 26 The Mall (above *Baljees*.). Indian and Chinese. Comfortable, fairly smart. *Himani*, The Mall. Indian. Restaurant above, tasty Mughlai, bar below. *Nalini*, The Mall, T207892. International. New, pleasant, good service but poor china, 0830-2200; also ice creams and sweets counters.

Top hotels have pleasant bars; not so good in town

Cheap Below the Mall, towards Lower Bazar, good cheap dhabas sell snacks (eg *tikki channa*). *Choice*, Middle Bazar, down steps from Fire Station. Chinese. Wide choice. Recommended. *Indian Coffee House*, The Mall. International. Cheap South Indian snacks, excellent coffee, some Western dishes, old world feel, uniformed waiters, spartan and dim. *Malook's* opposite Gaiety Theatre, down steps. Good Tibetan dishes. *New Plaza*, 60/61 Middle Bazar, down steps, T255438. Excellent value, friendly, simple but clean, serves a variety of western dishes.

Cafés and fast food *Baljees*, 26 The Mall, opposite Town Hall. Good snacks, justifiably packed, cakes and sweets from takeaway counter. *Goofa*, below Ashiana, The Ridge. Vegetarian. Dull, dimly lit but decent pizzas and thalis. *Park* just above Mall, beyond Scandal Point. Indian, Continental. Very popular traveller hangout (great pizzas). Recommended.

Cinema Bollywood films are shown at the *Rivoli*. **Sport Golf**: Naldera, 9-hole. Casual members: green fee and equipment, about Rs 100, see page 158. **Skating rink**: below Rivoli, on ice in winter, day's membership Rs 50 to skate to loud Indian film hits. **Skiing**: early Jan to mid-Mar. Ski courses at Narkanda (64 km) organized by Himachal Tourism, 7 and 15-day courses, Jan-Mar, Rs 1,700-3,000; see page 160 and also Manali.

Entertainment

Himachal Pradesh

Festivals In **Jun** the *Summer Festival* includes cultural programmes from Himachal and neighbouring states, and art and handicrafts exhibitions.

Shopping *Himachal Emporium*, The Mall, opposite Telegraph Office, for local woollen items.
Major shopping areas *Tibetan Self-Help Handicrafts Centre*, near Kusumpti, 6 km, produces carpets and
are The Mall, Lower woven goods, keeping Tibetan traditions alive, sold through other outlets in town.
Bazar, & Lakkar Bazar **Books**: *Maria Brothers*, 78 The Mall, good selection of antiquarian books, maps and
prints, 1030-1300, 1700-2000. *Minerva*, 46 The Mall, opposite Gaiety Theatre for
books and maps, good range.

Transport **Local Bus**: from Cart Rd. The 2-stage **lift** from the Taxi Stand on Cart Rd near *Hotel*
Cars are not allowed on *Samrat*, takes passengers to and from The Mall, Rs 5. **Taxi**: near lift on Cart Rd, T77645;
The Mall & The Ridge; fixed fares. Try private taxis, mini buses and Himachal RTC buses for local sightseeing
poor road signs in and around Shimla.

Long distance Air **Jabbarhatti airport** has daily flights from Delhi, Kullu and
Ludhiana by *Jagsons*, 58 The Mall, T/F225177. Flights can be badly disrupted by the
weather especially during the monsoon. Taxis charge Rs 300 to town (lift). Occasional
coach transfer. **Road Bus**: From **Main Bus Stand**, Cart Rd: *HP Tourism* coaches during
the season to **Chandigarh** 4 hrs, Rs 80, **Dehra Dun** 9 hrs, **Delhi** 10-12 hrs, Rs 200-225,
overnight to **Dharamshala** (10 hrs, Rs 135). **Manali** dep outside the 'Tunnel', 8-10 hrs, Rs
150, tickets from Main Bus Stand, *Span Travels*, deluxe, Rs 260 – a hair-raising journey
down to the Kullu Valley. HPRTC deluxe buses between Shimla and Delhi in the summer
(9 hrs). From **Rivoli (Lakkar Bazar)**: **Rampur** hourly from 0530, 8 hrs, and **Chitkul**, 2
daily; **Jeori** for Sarahan (8 hrs). **Taxi**: Union Stands near the lift and above the main Bus
Stand on Cart Road. **Chandigarh**, Rs 900; **Kalka** (90 km), Rs 700; **Mussoorie** Rs 2,500, 8
hrs, including stops; **Rekong-Peo**, Rs 2,500, 11 hours. 4 day round trip, Rs 6,000 (cheaper
hire from Haridwar). **Train** The main station has computerised reservation (T252915) for
all of India. The newer extension station is just below the Main bus stand, where some
trams start and terminate. T254289. Enquiry T210131. Travel to/from Shimla involves a
change of gauge at Kalka (see Box and Kalka below). It is quicker by bus but requires a
stronger stomach. **To Chandigarh** via Kalka: *Kalka-Howrah Mail, 2312* (change at Kalka
from *252*), 1745, 7 hrs; *Himalayan Queen, 4096* (change at Kalka from *256*), 1100, 6½ hrs.
To New Delhi via Kalka: *Himalayan Queen, 4096* (change at Kalka from *256*), 1100, total
11¼ hrs. **To Old Delhi**: *Kalka-Howrah Mail 2312* (change at Kalka from *252*), 1745, 12¾
hrs. **NB** The day train to Delhi recommended; **From New Delhi to Kalka** *Himalayan*
Queen, 4095, 0600, 5¼ hrs; *Howrah-Kalka Mail, 2311*, 2245, 5¾ hrs; then narrow gauge to
Shimla (see page 159). **By narrow gauge**: **To Kalka**: *Exp* (Season) *258*, 0955, 6¼ hrs; *Exp*
256, 1100, 5¼ hrs; *Rail Car* (Season, for minimum 6), *102*, 1220, 4¼ hrs, Rs 170; *KS Passen-*
ger 2, 1430, 6 hrs, Rs 14, Rs 140 (1st Class); *Exp 254* (Season), 1600, 5¼ hrs; *Sivalik Deluxe*
Exp 242, 0530, 5 hrs, Rs 305; *Mail 252*, 1800, 5½ hrs. For *Mail & Exp*, Rs 27, Rs 160 (1st
Class); reservation fee Rs 20.

Directory **Banks** Exchange procedure is awkward; photocopies of passport and visa needed. Shop around for
Changing foreign best rates (eg Standard Chartered charge up to Rs 195). *Indian Overseas Bank*, good rate on
currency outside Shimla minimum exchange of US$100. *UCO* good service and *Punjab* requires visiting 2 branches.
is not easy. **Communications Post**: Head GPO, The Mall (near Scandal Point). Open 1000-1600 Sun. **Poste**
Bank of Baroda in **Restante**: Counter 13 (separate entrance), chaotic. **CTO** nearby. Others near State Bank of India and
Mandi is one of the few Cambermere Bridge. **Internet**: Tourist office, The Mall, good facilities, 1 machine erratic opening hrs,
offering exchange Rs 100 per hr. Another above amusement arcade on the Mall. **Hospitals & medical**
facilities. **services** Chemists: many STD phone booths also stock a range of medical supplies. **Hospitals**:
Do not depend on credit *Kamala Nehru Hospital*, T. *Snowdon Hospital*. Dr Puri, Meghana Complex, The Mall, T201936/37,
cards for cash speaks fluent English, is efficient, and very reasonable (Rs 40). Recommended. **Tour companies &**
travel agents *Hi-Lander*, 62 The Mall, T201565, F204026 for adventure tours and treks. *Ibex*, Tara
Devi, T212255. *Span*, 4 The Mall, opposite GPO, T255279, F201300, comprehensive, efficient and

reliable, foreign exchange. **Tourist offices** *Himachal* (HPTDC), The Mall, T258302, F252557, hptdc@nde.vsnl.net.in 1000-1800, very helpful. Victory Tunnel, Cart Rd, T254589, 1000-1700. Directorate, 28 SDA Complex, Kasumpti Complex, T225924. Himachal Tourism has a/c and non-a/c cars and luxury coaches. Corporate Office, Ritz Annexe, T252704, F252206.

Around Shimla

The Hindusthan-Tibet road out of Shimla, after cutting through a tunnel at Dhali (8 km) to the dismal suburb of Sanjauli, passes some nearby holiday resorts. The interesting Sangye Choeling Tibetan monastery is about 1 km from the main bus stop (uphill, about 500m west of the junction). A road on the left leads to the attractive picnic spot of **Mashobra** (6 km; 2,150 m), with good forest walks and *Hotel Gables*, T480171, while 3 km further on is **Craignano** (2,280 m), which has a hilltop *Rest House*.

Kufri, 16 km from Shimla, hosts a winter sports festival; best in January and February. However, don't expect European or American resort slopes or facilities. At **Danes Folly** (2,550 m), 5 km away, is a government run orchard. A 10-minute walk uphill takes you to a mini zoo of Himalayan wildlife. Mahasu peak, 20 minutes from a path behind the cottages offers fabulous mountain views on a clear day; there is a small but interesting temple at the start of the walk.

Kufri
Phone code: 0177
Colour map 2, grid A1
Altitude: 2,500 m

Sleeping **B** *Kufri Holiday Resort*, T480300. 22 rooms and eight modern cottages (2 and 3-bedrooms) with limited hot water, attractive design and setting with flower-filled gardens, outstanding views from cottages above, good dining room, good walks, tours and treks organized. **B** *Shilon Resort*, at Shilon Bagh on Chail Rd, T483344. Upmarket, comfortable. **D** *Snow Shelter*, on main street in town centre, T480135. Very small, cramped, basic.

Transport Bus Rs 15

Chharabra is an enjoyable 3 km forest walk down from Kufri. The **Wildflower Hall** which once stood here was the residence of Lord Kitchener, Commander-in-Chief of the Indian Army. The original building was replaced; its

Chharabra
Altitude: 2,593 m

Around Shimla

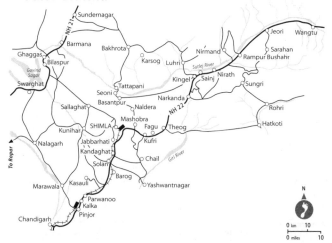

successor was converted into a hotel which burnt down in 1993. Oberoi is to open a new luxury **hotel**. The lovely gardens are surrounded by *deodar* forest with beautifully peaceful walks. **Fagu** (*phone code*: 0177), a small resort is an hour's trek from Kufri. Some 10 km further, the busy market town of **Theog** (2,250 m), is strung out on the hillside.

Naldera
Phone code: 0177
Colour map 2, grid A1
Altitude: 2,050 m

Off the Hindusthan-Tibet road, 26 km north of Shimla, Naldera has a nine-hole golf course, possibly the oldest in India and the beautiful Mahung temple. The colourful *Sipi Fair* in June attracts crowds from the surrounding villages who bring handicrafts to sell. **Sleeping B-C** *Log Huts*, T487739, six rooms. **C** *Golf Glade* (Himachal Tourism), T287739. Five rooms, restaurant, bar. **Tattapani** (*phone* code: 0177), 18 km north across the Sutlej River, has a hot spring flowing from the banks of the Sutlej River. **Sleeping E** *Tourist Inn* (Himachal Tourism), T485949. Four rooms, very basic dorm (Rs 30), meals.

Chail
Phone code: 01792
Colour map 2, grid A1
45 km SE of Shimla;
off the NH22
Altitude: 2,250 m

In a superb forest setting with fine snow views, Chail was once the Maharaja of Patiala's summer capital built on three adjacent hills and claimed to have the country's highest cricket ground at 2,444 m which is a 2 km walk from the bus stand! The old palace on Rajgarh Hill has been converted to a hotel while the old residency 'Snow view' and a Sikh temple stand on the other two hills. The **Chail Sanctuary**, once a private hunting reserve, is popular with birdwatchers. A *cheer* pheasant breeding programme was started here in 1988. It is an idyllic spot but not when the weekend day-trippers descend on the tiny resort. **Sleeping and eating B** *Chail Palace* (Himachal Tourism), T848343, F848383. 19 suites in old stone-built mansion, cottages (one to four bedrooms) and log huts, some antiques, billiards, tennis, orchards. **C** *Banjara Camp*, deluxe two-bed tents, bath tent, all meals, well organized. Recommended. Contact 17 Hauz Khas Village, New Delhi 110016, T011-6960509, F6967241, banjara@del2.vsnl.net.in **D** *Himneel* (Himachal Tourism). 16 rooms, restaurant, modest but full of character. *Kailash* restaurant serves good value breakfasts and lunches. ■ *Getting there: from Shimla, bus at 0830 takes 2½ hrs ; you can return by a different route.*

Solan
Phone code: 01792
Colour map 2, grid A1
Population: 22,000
Altitude: 1,450 m

Further along, and half way to Kalka on both the road and railway line, Solan is noted for its brewery and mineral water springs. **Sleeping D** *Gourmet's Paradise*, T20205. 14 rooms, restaurant. **E** *Tourist Bungalow* (Himachal Tourism), T23733. Nine rooms, dorm (Rs 75), restaurant with TV; **F** *Railway Retiring Room.*

Jabli
Phone code: 01793

About 65 km from Shimla, the small town has the government HPMC Juice and Jam factory selling discounted factory-fresh produce. **Sleeping** 6 km away **C-D** *Bonzo's Rock Rose*, Mangotehi, on NH22, T64018, 15 comfortable rooms, restaurant, bar, garden, fine views.

Parwanoo
Phone code: 01792
Colour map 2, grid A1
Population: 5,800

The tourist centre with a cable-car is on the Haryana border. **Sleeping B** *Timber Trail Resort*, near Datyar 4 km away, T32340, F33119. 25 rooms, 10 tents, restaurant, café, bar. **B** *Timber Trail Heights*, Banasar, T32301, F33119, reached by cable-car, also with restaurant, excellent setting with gardens, open 24 hours. **B-C** *Shiwalik* (Himachal Tourism), above the highway entering town, T32295, F32574. 23 rooms (14 a/c), restaurant, bar, tourist office.

Kalka
Phone code: 01733
Colour map 1, grid C3

Kalka is the terminus for the narrow gauge railway from Shimla. **F** *Retiring Rooms*, good for early morning departures, can be in demand in season so reserve ahead at Kalka or Shimla.

Road Easily reached from Shimla, by **bus** or **taxi** (Rs 800), and from Chandigarh by taxi (Rs 400). **Train** 1st class waiting room for ticket holders only. It is essential (especially during the 'season') to have an advance reservation for the narrow gauge train to avoid a rush 1 hr before departure when tickets are sold. Season (for 254/257): 1 May-15 Jul (school holidays start at end-May); 15 Sep-30 Oct; 15 Dec-1 Jan. The daily *Sivalik Deluxe Express* (No *241/242*), the line's pride and joy boasts "Toilet fittings of latest variety" and "Curtains of latest design"! The pricier ticket (Rs 305) includes tea and breakfast/dinner at **Barog** where there is **B-C** *Pinewood* (HP Tourism), T01792-38825, with rooms and restaurant. **To Delhi (ND)**: the best option from Delhi (ND) is the *Himalayan Queen 4095*, 0600, 5 hrs which connects with the 1140 to Shimla. Otherwise you have a long wait in Kalka. *Shatabdi Exp*, *2006*, 0600, 3¾ hrs; *Kalka-Howrah Mail*, *2312*, 2330, 7 hrs; *Himalayan Queen*, *4096*, 1645, 5½ hrs. **By narrow gauge** to: **Shimla** from Plat 6 (end of Plat 1): *KS Passenger 1*, 0400, 5¼ hrs, Rs 14, Rs 140 (1st Class); *Sivalik Deluxe Exp 241*, 0530, 5 hrs, Rs 305; *Mail 251*, 0620, 5¼ hrs; *Exp 253* (Season), 0700, 5½ hrs; *Rail Car* (Season, for minimum 6), *101*, 1120, 4½ hrs, Rs 170; *Exp 255*, 1140, 5¼ hrs (only one with a good connection from Delhi); *Himalayan Queen Exp* (Season) *257*, 1210, 6¾ hrs. For *Mail & Exp*, Rs 27, Rs 160 (1st Class). Reservation fee Rs 20.

Transport
The train often arrives on the Kalka platform already full of locals who board it while it waits in the siding! Worth paying Rs 150-170 plus reservation fee of Rs 20, to guarantee a seat on 1st class

The attractive hill resort is only 16 km hike from Kalka (35 km by road). **Sleeping C-D** *Roscommon* (Himachal Tourism), off the highway, T72005. Nine rooms, some in annexe, hot water, restaurant, run down, disappointing service. Several other **E-F** hotels.

Kasauli
Phone code: 017912
Colour map 1, grid C3
Altitude: 1,927 m

The area around Nalagarh was once ruled by the Chandela Rajputs. The fort commands wonderful views above an estate of forests and orchards, rich in birdlife, and is built on five levels around manicured grassy courts. Originally built in the 15th century; the Diwan-i-Khas (1618) is now the Banquet Hall. The present Raja has opened his home to guests. **Ramgarh Fort** (circa 1540) on the ridgetop, 21 km north (*altitude*: 1,200 m) with good views to the Himalaya, overlooks the valley which saw the westernmost activity in the Gurkha Wars of the early to mid-19th century.

Nalagarh
40 km NW of Kalka; on the Shimla-Ropar Rd

Sleeping B *Nalagarh Resort* (WelcomHeritage), T01795-23009, F23021. 15 comfortable rooms (some charming suites), with modern baths, traditional furniture, good food (buffets only), small pool, tennis, rural surroundings, run by Raja's family who meet guests, friendly and welcoming, plenty of atmosphere. Recommended. Reserve ahead direct or T011-4690741). **Transport** On request, hotel pick-up from Ropar (20 km) or Kalka (40 km). Car from Chandigarh, 45 mins; Delhi, about 5 hrs (drivers accommodated).

Shimla to Kinnaur and Spiti

★ Old Hindustan Tibet Road

The road east from Shimla to the Tibetan border (520 km), runs fairly level along the upper part of the slopes at about 2,500 m connecting a string of prosperous looking farms, villages and towns. The terraced slopes beyond are covered by well tended orchards. It passes through some dramatic scenery through Kinnaur and Spiti before joining the main Manali-Leh highway. You need a good head for heights. The narrow, winding roads with precipitous, unprotected drops are often subject to serious landslides.

The road may be severely damaged in the rains

Himachal Pradesh

Human sacrifice in the Himalaya

Human sacrifice was practised for centuries in the original Bhimkali temple in Sarahan. During the 16th and 17th centuries this was carried out with elaborate rituals. The sacrificial victim would be kept in the adjoining Narasimha Temple. After the ritual offering his blood would be placed on Bhimakali's tongue for her to 'drink' and *would then be used to wash the feet of a second deity Ushadevi. The priest would also place a mark of blood on the forehead of each worshipper. The sacrificed head would finally be thrown into the Sutlej river and the body into the well in the courtyard which is now blocked.*

Inner Line Permits (ILP)
Virtually impossible to get foreign exchange in this area

Inner Line Permits are needed for travel close to the Tibetan border (eg between Sumdo and Jangi) but are easy to get. The 'Inner Line' runs parallel to and 40 km inside the border; all visitors are barred, except from places like Kaza which are specifically exempt. Overnight stay is not permitted in Puh, Khabo and Sumdo. Rules may be further relaxed, so check with the tourist office. Permits are issued free to individuals, for seven days from the date (easily renewable for three days at Kaza or Recong Peo). Take three passport photos, your valid passport, two copies of the front page of passport and Indian Visa and complete the form from Sub-Divisional Magistrate's office (SDM) in Shimla, Recong Peo or Kaza (difficult in the last). Permits say "no overnight halts and no photography" though rules have been relaxed considerably. In Shimla, travel agents charge Rs 150. In Kaza, you need the additional 'No Objection' certificate from the Chief of Police – a mere formality of a stamp and signature. In Recong Peo, the whole process takes about an hour (which may include 'chai' or breakfast with the SDM!). **Sleeping and eating** Mainly in simple rest houses and lodges or in tents. In some places enterprising local families are opening their modest homes to paying guests. Local village shops often stock canned food and bottled water, and you may be surprised by the advent of television even in remote villages.

Narkanda
Phone code: 01782
Colour map 2, grid A1

The small market town at 2,700 m (*population*: 700) occupies a superb position on the col. **Sleeping C** *Hatu* (Himachal Tourism), T8430. 16 rooms, restaurant, commanding views. A small restaurant down lane near bazar has limited menu.

Routes

The road drops sharply through woodland interspersed with apple orchards from Narkanda, down to Kingel (33 km). From here it zig-zags down to Sainj (8 km). Some 5 km beyond Sainj there are superb views across the valley, and of a wall of eroded outwash deposits at least 50 m thick. A left turn goes to **Luhri** (800 m), where a minor road runs west, then north across the Sutlej to the **Jalori Pass**, Shoja and Aut. This seasonal route is best by four-wheel drive, though buses cover this route very carefully. See page 174. The main road east passes **Nirath** where there is a Surya Temple believed to date from the 8th century which still has some fine carving preserved on the outer walls and has carved wooden panels within. At an altitude of between 800-900 m the Sutlej valley towards Rampur has a subtropical summer climate, with mango trees and bananas replacing apples.

Rampur Bushahr
Phone code: 01782
Colour map 2, grid A1
Population: 4300
Altitude: 924 m

This is one of Himachal's most important market towns. The only ancient monastery in this tract has been pulled down and is being rebuilt. Padam Palace (1920s), opposite the bus stand, once the residence of the Raja, has interesting carved wooden panels and wall murals, but is difficult to enter. The gardens are shaded and peaceful and the curious summerhouse has Tibetan

Himachal Pradesh

murals. The Sat Narain Temple in the main bazar (1926) has a beautiful but decaying façade. The *Lavi Fair* (11-14 November) draws large crowds of colourful hill people who bring their produce (handicrafts, carpets, rugs, fruit and nuts and animals), to the special market. There are sporting competitions in the day, and dancing and making music around bonfires after dark. The fair which coincides with the return of the shepherds from high pastures has been held here for over 300 years.

Sleeping and eating B-D *Bushehar Regency*, T34103. 20 rooms, some a/c, well positioned, restaurant, bar 150 m away. **E-F** *Bhagwati*, below bus stand near river, T33117. Clean rooms with bath (hot water), TV, restaurant, friendly staff. Recommended. **E-F** *Narendra* Indira Market near bus stand, on the river, T33155, F34055. 15 rooms, with bath, TV (**D** a/c after mid-May), restaurant (wide choice), bar. Others with shared bath: **F** *Bodh*, near bus stand, T33302. 5 rooms, dorm (Rs 20), Tibetan/Chinese restaurant, friendly, helpful owner. **F** *Highway Home*, on main road west of town centre, T33063. 6 rooms, dusty and noisy. **F** *Kainthla*, near *Bhagwati*. Newish and clean. **F** *Rama*, next to bus stand. 9 rooms and dorm (Rs 20). *Sutlej View* (restaurant of Himachal Tourism), on main road overlooking river, 1 km west of town centre. Clean, limited menu but good food, attractive terrace and indoor a/c restaurant, open 0900-2200.

Transport Bus: the bus station is quite chaotic and timetables are not followed. To **Chandigarh** 0730; **Delhi** 1330; **Mandi** 0730, 1830 (9 hrs); **Recong Peo** 0500, 0930, 1330, 1600 (5 hrs) and **Puh**; **Sarahan** 1000, 1630, 1800 (2-3 hrs), better to change at Jeori; **Shimla**, several, 0430 to 2100 (5-6 hrs); **Tapri** (and Kalpa) 0545 (3¾ hrs), change at Karchham for Sangla and Chitkul. Buses are often late and overcrowded; seats are hard to get.

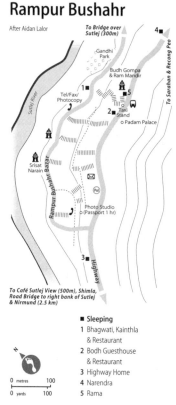

Rampur Bushahr

After Aidan Lalor

To Bridge over Sutlej (300m)

Gandhi Park

Budh Gompa & Ram Mandir

Tel/Fax/ Photocopy

Taxi Stand

Padam Palace

Srisai Narain

Photo Studio (Passport 1 hr)

To Café Sutlej View (500m), Shimla, Road Bridge to right bank of Sutlej & Nirmund (2.5 km)

To Sarahan & Recong Peo

Sutlej River

Rampur Bushahr Bazar

Highway

■ Sleeping
1 Bhagwati, Kainthla & Restaurant
2 Bodh Guesthouse & Restaurant
3 Highway Home
4 Narendra
5 Rama

0 metres 100
0 yards 100

Himachal Pradesh

From Rampur the highway enters one of the most exciting, and geologically **Routes** active, stretches of road in the region. During the rains the Sutlej is a surging torrent of muddy water, dropping over 450 m in under 30 km and passing through gorges and deeply incised valleys. Although an ancient trade route, the road is comparatively recent and is constantly being upgraded particularly in connection with the **Nathpa-Jhakhri** HEP scheme, with a 28 km long tunnel from Nathpa, near Wangtu, to Jhakhri, about 10 km beyond Rampur. When completed this will be one of the largest Hydel schemes in the world. The blasting both for the shafts and for road widening has further destabilized the already landslide-prone hillsides and during the rains the road may be blocked. Blockages are usually cleared within hours, though travelling times are wholly unpredictable. You also need a strong stomach, both for the main road and for diversions, especially up the Baspa Valley to Sangla. 9 km west of Jeori the river passes through a dramatic gorge. On the north side of the river isolated tiny pockets of cultivated land cling to the hillside.

Jeori
160 km from Shimla

Jeori is the junction for Sarahan, one hour away. **NB** Sarahan has very limited supplies. You can pick up bottled water in Jeori at *RS Stores* on the Sarahan road just above the junction with the main road.

★ Sarahan

Phone code: 01782
Colour map 2, grid A1
Population: 1,200
Altitude: 1,850 m

An important market for traders of neighbouring regions, 21 km south of Jeori. It is an attractive town with a pheasant breeding centre nearby. The bazar is interesting: friendly villagers greet travellers; shops sell flowers, bright red and gold scarves and other offerings for worshippers among local produce, fancy goods and jewellery, while numerous tailors' shops turn out garments for villagers around. It is also a stop on the trekkers' route.

Sights

Sarahan was the old capital of the local Rampur Bushahr rulers and has a palace complex containing the strikingly carved wood-bonded **Bhimakali Temple** (rebuilt circa 1927), in a mixture of Hindu and Buddhist styles. The two temples stand on a slope among apple and apricot orchards behind the bazar. Usually, the hilltop Himachali temples differ in style from those on the plains in being dedicated to local gods and goddesses instead of to the major deities, and in being built by local rulers instead of kings. Here it is dedicated to Durga as the destroyer of the *asuras* (demons) and has a Brahmin priest in attendance. Plan for an early morning visit to the temple to see morning prayers; evening prayers are around 1900. Pilgrim restrooms have been built around the outer courtyard. Before you enter the temple court, leave shoes and leather objects with the attendant; you are expected to wear the saffron cap offered to you before entering. The donation box is inside the temple. You may only photograph the outside of the temples; it is worth climbing around the back of the complex afterwards for a picturesque view.

According to some sources the ancient temple on the right (closed for safety reasons), is many centuries old (see box). The renovated temple is three-storeyed, with the lowest housing the stairs; the pagoda-style roof shape is borrowed from a Tibetan *gompa*. Built in traditional timber-bonded style it has white-washed dry stone and rubble masonry alternating with horizontal deodar or spruce beams to withstand earthquakes. Strangely, a severe quake earlier in the century had caused the older temple to lean precariously towards the newer, but miraculously a subsequent tremor has returned it to an almost upright line. The upper floors have balconies and windows with superb ornamental woodcarving; the silver repoussée work doors are also impressive. The first floor has a 200-year-old gold image of goddess Bhimkali which is actively worshipped only during the *Dasara* festival when animals and birds are sacrificed in the courtyard, while on the second floor daily early morning *puja* is carried out to a second image. The three other shrines around the courtyard (on your right as you enter), are to Raghunath, Narsimha and Sri Lanka Bir; the sacrificial altar and the old well are nearby.

Sarahan is surrounded by high peaks. A pilgrimage route encircles **Shrikhand Mahadev** peak (5,227 m), which takes pilgrims seven days to go round. On a clear day you get fantastic panoramic views of the snow covered peaks.

Daranghati Sanctuary, which is rich in birdlife, was the former hunting reserve of the Raja of Bushahr State. On either side of Dhaula Dhar range just

Himachal Pradesh

east of Rampur, it is particularly important for harbouring western tragopan and monal pheasants, and also musk deer and Himalayan tahr. There are *Forest Rest Houses*; contact Range Officer at Mashnoo.

C-D *Srikhand* (Himachal Tourism), T74234, on a superb hilltop site, overlooking the Sutlej valley, Srikhand peak and the range beyond. 19 rooms with bath and hot water (4 in annexe cheaper), dorm (Rs 75), unsatisfactory restaurant, erratic service, inefficient management. **D** *PWD Rest House*, near Temple. Small, quite basic but adequate. **F** *Temple rooms*, Rs 100, dorm Rs 25. Ask locally for cheap rooms in family houses. Srikhand has a restaurant with good views and a limited menu. Dhabas in town have basic food (rice, daal and snacks). **Sleeping & eating**

Bus: daily between **Shimla** (Rivoli Bus Stand) and **Jeori** on the Highway (6 hrs), quicker by car. Local buses run between Jeori and the army cantonment below Sarahan. **Transport**

Kinnaur and Spiti

The regions of Kinnaur and Spiti lie in the rainshadow of the outer Himalayan ranges. The climate in Spiti is much drier than in the Kullu valley and is similar to that of Ladakh. The temperatures are more extreme both in summer and winter and most of the landscape is barren and bleak. The wind can be bitingly cold even when the sun is hot. The annual rainfall is very low so cultivation is restricted to the ribbons of land that fringe rivers with irrigation potential. The crops include potatoes, wheat, barley and millet. The people are of Mongol origin and almost everyone follows a Tibetan form of Buddhism.

During the British period Spiti was part of the Maharaja of Kashmir's state of Kashmir and Ladakh but was later exchanged for territories formerly belonging to Kangra. The British improved communications but little else. **Suggested reading**: *Himalayan Circuit* by GD Khosla. 1989 OUP. An early account of travel into this then virtually unknown region of Kinnaur and Spiti. *The Ochre Border* by Justine Hardy. 1995, Constable, London. An account of crossing the Puri Parvati Pass from Kullu to Spiti. *Spiti: Adventures in the Trans-Himalaya* by Harish Kapadia, 1996, Indus. *Exploring Kinnaur and Spiti in the Trans-Himalaya* by Dhanu Swadi and Deepak Sanan, 1998, Indus. **Background**

Kinnaur किन्नौर

An exciting mountain road runs through cliffside cuttings along the left bank of the Sutlej, which is frequently blocked by rockfalls and landslides during the monsoons. At **Choling** the Sutlej roars through a narrow force, and at **Wangtu** the road re-crosses the river where vehicle details are checked. Immediately after crossing the Wangtu bridge a narrow side road goes to **Kafnoo** village (2,427 m), in the **Bhabha Valley**. It is a 5-hour drive from Sarahan to Kafnoo which is a camping site and the start for an attractive 10-day trek to the Pin Valley. **Routes**

For treks, see page 216. From Wangtu the road route runs to **Tapri** (1,870 m) and **Karchham** (1,899 m), where there are hot springs. At Karcham it issues straight on to the road so it is not convenient to bathe. Here the Baspa River joins the Sutlej from the south. A hair-raising excursion by a precipitous winding rough road leads 16 km up the Baspa Valley to Sangla; buses take approximately 1½ hours.

★ **Baspa Valley** The valley carries the marks of a succession of glacial events which have shaped it, although the glaciers which formed the valley have now retreated to the high slopes above Chitkul at over 4,500 m. All villages in Baspa are characterized by exaggerated steeply sloping slate roofs, rich wood carving and elaborate pagoda temples. Although Kinner Kailash (sacred to Hindus and Buddhists), is not visible from here, the valley is on the circumambulating *Parikrama/Kora* route which encircles the massif. Fields of the pink coloured *ogla*, a small flower seed grown specifically in the Baspa Valley for grinding into grain, add a beautiful colouring in the season.

Sangla

Phone code: 017864
Colour map 2, grid A2
Altitude: 2,680 m

Sangla is built on the massive buttress of a terminal moraine which marked one of the major glacial advances about 50,000 years ago. The Baspa River has cut a deep trench on its south flank. Immediately above is the flat valley floor, formed on the lake bed which was once dammed behind the moraine. There is a **saffron** farm just north of Sangla (claimed to be better than at Pampore, Kashmir) and it is famous for its apples; the climate is ideal, especially as there is no hail damage.

In many Kinnauri temples one must wear a hat & a special belt

The old seven-storey **Killa** (Fort), where the Kinnaur rajas were once crowned, is 1 km north of new Sangla just before the road enters the village. It was occupied by the local rulers for centuries. It now has a temple to Kamakshi where the idol is from Guwahati, Assam318. Sangla village has excellent carving and is full of character. ■ *0800-0900, 1800-1900.*

Sleeping C *Banjara Camps*, VPO Barseri, via Sangla, superb riverside site 8 km beyond Sangla. 2 and 4-bed deluxe tents, separate (or attached) bath tents, excellent varied food included, very friendly, excellent site, trekking, Ladakh tours. Highly recommended. Buses stop 2 km from the campsite (6 km out of Sangla), where road drops down to right, car park at foot of hill is 500 m walk from camp (horn will summon porters!), reservations: 17 Hauz Khas Village, New Delhi T011-6960509, F6857241. **D** *Farm House*, walking distance of main road. Five rooms, common toilet, and 10 double *Tents* (Himachal Tourism), on spare land by main road in Sangla centre, good tents, meals included. **E-F** *Mount Kailash*, T22227. Clean pleasant rooms (hot shower). **F** *Sangla Guest House*, near shops. Clean rooms with bath (hot water), restaurant. **F** *Trekker's Lodge* going out of town towards Chitkul.

Transport Bus: to Chitkul (often 2 to 3 hrs late); **Shimla** via Tapri (10 hrs); **Recong Peo**, 0630; from Tapri, 0930. 4WD recommended between Karchham and Chitkul in bad weather.

Directory Useful services Shops with basic provisions; ISD/Fax; no foreign exchange.

Barseri

Most Kinnauri Buddhist temples only accept visitors at around 0700 & 1900

Barseri, 8 km from Sangla, is situated on an outwash cone which has engulfed part of the Baspa's valley floor. This well kept "green village" is happy to show visitors its solar heaters, *chakkis* (water mills) and water driven prayer wheels. The Buddha Mandir with *Shakyamuni* and other images and a large prayer wheel is beautiful inside.

Rakcham The pagoda-style temple with beautiful wood carving is to Shamshir Debta, Devi and Naga, combining Buddhist and Hindu deities. The ibex horns on the roof are ancient male fertility symbols. There is also a pre-Buddist, animist Bon cho shrine and a Siva temple. **Sleeping F** *Rupin* guest house is along the road.

Chitkul with its typical houses, Buddhist temple and a small tower, is the furthest point foreigners can travel without special permits. The Kagyupa (Oral Transmission School), has a highly valued, old image of the Shakyamuni Buddha. There are four directional kings on either side of the door as well as a Wheel of Life. You can walk along the Baspa River which has paths on both sides. **Warning** The rough path along the tributary starting at the bridge across the river, below the bus stand, is very steep in places with loose stones. Do not attempt alone.

Chitkul
Colour map 2, grid A2
18 km from Barseri
Altitude: 3,450 m

Sleeping and eating D *Timberline Camps* (Delhi) T626292. Provides deluxe tents, chemical toilets. F *Amar Guest House*, in village. Clean double rooms (Rs 100), hot water, friendly family atmosphere. Recommended. F *Chirangan Guest House*, two to five rooms (Rs 100), hot water. One basic shop sells a few provisions. Carry your own or eat in guesthouse. **Transport** 2 buses a day to/from **Karchham** (0930) via Sangla (1100) and Rakcham; from **Tapri**, 0930; from **Recong Peo** 0600 (prompt).

Also called 'Peo', the District HQ is a busy little market town but there is no foreign exchange facility. The Sub-Divisional Magistrate's (SDM's) office in a three-storey building below the bus stand deals with Inner Line Permits (see page 160). A short walk above the town takes you to the Kalachakra Temple with a large Buddha statue outside – good views of Kinner Kailash.

Recong Peo
Phone code: 017852
Colour map , grid
Altitude: 2,290 m

Himachal Pradesh

Kinnaur & Spiti

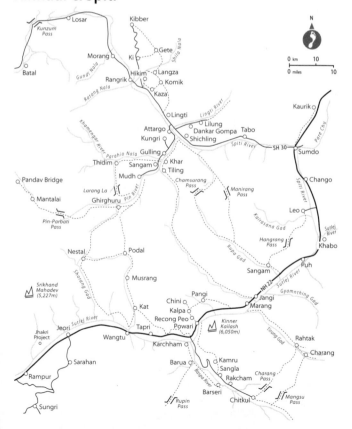

The stuff to record the epics

The **bhoj patra**, found distinctively in the Sangla Valley is a revered product. The extraordinarily fine waterproof layers just beneath the bark of the bhoj patra tree were used for writing centuries ago, particularly where palm leaves were not available. Renowned for its suppleness, strength and apparent indestructibility, leaves from this valley were used for some of Hinduism's most ancient writings, including the epics, and it is still highly valued for copying sacred texts. Genealogies which trace the descent of some families in the Sangla Valley to the legendary Pandavas are still widely accepted, and connections between the residents of the valley and the early roots of Hinduism are treasured.

Kothi village, reached by a path from the Kalachakra Temple, has ancient Hindu temples associated with the Pandavas. One has a tank of sacred fish, 30 minutes' walk from the bazar.

Sleeping and eating C *Banjara Camp*, of Sangla, plans to lease a hotel; contact 17 Hauz Khas Village, New Delhi 110016, T011-6960509, F6967241, banjara@del2.Vsnl.net.in **E** *Fairyland*, T2477. 8 rooms with bath (hot shower), restaurant with great view of Kinner Kailash, good food but disinterested management. **E** *Shivling Guest House* near bus Stand, T2477. 4 rooms with bath (hot shower), restaurant, good view of Shivling peak. **F** *Mayur*, 3 rooms with bath, dorm (Rs 30). **F** *Rangeen*, 3 rooms, dorm (Rs 35), restaurant. **F** *Snowview*, opposite bus stop in main bazar. Between the bazar and bus stand, stalls serve **cheap** Chinese/Tibetan.

Transport Reserve ticket from booth shortly before departure. **Bus** to **Chandigarh**; **Delhi** 1030; **Kalpa**, occasional; **Kaza** (9 hrs), gets very crowded so reserve seat before 0700; **Puh**; **Rampur**, frequent (5 hrs); **Sangla/Chitkul** (4 hrs); **Shimla**; **Tabo**, via Kaza, 9-10 hrs, Rs 65.

Kalpa
Phone code: 017852
Colour map 2, grid A2

Kalpa (Chini), 12 km from Recong Peo at 2,960 m, is reached after a stiff climb. It has an interesting temple complex and Budh mandir and is surrounded by apple, *bemi* (wild apricot) and plum orchards and chilgoza pine forests.

Sleeping D *Timberline Camps* T (Delhi) 626292. Provides deluxe tents, chemical toilets. **C** *Kinner Kailash* (open May-Nov) in commanding position, from suites (with bath tub, Rs 1100), to rooms, catering, camping, taxis. **E** *Forest Rest House* (2 km), caretaker can prepare meals, modern building with superb views over valleys and Kinner Kailash range, camping overnight (with permission), in school grounds from 1600-1000. **F** *Aucktong Guest House*, near Circuit House, 1 km north on Pangi road, T6019. 4 clean spacious rooms (more promised), large windows, superb views of mountains, restaurant, pleasant, very friendly ("we arrived for one night and stayed a week!"). Recommended.

Transport Bus to Shimla, 0730; Chitkul, 1300. To get to Peo for Kaza bus at 0730, walk down (40 mins) or arrange taxi from Peo. **NB** Travellers may not be allowed beyond Jangi without an 'Inner Line' permit. Contact SDM in Recong Peo a day ahead, see page 160.

Route A high road from Kalpa/Recong Peo with little or no traffic passes through Chilgoza pine forests (edible nuts), north to the hamlet of Pangi (10 km). Pangi is surrounded by apple orchards. The colourful Sheshri Nag temple at the top of the village has an inscription in a strange script above the entrance and standing stones in the courtyard. Apart from two Buddhist temples, the carved pagoda temple to Sheshri's mother encloses a huge boulder representing the Devi.

The road then goes over bare and rugged hills beyond to **Morang** which has impressive monasteries with wood carvings and sculptures. **Sleeping** F *Forest Rest House* and a provision store.

It continues to **Jangi** where there is a check post and to Puh. Khabo (2,831 m), a morning's drive from Kalpa, is at the confluence of the Sutlej and Spiti rivers, just south of Kah which is a steep climb with hairpin bends. The road follows the Spiti while the Sutlej valley disappears to the east towards the Tibet border. **Sumdo**, the last village of Kinnaur at the divide between the Hangrang and the Spiti Valleys, has a Border Police check post and a tea shop.

★ Spiti

The entry into the Spiti valley at Khabo is a rare example of crossing from the Himalaya to the Trans-Himalaya without going over a major pass. The 180 km State Highway 30, which joins Sumdo with Batal, passes through an arid valley with small patches of cultivation of peas and barley near the snow melt streams, to Tabo (31 km).

For treks in this area, see page 215

Himachal Pradesh

Tabo

At the crossroads of two ancient trade routes, Tabo was one of the great centres of Buddhist learning and culture. Founded in 996, the monastery is the oldest living Buddhist establishment in this part of the world. Today, the small town is rapidly being modernized with paved streets and electric lights. Government offices have appeared alongside traditional mud homes and the local shops stock basic provisions for trekkers. There is a post office.

*Colour map 2, grid A2
Altitude: 3,050 m*

Founded in 996 as a scholastic institution, the Gompa's original layout was planned as a *mandala* centred around a **Du khang** (Assembly Hall). The deodar wood used was imported from Kullu, Kinnaur, Chamba and Kashmir while the lack of quality structural stone resulted in the extensive use of earth, strengthened with gypsum for the high walls. Today the gompa houses 60 lamas and has a good collection of scriptures, *thangkas* and art pieces. Many of the colourful murals come close to the pure Indian style identified with Ajanta. The technique required the surface to be coated with several thin layers of lime and yak-skin glue and burnished vigorously to provide the 'ground' which was then smoothed and freshened with animal fat and butter. Natural vegetable dyes and powdered stone colours were mixed with *dzo* milk and yak urine for painting. The early Indian style murals used a profusion of reds and yellows with little stress on landscaping, the area around the principal figures being filled with small divinities. These images wear seraphic smiles and have half-shut dreamy eyes depicting introspective meditation. The later 17th-century paintings illustrate the Central Tibetan/Chinese art form where ultramarine takes over from the earlier dominance of reds and yellows, and landscapes become lively and vivid with the appearance of cliffs, swirling clouds, stylized flames, flora and fauna. Here the twists and turns of the limbs and the flowing elaborate drapery show great fluency. This is one of the few gompas in the Tibetan Buddhist influenced areas of Ladakh, Lahaul and Spiti where the highly structured art of painting the complex Tibetan religious iconography is

★ Chos Khor Gompa
The most important, it has an immense sense of the spiritual. Carry a torch. No photography allowed

taught. What appears outwardly as a free art form is actually taught on lined grid paper where each shape and form is closely measured.

Nine temples Tsuglhakhang ('academy') The 'resplendent' central *Mahavairochana* – a composite of four figures, each facing a cardinal direction, represents the unity of all Buddhas. On the walls inside are stucco figures (restored in the 17th century), of different Buddhas and Bodhisattvas. The frieze directly under the clay images describes (clockwise) Sudhana's path to Enlightenment while to the right is Shakyamuni's advance to Buddhahood. The floral ceiling decorations are in the Ajanta style.

Dri Tsang khang (Inner Sanctum) and **Kora** (Circumambulatory Path) At the centre of the 'mandala', the five *Dhyani* Buddhas escorted by four Bodhisattvas here, emerge from the darkness lit by a shaft of sunlight. The walls of the kora representing the 1,000 Buddhas, lend a sublime air. Snellgrove in *Buddhist Pilgrimage* equates Tabo to a 3-D mandala where each image in the circle of divinities is a part of an integrated whole, "a symbolic expression of the goal of spiritual striving and the means that lead to it".

Masks, weapons and ritual costumes are stored in the **Gon Khang** which is closed to visitors. **Zhalma** (Picture Hall) has a 17th-century entrance temple where the murals of the Buddha, his disciples, protective deities and Tara, are recent and in pure Tibetan style.

Dromton Lhakhang Chenpo (17th century) is dominated by Medicine Buddhas. The ceiling, in high Tibetan style, is exceptional, depicting nagas, titans, peacocks and parrots amongst rainbows with exquisite details of floral motifs and geometrical designs.

Ser Khang (Golden Temple) The walls were believed to have been coated with a layer of gold dust as thick as a yak's skin for painting the numerous larger-than-life figures; they were renewed in 16-17th centuries. The brilliant murals show Indian influence. Note specially the beautiful green Tara and goddess Usnishvijaya on the north wall.

Of the remaining temples the **Chamba Chenpo La Khang**, dedicated to the Maitreya (Future) Buddha, has a 6-metre high seated statue which symbolizes the redefining of the Dharma to be relevant in the next epoch. The murals of the eight Buddhas may be some of the earliest in Tabo. Later 16th-17th century murals show the fusion of Indian and High Central Tibetan styles after which Tibetan (Chinese) art flourished.

To the north, the small natural caves above the road were an integral part of the monastic complex. Pho Gompa, the only surviving, with early murals showing pure Indian influence, has been restored. These post Ajantan paintings, however, are already fading. On open ground to the east, on both sides of a dyke, there are pre-Buddhist rock carvings on metamorphosed igneous rocks showing ibex, swastikas, yonis, horses, panthers and human figures.

A large *Mala* (sacrificial wood) tree at the northwest corner of the enclave, the only one of four to survive, is held sacred by the villagers, while the monastery courtyard has *Ganday* trees which bear yellow, sweetly-scented flowers in the spring.

Sleeping C *Banjara Camp*, 11 deluxe 2-bed tents, bath tent, all meals, well organized. Recommended. Contact 17 Hauz Khas Village, New Delhi 110016, T011-6960509, F6967241, banjara@del2.vsnl.net.in **D-E** *Millennium Guest House*, run by monks in the complex, 13 colourful rooms, most with clean, shared toilets, hot water on request, meals. Also cheaper guesthouses in the village, many allowing camping. **Eating** *Tanzin*, near monastery. Tibetan food, friendly, family run, best in village. **Transport** Bus: to Chandigarh via Kinnaur, 0900; Kaza, 1000.

Once the capital of Spiti, Dankar is a tiny village. The early 16th-century fort/monastery **Dankar Gompa** (3,890 m), which once served as a jail, stands on an impressive overhang, perched on crumbling towers. Today it has over 160 lamas in residence. The 'highest temple' has a collection of Bhotia Buddhist scriptures, a four-in-one *Dhyani Buddha* and interesting murals of Medicine Buddhas and protector deities. The gompa is a two hours' very steep climb from a point 2 km away, beyond Shichling on the main road. The jeepable road from the SH30, about 1 km west of Shichling, winds up 8 km to Dankar (also two hours' walk) and is easier. A beautiful large pond at just under 4,100 m is reached by a 2½ km track. **Sleeping** Very limited. The Gompa has two rooms; only one has a bed.

Dankar
Colour map 2, grid A2

Lalung Gompa, known for its carved wood panelling, is off the SH30, 22 km from Kaza, reached by 8 km narrow, motorable track. From Dankar Gompa this is a two-hour trek. Carry plenty of water as there are no streams and it can get very hot.

About 5 km from Dankar is a sign for the Pin Valley National Park which is on the other side of the river; the Pin River joins the Spiti at **Attargo**, 9 km beyond Shichling and 15 km from Kaza. Above Attargo, 10 km along the Pin Valley, is the **Kungri (or Gungri) Gompa** (circa1330), which though not old is in an established monastic site with old carved wooden sculptures and is commonly understood to be a Bon monastery still practising elements of the pre Buddhist Bon religion. (The trek from the Bhabha Valley ends at the road head at Kungri.) One bus a day departs from Kaza at 1200, goes along the Pin Valley as far as **Mikkim** and turns straight back at 1400, not allowing enough time to visit the Gompa. You therefore face a long walk unless you can hitch a lift on a rare passing tractor or truck.

Pin Valley

At the confluence of the Pin River and one of its tributaries, 1 km from Mikkim, Sangam can be reached by one of two pulley systems. The one nearest the bus stop, across a bridge, requires your own rope harness. The other, 750 m west along the river has a person-size bucket. Both require a reasonable degree of fitness to negotiate, especially if crossing alone. (Local greeting is *joolay, joolay!*) **Sleeping** *Norzang Guest House*, rooms for Rs 100; *PWD Rest House*. There is a sub-post office but no provisions available.

Sangam

The Pin Valley is described as the 'land of ibex and snow leopard' and was created to conserve the flora and fauna of the cold desert. It adjoins the Great Himalayan National Park (southwest), and Rupi Bhabha Sanctuary (south) with the Bara Shigri Glacier forming its north boundary. The park covers 675 sq km with a buffer zone of 1,150 sq km mainly to its east where there are villages, and varies in altitude from 3,600 m to 6,630 m. Although the scenery is rugged, the summer brings a little more rain here than the rest of Spiti, resulting in a profusion of wild flowers.

Pin Valley National Park

The **wildlife** includes Siberian ibex, snow leopard, red fox, pika, weasels, lammergeier, Himalayan griffon, golden eagle, Chakor partridge, Himalayan snow cock and a variety of rose finches. The **Siberian ibex** can be sighted at high altitudes, beyond Hikim and Thango village. From July to September the young ibex kids need protection; the females move up to the higher pastures near cliffs while the adult males concentrate on feeding lower down.

Himachal Pradesh

The 60 km long **Lingti Valley** is famous for its **fossils**; **Shilla** peak (6,111 m), one of the highest in Himachal, is at the northern head of the valley; the highest is Chau Chau Kang Nilda or CCKN (6,303 m). The road continues to climb to Kaza following the Spiti River which in places makes a very wide valley.

Kaza
Phone code: 01906
Colour map 2, grid A2

Kaza (3,600 m) is 13 km from Lingti village. Old Kaza has village homes while New Kaza sports government offices. It is a busy bus terminus with a small market, a basic health centre and jeeps for hire. Inner Line Permits are issued (with difficulty), by the SDM's office. No foreign exchange is available.

There is an attractive one-day circular trek from here to **Hikim** and Komik villages visiting the monastery midway. Hikim gompa (early 14th century), modelled on a Chinese castle, was built under Mongol patronage.

Sleeping and eating Open May-Oct. **D-E** *Sakya 's Abode*, simple, varied rooms with bath, hot water on request, good meals. **E** *Tourist Lodge* (Himachal Tourism), 4 rooms, tents, catering. **F** *Mahabhadra*, basic but large room, shared bath, very clean, meals. Recommended. **F** *Snow Lion*, basic rooms with bath. Kaza is also ideal for **camping**. *Electricity Board*. PWD *Rest Houses*. Irrigation Dept *Bungalow* at Rangrik (4 km). *Layul*, a restaurant, does Chinese, Tibetan and Indian dishes, and cold beer. Also several bakeries and cafés.

Reserve a seat at least 1 hr ahead or night before

Transport The road via Kunzum-La and Rhotang Pass can be blocked well into Jul. **Bus**: New Bus Stand, bottom end of village. In summer: from **Manali** (201 km), 12 hrs via Rohtang Pass and Kunzum La; **Shimla** (412 km) on the route described, 2 days. Approximate times shown: daily to **Chango**, 1400; **Kibber** 0900, **Losar** 0900; **Mikkim** (19 km from Attargo), in the Pin Valley, 1200 (2 hrs); returns 1400. Long distance buses to **Kullu**, 0400; **Manali** (from Tabo), 0500; **Chandigarh** 0630. The last three are heavily used.

Routes
From Kaza, a road to the northeast goes to **Kibber** (19 km; 4,205 m), which has a school, post office and a bank. **Tashigang**, 18 km away; is one of the highest villages in the world connected by road. **Ki Monastery** on the way is the largest in Spiti and houses 300 lamas. Although it has suffered from wars, fires and earthquakes it still has a good collection of *thangkas* and *kangyurs* (scriptures). Although no permit is needed, the monks have instituted their private 'entrance fee' system which, by all accounts, appears quite flexible and linked to the visitors perceived ability to pay. There are a few cheap guest houses and camping is possible. If you cannot stay take a bus up and walk down via the Ki Monastery (11 km from Kaza).

Losar (4,079 m), 55 km from Kaza, the last village in Spiti is reached after driving through fields growing peas and cabbage among poplars, willows and apple orchards.

The road continues up to the **Kunzum La** (Pass) (18 km; 4,551 m), meaning 'meeting place for ibex', which gives access to Lahul and good views of some of the highest peaks of the Chandrabhaga (CB) group notably CB 14, 16 and 17 that lie immediately opposite the Kunzum La to the west, while to the southeast is the Karcha Peak (6,271 m). The pass has an ancient chorten marker. The temple to **Gyephang**, the presiding deity, is circumambulated by those crossing the pass; the giver of any offering in cash which sticks to the stone image receives special blessing.

The road does 19 hairpin bends to descend down the rock strewn terrain to the valley of the river Chandra to **Batal**, and on to **Chhota Dhara** and **Chhatru** (both have 2-room PWD *Rest Houses*), and **Gramphoo** joining the Manali-Keylong-Leh highway (3 hrs journey from the pass), see page 215. Gramphoo is 62 km from Manali.

Shimla to Kullu Valley

Bilaspur used to be the centre of a district in which the tribal Daora peoples panned in the silts of the Beas and Sutlej for gold. Their main source, the Seer Khud, has now been flooded by the Bhakra Nangal Lake, and they have shifted their area of search upstream. **Eating** *Lake View Café*, with clean toilets.

Bilaspur
Colour map 1, grid C3
Population: 10,600

The dam on the river **Sutlej**, is one of the highest dams in the world at 225 m and was built as part of the Indus Waters Treaty between India and Pakistan (1960).

Bhakra-Nangal Dam

The Treaty allocated the water of the rivers Sutlej, Beas and Ravi to India. The dam provides electricity for Punjab, Haryana and Delhi. It is also the source for the Rajasthan Canal project, which takes water over 1,500 km south to the Thar desert. **Sleeping D** *Kadamba Tourist Complex* (Punjab Tourism), near Main Market, Nangal, T2122. 16 rooms, some a/c, dorm, restaurant, beer bar, garden. **D** *Motel* (Punjab Tourism), is at **Abub Sahar**.

The town along the main bus route has reasonably priced guesthouses and small hotels near the bus station. **Sleeping D-E** *Maya Deluxe*. Range of rooms (some a/c), large and clean, decent food (but staff walk in without knocking)

Una

Ghanahatti (18 km) has the adequate *Monal Restaurant*. There are some magnificent views, sometimes across intensively cultivated land, sometimes through plantations of chilgoza, khir and other species. In **Shalaghat Sleeping D** *Mehman* and restaurant occupies an extraordinarily bold setting. **Darla Ghat** is now quite a bustling town, its modern prosperity based on the cement works. 4 km before Darlaghat **D** *Baghal* (Himachal Tourism), T01796-48116, 16 rooms, restaurant. A Punjabi *dhaba* 2 km east of Darla Ghat offers snacks and meals.

The road descends into a deep valley before climbing again to the small market town of **Bhararighat**. A jeep can take over 2 hrs for this part of the journey. In **Brahmpukar** the road to Beri and Mandi is a very attractive country lane. The more heavily used though still quiet road to the main Bilaspur-Manali road joins it at Ghaghas. **NB** During the monsoons landslides on the NH 21 may result in very long delays. Carry plenty of water and some food .

Routes

Ghaghas (Ghagus) is a small but important junction town, standing on a deep ravine. **Sleeping D-E** *Chiterkoot*, by the bridge, T4196, reasonable restaurant and bar. There are a couple of tea shops nearby.

Ghaghas
Colour map 1, grid C3

The huge limsetone quarries and cement factory at Barmana, with a capacity of 10,000 bags a day, are serviced by hundreds of heavy lorries, sometimes causing long queues. The road runs along the left bank of the Sutlej just before the river enters the huge Govind Sagar.

Routes

The tree-lined and attractive approach to the town from the south gives some indication of the town's rapid growth and prosperity. **Sleeping D** *Relax Inn*, on Mandi side of town, modern, clean; *Chinar Restaurant*, on NH21, south of centre is modern and decent. North of Sundernagar the road passes through the small lorry halt and repair town of **Ner Chowk** before continuing to Mandi. The *Roadside Milk Bar*, 8 km south of Mandi serves excellent milkshakes.

Sundernagar
Colour map 1, grid C3
Population: 21,000
Altitude: 1,174 m

Himachal Pradesh

★ *Dasara in Kullu*

Dasara celebrates Rama's victory over the demon Ravana. From their various high mountain homes about 360 gods come to Kullu, drawn in their raths (chariots) by villagers to pay homage to Raghunathji who is ceremoniously brought from his temple in Kullu.

The goddess Hadimba, patron deity of the Kullu Rajas has to come before any other lesser deities are allowed near. Her chariot is the fastest and her departure marks the end of the festivities. All converge on the maidan on the first evening of the festival in a long procession

accompanied by shrill trumpeters. Thereafter there are dances, music and a market. During the high point of the fair a buffalo is sacrificed in front of a jostling crowd. Jamlu, the village God of Malana, high up in the hills, follows an old tradition. He watches the festivities from across the river, but refuses to take part! (see page 218). On the last day Raghunathji's rath is taken to the river bank where a small bonfire is lit to symbolize the burning of Ravana, before Ragunathji is returned to his temple in a wooden palanquin.

Mandi (Sahor) मण्डी

Phone code: 01905
Colour map 1, grid C3
Population: 23,000
Altitude: 760 m

Founded by a Rajput prince in circa 1520, Mandi is held sacred by both Hindus and Buddhists. The old town with the main bazar is huddled on the left bank of the Beas at the southern end of the Kullu Valley, just below its junction with the Uhl River. The Beas bridge is across Sukheti Khad at the east end of town. The main bus station is just above an open playing field. It is worth stopping a night in this quaint town with 81 temples, a 17th-century palace and a colourful bazar.

Sights The **Triloknath Temple** (1520) on the river bank, built in the Nagari style with a tiled roof, has a life-size three-faced Siva image (Lord of three worlds), riding a bull with Parvati on his lap. It is at the centre of a group of 13th-16th century sculpted stone shrines. The Kali Devi statue which emphasizes the natural shape of the stone, illustrates the ancient Himalayan practice of stone worship.

The **Panchavaktra Temple** at the confluence of the Beas and a tributary with views of the Trilokinath, has a five-faced image (*Panchanana*) of Siva. The image is unusually conceived like a temple *shikhara* on an altar plinth. Note the interesting frieze of yogis on a small temple alongside.

The **Bhutnath Temple** (circa 1520) by the river in the town centre is the focus at *Sivaratri* festival (see below). The modern shrines nearby are brightly painted.

In lower **Sumkhetar**, west of the main bazar is the 16th-century **Ardhanarishvara Temple** where the Siva image is a composite male/female form combining the passive Siva (right) and the activating energy of Parvati (left). Although the *mandapa* is ruined, the carvings on the *shikhara* tower and above the inner sanctum door, are particularly fine.

From the old suspension bridge on the Dharamshala road, if you follow a narrow lane up into the main market, you will see the slate roof over a deep spring which is the **Mata Kuan Rani Temple**, dedicated to the 'Princess of the Well'. The story of this Princess of Sahor (Mandi) and her consort **Padmasambhava** (who introduced Mahayana Buddhism in Tibet), describes how the angry king condemned the two to die in a fire which raged for seven days and when the smoke cleared a lake appeared with a lotus – Rewalsar or *Tso Pema* (Tibetan 'Lotus Lake').

Rewalsar Lake (*phone code*: 01905) The small dark lake, 24 km southeast, with **Excursions** its floating reed islands is a popular pilgrimage centre. The colourful Tibetan Buddhist monastery was founded in the 14th century though the pagoda-like structure is late 19th century. The Gurudwara commemorates Guru Gobind Singh's stay here. Start early for the hilltop temples by the transmission tower as it is a steep and hot climb. The *Sisu* fair is held in February/March. **Sleeping and eating** E *Rawalsar Inn* (Himachal Tourism), on high ground with views, T80252, 13 rooms with bath, dorm (Rs 75). F *Peace Memorial Inn.* Clean rooms, some with bath (Rs 130), friendly. *Gomush Tibetan Restaurant*, near Gompa, does excellent momos. Other *dhabas* are by the bus terminal. **Transport** Buses from Mandi, one hour, Rs 12.

Prashar The three-tiered pagoda **Rishi temple** by a sacred lake is in a basin surrounded by high mountains with fantastic views of the Pir Panjal range. Dedicated to a deified Vedic sage, the rich woodcarvings here suggest a date earlier than the Manali Dhungri Temple (1553) which is not as fine. No smoking, alcohol or leather items are allowed near the temple or lake. **Sleeping and eating** Basic *Pilgrim Rest Houses*, drinking water from the lake. *Forest Rest House*, 1 km west of temple. **Transport** Daily bus to **Kataula** (20 km, with an attractive pagoda temple), and onto Bagi (8 km). Follow a steep trail through the forest of rhododendron, oak, deodar and *kail* (three hours). After arriving at a group of large shepherd huts the trail to the left goes to the temple, the right to the *Forest Rest House*.

Aut (see below) You can walk to Aut from Prashar in six to seven hours. A level trail east crosses a col in under 1 km; take the good path down to the right side of the nullah (valley) and cross the stream on a clear path. Climb a little and then follow a broad path on the left bank to the road. Turn right and down to Peon village in the Chir nullah and continue to Aut.

D *Ashoka Holiday Inn*, near Chohatta Bazar, Gandhi Chowk, T22800. Reasonable **Sleeping** rooms, restaurant. **D** *Mandav* (Himachal Tourism), above Main Bus Stand, T35503, F35551. 13 clean rooms with bath (cheaper in annexe), 2 **C** a/c, restaurant, beer, good value. **D** *Mayfair*, Seri Bazar, T22570. 60 a/c or air-cooled rooms with bath, restaurant, exchange. **D** *Munish Resorts*, on hillside 3 km from Main Bus Stand, T22330, above New Beas Bridge (Rs 30 by taxi from bus stand). Clean rooms with bath (need revamp), restaurant, lovely views, colourful garden with tempting fruit (signed 'do not pick!'), friendly family, personal attention. **D** *Standard*, opposite Old Bus Stand, Main Bazar, T22948. 15 rooms with bath, restaurant, terrace garden. **D-E** *Raj Mahal*, near Court, Main Bazar, T22401, F62308. 16 rooms, deluxe rooms with bath (sharpened sword in one might be mistaken for a towel rail!), 4 'special' rooms, period furniture and paintings, others **F**, former 'Palace' has character but in need of attention, decent restaurant, bar, garden temple with huge old Mahadev statue, a fine example of Pahari art – "like staying at a great aunt's", run by the polite 'raja'. In town: **D-F** *Evening Plaza*, opposite old bus stand. 11 rooms, some a/c, changes money at a good rate. **E** *Beas Guest House*, near bus stand, T23409. 4 rooms, cheap dorm. **F** *Adarsh*, adequate rooms with bath. *Shiva* and *Standard* are filthy.

Himachal Tourism *Café Shiraz*, near Bhutnath Temple. *Raj Mahal.* Quiet, peaceful **Eating** (interesting photos and antiques), pleasant garden, good value but surly waiters.

Feb/Mar *Sivaratri Fair*, a week of dance, music and drama as temple deities from sur- **Festivals** rounding hills are taken in procession with chariots and palanquins to visit the Madho Rai and Bhutnath Temples.

Shopping *Indra Bazar* below the palace is a modern shopping centre. *Handicrafts*: near Bhutnath Temple and in Seri Bazar.

Transport **Bus**: Chandigarh (203 km, 5 hrs); **Delhi**; **Dharamshala**; **Manali** (4 hrs, Rs 55); **Shimla** (5½ hrs, Rs 100). Book private buses in town or opposite the bus stand at least **one day in advance**; they do not originate in Mandi. **Taxi**: Rs 300 to **Kullu**. **Trains** Jogindernagar (55 km) is on the narrow gauge from Pathankot.

Directory **Banks** *Bank of Baroda*, Hospital Rd, in the old town centre, can take over an hour to change Visa; *Indian Overseas Bank* changes TCs. *Evening Plaza Hotel* is the only place to change cash (see above). **NB** Mandi has one of the few banks in Himachal able to give cash on Master/Visa cards.

Tirthan Valley and Jalori Pass

From Mandi the **NH21** runs east then south along the left bank of the Beas, much diminished in size by the dam at **Pandoh** (19 km) from which water is channelled to the Sutlej. The dam site is on a spectacular meander of the Beas (photography strictly prohibited). The NH21 crosses over the dam to the right bank of the Beas then follows the superb **Larji gorge**, in which the Beas now forms a lake for a large part of the way upstream to Aut. At **Aut**, pronounced 'out', there is trout fishing (best, March and April). The tourist office issues licences. The main bazar road has a few cheap hotels and eating places. From Aut, a road branches off across the Beas into the **Tirthan Valley** climbing through beautiful wooded scenery with deodar and larch up to the Jalori Pass. Allow at least 1½ hours by jeep to **Shoja** (42 km) and another 30 minutes to Jalori.

Banjar, with attractive wood fronted shops lining the narrow street, has the best examples in the area of timber bonded Himalayan architecture in the fort-like rectangular temple of Murlidhar (Krishna). Half way to **Chaini** (3 km), the large Shring Rishi temple to the deified local sage is very colourful with beautiful wooden balconies and an impressive 45 m tall tower which was damaged in the last earthquake. The entrance, 7 m above ground, is reached by climbing a notched tree trunk. Such free standing temple towers found in eastern Tibet, were sometimes used for defence and incorporated into Thakur's castles in the western Himalaya. The fortified villages here even have farmhouses like towers. **Sleeping** **F** PWD *Guest House* in Banjar. From Banjar the road climbs increasingly steeply through **Jibhi** (9 km). **Sleeping** **F** *Doli Guest House*, rooms with bath, restaurant (fresh brown bread), knowledgeable owner, Mr BS Rana organizes local treks with guides (Rs 200 per day).

Ghayaghi is 2 km beyond. **Sleeping** **F** *Gulbahar* guesthouse, also rooms in family house. **Transport** The last few kilometres above Jibhi are extremely steep and narrow, though astonishingly, local buses ply the route. Bus to Jalori can take one hour (Rs 5). Some go via Ghayaghi (approximate times): Kulla-Bagipul, 0800; Manali-Rampur, 1000; Kullu-Dalash, 1100; Manali-Ani, 1100. If heading for Shimla or Kinnaur, change buses at Sainj on NH22.

In **Shoja Sleeping** **D** *Lamergier's Camp*, with self-contained tents, hot showers and toilets (basic two-person tent Rs 150), dining tent, treks and mountain biking, contact Snowflakes, Shimla, T0177-213535 or North West Safaries, Ahmadabad, T079-441511. **F** *Forest Rest House* enjoys a spectacular and isolated position just below the Jalori Pass, reserve in advance.

Jalori Pass A ruined fort sits high to the west of the pass and from the meadows there are
Altitude: 3,350 m fantastic views, especially of the Pir Panjal range. It is a metalled road, most suitable for four-wheel drive vehicles. ■ *Only open in good weather, from*

Himachal Pradesh

mid-Apr. You may wish to take the bus up to the Pass and walk down, or even camp one night at the Pass.

There is a very pleasant, gradual walk, 5 km east, through woodland (one hour), starting at the path to the right of the temple. It is easy to follow. **Sereuil Lake** ('Pure Water'), is where local women worship Burhi Nagini Devi (snake goddess) and walk around the lake pouring a line of *ghee*.

Sleeping and eating Dhabas provide simple refreshments and one has 2 very basic cheap rooms at the Pass. Camping possible. **Transport Road** A bus from Ani and Khanag to the south, runs to the Pass and back. 4 buses daily traverse the pass in each direction when it is open (8-9 months). See Ghayaghi above. Bus to Sainj, 3½ hrs, and on to Shimla, 5 hrs.

The park (60,561 ha) and sanctuary (6,825 ha) (*altitude*: 1,500-5,800 m) lie southeast of Kullu town in the Seraj Forest Division, an area bounded by mountain ridges (except to the west) and watered by the upper reaches of the rivers Jiwa, Sainj and Tirthan. The National Park, created in 1984, has its headquarters in Shamshi. The hills are covered in part by dense forest of blue pine, deciduous broadleaved and fir trees and also shrubs and grassland; thickets of bamboo make it impenetrable in places. Attractive species of iris, frittilaria, gagea and primula are found in the high altitude meadows. Wildlife include the panther, Himalayan black bear, brown bear, tahr, goral and bharal. The rich birdlife includes five species of pheasant.

Great Himalayan National Park & Tirthan Sanctuary

Himachal Pradesh

★ The Kullu Valley: Valley of the Gods

The Beas Valley was the gateway to Lahul for the Central Asian trade in wool and borax. It is enclosed to the north by the Pir Panjal range, to the west by the Bara Bangahal and to the east by the Parvati range. The approach is through a narrow funnel or gorge but in the upper part it extends outwards. The name Kullu is derived from Kulantapith 'the end of the habitable world'. It is steeped in Hindu religious tradition, every stream, rock and blade of grass seemingly imbued with some religious significance.

History For a long time the **Kullu Kingdom** was restricted to the upper Beas Valley. The original capital was at Jagatsukh, 5 km to the south of Manali. In the 15th century it was extended south to Mandi. In the 17th century the capital was shifted to Kullu and the kingdom's boundaries extended into Lahul and Spiti and as far east as the Sutlej. Kullu was strategically located on trade routes from North India to Ladakh and beyond, so was bound to attract outside interest. The Sikhs, for example, contested Kullu's control of this section of the trade route. In 1847, Kullu came under British control and was governed from Dharamshala.

Kullu कुल्लू

Phone code: 01902
Colour map 1, grid B3
Population: 14,500
Altitude: 1,219 m

Sprawling along the grassy west bank of the Beas, Kullu, the district headquarters, hosts the dramatically colourful Dasara festival. Less commercialized than its neighbour Manali, it is known across India as the home of apple growing.

Ins & outs **Getting there** Bhuntar airport, 10 km south, has flights from Delhi, Shimla and Ludhiana; transfer by bus or taxi. For buses from the south, get off at Dhalpur Bus Stand if you choose a nearby hotel. **Getting around** The Main Bus Stand and Dhalpur with ample hotels and restaurants are close enough for walking. Buses and taxis go to nearby sights. **Best time to visit** Climate: Mid-Sep-mid-Nov are the best seasons. May and Jun are hot but offer good trekking options. Mar-mid-Apr can be cold with occasional heavy rain.

Sights The bulky curvilinear temples seem to resemble the huge boulders found in river beds and on hillsides. A peculiar feature of the Nagari temples is the umbrella-shaped covering made of wood or zinc sheets placed over and around the *amalaka* stone at the top of the spire.

The **Raghunathji Temple** is the temple of the principal god of the Dasara festival. The shrine houses an image of Shri Raghunath (brought here from Ayodhya in circa 1657), in his chariot. **Bhekhli**, a 3 km climb away, has excellent views from the **Jagannathi Temple**. The copper 16th-17th-century mask of the Devi inside has local Gaddi tribal features while the copper one shows Rajasthani influence. The wall painting of Durga is in traditional folk style.

There are also superb views on the steep but poorly marked climb to the tiny **Vaishno Devi Temple**, 4 km north, on Kullu-Manali road, where a small cave has an image of the goddess Vaishno.

Bijli Mahadev, 11 km from Kullu at 2,435 m, is being connected by road all the way. There should only be a 2 km walk up steps from the road head. The temple on a steep hill has a 20 m rod on top which is reputedly struck by *bijli* (lightning), shattering the stone *lingam* inside. The priests put the lingam together each time with *ghee* (clarified butter) and a grain mixture until the next strike breaks it apart again. ■ *Getting there: several buses until late afternoon from Left Bank Bus Stand. The road to Bijli is very rough and the buses are in a poor state.*

Excursions

    Bajaura Temple on the banks of the Beas River, about 200 m off the NH21 at **Hat** (Hatta), is one of the oldest in the valley. The massive pyramidal structure is magnificently decorated with stone images of Vishnu, Ganesh and Mahishasuramardini (Durga as the Slayer of the Buffalo Demon, see page 367) in the outer three-sided shrines. The last is beautifully composed. The slender bodies, elongated faces and limbs suggest East Indian Pala influence. Floriated scrollwork decorate the exterior walls. Inside this Siva temple is a large *yoni-lingam*.

A *Apple Valley Resorts*, Mohal, NH21, on the Beas River, 6 km from airport, T22310, F24116. 36 comfortable, very well designed modern chalets in landscaped grounds, excellent food, friendly reception, rafting nearby. **C** *Silver Moon* (Himachal Tourism), perched on a hill, 2 km south of centre, T22488 (taxis Rs 50 from Kullu centre, buses stop at gate if requested – ask for the last barrier south out of Kullu). 6 rooms with bath and heaters, each with a small sitting room in traditional style, very clean, good food, once the State Guest House it still has character, pleasant staff, possibly enhanced because Mahatma Gandhi stayed here. **C** *Vaishali*, Gandhinagar, 1 km south of bus stand No 2, T24425, F23073. 33 rooms, excellent restaurant, modern immaculate kitchen, pleasant small garden running down to river, now expanding, near Institution of Meditation and Swami Shyam Ashram, rafting 4 km south. **C-D** *Sarwari* (Himachal Tourism), 10 mins' walk south of Dhalpur Bus Stand, T22471. 16 rooms (10 in more spacious wing), 8-bed dorm (Rs 75), good value restaurant, beer, pleasant gardens, elevated with good views, peaceful. **C-D** *Shobla*, T22800. 25 rooms, central, clean, pleasant atmosphere, airy restaurant, overlooking river.

Sleeping
■ *on map*
Price codes:
see inside front cover

The choice is widening, some good accommodation in all ranges, though very full during Dasara. Large off-season discounts (30-50%)

D-E *Aaditya*, Lower Dhalpur, on river bank, T24263. Decently furnished rooms with bath (hot shower), some with river-facing balcony, others cheaper, smart, room service meals, bar. **D-E** *Ramneek*, Dhalpur, just west of taxi stand, T24449. 21 clean rooms with bath (hot water), TV, decently maintained. **E** *Bijleshwar View*, near Tourist Office, T22857. Rooms with fireplace, TV, bath (hot water), only moderately clean, restaurant, peaceful garden, friendly. **E** *Madhu Chandrika*, near Lower Dhalpur Bazar, T24395, F22720. Rooms and dorm, quiet area. **E** *Rohtang*, Dhalpur, T22303. 12 rooms with bath, restaurant (Indian, Chinese), simple, clean and good value. **E-F** *Kullu Valley Hotel*, Akhara Bazar, T22223. Rooms with TV, phone, bath tub, restaurant.

In hotels *Shobla* has a pleasant restaurant (serves beer). *Vaishali's* a/c *Shabnam*, is excellent. *Silver Moon* and *Rohtang* are recommended. *Ashiyana*, Sarvari Bazar. Clean, good south Indian. Recommended. *Hot Stuff Food Junction*, near tourist information. Good for snacks, light meals, outdoor seating. *Monal Café*, near tourist office. Simple meals. *Sapna Sweets*, Akhara Rd. Good for snacks early in the day.

Eating
● *on map*
Price codes:
see inside front cover

End-Apr Colourful 3-day *Cattle Fair* attracts villagers from the surrounding area. Numerous cultural events accompany. *Dasara* is sacred to the goddess Durga which, elsewhere in India, tends to be overshadowed by *Diwali* which follows a few weeks

Festivals

Himachal Pradesh

later. In this part of the Himalaya it is a great social event and a get-together of the Gods. Every village has a deity, and they all come to Kullu.

Shopping Best buys are shawls, caps, *gadmas*. The state weaving co-operative, *Bhutti Weavers Colony*, 6 km south, has retail outlets, *Bhuttico*; one store 2 km south of *Apple Valley Resorts*. Akhara Bazar has a *Govt Handicrafts Emporium*, *Himachal Khadi Emporium* and *Khadi Gramudyog*. *Charm Shilp* is good for sandals.

Transport **Air** A bank is open at flight times. Transport to town: buses and taxis at the airport. **Jagson**, Dhalpur Maidan, T66187, Apt T65303, to **Delhi, Shimla**, flights often cancelled. *Trans Bharat*: Delhi, twice weekly. **Road** **Bus**: Main Bus Stand, Sarvari Khad with a booking office: for long distance and to **Manali**; Left Bank Bus Stand across the bridge (from town, turn east at sign for *Gupta Shawls/Municipal Resthouse*, opposite telegraph office): buses for **Naggar** (half hourly in summer, Rs 14) and **Bijli Mahadev**; some go to **Manali**; Dhalpur Bus Stand for buses to the south but board these at the Main Bus Stand to be sure of a seat. HP Tourism deluxe bus to **Chandigarh** (270 km), 0700, 8 hrs, Rs 250; **Delhi** (512 km) 15 hrs, government and *HP Tourism* are better than some private ones, leaves Delhi 1600, Rs 400 (a/c Rs 600); **Dharamshala**, 0800-0900, 8 hrs, Rs 200; **Shimla** (235 km), 0800, 8 hrs, Rs 225. Tickets from Tourist Office. Most buses coming to Kullu continue to **Manali**. **Taxi**: opposite Dhalpur Bus Stand.

Kullu

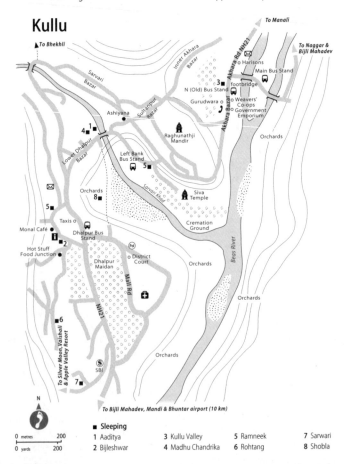

■ Sleeping			
1 Aaditya	3 Kullu Valley	5 Ramneek	7 Sarwari
2 Bijleshwar	4 Madhu Chandrika	6 Rohtang	8 Shobla

Banks *State Bank of Patiala* (1100-1400), Akhara Bazar (north of town) for foreign exchange (cash and TCs only); not at *State Bank of India*, off NH21, south of town. Nearest Visa exchange at Mandi. **Communications** Near petrol pump, Akhara Bazar. International fax only; sign "send a fax and relax"! – bureaucratic office, takes time. **Tour companies & travel agents** *Look East*, c/o Bajaj Autos, Manikaran Chowk, Shamshi, T65771, recommended for river rafting and bike hire. *Harisons*, Akhara Bazar, T24893, has had some bad reports. **Tourist offices** *Himachal*, T22349, near Maidan, 1000-1700, local maps available, very helpful officer, advises on exchange.

Directory

★ Parvati Valley

The Parvati (Parbati) valley runs northeast from Bhuntar. Attractive orchards and the fresh green of terraced rice cultivation line the route. Known for its hot springs at Manikaran, more recently the valley has become infamous with reported cases of missing travellers. Posters of the missing are everywhere. ■ *Getting there: several local buses (and jeep taxis), travel daily to the valley from Kullu via Bhuntar, taking about 2 hrs to Manikaran, which also has buses from Manali. It is best not to travel alone.*

Take special care as the area is prone to landslides & flash floods. The intense cultivation of narcotics attracts a large influx of interested travellers

Jari, is at the point where the deep Malana Nala joins the Parvati River. It is a popular resting place for trekkers but also for drug users. The guest houses vary; a few away from the village centre have better views.

Jari

Kasol is en route to Manikaran. The quiet little village has spread on both sides of the road bridge which crosses a tributary that flows into the Parvati not far from the village itself. About half a kilometre beyond the village, a narrow side road leads to the river and the location of a fine hot spring on the river bank. **Sleeping E** *Tourist Huts* (Himachal Tourism), 3 rooms, no catering. Many long stay visitors congregate in the cheap guest houses here. **Chhalal** is a 20-minute walk from Kasol. It is a quiet village where families take in guests. See also Malana Valley Treks (page 219).

Kasol
Colour map 1, grid B3

Manikaran is at the bottom of a dark gorge with **hot sulphur springs** emerging from the rock strewn banks of the Parvati. The local legend describes how while Parvati bathed in the river, Naga, the serpent god stole her *manikaran* (earrings). At Siva's command Naga angrily blew them back from underground causing a spring to flow. Hindu and Sikh pilgrims come to the Rama temple and the gurdwara and gather to cook their food by the springs, purportedly the hottest in the world. There are separate baths for men and women. Short treks go to Pulga and Khirganga beyond while a footpath (affected by landslips in places), leads to the Pin Valley in Spiti. Manikaran, though not attractive in itself, provides a brief halt for trekkers. It has also become a popular place for dropouts. **Sleeping D** *Parvati* (Himachal Tourism), near the temple, T01902-73735, 10 simple rooms, sulphur baths, restaurant. A cheaper guest house on the square has clean rooms. Local families also take paying guests. **Eating** The Sikh Gurudwara does excellent meals, steam cooked at the springs (donation only). There are wayside stalls serving local food, while some near the springs cater for Westerners.

Manikaran
45 km from Kullu

Pulga, a noisy village, seemingly overrun by giggling children, is in a beautiful location with some cheap guest houses. It is a good four hour walk east of Manikaran, though the new road will make it possible to get here by four-wheel drive. **Sleeping and eating** Some longstay travellers prefer the basic airy guest houses outside the village proper which offer meals. **F** *Trimurti* is recommended. Avoid *Rama Guest House* where some rooms are dark and

Pulga

Himachal Pradesh

A Russian in the Kullu Valley

Nicholas Roerich was born in St Petersburg in 1874. In Russia he achieved great renown as an artist and set and costume designer.

Roerich travelled to Sikkim and Bhutan where, while researching Buddhist manuscripts and planning his mammoth expedition across Central Asia, he began to paint the Himalaya. In 1929 he returned to India and settled in Naggar where the family set up the Uruswati Institute of Himalayan Research and where he lived until his death in December 1947.

cramped. *Paradise Restaurant*, in the village, does great vegetarian dishes. Also has information on guides and equipment for treks up the valley and over the Pin-Parvati Pass (5,300 m). If you are lucky, you may be able to persuade the watchman of the old Forest Rest House to let you in. The 'visitors's registration book' contains entries that date back to the 1930's and include several well known mountaineers who have passed by.

Khirganga Khirganga is along the trek which winds through the lush Parvati valley, east of Pulga. It is known for its sacred ancient hot springs marking the place where Siva is thought to have meditated for 2,000 years. There is an open bathing pool for men and an enclosed pool for women, next to the humble shrine at the source. **Sleeping and eating** A few tents may be hired. *Dhabas* sell vegetarian food.

Kullu to Manali The NH21 continues north along the west side of the Beas. The older road to the east of the river goes through terraced rice fields and endless apple orchards, and is rougher and more circuitous but more interesting. Sections of both roads can be washed away during the monsoon. The NH21 winds out of the centre of Kullu along the right bank of the Beas passing the **Sitaramata Temple**, embedded in the conglomerate cliff. **Raison** (*phone code*: 01902), is a grassy meadow favoured by trekking groups. **Sleeping D** *Adventure Resort* (Himachal Tourism), 4 km north, T40516. 14 camp huts by Beas River, camping, restaurant, peaceful setting.

Katrain
Phone code: 01902
Colour map 1, grid B3

Katrain, in the widest part of the Kullu Valley mid-way between Kullu and Manali, is overlooked by Baragarh Peak (3,325 m). **Sleeping A** *Span Resort*, Kullu-Manali Highway, T40138, F40140. Eight attractive stone cottages with 25 rooms, overlooking the river, sports, riding, good views, trout hatchery nearby ensures good river fishing, very comfortable, but some **C** category facilities. **C** *River Bank*, attractive décor, comfortable rooms. Himachal Tourism's **D** *River View*, T40136, two family rooms with bath, meals, contact tourist office, Kullu, and cheaper **D** *Anglers' Bungalow*, T40136. Seven rooms with baths in four stone cottages and dorm (Rs 50), meals, superb views, spartan inside. Katrain and Naggar, are on opposite sides of the river. Across the bridge at **Patli Kuhl**, the road climbs through apple orchards to Naggar.

★ Naggar
Phone code: 01902
Colour map 1, grid B3

Naggar's (Nagar) interesting castle sits high above Katrain. With a pleasant, unhurried atmosphere, it is a good place to stop a while. It is also an entry for treks to Malana, see page 219.

Sights The **castle** (early 16th century), withstood the earthquake of 1905, and is a fine example of timber-bonded building of West Himalaya. Probably built by Raja Sidh Singh, it was used as a royal residence and state headquarters until the 17th century when the capital was transferred to Sultanpur (see Kullu). It continued as a summer palace until the British arrived in 1846, when it was sold to Major Hay, the first Assistant Commissioner who Europeanized part of it, fitting staircases, fireplaces et cetera. This quaint castle/fort is built round a courtyard with verandahs which have enchanting views over the valley. Extensive renovations have produced fine results, especially in the intricately carved woodwork.

In the first courtyard are several black *barselas* (sati stones) with primitive carvings. Beyond the courtyard and overlooking the valley the **Jagti Pat temple** houses a cracked stone slab measuring 2½ m by 1½ m by 2 m believed to be a piece of Deo Tibba which represents the deity in 'the celestial seat of all the gods'. A priest visits the slab every day.

The small **museum** has some interesting exhibits, including examples of local women's dress and headdress (*pattu* and *thippu*) and folk dance costumes (*chola*). There are also local implements for butter and tea making, and musical instruments like the broad bell horn (*karnal*) and long curled horn (*singa*).

Roerich Art Gallery A short climb from the castle is Nicholas Roerich's old home in a peaceful garden with excellent views. The small museum downstairs has a collection of photos and his distinctive stylized paintings of the Himalayas using striking colours. ■ *Rs 10 (includes Folk Museum). 0900-1300, 1400-1700. Closed Mon.*

Uruswati Institue, uphill from the main house, was set up in 1993. The Himalayan Folk and Tribal Art Museum is well presented, with contemporary art upstairs. One room upstairs is devoted to a charming collection of Russian traditional costumes, dolls, musical instruments. ■ *Rs 15.*

There are a number of **temples** around the castle including the 11th-century **Gauri Shankar Siva** near the bazar, with some fine stone carving. Facing the castle is the **Chaturbhuj** to Vishnu. Higher up, the wooden **Tripura Sundari** with a multi-level pagoda roof in the Himachal style celebrates its fair around mid-May. Above that is the **Murlidhar Krishna** at Thawa, claimed as the oldest in the area which has a beautifully carved stone base. Damaged in the 1905 earthquake, it is now well restored. There are fine mountain views from here.

Sleeping C-D *Castle* (Heritage Hotel), T47816. A guest house and then a hotel since 1978, 14 rooms (vary), stylish but traditional decor and furniture, comfortable beds, fireplaces, modernized baths, best **B** overlook valley, some share bath (**E**), dorm (Rs 75), "beautifully renovated, enchanting", restaurant, good service. **D-E** *Sheetal*, Roerich Marg near Castle, T47819. 10 very pleasant rooms with bath, overlooking valley, clean and spacious, use of kitchen. **E** *Ragini*, T47855, F47793. 9 smart rooms with modernized baths (hot water), some Rs 450, nice décor, large windows, good views from rooftop restaurant, good value. **E-F** *Poonam Mountain Lodge*, T47747. Spotless rooms, constant hot water, very good food, but avoid insistence on booking treks. **E-F** *Snow View*, down steps past Tripura Sundari Temple, T47735, rooms and restaurant, weaving co-op outlet. **F** *Alliance*, 200m above Castle, T47763. 6 rooms, hot water, meals, clean, simple, homely, very good value. **F** *Chand Kulvi*, near Bus Stand, T47713. 8 rooms, some with bath, away from road, lovely garden. **F** *Uttam*, near bus stand. Pleasant clean rooms with hot shower.

Eating *Chandrakhani Himalayan Health Food*, Roerich Marg, above Tripura Sundari temple. Serves local food – millet, brown rice, tofu, fresh pasta and cheese. *Nightingale* 200m above bus stand, does trout. *Ristorante Italiano*, bus stand. Open in season, Fri-Sun.

Freedom walking

'Freedom' walking, popular in Nepal, is not really feasible here and porters and/or horses are required; these are not always easily available and prices fluctuate considerably. A good arrangement is to go on an organized trek with a group. You can do it independently but it requires greater planning. The trek into or from Zanskar is only recommended for the vigorously fit.

The area is becoming littered with rubbish so please take care when disposing of litter.

Trekking For Malana, it is best to employ a local guide. Pawan, from the old *chai* shop in the main village, is recommended. Avoid *Poonam's*.

Transport The **bus** stop is in the Bazar, below the castle. Daily bus between Kullu and Manali via Naggar by the scenic east bank route; Kullu and Manali (1½ hrs each, Rs 5). Manali to Patli Kuhl (6 km from Naggar, 45 mins, Rs 10); where you can get a local bus (half hourly in summer), rickshaw (Rs 60).

Routes Travelling on the old road 5 km south of Manali, is **Jagatsukh**, the capital of Kullu before Naggar. There are some old stone temples just above the road including one of the late 13th century.

★ Manali

Phone code: 01902
Colour map 1, grid B3
Population: 2,600
Altitude: 1,926 m

Manali occupies the valley with the once unspoilt Old Village to the north and Vashisht, up on the opposite hillside across the river. Set amidst picturesque apple orchards, Manali is packed with Pahari-speaking Kullus, Lahaulis, Nepali labourers and enterprising Tibetan refugees who have opened guest houses, restaurants and craft shops. The town has become increasingly built-up with dozens of new hotel blocks. It is also a major tourist destination for Indian holidaymakers. Others, together with adventure seeking foreigners, are attracted by the culturally different hill people and the scenic treks this part of the Himalaya offers. It is the start of the recommended two-day road route to Leh in the summer months.

Ins & outs   **Getting there** Bhuntar airport (near Kullu) is 50 km away with bus and taxi transfers. The Bus and Taxi Stands are right in the centre of Manali town, within easy reach of some budget hotels though many upmarket ones are a taxi ride away. **Getting around** Manali and the area around, though hilly, is ideal for walking. For journeys outside, taxi rates are high. **Climate** Best season is Mar-Apr, but can have occasional heavy rain and be cold with snow in the villages. May-Jun offer better trekking; also post monsoon mid-Sep-mid-Nov.

The town
Manali is named after Manu, the Law Giver, who legend tells arrived here by boat when fleeing from a great flood centuries ago

The **Tibetan Monastery** built by refugees, is not old but is attractive and is the centre of a small carpet making industry. Rugs and other handicrafts are for sale. The colourful **bazar** sells Kullu shawls, caps and Tibetan souvenirs.

Old Manali is 3 km away, across Manalsu Nala. The road from newer Manali crosses Manalsu Nala and climbs uphill and through the virtually unspoilt village and continues to a 'new' Hindu temple (visitors may have to abandon their aged rickshaws and walk up part of the hill). The last few years have seen continuing building work in the lower reaches of the village. Higher up, newer guest houses mingle with attractive old farmsteads with wooden balconies and thick stone tiled roofs. While out of season Old Manali retains a

Manali

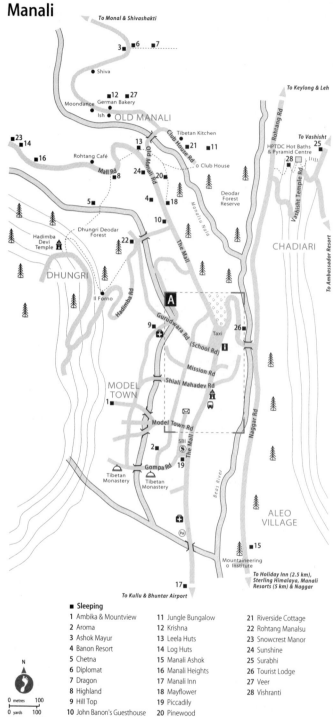

To Monal & Shivashakti

Shiva

Moondance
German Bakery
Ish

OLD MANALI

Tibetan Kitchen

To Keylong & Leh

To Vashisht

HPTDC Hot Baths
& Pyramid Centre

Rohtang Café

Mall Rd

o Club House

Deodar
Forest
Reserve

CHADIARI

Hadimba Devi
Temple

Dhungri Deodar
Forest

DHUNGRI

Il Forno

Hadimba Rd

To Ambassador Resort

A

Gurudwara Rd

(School Rd)

Taxi

Mission Rd

Shiali Mahadev Rd

MODEL
TOWN

Naggar Rd

Model Town Rd

SBI

Gompa Rd

Tibetan
Monastery

Tibetan
Monastery

Beas River

ALEO
VILLAGE

Pol

Mountaineering
o Institute

To Holiday Inn (2.5 km),
Sterling Himalaya, Manali
Resorts (5 km) & Naggar

To Kullu & Bhuntar Airport

N

0 metres   100
0 yards   100

Himachal Pradesh

■ **Sleeping**

1 Ambika & Mountview	11 Jungle Bungalow	21 Riverside Cottage
2 Aroma	12 Krishna	22 Rohtang Manalsu
3 Ashok Mayur	13 Leela Huts	23 Snowcrest Manor
4 Banon Resort	14 Log Huts	24 Sunshine
5 Chetna	15 Manali Ashok	25 Surabhi
6 Diplomat	16 Manali Heights	26 Tourist Lodge
7 Dragon	17 Manali Inn	27 Veer
8 Highland	18 Mayflower	28 Vishranti
9 Hill Top	19 Piccadily	
10 John Banon's Guesthouse	20 Pinewood	

Related map
A Manali centre,
page 185

quiet charm, in the view of some, that is diminished during the tourist season by the arrival of techno music and the drug scene.

Vashisht (2,200 m), is a small hillside village that can be reached by road or a footpath (30-40 minutes' walk from tourist office). Note the carvings on the houses of the wealthy farmers. Below the village, there is a **temple** to Rama and Vashisht, with sulphur springs; remove shoes at the entrance (small fee). Hot springs at the top of the hill lead to free communal baths in the village centre where one washes in other people's dirty water! It can get filthy later in the day so it is best to go early. The HPTDC Bath Complex remained closed in mid-2000. The village with its messy jumble of old village houses and newer buildings has cheap places to stay which attract a new generation of young travellers.

Dhungri Village is at the top of Hadimba Road. Follow the road uphill, past the gates leading to the temple and take the path 50 m further to arrive at the village centre. The village houses have cedar wood carving and balconies with superb views across the valley. Travellers are welcomed into family homes and traditional village life carries on around the guests.

★ **Hadimba Devi Temple** The Dhungri temple (1553), in a clearing among ancient *deodars*, is a 2 km pleasant walk from the tourist office. Built by Maharaja Bahadur Singh, the 27 m high pagoda temple has a three-tier roof and some fine naturalistic wood carving of animals and plants, especially around the doorway. The structure itself is relatively crude, and the pagoda is far from perfectly perpendicular. Massive deodar planks form the roof, but in contrast to the scale of the structure the brass image of the goddess Hadimba inside, is tiny. A legend tells how the God Bhima fell in love with **Hadimba**, the sister of the demon Tandi. Bhima killed Tandi in battle and married Hadimba, whose spirituality, coupled with her marriage to a god led to her being worshipped as a goddess. Today she is seen as an incarnation of Kali.

The small doorway, less than 1 m high, is surrounded by wood-carved panels of animals, mythical beasts, scrolls, a row of foot soldiers and deities, while inside against a natural rock is the small black image of the Devi. To the left is a natural rock shelter where legend has it that Hadimba took refuge and prayed before she was deified. The greatly enlarged footprints imprinted on a black rock are believed to be hers. Hadimba Devi plays a central part in the annual festival in May, at both Kullu and Manali.

To prevent the **master craftsman** producing another temple to equal this elsewhere, the king ordered his right hand to be cut off. The artist is believed to have mastered the technique with his left hand and reproduced a similar work of excellence at Trilokinath in the Pattan Valley. Unfortunately, his new master became equally jealous and had his head cut off, see page 194.

A **feast and sacrifice** is held in mid-July when the image from the new temple in Old Manali is carried to the Hadimba temple where 18 ritual blood sacrifices are performed. Sacrifices include a fish and a vegetable but ends with the beheading of an ox in front of a frenzied crowd. **NB** This ceremony is not for the faint-hearted. Pickpockets are rife, and known to take advantage of awestruck tourists, so take care.

★ **Walks**
Manali is the trail-head for a number of interesting & popular treks. There are also some very pleasant short hikes around Manali

Beyond Old Manali The shepherd trail which winds its way up and down the hillside, allows you to capture a picture of Himalayan life as well as see some superb birdlife. The path starts at some concrete steps on the first hairpin bend along the paved road to Old Manali, or you can pick it up where the road ends and taxis turn around at the top of the hill and continue along the cemented path which turns into a dirt trail, for four to five hours.

Towards Solang In Old Manali Village, take the right fork and then turn left in front of the new temple. This trail is a classic, following the right bank of the Beas River up towards the Solang Valley passing the villages of **Goshal**, **Shanag**, **Buruwa** to **Solang** (2,480 m), a small ski resort with all of 2½ km of runs! You can get tea, biscuits and nuts along the walk and even be tempted by steaming spicy noodles. To return to Manali it is a steady walk down the valley side to the main Rohtang Pass-Manali Highway where you can pick up a bus (Rs 5) or shared jeep (Rs 10).

Beyond the Hadimba Temple Keeping the temple on your right follow the contour of the hill and bear right to pick up a clear pack-horse trail which heads up the steep valley. This is a steady uphill climb through woodland giving superb views of the river below, abundant Himalayan birdlife and a chance to see all manner of activity in the woods (chopping, cutting, burning). Go prepared for cold.

Towards Sethan Take a local bus to the *Holiday Inn* (3 km) on the Naggar road. With the hotel behind you, cross the road and through the orchard and

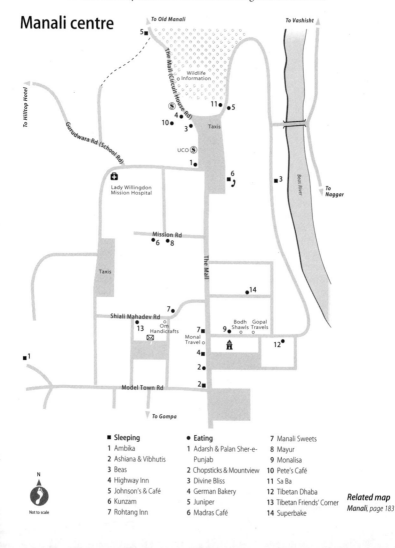

Manali centre

Himachal Pradesh

■ Sleeping	● Eating	7 Manali Sweets
1 Ambika	1 Adarsh & Palan Sher-e-	8 Mayur
2 Ashiana & Vibhutis	Punjab	9 Monalisa
3 Beas	2 Chopsticks & Mountview	10 Pete's Café
4 Highway Inn	3 Divine Bliss	11 Sa Ba
5 Johnson's & Café	4 German Bakery	12 Tibetan Dhaba
6 Kunzam	5 Juniper	13 Tibetan Friends' Corner
7 Rohtang Inn	6 Madras Café	14 Superbake

N

Not to scale

Related map
Manali, page 183

fields which have low mud walls all round which can be walked on. Bear east till you come to a disused track and then bear right and follow it to the once untouched village of **Prini** which now has several five-star hotels! – if you are lucky the *chai* shop will be open. Further east, the trail to Sethan village becomes somewhat in distinct though local people are at hand to point you in the right direction. It is a superb three-hour hike up a wooded valley to Sethan (3,000 m), which is well off the tourist trail. **Nehru Kund** (6 km), is on the Keylong Road.

Beyond Vashisht Walk past the village, up the hillside to a waterfall. About two hours.

Tours **Himachal Tourism**, T52116. Daily, in season by luxury coach or car for five: to Nehru Kund, Rahla Falls, Marhi, Rohtang Pass; to Solang, Jagatsukh and Naggar; 0900-1600, Rs 135 (Rs 700 car); to Manikaran, 0900-1700, Rs 150 (Rs 800 car).

Essentials

Sleeping
■ *on maps,*
pages 183 & 185
Price codes:
see inside front cover

New hotels continue to be built to cater for the heavy demand in season. Hotels are often full, particularly in May and Jun, so better to visit off-season when most offer discounts. Winter heating is a definite bonus. (The helpful Private Hoteliers' Information Centre is near the Taxi Stand).

AL *Holiday Inn*, 2.5 km south of Manali on Naggar Rd, T52262, F52562. Luxury hotel. **AL** *Manali Resorts*, 5 km south of Manali on Kullu Rd, T52274, F52174. 50 rooms, a luxury base for winter sports, Helipad for heli-skiing, lovely position with landscaped gardens by Beas River. **AL** *Snowcrest Manor* (was *Panchratan*) beyond *Log Huts*, T53354, F53188. 30 rooms in modern hotel on steep hillside with great views. **A** *Ambassador Resort*, Sunny Side, Chadiari, overlooking Old Manali, T52235, F52173. 40 rooms, interesting design, good views. **A** *Leela Huts*, Sunshine Orchards,The Mall (N), T52464. Luxury huts, sitting room, kitchen. **A** *Sterling Himalayan Continental*, Prini, Naggar Rd, T53011, F52494. 35 immaculate, very comfortable rooms, airport transfer, taxi Rs 50 from centre, 2½ km.

B *Manali Ashok* (ITDC), Naggar Rd (1.5 km from centre), Aleo, T52331, F53108. 29 rooms and suites with bath, restaurant, quiet with superb views, good value. **B** *Manali Heights*, near Log Huts, T52621, F52618. 27 centrally heated rooms, bath tubs, direct dialling, all comforts, stylish décor. **B** *Manali Inn*, Rangree, south of town, T53551, F52582, puneet@ giardl01.vsnl.net.in 25 comfortable rooms on 5 storeys. **B** *Piccadily*, The Mall, T52152, F52113. 44 rooms, clean, modern though signs of wear, welcoming reception, good restaurant but very slow service. Himachal Tourism's **B-C** *Kunzam*, The Mall (next to Tourist Office), T53197. 47 rooms, restaurant, bar. **B-C** *Log Huts*, top of Circuit House Rd high above Manalsu Nala, T52407, F52325. 2-bedroom cottages, 6 newer and modern, 6 spacious though dated, kitchen, attractive views, cafeteria nearby and room service, peaceful.

D *Aroma*, Model Town, near Tibetan monastery, T52159, F52694. 12 rooms with bath, restaurant. **D** *Ashiana*, T52232. Clean, comfortable rooms with hot shower, good restaurant. **D** *Chetna*, near *Log Huts*, T52624. 13 comfortable rooms with balconies, hot water, good open-air restaurant, lawns, elevated, with beautiful views. **D** *Highland*, near *Log Huts*, T52399. 34 rooms some with balcony, hot showers, restaurant (mainly Chinese), pleasant garden, stone building with bright, clean, comfortable rooms (20 in newer block well-appointed, old block has character). **D** *Highway Inn*, opposite Main Bus Stand, T52200. 22 rooms with bath, restaurant, credit cards. **D** *Rohtang Inn*, opposite Bus Stand, The Mall, T52441. 12 modern rooms, bath tubs, meals.

D *Rohtang Manalsu* (Himachal Tourism), near Circuit House, The Mall, T52332. 27 large rooms, good restaurant, garden, superb views. **D** *Sunshine*, The Mall, T52320. 9 rooms in old traditional house, others in newer cottage, log fires, lot of character, restaurant, lovely garden, peaceful, family atmosphere, friendly, good value. **D-E** *Beas* (Himachal Tourism), near Tourist Office, T52832. 31 rooms with bath, TV, breakfast, room service meals, magnificent river views. **D-E** *Johnson's*, The Mall, near SBI. Fully furnished, kitchen (gas, fridge, etc), full of character, old but clean, orchard gardens, café nearby. **D-E** *Jungle Bungalow*, above Club House (turn right after Manalsu bridge). Clean rooms, common hot shower, good service, friendly, pleasant atmosphere. Recommended.

E *Tourist Lodge*, on river bank. Spartan 4-bed rooms, no towels. **E** *Ambika*, Model Town, T52203, F53993, large and airy rooms with clean bath, mountain views, average meals, use of kitchen, excellent value. **E** *Mountview*, end of Model Town Rd, T52465. Large rooms, shower and Western toilet, some with great views, heater Rs 50, discounts off-season (Rs 200) when restaurant is closed (breakfast and *thalis* only), very secure, friendly and helpful, excellent value. Highly recommended. **E** *Hill Top*, School Rd, T52140. 9 simple rooms, room service. **E** *Snow Lion*, Circuit House Rd. Rooms with bath, room service, helpful staff.

Many cheap hotels on School Rd. Model Town offer modest rooms, often shared baths, some have restaurants, some room service. May only provide hot water in buckets

The Banon family has been in the valley for the last century and now run several guesthouses: **B** *Banon Resort*, New Hope Orchards, The Mall, T52490, F52378. 32 rooms (mostly 1 and 2-bedroom suites) some with good mountain views, grandiose, wood panels and marble, but poor service, reception keener to watch TV, restaurant good in the evening but 'bar' nearby "a raucous den" (now no longer in Banon hands so standards slipping). **B-C** *John Banon's Hotel*, Manali Orchards, T52335, F52392. 12 rooms with snow views (6 newer **B**), full board (good Continental), garden, peaceful, simple, rustic but very pleasant. **D** *Pinewood*, The Mall, T52518. 10 heated rooms, restaurant, gardens, attractive rooms (best upstairs), good views, quiet. **C** *Mayflower*, The Mall, opposite Circuit House, T52104, F52182. 18 rooms, spacious, tastefully decorated wood-panelled suites (cold in winter but log fires fill the room with smoke), no TV, no restaurant. **C-D** *Holiday Home International*, Circuit House Rd, T52010. 16 rooms with good baths, restaurant, good views.

Dhungri Village Many families offer rooms with basic facilities (Rs 50-70). Several are in traditional houses, clean rooms, covered in wood carving, basic bedding, small stove (fuel can be bought), some have balconies with fantastic views. **F** *Freedom Café* takes guests. **F** *Scenic Cottage*, some rooms with baths.

Old Manali Uphill on the village outskirts: **D-E** *Ashok Mayur*, about 300m from bridge (opposite *Shiva Café*). Few comfortable rooms, terrace, restaurant. **D-E** *Dragon*, T52290. Comfortable rooms with bath, traditional construction (wood-bonded stone), internet, fine mountain views, garden, apple orchard. **E-F** *Diplomat*. A newish guest house; **E-F** *Krishna*, T53071. Well established, few simple, clean rooms, some with baths (hot water), good *Blue Diamond* café, verandah with great views of snowy peaks. Beyond the village, along the cemented path: **E-F** *Shivshakti*, T54170. Pleasant, rooms and *café*, friendly farming family, fine views across valley and mountains beyond. **E-F** *Monal*, a little further, up steep cemented steps, on a hilltop. Rooms with hot showers, café, pretty garden, superb views all round. **E-F** *Veer*, T52410. Large rooms, some with bath (bucket hot water), great views, friendly, very good value.

Vashisht **D** *Bhrigu*, just above HPTDC Baths. Comfortable, if dated rooms with bath, some with good views, restaurant. **D** *Valley View*, close by, is similar. **D** *Surabhi* below

Himachal Pradesh

the village. Clean, attractive rooms, modern bath fittings (real tubs!), big windows facing mountains, cable TV, restaurant, exchange, exceptional value off-season (Rs 350). **E-F** *Bodh*, Village Centre, T54165, bunteee23@hotmail.com 5 clean, tidy rooms, shared bath (hot shower), good views from terrace.

Eating

Hotels may need advance notice from non-residents. Some close in the off-season

● *on maps*
Price codes:
see inside front cover

Expensive *Chopsticks* (*Highland Hotel*), The Mall, opposite Bus Stand, T52539. Tibetan, Chinese, Japanese. Very good food, large helpings, very good curd and pancakes, also good breakfast (porridge), friendly, warm (wood-burning stoves), welcoming. *Johnson's Café*, Circuit House Rd. Western (varied menu). Elegant restaurant in a large garden, specializes in trout, excellent home made pasta, good filter coffee, delicious icecreams. Recommended. *Mayur*, Mission Rd. Vast international menu. Excellent food, smart, efficient service, subdued decor, very pleasant with linen table cloths and candles on tables, Indian classical music, great ambience, cosy with wood-burning stove and generator. Highly recommended.

Mid-range *Adarsh*, The Mall (opposite Kunzam). One of many Punjabi places, but has more style and better menu than others. *Juniper*, near Nehru Park. Good Indian, Chinese. *Il Forno*, Hadimba Rd. Italian. Attractive pizzeria, half way up hill. *Italiano*, corner of Mall and Circuit House Rd, 1st Flr. Well cooked selection of pizza, pasta and fish, good value. *Monalisa* in Bazar. International. Renovated in early 2000, friendly, smallish, good choice, popular. *Mountview*, The Mall, opposite Bus Stand. Good Tibetan, Japanese, some Chinese. Unpretentious, pleasant, warm (wood-burning stove), friendly amiable owner. *Sa Ba*, Nehru Park. Mixed. Excellent Indian, snacks, pizzas, cakes, some outdoor seating to people-watch, highly recommended (no toilet). *Vibhuti's*, The Mall, corner of Model Town Rd, up short flight of steps. South Indian vegetarian. Delicious *masala dosas*.

Cheap *Madras Café*, Mission Rd. South Indian. Simple and a bit shabby, veg *thalis* and snacks. *Manali Sweets*, Shiali Mahadev Rd. Excellent Indian sweets (superb *gulab jamuns*!), also good *thalis* (Rs 40). *Mountview*, end of Model Town Rd. Italian, Indian. Good pizzas, spaghetti, opens 0600 for breakfast. *Palan Sher-e-Punjab*, near Taxis, The Mall. Good Punjabi vegetarian. *Tibet Kitchen*, across Manalsu bridge, Club House Rd. Tasty momos, pleasant ambience, friendly service. *Tibetan Dhaba*, back of bus station (behind *Bookworm*). Very small and cosy, great *momos*, bring your own container for "take- away"! *Tibetan Friends' Corner*, behind the post office. Shop with café above. Excellent *momos* and Tibetan dishes, good value. Recommended.

Cafés and fast food *Divine Bliss*, The Mall, opposite Nehru Park, in basement. Cakes (try cainnamon rolls) and vegetarian burgers. *German Bakery*, opposite Nehru Park, has good cakes, breads, real coffee, not cheap but popular. *Peter and Sadhana's Garden Café*, behind German Bakery. Quiches, fresh bread, cakes (try French toast with honey), excellent muesli, good filter coffee, home made jams and peanut butter sold, garden, interesting owner. Try the *chai* stall at the entrance to the NAC market, behind the bus station.

Dhungri Village There is a bakery and restaurant opposite the temple. Stalls sell snacks, drinks and bare necessities. *Green Forest*, on the forest path, past temple down towards Old Manali, just after leaving the forest. Vegetarian. Excellent breakfasts and meals. The path downhill leads to the *Il Forno* Pizzeria.

Old Manali Plenty of Israeli dishes and music which can range from techno to Tibetan. *Tibetan Kitchen* , *German Bakery*, over-the-counter branch, just beyond Manalsu bridge, and left. Reasonably priced cakes, breads, real coffee, trekkers' supplies. *Shiva Garden Café* , 100 m further uphill. Good food with an adventurous international flavour plus 'German bakery', delightful spot, pleasant ambience with open-air seating, restful music (Tibetan enterprise) good views over Manalsu Nala, very reasonable. *Moondance*, opposite. Good choice of western favourites. Recommended. *Ish*, on left past shops going uphill (before road swings to right). Great fruit muesli, pizzas.

Vashisht *Lhasa Café*, in village centre, above *Vashisht Video Hall* (which shows 2-3 films daily). *Pyramid Centre*, path below HPTDC Baths. Western. Set in a beautiful relaxing garden with wonereful views across the valley, hot/cold drinks, cakes, 0700-2200; glassed-in section offers tasty and varied vegetarian dishes (Italian manager), massage, London trained hairdresser in summer, local information on activities. *Zodiac Café*, village centre, for food, music and wonderful cinnamon *chai*, great for meeting other travellers, entertaining. *Rainbow* and German Bakery and *Bhola's Tibetan Café*, have great views from the rooftop. *Superbake*, has some good bread, cakes, biscuits and chilled drinks.

★ **Hot Baths** (Himachal Tourism), half way up the hill towards Vashisht (long flight of steps) where natural sulphur spring water is piped into a clean tiled bath-house. **NB** Closed since Oct 1999 due to objections by villagers to allow the government to use the spring water free of charge. Normally open 0800-1300, 1400-1600, 1800-2200, Rs 40-120 for 30 mins. Baths of different sizes (may be shared), and showers, towels available. Popular, so you need to queue when busy or book a slot later. Baths are well maintained, offer privacy and are very refreshing; highly recommended early morning or after a long walk. Himachal Tourism **Utopia Complex,** Club House Road, on river bank, has snooker, billiard, badminton, table tennis, well appointed restaurant and bar, Rs 5. Also a small museum on Himachali culture. A gym and steam bath are planned. **Skiing/Mountaineering**: *Mountaineering and Allied Sports Institute*, 1.5 km out of town, organizes courses in mountaineering, skiing, watersports, high altitude trekking and mountain-rescue courses; 5 and 7-day ski courses, Rs 3,000 for the latter, Jan-Mar. There is a hostel, an exhibition of equipment and an auditorium. | **Sport & activities**

Mid-Feb Week-long *Winter Sports Carnival*. May 3-day colourful *Dhungri Forest festival* at Hadimba Devi Temple, celebrated by hill women. | **Festivals**

At NAC Market, behind Bus Station: **Books** *Bookworm*, huge stock of quality paperbacks, reasonably priced. Highly recommended. **Crafts and local curios** Also in the market: *Manushi*, women's co-op producing good quality shawls, hats, socks etc. *Shree-la Crafts*, friendly owner, good value silver jewellery. Tibetan Bazaar and Tibetan Carpet Centre. On The Mall: try the government shop; *Charitable Trust Tibetan Handicrafts*. For shalws: *Bhutico*; *Bodh*, along the Hindu Temple in bazaar, T52269, has a good range of shalws. *Om Collection*, good Tibetan T-shirts, dresses, jewellery, jumbers. **Tailors** *Gulati Traders*, Gulati Complex, Sikh tailors, quick, good quality, copies and originals (caps to order, ready in hrs, Rs 75). | **Shopping**

Local Taxi: the local union is very strong, office near tourist office, T52450; outsiders need a permit to operate in the area. Fares tend to be high; from bus stand: Rs 50 for hotels (2-3 km). To Vashisht or top of Old Manali Rd, Rs 60; auto-rickshaws Rs 30. **Motorbike**: Enfields and Hondas for hire; reasonable charges at *Enfield Club,* Vashisht Road, T54090. Passport must be left as a deposit; reserve ahead in high season. The uncrowded Kullu-Manali road via Naggar is ideal. | **Transport**

Long distance Air: Flights connect Bhuntar near Kullu, with Delhi, Shimla and Ludhiana.Jagsons, T52843. Transport to town: taxi to Manali, Rs 650 for 4 persons. Himachal Transport (green) bus, every 15 mins, Rs 25 (allow 2½ hrs travel time from

Manali). **Bus**: (see page 88). Himachal Tourism coaches in season (fewer in winter); Deluxe have 2 seats on either side: *Harisons* and *Swagatam* (see directory), run own buses. **Chandigarh** dep 0700, 10 hrs, Rs 200; **Delhi** a/c 1530, 15 hrs, Rs 500; non a/c 1700, Rs 350. **Dharamshala** 0530, 0810, Rs 130, Private coach dep 1900, 2230, 10-11 hrs, Rs 250, year round; **Keylong** 0600, 6 hrs, Rs 70. **Kullu** via **Naggar**: 2 daily, Rs 20, 1hr; other Kullu buses via NH stop at **Patli Kuhl** (see Naggar above). **Mandi**, Rs 70. **Rohtang Pass** 0900, day trip with photo-stops, striking scenery (take sweater/jacket), 1½ hrs at pass, Rs 100. **Shimla** (280 km), 0800, 9 hrs, Rs 200; 2000, 10 hrs. **To Leh** Himachal Tourism and private coaches run ordinary and luxury buses during the season (mid-Jun to end-Sep), but not always daily; usually based on demand. Seats should be reserved ahead. Front seats are best though the cab gets filled by locals wanting a 'lift'. Those joining the bus in Keylong must reserve from Manali to be certain of a seat. Rs 350-800 (Rs 1,100 including tent and meals); usual overnight stop is at Sarchu where other cheaper tents may be available (some choose to sleep on the bus). The 530 km takes about 24-28 hrs on the road, dep 0600, arr Leh next afternoon. See page 196 for further details. Various State RTCs offer direct services to major towns. HRTC Bus Stand, The Mall, reservations, 1000-1200, 1400-1600. Reports of some drivers getting drunk, hence unsafe. **Taxi**: **Aut**, Rs 800, Rs 1,000 (return); **Darcha**, Rs 3,000; **Keylong**, Rs 2,400; **Kullu**, Rs 500 (Rs 700 return); **Mandi** Rs 1,200 (Rs 1,500 return); **Naggar**, Rs 300 (Rs 400 return); **Rohtang Pass**, Rs 900, Rs 11,000 (return). **Train**: From Delhi, up to Chandigarh or Shimla, or via Pathankot to Jogindernagar, and then bus transfers, see page 88.

Directory

Banks *State Bank of India*, The Mall, 100 m above *Picadilly Hotel*. Only changes AmEx TCs *UCO Bank*, The Mall, opp Nehru Park (1000-1430, closed Wed and Sun), changes TCs (Rs 50 for $500), quicker and more polite than the SBI. Signs indicate exchanges on The Mall; try *Swagatam* opp Kunzam, changes major TCs, cash against Visa. **Communications** Post: GPO, off Model Town Rd. 0900-1700, Mon-Sat. Very efficient. **Telephone**: telecom office, south of Shiali Mahadev Rd. *Gopal Travels*, opp temple in bazar. Friendly ISD phone (charges per second), receives faxes, photocopies. **Internet**: *Nirvana Café*, Old Manali, cheap, well run. **Hospitals & medical services** Mission Hospital, T52379. *Men Tsee Khang*, Gompa Rd, highly recommended for Tibetan herbal/mineral treatments. **Chemists**: opp NAC Market.

Tour companies & travel agents *Valleycon*, NAC Market. Friendly and helpful. *Himalayan Adventurers*, opp *Kunzam*, T52750, F52182. Recommended. *Swagatam* opp *Kunzam*, The Mall, T52990, F54290. Long distance buses, trekking, rafting, very efficient. Recommended. **Trekking**: Clarify details and number of trekkers involved. *Himalayan Journeys*, near German Bakery, T52365, F53065, www.himalayanjourneysindia.com *Monal Himalayan Travels* opp Bus Stand, T52715. Shambala, NAC Market, Shop 40 (opposite *Bookworm*), T52760, F52690. Excellent guide, horses and food. *Shangri-la Adventures*, Tibetan Colony, Rohtang Rd, T52734, F52404, shang-adv@hotmail.com Treks to Zanskar, Ladakh, Spiti, fishing, rafting, experienced Tibetan guides, competitive pricing for small groups, excellent service from Jigme, honest, friendly. *WH Adventure*, opposite Rambagh Taxi Stand, The Mall, T52176, F52531, Mr Ghosh is very knowledgeable, advises on routes and equipment. **Tourist offices** Himachal, next to *Kunzam Hotel*, The Mall, T53531, F52325, helpful for bus and hotel bookings, T52116.

Lahul लाहौल

The arid mountainous landscapes of Lahul (also referred to as Lahaul), lying in Colour map 1, grid B3
*the rain shadow north of the Himalayan axis, offer a stark contrast to the lushness
of the Kullu Valley. Upper Lahul comprises the Bhaga and Chandra valleys,
Lower Lahul the region below the confluence where the rivers merge to become the
Chenab.*

The whole region can be approached by road from three directions: from **Shimla** via **Ins & outs**
the Spiti Valley; from **Manali** over the Rohtang Pass (3,985 m), into Upper Lahul; and
from **Zanskar** and **Ladakh** over the Shingo La and Baralacha La (passes). The Shingo
La gives access to Lahul from Zanskar (see page 260), while the Baralacha La (4,880 m)
on the Leh-Manali road provides access from Ladakh. There is a trekking route from
Manali to Zanskar.

Lying in the transition zone between the green alpine slopes of the Kullu and **A region in**
Chamba valleys to the south and the dry, arid plateau of Ladakh, Lahul gets **transition**
enough rain during the monsoon months to allow extensive cultivation, particularly on terraces, of potatoes, green peas and hops (for beer making). Lahul
potatoes are some of the best in the country and are used as seed for propaga-
tion. These and rare herbs have brought wealth to the area.

Most people follow a curious blend of both Hindu and Buddhist customs
though there are a few who belong wholly to one or the other religion.

Historically there are similarities between this region and Ladakh since in the **History**
10th century Lahul, Spiti and Zanskar were part of the Ladakh Kingdom. The
Hindu Rajas in Kullu paid tribute to Ladakh. In the 17th century Ladakh was
defeated by a combined Mongol-Tibetan force. Later Lahul was separated into
Upper Lahul which fell under the control of Kullu, and Lower Lahul which
came under the Chamba Rajas. The whole region came under the Sikhs as their
empire expanded, whilst under the British Lahul and Kullu were part of the
administrative area centred on Kangra.

Manali to Leh

This is currently the main route for foreigners into the region of Lahul and on
to Leh. The 530 km highway is usually open from July to September, depending on snow fall; most buses stop in mid-September. The first 52 km runs up
the Kullu valley, then climbs through the Rohtang Pass into Lahul. The Pass
itself normally opens at the end of May, but in 2000 was opened on 30 April
and only closed at the end of the previous December. The journey, which has
memorable mountain scenery but some scary roads, is best done with two
night stops, possible at Keylong (see below), Darcha, Sarchu or Pang. The last
three are campsites with tents on terraces above the river valley. The highest
pass on the route is the 5,370 m Taglang La. No permits necessary.

From Manali the **NH21** runs north along the left bank of the Beas through **To Keylong**
small settlements such as the village of **Palchan** (10 km). **Eating** The

Himachal Pradesh

Only for the determined

Streams cross the road at several places. These may be impassable during heavy rain, and those fed by glaciers swell significantly during the day as meltwater increases, so travel in the late afternoon can be more difficult than in the early morning when the flow is at its lowest. Rockfalls are also a common hazard.

e *Vegetable Hot Shoppe* on the bridge and *Whispering Park*, just to the north.

The road begins to climb sharply through **Kothi Kodi** (4 km; 2,530 m), set below towering cliffs which has a rest house. Beautiful views of coniferous hillsides and meadows unwind as the road climbs through 2,800 m, conifers giving way to poplars and then banks of flowers. The 70 m high **Rohalla Falls** (19 km) at an altitude of 3,500 m are a spectacular sight just 9 km before the seasonal settlement of Marrhi, a widely used restaurant 'stop'.

The landscape, covered in snow for up to eight months of the year, becomes totally devoid of trees above Marrhi as the road climbs through a series of tight hairpins to the Rohtang Pass (17 km; 3,985 m).

★ Rohtang Pass
Colour map 1, grid B3

From the pass you get spectacular views of precipitous cliffs, deep ravines, large glaciers and moraines. Buses stop for photos. Do not expect a quiet and remote mountain pass during the summer season. From June until mid October (when Himachal Tourism runs a daily bus tour from Manali), the pass becomes the tempory home to a dozen or more noisy roadside 'cafes'. They compete with loud Indian film music to attract the visiting Indian honeymooners and tourists who come up here to see and feel snow.

The descent to **Gramphoo** (Gramphu), which is no more than a couple of houses at the junction of the road from Tabo and Kaza, offers superb views of the glaciated valley of the Chandra River, source of the Chenab. To the north and east rise the peaks of Lahul, averaging around 6,000 m and with the highest, Mulkila, reaching 6,520 m. As the road descends towards Khoksar there is an excellent view of the Lumphu Nala coming down from the Tempo La glacier. An earlier glacial maximum is indicated by the huge terminal moraine visible half way up the valley. At the base of the south facing slope isolated pockets of potato cultivation form dark green patches on the otherwise bare mountainside.

There is a police check post in **Khoksar** (3,140 m) where you may be required to show your passport and sign a register. This can take

Manali to Leh

To Pangong Tso

LADAKH

Choglamsar
LEH *(3,500m)* — Shey — Thikse — Sakti
Kharu
Hemis — Upshi — Rumtse — *Indus River*
Taglang La *(5,370m)*

Debring

Moray Plains

ZANSKAR

To Tsokar

Pang *(4,630m)*

Lachalung La *(5,065m)*
Brandy Nullah

Sarchu

Baralacha La *(4,880m)*

Trek to Leh via Padum

Patseo — Zingzingbar

Bhaga River

To Chandratal Lake

Jespa *(3,200m)*
Darcha

LAHUL

Keylong *(3,350m)*

To Pattan Valley

Tandi
Chenab River Gondhla
Rapsang — *Chandra River*

Sissu *(3,130m)* — Khoksar
Gramphoo

Rohtang Pass *(3,985m)*

Marhi

Jeep road to SPITI

Kothi

N

MANALI *(2,050m)*

Beas River

Not to scale

some time if more than one bus arrives at once. There is a small café and drinks stall. The road crosses the Chandra by a Bailey Bridge to the right bank running east-northeast past fields of peas and potatoes. About 8 km west of Khoksar work has started on the proposed Rohtang tunnel to link the Solang Valley with the Chandra Valley. In **Sissu** (15 km from Khoksar; 3,120 m) there is a power house and an **F** PWD *Rest House*, very near checkpoint, basic but clean, helpful staff. You can cross the bridge to see the attractive waterfall. The road then passes through Gompathong to Gondhla (8 km).

It is worth stopping here to see the 'castle' belonging to the local *thakur* (ruler), built around 1700. The seven-storey house with staircases made of wooden logs has a verandah running around the top and numerous apartments on the various floors. The fourth floor was for private prayer, while the Thakur held court from the verandah. There is much to see in this neglected, ramshackle house, part- icularly old weapons, statues, costumes and furniture. The 'sword of wisdom' believed to be a gift from the Dalai Lama some time ago, is of special interest. On close inspection you will notice thin wires have been hammered together to form the blade, a technique from Toledo, Spain! The huge rock near the Government School, which some claim to be of ancient origin, has larger-than-life figures of *Bodhisattvas* carved on it.

Gondhla
Colour map 1, grid B3
Altitude: 3,160 m

As the road turns north approaching **Tandi** the Chandra rushes through a gorge, giving a superb view of the massively contorted, folded and faulted rocks of the Himalaya. Tandi itself is at the confluence of the Chandra and Bhaga rivers, forming the Chandrabhaga or Chenab. **Keylong** is 8 km (see below). A roadside café serves rice and lentils.

Pattan Valley

The Pattan Valley has a highly distinctive agricultural system which despite its isolated situation is closely tied in to the Indian market. Pollarded willows are crowded together all around the villages, offering roofing material for the flat-roofed houses and fodder for the cattle during the six-month winter. Introduced by a British missionary in the 19th century to try and help stabilize the deeply eroded slopes, willows have become a vital part of the valley's village life, with the additional benefit of offering shade from the hot summer sun along the roads and family compounds. Equally important are the three commercial crops which dominate farming, hops, potatoes and peas, all exported from the valley, while wheat and barley are the most common subsistence grain crops.

Just out of Tandi after crossing the Bhaga River on the Keylong road, the Udeypur road doubles back along the right bank of the Chenab. It runs close to but high above the river, through a series of small settlements clustered on intensively cultivated outwash fans.

Routes

The road passes through **Ruding** (10 km from Tandi) and **Shansha** (5 km), a well-built village surrounded by wheat, hops and potatoes. **Jahlma** (6 km) has a post office and the road continues to **Thirot** (11 km), where there is a PWD *Rest House*. A bridge at Jhooling crosses the Chenab. Some 6 km further on, the road enters a striking gorge where a bridge crosses the river before taking the road up to Trilokinath (6 km).

Trilokinath (2,760 m) is approached by a very attractive road which climbs up the left bank of the Chenab. Several intensively cultivated areas and clustered villages on glacial deposits are interspersed with forests and open hillside. The glitteringly white-painted Trilokinath temple stands at the end of the village

★ Trilokinath
Colour map 1, grid B3

Himachal Pradesh

street on top of a cliff formed by the eroded edge of a glacial outwash fan over-looking the Chenab far below.

The Siva **temple** has been restored by Tibetan Buddhists, whose influence is far stronger than the Hindu. Tibetan prayer-flags decorate the entrance to the temple which is in the ancient wooden pagoda style. In the courtyard is a tiny stone Nandi and a granite lingam, Saivite symbols which are dwarfed in significance by the Buddhist symbols of the sanctuary: typical prayer-wheels constantly being turned by pilgrims, and a 12th-century six-armed white marble Avalokiteshwara image (Bodhisattva) in the shrine along with other Buddhist images. The original columns date from Lalitaditya's reign in the eighth century, but there has been considerable modernization as well as restoration, with the installation of bright electric lights including a strikingly garish and flickering chakra on the ceiling. Hindus and Buddhists celebrate the three-day *Pauri Festival* in **August**.

Udeypur
Colour map 1, grid B3
Trekking routes cross the
valley here & further
west, see
page 216

Ten kilometres from the junction with the Trilokinath road is Udeypur (Udaipur); the name was changed from Markul in about 1695 when Raja Udai Singh gave it the status of a district in his administration. Visited in the summer it is difficult to imagine that the area is completely isolated by sometimes over 2 m of snow during the six winter months. It is supplied by weekly helicopter flights (weather permitting); the helipad is at the entrance to the village.

The unique **Mrikula** (Markula) **Devi temple** (AD1028-63) is above the bazar. The temple dedicated to Kali looks wholly unimposing from the outside with a battered looking wood-tiled 'conical' roof and crude outside walls. However, inside are some beautiful, intricate deodar-wood carvings belonging to two periods. The façade of the shrine, the mandapa (hall) ceiling and the pillars supporting it are earlier than those beside the window, the architraves and two western pillars. Scenes from the *Mahabharata* and the *Ramayana* epics decorate the architraves, while the two door guardians (*dvarapalas*), which are relatively crude, are stained with the blood of sacrificed goats and rams. The wood carvings here closely resemble those of the Hadimba Temple at Manali and some believe it was the work of the same 16th century craftsman. See page 184. The silver image of Kali (*Mahishashurmardini*) 1570, inside, is a strange mixture of Rajasthani and Tibetan styles (note the Lama-like headcovering), with an oddly proportioned body. **Sleeping E** *Forest Rest House*, off the road in a pleasant raised position, two rooms with bath, very basic, bring your own sleeping bag. **Camping** is possible in an attractive site abut 4 km beyond the town (permission from Forest Officer) but since there is no water supply nearby water has to be carried in from a spring about 300 m further up the road. Carry provisions as there is little in the bazar.

Keylong

Phone code: 019002
Colour map 1, grid B3
Altitude: 3,350 m

The principal town of the district of Lahul, Keylong is set amidst fields of barley and buckwheat surrounded by brown hills and snowy peaks and was once the home of Moravian missionaries. The local deity 'Kelang Wazir' is kept in Shri Nawang Dorje's home which you are welcome to visit. There is a Tibetan Centre for Performing Arts. Only traders and trekkers can negotiate the pass out of season.

The town

The bus stand with a few tea stalls alongside is on the NH21 which by-passes the town. Tracks run down into the town centre. It has little to offer, though the views are very attractive and there are pleasant walks. There is a pleasant circuit of the town by road which can be done comfortably in under two hours.

Keylong is an increasingly widely used stopping point for people en route to Leh or trekking in the Lahul Spiti area. Landslides on the Leh-Manali road can cause quite long delays and the town can be an unintended rest halt for a couple of days.

A statue in the centre of Keylong commemorates the Indian nationalist **Rash Behari Bose** (born 15 May 1886 near Calcutta). As the memorial tablet relates, he was arrested for throwing a bomb at the Viceroy, Lord Hardinge, in Calcutta on 23 December 1912 which 'explained his subsequent visit to Keylong' – as a prisoner. In 1915 he went to Japan where he settled and learned Japanese. Founder of the Pan Asian League, he remained dedicated to the overthrow of British colonial rule in India. In 1941 he declared war on England from his home in Tokyo, laying the foundations for the subsequent formation of the Indian National Army by Subhas Chandra Bose.

Excursions

Three monasteries are within hiking distance of Keylong

Khardong Monastery (3.5 km), across the Chandra River up a steep tree-shaded path, is the most important in the area. It is believed to have been founded 900 years ago and was renovated in 1912. Nuns and monks enjoy equality; married lamas spend the summer months at home cultivating their fields and return to the monastery in winter. The monastery, with its four temples, contains a huge barrel drum, a valuable library and collections of *thangkas*, Buddha statues, musical instruments, costumes and ancient weapons. **Sha-Shur Monastery** (1 km), was in legend reputedly founded as early as 17 AD by a Buddhist missionary from Zanskar, Lama Deva Tyatsho who was sent by the Bhutanese king. It has ancient connections with Bhutan and contains numerous wall paintings and a 4½ m *thangka*. The annual festival is held in June/July. **Tayul Monastery**, above Satingri village, has a 4-m high statue of Padma Sambhava, wall paintings and a library containing valuable scriptures and *thangkas*. The mani wheel here is supposed to turn on its own marking specially auspicious occasions, the last time having been in 1986.

At the confluence of the Chandra and Bhaga rivers, near Tandi 8 km to the west, **Guru Ghantal** on a hill above Tupchiling village (where there is a caretaker), was founded by Padma Sambhava 800 years ago. The images are made of wood instead of clay; a black Kali image in stone suggests its Hindu origin. Sadly the damp is taking its toll on the wall paintings in the monastery; Tupchiling now houses some of its treasures.

Himachal Pradesh

Keylong

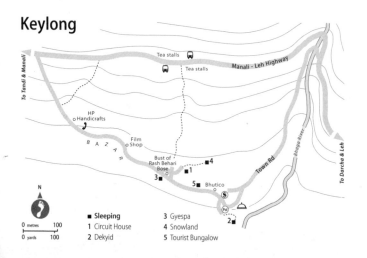

To Tandi & Manali

Tea stalls

Manali - Leh Highway

Tea stalls

HP Handicrafts

B A Z A R

Film Shop

Bust of Rash Behari Bose

Bhaga River

Town Rd

To Darcha & Leh

■1

■4

3 ■

5 ■ Bhutico

Ⓢ

2 ■

N

0 metres 100
0 yards 100

■ **Sleeping**
1 Circuit House
2 Dekyid

3 Gyespa
4 Snowland
5 Tourist Bungalow

Essentials

Sleeping & eating
Price codes:
see inside front cover

D *Dekyid*, below police station. 3-storey hotel, friendly, helpful reception, decent sized rooms with bath, quiet, excellent views over fields, good restaurant but service very slow. **D** *Snowland*, above Circuit House, T2219. 15 rooms with bath, modest but adequate, friendly reception. **E** *Rest House*, mainly for officials, rooms with shared bath may be available (bring sleeping bag), reservations, Deputy Commissioner, Keylong. **E** *Tourist Bungalow* (Himachal Tourism), T22247. 3 rooms with bath, 2-bed tents, dorm (Rs 75), meals to order, solar heated pool, reserve ahead, open mid-Jun to mid-Oct. **F** *Gyespa*, in bazar close to footpath from bus stand. Small rooms, basic but adequate, good restaurant. Several local restaurants on main road including *Vikrant*, recommended (good curry).

Transport

Road Interruptions (including passport check) and long delays are common during the monsoon and uncertainty is one of the hallmarks of the route from Manali through to Leh. To **Manali** by jeep, 4 hrs, weather permitting; **Sarchu** 6 hrs, **Leh** 14 hrs. **Bus**: state and private luxury buses are most comfortable but charge more than double the 'B' class fare (see below). To **Manali** (6-8 hrs); to Leh (18 hrs, Rs 300-375). **NB** To board deluxe buses to Leh in Keylong, reserve ahead and pay full fare from Manali (Rs 700, plus Rs 300 for tent and meals in Sarchu).

Directory

Banks *State Bank of India*; no foreign exchange.

★ Keylong to Leh

Jespa (21 km; 3,200 m), has a campsite, a few tea stalls and a mountaineering institute. Himachal Tourism's ugly concrete *'Lodge'* with three basic rooms with toilets (to get hot water and the plumbing to work needs much persuasion in cash and kind), large dining room, kitchen area, cheap camping in the yard. **Sleeping** 2 km beyond Jespa in **Teh**. **C** *Ibex Hotel*, completely glass and whitewashed cement, out of place in the rural setting, comfortable rooms, ISD, reserve (Manali) T01901-2480.

All vehicles must stop for passport checks at **Darcha** check post where the Bhaga River is bridged. You can walk across the causeway and get a cup of tea or soup and basic provisions at the roadside stone huts. Tents appear on the grassy river bank in the summer to provide a halt for trekkers to Zanskar. The road climbs to **Patseo** where you can get a view back of Darcha. A little further is **Zingzingbar**. Icy streams flow across the road while grey and red-brown scree reach down from the bare mountainside to the road edge. The road then goes over the **Baralacha La** (54 km; 4,880 m), 107 km from Keylong, at the crossroads of Lahul, Zanskar, Spiti and Ladakh regions before dropping to **Sarchu** (HP border). **Sleeping** *Tented Camp* (Himachal Tourism), on roadside, mostly two-bed tents (sometimes reported dirty), communal toilet tents, late night Indian meal and breakfast; private bus passengers without reservations are accommodated whenever possible (Rs 120-150 per person plus Rs 45 each meal, instead of the official Tourism charge of Rs 300!); open mid-June to mid-September. Occasionally other tents are set up which may be cheaper.

The road runs beyond Brandy Nala by the Tsarap River before negotiating 22 spectacular hairpin bends to climb up to the **Nakli La** (4,950 m) and **Lachalung La** (5,065 m). It then descends past tall earth and rock pillars to **Pang**, a summer settlement in a narrow valley where you can stop for an expensive 'breakfast' (usually roti, vegetables and omlettes to order). The camp remains open beyond 15 September; overnight stop is possible in communal tents. The 40 km wide Moray plains (4,400 m) provide a change from the slower mountain road. The road then climbs to **Taglang La** (5,370 m), the highest motorable pass along this route and the second highest in the world; the altitude is likely to affect many travellers at this point. You descend slowly towards the valley, passing small villages, before entering a narrow gorge with purple coloured cliffs. The road turns left to continue along the Indus basin passing **Upshi** with a sheep farm and a check post, and then **Thikse**, before reaching **Leh**.

Motorcycling from Manali to Leh

Allow 4 days on the way up, to help acclimatize as the 500 km road will take you from 2,000 m to 5,420 m and down to 3,500 m (Leh). The last petrol station is in Tandi, 7 km before Keylong, A full tank plus 5 to 10 litres of spare petrol will take you to Leh. Above 3,500 m, you should open the air intake on your carb to compensate for the loss of power.

Apart from Keylong, there are no hotels, only a few tented camps, providing basic food and shelter from mid-June to mid-September. Some will be noisy and drafty. The lack of toilet facilities leads to pollution near the camps (don't forget your lighter for waste paper). A tent and mini stove plus pot, soups, tea, biscuits, muesli, will add extra comfort, allowing you to camp in the wild expanses of the Moray Plains (4,700 m).

Unless you plan to sleep in the camp there, you must reach Pang before 1300 on the way up, 1500 on the way down, as the police will not allow you to proceed beyond the checkpoint after these times. The army camp in Pang has helpful officers and some medical facilities.

Himachal Pradesh

Dharamshala and Northern Himachal

★ Dharamshala

Phone code: 01892
Colour map 1, grid B2
Population: 8,600
Altitude: 1,250-1,980m

Dharamshala has a spectacular setting along a spur of the Dhauladhar range, varying in height from 1,250 m at the 'Lower Town' bazar to pleasanter McLeodganj at 1,768 m. Surrounded by forests of chir pine, rhododendron and Himalayan Oak, it is set against a backdrop of high peaks on three sides, with superb views over the Kangra Valley and Shiwaliks and of the great granite mountains that almost overhang the town.

Ins & outs

For trekking in Northern Himachal, see page 219

Getting there Lower Dharamshala is well connected by bus with towns near and far. You can travel from Shimla to the southeast or from Hoshiarpur to the southwest along the fastest route from Delhi. The nearest station on the scenic mountain railway is at Kangra while Pathankot to the west is on the broad gauge. **Getting around** From Dharamshala, it is almost 10 km by the bus route to McLeodganj but a shorter, steeper path (3 km), takes about 45 mins on foot. Local jeeps use this bumpy, potholed shortcut. Compact McLeodganj itself, and its surroundings, are ideal for walking.

History

The hill station was established by the British between 1815 and 1847, but remained a minor town until the **Dalai Lama** settled here after Chinese invasion of Tibet in October 1959. There is an obvious Tibetan influence in McLeodganj. It is this 'Upper' and more attractive part of town that attracts the bulk of visitors. The Tibetan community has tended to take over the hospitality business (sometimes a cause of friction with the local population) and provides cheap but clean hotels and small friendly restaurants. Now many Westerners come here because they are particularly interested in Buddhism, meditation or the Tibetan cause.

The Norbulingka Institute (see below) offers classes for those with a special interest in the **Tibetan language**. A visitor's attempt to use a few phrases in Tibetan is always warmly responded to: *tashi delek* (hello, good luck), *thukje-chey* (thank you), *thukje-sik* (please), *gong-thag* (sorry), *shoo-den-jaa-go* (goodbye) and reply *chipgyu nang-go*!

Suggested reading *My land and my people* and *Freedom in Exile* by the Dalai Lama; *In exile from the land of the snows* by Avedon; *Tibet: Its history, religion and people* by Norbu and Turnbull.

Sights

The **Church of St John-in-the-Wilderness** (1860), with attractive stained glass windows, is a short distance below McLeodganj. Along with other buildings in the area, it was destroyed by the earthquake of 1905 but has been rebuilt. In April 1998 thieves tried to steal the old bell, cast in London, which was installed in 1915, but could only move it 300 m. The Eighth **Lord Elgin**,

● ●

Fight over the flight of the living Buddha

Rival claims by two boy-gods to the position of the 17th Karmapa, the head of the Kagyu Buddhist sect and the inheritor of the coveted black hat 'woven from the hair of 10,000 angels', has created a rift in high Buddhist clerical circles. The Indian headquarters of the powerful and affluent Kagyu sect is in Rumtek in Sikkim. On 5 January 2000, the dramatic appearance of the 14 year old Urgyen Thinley in Dharamshala after a strenuous mountain crossing after escaping from captivity in Tibet, has put the cat among the pigeons. The older claimant, Thaye

Dorje now 17, who escaped from Tibet as the 17th incarnation of a 12th century spiritual leader in 1994, is being groomed in the quiet backwaters of Kalimpong, away from the warring monks of Rumtek, for the third highest position (after the Dalai Lama and the Panchen Lama) in Tibetan Buddhism. Thaye Dorje's supporters are ready to oppose any move by the new arrival, who has the blessing of the Chinese authorities and His Holiness the Dalai Lama, to usurp the 'throne' they feel rightfully belongs to their earlier find.

● ●

one of the few Viceroys to die in office, is buried here according to his wish as it reminded him of his native Scotland. ■ *1000-1700.*

The **Namgyal Monastery** at McLeodganj with the Buddhist School of Dialectics, mostly attended by monks, is known as Little Lhasa. This Tsuglagkhang ('cathedral') opposite the Dalai Lama's residence, resembles the centre of the one in Lhasa and is five minutes' walk from the main bazar. It contains large gilded bronzes of the Buddha, Avalokitesvara and Padmasambhava and is a good place to see small groups of animated monks 'debating'! To the left of the Tsuglagkhang is the **Kalachakra Temple** with very good modern murals of *mandalas*, protectors of the Dharma, and Buddhist masters of different lineages of Tibetan Buddhism, with the central image of Shakyamuni. Sand mandalas (which can be viewed on completion), are constructed throughout the year, accompanied by ceremonies. The temple is very important as the practice of Kalachakra Tantra is instrumental in bringing about world peace and harmony.

The Dalai Lama usually leads the prayers on special occasions – 10 days for *Monlam Chenmo* following *Losar, Saga Dawa* (May) and his own birthday (6th July). If you wish to have an audience with him, you need to sign up at the Security Office by *Hotel Tibet*. **NB** His Holiness is a Head of State and the incarnation of Avalokitesvara, the Bodhisattva of Love and Great Compassion; please show respect by dressing appropriately (no shorts, sleeveless tops, dirty or torn clothes); monks may 'monitor' visitors. See page 28. **Dip Thekchen Choeling Monastery** with its golden roof in a wooded valley, can be seen from above. See sleeping below. Further down the 3 km steep motorable road to Dharamshala is the Nechung Monastery in **Gangchen Kyishong** with the Central Tibetan Administration (CTA) which began work in 1988.

The **Norbulingka Institute** is becoming a major centre for Buddhist teaching and practical work. Named after the summer residence of the Seventh Dalai Lama built in 1754, it was set up to ensure the survival of Tibetan Buddhism's cultural heritage. Over 100 students are engaged in a variety of crafts in wood, metal, silk and metal, and *thangka* painting (some excellent). The temple has a 4.5-metre high gilded statue of the Buddha and over 1,000 painted images. For **B** *Chonor House* and *Norling* (see sleeping below). There is a small **museum** of traditional 'dolls' made by monks and a **Tibetan Library** with a good range of books and magazines. You can attend lectures and classes on Tibetan culture and Buddhism or attend two **meditation** classes free

Himachal Pradesh

(please leave a donation); those attending regularly pay Rs 100 per meditation session.

Foreign volunteers are often accepted at the hospital and other units here. Also ask at *Hotel Tibet* for the free monthly '*Contact*' which carries news of opportunities.

Walks around McLeodganj

Outside the rainy season lovely walks are possible

Bhagsu, a 2 km stroll east, has a temple to Bhagsunath (Siva). The mountain stream here, channelled through three spouts, feeds a small pool for pilgrims, while there is an attractive waterfall beyond. It is a quiet, relaxing place with great views, and so attracts some to stay here. **Sleeping and eating** Local families rent out rooms on the hill above; enquire locally. **E** *Meghawan*, rooms and restaurant. **E-F** *Pink and White*, variety of rooms, some with bath, meals, friendly, clean, TV, ISD. *Sri Guru Kirpa Restaurant* is recommended for vegetarian Indian and Chinese meals, or pizzas, though the spices can make you hit the roof. Places by the temple also sell food.

Dharamkot, 3 km away, has very fine views and you can continue on towards the snowline. In September, an annual fair is held at **Dal Lake** (1,837 m), 3 km from McLeodganj bus stand; it is a pleasant walk but the 'lake', no more than a small pond, is disappointing.

Naddi Gaon, 1½ km further uphill from the bridge by Dal Lake, has superb

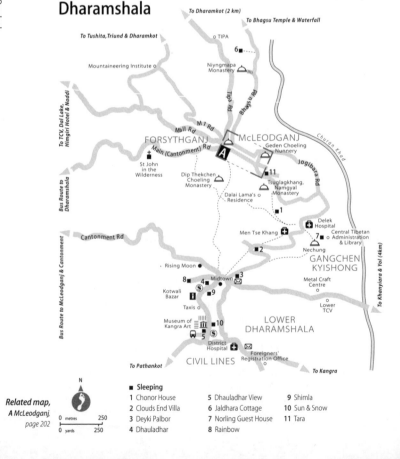

Dharamshala

To Dharamkot (2 km)
To Bhagsu Temple & Waterfall
To Tushita, Triund & Dharamkot
o TIPA
6 ■
Mountaineering Institute o
Niyngmapa Monastery
To TCV, Dal Lake, Himgiri Hotel & Naddi
Tipa Rd
Bhagsu Rd
Mall Rd
M T Rd
FORSYTHGANJ
Main (Cantonment) Rd
McLEODGANJ
Chuan Khod
A
Geden Choeling Nunnery
St John in the Wilderness
Dip Thekchen Choeling Monastery
11
Jogibara Rd
Dalai Lama's o Residence
Tsuglagkhang, Namgyal Monastery
Bus Route to Dharamshala
1
Delek Hospital
Cantonment Rd
Men Tse Khang
7 ■
Central Tibetan Administration & Library
To Khaniyara & Yol (4km)
Nechung
GANGCHEN KYISHONG
Rising Moon
2
Metal Craft Centre
Bus Route to McLeodganj & Cantonment
8 ■
4
Midtown
3
o Lower TCV
Kotwali Bazar
9
Taxis o
Museum of Kangra Art
10
LOWER DHARAMSHALA
5
District Hospital
Foreigners' Registration Office
To Pathankot
CIVIL LINES
To Kangra

N
Related map, A McLeodganj, page 202
0 metres 250
0 yards 250

■ Sleeping
1 Chonor House
2 Clouds End Villa
3 Deyki Palbor
4 Dhauladhar
5 Dhauladhar View
6 Jaldhara Cottage
7 Norling Guest House
8 Rainbow
9 Shimla
10 Sun & Snow
11 Tara

views of the Dhauladhar Range; **Kareri Lake** (3,048 m) is further. The **TCV** (Tibetan Childrens' Village) nearby educates and trains children in traditional handicrafts. Big hotels are rapidly appearing next to the traditional Naddi village. **Sleeping** Most enjoy excellent views. **C-D** *Him Giri*, T22998. Cottages, Indian and Chinese restaurant, friendly, good value. **C-D** *Udechee Huts*, Talnu View Pt, 500 m above Dal Lake, T24781. Eight pleasantly furnished circular huts with bath (hot water), blending in with local style, restaurant, well kept, friendly hosts. Recommended. **C-D** *Nishaad Resorts*, Cantt area, T21707. Modern smart, wood-panelled units with bath, some apartments with kitchen, TV room, treks, family run, good value. **E-F** *Annapurna*, T21336, eight rooms, some with bath, TV. ■ *Getting there: buses from Dharamshala, 0800-1900.*

The **Bhagsu temple** and waterfall is a pleasant easy walk. It is an 8 km trek to **Triund** (2,827 m) at the foot of the Dhauladhar where there is a *Forest Lodge* on a hill top. A further 5 km (one hour walk), brings you to **Ilaka**.

Museum of Kangra Art

The museum collection includes regional jewellery, paintings, carvings, a reminder of the rich local heritage contrasted with the celebrated Tibetan presence. Copies of Roerich paintings will be of interest to those not planning to visit Naggar. ■ *Closed Mon. Main Road.*

Tours

Himachal Tourism luxury coach, in season: Dharamshala to McLeodganj, Kangra Temple and Fort, Jawalamukhi, 1000-1900, Rs 100; Dharamshala to McLeodganj, Bhagsunath, Dal Lake, Talnu, Tapovan, Chamunda, 0900-1700, Rs 60.

Essentials

Sleeping
■ *on map below & page 202*
Price codes:
see inside front cover

Most visitors stay in McLeodganj.
In Mar, May & early Jun, accommodation may be difficult to find. Many offer seasonal discounts (40% from mid-Jun to Aug)

Dharamshala B *Chonor House*, Thekchen Choeling Rd, T21006, F21468, chonorhs@vsnl.com 12 very comfortable rooms furnished in Tibetan style (murals of lost monasteries and mythical beasts), good restaurant, clean, well managed, popular with foreign diplomats, a quiet and lovely place. **C** *Norling Guest House*, Gangchen Kyishong, norling@vsnl.com With traditionally furnished rooms. Both accept Master/Visa cards. Book well ahead. **B-C** *Clouds End Villa*, steep approach off road to CTA (signed to District Commissioner's), T22109. Rooms in Raja of Lambagraon's bungalow (Raj period), not luxurious but very clean, annexe has excellent valley views, authentic local cuisine (everything home made), tours, peaceful, very friendly, excellent service, good value. Highly recommended. **C-D** *Dhauladhar* (Himachal Tourism), Kotwali Bazar, T24926, F24212. 23 rooms (3 **B** suites), restaurant, bar, pleasant garden, billiard table, terrace for meals. **D** *Dhauladhar View*, near Museum, T22889. With 9 decent rooms. **D** *Yatri Niwas*, near Bus Stand, T23163. 14 rooms (3 deluxe), restaurant. The cheap **E** and **F** hotels are Tibetan run: **E** *Rainbow*, Old Charri Rd, Kotwali Bazar, T22647. 8 clean rooms, some with bath (**D**), TV. *Deyki Palbor*, near the fountain, *Shimla*, opposite Tourist Office, and *Sun and Snow* past steps, near bank, are similar.

McLeodganj B *Glenmore Cottages*, off Mall Rd, T21010, F21528. 5 'cottages' with bedroom, kitchen, verandah, secluded old colonial house surrounded by forest, good valley views, great walks from doorstep.

South of Bazar B-C *Bhagsu* (Himachal Tourism), T21091. 20 rooms (damp), restaurant, pleasant garden, good views, overpriced. **B-C** *Surya*, T21868, F22768. 40 large rooms, tastefully furnished, comfortable, quiet, good views, good restaurant with occasional live music/cultural show, bar, exchange, friendly. **C-D** *Him Queen*, T24961, F21184. 35 rooms, pleasantly furnished, homely, friendly, best rooms with view, good

Himachal Pradesh

seasonal discount. **D** *Kareri*, T21132, F21528. 4 rooms with bath (tub), phone, friendly, good value. **D** *Tibet* behind Bus Stand, T22587, F22427. 20 renovated rooms with bath and TV (from Rs 450), good restaurant, credit cards. Recommended. **D-E** *Cheryton Cottage*, Jogibara Road, next to *Chocolate Log*, 4 very smart rooms with bath, garden. **E** *Ladies Venture*, Jogibara Rd, T22559. Clean rooms, some with bath (bucket hot water), good dorm (Rs 50), peaceful, small restaurant (good Chinese and Western), terrace very friendly. **E** *Om*, western edge of bazar, T21313. 10 clean, smart rooms with phone, excellent shower, very good restaurant, great views at sunset. **E** *Snow Lion*, near prayer wheels. 8 rooms with bath, friendly. **E** Tara, near Bhagsu,

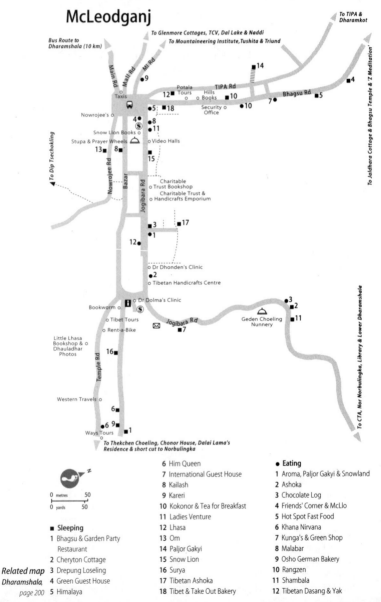

McLeodganj

Himachal Pradesh *(side margin)*

Sleeping
1 Bhagsu & Garden Party Restaurant
2 Cheryton Cottage
3 Drepung Loseling
4 Green Guest House
5 Himalaya
6 Him Queen
7 International Guest House
8 Kailash
9 Kareri
10 Kokonor & Tea for Breakfast
11 Ladies Venture
12 Lhasa
13 Om
14 Paljor Gakyi
15 Snow Lion
16 Surya
17 Tibetan Ashoka
18 Tibet & Take Out Bakery

● **Eating**
1 Aroma, Paljor Gakyi & Snowland
2 Ashoka
3 Chocolate Log
4 Friends' Corner & McLlo
5 Hot Spot Fast Food
6 Khana Nirvana
7 Kunga's & Green Shop
8 Malabar
9 Osho German Bakery
10 Rangzen
11 Shambala
12 Tibetan Dasang & Yak

Related map *Dharamshala* page 200

T21181, tamdintara@hotmail.com 12 large clean rooms, comfortable and safe, with bath and 24 hr hot water, lovely views, warm friendly family, home cooked snacks, internet, all in a new guesthouse so everything works. Recommended. **E-F** *Dip Thekchen Choeling Monastery*, below McLeodganj, climb down 300 steps. Clean rooms, shared toilets, hot showers, breakfast and dinner at set times, "wonderfully peaceful". Recommended. **E-F** *Drepung Loseling*, Jogibara Rd, T21087. Clean rooms with bath (some with hot water), dorm (Rs 30). **E-F** *Green Guest House*, T21200. 19 variable rooms, restaurant (good capuccinos and desserts), crowded with backpackers. **E-F** *Himalaya*, Bhagsu Rd, T21223. 8 rooms, some with bath (hot shower), restaurant (good Tibetan brown bread, muesli, pancakes). **E-F** *Lhasa*, TIPA Rd, T21824. 7 clean rooms, some with bath, good restaurant. **E-F** *Paljor Gakyi*, T23143, TIPA Rd, up steps. 14 clean rooms with bath (hot shower), dorm (Rs 25), very friendly, excellent views. Recommended. **E-F** *Tibetan Ashoka*, T22763. 37 very clean rooms, some with hot shower and good views (cheapest Rs 90, shared shower, bucket hot water extra, no views), strict on check-out time, nice owners. Highly recommended. **F** *International Guest House*, Jogibara Rd, just below PO, T22476. 10 fairly clean rooms with hot shower. **F** *Kailash*, Jogibara Rd, T21044. 10 rooms, shared bath, good restaurant (one of the oldest in town), popular with Tibetans. **F** *Kokonor*, opposite Security office, T21011. 5 basic rooms, shared hot shower, good restaurant (Tibetan, Chinese, Italian, excellent cakes).

Enterprising Tibetans in the upper town offer good traveller favourites for those tired of curries; some serve beer. Be adventurous and try Tibetan soups (*thukpa*), noodle dishes, steamed or fried *momos* and *shabakleb*. Consider refilling your bottles with safe filtered, boiled water at the eco-friendly *Green shop* on Bhagsu Rd, Rs 6.

Eating
● *on map, pages 200 & 202*
Price codes: see inside front cover

Dharamshala, in Kotwali Bazar *Midtown*. Indian. Mainly non-veg dishes. *Rising Moon*. Tibetan, Chinese.

McLeodganj *McLlo*, near Bus Stand. Indian, Western. Glassed in, 1st floor, beer, good value, recommended. **Mid-range** *Amdo Chachung*, Jogibara Rd. Good Tibetan. Nice terrace, cable TV. *Aroma*, Jogibara Rd, by Dr Dhonden's clinic. Israeli plus. Houmus, falafel etc. *Ashoka*, Jogibara Rd. Varied. Pleasant atmosphere, very good curry. *Khana Nirvana*, Temple Rd. International. Well prepared Mexican/Italian dishes 'smoothies' (fruit juices), organic coffee, herb teas, American run, excellent ambience, good service. Highly recommended. *Yak* and *Snowland* Jogibara Rd. Tibetan. Highly recommended for cheese momos. *Tibetan Dasang*, Jogibara Rd. Tibetan plus. Also excellent porridge, fruit muesli and wholewheat bread. **Cheap** *Friends Corner*, near Bus Stand. Good breakfasts, dim but popular. *Garden Party*, near *Bhagsu Hotel*. South Indian. *Om*, west end of bazar. Indian. Very good meals from Rs 35. *Shambala* Indian. Excellent meals (Rs 50), and western cakes and pancakes, "best apple pie", good portions, very good value, pleasant atmosphere (records on request). Recommended. *Shangrila*, near prayer-wheels. Meal (Rs 25), delicious cakes. *Hotel Tibet*, good Tibetan/Japanese restaurant and '*Take Out*' bakery for cakes and breads. *Tibetan Kitchen*, Temple Rd. Good meals.

Cafés and fast food Mid-range: *Chocolate Log*, Jogibara Rd. International. Log-shaped, deceptively shack-like is a pleasant surprise, excellent cakes and snacks, clean, terrace or indoor seating below (closed Mon). Recommended. *German Bakery*, MI Rd (steep road to Dharamkot), best bread and brown rice, open till 0100. *Kunga's*, Bhagsu Rd. Quiches, pies etc. *Hot Spot*, near Bus Stand, for fast food. *Rangzen* (Freedom), Bhagsu Rd. Good health food, cakes. **Cheap**: *Tea for Breakfast*, Bhagsu Rd. Huge pancakes, friendly. Recommended.

Himachal Pradesh

Entertainment

'Contact' (monthly, free from Hotel Tibet, Green shop) lists details of courses, events etc

Meditation *Tushita Meditation Centre*, T24366, quietly located in Dharamkot village 2 km north of McLeodganj, offers individual and group meditation; 10-day 'Introduction to Buddhism' including lectures and meditation, Rs 2,500 (residential courses get fully subscribed); simple accommodation on site. *Upassna*, next to Tushita, 10-day retreat, meditation in silence, donations only, reserve in advance through 'Michael' at the centre. Interesting **"Z Meditation"** course including yoga and naturopathy; meditation and yoga retreats offered in silence with separate discussion sessions, 3 days (starting Mon and Thu 0625-1230), Rs 650 includes a 'humble' breakfast; also evening yoga classes (1730-1900) Rs 50, daily except Sun, highly recommended for beginners, run by friendly couple in peaceful location with beautiful views. Contact *Hotel Pink and White*, Rooms 305, Bhagsunath, 2 km northeast of McLeoganj, at least one day in advance, 1230-1400, except Sun. See also *Tibetan Library* above and *Tibet* travel agent below. **Music and dance** *TIPA* (*Tibetan Institute of Performing Arts*), McLeodganj, stages occasional music and dance performances; details at Tourist Office. **Sports** **Trekking**: best season Apr-Jun and Sep-Oct. Equipment and porters can be hired from a branch of the *Mountaineering Institute* on Dharamkot Rd, reasonable charges; *Yeti Trekking* organizes treks. **Video halls** 2 on Jogibara Road, show western films; also documentaries on Tibet (look for posters).

Shopping

It is pleasantly relaxed to shop here. You are usually quoted a fair price from the start by the Tibetans. McLeodganj Bazar is good for Tibetan handicrafts (carpets, metalware, jewellery, jackets, handknitted cardigans, gloves); special Sunday market. *Green shop* Bhagsu Rd, sells recycled and handmade goods including cards and paper; *Tibetan Handicrafts Centre*, ask at office for permission to watch artisans working on carpets, thangkas etc, very informative, reasonable prices; *Tibetan Children's Villages (TCVs)* outlets. The Dickensian *Nowrojee Store*, near the Bus Stand, with its wooden counters, is a curiosity. **Books and film** *Bookworm*, near *Surya Resort*, has a good selection of paperbacks, some second-hand; *Charitable Trust Bookshop* and *DIIR* for cards, books on Tibet and Buddhism. *Little Lhasa Bookshop* and *Dhauladhar Photo Lab* on Temple Rd, 1-day service (quality OK but below Western standards).

Transport

Local **Bus**: between Dharamshala and McLeodganj, 10 km, 30 mins' bus ride, Rs 6. **Taxi**: shared by 4, pick up shuttle taxi at Kotwali Bazar on its way down before it turns around at the bus stand as it is usually full when it passes the taxi stand.

Long distance **Air** Nearest airport at Gaggal, 13 km (closed at present). **Road NB** It is dangerous to drive at night in the hills. The roads are not lit and the risks of running off the edge are great. **Bus**: many originate in Dharamshala but some super and semi-deluxe buses leave from McLeodganj bus stand or travel agencies. Himachal Tourism luxury coach (in season): to **Dalhousie and Chamba**: 0730, 7 hrs, Rs 80, Rs 120, 9 hrs; **Manali**: 0900, Rs 200; **Shimla**, 0700, Rs 140. Buses to **Baijnath** 2½ hrs, Rs 25; **Chandigarh** (248 km) 9 hrs, via Una (overnight stop possible); **Delhi** (Kashmir Gate, 521 km), semi-deluxe coach dep McLeodganj 1700, 2030, 14 hrs, Rs 250 (Rs 280 from agents); dep Delhi 1930, arr Lower Dharamshala 1000, recommended for best morning views of the foothills (stops en route); Deluxe Coach to Connaught Pl, dep 1800, Rs 350. **Kangra**: 50 mins, Rs 11; **Kullu** (214 km) 10 hrs; **Manali** (253 km) 11 hrs, Rs 130 (private Rs 250); best to travel by day (dep 0800), fabulous views but bus gets overcrowded; avoid sitting by door where people start to sit on your lap! Always keep baggage with you; **Pathankot** (90 km) 4 hrs, with connection for Amritsar, 3 hrs; **Shimla** (317 km, via Hamirpur/Bilaspur) 10 hrs. **Taxis** can be hired from the bus stands. Full day (80 km), Rs 800. Between Dharamshala and McLeodganj, Rs 90. **Train** Nearest broad gauge railhead is at Pathankot; booking office at bus stand, 1000-1100 (no computer). For narrow gauge, see page 207.

Directory

Banks *Bank of Baroda*, Kotwali Bazar. For Visa cash advances, order or ring T23175 with details, collect on next working day. *State Bank of India*, Dharamshala and McLeodganj, changes TCs, 1030-1430, Sat 1030-1230. Private exchange at *Friends Corner* near Bus Stand, friendly, open Sun days, no hassle but large commission on cash against credit card. **Communications** Post: GPO, 1 km below tourist office on Main Rd, Mon-Sat, 1000-1630, another in Kotwali Bazar. In McLeodganj, the post office, Jogibara Rd, has poste restante (0900-1700, Sat 0900-1500) but doesn't check collector's identity carefully. **Internet:** *Skyline*, outside *Tibetan Ashoka Hotel*, email, send Rs 50, receive Rs 15, 1 machine, quiet, slow but friendly, internet typically Rs 100 per hr, cheap word processing. Recommended. *Computer Centre* at Gangchen Kyishong, offers a similar service. *Green Cyber Café*, next to Green Hotel, 8 machines, well run, own generator (café and cake shop serve the long queues). *Himalaya Café* next door, 3 pcs. *Tibtronic*, next to post office, 6 machines, quieter, no café. **Hospitals & medical services** *Delek Hospital* above Gangchen Kyishong, often has foreign volunteer doctors, good for dentistry. *District Hospital*, Dharamshala, T22333. *Men Tse Khang* (Tibetan Medical Inst) T22484, Gangchen Kyishong, for Tibetan herbal medicine. *Dr Dolma's* and *Dr Dhonden's* clinics, near McLeodganj Bazar for Tibetan treatment. **Tour companies & travel agents** In McLeodganj: *Bhagsu*, Bazar, STD/ISD, fax. *Potala*, Bhagsu Rd, T22578 (Delhi T3713309, F6461914), helpful staff. *Tibet Tours*, Temple Rd, T21539, F21528, pilgrimage tours, with lectures by eminent Buddhist lamas, meditation classes. Recommended. *Ways & Tours*, Temple Rd, T25070, F24475, most reliable, Mr Gupta is very experienced, offers professional service. *Western Travels*, Temple Rd, T21926, F21252, good 24-hr Fax receiving service. In Dharamshala: *Tulip*, Kotwali Bazar, Cantt Rd, T23095. **Tourist offices** *HP*, Kotwali Bazar, near Bus Stand, T24928, F24212. *Tourism Dept*, T23107. *Hotel Tibet* also has good information. **Useful addresses** Foreigners' Registration Office: Civil Lines, Dharamshala, beyond GPO. **Police:** T22303.

Stops along the Kangra Valley Railway

Jogindernagar is the terminus of the beautiful journey by narrow gauge rail from Pathankot via Kangra. The hydel power scheme here and at nearby Bassi channels water from the River Uhl. **Sleeping D** *Uhl* (Himachal Tourism), on hill out of town, T22002, 16 rooms with bath, best upstairs with balcony, simple, clean and peaceful, restaurant. ■ *Getting there: train from Pathankot, 0920, daily, 8½ hrs.*

Jogindernagar
Phone code: 01908
Colour map 1, grid B3
Altitude: 1,220 m

The temples are old by hill standards, dating from at least 1204. The **Vaidyanatha Temple** (originally circa 800), which contains one of 12 *jyotirlingas* stands by the roadside on the Mandi-Palampur road, within a vast rectangular enclosure. Originally known as **Kirangama**, its name was changed after the temple was built to **Siva** in his form as the Lord of Physicians. It is a good example of the Nagari style; the walls have the characteristic niches enshrining images of Chamunda, Surya and Karttikeya and the *sikhara* tower is topped with an *amalaka* and pot. A life-size stone Nandi stands at the entrance. Note the Lakshmi/Vishnu figure and the graceful balcony window on the north wall. **Sleeping F** *Standard*, behind bus station. Fairly clean and surprisingly tidy rooms with bath and hot water. HP Tourism's *Café Bhairav* on left along road to Palampur, is decent and good value. ■ *Getting there: train from Pathankot or Jogindernagar and bus to/from Mandi, 3½ hrs, Rs 40.*

Baijnath
Colour map 1, grid B3

This is a pleasant little town for walking, 16 km from Baijnath, 40 km from Dharamshala (via Yol), with beautiful snow views, surrounded by old British tea plantations, thriving on horticulture. The Neughal Khad, a 300 m wide chasm through which the Bundla flows is very impressive when the river swells during the monsoons; Himachal Tourism has a café. Palampur is a popular stop with trekkers; see page 219. It also claims to hold a record for rainfall in the area! ■ *Getting there: the town is 5 km from the railway station (taxi Rs 50).*

Palampur
Population: 3,600
Phone code: 01894
Colour map 1, grid B3
Altitude: 1,260 m

Taxis are needed for first 3 hotels from bus or train station

Sleeping B-C *Taragarh Palace* (WelcomHeritage), in Al-hilal, 11 km southeast, T63034, taragarh@ vsnl.com 12 rooms in 1930s summer resort, period furniture, atmospheric, tastefully decorated, good restaurant (worth stopping en route), tennis, pool, lovely gardens and mango orchards, luxury Swiss tents in summer. **C** *Masand*, Bandla, 2 km bus stand, T30623. 8 rooms, restaurant, clean, on hill away from bazar, often booked. **C** *Silver Oaks*, Bandla Tea Estate, on a hill 3 km from bus stand (past *Masand*), T30747, F30530. 14 large rooms, dorm for budget travellers, impressive reception area, welcoming, quiet, scenic location with views of snowcapped Dhaula Dhar peaks. Himachal Tourism **C-D** *T-Bud*, 1 km from bus stand, T31298 (tea pickers pick 'a bud and 2 leaves'). In a beautiful setting, adequate, but lacks maintenance, 23 rooms (some big, airy), hot water, restaurant, pleasant lawn, clean and quiet. **C-E** *Yamini*, Ghaggar Rd, in town, T30631. 25 rooms, 8-bed dorm (Rs 75).

Transport Air The nearest airport is at Gaggal, 28 km (closed at present). **Road** Chandigarh, 265 km (via Nangal, Una, Kangra), 5½ hrs; Delhi, 535 km, 10 hrs. **Bus**: from **Delhi ISBT**, overnight deluxe bus. To **Andretta** (Private) from the bus station. **Dharamshala**, State buses from near the Nehru statue at the top of the main street. **Train** From Pathankot (narrow gauge) *Kangra Queen*, 0820, 4 hrs 30 mins, return departs Palampur 1345, via Kangra and Jawalamukhi, Rs 330 or Rs 190; see box above.

Directory Bank None changes money. **Tour operator** *Golden Oriole*, Nachhir, T/F32151, for treks.

Andretta

Andretta is an attractive village surrounded by orchards and tea gardens (13 km from Palampur) associated with **Norah Richards**, a follower of Mahatma Gandhi, who popularized rural theatre, and with the artist **Sardar Sobha Singh** who revived the Kangra School of painting. His paintings are big, brightly coloured, ultra-realistic and often devotional incorporating Sikh, Christian and Hindu images. There is an art gallery dedicated to his work and memory.

The Andretta Pottery (signposted from the main road), is charming. It is run by an artist couple (Indian/English), who combine village pottery with 'slipware'. The Sikh partner is the son of Gurcharan Singh (of Delhi Blue Pottery fame) and is furthering the tradition of studio pottery ; works are for sale. There is a Writers' Retreat run by the University of Punjab. ■ *Getting there: Panchruki (3 km) is a stop on the Kangra Valley Railway.*

Kangra Valley

The Kangra Valley, between the Dhaula Dhar and the Shiwalik foothills, starts near Mandi and runs northwest to Pathankot. It is named after the town of Kangra but now the largest and main centre is Dharamshala. Chamba State, to its north, occupies part of the Ravi River valley and some of the Chenab Valley.

History In 1620 Shah Jahan captured Kangra fort for his father Jahangir, and Kangra became a Mughal province. Many of the court artists fled to neighbouring Chamba and Kullu as the Rajas submitted to Mughal rule. When Mughal power weakened, the 16-year-old **Sansar Chand Katoch II** (1775-1823) recaptured the fort and the Rajas reasserted their independence. Under his powerful leadership, Kangra sought to extend its boundaries into the Chamba and Kullu Valleys but this was forestalled by the powerful Gurkhas from Nepal who conquered what is now the hill region of UP and HP. With the rise of the

The little-known 'mountain' railway

A superb narrow gauge railway links Pathankot in the west with Jogindernagar via Kangra (near Dharamshala) and Baijnath. The views of the Kangra Valley are quite spectacular. This is very much a working service and not a 'relic' (this train can be packed with ordinary users). Sadly, it is often very late as it is incredibly slow, *and very uncomfortable because of the hard seats. 'Tourists' would do better to sample short sections of the line, and allow for delays – any purposeful journey is better done by bus. See page 208 for an optimistic timetable.*

Sikh Empire, the valley was occupied until the Treaty of Amritsar. Then under the British, Dharamshala was made the administrative capital of the region which led to the decline of Kangra.

Kangra School of Painting Raja Goverdhan Singh (1744-1773) of Guler gave shelter to many artists who had fled from the Mughals, and during the mid-18th century a new style of miniature painting developed. Based on Mughal miniature style, the subject matter derived from Radha/Krishna legends, the rajas and gods being depicted in a local setting. Under Sansar Chand II the region prospered and the **Kangra School** flourished. Kangra fort where he held court for nearly 25 years was adorned with paintings and attracted art lovers from great distances. Later he moved his capital to Nadaun and finally to **Sujanpur Tira** (80 km) and at each place the temples and palaces were enriched by artists. The 1905 earthquake damaged many of these buildings though you can still see some miniature wall paintings.

Kangra कांगड़ा

Kangra was once the second most important kingdom in the West Himalaya after Kashmir. Kangra town, the capital, was also known as Bhawan or Nagarkot, and overlooks the Banganga River. It claims to have existed since the Vedic period with historical reference in Alexander's war records.

Phone code: 018926
Colour map 1, grid B2
Altitude: 615 m
18 km S of Dharamshala

Kangra fort stands on a steep rock dominating the valley. A narrow path leads up to the fort which was once protected by several gates and had the palace of the Katoch kings at the top. The fort, a 15 minute walk from the road bridge, is worth the effort. At its foot is a large modern Jain temple which has pilgrim accommodation (worth considering for its peaceful location). There is also a British Cemetery nearby. Inside the Fort itself is an old Jain temple which is still in use. At the very top, the remains of Sansar Chand's palace offer commanding views. ■ *US$5, Indians Rs 5.*

Sights

Brajesvari Devi Temple, in Kangra Town, achieved a reputation for wealth in gold, pearls and diamonds and attracted many Muslim invaders from the 11th century including Mahmud of Ghazni, the Tughlaqs and the Lodis who periodically plundered its treasures and destroyed the idols. In the intervening years the temple was rebuilt and refurbished several times but in the great earthquake of 1905 both the temple and the fort were badly damaged. The Devi received unusual offerings from devotees. According to Abul Fazal, the pilgrims "cut out their tongues which grew again in the course of two or three days and sometimes in a few hours"!

The present temple in which the deity sits under a silver dome with silver *chhatras* (umbrellas) was built in 1920 and stands behind the crowded,

Himachal Pradesh

colourful bazar. The State Government maintains the temple; the priests are expected to receive gifts in kind only. The area is busy and quite dirty, with mostly pilgrim-oriented stalls. Above these is St Paul's Church and a Christian community. Along the river between Old Kangra and Kangra Mandir is a pleasant trail, mostly following long-disused roads past ruined houses and temples which evidence a once sizeable town.

Excursions
34 km SW of Dharamshala
Altitude: 800 m

A sandstone ridge to the northeast of the village, **Masrur**, has 15, nineth to 10th century *sikhara* temples excavated out of solid rock. They are badly eroded and partly ruined. Even in this state they have been compared with the larger rock cut temples at Ellora in Maharashtra and at Mamallapuram south of Chennai. Their ridge-top position commands a superb view over the surrounding fertile countryside, but few of the original *shikharas* stand, and some of the most beautifully carved panels are now in the State Museum, Shimla. **Getting there** buses from Kangra.

Jawalamukhi is one of the most popular Hindu pilgrimage sites in HP and is recognized as one of 51 *Shakti pitha*. The **Devi temple** tended by the followers of Gorakhnath is set against a cliff and from a fissure comes a natural inflammable gas which accounts for the blue 'Eternal Flame'. Natural springs feed the two small pools of water; one appears to boil, the other with the flame flaring above the surface contains surprisingly cold water. Emperor Akbar's gift of gold leaf cover of the dome. In March/April there are colourful celebrations during the *Shakti Festival*; another in mid-October. **Sleeping C-D** *Jwalaji* (Himachal Tourism), T019705-22280. 25 rooms, some a/c, dorm (Rs 75), simple restaurant. **D** *Mata Shree*, 15 rooms, few a/c. *Matri Chhaya*, T22281. 32 rooms, dorm (Rs 40), restaurant. **Getting there** buses from Kangra.

Pragpur across the river Beas, 20 km southwest of Jawalamukhi, is a medieval 'Heritage' village with cobbled streets and slate-roofed houses which has a 300-year-old country home by an ornamental pond. The fine 'Judges Court' (1918) nearby has been carefully restored using traditional techniques. **Sleeping B** *Judge's Court* (Heritage), set in a large orchard, T01970-45035, F011-6885970, eries@del2. vsnl.net.in seven tastefully decorated rooms in a fine mansion, one in annexe, one large private modernized suite in the 'ancestral courtyard' with verandah overlooking the Dhauladhar, family hospitality, home grown vegetables and fruit, traditional meals, tours of Kangra Fort and other sights included (a ride on a part of the narrow-gauge mountain railway is possible), three to four day stay recommended, reserve ahead.

Sleeping & eating

Most on the main busy road are noisy – even at night. **D-E** *Maurya*, Dharamshala Rd, T25244. Clean but characterless rooms with bath, dorm, no restaurant or room service, disappointing. **E** *Anand*, Nehru Bazar, above shops, T25243. 10 rooms, dining hall. *Gupt Ganga Dharamshala*, 30 rooms and 3 halls, please leave a donation. *Chicken Corner*, Dharamshala Rd near the main bazar, an eccentric though fairly clean little hut does chicken dinners and acceptable breakfasts (tea with "sugar lumps for VIP's! If the toast takes long to arrive, it's because the enthusiastic owner is cutting the crusts off").

Transport

Air Gaggal airport (closed at present) is 7 km away. **Road Bus** Dharamshala: you can cross the railway track and follow the path all the way down to the road bridge, way below; stop the bus to Dharamshala on the opposite side of the bridge under 1 hr. **Taxi**: Dharamshala Rs 400. **Train** Narrow gauge: to **Pathankot**: 0620, 0957, 1326, 1618, 1845, 2024, 4½ hrs; from Pathankot: 0435, 0835, 0921, 1300, 1600, 1800, 5 hrs (often 1 hr late!); continues to Baijnath, 2¼ hrs. The faster *Kangra Queen* from Pathankot, 0820, goes to Palampur. **Kangra** station serves Old Kangra with the fort, near the main road, while **Kangra Mandir** station is near the temple, bazar and most of the hotels. Avoid arriving at either after dark as both stations are isolated.

To travel west from Dharamshala or Kangra take the Mandi-Pathankot road at Gaggal. From Gaggal the road drops steadily to Nurpur.

Dharamshala to Dalhousie

Nurpur Emperor Jahangir named this after his wife in 1622, two years after Kangra had been taken from him by his son Shah Jahan. The fort is now in ruins. Some fine carving remains visible along with a Krishna temple, also in ruins. The town is known for its *pashmina* shawls. Nurpur has a PWD *Rest House*.

16 km E of Pathankot
Population: 8,000
Colour map 1, grid B2
Altitude: 420 m

From Nurpur continue to **Chakki** (13 km. *Altitude*: 370 m). The main road continues to Pathankot (11 km). From Chakki the road climbs to **Dhar** (14 km, *altitude*: 680 m), where a road to the left leads to **Udhampur** and Kashmir. At Dunera (17 km) there is a barrier gate to keep traffic to a one way system for the next 28 km to **Banikhet** (1,680 m). The road continues 8 km to Dalhousie.

Chamba Valley

Dalhousie

Dalhousie, named after the Governor-General (1848-56), was developed on land purchased by the British in 1853 from the Raja of Chamba. It sprawls out over five hills ranging from 1,600-2,400 m, just east of the Ravi River. By 1867 it was a sanatorium and reached its zenith in the 1920s and 30s as a cheaper alternative to Shimla. Rabindranath Tagore wrote his first poem in Dalhousie as a boy and Subhash Chandra Bose came secretly to plan his strategies during the Second World War. Its popularity declined after 1947 and it became a quiet hill station with old colonial bungalows, surrounded by thick pine forests interspersed with oak and rhododendron. It remains a popular bolt hole for tourists from the plains but its importance today is due to the number of good schools and the presence of the army.

Phone code: 01899
Colour map 1, grid B2
Population: 8,600
Altitude: 2,030 m

The three Malls laid out for level walks are around Moti Tibba, Potreyn Hill and Upper Bakrota. The last, the finest, is about 330 m above **Gandhi Chowk** (formerly Post Office Square) around which the town centres. From there two rounds of the Mall lead to Subhash Chowk. Tibetans make and sell handicrafts, woollens, jackets, cardigans and rugs. Their paintings and rock carvings can be seen along Garam Sarak Mall.

Sights

Just over 2 km from Gandhi Chowk is **Martyr's Memorial** at Panchpulla (five bridges), which commemorates Ajit Singh, a supporter of Subhash Bose and the Indian National Army during the Second World War. On the way you can see the **Satdhara** (seven springs), said to contain mica and medicinal properties. **Subhash Baoli** (1½ km from the square), is another spring. It is an easy climb and offers good views of the snows. ½ km away **Jhandri Ghat**, the old palace of Chamba rulers, is set among tall pine trees (not open to the public). For a longer walk try the Bakrota Round (5 km), which gives good views of the mountains and takes you through the Tibetan settlement.

Kalatope (9 km; 2,500 m), with good mountain views, is a level walk through a forest sanctuary with an **E** *Tourist Lodge*. The road is jeepable.

Excursions

Khajjiar (*phone code*: 018992), 22 km further along the motorable road, is a long, wide glade ringed by cedars with a small lake. You can explore the area in a pleasant three-day walk. Alternatively you can extend the day's walk to Khajjiar into a short trek to Dharamshala over two days. A 30-km path through dense deodar forest leads to Chamba. **C** *Mini Swiss*, T36365. Comfortable, very clean rooms (singles 50% less), great views, good restaurant. **C-D** *Devdar* (Himachal Tourism), T36333. 12 clean rooms, dorm and beds in cottage (Rs 75), simple restaurant, horse riding, beautiful setting. ■ *Getting there: buses from Dalhousie, 0930, return 1530, 1 hr, Rs 13.*

Tours Himachal Tourism have daily tours during the tourist season to Khajjiar, 0900-1500, Rs 500 (car for five) or Rs 75 by luxury coach; to Chamba, 1000-1900, Rs 100 by luxury coach; to Pathankot (one way) by luxury coach, Rs 100.

Sleeping
■ *on map*
Price codes:
see inside front cover

Unfortunately some hotels look neglected and rundown, often because the cost of maintaining the Raj-built structures is prohibitive. Nearly all however have good mountain views and offer discounts out-of-season. **B-C** *Silverton*, near Circuit House, The Mall (Thandi Sarak), T42329. Old colonial building in large grounds, rooms with phone, TV. **C** *Grand View*, near Bus Stand, T42823, F40609. 26 spacious rooms, restaurant, rather run down but better than some, overpriced. **C** *Alps Holiday Resort*, Khajjiar Rd, Bakrota Hills, T40775, F40721, vacations@valvalue.dhl.sml 16 smart rooms in modern hotel, 2 km climb from centre. **C-D** *Aroma-n-Claire*, Court Rd, T42199. 20 rooms with bath, large but spartan, some with good views, restaurant, exchange, library, rather dated. **D** *Fair View*, Mall Rd (Garam Sarak), T42206. 13 rooms, mosquitos galore. **D-E** *Geetanjali* (Himachal Tourism), Thandi Sarak, near Bus Stand, T42155. 10 rooms (some 4-bed) with bath, simple restaurant. **E-F** *Crags*, off The Mall (Garam Sarak), T42124. Tired but large, clean rooms with bath (hot water), meals, good views down valley, friendly, but check bill carefully. **E-F** *Glory*, near Bus Stand, T42533. 5 rooms with bath, good restaurant, **E-F** *Mehar's*, The Mall (Thandi Sarak), T42179. 43 rooms. **E-F** *New Metro*, Subhash Chowk. **F** *Youth Hostel*, T42159. Good discounts for YHAI Members, reservations: tourist office, T42136.

Dalhousie

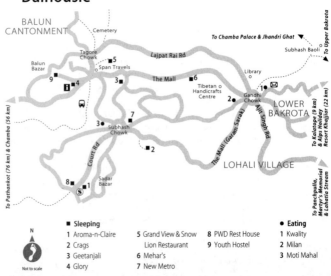

■ Sleeping		● Eating
1 Aroma-n-Claire	5 Grand View & Snow	8 PWD Rest House	1 Kwality
2 Crags	Lion Restaurant	9 Youth Hostel	2 Milan
3 Geetanjali	6 Mehar's		3 Moti Mahal
4 Glory	7 New Metro		

N
Not to scale

Moti Mahal, *New Metro* and *Lovely*, on Subhash Chowk. Several near GPO, include **Eating**
Kwality. Good Indian and Chinese if a bit pricey. Pleasant place with TV. Also *Milan* is
similar. Very friendly, serves large portions. *Punjab*, Garam Sarak, just off Gandhi
Chowk. Popular, good value. *Snow Lion*, near *Grand View*, does Tibetan dishes.

Pony hire: from Subhash and Gandhi Chowks. **Entertainment**

Handicrafts *Tibetan Handicrafts Centre*, Gandhi Chowk. *Himachal Handicrafts* **Shopping**
Emporium.

Dalhousie is on NH1A. From: **Delhi** (559 km); **Chandigarh** (336 km); **Shimla** (414 km). **Transport**
Local Jeeps from bus stand, up to Gandhi Chowk, Rs 30, Bakrota Rs 70. **Long dis-
tance Air** Nearest airport is at Amritsar (200 km). **Train** Nearest station is at
Pathankot, 2 hrs by taxi. **Road** Return **taxis**, Rs 300, 4 hrs; Chamba, Rs 550. **Bus**:
Chamba (56 km via Khajjiar) 1½ hrs; **Dharamshala** (180 km, 7 hrs via Gaggal on the
Shimla bus, change at Gaggal, 30 mins from Dharamshala); **Pathankot** 120 km, 3 hrs.

Banks *Punjab Bank*, Court Rd, changes TCs. **Communications** GPO: Gandhi Chowk. **Directory**
Hospitals & medical services Chemists at Subhash and Gandhi Chowks. *Civil Hospital*, T42126.
Tourist offices *HP*, near Bus Stand, T42136, 1000-1700, but opening irregular. **Travel
agent** *Span*, nr Bus Stand.

★ Chamba चम्बा

Picturesque Chamba (996 m), is on the south bank of the Iravati (Ravi), its stone   Phone code: 018992
houses clinging to the hillside. Some see the town as having an almost Italian feel,   Colour map 1, grid B2
surrounded by lush forests and with its Chaugan or grassy meadow in the centre.

Getting there From Dalhousie it is a very pleasant drive to the medieval town of **Ins & outs**
Chamba. The higher road, at about 1,800 m, passes through some beautiful forests
while the winter road takes a lower route. **Getting around** Buses arrive at the north
end of the *Chaugan*. Most hotels, temples and palaces are within walking distance of
the bus stand.

Founded in the 10th century, **Chamba State** was on an important trade route **History**
from Lahul to Kashmir and was known as 'The Middle Kingdom'. Though
Mughal suzerainty was accepted by the local Rajas, the kingdom remained
autonomous though it came under Sikh rule from 1810-46. Its relative isolation led to the nurturing of the arts – painting, temple sculpture, handicrafts
and unique *rumal*. The pieces of silk/cotton with fine embroidery imitate miniature paintings; the reverse is as good as the front.

Chamba is the centre of the **Gaddis**, shepherds who move their flocks of sheep **The town**
and goats, numbering from a couple of hundred to a thousand, from lower
pastures at around 1,500 m during winter to higher slopes at over 3,500 m,
after snowmelt. They are usually only found in the Dhaula Dhar range which
separates Kangra from Chamba. Some believe that these herdsmen first
arrived in this part of Himachal in the 10th century though some moved from
the area around Lahore (Pakistan) in the 18th century, during the Mughal
period. Their religious belief combines animism with the worship of Siva;
Bahrmaur with its distinctive Manimahesh temple is their principal centre of
worship (see below).

In the winter the Gaddis can be seen round Kangra, Mandi and Bilaspur and in the small villages between Baijnath and Palampur.The men traditionally wear a *chola* (a loose white woollen garment), tied at the waist with a black wool rope and a white embroidered cap.

Sights The Chaugan, under a kilometre long, is the central hub of the town but sadly, over the last two decades, shops have encroached into the open space; an underground shopping complex may be built to save it.

There are several ancient Pahari temples with attractive curvilinear stone towers. The **Lakshmi Narayana** Temple Complex (ninth to 11th centuries), contains six *sikhara* temples with deep wooden eaves, several smaller shrines and a tank. These are dedicated to Vishnu and Siva, with some of the brass images inlaid with copper and silver. The **Hari Rai Temple** (14th century), contains a fine 11th-century bronze Chaturmurti (four-armed Vishnu), rarely visible as it is usually 'dressed'. The 10th-century wooden **Chamunda Devi Temple** to the north (1 km uphill from the bus stand), with some interesting wood carvings, stands over the river with commanding views. Others of note are the Bajreshwari, Bansigopal and Champavati.

The Akhand Chandi, the Chamba Maharajas' palace, beyond the Lakshmi Narayan complex, is now a college. The old **Rang Mahal** (Painted Palace) in the Surara Mohalla, was built by Raja Umed Singh in the mid 18th-century. A prisoner of the Mughals for 16 years, he was influenced by their architectural style. The wall paintings in one room are splendid. The theme is usually religious, Krishna stories being particularly popular. Some of these were removed to the Bhuri Singh Museum after a fire, together with wood carvings and manuscripts.

Museums The **Bhuri Singh Museum** near the Chaugan in a three-storey building houses a heritage collection, craft items including some excellent *rumals*, carvings and fine examples of Chamba, Kangra and Basholi schools of miniature paintings. ■ *Daily except Sun, 1000-1700.*

Sleeping & eating **C-D** *Iravati* (Himachal Tourism), Court Rd near Bus Stand, T22671, F22565. 17, mostly clean rooms with bath and hot water, restaurant (very slow, surly service but reasonably priced). **E** *Akhand Chandi*, College Rd, Dogra Bazar, T22371. 9 rooms, some a/c, restaurant. **E** *Champak* (Himachal Tourism), T22774. 7 depressing rooms, some with bath, dorm (Rs 50). **E** *Rishi*, opposite Lakshmi Narayana Temple, T24343. Rooms with bath (hot water), colour TV, good value meals, friendly owner, pleasant place. Avoid *Jimmy's Inn*. Several tea shops and *Ravi View Café*.

Festivals April *Suhi Mela* lasts three days. **July-August**: *Minjar*, seven-day harvest festival when people offer thanks to Varuna the rain god. Decorated horses and banners are taken out in procession through the streets to mark its start. Sri Raghuvira is followed by other images of gods in palanquins and the festival ends at the river Irawati where people float *minjars* (tassels of corn and coconut). Gaddis and Gujjars take part in many cultural events to mark the start of harvesting.

Shopping *Rumal* embroidery and leather goods from *Handicrafts Centre*, Rang Mahal.

Transport **Train** Pathankot, the nearest railhead is 3 hrs drive. **Bus**: Dalhousie (2 hrs plus stop in Khajjiar), Rs28; direct to Amritsar, 0745, 8 hrs, Rs 105. **Jeep** hire is relatively expensive. Special service during Manimahesh Yatra (see below).

Directory **Bank** *State bank of India*, Court Rd, changes AmEx TC's. **District Commissioner**,T22221. **Travel agents** *Manimahesh*, Lakshminarayan Temple Lane, T22507. *Thakur Taxis*, near Bus Stand, T2755, for sightseeing and touring. **Tourist office** *Hotel Iravati*, T22671.

★ Trekking in Himachal Pradesh

Trekking from Shimla

From Shimla on the Hindustan-Tibet Highway, there are opportunities for short and long treks. These include **Chharabra**, 13 km beyond Shimla at 2,593 m and **Naldera**, 23 km from Shimla, which was Curzon's summer retreat (for these, see page 158).

Still further on at **Narkanda**, 64 km from Shimla, is another trek with very good walks, especially up Hattu Peak. From Narkanda the road runs down to the Sutlej valley and enters Kinnaur and Spiti. Foreigners are allowed into Spiti with permits.

From just beyond Narkanda you can trek northwest over the **Jalori Pass** (3,350 m) in the **Seraj** region. Starting from Ani village reached by bus/jeep from Luhri in the Sutlej Valley below Narkanda, you trek into the lower part of the Kullu Valley, joining the Kullu-Manali road at Aut. There is a jeepable road over much of this route. An alternative is to proceed 65 km from Narkanda to **Rampur** and then trek into the Kullu Valley via the **Bashleo Pass** (3,600 m). There are *Forest Rest Houses* en route so a tent is not essential. The pass is crossed on the third day of this five-day trek. Both treks end at **Banjar** in the Tirthan Valley from where there are buses to Kullu.

Trekking from Chamba

Season The Chamba region receives less rain than the Kangra Valley to the south. A trek, particularly over the Pir Panjal into Lahul is possible during the monsoon months (June-September). The ideal season, though, is just after the monsoon.

There are several short and longer treks from Chamba and Bahrmaur in the Upper Ravi Valley. **Suggested reading** *Trekking in Himachal Pradesh* by G & M Puri.

To the north there are three main passes over the Pir Panjal into Lahul: the **Pir Panjal** Kalicho, Kugti and Chobia Passes. At least five days should be allowed for crossing them as their heights are around 5,000 m and acclimatization is highly desirable. All the first stages of the walks are along the Budhil River, which flows through Bahrmaur and is a tributary of the Ravi River. After the first two days, the services of a guide or porters are recommended for picking the right trail. Views from the passes are very good both of the Himalaya to the north and the Chenab Valley to the south. The descent from the passes is very steep. On reaching the road you can take a bus from **Udeypur** or **Trilokinath** in the Pattan Valley, to the Kullu Valley over Rohtang Pass. Several trails cross the high passes over the Pir Panjal range to give access to the Pattan valley of

Lahaul. The semi nomadic gaddi shepherds regularly use these to take their flocks across to the summer grazing grounds located in the high side valleys of Lahaul.

Bahrmaur
Colour map 1, grid B3
Altitude: 1,981 m

Bahrmaur, also spelt Brahmaur or Bharmaur, is 65 km from Chamba. It can be reached by bus. It was the original capital Brahmapura for four centuries and has eighth to 10th-century *Pahari* (hill) style temples. The best known are the Lakshminarayan group (Chaurasi) which is the centre of worship for the semi-nomadic Gaddi tribe. From Bahrmaur a three-day trek is possible to **Manimahesh Lake** (3,950 m) 34 km, in the Manimahesh Kailash (5,575 m), a spur running off the Pir Panjal.

The **Manimahesh Yatra** begins in Chamba and ends at the lake, revered by local people as a resting place of Siva; pilgrims arrive at the Manimahesh temple here and take a holy bath a fortnight after *Janmashtami* (September/October). The temple has a brass *Mahisasuramardini* image. During the *yatra* period buses, minibuses and taxis are laid on from Chamba to Bahrmaur. Many pilgrims trek the next 12 km to Hadsar although jeeps are available; from there it is two-days' climb to the lake with a night halt at Dhanchho. **Sleeping** Himachal Tourism tents available at Bahmaur (where there is also a Tourist Rest House), Hadsar, Dhanchho and Manimahesh; contact tourist office, Dalhousie, T2136. Ponies and porters can be hired at each place.

Kullu Valley treks

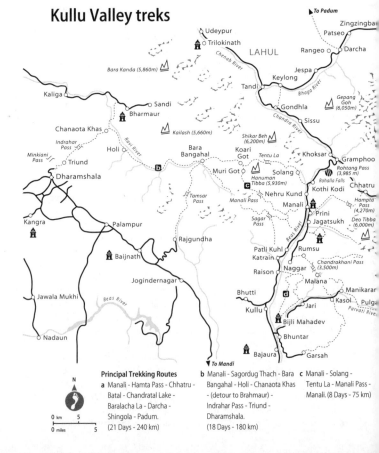

Principal Trekking Routes

a Manali - Hamta Pass - Chhatru - Batal - Chandratal Lake - Baralacha La - Darcha - Shingola - Padum. (21 Days - 240 km)

b Manali - Sagordug Thach - Bara Bangahal - Holi - Chanaota Khas - (detour to Brahmaur) - Indrahar Pass - Triund - Dharamshala. (18 Days - 180 km)

c Manali - Solang - Tentu La - Manali Pass - Manali. (8 Days - 75 km)

The nine-day trek starting from Chamba includes **Rakh** (20 km) on Day 1, Bahrmaur on Day 2, a rest stop there, then continuing to **Hadsar** (12 km), **Dhanchho** (7 km) and **Manimahesh** (7½ km) with a brief halt at **Bhairon Ghati**. The return is by the same route.

Trekking in Lahul, Kinnaur and Spiti

The border areas are being opened to trekkers with permits. At the same time the local tribal people are being exposed to outside influences which started with the introduction of television in these valleys. Now enterprising families open their homes to paying guests, youths offer their services as guides and muleteers and shops stock bottled drinks and canned food; however, anyone trekking in this region is advised to carry food, tents and all essentials.

Season Lahul (and Zanskar and Ladakh) are ideal trekking destinations during the monsoon as they are not nearly as wet as most other regions. Best: mid-June to mid-October but some passes (eg Shingo-La, Parvati Pass), may remain snow bound until mid-July or even later.

Lahul
Colour map 1, grid B3

You can take a trek from **Darcha**, see page 194, up the valley over the **Shingo La** and on to **Padum**, the capital of the Zanskar region. Padum is linked with Leh. Shingo La is over 5,000 m so some acclimatization is desirable. The route is well marked.

An alternative route to Zanskar is up the Chandra valley and over **Baralacha La**. From here a trail leads over a high pass to Phuktal, where you join the main trail coming from Darcha. Most travellers drive into Darcha; however, a fine trek past the 'Lake of the Moon' or Chandratal makes a nice and less known addition for those with a little more time. The route taken from **Manali** is over the **Hamta Pass** with good views of Deo Tibba (6,001 m), weather permitting, to **Chhatru** village in the Chandra Valley where a rest house has camping in the grounds and local families accommodate visitors in very basic homes. It is four days' trek from Manali. Two days along the dirt road brings you to **Batal** (to save time you can take the bus from Manali over the Rohtang Pass). The next stage of both variations is to Chandratal.

Chandratal (4,270 m), is 18 km from Batal. The first section up to Kunzum Pass is on the bus route. The remaining 8½ km trail is open June-October and brings you to the beautiful clear blue water lake, about a kilometre long and half a kilometre

d Manali - Naggar - Malana - Manikaran - Kasol - Jari - Bijli Mahadev - Naggar - Manali. (9 Days - 140 km)

Himachal Pradesh

wide which lies on a glacial bowl. Carry your own tent and provisions. The lake can also be reached on a lower 14 km trail that directly runs from Batal (no regular buses from Manali).

From Chandratal the route crosses several fast flowing stream before reaching the Baralacha La (usually three days). You need to be very careful and take adequate safety precautions while negotiating these stream crossings. It then goes over another pass along the same ridge as the Shingo La, to join the main Darcha-Padum trail. From here you can continue on to **Padum** or return to Darcha in Lahul. This second option makes for a very good circular trek.

A third possibility is to trek down the Chenab Valley and either cross the Pir Panjal by one of a number of passes into the Ravi Valley via Bahrmaur, to Chamba or carry on to Kishtwar.

Lower Lahul You can trek from the district town of **Udeypur** at the base of the Miyar Nullah, the upper section of which is glaciated. To the east, high passes give access to the Bhaga valley and to the west to the Saichu Nala (Chenab tributary). The Trilokinath Temple nearby is well worth a visit (see page 193).

Trails run into the Miyar Nullah, renowned for flowers, then over the 5,100 m Kang La pass to Padum. Alternatively, you can follow the Chandrabhaga River to the scarcely visited Pangi valley with its rugged scenery and then over the 4,240 m Sach Pass leading to Chamba District.

Pangi valley The Chandrabhaga flows at over 2,400 m after the two rivers meet in this desolate and craggy region. The cheerful and good-looking Pangiwals keep their unique heritage alive through their singing and dancing. The Mindhal temple to Devi is their focus of worship. **Kilar** is the HQ which has a *Rest House* and the Detnag Temple nearby. From Kilar a wide trail follows the steep slopes above the Chandrabhaga (Chenab) River to Dharwas on the Himachal/Kashmir border and then onwards to **Atholi** in the Paddar region of Kishtwar, known for its sapphire mines.

Kinnaur Close to the Tibetan border on its east, Kinnaur has the Sutlej flowing through it. Garhwal is to the south, Spiti Valley to the north and Kullu to the west. See page 163. The rugged mountains and sparse rainfall makes Kinnaur resemble Lahul. The Kinners are Hindu but the Tibetan Buddhist influence is evident in the numerous gompas that can be seen alongside the temples. The *Phulaich* (*Festival of Flowers*), takes place in September when some villagers leave for the mountains for two days and nights to collect scented blossoms, then return on the third day to celebrate with singing and dancing.

Kinnaur, including the lovely side valleys of **Sangla** and **Bhabha**, is now open with permits easily available from the District Magistrates in Shimla, Kullu or Keylong. These treks are immensely enjoyable; although there are stone huts and the occasional PWD or *Forest Rest House*, always carry a tent in this area.

Baspa Valley Starting from **Sangla** (2,680 m), you can take a fairly level forest walk up to Barseri (5 km), then along the road up to Rakcham (8 km; 3,130 m) and climb gradually to reach **Chitkul** (18 km; 3,450 m), passing through Mastrang. Another option is to start at **Morang**, see page 167, which has a bus from Kalpa. The trail follows the Sutlej River bank for a short distance until the Tirung Gad meets it. Here it turns southeast and after going through a narrow valley reaches **Thangi**, a village connected to Morang by jeepable road where mules are available for hire. The track continues along barren hills to Rahtak (camping possible), before rising steeply to Charang Pass (5,266 m), then drops down following a mountain stream to Chitkul.

Another beautiful valley to trek, starting from **Kafnoo** (*altitude*: 2,427 m), 22 **Bhabha Valley**
km from Wangtu. Permit details have to be entered and stamped at the police
post 1 km before Kafnoo reservoir. They are checked at Tabo.

There is level ground at the end of the road by the reservoir suitable for
camping, but it can get flooded. Local guides available. From Kafnoo, the trail
follows the right bank of the river for about a kilometre before crossing over to
the left bank over a new bridge. From here, the trail gradually ascends to
Chokhapani (known locally as Sholti), about a five-hour walk away. The riverside trail is slippery and not recommended. The upper trail climbs past
Yangpa II then through fields around Musrang hamlet. There is an adequate
campsite at Chokhapani (10 km *altitude*: 3,000 m).

From Chokhapani to **Upper Mulling** (*altitude*: 3,470 m), is a beautiful 8 km,
four hours' walk (include lunch stop), following the left bank of the Bhabha
stream. Initially going through forests the track then crosses open meadows. At
the far end of the meadows is an ideal camping site by the river. The trail from
Mulling enters a forested section leading to a snow bridge across the stream.
Cross the stream and follow the steeply rising trail to the **Kara** meadows where
the Government Animal Husbandry Department has a Merino sheep breeding
centre. Ford the Bhabha River with care (either on horseback or by wading
across with support from a fixed line), to the campsite at Pasha. This section
takes three hours, so you can continue to the **Kara-Taria Pass Base**. The 5 km
walk up a steep trail along the right fork of the Bhabha stream takes another four
hours. Taria Base Pass (*altitude*: 4,290 m) camp is below the steep slope leading
to the Pass. Camp well away from the slope as it is prone to rock falls.

There is a steep descent over scree for the first kilometre from **Taria Pass**, fol- **Pin Valley**
lowed by a five-hour 15 km walk along a narrow but clear trail to the first camp
in the Pin Valley. None of the apparently promising campsites on the way has a
good water source. The **Bara Boulder** site has a stream and good grazing for
horses.

Mudh (*altitude*: 3,925 m) The 11 km stretch from Bara Boulder to Mudh
takes four hours. It is the highest permanently inhabited village in the Pin Valley and is surrounded by summer cultivation. Log bridges cross several
streams feeding into the Pin River. There are places to stay and food is available
but some villagers charge up to Rs 200-300 for a room. It is possible to camp
outside the village. One campsite is on the flat plateau overlooking the river
near the summer hut of the lay lama (before crossing the narrow foot bridge on
the river), another is near the fields immediately below the village about the
place where a side stream runs below the old monastery into the Pin. It is worth
visiting the old gompas in the village.

From Mudh to **Gulling** is a gentle five-hour trek (15 km) along the right
bank of the Pin. A single log bridge takes the path into Tilling village, followed
by a gentle climb to the big village of **Sangam** on the opposite bank (see page
169). The track crosses a rocky spur and descends steeply to some small fields
beside the river. Descend to the sandy river bed and cross diagonally to the single wire rope strung across the river. A makeshift pulley and harness crossing
has to be rigged up here unless a suitable shallow spot can be found further
downstream. Camp can be set up in the fields just below the road immediately
above the crossing point.

From this point arrange to be picked up to drive to Spiti. You can visit the
small but locally important Nyingmapa Gompa of Kungri (Ghungri), just
above the road, and if you have an extra day based here you can walk up the
short stretch of dirt road towards Sangam, then turn right into the virtually
unknown Parahio River valley, an important tributary of the Pin.

Himachal Pradesh

The valley of the Gods

No one knows the origin of the village of Malana. People believe that a band of renegade soldiers who deserted Alexander's army in the 4th century BC settled here (some wooden houses have soldiers carved on them); it is more probable that their antecedents were from the Indian plains. Their language, Kanashi, has no script but is linked to Tibetan. The villagers are directly involved in taking decisions on important matters affecting them, thus operating as an ancient democratic 'city state'. Language, customs and religious practices too differ from neighbouring hill tribes, polygamy being permitted.

A charming myth is associated with Jamlu, the principal deity in the valley. Jamlu, possibly of pre-Aryan origin, was carrying a casket containing all the important deities of Hinduism and while crossing the mountains through the Chandrakhani Pass into Kullu, a strong gust of wind blew open the box and spread the deities all over the valley. Since then Malana has been known as 'The Valley of the Gods'.

Spiti Meaning literally 'the place of Mani', Spiti is a high altitude desert, bare, rugged and inhospitable, with the Spiti River running from the slopes of Kunzum La (4,551 m) to Sumdo (3,230 m). Kunzum La offers seasonal access by road to Kullu from the valley, and it is also directly connected with Shimla via the NH22 and the SH30.

Like neighbouring Lahul, Spiti is famous for its *gompas* (monasteries). See page 167. At **Tabo**, 42 km from Kaza, the Buddhist monastery is one of the region's most famous. There is a dispensary and two adequate teashops. Foreigners are now allowed to stay overnight in Tabo. There are other important gompas at **Dankar**, **Ki**, **Kungri** and **Lalung**.

Trekkers interested in **fossils** choose a trail starting at **Kaza** and travel to **Langza** (8½ km), which has a narrow motorable track. The trek goes to Hikim, the Tangyut monastery, Komik (8 km) and returns to Kaza (6 km).

From Kibber (4,205 m) there is a 6 km track through alpine meadows to **Gete** (4,520 m), which claims to be one of the highest permanent settlements in the world only reached on foot.

NB Foreigners are now permitted to trek in this region going up to **Kibber**, one of the highest villages in the world. For details of 'Inner Line' permits see pages 53 and 160.

Trekking in the Kullu and Parvati Valleys

Treks here vary in duration and degree of difficulty. There are pleasant walks up the subsidiary valleys from Aut and Katrain with the opportunity to camp in spectacular and high locations without having to spend very long getting there. An option is to take the bus up to the Rohtang Pass, 51 km from Manali, which is very spectacular and then walk down. There is a path, and it only takes a few hours. **Recommended reading** *Kulu, to the end of the habitable world* by Penelope Chetwode. John Murray, 1972. It chronicles her travels from Narkanda to Ani and then over the Jalori Pass to Banjar and Aut in the Tirthan valley with a recalcitrant mule. Penelope Chetwode died a peaceful and natural death near Khanag while travelling along this route during the early 1990s.

Season The post-monsoon period (September to mid-November), is the most reliable season. Longer treks with crossings of high passes can be undertaken then, before the winter snows arrive. During the monsoon (June-September) it is wet but the rain is not continuous. It may rain all day or for only an hour or two. Visibility is affected and glimpses of mountains through the clouds are more likely than broad clear panoramic views. However, many flowering plants are at their best. There is trekking in the spring, that is April-May, but the weather is more unsettled and the higher passes may still have quite a lot of snow on them. There can be very good spells of fine weather during this period and it can get quite hot in May.

Equipment You will need to take your own since equipment hired out by local agencies is often of an inferior quality. Kullu now has pony unions with fixed rates for guides, porters and horses. Ask at the Tourist Office and the Mountaineering Institute for information and assistance, see page 58.

From **Manali** you can go north into **Lahul** (Map trek **a**) and **Spiti** Valleys by crossing the Rohtang (3,985 m) or the Hampta Pass (4,270 m). Once over the great divide of the Pir Panjal the treks are as briefly described – see Trekking in Lahul, Kinnaur and Spiti above. West of Manali there are routes into the **Chamba** and **Kangra** Valleys (Map trek **b**).

The trek to Malana Valley offers an opportunity to see a relatively isolated and comparatively unspoilt hill community. From Manali you go to Naggar (28 km, which can also be reached by bus) and stay at **Rumsu** (2,377 m) which is higher. The Chandrakhani Pass (3,500 m) takes you into the Malana Valley at the head of which is the glacier. On the third day you can reach **Malana** (2,650 m, 20 km from Naggar), which has two guest houses. In the past you could only enter with permission from the villagers but this is no longer needed. On the fourth day you trek to **Jari** (1,500 m) where you can catch a bus to Kullu. The road from Jari to Malana may destroy the uniqueness of the community. The whole of the Malana Valley is dominated by **Deo Tibba** peak in the north.

Malana Valley

To extend the trek from Malana it is possible to continue to **Manikaran** and onwards to Pulga and beyond in the scenic Parvati Valley. You can also get to Manikaran by bus from Kullu (see page 179). Up to Khirganga the trail is fairly clear but take care since the area is prone to heavy rain and land slips. Beyond Khirganga, the trek follows the valley up-river passing the tree line to Pandav Bridge and eventually arriving at the sacred lake and shrine at Mantalai. Here it splits leading up and over the Pin-Parvati Pass, and down into the dry Pin Valley.
    Alternatively, you can explore the lower Parvati Valley by walking to **Kasol** on the river with a *Tourist Hut* (no catering), and then to Jari and Naggar via the temple of Bijli Mahadev (Map trek **d**).

Parvati Valley

The difference between the Parvati and the **Pin Valley** is striking. Immense glaciers and bizarre moonscape rock formations here contrast with the verdant pastures and evergreen forests of the Parvati valley behind. The trek leads down to the traditional village of **Mudh** (see page 217). The road to Mudh is still incomplete so it takes about five hours to walk to Sangam and Chatral, leading to Kinnaur and Spiti. There are buses from Chatral to Kaza (see page 170). The trek from Manikaran to Kaza with passes over 5,300 m, can take 10-14 days.

Pin Valley
Guides & porters are necessary

Trekking in Kangra

There are very pleasant day walks throughout the Kangra Valley. Longer, more arduous treks are north over the Dhaula Dhar to Chamba or the Kullu Valley.
    Baijnath, **Palampur** and **Dharamshala** are popular starting points. See page 198. From here you go over the **Dhaula Dhar** at passes such as the

Himachal Pradesh (side margin)

Indrahar and Minkiani (both from Dharamshala) and the Waru (from Palampur), then enter a feeder of the Upper Ravi Valley.

Midway up the valley which lies between the Manimahesh Dhar and Dhaula Dhar ranges is Bara Bangahal. From there you can go downstream to **Chamba** or upstream which offers the choice of at least three passes for crossing into the Kullu Valley. The northernmost of these is the Sòlang Pass which passes Beas Kund beneath Hanuman Tibba. In the middle is the Manali Pass whilst the southernmost is Sagar Pass. A good trip which includes the upper part of this valley is the round trip trek from Manali, see page 219.

Jammu & Kashmir

5

Jammu & Kashmir

224 Background

227 Srinagar
230 Jammu
233 Trekking in Jammu & Kashmir
234 Srinagar to Leh Road

235 Ladakh
238 Leh
247 Monasteries along the Leh Manali Highway
250 Monasteries along the Srinagar Road
253 Nubra Valley, Nyoma and Drokhpa area
255 Trekking in Ladakh

258 Zanskar
259 Trekking in Zanskar

Jammu and Kashmir, the contested jewel of South Asia's northernmost region, has seen its astonishingly beautiful valleys and mountains repeatedly scarred by political dispute. Its lakes, fertile valleys and remote, snow-covered peaks have drawn rulers, pilgrims and ordinary travellers from the Mughals onwards.

Tragically, the beauty of the Vale of Kashmir has been effectively out of bounds for over ten years. However, the state has other fascinating and accessible regions, set in some of the world's most beautiful scenery.

The spectacular high altitude deserts of Ladakh and Zanskar provide the setting for a hardy Buddhist culture, whose villages and monasteries retain strong links with Tibet. Alchi, Hemis and Thikse are just three of the most striking of the many monasteries clinging to mountainsides, and some of the highest altitude passes in the world allow entry to one of India's least known regions.

All foreigners entering the Vale of Kashmir and Ladakh are required to register their arrival. Despite the fact that visitors still go to the Vale of Kashmir there is a very obvious military presence and frequent acts of violence.

Background

The land
Population: 9,000,000
Area 222,000 sq km

The largest of India's Himalayan states comprises three regions: **Jammu**, the mainly Hindu foothills in the south; the **Vale of Kashmir**, overwhelmingly Muslim in the centre; **Ladakh** and **Zanskar**, the western highlands of the great Himalayan axis, predominantly Buddhist.

Jammu is the borderland with the Punjab, and the transitional zone between the plains and the mountains. To the north the Shiwaliks give onto the Pir Panjal which attain heights of 5,000 m.

The Vale of Kashmir, lies between the Pir Panjal and the High Himalaya, at an average altitude of 1,580 m. Rising behind the Vale are the Great Himalaya which culminate in the west with Nanga Parbat ('Naked Mount' – 8,125 m). The Nagin and Dal lakes dominate Srinagar. Nearby is Anchar Lake.

The Trans-Himalaya form a rugged zone of transition, the **Zanskar** range to the south and the **Ladakh** range to the north, with an average altitude of 5,000 m. Leh, the capital, is at an altitude of 3,520 m. As the mountains were raised the Indus maintained its course, carving very deep gorges.

Climate Even in the Vale, the air in summer is fresh and at night can even be quite brisk. The highest daytime temperatures in July rarely exceed 35°C in July but may fall as low as -11°C in winter. A short climb quickly reduces these temperatures. In Ladakh the sun cuts through the thin atmosphere, and daily and seasonal temperature variations are even wider. The rain-bearing clouds drifting in from the Arabian Sea never reach Ladakh. Srinagar receives over 650 mm per annum whereas Leh has only 85 mm, much as snow. Over half Srinagar's rain comes with westerly depressions in the winter.

History Ruled for many years by Scythian and then Tartar princes, Kashmir was captured by Shams ud Din in 1341 who spread Islam across the Vale which subsequently became popular with the Mughals. Babur longed for the streams and cool mountain air of the Hindu Kush. In 1588 the Mughal Emperor Akbar conquered Kashmir and his son **Jahangir** (1605-27), captivated by the beauty of the Vale of Kashmir, planted *chenar* trees and constructed pleasure gardens. At the close of the first Sikh War in 1846 Jammu, the Vale of Kashmir, Ladakh, Baltistan and Gilgit were assigned to the Maharaja **Gulab Singh of Jammu**, who founded a dynasty of Dogra Rajputs, descended from the Katoch branch of the lunar race of **Rajputs**. Thus, Hindus ruled a mainly Muslim population.

Independence Kashmir's future remained unresolved at Independence. Eighteen months of fighting in 1948-49 left the state split by a UN monitored ceasefire line which remains the *de facto* border between India and Pakistan. Kashmir has remained the single most important cause of conflict between the two countries ever since, while arguments for autonomy within the Kashmir Valley have periodically dominated the political agenda. Since 1989 the Indian army has struggled to keep control against a Pakistan-backed militia.

The current political situation In mid-2000 India and Pakistan still showed no sign of resolving the Kashmir dispute. The conflict over the northern border town of Kargil in summer 1999 has left a heightened state of tension. Pakistan remains committed to a referendum allowing Kashmiris a vote on whether to join Pakistan or stay with India, but without the option to vote for Independence. India continues to be determined to face down opposition to its control of the state. An estimated 300,000 troops remain in the region and

Warning

Visitors to India have been advised not to travel to the Kashmir Valley. Several of the splinter groups opposed to the Indian Government have taken hostages as a means of putting pressure on the Government so the risks of travel to Kashmir are still real.

Travel agents, especially in Delhi, try to persuade tourists that everything is normal. Since an increasing number of domestic tourists are visiting the valley. Take advice from your own consulate.

despite some sources urging tourists to start visiting again most foreign consulates still advise visitors to stay away.

People and language Culturally the people of Jammu, Kashmir and Ladakh could scarcely be more different from each other. The nine million people are unevenly scattered. The Vale of Kashmir has over half, whilst Ladakh is the most sparsely populated. Jammu was traditionally the seat of Dogra power and serves a largely Hindu population with its affinities more with the Punjab than the Vale. Kashmir marks the northernmost advance of Islam in the Himalaya while Ladakh is aptly named 'Little Tibet'. Ethnically the Ladakhis are of Tibetan stock. Indeed, it was once a province of Tibet and was governed in secular matters by an independent prince and in spiritual affairs by the Dalai Lama. Kashmiri is influenced by Sanskrit and belongs to the Dardic branch of the Indo-Aryan languages. Linguistically and physically Kashmiris are similar to the tribes around Gilgit in Pakistan. The Ladakhis physically reveal Tibetan-Mongolian and Indo-Aryan origins while their language belongs to the Tibetan-Burmese group.

Culture

Jammu & Kashmir

Handicrafts Kashmir is renowned for its distinctive and fine handicrafts. Many of these developed when Srinagar was an entrepôt on the ancient trans-Himalayan trade route. High quality craftsmanship in India initially owed much to the patronage of the court and Kashmir was no exception. From the 15th century onwards, carpet making, shawl weaving and embroidery and decorative techniques were actively encouraged and the tradition grew to demands made at home and abroad. Since tourism has been severely affected in the Vale since 1989, Kashmiri tradesmen have sought markets in other parts of India.

NB All trade in Shahtush & articles made from the wool of the Chiru is banned, hence buying & exporting an article is illegal

Kashmir shawls are world renowned for their softness and warmth. The best are *pashmina* and *shahtush*, the latter being the warmest, the rarest and, consequently, the most expensive. Prized by Moghuls and Maharajas they found their way to Europe and through Napoleon's Egyptian campaign became an item of fashion in France. The craft was possibly introduced from Persia in the 15th century. Originally a fine shawl would take months to complete especially if up to 100 colours were used. The soft fleece of the pashmina goat or the fine under hairs of the Tibetan antelope were used, the former for cashmere shawls, the latter for *shahtush*. The very best were soft and warm and yet so fine that they could be drawn through a finger ring. The designs changed over the years from floral patterns in the 17th century to Paisley in the 19th century. The Mughals, especially Akbar, used them as gifts. However, with the introduction of the Jacquard loom, cheap imitations were mass produced at a fraction of the price. The Kashmir shawls thus became luxury items, their manufacture remaining an important source of employment in the Vale, but they ceased to be the major export. See warning in margin.

Carpets Hand knotted carpets are available in pure wool and mixed with cotton or silk. The patterns tend to the traditional, the Persian and Bukhara

Pashmina and Shahtush

Kashmir shawls are world renowned for their softness and warmth. The best are pashmina and shahtush, the latter being the warmest, the rarest and, consequently, the most expensive. Prized by Moghuls and Maharajas they found their way to Europe, and through Napoleon's Egyptian campaign, became an item of fashion in France.

The craft was possibly introduced from Persia in the 15th century. Originally a fine shawl would take months to complete especially if up to 100 colours were used. The soft fleece of the pashmina goat or the fine under hairs of the Tibetan antelope were used, the former for

cashmere shawls, the latter for shahtush. The very best were soft and warm and yet so fine that they wcould be drawn through a finger ring. The designs changed over the year s from floral patterns in the 17th century to Paisley in the 19th century. The Mughals, especially Akbar, used them as gifts. However, with the introduction of the Jacquard loom, cheap imitations were mass produced at a fraction of the price. The Kashmir shawls thus became luxury items, their manufacture remaining an important source of employment in the Vale, but they ceased to be the major export.

styles being common, though figurative designs such as The Tree of Life are becoming increasingly popular. Young boys work with a master and it is common to hear them calling out the colour changes in a chant. Child labour in carpet making across North India is increasingly widely criticized. Government attempts to insist on limiting hours of work and the provision of schooling often seem to be ignored. A large carpet will take months to complete, the price depending on the density of knots and the material used, silk being by far the most expensive. The salesmen usually claim that only vegetable dyes are used and whilst this is true in some instances, more readily available and cheaper chemical dyes are commonplace. After knotting, the pile is trimmed with scissors, loose threads burnt off and the carpet washed and dried.

Papier mâché boxes, trays, coasters make ideal gifts. Paper is soaked, dried in a mould, then painted and lacquered. Traditionally, natural colouring was used (lapis lazuli for blue, gold leaf for gold, charcoal for black) but this is unlikely today. The patterns can be highly intricate and the finish exquisite.

Other crafts include crewel work (chain stitching) on fabric, fur coats and 'Kashmiri silver' jewellery, silk and fine woodcarving, particularly on walnut wood.

Modern Jammu & Kashmir **Government** The state enjoys a special status within the union. As defined in Article 370 of the constitution, since 1956 Jammu and Kashmir has had its own constitution affirming its integrity. The central government has direct control over defence, external affairs and communications within the state and indirect influence over citizenship, Supreme Court jurisdiction and emergency powers. In normal times the state sends six representatives to the Lok Sabha and two members who are nominated by the governor to the Rajya Sabha.

Srinagar श्रीनगर

Founded by Raja Pravarasen in the sixth century and beautifully located around a number of lakes, Srinagar, 'the beautiful city', is divided in two by the river Jhelum which is crossed by a number of bridges (kadal). *Despite the name, the beauty of Kashmir has never been reflected in that of its main town. The city's daily life revolves around the river and Dal and Nagin lakes but the lack of tourists has led to neglect.*

Colour map 1, grid A1
Population:
570,000 (1981)
Altitude: 1,730 m

Getting there Srinagar has daily flights from Delhi via Jammu and weekly flights from Leh. The taxi transfer takes 45 mins. Buses from Delhi and Jammu arrive after a tediously slow trip with army escorts. This journey must be undertaken in daylight.

Ins & outs

Legend suggests that hill **Hari Parbat** was once a lake as large as a sea, inhabited by the abominable demon Jalobhava. The gods called on Sati Mata for help, who taking the form of a bird dropped a pebble on the demon's head. The pebble increased in size as it descended and crushed him. Hari Parbat is revered as that pebble and it became the home for all 33 crore (330 million) gods of the Hindu pantheon. There is a 16th-century fort on the hill.

Background

The **Jama Masjid** (1674), is notable for the wooden pillars supporting the roof, each made from a single *deodar* tree. To the southeast is the **Rozahbal mosque**, which has the 'tomb of Jesus' (Holger Kersten's *Jesus Lived in India* recounts the legend). Across the river is the **Pattar Masjid** (1623) built for the Empress Nur Jahan and renamed Shahi Mosque. **Shankaracharya Hill** is behind the Boulevard. The temple was built during Jahangir's reign but is said to be over a second century BC temple built by Asoka's son. The hill was known as Takht-i-Sulaiman – The Throne of Solomon.

Sights
Dusk-to-dawn curfews are not uncommon. In 2000-01 it still may not be possible to visit some of the sites outlined below

The lake is 6.4 km long and 4 km wide and is divided into three parts by man-made causeways. The small islands are willow covered, while round the lake are groves of *chinar*, poplar and willow. The **Mihrbahri** people have lived around the lakes for centuries and are market gardeners, tending the floating beds of vegetables and flowers that they have made and cleverly shielded with weeds to make them unobtrusive.

Dal Lake

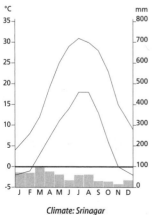

Climate: Srinagar
Best time to visit: May-Sep

Set in front of a triangle of the lake created by the intersecting causeways with a slender bridge at the centre lies the famous **Nishat Bagh** (Garden of Gladness). Sandwiched between the hills and the lake, it was laid out by Asaf Khan, Nur Jahan's brother, in 1632.

Shalimar Bagh is about 4 km away and set back from the lake. A channel extends up to their edge. Built by

Exercise caution

Travellers continue to visit Srinagar, some using the road to Leh to enter Ladakh. It is essential to be extremely careful. Moving around the town can be hazardous, especially after dark – only a few suitable hotels and houseboats are open; there are no bars, beer shops or cinemas and phone links with the rest of India, let alone overseas, are poor.

Jahangir for his wife, Nur Jahan, the gardens are distinguished by a series of terraces linked by a water channel. These are surrounded by decorative pools which can only be reached by stepping stones. The uppermost pavilion has elegant black marble pillars and niches in the walls for flowers during the day and candles or lamps at night.

Chashma Shahi (Royal Spring, 1632) This much smaller garden was built around the course of a renowned spring and is attributed to Shah Jahan though it has been altered over the centuries.

Hazratbal (Majestic Place) is on the western shore of the lake and commands excellent views. The modern mosque has a special sanctity as a hair of the **prophet Mohammad** is preserved here. Just beyond is the **Nazim Bagh** (Garden of the Morning Breeze), one of the earliest Mughal Gardens and attributed to Akbar.

Museum **Pratap Singh Museum**, Lal Mandi (between Amira Kadal and Zero Bridge)

Srinagar

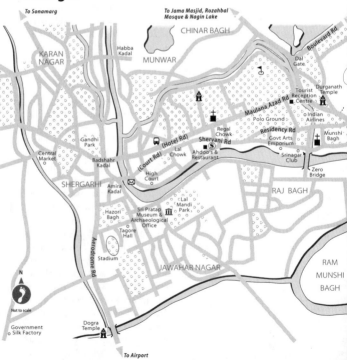

Jammu & Kashmir

The most expensive spice in the world

Pampore, 16 km from Srinagar, is the centre of Kashmir's saffron industry. Saffron, a species of crocus (Crocus sativus), grows here in abundance and in a few other places in the world, and is harvested by hand. Within each purple bloom, the three orange-red anthers yield pure saffron. Over 4,500 blooms make one ounce (28 grms) of the spice, so the price of this delicate flavouring and colouring in cooking is high (once far more valuable than gold). Its value has led the Indian Government to set up a saffron research farm at Sangla in Himachal Pradesh.

The precious orange coloured dye was used by royalty and the colour saffron was chosen by monks for their robes after the Buddha's death. In 631 AD Hiuen Tsang commented on how rich the country was agriculturally, noting the abundant fruits and flowers as well as the medicinal herbs and saffron. He admired the Kashmiris' good looks and their love of learning, but also felt that they were too frivolous and given to cunning.

has a fine collection of miniature paintings, weapons, tapestries and sculpture but rather poorly displayed. ■ *1000-1700, closed Mon, Fri lunchtime. Free (small donation is appreciated).*

In view of the present political situation this edition of the Handbook does not carry details of places to visit outside Srinagar.

Around Srinagar

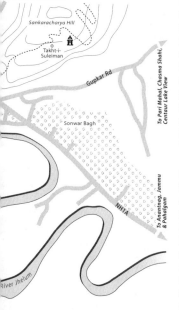

To Dal Lake & Nehru Park

Sankaracharya Hill

Takht-i-Suleiman

Gupkar Rd

To Pari Mahal, Chasma Shahi, Centaur Lake View

Sonwar Bagh

NH1A

To Anantnag, Jammu

To Anantnag, Jammu & Pahalgam

River Jhelum

Jammu & Kashmir

Essentials

Sleeping

■ on map
*Price codes:
see inside front cover*

Since the clampdown in Kashmir many hotels are occupied by military personnel. It is impossible to give reliable information

A-L *Centaur Lake View*, Chashma Shahi (5 km centre), T475731, F471877. 248 modern rooms. **A-L** *Grand Palace*, Gupkar Rd, T470101, F453794. 60 rooms in re-opened palace. **A** *Shah Abbas*, Boulevard Rd, T479334, F476553, www.shahabbashotel. com 84 rooms facing lake or mountains. **C-D** *Ahdoo's*, Shervani Rd. Established. **D** *Tourist Reception Centre*, Maulana Azad and Sherwani Rds, T474060, F476107. Rooms and dorm in *Hostel*. **E** hotels in Khonkhun, Dal Gate include *Cathay*, T474014, and *Shabnam*, T451813.

Houseboats These are peculiar to Srinagar and are moored along the shores of the Dal Lake (the target of pushy salesmen), the quieter and distant Nagin Lake and along the busy Jhelum. In the valley's hey day the boats were well kept and delightfully cosy. Still mostly family run, they usually include all meals. It is best to see the boat and make sure what services are included before hiring. Travellers have recommended: *Bambri Palace*, Dal Lake, Gate 2, F475774, immaculate, Md Yusuf

Khankashi takes excellent care, well-furnished. On the Dal Lake ***Garden of Eden***, T475407. Owned by a reliable family who also have ***Beauty Star***. For luxury, try, ***New Moon*** which is run by 'Carefree Travelo'. ***Happy Day***, with a considerate owner, and ***New Manila***, on the Dal Lake, T472787, for good food, helpful service including tours.

Eating ***Ahdoo's***, Residency Rd. ***Shah-en-Shah***, Boulevard Rd, garden seating in summer.

Transport **Local Shikaras** (boats): Rs 20 per hr but some ask Rs 60. **Long distance Air** Srinagar Airport, 14 km, T430334. ***Indian Airlines*** T452328, airport T430194, flies to **Delhi** and **Jammu** daily; **Amritsar**, Tue, Thu, Sat; **Leh**, Sat. ***Jet Airways*** T475555, airport T433007: **Delhi** and **Jammu** daily. ***Pawan Hans*** may offer helicopter services to Amarnath in Aug. **Road** Srinagar on NH1A, is linked to the rest of India by all-weather roads, some through superb scenery. To **Jammu** (293 km), by a narrow mountain road, often full of lorries and military convoys, takes 12 hrs; few stops for food and facilities. **Bus**: State Roadways buses run to Jammu from Delhi, Chandigarh and Amritsar; some continue to Srinagar. J&KSRTC, TRC, Srinagar, T72698. Summer 0600-1800, winter 0700-1700. Bus to **Kargil** (alternate days in summer, Rs 90-170), **Leh** (434 km, Rs 180-340). **Train** The nearest railhead is Jammu Tawi with coach (12 hrs) and taxi transfer (9 hrs). Govt TRC, 0700-1900. T72698 for reservation of 2nd-Class Sleeper and a/c only. Summer 0830-1900, winter 1000-1800. Also at *Radhakrishnan*, Budhah Chowk, T72929.

Directory **Banks** *Grindlays* and *State Bank of India* on Shervani Rd. **Travel agent** *Sita*, *Hotel Broadway*, Maulana Azad Rd, T477186, F452600. **Tourist Office** *J&K*, TRC, T452690, F479548. **Useful addresses** Ambulance: T474591. **Fire:** T472222. **Police:** T100.

Jammu जम्मू

Colour map 1, grid B1
Population: 223,361 (1981)
Altitude: 305 m

Jammu, the second largest city in the state, is the winter capital of government and main entry point for Kashmir by rail. Not an attractive city, with few open spaces and too much traffic, it is chaotic with little to recommend it.

Ins & outs **Getting there** The railway station is in the New Town, across the Tawi River, and a few kilometres from the old hilltop town where most of the budget hotels are located. The General Bus Stand where inter-state buses come in, is at the foot of the steps off the Srinagar Road in the Old Town. **Getting around** The frequent, cheap city bus service or an auto-rickshaw comes in handy as the two parts of the town and some sights, are far apart.

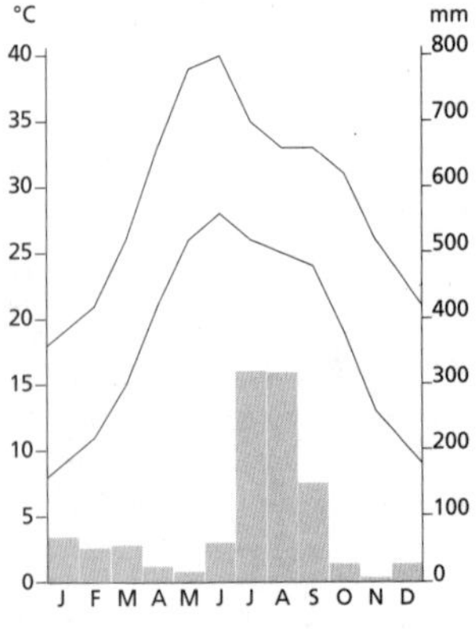

Climate: Jammu
Best time to visit: Nov-Mar

Sights The **Raghunath Temple** (1857) in the old centre, is one of the largest temple complexes in North India. The temple has seven shrines, with gold plated interiors. The most important houses the Dogras' patron deity, Rama, Vishnu's eighth incarnation. The arches and architectural details show Mughal influence.

Morning and evening *aartis* are ritually attended and there is also a stone lingam here and in the other shrines, for this is a centre for Shakti worship. A portrait of Ranbir Singh, the temple patron and a sculpture of Hanuman are at the entrance. The other shrines have images of Vishnu in various incarnations, Siva and Surya. The **Sanskrit Library** here contains numerous rare manuscripts.

The **Rambiresvar Temple** (1883), centrally located about 500 m from the Dogra Art Gallery on the Shalimar Road, is dedicated to Siva. It has a 75-metre tower and extraordinary crystal lingams and is the largest Siva temple in North India.

The **Bahu Fort** with its ruined ramparts stands on a rock face overlooking the river south of the city, the oldest remaining building in the region. The original structure was improved and rebuilt as the Mondi Palace (circa 1880) by the Dogra rulers. Bagh-e-Bahu gardens around the fort has a *cafetería*. The **Kali Temple** inside the fort attracts large crowds at a festival held twice a year in March/April and September/October. The Old Palace is now the **High Court**.

Jammu

Not to scale

■ **Sleeping**
1 Arjuna Jewel & Cultural Academy
2 Cosmopolitan
3 Jammu Ashok
4 KC Residency
5 Mansar & Tawi View
6 Picnic
7 Premier & Chinese Room Restaurant

Jammu & Kashmir

Amar Mahal Museum, superbly sited on the bend of the Tawi, is just off Srinagar Road. There is a portrait gallery, Pahari paintings of *Mahabharata* scenes and royal memorabilia. The early 20th century palace is a curiosity; its French designer gave it château-like sloping roofs and turrets. Four rooms are open but you can look into others through the windows. ■ *Winter 0900-1230, 1330-1700, summer 0900-1230, 1330-1800, Sun 1000-1200, closed Mon. Fine views of the river but no photography. Getting there: Rs 25 by auto-rickshaw.Rs 5.*
Dogra Art Gallery, Gandhi Bhawan, near New Secretariat, in a part of the Old Palace. Collection of Pahari miniatures (four good Kangra School paintings), terracottas, manuscripts and sculptures including sixth century terracotta heads. Sadly, it is poorly maintained and dimly lit. ■ *Winter 1100-1700, summer 0800-1330, closed Mon. Free.*

Museums

Akhnoor, 32 km northwest of Jammu, is where the Chenab River meets the plains and was on the route to Kashmir in Mughal times. **Surinsar** and **Mansar Lakes**, 80 km and 42 km east of Jammu are picturesque forest fringed lakes. **Sleeping** *Tourist Bungalow* and *Huts*.

Excursions

B *Asia Jammu-Tawi*, Nehru Market, north of town, T535757, F535756. 44 rooms, restaurant, exchange, pool, clean, comfortable. Recommended. **C** *Hari Niwas Palace* (Heritage Hotel), 3.5 km from centre, T543303. 18 a/c rooms. **C** *Jammu Ashok*, opposite Amar Mahal. 48 rooms, restaurant, pool. **C** *KC Residency*, Vir Marg, T542773, F542779. 61 a/c rooms, excellent restaurant , exchange, pool. **D** *Cosmopolitan*, Vir Marg, T547561. 28 rooms, some a/c, good restaurant, bar. **D** *Jewel*, Jewel Chowk,

Sleeping
■ *on map, page 231*
Price codes:
see inside front cover

T547630. 18 rooms, some air-cooled, restaurant. **D** *Premier*, Vir Marg, T543234. 21 rooms, some a/c, restaurants, bar. Recommended. **D-E** *Tourist Reception Centre*, Vir Marg, T549554. 128 rooms with bath, a few air-cooled, good value with best in Blocks NA and A, poor dorm restaurant. **E** *Picnic*, Idgah Rd, T543931. 20 rooms. **E** *Tawi View*, below Gummat, T543752. Few air-cooled rooms. **F** *Arjuna*, Jewel Chowk, T578211. Convenient for buses. **F** *Shankar* (5 minute walk past post office on right of Reservations at bus station, after 8 minute walk, right again), basic rooms (2-3 beds), fan, bucket bath, limited restaurant but reasonable food.

Eating

● *on map, page 231*
Price codes:
see inside front cover

Expensive Hotels: *Asia Jammu-Tawi's* outdoor *Bar-e-Kabab*. International. Good food, evening entertainment. *KC Residency* . International. Bizarre revolving restaurant, trundles round with an occasional jolt but serves excellent food, good views especially at night when you can see the lights on the pilgrimage trail at Vaishno Devi. **Mid-range** *Cosmopolitan*. Good Chinese and Kashmiri. **Cheap** Several on Vir Marg.*India Coffee House*, Exhibition Ground. *Kailash* and *Amritsarian* in Raghunath Bazar are recommended for veg. *Jewel*. Mainly fast food.

Entertainment **Sport** **Swimming**: *Jammu Tawi Hotel* (non-residents pay). *Maulana Azad Stadium Complex* has a large pool, T542038. **Festivals** Jan *Lohri* is an important festival throughout North India and is celebrated with *havan yagnas* in temples and houses. Apr *Baisakhi* is the harvest festival. A large celebration is held at Nagbani temple.

Shopping Wool tunics (*pherans*), fine pashmina shawls (from Rs 8,000) and woodcarvings are good, as well as dried fruit and nuts. Main shopping areas: Raghunath Bazar, Hari Bazar, Upper Gummat. *J&K Govt Arts Emporium* and *Khadi Gramudyog* are both on Vir Marg.

Transport **Local** **Bus**: frequent, on fixed routes; low fares. **Mini-buses**, **tempos** and **auto-rickshaws**. **Taxis**: un-metered, T533485. Tourist taxis, T542231.

Long distance **Air** Airport, 6 km. **Transport to town** taxis and auto-rickshaws; fix fares beforehand. **Indian Airlines**, TRC, Vir Marg, T542735, Apt T531433, flies to **Delhi** and **Srinagar** daily; **Leh** (Thu, Sun). **Jet Airways**, KC Residency Hotel, T574312, Apt T453999; to **Delhi** and **Srinagar** daily. **Helicopter** *Pawan Hans* may resume services to Katra for Vaishno Devi, Mar-Jul. **Train** Station, T531085. To **Old Delhi**: *Jammu Tawi Mail*, 4034, 1545, 14_ hrs; *Jammu Tawi Delhi Exp*, 2404, 1835, 10 hrs. **New Delhi**: *Jhelum Exp*, 1078, 2145, 12_ hrs; *Shalimar Exp*, 4646, 2055, 14_ hrs; *Rajdhani Exp*, 2426, Sun, 2030, 9 hrs. **Kolkata** (South): *Jammu Tawi Exp*, 3152, 1815, 45 hrs. **Road** Sumos run to Katra from the station. **Bus** J&K SRTC, TRC, Vir Marg , T546851 (1000-1700), General Bus Stand, T542666 (0400-2000) direct buses to **Srinagar** (293 km), **Katra (for Vaishno Devi)**, **Pathankot and Kishtwar**. Punjab Roadways T542782 . To **Delhi** (586 km), daily. Super deluxe, video and A-class coaches to Srinagar leave from the railway station, usually between 0600 and 0700. B-class buses to Srinagar from the General Bus Stand go via the station but may get full.

Directory **Banks** *State Bank of India*, Hari Market, among several. **Communications** GPO: Pacca Danga. Post Offices in Old Palaces, near Dogra Art Gallery and Raghunath Temple. **Tourist offices** *J&K Tourism*, Tourist Reception Centre, Vir Marg, T548172. *Jammu Tawi*, Railway Station, T544842. *JKTDC*, T546412. Tour operator on On Vir Marg. **Useful addresses** Fire: T101. Hospital:, T547637. **Police**: T100. **Foreigners' Registration Office**: Supt of Police, Canal Rd, T542676. **NB** Foreigners must register.

exodus
9 Weir Road
LONDON
SW12 0BR

BUSINESS REPLY SERVICE
Licence No SW4909

getaway tonight on

www.exodus.co.uk

exodus
The Different Holiday

Around Jammu

The Vaishno Devi cave is one of the region's most important pilgrim sites. As the temple draws near you hear cries of Jai Matadi (Victory to the Mother Goddess). Then at the shrine entrance, pilgrims walk in batches through cold ankle-deep water to the low and narrow cave entrance to get a glimpse of the deity. Visitors joining the yatra find it a very moving and exhilarating experience.

Vaishno Devi
Phone code: 01991
Colour map 1, grid B1

The Vaishno Devi cave is at 1,700 m (30 m long and only 1½ m high), 61 km north of Jammu. It is dedicated to Mahakali, Mahalaxmi and Mahasaraswati, the three mother goddesses of Hinduism. According to legend Vaishno Devi used the cave as a refuge when she was fleeing from the demon Bhairon who wanted to marry her. She would have nothing to do with this and killed him. Pilgrims usually visit the temple to Bhairon who was absolved of his sins before he died.

The main pilgrimage season is March to July. The arduous climb along the 13 km track to the cave temple has been re-laid, widened and tiled, and railings provided. Another road from Lower Sanjichat to the Darbar brings you 2 km closer with 300 m less to climb. Ponies, *dandies* and porters are available from Katra at fixed rates. Auto-rickshaws and taxis can go as far as the Banganga. Yatra slips issued by the Shrine Board in Katra must be presented at Banganga checkpoint within six hours. Tea, drinks and snacks are available on the route.

Visitors should leave all leather items in a cloakroom at Vaishno Devi before entering the cave; carry bottled water and waterproofs. If you are on your own or in a small group, to avoid a wait for a group allocation, present yourself at Gates 1 or 2, and smile. **Katra** (*phone code*: 01991) is an attractive town at the foot of the Trikuta Hills.

B *Country Inn*, modern hotel to open by 2000. **C** *Asia Vaishnodevi*, T32061, F33344. 37 rooms, some a/c, restaurant, transport to Banganga. **C-D** *Ambica*, T32062. 50 rooms, some a/c. **D** *Durga*, 30 rooms, restaurant. Among several cheap hotels: **E** *Prem*, Main Bazaar, T32014. Rooms with hot water and a fire, adequate. J&K Tourism **E** *Tourist Bungalow*, T32009, 42 rooms, and **E-F** *Retiring Centre*, T32309. With rooms and dorm, are near the bus stand. At the half-way point to Vaishno Devi: **F** *Dormitories* and simple rooms provide sheets and blankets.

Sleeping
This is a selection of over 50 places

Excellent vegetarian food is available – curd and *panir* (curd cheese) dishes are especially good for non-*dhaba* food try the 2 vegetarian fast food places on the main street. Both clean and good. No alcohol.

Eating

Long distance Air *Pawan Hans* may resume helicopter to Sanjichat. **Road Buses & taxis** leave from General Bus Stand, Jammu (or the railway station at peak season) and go to Katra (48 km); Rs 25, a/c Rs 55; taxi Rs 500 for 4.

Transport

Trekking in Jammu & Kashmir

Although the major pilgrimage to Amarnath is massively guarded by the army, treks in the region cannot be regarded as safe. It is currently almost impossible to trek in Jammu and Kashmir, though it is still possible to get into Ladakh. The government is making great efforts to develop alternatives to Kashmir in Himachal Pradesh, see page 213.

Jammu & Kashmir

Srinagar to Leh Road

The alternative route to Leh from Manali is equally fascinating, see page 191

*The road to Leh from Srinagar must be one of the most fascinating journeys in the world as it negotiates high passes and fragile mountainsides. There are dramatic scenic and cultural changes as you go from Muslim, verdant Kashmir to Buddhist, ascetic Ladakh. **NB** Because of political unrest in Kashmir, the route, which runs very close to the Line of Control, was closed to travellers in 2000.*

Sonamarg ('Path of Gold'), 84 km from Srinagar at an altitude of 2,740 m, is the last major town in Kashmir before the Zoji La and Ladakh. From Zoji La the road descends to **Minamarg** meadow and Dras. The winter temperatures go down to -50°C, and heavy snow and strong winds cut off the town. The broad Kargil basin and its wide terraces are separated from the Mulbekh valley by the 12 km long **Wakha Gorge**.

On the bank of the river Suru, **Kargil** (*altitude*: 2,740 m), was an important trading post on two routes, from Srinagar to Leh, and to Gilgit and the lower Indus Valley. Before 1990 it was the overnight stop on the Srinagar-Leh highway, and in 1999 the Pakistan army took control briefly of the heights surrounding the town before being forced to retreat.

From Kargil the road goes on to **Shergol** (30 km), the cultural boundary between Muslim and Buddhist areas and then passes **Mulbekh** (9 km) with its and **Namika La** (13 km; 3,720 m), known as the Pillar in the Sky. It climbs to **Photu La** (4,093 m), the highest pass on the route. From here you can catch sight of the monastery at Lamayuru. The road does a series of loops to descend to **Khaltse** (Khalsi) (36 km) where it meets the milky green Indus River.

In **Lamayuru**, the monastery, 10 km from Khaltse, is perched on a crag overlooking the Indus in a striking setting between a drained lake and high mountains.

The complex, which includes a library, thought to be the oldest in the region, was founded in the 11th century and belongs to the Tibetan Kagyupa sect. The present monastery dating from the 16th century was partly destroyed in the 19th. You can still see some of the murals, the 11-headed and 1,000-armed Avalokiteshvara image, along with the redecorated *dukhang* (assembly hall). There are caves carved out of the mountain wall and some of the rooms are richly furnished with carpets, Tibetan tables and butter lamps. Festivals are in February/March and July. There are buses from Leh. **Sleeping** *Monastery Hotel* or few guest houses. They do meals too. Camp near the stream in a willow grove.

Rizong (53 km) has a monastery and nunnery, which may accommodate visitors. **Saspul** village marks the wide valley from which you can reach **Alchi** by taking a branch road across the Indus after passing some caves. **Lekir** is off the main road, 8 km after Saspul. Further along the road you catch sight of the ruins of **Basgo** before it crosses the Chargyal Thang plain with chortens and *mani* walls and enters **Nimmu**. The road rejoins the Indus valley and rises to another bare plateau to give you the first glimpse of Leh, 30 km away. **Phyang** is on a hill and finally **Spituk** is reached (see page 247 for details of monasteries).

There are check points on some routes and foreigners will need to register at Upshi (Manali-Leh) or Khaltse (Srinagar-Leh) and pay an entry tax of US$10. Visitors from Leh approach Lamayaru along this road.

Ladakh

The mountains of Ladakh – literally 'many passes' – may not be as spectacular as some parts of the high Himalaya, as even the valleys are at an altitude of 3,500 m with the summits only 3,000 m higher. Because it is desert there is little snow on them and they look like big brown hills, dry and dusty, with clusters of willows and desert roses along the streams. Yet for thousands of visitors Ladakh is a completely magical place, remote, with delightful, gentle, ungrasping people.

Until very recently Ladakhi society has generally been very introverted and the economy surprisingly self-sufficient. Ladakh also developed a very distinct culture. Polyandry (where women have more than one husband) was common, but many men became *lamas* (monks) and a few women *chomos* (nuns). Most people depended on subsistence agriculture but the harsh climate contributed to very high death rates and a stable population. That is rapidly changing. Imported goods are increasingly widely available and more and more people are taking part in the monetary economy. Ladakh and its capital Leh have only been open to tourists since 1974 but some argue that already there are too many.

Entry Taxes Foreign visitors to the valley pay US$10 at the point of entry into Ladakh. For the newly opened areas of Nubra and Shyok Valleys and Drokhpa, Tso-moriri and Pangong Tso, the permit costs US$20, while trekkers in the Hemis High Altitude Park must pay Rs 25 (Indians Rs 10) per day. **Inner Line Permits** Areas which would normally be restricted but are open to tourists include Rizong, Likir, Phyang, Shey, Thikse, Chemrey and Tak-thok gompas. A permit is needed to visit the newly opened areas.

Four mountain ranges cross Ladakh – Gt Himalaya, Zanskar, Ladakh and Karakoram – as do the river Indus and its tributaries the Zanskar, Shingo and Shyok. The Zanskar runs its course of 120 km before joining the Indus at Nimmu near Leh. During the winter months the frozen Zanskar provides the only access for Zanskaris into Ladakh. Ladakh also has the world's largest glaciers outside the polar regions, and the large and beautiful lake Pangong Tso, 150 km long and 4 km wide, at a height of over 4,000 m.

   Flora and fauna Willow and poplar grow in profusion and provide fuel and timber, as well as fodder and material for basket making. The fragrant juniper is reserved for religious ceremonies. The area supports some rare species of animals and birds – red foxes, wolves, ibex, mouse hare and marmots and among the 100 or so species of birds are black necked cranes, Bactrian magpies, Turkoman rock pigeon, desert wheatears, buntings, larks, kite, kestrel and many kinds of finches, ducks and geese. Some rare mammals found in Ladakh include the *brong drong* (wild yak), *kyang* (wild horse) and *nyan* (the large-horned sheep). The snow leopard is the rarest wild animal and you are unlikely to see some of the others, like the musk deer, the Tibetan gazelle or the *chiru* antelope which is prized for its fleece which produces *shahtush*, the very best wool.

Rock carvings indicate that the region has been used for thousands of years by

Background
As a matter of course, you should carry your passport with you since Ladakh is a sensitive border region

The land

History

Colour map 1, grid A3
Population: 175,000
Altitude: 2,500-4,500 m, passes at 4,000-6,000 m, peaks up to 7,500 m

Jammu & Kashmir

nomadic tribesmen who include the Mons of North India, the Dards, the Mongols and Changpa shepherds from Tibet. In Roman times Kashmir and Ladakh lay on a feeder of the great Silk Road that ran from China to the Mediterranean.

Early political development By the end of the 10th century, Ladakh was controlled by the Thi Dynasty which founded a capital at Shey and built many forts. Tibetan Lamaistic Buddhism took hold at the same time and over 100 gompas were built. In 1533 Soyang Namgyal united the whole region up to the outskirts of Lhasa and made his capital at Leh. The Namgyal Dynasty still exists today and the Rani (Queen) of Stok was elected to the Indian Parliament.

Medieval expansion During the reigns of Senge Namgyal (circa 1570-1620) and Deldan Namgyal (circa 1620-60) Ladakh was threatened from the south and west by the Baltis, who had enlisted the assistance of the Mughals. They were beaten back and the Namgyals extended Ladakhi power. The expansionist era came to an end when the fifth Dalai Lama of Tibet, Nawang Lobsang Gyatso (1617-82) persuaded the Mongols, whom he had converted to Buddhism, to enter a military campaign against West Tibet and Ladakh. The Ladakhis were unable to repel the invading Mongol forces and in desperation Delegs Namgyal turned to Kashmir for help. The Mughal Governor of Kashmir sent troops to help the King of Leh regain his throne but in return he had to pay regular tribute and build a mosque. From then on the country became an extension of the Mughal Empire. In 1834 Zorwar Singh, an Army General, conquered Ladakh and brought the area under the control of the Dogra Maharajah of Kashmir. The dethroned royal family received the Stok Palace where they still live today.

Culture **People** There are four main groups. Tibetan **Changpas** form the bulk of the population in central and eastern Ladakh, over several generations gradually assuming the Ladakhi identity. These nomadic herdsmen can be seen living in black yak-hair tents on the mountains with their yaks, goats and sheep. They still provide the fine *pashm* goat wool but the finer *shahtush* is now very rare. The **Mons**, nomads of Aryan stock, introduced Buddhism and established settlements in the valleys; some are professional entertainers and musicians. The **Droks** or Dards from the Gilgit area settled along the Indus valley and introduced irrigation; many converted to Islam 300 years ago though some remained Buddhist. Most are cultivators speaking a language based on Sanskrit. The **Baltis** with Central Asian Saka origins mostly live in the Kargil region. Ladakhis have developed the ability to survive in a very harsh environment, whilst remaining remarkably cheerful.

Ladakhis **dress** in *gonchas*, loose woollen robes tied at the waist with a wide coloured band. Buddhists usually wear dark red while Muslims and nomadic tribes often use undyed material. The head dress varies from the simple Balti woollen cap with a rolled brim and the traditional *gonda* (a high embroidered hat) to the snake-shaped ornate black lambskin *perak* worn by some women. Studded with turquoise and lapis lazuli these are precious enough to be handed down as heirlooms.

Religion 52% of Ladakh's population are Lamaistic Buddhists. Most follow Mahayana **Buddhism** of the *Vajrayana*) sect with a mixture of Bon animism and Tantric practices. The Red Hat Drukpa (or Kagyupa) sect of Tibetan monastic Buddhists enjoy royal patronage. The reformist Yellow Hat sect are Gelugpa Buddhists, and like the Dalai Lama, wear a yellow head-dress with their maroon robes. The more ancient Nyingmapa Buddhist have their seat in Tak-thok. Ladakhi lamas may also be physicians, teachers and

Running hot and cold

The temperature can go down to -30°C in Leh and Kargil and -50°C in Dras, remaining sub-zero from December to February. Yet on clear sunny days in the summer, it can be scorching hot and you can easily get sunburnt. Rainfall is only 50 millimetres annually and there are even occasional dust storms. Take plenty of skin cream.

astrologers; they also work in the fields, as do the *chomos* (nuns). Nearly every family has a member who chooses to become a lama (often the third son) or a chomo. The most important in the Tibetan tradition are recognized reincarnate lamas (*Trulku*), who are born to the position. The Buddhist *gompas* (monasteries) are places of worship, meditation and religious instruction and the structures, often sited on spectacular mountain ridges, add to the attraction of the landscape while remaining a central part of Ladakhi life. Travellers to Ladakh will find visits to *gompas* a rewarding experience, and there are several within easy reach of Leh.

Ladakh also has a large number of Shi'a **Muslims** many being immigrant Kashmiris and Dards. Their mosques and imambaras influenced by Persian architecture can be found in Leh proper and villages nearby. The famous imambara of Chochot Yugma on the bank of the Indus River, a few minutes' walk from Choglamsar bridge, is the oldest in the region and is worth a visit. The majority of the Shi'a Muslims are in Kargil District which also has a number of interesting mosques and imambaras.

Food Barley is turned into *tsampa* after roasting and grinding or *chang*, a sour alcoholic drink, also commonly made from fermented rice. Tsampa is mixed with yoghurt, cheese or chang to make it more tasty. *Gur gur* (tea) is the staple drink, made with a mixture of tea leaves, soda-bicarbonate and salt which is boiled before churning with butter until it thickens. *Momos* are balls of dough which are steamed with a minced meat filling. *Khotays* are fried *momos*.

Festivals The Buddhist festivals usually take place in the bleak winter months when villagers gather together, stalls spring up around the *gompas* and colourful dance dramas and masked dances are performed in the courtyard. Musical instruments, weapons and religious objects are brought out during these dance performances. The *Kushak* (the high priest) is accompanied by monks in monotonous recitation while others play large cymbals, trumpets and drums. The serious theme of the victory of Good over Evil is lightened by comic interludes. A few monasteries celebrate their festivals in the summer months for example Lamayuru, Hemis, Phyang. The *Ladakh Festival* from 1-15 September.

Recent history Following India's independence and partition in 1947 Ladakh, like Kashmir, was divided. Indian and Chinese troops have been stationed on the eastern border since the Chinese invasion of Tibet in 1950-51. From the early 1950s Chinese troops were stationed in the Aksai Chin, which India also claimed, and without Indian knowledge built a road linking Tibet with Xinjiang. This was one of the two fronts in China's war with India in 1962, which confirmed China's de facto hold on the territory. India still disputes its legality. Since the 1962 war the Indian army has maintained a very strong presence in Ladakh. The strategic requirements of better links with the rest of India were primarily responsible for Ladakh being 'opened up' to some influences from outside. Very recently, the local government body, the Ladakh Hill Council, has once again put forth a demand to the Indian Government to separate the district from the rest of the state of Jammu and Kashmir. Citing

Modern Ladakh

Jammu & Kashmir

reasons of cultural uniqueness and the fact that they do not wish to be part of any separatist movement in Kashmir, the Ladakhis demand being made into an 'Union Territory' directly funded by the central government.

Economy Out of necessity, the people, particularly the Baltis, are expert irrigation engineers, cutting granite to channel melt water to the fields. Ladakh has retained cultural links with its neighbouring regions in Himachal Pradesh, Kashmir, Tibet and Central Asia and traded in valuable *pashm*, carpets, apricots, tea, and small amounts of salt, borax, sulphur, pearls and metals. However, today military spending and tourism provide the largest sources of external income, the latter strikingly visible in the bustling population of Leh during the summer months. Solar and water-power have provided basic comforts to some villages.

Cultivation in Ladakh is restricted to the areas immediately around streams and rivers, and altitude and topography determine the choice of crop. Barley forms the staple food while peas are the most common vegetable and apples and apricots the most popular fruits. Because of the harshness of the climate and lack of rain, the cropping season usually lasts from April to October. Apple and apricots grow well, with the latter being dried for the winter, the kernel yielding oil for burning in prayer-lamps. At lower altitudes, grape, mulberry and walnut are grown. Travellers venturing out of Leh are likely to see villagers using traditional methods of cultivation with the help of dzos and donkeys and implements that have not changed for centuries.

Livestock is precious, especially the *yak* which provides meat, milk for butter, hair and hide for tents, boots, ropes and dung for fuel. Goats, especially in the eastern region, produce fine *pashm* for export. The Zanskar pony is fast and strong and therefore used for transport – and for the special game of Ladakhi polo! Nomadic herdsmen move their animals to alpine pastures at altitudes of 4,000 m and more over the summer months.

Communication The area is virtually cut off for six months when roads become impassable; the only link with the outside world is by air. The frozen Zanskar River, the "Tchadar", links Padum with Nimmu near Leh. Animal transport is provided by yaks, ponies, Bactrian camels and the broad backed *hunia* sheep.

Recommended reading *Ladakh* by H Harres, Innsbruck, 1980; *A Journey in Ladakh* by Andrew Harvey, Cape, London, 1983; *Ancient Futures:* Learning from Ladakh by Helena Norberg-Hodge, Rider, London, 1992; *Ladakh, Crossroads of High Asia* by J Rizvi, OUP, Delhi, 1983; *That Untravelled World* by Eric Shipton. See also under **Excursions** below.

★ Leh

Phone code: 09182
Colour map 1, grid A3
Population: 90,000
Altitude: 3,500 m

Mysterious dust-covered Leh sits in a fertile side valley of the Indus, about 10 km from the river. Encircled by stark awe-inspiring mountains with the cold desert beyond, it is the nearest experience of Tibet in India.

Ins & outs   **Getting there** For 7-8 months in the year Leh's sole link with the outside world is by air. Tickets are in heavy demand so it is essential to book well ahead (you can do this on the internet from home). From mid-Jun to end-Sep (weather permitting), in addition to air passengers and trekkers, the Manali-Leh Highway opens to traffic bringing travellers to the New Bus Stand, south of town. There are jeeps from here as well as from the airport. **Getting around** Most hotels are within a few minutes' walk of the Main Bazar Street around which Leh's activities are concentrated. All the places of interest in Leh itself can also be tackled on foot by most visitors though those arriving

Prepare for a different lifestyle in Leh

The whitewashed sun-dried brick walls of a typical two-storey, flat-roofed Ladakhi house, often with decorative woodwork around doors and windows and a carefully nurtured garden, look inviting to a traveller after a very long hard journey, whether by road or air. Local families are opening their homes to provide for the increasing demand for accommodation for a very short peak season and new hotels are springing up. These are listed by the Tourism Department as **A-D** class hotels or as guest houses and must charge fixed rates. However, prices do not reflect the type of furniture, furnishings and plumbing you might expect elsewhere in India although on the whole the rooms are kept clean. There is usually a space for sitting out – a 'garden' with a tree or two, some flower beds and some grass struggling to establish itself.

Electricity is limited, so expect power cuts which are random and unpredictable. Some hotels have generators. Those without may run out of tap water but buckets are always at hand. Hot water is a luxury, available only during mornings and evenings. Plumbing allows for flush WCs in at least **D** category hotels but the water from the basin disappears down the plughole only to emerge around your feet as there is only one drain in a corner of the bathroom!

Guests are encouraged to economize on water and electricity – you will notice the low-power bulbs and scarcity of lights in rooms and public areas, so put away your reading until sunrise.

Drinking water is limited. A few hotels, eg Kang-lha Chhen, have a spring within their grounds; some hotels tap in to the water intended for cultivation. You can help by visiting Dzomsa for water and laundry and by using the local earth/compost toilets.

The pace is slow and relaxed – though barking dogs in some parts of town may make the nights a little less restful than you might have hoped.

by air are urged to acclimatize for 48 hrs before exerting themselves. For visiting monasteries and spots out-of-town arrange a jeep or taxi.

Leh developed as a trading post and market, attracting a wide variety of merchants – from Yarkand, Kashgar, Kashmir, Tibet and North India. Tea, salt, household articles, wool and semi-precious stones were all traded in the market. Buddhism travelled along the Silk Road and the Kashmir and Ladakh feeder, which has also seen the passage of soldiers, explorers and pilgrims, forerunners of the tourists who today contribute most to the urban economy.

History

The old Palace sits precariously on the hill to the north and looms over Leh. The wide Main Bazar Street (circa 1840s) which once accommodated caravans, with two old gates at each end has a colourful vegetable market where remarkably unpushy Ladakhi women sell local produce on the street side while they knit or chat. Makeshift craft and jewellery stalls line parts of Fort Road to the east to attract summer visitors along with Kashmiri shopkeepers who have come in search of greener pastures. The Old Village, mainly to the east of the Main Street, with its maze of narrow lanes, sits on the hillside below the Palace and can be fun to explore.

Sights
Given the darkness of many buildings even at midday it is well worth taking a torch wherever you go; a must at night

Leh Palace has been described as a miniature version of Lhasa's Potala Palace. Built in the mid-16th century, the Palace was partly in ruins by the 19th. It has nine storeys, sloping buttresses and projecting wooden balconies. From the town below it is dazzling in the morning sun and ghostly at night. Built by King Singe Namgyal and still owned by the royal family, it is now unoccupied – they live in the palace at Stok. Visible damage was caused during Zorawar

Jammu & Kashmir

Singh's invasion from Kashmir in the last century. Be careful of the hazardous holes in the floor. After a steep climb some find the Palace disappointing, but the views from the roof are exceptional. ■ *Summer 0700-0930, and also sometimes 1500-1800.*

A part of the palace is a **museum**. Like the Lhasa Potala Palace it has numerous rooms, steps and narrow passages lined with old *thangkas*, paintings and arms. The central prayer room (not in use), usually locked but opened on request, has religious texts lining the walls. The Archaeological Survey of India is responsible for restoration and you may be able to watch work in progress.

There are many painted scrolls, murals and old manuscripts in the ruined **Palace/Fort**, while the remains of the **Leh Gompa** houses a large golden Buddha. **Tsemo** (Red) **Gompa** (15th century) is a strenuous walk north of the city and has a colossal two-storey high image of *Maitreya*, flanked by figures of *Avalokitesvara* (right) and *Manjusri* (left). It was founded by the Namgyal rulers and a portrait of Tashi Namgyal hangs on the left at the entrance. ■ *0700-0900, Rs 10.*

Of the monasteries, the **Soma Gompa** or the New Monastery (1957) in the main street of the Old Village was built to commemorate the 2,500th anniversary of the birth of Buddha.

Visit the ★ **Ecological Centre** of LEDeG (Ladakh Ecological Development Group), T/F52884, and Craft Shop (next to *Tsemo La Hotel*) which opened in 1984 to spread awareness of Ladakhi environmental issues, encourage self-help and use of alternative technology. It has a library of books on Ladakhi culture, Buddhism, the environment. An interesting video 'Ancient Futures' tracing ecologically sensitive Ladakh's changing face over two decades, is shown daily except Sunday, at 1630 (minimum 10 people); highly recommended. The full 'Appropriate Technology' display is at the **New Ecology Centre** below the Shanti Stupa. There is also a handicrafts centre, a technical workshop, and an organic vegetable garden there.

The non-profit making **SECMOL** (Students' Educational & Cultural Movement in Ladakh), PO Box 4, is in Karzoo with an office in the Old Leh Road. It encourages the teaching of Ladakhi history, culture and crafts. ■ *Mon-Sat, 1400-1800. T3585.*

Women's Alliance of Ladakh Centre, off Sankar Road, is an alliance of 3,500 Ladakhi women, concerned with raising the status of traditional agriculture, preserving the traditionally high status of women which is being eroded in the modern sector, and creating an alternative development model based on self-reliance for Ladakh. The Centre will have a restaurant selling local and organic foods, and a craft shop. They hold spectacular festivals, cultural shows, dances et cetera which are advertised around Leh; mainly aimed at local people, but others are welcome. WAL, in conjunction with the Ladakh Project, runs a Farm Volunteer Scheme. Western volunteers live and work on a Ladakhi farm, helping to boost the status of traditional agriculture.

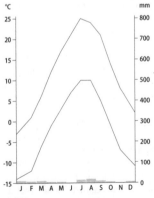

Climate: Leh
Best time to visit:
May-Sep

On the Changspa Lane across the stream, you reach the start of the stiff climb up to the white Japanese **Shanti Stupa** (1989). This is one of a series of Peace Pagodas built by the Japanese around the world. There are good views from the top where a tea room offers a welcome sight after the climb. There is also a jeepable road.

Sankar Gompa (17th-18th centuries), of the Yellow Hat Sect, is one of the few gompas built in the valley bottom. It is a 3 km pleasant walk past the *Himalayan Hotel* through fields. It houses the chief lama of Spituk and 20 others. The newer monks' quarters are on three sides of the courtyard with steps leading up to the Du-Khang (Assembly Hall). There are a number of gold statues, numerous wall paintings and sculptures including a large one of the 11 headed, 1,000-armed *Avalokitesvara*. ■ *0700-1000, 1700-1900, Prayers at 1800 (before visiting, check at the Tourist Office). Rs 250.*

The architecturally striking **Leh Mosque**, in the main bazar is worth visiting (the inner section is not open to woman visitors). The Sunni Muslim mosque is believed to stand on land granted by King Deldan Namgyal in the 1660s; his

Leh orientation

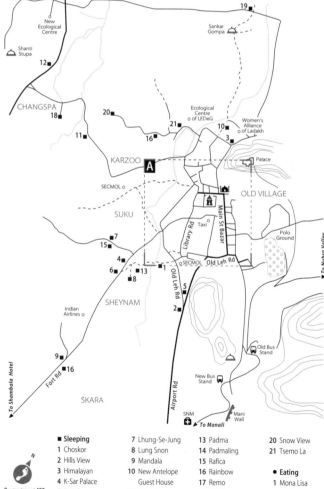

Jammu & Kashmir

■ Sleeping	7 Lhung-Se-Jung	13 Padma	20 Snow View
1 Choskor	8 Lung Snon	14 Padmaling	21 Tsemo La
2 Hills View	9 Mandala	15 Rafica	
3 Himalayan	10 New Antelope	16 Rainbow	● Eating
4 K-Sar Palace	Guest House	17 Remo	1 Mona Lisa
5 Kangla	11 Omasila	18 Ri-Rab	
6 Lharimo	12 Oriental	19 Silver Cloud	

0 metres (approx) 400
0 yards (approx) 400

Related map
A Leh centre,
page 243

Conversation to construction

*If you are interested in **voluntary work**, get in touch with the different organizations in Leh direct (SECMOL, LEDeG). There is a range of possibilities around Leh for potential volunteers – from teaching English to construction work. Alternatively, contact Ladakh Project, Apple Barn, Week, Dartington, Devon TQ9*

6JP, UK, or 850 Talbot Ave, Albany, CA 94796, USA. Farm volunteers with the Ladakh Project are welcome from May-October, for a minimum of one month to stay and work with a Ladakh farming family. A contribution of about $200 plus a nominal daily lodging is expected.

grandmother was the Muslim Queen of Ladakh. The **Mahabodhi Society International Meditation Centre** is in town; enquire about short courses.

Polo (the 'national' sport) is popular in the summer and is played in the polo ground beyond the main Bus Stand. The local version which is fast and rough appears to follow no rules! The Archery Stadium is nearby where winter competitions attract large crowds; the target is a hanging white clay tablet.

From the radio station there are two long **mani walls**. *Rongo Tajng* is in the centre of the open plain and was built as a memorial to Queen Skalzang Dolma by her son Dalden Namgyal. It is about 500 m long and was built in 1635. The stones have been meticulously carved. The other, a 350 m wall down the hill and is believed to have been built by Tsetan Namgyal in 1785 as a memorial to his father the king.

Essentials

Sleeping
■ *on maps, pages 241 & 243*

Price codes: see inside front cover

Advance reservations in **B** and **C** grade hotels may not be honoured in the peak season (mid-Jul to end-Aug) since they cater for tour/trekking groups whose arrival and departure can be unpredictable. Hotel touts can be a nuisance during the 14-day Ladakh festival. Outside the peak period expect discounts though few places remain open in the winter, eg *Siachen, Kangri* and *Yak Tail*. Many traditional Ladakhi homes (see box, page 239) offer rooms during the summer. Those in Karzoo and Changspa (some way from the bus stand) are quieter and preferable to those near the bazar.

A-B *Galdan Continental*, off Fort Rd, T52173. 25 comfortable rooms, some with bath tub, around a grassy quad. **A-B** *K-Sar Palace*, T/F52348. Large rooms with pleasant views, exchange. **B** *Bijoo*, near Library, 100 m from Bazar, T52131. 2-storey white building hidden by wall, 18 good rooms with bath, good restaurant (fixed buffet during high season, ringing the changes), pleasant flower-filled garden and shady seating, treks and tours, very helpful staff. **B** *Kang-lha Chen*, T52144. 25 rooms, most with baths, good restaurant, pleasant shaded inner courtyard garden, own spring, quiet and peaceful, old fashioned but well maintained, open May-Oct. **B** *Kangri*, Nehru Park, T52051. 22 rooms with bath, restaurant (Indian, Chinese, Ladakhi), loud generator nearby a nuisance until 2300, indifferent service and quality. **B** *Ladakh Serai*, at Sabu (northeast of Leh), sT52777, 15 *yurts* (luxury circular tents) set among willows, very peaceful, convenient for short treks, visiting monasteries and river rafting, reservations: *Mountain Travels*, 1/1 Rani Jhansi Rd, Delhi, T7523057, F7777483.

B *Lharimo*, T52101. 30 simple but comfortable rooms with baths, good views from balconies, restaurant, attractive, old building with prayer flags, central. Recommended. **B** *Shambala*, Skara, T52607. 24 large airy rooms, good restaurant (often catering for German packages), meals included, very pleasant, friendly staff, peaceful away from crowds, attractive garden with hammocks, free transport to centre (taxis, Rs 50).

C *Choskor*, near Library, T52426. 13 simple rooms. **C** *Omasila*, Changspa, T52119. 26 rooms, restaurant (fresh garden vegetables), pleasant quiet location, own spring water. **C** *Tsemo La*, Karzoo, T52790. 2 old resthouses, now almost derelict. **C** *Yak Tail*, Fort Rd, T52218. 14 rooms (newer have balconies), nice garden restaurant (good, reasonably priced Indian), exchange, open in winter, pleasant atmosphere. **C-D** *Rafica*, off Fort Rd (5 mins walk from Main Bazar, 10 mins from Bus Stand), T52258. 24 rooms, some large, those on 1st flr have good views, restaurant recommended, friendly, quiet, among fields, treks and tours, good value. **C-D** *Mandala*, towards Shambala, T52130. 20 rooms, far from centre, old hotel now extended, rooms in extension better and have views, pleasant terrace, sadly very unwelcoming, temperamental reception. **C-D** *Snow View*, Karzoo, past Ecological Centre, T52336. 10 rooms (upstairs with good views), peaceful, far from bazar. **C-E** *Silver Cloud*, on road opposite Sankar Gompa, 15 min walk from centre, T53128, F52572. 15 very clean rooms, 9 with baths, in Ladakhi guest house, excellent food, large garden, friendly, helpful family. **D** *Dragon*, T52139. 16 rooms with bath, improved, almost always filled with trekking parties (porters camp in garden!) **D** *Himalayan*, Sankar Gompa Rd, T52104. 26 rooms, most with bath, old building in a quiet, shady willow grove by a stream, restaurant, camping. **D** *Ibex*, Fort Rd, T52212. 14 rooms, near the bazar. **D** *Lhung-Se-Jung*, Fort Rd, T52193. 18 smallish rooms with bath, 2-storey old building and small annexe, upstairs better, restaurant, small garden, quiet location, student discount, good service. **D** *Padmaling*, Changspa, T52933. 10 clean rooms with bath, hotwater morning and evening, helpful manager, *Mona Lisa* restaurant next door, pleasant garden, good views over Stok Kangri. **D** *Ri-Rab*, Changspa, T52239. 10 clean simple rooms with baths, restaurant (own fresh garden vegetables).

There is some budget accommodation along the Old Road and in the Changspa area; some are very basic with cold water only. Fleas and bed bugs can be a problem; use your own sleeping bag if possible. Among many: **E** *Bimla Guest House*, Suku, T52754. 18 rooms, sitting area, welcoming. **E** *Dehlux*, Suku. 9 rooms (hot water in buckets), garden, quiet. **E** *Hills View*, near Tourist Office, T52058. 12 clean rooms (sharing bath between 2 rooms) some with good views, breakfast and snacks, pleasant staff, pretty garden, relaxing, safe, stores luggage. **E** *Indus*, Suku. 17 large rooms some with bath (hot water in buckets), better upstairs, good food. **E** *Kangla*, Airport Rd, near Dragon, T52670. 14 rooms, very friendly, helpful, organize treks. Recommended. **E** *New Antelope Guest House*, Main St, T52086. 11 simple, clean rooms, some with bath, good food, quiet, shady garden. **E** *Old Ladakh*, in the Old Town. 8 rooms, varying in comfort, has character,

Leh centre

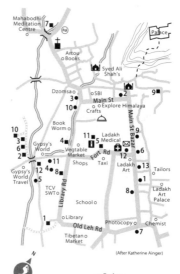

(After Katherine Ainger)

Not to scale

■ **Sleeping**
1 Bijoo
2 Bimla Guest House
3 Dehlux
4 Galdan Continental
5 Ibex
6 Indus
7 Kang-lha Chen
8 Kangri & Exchange
9 Old Ladakh
10 Ti-Sei Guest House
11 Tourist Lodge
12 Yak Tail

● **Eating**
1 Amdo II
2 Budshah Inn & Tailors
3 Devi Tibetan
4 Dreamland
5 In-Style & Bakery
6 Kokonor
7 Kyishong
8 La Montessori
9 Nepali
10 Pumpernickel German Bakery
11 Summer Harvest
12 Tibetan Friend's Corner
13 Wok Tibetan Kitchen

Related map
Leh orientation,
page 241

Jammu & Kashmir

Unlucky in Leh

The supply of clean water and the sewage system can come under heavy pressure in the tourist season. Drink pressure boiled water from Dzomsa (see map) only or use water purification tablets. Bottled water can sometimes be more than a year old and doesn't always conform to safety standards. Meat is sometimes brought in unrefrigerated lorries having travelled two days, so is best avoided.

pleasant atmosphere, good place to meet other travellers. **E** *Oriental*, end of Changspa Lane, below Shanti Stupa. Very clean rooms in traditional family home, good home cooking, great views across the valley, friendly. **E** *Rainbow*, Karzoo. Big clean rooms with wonderful views of mountains and Shanti Stupa, hot water in buckets, great hospitality, good breakfasts. Recommended. **E-F** *Tourist Bungalow* (J&K Tourism), have a few rooms with bath (VIP room best), book in advance through Tourist Office with 50% deposit. **F** *Lung Snon*, Sheynam Chulli Chan. 8 rooms, delightful guest house in peaceful countryside, 1 km from bazar, clean and friendly, but simple, earth toilet. **F** *Padma*, off Fort Rd, 8 mins walk from bazar. 6 clean rooms, upstairs has mountain views, earth toilets, peaceful garden, cheap meals to order. **F** *Remo*, Fort Rd (opposite Mandala), T53336. Clean, quiet, simple rooms, shared toilets, bucket hot water (no charge), very kind family. **F** *Ti-Sei Guest House*, Suku. Good value rooms in peaceful location, 'glass room' (**E**), meals, terrace.

Eating
● on maps, pages 241 & 243
Price codes:
see inside front cover

Top hotels often include meals in the room rate. **Expensive** *Mona Lisa*, Changopar, T52687. International. Good atmosphere, quiet garden with shady trees, hanging lanterns, excellent food (try pizzas, momos, garlic cheese with bread, apricot pie), service can be indifferent though.

Mid-range *Dreamland* (separate from hotel). International. Good atmosphere and food especially Chinese, excellent breakfasts. *In-Style*, Fort Rd. International. Al fresco at back, popular for breakfast, takeaway snacks, also Chinese menu. Both have 'notice boards'. *Kokonor*, entrance on alley off Main St, 2nd Flr. "Chinese and Tibetan specialities and Western encouragements served with generosity and flair", very popular, good value. Recommended. *La Montessori*, Main St Bazar. Excellent Tibetan and Chinese. Filling soups, interesting local clientele. *Summer Harvest*, Fort Rd, 1st Flr, next to *Dreamland*. Mainly Indian, also Chinese, Tibetan. Extensive menu of local and 'tourist' dishes from mutton *thukpa* (Rs 30) to tandoori chicken (Rs 160). *Yak Tail*. International. In a pleasant courtyard garden.

Cheap *Amdo II*, Main Bazar. Tibetan. Good fried momos, Rs 25-35 per dish, friendly (better than *Amdo Café* opposite). *Budshah Inn*, Lal Chowk, top Flr. North Indian. Lacks ambience but excellent Kashmiri (Rs 45, dish). *Devi Tibetan*. Traditional meals, refreshing spiced teas. *Kyishong*, Old Leh Rd. Tibetan. Very good, traditional meals (tsampa, bamboo shoots etc), popular. *Nepali*. Nepali, Tibetan. Excellent veg *momos*. *Tibetan Friend's Corner*. Clean, simple, delicious *kothay* (fried *momos*) Rs 25, huge pancakes, friendly, locally popular. *Wok Tibetan Kitchen*, Main St, 1st Flr. Mainly Tibetan. Good food and prices, very popular.

Confectionery 4 *German Bakeries* sell good bread (trekking bread keeps for a week) and excellent cakes and muesli; *Pumpernickel* , Main St Bazar, the original German bakery is the best and friendliest, indoor/outdoor seating, excellent apricot pie and apple crumble, message board for trekkers; others with similar fare are *Mona Lisa* and *In Style*.

Jammu & Kashmir

To fly or not to fly

Travel by road gives you an advantage over flying into Leh as it enables you to **acclimatize** to a high altitude plateau and if you are able to hire a jeep or car it will give you the flexibility of stopping to see the several sights on the way. However, some people find the bus journey from Manali (or Srinagar)

terrifying and very uncomfortable, and most healthy people find that if they relax completely for two days after flying in, they acclimatize without difficulty (see note under air, transport above). If you have a heart condition, consult your doctor on the advisability of your going to Leh.

Entertainment

The Ecological Centre shows occasional films (see page 240). Ladakhi dancing and singing, below entrance to Palace, 1800 (1 hour), Rs 50 (take warm clothes). **Sport Mountaineering**: information on trekking and mountaineering from Indian Mountaineering Federation, Benito Juarez Marg, New Delhi; *Adventure Institutes in India* c/o Tourist Office. Local tour companies offer treks and mountain climbing. **Polo**: The Polo Club (the highest in the world); worth a visit. **White-water rafting and kayaking**: is possible on the Tsarap Chu and Zans rivers from mid-Jun; the upper reaches of the former (grade 4 rapids) are suitable for professionals only, though the remaining stretch can be enjoyed by the inexperienced. Along the Indus: Hemis to Choglamsar (easy, very scenic); Phey-Nimmu (grade 3); Nimmu-Khaltse (professional). Ensure the trip is organized by a well-experienced rafter and that life jackets and wet suits are provided. ½ to full day, including transport and lunch, Rs 800-1,400. See Tour companies below.

Festivals

A few monasteries (Hemis, Lamayaru, Phyang) hold colourful festivals in the summer – see page 237, under Ladakh Religion above. Dates vary depending on the lunar calendar.

Losar which originated in the 15th century to protect people before going to battle is celebrated in **Dec**. The main events ot the *Ladakh Festival* (1-15 Sep) are held in the Leh Polo grounds with smaller events arranged in other districts. Arranged by the State Government usually during the first week in September, there are four days of dances, displays of traditional costumes, Ladakhi plays and polo matches. *Buddha Purnima* (**Apr-May** full moon) marks the Buddha's birth.

Shopping

Please use your own bags. Plastic bags are not allowed in the bazar.

They are not biodegradable & were finding their way into streams when not piled on unsightly heaps

Leh Bazar is full of shops selling curios, clothes and knick-knacks. Tea and *chang* (local barley brew) vessels, cups, butter churns, knitted carpets with Tibetan designs, Tibetan jewellery, prayer flags, musical bowls, are all available. Prices are high especially in Kashmiri shops so bargain vigorously. It is usually better to buy Ladakhi jewellery and souvenirs from Ladakhis who generally ask a fair price. **Books** *Artou Books*, opposite Post Office, Zangsti and in Main Bazar has a good selection, especially on trekking and the region. Also fax and international phone; *Book Worm*, near Gandan Hotel, good for second-hand. **Crafts** *Cottage Emporium*, opposite *Dreamland Hotel* has a large selection of carpets. *LEDeG Craft Shop* at the Ecology Centre, and opposite the State Bank in the Main Bazar, recommended. *Chan Gali* is worth exploring for curios and local jewellery. *Tibetan Arts* and *Ladakhi Village Curios* have a selection of *thangkas*, inlaid bowls, baubles, bangles and beads. *Sonam Bongo*, top of Main Bazar St, has local costumes; *Ladakh Arts & Craft House*, top of Fort Rd, opposite PO has a few interesting bric-a-bracs; group of Ladakhis have stalls off the Fort Road selling jewellery; others do business along the road. **Fruit and nuts** Available in season. Dried apricots can be bought along any roadside in Aug-Sep. Bottled juice is sold by the '*Dzomsa*' Laundry. **Photography**: *Syed Ali Shah's Postcard Shop*, Choterantag St, is worth a visit. An authentic photographer's studio; collection of old photos—copies sold (personalities, festivals etc), postcards, camera films. **Tailor**: next to *Budshah Inn*

Jammu & Kashmir

Be ecology conscious

The **Dzomsa** shop, a self-help co-operative, just past the German Bakery on the main street in Leh, has attempted to put into practise some of the ideals of LEDeG. It sells pressure-boiled drinking water for tourists, refilling a small plastic bottle for Rs 7. It also sells local apricot juice and runs a laundry service that does not pollute local streams used for drinking. We urge all travellers to use their services.

near mosque, excellent shirt maker, made-to-measure. Also several in Nowshara Gali.

NB There are tight restrictions on the export of anything over 100 years old. Baggage is checked at the airport partly for this reason. However, even though most items are antique looking, they are, in fact, fresh from the backstreet workshops. If you walk down the narrow lanes, you will probably find an artisan at work from whom you can buy direct.

Transport

If you have travelled by road you will have come over some high passes & may already be better acclimatized, but a mild headache is common & can be treated with aspirin or paracetamol. Drink ample non-alcoholic fluids on the journey

Leh is connected to Manali via Keylong (closed Oct to mid-Jun or longer) and to Srinagar, via Kargil, by a State Highway. **NB** Both can be seriously affected by landslides, causing long delays. The Leh-Srinagar Road is also often blocked by army convoys. Information on road conditions from the Traffic Police HQ, Maulana Azad Rd, Srinagar.

Local Bus: the New Bus Stand is near the cemetery (use a short cut). The vehicles are ramshackle but the fares are low. See under monasteries for details. Enquiries J&KSRTC, T52285. **Tourist taxi & jeep**: *Ladakh Taxi Operators' Union*, Fort Rd. Fixed fares point-to-point. From the airport, about Rs 80; from Bus Stand Rs 60. A day's taxi hire to visit nearby *gompas* costs about Rs 1,000-1,200; Nubra Rs 6,000. **Bike hire**: opposite *Yak Tail*.

Long distance Air The small airport is 5 km away on Srinagar Rd. It is surrounded by hills on 3 sides and the flight over the mountain ranges is spectacular. Transport to town: buses, and jeep-taxis (Rs 80), for sharing. Weather conditions may deteriorate rapidly even in the summer resulting in flight cancellations (especially outside Jul and Aug) so always be prepared for a delay or to take alternative road transport out of Ladakh. Furthermore, the airlines fly quite full planes into Leh but can take fewer passengers out because of the high altitude take-off. This adds to the difficulty of getting a flight out. **Book your tickets as soon as possible** (several months ahead for Jul and Aug). You can book on the Internet before you leave for India See page 34. Tickets bought in Leh may not be 'confirmed'. The *Indian Airlines* office is near *Shambala Hotel* and is often chaotic. **NB** Avoid connecting with an onward flight or train immediately after your visit to Ladakh. If you fail to get on the outward flight, you do not get an immediate refund from the airline but have to reclaim it from the travel agent. It is therefore essential to have enough money to travel out by road if your return is imperative; remember, a taxi to Manali takes 2 days and to Delhi, up to 4 days. Despite the difficulties, even if you do not have a firm outward booking and have been 'wait-listed' you may sometimes get on a flight at short notice, eg if weather conditions improve. It is worth asking. Patience, persistence, a steady nerve and flexibility for your onward arrangements are all you need! Check-in time can be 2 hrs ahead. *Indian Airlines*, T52255), flies from *Delhi*, 0610, returns 0815, daily in season (Jul-Sep); less frequently at other times (in winter, this is the only link between Ladakh and the outside world); to **Jammu**, Thu, Sun; **Chandigarh**, Tue; **Srinagar**, Sat.

Road The road to **Manali**, crossing some very high passes, is open mid-Jun or early Jul, until end-Sep (depending on the weather) and takes 2 days. Road conditions may be poor in places. Departure from Leh can be early (0400) with overnight stop in Keylong; next day to Manali. Alternatively, camp in Sarchu (10 hrs from Leh), or Jespa; next day 14 hrs to Manali (Rs 150 each in Sarchu, camp). **NB** Journeys can take longer early and late in the season. Roadside tents provide food *en route* during the tourist season; carry snacks, water and a good sleeping bag when planning to camp. To reduce the ill-effects of high altitude, avoid rushing around and take plenty of non-alcoholic drinks. Many travellers find the mountain roads extremely frightening and they are comparatively dangerous. Some are cut out of extremely unstable hillsides, usually with nothing between the road's edge and the nearly vertical drop below. Although 'Himank' road-building gangs, working under exceptionally harsh conditions, constantly repair and improve the Highway, parts remain rough and pot-holed and during the monsoons (especially Jul) landslides and rivers can make it impassable for 2-3 days. It is also a long and uncomfortable journey, but there is some spectacular scenery.

Bus: Himachal Tourism runs regular (not daily) Deluxe and Ordinary buses between Manali and Leh, usually mid-Jun to end-Sep, 2 days. To **Manali**, 530 km, 'Deluxe', booked at HPTDC, Fort Rd, or at travel agents, Rs 800 (Rs 1,100 includes camp bed and meals in Sarchu). Ordinary (Private) booked at bus stand, 'A' Rs 500, and 'B', Rs 350, stop overnight at Keylong. J&KSRTC bus **Kargil**, 230 km, (alternate days in summer) Rs 110-180, **Srinagar** 434 km, Rs 200-360. **Taxi**: Four-wheel drive (Jeep or Gypsy) between Leh and Manali are expensive but recommended if you want to stop en route to visit monasteries. 2-day trip, about Rs 13,000. Taxis often return empty to Manali (since some choose to fly out of Leh) so may agree a much reduced fare for the return leg. Officially, Manali (or Srinagar) taxis are allowed to carry their passengers to and from Leh but are not permitted to do local tours, a rule fiercely monitored by the Leh Taxi Operators' Union (see local transport).

Tour operators *Alpine Trek and Tour*, PO Box 54, recommended. *Explore Himalayas*, PO Box 45, Main Bazar (opp SBI), T/F53354, wangchuks@hotmail.com "well informed, highly recommended for treks and tours, excellent crew, friendly, good to animals, environment conscious, food incredible!", good value (eg Nubra Valley, $25 per day); *Gypsy*, Old Fort; *Indus Himalayan*, opp Taxi stand, T52735; *Rimo Expeditions*, Kang-lha Chhen Hotel, T53644, treks and rafting. **Tourist offices** *J&K*, 2 km south, on Airport Rd, T52297, with Trekking equipment hire shop. **Useful addresses** Ambulance: T52014. **Police:** T52018. **Foreigners' Registration Office:** T52200.

Directory Banks **NB** It is not possible to get money on credit cards anywhere in Ladakh. Get TCs before you arrive. *State Bank of India*, exchange counter only next to tourist office (opposite Taxi Stand, but slow. Fast, convenient service at moneychangers next door; *Ladakh Art Palace* (signposted from bazaar) changes money; poorer rate. Large hotels and *AmEx* (1030-1430, Sat 1030-1230) in Kangri and *Yak Tail*, charges a steep commission. Avoid banks (and market) on army pay-day! **Communications** Post: Head Post Office & Telegraph Office: Airport Rd, 3 km from Leh centre (1000-1500); parcels often disappear. Mail may be sent via *Gypsy's World*, Fort Rd, T52935, 52220, F52735 (not fail safe; staff need persuading to collect mail from GPO regularly); make sure your name is prominently written, and addressed c/o Gypsy's World, PO Box 160, Leh, Ladakh 194101, India. **Telephone:** Pick up **faxes** here for a small fee (staff will hold them for a few weeks); **email** services too. Phone and fax connections with the rest of India are unpredictable. **Medical services** Hospitals: SNM Hospital, T52014 (also for advice on *mountain sickness*), after hrs, T52360). During the day, doctors at the crowded hospital have little time; better at clinics in the evenings. *Soway Clinic*, in Bazar; *Kunfan Octsnang Clinic*; *Ladakh Medicate*, behind post office (ask for Dr Norbu, Old Leh Rd, recommended). A traditional Tibetan doctor (amchi) can be consulted at the *Ecological Centre*. In an emergency call T52360 for a doctor.

Women on their own should take special care when arranging a tour with a driver/guide

Monasteries along the Leh Manali Highway

You must take a local Ladakhi guide as the Lamas can refuse admission if unaccompanied. Carry a torch. Camera flash is usually not allowed in monasteries to reduce damage to wall paintings and *thangkas*. If you hire a car or jeep (good value when shared by four) you can visit the places below in a day. If you are short of time, try to see Thikse and Hemis, at least. **Recommended reading** *Monasteries*

Jammu & Kashmir

of Ladakh by Paldang; *The Cultural Heritage of Ladakh* by DL Snellgrove and T Skorupski, Aris & Phillips, Delhi, 1977, 1980; *Himalayan art* by M Singh, UNESCO, 1971.

Choglamsar Choglamsar, south of Leh (on the east bank of the Indus), is a green oasis with poplars and willows where there are golf links and a polo ground as well as horticultural nurseries. Some village houses use solar energy. The Central Institute of Buddhist Studies is here with a specialist library. Past the Tibetan Refugee Camps, Children's Village and the Arts and Crafts Centre, the Choglamsar Bridge crosses the Indus. ■ *Getting there: hourly buses, 0800-1800.*

★ Stok
Colour map 1, grid A3

Across Choglamsar Bridge, 10 km south of Leh, is the royal palace dating from the 1840s when the King of Ladakh was deposed by the invading Dogra forces. The last king died in 1974 but his widow continues to live here; his son continues the royal line and ascended the throne in July 1993. The palace is a rambling building where only a dozen of the 80 rooms are used. The small **Palace Museum** (three rooms) is worth visiting. It is a showpiece for the royal *thangkas* (many 400 years old), crown jewels, dresses, coins, *peraks* encrusted with turquoise and lapis lazuli as well as religious objects. ■ *May-Oct, 0800-1900. Rs 25.*

There is an **archery** contest in July. The **gompa**, a short distance away, has some ritual dance masks. The *Tsechu* is in February. A three hour **walk** up the valley behind Stok takes you to some extraordinary mountain scenery dominated by the 6,121 m high Stok Kangri.

■ *Getting there: Taxis from the Leh central taxi stand are available at fixed rates at any time.*

Sleeping **C-D** *Highland,* below Museum, comfortable rooms with bath, good views. Getting there: 2 buses, 0730, 1700.

Shey
Colour map 1, grid A3
15 km southeast of Leh on the Indus River (also along a stone path from Thikse)

Until the 16th century, Shey was the royal residence, located at an important vantage point in the Indus Valley. Kings of Leh were supposed to be born in the monastery. The royal family moved to Stok in order to escape advancing Dogra forces from Kashmir who came to exploit the trade in pashmina wool. Shey, along with Thikse, is also regarded as an auspicious place for cremation.

Much of the palace and the fort high above it have fallen into disrepair though the soot covered wall paintings in the palace have now been restored. The palace gompa with its 17.5-metre high blue-haired Maitreya Buddha (imitating the one at Tsemo Gompa) is attended by Drukpa monks from Hemis. It is made of copper and brass but splendidly gilded and studded with precious gem stones. The large victory *stupa* is topped with gold.

There are extensive grounds to the east (which once was a lake) with a large number of *chortens* in which cremated ashes of important monks, members of the royal family and the devout were buried. A newer temple houses another old giant Buddha statue. There are several rock carvings; particularly noteworthy is that of five *dhyani* Buddhas (circa 8th century) at the bottom of the hill. **Sleeping** The small hotel below the gompa has spartan but clean rooms. ■ *All day; try to be there 0700-0900, 1700-1800 when prayers are chanted. Rs 15. Getting there: hourly buses, 0800-1800.*

★ Thikse This is one of the most imposing monasteries in Ladakh and was part of the original Gelugpa order in the 15th century. It is situated 25 km south of Leh on a crag overlooking the flood plain on the east bank of the Indus.

The 12-storey monastery painted deep red, ochre and white, with typical tapering walls has 10 temples, a nunnery and 60 lamas in residence whose houses cling to the hillside below. The complex contains numerous *stupas*, statues, *thangkas*, wall paintings (note the fresco of the 84 *Mahasiddhas*, high above), swords and a large pillar engraved with the Buddha's teachings.

The new temple interior is dominated by a giant 15 metre-high Buddha figure near the entrance. The principal *Dukhang* (assembly hall) right at the top of the building has holes in the wall for storing religious texts; good views from roof. The temple with the Guardian Deities (which in other monasteries may be closed to women) is open to all since parts of the offending figures are covered. The *Dukhang* lower down has Tibetan style wall paintings.

Thikse is a good place to watch religious ceremonies, usually 0630 or 1200; an early start by taxi makes even the first possible. They are preceded by the playing of large standing drums and long horns similar to *alpenstock*. Masked dances are performed during special festivals. **Sleeping** E *Shalzang Chamba Hotel* has an outdoor restaurant. ■ *Rs 20 (mostly for restoration and maintenance). Drinks kiosk at entrance. Getting there: hourly buses, 0800-1800.*

Across the valley on a hill is the earliest Drukpa monastery which was built before Hemis, though its decorations are not as ancient. It is also called 'Tiger's nose' because of the shape of the hill site. This small but well kept monastery has a beautiful silver-gilt chorten in the Assembly Hall which was installed around 1955 and some interesting paintings in the dark temple at the back (bring a torch). There are excellent views of the Indus valley and the Zanskar range. No need for a local guide as the lamas are always willing to open the doors.

Stakna

On the west bank of the Indus, 45 km south of Leh, the monastery, built on a green hillside surrounded by spectacular mountain scenery, is hidden in a gorge. It is the biggest and wealthiest in Ladakh and is a 'must' for visitors. You walk past chortens and sections of *mani* walls to enter the complex through the east gate which leads into a large 40 m x 20 m courtyard where sacred dances are performed during the *Hemis Tsechu* (end June-early July). It commemorates the birth of Guru Padmasambhava who is believed to have fought local demons to protect the people. Young and old of both sexes, and lamas take part in masked dance-dramas while stalls sell handicrafts.

★ Hemis
Colour map 1, grid A3

The Drukpa monastery was founded by Stagsang Raspa during the reign of Senge Namgyal (circa 1630). Colourful flags flutter in the breeze from the four posts against the white walls of the buildings. On the north side are two assembly halls approached by a flight of steep stone steps. The large Dukhang to the right used for ceremonies is rather plain; the smaller Tshogskhang (the main temple) contains some silver gilt chortens and a Kashmiri lacquered-wood throne. The murals in the verandas depicting guardian deities, the *kalachakra* (wheel of life) and 'Lords of the four quarters' are well preserved.

A staircase alongside the Tshogskhang leads to a roof terrace where there are a number of shrines including a bust of the founder. The *Lakhang* (chapel) has ancient Kashmiri bronzes and silver *chortens*, an important library of Tibetan style books and an impressive collection of *thangkas*, the largest of which is displayed every 12 years (next 2004). The heavy silk *thangka* is beautifully embroidered in bright coloured threads and pearls.

There is a pleasant 3 km walk uphill to another gompa. A stay in Hemis overnight enables you to attend early morning prayers, a moving experience and strongly recommended. **Sleeping and eating** Many householders take in guests. F *Tourist*. Camp or sleep on the floor, own sleeping bag, Rs 25. The tented restaurant is basic and grubby. ■ *Getting there: bus services have improved making a day trip possible.*

Jammu & Kashmir

Monasteries along the Srinagar Road

The Srinagar road out of Leh passes through a flat dusty basin mostly occupied by Army encampments with mile after mile of wire fencing. See also page 234.

Spituk
Colour map 1, grid A3
8 km from Leh

The monastery standing on a conical hill with three chapels was founded in the 11th century but the buildings, in a series of tiers with courtyards and steps, date from the 15th century. The newest is electrified. The Yellow-Hat Gelugpa monks created the precedent in Ladakh of building on mountain tops rather than valley floors; you can get good views of the countryside around.

The long 16th to 17th-century **Du-khang** is the largest building and has two rows of seats along the length of the walls to a throne at the far end. Sculptures and miniature chortens are displayed on the altar. Spituk has a collection of ancient Jelbagh masks, icons and arms including some rescued from the Potala Palace in Lhasa.

The **Mahakal Temple** (16th-17th century) higher up the hill contains a shrine of Vajrabhairava, often mistaken for the goddess Kali. The terrifying face is only unveiled in January, during the Gustor festival. ■ *Getting there: Srinagar buses drop you on the highway, 4 daily, 20 minutes.*

★ Phyang
Colour map 1, grid A3
16 km from Leh

The gompa dominates a side valley with a village close by. It belongs to the Red Hat Kagyupa sect, with its 16th-century Gouon monastery built by the founder of the Namgyal Dynasty which is marked by a flagstaff at the entrance. It houses hundreds of statues including some Kashmiri bronzes (circa 14th century), *thangkas* and manuscript copies of the Kangyur and Tengyur; temple walls have colourful paintings centering on the eight emblems of happiness which have been restored. It is the setting for a spectacular Tseruk festival with masked dancing (July). ■ *Getting there: 3 buses daily, 1 hr; the morning bus allows you to explore the valley and walk back to Leh, but the afternoon bus only allows 20 mins for visit (last return, around 1700).*

Routes

Two kilometres before Nimmu the Indus enters an impressive canyon before the Zanskar joins it (a good place to photograph). As the road bends a lush green oasis with lines of poplars comes into view. The mud brick houses of Nimmu have grass drying on the flat rooftops to provide fodder for the winter. A dry stone *mani* wall runs along the road; beyond Nimmu the walls become 2-metre wide in places with innumerable chortens alongside. The rocky outcrops on the hills to the right appear like a natural fortress.

Basgo

The road passes through Basgo village with the ruins of a Buddhist citadel impressively sited on a spur overlooking the Indus Valley. It served as a royal residence for several periods between the 15th and 17th centuries. The Fort Palace was once considered almost impregnable having survived a three-year siege by Tibetan and Mongol armies in the 17th century.

Among the ruins only two temples have survived. The higher Maitreya Temple (mid-16th century) built by Tashi Namgyal's son contains a very fine Maitreya statue at the rear of the hall, flanked by *bodhisattvas*. Some murals from the early period illustrating the Tibetan Buddhist style have also survived on the walls and ceiling; among the Buddhas and *bodhisattvas* infilled with details of animals, birds and mermaids, appear images of Hindu divinities. The Serzang (Gold and Copper) Temple (17th century), with a carved doorway, is the other and contains another large Maitreya image whose head rises through the ceiling into a windowed box-like structure which can be seen by climbing up to the gallery above. The murals look faded and have been damaged by water; the scriptures are stored along the walls. A smaller shrine nearby contains another Buddha image. ■ *Getting there: see Alchi below.*

Lekir (Likir)

Five and a half kilometres from Basgo, a road on the right leads to Lekir by a scenic route. The picturesque white-washed monastery buildings rise in different levels on the hillside across the Lekir River.

Lekir was built during the reign of Lachen Gyalpo who installed 600 monks here, headed by Lhawang Chosje (circa 1088). The gompa was invested with a collection of fine images, thangkas and murals to vie with those at Alchi. The present buildings date mainly from the 18th century since the original were destroyed by fire.

A rough path up leads to the courtyard where a board explains the origin of the name: Klu-Khyil (snake coil) refers to the *nagas* here, reflected in the shape of the hill. Lekir was converted to the Gelugpa sect in the 15th century. The head lama, the younger brother of the Dalai Lama, has his apartments here, which were extended in the mid 1990s.

The **Du-khang** contains huge clay images of the Buddhas (past, present and future) and Kangyur and Tengyur manuscripts, the Kangyur having been first compiled in Ladakh during Lachen Gyalpo's reign. The **Nyenes-Khang** contains beautiful murals of the 35 confessional Buddhas and 16 arahats. The **Gon-Khang** houses a statue of the guardian deity here, Se-Ta-Pa and Yaman-taka. A small but very interesting **museum** of *thangkas*, old religious and domestic implements, costumes et cetera which are labelled in English. ■ *Rs 15. Opened on request (climb up to a hall above, up steep wooden stairs).*

Village craftsmen produce *thangkas*, carved wooden folding seats and clay pottery. **Sleeping** *Norbu Spon Guest House*, 3 km off main road towards Lekir, also allows camping; the two-storeyed white-washed *Lhankay Guest House* stands in fields. ■ *Getting there: bus from Leh each afternoon, return each morning; see Alchi.*

★ Alchi

Alchi's large temple complex is regarded as one of the most important Buddhist centres in Ladakh & a jewel of monastic skill

The road enters Saspul, 8 km from the Lekir turn-off. About 2 km beyond the village, a link road with a suspension bridge over the river leads to Alchi which is hidden from view as you approach; a patchwork of cultivated fields surround the complex. The flood plain at Alchi is very fertile and provides good and relatively extensive agricultural land.

A narrow path from the car park winds past village houses, donkeys and apricot trees to lead to the Dharma Chakra monastery. You will be expected to buy a ticket from one of the lamas on duty. The whole complex, about 100 m long and 60 m wide is enclosed by a white-washed mud and straw wall. A path on the right past two large prayer wheels and a row of smaller ones leads to the river which attracts deer down to the opposite bank in the evenings. At the rear small chortens with inscribed stones strewn around them, line the wall. From here, you get a beautiful view of the Indus River with mountains as a backdrop.

Use of camera flash is forbidden

Founded in the 11th century by **Rinchen Zangpo** the 'Great Translator', it was richly decorated by artists from Kashmir and Tibet. Paintings of the mandalas which have deep Tantric significance are particularly fine; some decorations are reminiscent of Byzantine art. The monastery is maintained by monks from Lekir and is no longer a place for active worship.

The three **entrance chortens** are worth looking in to. Each has vividly coloured paintings within, both along the interior walls as well as in the small chorten-like openings on the ceilings. The first and largest of these has a portrait of the founder Rinchen Zangpo. Some of the paintings here are being restored by foreign researchers.

The Choskor (religious enclave) comprises 5 principal temples

The **Du-khang** is the oldest temple, which has a courtyard (partially open to the sky) with wooden pillars and painted walls; the left wall shows two rowing boats with fluttering flags, a reminder perhaps of the presence in ancient times of lakes in this desert. The brightly painted door to the Du-khang (about 1½ m high) and the entrance archway has some fine woodcarving; note the dozen or so blue pottery Buddhas stuck to the wall! The subsidiary shrines on either side of the doorway contain *Avalokitesvaras* and *bodhisattvas* including a giant four-armed Maitreya figure to the extreme right.

This main Assembly Hall which was the principal place of worship suffers from having very little natural light so visitors need a good torch. The 'shrine' holds the principal gilded *Vairocana* (Resplendent) Buddha (traditionally white, accompanied by the lion) with ornate decorations behind, flanked by four important Buddha postures among others. The walls on either side are devoted to fine *Mandala* paintings illustrating the four principal manifestations of the *Sarvavid* (Omniscient) Buddha – *Vairocana*, *Sakyamuni* (the Preacher), *Manjusri* (Lord of Wisdom) and as *Prajna Paramita* (Perfection of Wisdom) described in detail by Snellgrove and Skorupski. There are interesting subsidiary panels, friezes and inscriptions. Note the terrifying figure of *Mahakala* the guardian deity above the door with miniature panels of royal and military scenes. The one portraying a drinking scene shows the royal pair sanctified with haloes with wine-cups in hand, accompanied by the prince and attendants – the detail of the clothing clearly shows Persian influence.

There are two small temples beyond. The **Lotsawa** (Translator's) and **Jampang** (Manjusri) Lhakhangs were built later and probably neglected for some time. The former contains a portrait of Rinchen Zangpo along with a seated Buddha while the latter has *Manjusri* where each directional face is painted in the colour associated with the cardinal directions of north (dark green), south (yellow), east (blue) and west (red).

Alchi Choskor

Sum-stek, the three-tier temple with a carved wooden gallery on the façade, has triple arches. Inside are three giant four-armed, garlanded stucco figures of *bodhisattvas*: the white *Avalokitesvara* on the left, the principal terracotta-red *Maitreya* in the centre at the back, and the ochre-yellow *Manjusri* on the right; their heads project to the upper storey which is reached by a rustic ladder. The remarkable features here are the brightly painted and gilded decorations on the clothing of the figures which include historical incidents, musicians, palaces and places of pilgrimage. Quite incongruous court scenes and Persian features appear on *Avalokitesvara* while the figures on *Maitreya* have Tantric connotations illustrating the very different styles of ornamentation on the three figures. The walls have numerous mandalas and inscriptions.

Lhakhang Soma (New temple) is a square hall with a chorten within; its walls are totally covered with mandalas and paintings portraying incidents from the Buddha's life and historic figures; the main figure here is the preaching Buddha. There is an interesting panel of warriors on horseback near the door. **Kanjyur Lhakhang** in front of the Lhakhang Soma houses the scriptures.

Near Alchi car/bus park there are tea stalls and a few guest houses: **E-F** simple *Lotsava* on the path. *Zimskhang*, very basic rooms, walled-in open-air restaurant for light meals and snacks, camping. *Uley Tokpo Camp* is a few kilometres before Alchi. **Saspul** has the *Carefree Travels Camp* and *Worldroof Camping Resort and Restaurant*. **Sleeping & eating**

Road Srinagar bound buses stop at Saspul; from there it is a 2.5 km walk across the bridge. Buses dep Leh for Alchi, around 0630, 1500, nearly 3 hrs. **Taxi**: (for 4/5) to visit **Alchi, Lekir** and **Basgo** (8 hrs), Rs 1,000. **Transport**

For **Lamayaru,** see page 234.

Nubra Valley, Nyoma and Drokhpa area

These once restricted areas are now open to visitors. Permits are freely issued by the District Magistrate (District Development Commissioner) in Leh to groups of four or more travelling together by jeep, for a maximum of seven days. Allow a day to get a permit which costs RS 250. A lot of ground can be covered in the period but it is necessary to consult a Leh-based trekking and travel agent. You need to go fully equipped with tents, food and sleeping bags although there are a few rest houses and temporary lakeside tented camps are occasionally set up by tour companies.

The Rupshu area, a dry, high altitude plateau to the east of the Leh-Manali Highway is where the nomadic Changpas live (see page 236) in the bleak and windswept **Chamathang** highlands bordering Tibet. The route to the beautiful Tso-Moriri (Lake) which is the only nesting place of the bar-headed geese on the Indus (where the Brahminy duck and black-necked crane also breed), has now been opened to visitors. To the south of the 27 km long lake is the land of the Tibetan wild ass, the *kiang*. **★ Tso-Moriri**
220 km from Leh

You can travel either via **Chhumathang** (140 km) visiting the hot spring there or by crossing the high pass at Taglang La, leaving the Manali-Leh Highway at Debring. The route takes you past **Tsokar** basin (154 km) where salt cakes the edges. A campsite along the lake with access to fresh water is opposite **Thukje** village which has a gompa and a 'wolf catching trap'! The road then reaches the hot sulphur springs at **Puga** before reaching the beautiful Tso-Moriri (about four hours drive from Tsokar). You can follow the lake bank and visit the solitary village of **Karzog** (4,500 m), north of the lake, which has a gompa. **Sleeping** PWD *Rest Houses* at Chhumathang and Karzog. Guest houses at Karzog. Camping at Tsokar and Karzog. tented camp at Chhumathang. **Transport** Jeep from Leh.

Jammu & Kashmir

★ **Pangong-Tso**
Colour map 1, grid A4

(4,250 m) From Leh you can also get a permit to visit the narrow 130 km long Pangong-Tso (*tso* – lake) the greater part of which lies in Tibet. The road, which is only suitable with four-wheel drive in places, is via Karu on the Manali-Leh Highway, where the road east goes through **Zingral** and over the Chang La pass. Beyond are **Durbuk** a small village with low-roofed houses and **Tangste**, the 'abode of Chishul warriors' with a Lotswa Temple, which is also an army base with a small bank. The rough jeep track takes you through an impressive rocky gorge which opens out to a valley which has camping by a fresh water stream in the hamlet of **Mugleb** and then on to **Lukung**, the last check-point and finally **Spangmik** (153 km from Leh). On the way you will be able to see some Himalayan birds including *chikhor* (quail) which may end up in the cooking pot.

An overnight stop on the lake shore allows you to see the lake in different lights. You can walk between Lukung and Spangmik (7 km) on this second day, passing small settlements growing barley and peas along the lake shore. Both villages have yaks which you can experience a ride on! You return to Leh on the third day. **Sleeping** *Tented Camps* at Durbuk, Tangtse, Lukung and Spangmik. **Medical services** Dispensary at Tangtse. **Transport** Jeep from Leh.

★ **Nubra Valley**
Colour map 1, grid A4

North of Leh, travel across the Ladakh range over the 5,600 m **Khardung La**, possibly the highest motorable pass in the world for an exhilarating high-altitude experience (best after mid-June). This is along the old Silk Route to the lush green Nubra valley up to **Panamik** (140 km from Leh) which has reddish, sulphurous hot springs nearby. **Permits** needed; not given to diplomats (!), Pakistanis and Chinese.

Once camel caravans transported Chinese goods for exchanging with Indian produce. Camels which are now rare and prized can occasionally be seen on the sand dunes near Nubra (see also Trekking in 'Nubra & Shyok Valleys' below). The relatively gentler climate here allows crops, fruit and nuts to grow, so some call it 'Ldumra' (orchard). You can visit the **Samstanling**, **Sumur** and **Deskit** gompas. **Sleeping** PWD rest houses at **Deskit**, **Panamik** and **Khardung** village with permission from Exec Engineer, PWD, Deskit. Local families take in guests and tented camps are sometimes set up by tour companies (double tents Rs 800 including food) during the season. **Medical services** *Primary Health Centre* at Deskit; Dispensary at Panamik. **Transport** From Leh two buses per week Jun-Sep; 8 hours. A few have tried a bike (which you can transport on top of a bus for the outward journey if you can't face the hard pedalling!)

Drokhpa area

Dah and **Biama**(Bema) are two Drokhpa villages where the so-called pure Aryan tribe, speaking a distinct dialect, live in a fair degree of isolation; Buddhism here is mixed with animist practices. You may reach these Indus valley villages from **Khaltse** on the Leh-Srinagar road via Dumkhar, Tirit, Skurbuchan and Hanudo. **Sleeping** PWD *Rest House* at Biama; local *Guest Houses* and a *Campsite*. **Transport** Jeep from Leh.

Trekking in Ladakh

Some treks in the Indus Valley and the Nubra and Shyok Valleys are described in brief here. See page 53 for travellers for general advice. Make sure your trekking guide is experienced and competent. **Recommended reading** *Leh & Trekking in Ladakh* by Charlie Loram. 1996. Trailblazer, Hindhead, Surrey.

Leh is the major town in this valley. For trekking, July and August are pleasant months. Go earlier and you will be trudging through snow much of the time. September and October are also good months, though colder at night.

Trekking in the Indus Valley

Both places are in the Indus Valley, only 30 km apart. A very satisfying 9-10 days can be undertaken by traversing the Stok range to the Markha Valley, walking up the valley and then back over the Zanskar range to Hemis. **NB** Charge: Rs 25 per person per day in the Hemis High Altitude Park (Indians Rs 10 per day). Since all of the Spituk-Hemis Markha Valley trek falls within the park boundary, a typical 10 day trek costs Rs 250 per person. The charge is payable at small trailside posts located a couple of hours walk from the trek start points at Spituk and Martselang.

★ **Spituk to Hemis**

There is an interesting monastery at **Spituk**, a short drive from Leh (see

Jammu & Kashmir

Ladakh & Zanskar treks

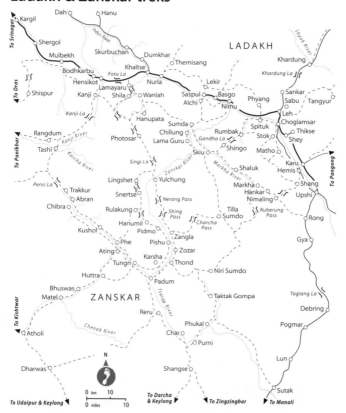

page 250). From Spituk proceed southwest of the Indus along a trail passing through barren countryside. After about 7 km you reach the **Jinchan Valley** and in a further five hours, the beautiful Rumbak village. Camp below the settlement. You can also trek here from Stok which takes two days and a steep ascent of the **Namlung La** (4,570 m).

From Rumbak it is a five-hour walk to Utse village. The camp is two hours further on at the base of the bleak **Gandha La** (4,700 m), open, bare and windswept. To go over the pass takes about three hours, then the same time again to negotiate the wooded ravine to Skiu. Here the path meets the Markha Valley. You can make a half day round trip from Skiu to see the impressive gorges on the Zanskar River. The stage to Markha where there is an impressive fort, is a six-hour walk. The monastery, which is not particularly impressive from the outside, has some superb wall paintings and *thangkas*, some dating from the 13th century. You need to take a torch.

The next destination is **Hankar** village, whose ruined fort forms an astonishing extension of the natural rock face, an extremely impressive ruin. From here the path climbs quite steeply to a plateau. There are good views of Nimaling Peak (6,000 m) and a number of *mani* walls en route. From **Nimaling** it is a two-hour climb to **Gongmaru La** (5,030 m) with views of the Stok range and the Indus Valley. The descent is arduous and involves stream crossings. There is a lovely campsite at **Shogdu** and another at **Sumda** village, 3 km further on. The final stage is down the valley to Martselang from where you can walk down 5 km to **Karu** village on the Leh-Manali road or take a 2 km diversion to visit Hemis monastery. The daily walking time on this trek is five to six hours so you must be fit.

Hemis High Altitude National Park Set up in 1981, the park adjoining the monastery covers 600 sq km comprises the catchments of Markha, Rumbak and Sumda nalas, with plans to extend across another 1,670 sq km. The rugged terrain with valleys often littered with rocks and rimmed by high peaks (some over 6,000 m), supports limited vegetation but contains some rare species of flora and fauna. ■ *Rs 25 per person per day; Indian Rs 10 per day.*

Wildlife Some are rare, for example ibex, Pallas's cat, *bharal* and *shapu* while a reserve to protect the endangered snow leopard (*Panthera unica*) is planned. It is hoped to restrict the activities of local villagers who graze livestock within the park, to a buffer zone so that their animals can be kept safe from attack by wolves and snow leopards.

There are camping sites which you can reserve through the Div Forest Officer, Wildlife Warden, Leh. **NB** Since most of the Park lies within 'Restricted' areas, you need a special Group Permit for entry, also issued in Leh. Contact local travel agent for advice.

Trekking from Lamayaru to Alchi This is a shorter trek of five to six days. The average daily walking time is 6½ hours so do not imagine that the shortness of the trek means less effort. Three passes, the **Printiki La** (3,500 m), **Konke La** (4,570 m) and **Stapski La** (5,200 m) are crossed rewarding the exertion of reaching them with excellent views.

The first stage involves walking from the usual campsite just below the monastery down the valley for 2 km then over the **Printiki La**. You then descend the Shillakong Valley and climb to **Phangi** village, passing huge boulders brought down by a landslide, and impressive irrigation in such a forbidding landscape. From Phangi you walk up the Ripchar Valley to **Khaltse**, crossing the river a number of times. There are a number of small settlements until you reach the summer grazing ground a few kilometres below the pass. The **Konke La** is a steep two hours climb. From here you will see the Zanskar River and gorge and the Stok range.

The fourth stage should be with a guide since the trail splits, one leading to **Chillung** on the Zanskar River, the other to **Sumdahchenmo**, the latter being quite treacherous as it involves many river crossings (about three hours below Sumdahchenmo there is a path which climbs the ridge above the river; it is quite easy to miss this, hence the guide). There is a monastery here with an impressive statue of the Buddha and some attractive wall paintings. A camping site lies just beyond the village. The last stage of the trek is long, about eight hours walking, and takes you over the **Stapski La** to **Alchi**. The views from the top are superb. From Alchi you can get a bus to Leh.

The gradual easing up of controls to visit the Nubra-Shyok valleys has now made possible treks that start from points in the Indus valley not far from Leh, cross the Ladakh Range to enter the Shyok River valley and then recross the Ladakh range further to the west to re-enter the Indus valley near Phyang monastery.

Trekking in the Nubra & Shyok Valleys
Ask a good local trekking agent for advice on how to get required 'Restricted Area Permits'

Day 1 Drive from Leh south along the Manali road to **Karu**, near Hemis, where you turn left and drive about 10 km to the roadhead at the village of Sakti, just past **Takthak monastery**. Trek about 90 minutes to **Chumchar** and camp.

Day 2 Cross the Ladakh range at the **Wari La** pass (4,400 m) and descend to Junlez on the northern flank.

Day 3 Walk downhill to **Tangyar** (3,700 m), with a nice gompa.

Days 4, 5, 6 A level walk along the **Shyok** River valley takes you to **Khalsar** from where you follow the military road west to the confluence of the Shyok and Nubra rivers at **Deskit**. On a hill above the village is a Gelugpa sect **monastery** (the largest in Nubra) built by the Ladakhi king Sohrab Zangpo in the early 1700's. There is large statue of Tsongkhapa and the Rimpoche of Thikse monastery south of Leh oversees this monastery also. The Rimpoche was nominated to the Rajya Sabha in 1998. The next biggest monastery in Nubra is near **Tiggur** halfway along the road north of Deskit to **Panamik** in the Nubra Valley. Called the **Samtanling** gompa, it was founded in 1842 and belongs to the Gelugpa sect. The Permit alows travel only up to the village of Panamik (see Nubra Valley above).

Days 7,8,9 Three days to gradually ascend the northern flanks of the Ladakh Range passing the hamlets of **Hundar, Wachan** and **Hundar Dok** to the high pastures of **Thanglasgo** (4,700 m).

Days 10 & 11 Trek back over the Ladakh Range via the Lasermo La pass (5,150 m) to a campsite on the southern base of the pass.

Day 12 Camp at Phyang village about 1 km above Phyang monastery before driving back to Leh.

Jammu & Kashmir

Zanskar

Colour map 1,
grid B2

Zanskar can be cut off by snow for as much as seven months each year when access is solely along the frozen Zanskar River. This isolation has helped Zanskar to preserve its cultural identity, although this is now being eroded. Traditional values include a strong belief in Buddhism, frugal use of resources and population control. Values, which for centuries, have enabled Zanskaris to live in harmony with their hostile yet fragile environment.

The land Zanskar is a remote area of Ladakh contained by the Zanskar range to the north and the Himalaya to the south. There are two subsidiary valleys, the **Stod** (Doda Chu) and the Lung-Nak – Valley of darkness (Tsarap Chu) which converge below **Padum**, the capital. The Zanskar River flows along the valley from Padum to Zangla, then cuts through the Zanskar range in a series of impressive gorges to join the Indus. The main valley is approximately 300 km long and is ringed by mountains so access to it is over one of the high passes. The most important are the **Pensi La** connecting Zanskar with the Suru Valley in the west, the **Umasi La** with the Chenab Valley in the south and the **Shingo La** with Lahul in the east. This makes for very spectacular trekking country. The long Zanskar Valley was 'opened' up for tourism even later than the rest of Ladakh and quickly became popular with trekkers. There is now river rafting on the Zanskar River. The jeep road from Kargil to Padum over the Pensi La is usually open mid-June to mid-October.

History Zanskar became an administrative part of Ladakh under Senge NamgyaI whose three sons became the rulers of Ladakh, Guge and Zanskar/Spiti. This arrangement collapsed after Ladakh's war with Tibet and the Zanskar royal house divided, one part administering Padum, the other Zangla. Under the Dogras, the rulers were reduced to puppets as the marauding army wreaked havoc on the villages, monasteries and population. The present king of the Zanskar valley, Punchok Dawa who lives in his modest home in Padum, is held in high regard.

Culture **People** The Zanskaris are of the same stock as the Ladakhis and because of the sheer isolation of their homeland were able to preserve their Buddhist culture against the onslaughts of Islam. The majority of Zanskaris are Buddhist though there are Muslim families in Padum, the capital, dating from the Dogra invasion who consitute 40% of the town's population.

Religion The foundation of Sani in the 11th century is recognized as the first monastery in Zanskar. Phugtal and Karsha date from the same period. The sects developed alongside those in Ladakh. The **Gelugpa** (Yellow Hat) order was established in the 15th century and monasteries at Karsha, Lingshet and Mune belong to this. The **Drukpa** sect set up monasteries at Bardan and Zangla and 'occupied' that at Sani. These have links with Stakna near Leh and the Gelugpa is associated with the Lekir monastery.

Traditional Ladakhi and Zanskari life, even today, comes close to Gandhi's idealized vision of life in ancient India: small village 'republics', each self-sufficient, everyone playing a valuable part, with no crime and discrimination with regard to caste or religion and where disparities in wealth would not exist.

Economy **Agriculture** An almost total lack of precipitation has meant that cultivation must rely on irrigation. As in Ladakh, the rivers have been harnessed but with difficulty. The deep gorges presented a problem. Headworks were constructed and irrigation channels (yura) were contoured along to the fields, some up to 5 km away. **Barley** is the most suitable crop as it is very hardy, copes well with poor soils and can be roasted to form the staple *tsampa* (ngamphe) which can be eaten without cooking. This is useful in winter when fuel is scarce Peas are the only other crop. Animal husbandry complements agriculture which only produces one crop per year. Sheep and goats are taken to high meadows in the summer after the snow melt and grazed while the shepherds live in small stone huts.

Recommended reading *Zanskar, the Hidden Kingdom* by Michel Peissel. *Zanskar, a Himalayan Kingdom* by Oliver Folloni, with superb photos.

Padum has a population of about 1,000 of whom a sizeable minority are Sunni Muslim. On arrival you must report to the Tourist Officer. **Sleeping** is very limited, being mostly dormitory style. **F** *Tourist Complex* has basic rooms, meals available. You can camp. **Transport** Access is either by the jeep road over the **Pensi La**, generally open from mid-June to mid-October with a bus service on alternate days from Kargil (no Permit needed), 18 hours. The alternative method is to trek in.

Padum
Colour map 1, grid B3

Trekking in Zanskar

Trekking in Zanskar is not easy. The paths are often rough and steep, the passes high and the climate extreme. Provisions, fuel and camping equipment should be taken along from Kishtwar, Manali or Leh. You may get necessities such as dried milk, biscuits and sugar from Padum, though probably not at the beginning of the season. In Padum the Tourism Officer and Govt Development Officer will be able to advise and maybe even assist in hiring horses. Porters can be hired at **Sani** village for the traverse of the **Umasi La** into Kishtwar. Horses cannot use this pass. In Padum you may be able to hire porters with whom you can cover rougher terrain.

You can trek this three-day route before the road opens (June-October) when it is free of vehicles.

Pensi La to Padum

This is a demanding 9-day trek which includes seven passes, five of which are over 4,500 m. The highest is the Singi La (5,060 m). It is essential to be very fit before starting the trek. Each day's walking should take under six hours, but with time for rests and lunch this adds up to a full day. An extra day allows for flexibility.

Karsha to Lamayaru

The 16th-century monastery of the Tibetan Gelugpa (Yellow Hat) sect at **Karsha** is the largest and wealthiest in the Zanskar Valley and is occupied by nearly 200 monks. Karsha has an inn with dormitory beds and a vegetarian canteen.

This is another demanding trek which also takes about 10 days. Some are through the spectacular gorges between Markha and Zangla. A local guide is recommended as this is truly a wilderness area. The trek involves walking along stream beds and in July there is still too much snow melt to allow safe crossings. Recommended only for August/September.

Padum to Leh

It is seven hours walking from Padum to Zangla and this includes crossing the Zanskar River by a string and twig bridge that spans over 40 m. Ponies are not allowed on it and if it is windy sensible humans don't cross! At **Zangla** you can see the King's palace which has a collection of thangkas painted by the King's don who was once a monk. The third stage takes you over the **Charcha**

La (5,200 m). On the next stage river crossings are again necessary. This is time consuming and if you are travelling in mid-summer, an extra day may be called for.

You then follow the **Khurna River** to a narrow gorge that marks the ancient border between Zanskar and Ladakh, and end up below the Rubarung La. When you cross this you get good views of the Stok range. You then descend into the Markha valley and from here you can reach Leh in six stages by heading west into the heart of the valley and then crossing the Ganda La to Spituk, or in three stages by crossing the Gongmaru La and descending to Martselang and nearby Hemis.

★ **Padum to** This is a week long trek and starts with a walk along the Tsarap Chu to Bardan, **Darcha** which has stupas and interesting idols, and Reru.

After two stages you reach **Purni** with a couple of shops and a popular campsite, where you can stay two nights and make a side trip to the impressive 11th-century **Phugtal monastery** which is a 2 hour walk. On a spectacular site, it has been carved out of the mountainside round a limestone cave. Usually there are about 50 monks in attendance. From Purni you continue on to Kargya, the last village before the **Shingo La**. It's another day's walk to the camp below this high pass (5,200 m).

The mountain scenery is stunning with 6,000 m plus peaks all around. Once over the pass you can stop at **Rumjack** where there is a campsite used by shepherds or you can go further to the confluence of the **Shingo River** and the **Barai River** where there is now a bridge. From here the trail passes through grazing land and it is about 15 km from the river to Darcha, the end of the trek. Keen trekkers can combine this with a trek from **Darcha** to **Manali**. The average daily walking time of the Padum-Darcha trek is six hours so this is you have to be very fit.

Eastern Himalaya

262

Eastern Himalaya

264 Access from Kolkata

274 Darjeeling and North Bengal

293 Sikkim

313 Assam, Meghalaya and
Arunachal Pradesh

With the Kangchendzonga Ranges towering massively above Darjeeling the highest mountains of the Indian Himalaya are more accessible in the east than in the west. The contrasts from the plains are even more strking. The short steep climb from Bagdogra or Siliguri takes you straight up to the hill station of Darjeeling. A slightly longer journey takes you to the heart of Sikkim. From both you have the sense of being surrounded by gloriously untouched snow-capped pinnacles.

Yet for all their accessibility from the plains, the Eastern Himalaya are in many ways even more remote than the western ranges. Far from Delhi, India's main entry point for foreign visitors, it is a two hour flight even to Bagdogra and a day and night journey by train. (Kolkata is an hour's flight). Even then you are still far from the eastern limits of the Himalaya proper. The massive Brahmaputra River, which with the Ganges and the Indus is the third of the great Himalayan rivers, runs through the heart of Assam. To its north the Himalaya rise through one of India's newest and least accessible states, Arunachal Pradesh, while to its south is the Shillong Plateau. With access to Arunachal Pradesh restricted by the Government, the number of visitors who can see such treasures of Buddhism as the Tawang monastery, is tiny. Yet in Assam itself it is possible to see great National Parks such as Kaziranga, and if you feel you would really like to see rain, take an excursion to Mawsynram in the Shillong Hills, the wettest place on earth.

Access from Kolkata

★ Kolkata (Calcutta)

Phone code: 033
Population: 11.02 mn

To Bengalis Kolkata is the proud intellectual capital of India. It also has the nearest international airport for gaining access to the Eastern Himalaya.

Ins & outs
See page 271 for further details

Getting there The airport at Dum Dum serves both international and domestic flights with a taxi or coach transfer to the city centre taking 30 to 45 mins. **Haora (Howrah) station**, on the west bank of the Hugli, can be daunting and the taxi rank outside is often chaotic. Long distance buses arrive at Esplanade, within 15 to 20 mins' walk of most budget hotels. **Getting around** You can cover much of Central Kolkata on foot but for the rest you need transport. Buses and minibuses are often jam-packed and are best avoided. The electric trams can be slightly better outside peak periods. The city's showpiece Metro, though on a limited route, is worth a try. Taxis are relatively cheap but allow plenty of time to get through very congested traffic.

The city
Calcutta, as it came to be named, was founded by the remarkable English merchant trader **Job Charnock** in 1690. That year he selected three villages – Kalikata, Sutanuti and Govindpur – where Armenian and Portuguese traders had already settled, leased them from Emperor Aurangzeb and returned to what was to become the capital of British India. Charnock became the first Governor of Calcutta, where he lived with his Indian wife.

The first fort here, named after King William III (completed 1707), was on the site of the present BBD Bagh. In 1756, Siraj-ud-Daula, the then Nawab of Bengal, began to take note of Kolkata's growing wealth and found little difficulty in capturing the city. Within a year, however, Robert Clive took the city back. The new Fort William was built and in 1772 Calcutta became the capital of British administration in India with Warren Hastings as the first Governor of Bengal.

Colonial Calcutta grew as new traders, soldiers, administrators and their wives arrived establishing their exclusive social and sports clubs. Calcutta prospered as the commercial and political capital of British India up to 1911, when the capital was transferred to Delhi.

Some of the city's most impressive colonial buildings were built in the years that followed.

Independence & after
Kolkata had to absorb huge numbers of migrants immediately after Partition in 1947. In the late 1960s the election of the Communist Party of India Marxist (**CPM**) led to a period of stability. In the last decade the CPI (M) has become committed to a mixed economy and has actively sought foreign private investment.

A few interesting sights near the centre are briefly described here. For a fuller coverage, see Footprint's *India Handbook*.

Central Kolkata

Many historic Raj buildings surround the square which is quietest before 0900. Re-named Benoy Badal Dinesh (BBD) Bagh after three Bengali martyrs, the square has a small artificial lake, fed by natural springs. The **Writers' Building** (1780), designed by Thomas Lyon as the trading HQ of the East India Company, was refaced in 1880. It is now the state Government Secretariat. **Mission Row** (now RN Mukharji Road) is Kolkata's oldest street, and contains the **Old Mission Church** (consecrated 1770), built by the Swedish missionary Johann Kiernander.

★ **BBD Bagh (Dalhousie Sq)**
Sightseeing takes time, & Kolkata can be very hot outside Nov-early Mar. Asthma sufferers may find the traffic pollution very trying

The silver-domed **General Post Office**, built on the site of the original Fort William, was designed by Walter Granville (1868). The **Black Hole of Calcutta** was at the northeast corner of the post office. The sight of the Lyon's Range **stock exchange** in full swing, spilling out onto the street, confirms that commercially, Kolkata is still very much alive.

West side of BBD Bagh

The imposing **Raj Bhavan** (1799-1802) is the residence of the Governor of West Bengal. Entry is restricted. The **Town Hall** (1813) has been converted into a museum. The **High Court** (1872) was modelled on the medieval cloth merchants' hall at Ypres in Flanders.

The **Ochterlony Monument** (1828), re-named Shahid Minar (Martyrs' Memorial) in 1969, was built as a memorial to Sir David Ochterlony .

★ **St John's Church** (1787) (0900-1200, 1700-1800), like the later St Andrew's Kirk (1818), was modelled partially on St Martin-in-the-Fields, London. Inside are Warren Hastings' desk and chair and the tomb of Bishop Middleton, first Bishop of Calcutta. 'The Last Supper' by **Johann Zoffany** in the south aisle, shows the city's residents dressed as the Apostles. Job Charnock is buried in the old cemetery.

South of BBD Bagh

★ **South Park St Cemetery** The cemetery was opened in 1767 to accommodate the large number of the British who died serving their country. The heavily inscribed, decaying headstones, obelisks, pyramids and urns have been somewhat restored. The cemetery is a beautifully quiet space on the south side of one of Kolkata's busiest streets. Tombs include those of **Col Kyd**, founder of the Botanical Gardens, and the great oriental scholar **Sir William Jones**.

Park Street & Maidan Area
Travellers have reported attempted robbery; if alone, avoid going when it is deserted

Conveniently close to Chowringhee and the vast shopping arcade, New Market, Sudder Street is the focus for Kolkata's budget travellers.

This area, 200 years ago, was covered in dense jungle. Larger than New York's Central Park, it is perhaps the largest urban park in the world! Often called the 'lungs' of the city, it is a unique 'green' in which stands Fort William and several club houses and where thousands each day pursue a hundred different interests.

The Maidan

This is the city's main thoroughfare with shops, hotels, offices and residential buildings. You can still see some of the old imposing structures with pillared verandahs (designed by Italian architects as residences of prominent Englishmen) though modern high rise buildings have transformed the skyline of this ancient pilgrim route to Kalighat.

Chowringhee *(Jawaharlal Nehru Rd)*

St Paul's Cathedral (1847) is the original metropolitan church of British India. The cathedral has a fine altar piece, three 'Gothic' stained glass windows, two Florentine frescoes and the great West window by British Pre-Raphaelite artist **Sir Edward Burne-Jones**. ■ *0900-1200, 1500-1800; 5 services on Sun.*

Access from Kolkata

Kolkata

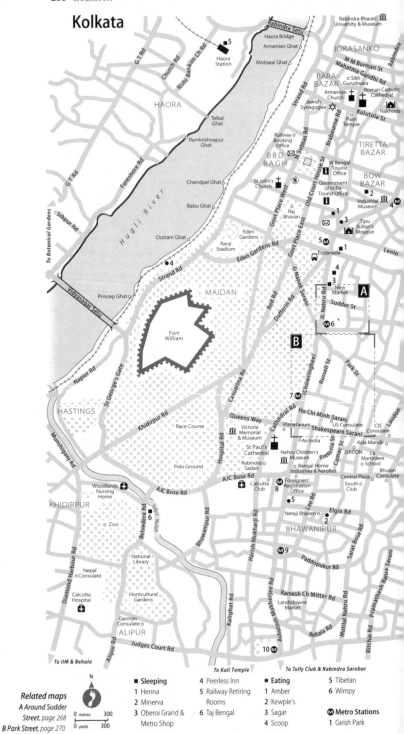

Access from Kolkata

Related maps
A Around Sudder
Street, page 268
B Park Street, page 270

0 metres 300
0 yards 300

■ **Sleeping**
1 Henna
2 Minerva
3 Oberoi Grand &
Metro Shop

4 Peerless Inn
5 Railway Retiring
Rooms
6 Taj Bengal

● **Eating**
1 Amber
2 Kewpie's
3 Sagar
4 Scoop

5 Tibetan
6 Wimpy

Ⓜ **Metro Stations**
1 Girish Park

2 MG Rd
3 Central
4 Chandni Chowk
5 Esplanade
6 Park St
7 Maidan
8 Rabindra Sadan
9 Bhawanipur
10 Jatindas Park

Lord Curzon's white marble monument to Queen Victoria and the Raj (1906-21) designed in Italian Renaissance-Mughal style stands in large well kept grounds with ornamental pools.

There is a wealth of Raj memorabilia: portraits, paintings, sculpture, arms and armoury, prints of old Calcutta, documents relating to the East India Company and watercolours and engravings of Indian scenes capturing moments of Empire. There are fine miniatures, a rare collection of Persian manuscripts, and paintings by Zoffany, T and W Daniells, Samuel Davis and Emily Eden (advance notice needed). Look out for the fascinating 'History of Calcutta' exhibition at the rear.

■ *Mar-Oct 1000-1630, Nov-Feb 1000-1530; Museum 1000-1530, closed Mon (very crowded on Sun). Rs 2. Guided tours at 1030 (allow at least 1 hr). Postcards and guidebooks available. Cameras are not permitted.*

★ Victoria Memorial

After the defeat in 1756 (see page 264) the British built a new massive fort on the site of the village of Govindapur, large enough to house all the Europeans in the city in case of an attack and the jungle around it was cleared to give a clear field of fire, which later became the Maidan.

Fort William
You need permission to enter

Mother Teresa, an Albanian by birth, came to India in 1931. She started her Order of the Missionaries of Charity in Kalighat to serve the destitute and dying, 19 years later. *Nirmal Hriday* ('Pure Heart'), near the Kali Temple, the first 'home' for the dying was opened in 1952. Mother Teresa died in 1997 but her work continues unabated. Anyone interested in **voluntary work** should write in advance to the office at 54A AJC Bose (Lower Circular) Road, T2497115. The Mother House here has a museum.
■ *0800-1200, 1500-1800, closed Thu. Charity Office, T2449267.*

Mother Teresa's Homes

Access from Kolkata

Essentials

Sleeping
■ *on maps*
Price codes:
see inside front cover

*Mid-priced hotels often
have a few a/c rooms
(extra tax) but may not
have a generator & so
have power cuts,
especially in summer.
Some include break-
fast, some a meal*

Watch out for 10% luxury tax, 10% service charge and 20% expenditure tax. For usual facilities in different categories, see page 33. Most hotels listed are about 15 km from the airport. The city centre, about 5 km from Haora railway station, has several medium price hotels with a/c rooms. The budget hotels are concentrated in the Sudder St/Mirza Ghalib St area. **Telephone number changes** T1952 (dial old number to get new). "Ask Me" T4746363, advises on local affairs, numbers, addresses etc.

Airport AL *Airport Ashok*, T5119111, F5119137, airportel@cal.vsnl.net.in 149 rooms, modern, soundproofed, restaurant with 'frontier cuisine', but unexciting. **D** *Rest House III*. Some a/c, doubles, and cheaper dorm beds. **E** *Airport Rest Rooms*, Old Terminal Building.

Kolkata City L-AL *Oberoi Grand*, 15 JL Nehru, T2492323, F2491217. Atmospheric Victorian building opposite the Maidan exquisitely restored, excellent restaurants

Around Sudder Street

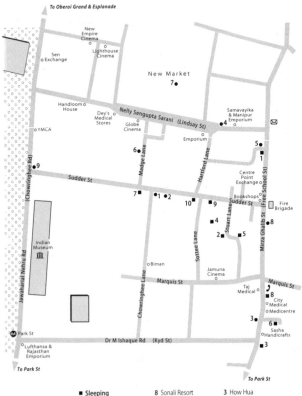

■ **Sleeping**	
1 Deeba Guest House	8 Sonali Resort
2 Galaxy & Paragon	9 Shilton & Jo-jo's
3 Khaja Habib	10 Tourist Inn
4 Maria	
5 Modern Lodge	● **Eating**
6 Omaira & Ruby	1 Blue Sky Café & Zurich
7 Red Shield Guest House	2 Curd Corner & STD/ISD phone

3 How Hua
4 Jimmy's
5 Kathleen's Bakery
6 Khalsa
7 Nahoum Bakery
8 Prince
9 Zaranj

including French, lovely pool (non-residents pay). **L-AL** *Taj Bengal*, 34B Belvedere Rd, Alipore, T2483939, F2481766. Opulent and modern. **AL** *Park*, 17 Park St, T2497336, F2497343.

B *Kenilworth* (Best Western), 1 & 2 Little Russell St, T2828394, F2825136. good restaurant (excellent lunch buffet), new 'Pub', quiet. **B-C** *Peerless Inn*, 12 JL Nehru Rd, T2430301, F2486650. Modern business hotel but drab exterior, excellent *Aaheli* restaurant.

C *Astor*, 15 Shakespeare Sarani, T2429917, F2427430. 32 rooms (inferior annexe), good open-air restaurant. **C** *Minerva*, 11 Ganesh Chandra Ave, T263365, F61082. Upgraded rooms, good a/c restaurants especially Chinese.**D** *CKT Inn*, 12 Lindsay St, T/F2440047. Clean, cosy rooms with bath despite dreary exterior, good service, friendly. **E** *Henna*, 6A SN Banerjee Rd, Gate 4, 2nd Floor, T244421.

Around Sudder Street **E** *Biman*, 8/1B Chowringhee Lane, T2461379. 20 rooms, some a/c (Rs 400), clean, friendly. **E** *Khaja Habib*, 33 Mirza Ghalib St, T293305. 14 rooms, clean, well maintained. **E** *Galaxy*, Stuart Lane, T2464565. 4 good rooms, new, clean, pleasant. **E** *Maria*, 5/1 Sudder St, T2450680. 21 rooms, some with bath, dorm, basic, not great, no drugs or alcohol, internet, STD. **E** *Ruby*, B33/H/4 Mirza Ghalib St, T2465994. 8 rooms with bath, pleasant, clean, but a bit noisy (TV in reception). **E** *Omaira*, B-33/H/4 Mirza Ghalib St, 2nd Floor (no sign, look for *Ruby*), T2291550. 16 rooms with bath, TV (Rs 325), clean, good value. **E** *Shilton*, 5A Sudder St, T2451512. 27 modest rooms with bath in old house. **E-F** *Modern Lodge*, 1 Stuart Lane, T2444960. 30 rooms, best on 1st floor and on roof with bath Manager ('a Sudder St institution') helpful for cheap flights, friendly. Salvation Army's **E-F** *Red Shield Guest House*, 2 Sudder St, T2450599. 7 modest rooms (5 with bath), segregated, dark 3-5 bed dorms Rs 60 (no late nights!), erratic water supply, bag storage, very friendly staff. **E-F** *Sonali Resort*, 21A Mirza Ghalib St via narrow alleyway, T2451844. 17 rooms with bath, friendly. **F** *Deeba Guest House*, 18 Mirza Ghalib St, T2448602. 12 rooms with bath, clean but claustrophobic, noisy. **F** *Tourist Inn*, 4/1 Sudder St, T2449818. 9 rooms some with bath small and basic.

Popular with backpackers, most have cheaper singles & dormitories

Haora **E** *Railway Retiring Rooms*. Some a/c, at both stations for passengers with tickets over 200 km or Rail Pass holders. **E** *Railway Yatri Niwas*, Haora, between old and new stations. 28 rooms, 8 a/c, 5-7 bed dorms, no reservations. restaurant, left luggage.

Thursdays are 'meatless' days but chicken and fish are available. Licensed restaurants serve alcohol (some are no longer pleasant places to eat in since the emphasis is on drink). **NB** Taxes, can double the price on the menu. Many restaurants do not accept credit cards.

Eating
● *on maps, pages 266, 268 & 270*

Expensive *Amber*, 11 Waterloo St, T2483018. North Indian. 3 floors of gourmet delights (try *tandoori*), generous helpings, fast service, bar *Bar-B-Q*, 43 Park St, T249116 (closed Thu). Good Indian, bar. *Blue Fox*, 55 Park St, T2494165. Bar, popular, excellent sizzlers. *Zaranj*, 26 JL Nehru Rd, T299344. Tasteful, stylish, excellent food.

Mid-range Around Sudder Street: *Gupta* 53C Mirza *Ghalib St*. Good Indian and Chinese. Small, intimate. *How Hua*, 10 Mirza Ghalib St. Chinese. Friendly service, excellent Chimney soup. *Jimmy's* 14D Lindsay St. Chinese. Small, a/c, good *momos*, Szechuan. *Kathleen's*, 12 Mirza Ghalib St (closed Thu). Comfortable, pleasant, '*Princess*' for families.
    Around Park Street: *Kwality*, 17 Park St (closed Thu) and 2 Gariahat Rd (closed Wed). Excellent Indian and Continental *Mocambo*, 25B Park St. International. A/c, pleasantoutstanding grilled *hilsa* served on banana leaf. *Peter Cat*, 18A Park St

Access from Kolkata

(closed Thu). International. Good kebabs and sizzlers. *Shenaz*, 2A Middleton Row. Good tandoori, bar. *Silver Grill* 18E Park St. Chinese. Try *Limkai* chicken and Thai prawns. **Bengali**: *Aaheli* at Peerless Inn, T2430222. Excellent, comfortable a/c, no alcohol. *Kewpie's*, 2 Elgin Lane, T4759880, closed Mon. Authentic Bengali. Tiny, a/c, open for lunch and dinnerreserve. *Suruchi*, 89 Eliot Rd. Bengali. Simple surroundings but carefully prepared by self-help Women's group at lunchtime.

Elsewhere: Connoisseurs of **Chinese** cuisine travel to South Tangra Rd (off the E Metropolitan Bypass) – basic eateries. *Lily's Kitchen,* very generous ; *Ka Fu Lok* and *Sin Fa*; *Eau Chew*, P32 Mission Row Extn; *Mayfair China Bowl*, 122A Meghnad Saha Sarani (South Kolkata). Chinese. Small and intimate, 'spicy Chinese. *Tibetan*, near Elgin Rd corner of JL Nehru Rd. Excellent dishes under Rs 50.

Cheap Around Sudder Street: *Badshah*, New Market. Well known for *kebab rolls*, bar. *Blue Sky Café*, 3 Sudder St. Western, Chinese, Continental. Popular travellers' meeting place, excellent food; *Curd Corner*, Sudder St. Excellent snacks. *Elfin*, near New Market. Cheap *thalis* and Chinese lunches. *Jo-jo's*, 30 Free School St (6 Sudder St). Good

Park Street

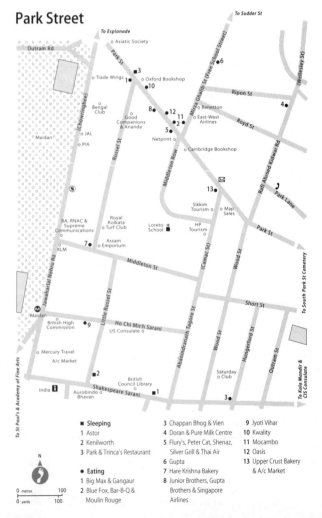

■ Sleeping	3 Chappan Bhog & Vien	9 Jyoti Vihar
1 Astor	4 Doran & Pure Milk Centre	10 Kwality
2 Kenilworth	5 Flury's, Peter Cat, Shenaz,	11 Mocambo
3 Park & Trinca's Restaurant	Silver Grill & Thai Air	12 Oasis
	6 Gupta	13 Upper Crust Bakery
● Eating	7 Hare Krishna Bakery	& A/c Market
1 Big Max & Gangaur	8 Junior Brothers, Gupta	
2 Blue Fox, Bar-B-Q &	Brothers & Singapore	
Moulin Rouge	Airlines	

Access from Kolkata

Indian snacks and meals. a/c. *Khalsa*, 4C Madge Lane. Punjabi. Also Western breakfasts and good *daals* (no smoking). *Prince*, 17 Mirza Ghalib St.Limited menu but praiseworthy Bengali dishes, clean. *Zurich*, 3 Sudder St. Relaxed, excellent snacks, breakfasts, clean.

Vegetarian *Gupta Brothers*, 18B Park St. *Thalis* and Indian sweets, stand-up. *Junior Brothers*, 18B Park St (1st Floor). Very large *thalis* and 'set office lunch'. *Jyoti Vihar*, 3A Ho Chi Minh Sarani. South Indian. A/c, busy at lunchtime. Recommended. Minerva Hotel's *Raj*. Excellent South Indian. A/c, small and simple.

Cafés and fast food *Big Max*, 1 Russell St (Park St corner). *Corner Café*, AJC Bose Rd. For pizzas and burgers. *Super Snack Bar*, 14 Old Court House St. Good *dosas*.

Kathi-rolls (Tender kebabs wrapped in *parathas*) are hard to beat. Try mutton/chicken *egg roll* (if you don't want raw onions and green chillis, order "no piaaz e mirchi"). *Nizam's*, off SN Bannerjee Rd (opposite Elite Cinema), and 22/25 New Market, and stalls in Zakaria St, Park Circus. *Rehmania*, Park St/AJC Bose Rd corner, and *Shiraz*, 56 Park St, for Mughlai food, and *Sagar*, 1 Meredith St.

Bengali sweets Worth sampling (often very sweet!) are *sandesh*, *roshogolla*, *barfi*, *roshomalai*, *pantua* and of course the honey-coloured curd, *mishti doi*. *Chappan Bhog*, 28B Shakespeare Sarani. *Vien* next door. *Doran* and *Pure Milk Centre* near Rafi Ahmed Kidwai St/Ripon St corner. Superb *mishti doi*. *Ganguram*, 46C JL Nehru Rd; *Mithai*, 48B Syed Amir Ali Ave. *KC Das*, 11 Esplanade East.

Bengali snacks Fresh every afternoon at most sweet shops (1600-1730): try *shingaras*, *kochuris* and *nimkis*. *Gangaur*, Russell St, AJC Bose Rd corner. *Krishna*, Camac St.

Confectionery *Flury's*, 18 Park St (closed Mon). English breakfasts, good afternoon teas. *Hare Krishna Bakery*, corner Russell/Middleton Streets. *Hot Breads*, Central Plaza, 2/6 Sarat Bose Rd. *Kathleen's*, several, including 12 Mirza Ghalib St and corner of Lord Sinha Rd/AJC Bose Rd. *Kookie Jar*, Rawdon St. One of the best; *Baker's Square*, next door. *Nahoum*, F20, New Market. *Upper Crust* 1/1 Camac St (and Judges Court Rd). A/c, clean, modern, delicious cakes, snacks. **Ice creams** Look out for *Rollicks*, *Vadilal's* and *Walls* outlets. *Icescapades*, Russell St. *Scoop*, 71 Strand Rd, Man-o-War Jetty.

Up-market restaurants serve alcohol. In Sudder St, *Fairlawn's* pleasant garden terrace for chilled beer. Independent bars, open usually until 2230, lack atmosphere; some are positively men only. **Bars**

Alliance Française, 5C Sukh Sagar, 2/5 Sarat Bose Road, T4757084, afcalcut@cal.vsnl.net *British Council* Library, 5 Shakespeare Sarani, T2425370. UK newspapers and journals,small café. *Max Mueller Bhavan*, 8 Ballygunge Circular Rd. *USIS*, 7 JL Nehru Rd. **Cultural centres & libraries**

American Express, 21 Old Court House St, T2486181. *Eastern Travels*, 26 Shakespeare Sarani, T2477773. *Mercury*, *TCI*, 46c JL Nehru Rd, T2423535. *Sita*, 3b Camac St, T297185. *Thomas Cook*, Chitrakut (2nd Flr), 230a AJC Bose Rd, T2475354. *Travel Bureau*, 50/1 SN Banerji Rd, T2450428. *Warren*, 31 JL Nehru Rd, T296611. **Tour operators**

Local Road Bus: State Transport services are usually overcrowded after 0830. Faster, minibuses cover major routes. **Private taxi**: Car hire with driver, from Rs 750-1,200 (a/c) for 8 hrs. *Gainwell*, 8 Ho Chi Minh Sarani, T2426667; *Mercury*, 46C JL Nehru Rd, T2423555; *Wenz*, at Oberoi Grand, and at Airport T2492323; *Wheels*, 150 Lenin Sarani, **Transport**

T273081. **Rickshaw**: Hand-pulled rickshaws go along congested lanes. **Taxi**: yellow-top: new meters start at Re 1; you multiply by 12. Old meters start at Rs 5; you pay double plus 20 (Rs 12) minimum. Drivers carry conversion charts. **River Ferry**: to cross the Hugli, eg from Haora station, except Sun. **Train** The **Metro** (unique in India) is usually clean, efficient and punctual. 0800-2115, Sun 1400-2000; fare Rs 3-5. Enquiries T2494750. **Tram**: Kolkata is the only Indian city to run the extensive network.

Long distance Air Enquiries T5266233, T140. A Reservation counter for rail (same day travel only) and one for hotels are in the arrivals hall. At the **International terminal**: *State Bank of India* (24 hrs, changes rupees into US$ only). **Transport to town**: the **pre-paid taxi** service (closes at 2200) from Dum Dum to the city centre is excellent value, Rs 100, about 40 mins (but Deluxe cars charge Rs 400-650). **A/c coach transfer** to *Indian Airlines'* city office, approximately 2 hourly from 0530, Rs 75. The public bus is a nightmare; strongly not recommended. The nearest **Metro station** is at Dum Dum (Rs 5 to city centre); auto-rickshaws to there, about Rs 60; total 40 mins. **Transit passengers** with onward flights may use the *Airport Rest Rooms* (some a/c, doubles, dorm). **Domestic**: *Indian Airlines*, T2204433, 0900-1900, chaotic (use travel agent). Airport, T5119841. *Indian Airlines*: flies to Delhi, Guwahati, Dibrugarh, Jorhat, Silchar, Tezpur. *Jet Airways*: flies to, Delhi, Guwahati, Jorhat.

Road   Bus: The Tourist Office, BBD Bagh, has timetables. Advance bookings at computerized office of Kolkata State Transport Corp (STC), Esplanade, T2481916. **Kolkata STC**, **North Bengal STC**, T2481916, to **Cooch Behar**; **Siliguri**, 12 hrs, and **Sikkim Govt**, Gangtok via Siliguri.

Train Kolkata is served by 2 railway stations, **Haora** ('Howrah'), and **Sealdah**. Haora station has a separate complex for platforms 18-21. Enquiries, Haora, T6602581, 'New' Complex, T6602217, Sealdah, T3503535. Central Enquiry, T2204025. Reservation, T136 (computerized). **Computerized Booking Office**, Rabindra Sadan, 61 JL Nehru Rd, T2472143. Rly Reservations, 6 Fairlie Place, BBD Bagh, T2206811; 0900-1300, 1330-1600, Sun 0900-1400 (best to go early). At Fairlie Place, Foreign Tourist Counter, upstairs for Indrail Passes, but downstairs can be much quicker. There are separate queues for Northern and South Eastern Railways. **NB Taxis**: At **Sealdah** ignore touts who quote Rs 80 for Sudder St; instead, join the queue for licensed cabs (rate Rs 25). At **Haora** there are prepaid taxis; or get the **ferry** across the river to Chandpal/Babu Ghat and hire a taxi or walk from there. Buses and minibuses get very crowded. Trains listed depart from Haora (Howrah), unless marked '**S**' for Sealdah (timings change every Apr and Oct). **Darjeeling**: (detrain at **New Jalpaigurï, NJP**) 13¾ hrs, and connect to toy train or take a bus) *Kamrup Exp*, *5659* (AC/II), 1735, continues to Guwahati; (**S**) *Darjeeling Mail*, *3143* (AC/CC&AC/II), 1915, NJP, 13 hrs. (**S**) *Kanchenjungha Exp*, *5657*, 0625, NJ, 11 hrs. **Delhi (ND)**: *Rajdhani Exp* (AC/CC), *2301*, 1700, Mon, Tue, Wed, Fri, 17 hrs; *2305*, via Patna, Thu, Sun, 1345, 20 hrs; *Kalka Mail*, *2311* (AC/II), 1915, 24 hrs; *Purva 2303* (AC/CC), Tues, Fri, Sat, 0915, 22 hrs; **Guwahati** *Seraighat-Guwahati 3045*, Wed, Thu, 2200, 18 hrs; *Bangalore-Guwahati Exp*, *5625* (AC/II), Mon, 1410, 22 hrs.

Directory **Airline offices** *Indian Airlines*, 39 Chittaranjan Ave, T266869, reservations, T5229633 and *Hotel Hindusthan International*, T2476606, Airport, T5529638. *Jet Airways*, 230A AJC Bose Rd, near *Hindusthan International*, T2408192, Airport, T5528836. *Sahara*, 2A Shakespeare Sarani, T2473297, Airport T5528442. **Communications** 1000-1700. **Post**: GPO: BBD Bagh (W). Poste Restante, 0700-2230. closed Sun and holidays. **Tourist offices** *Govt of India*, 4 Shakespeare Sarani, T2421402. *West Bengal*, WBTDC, Netaji Indoor Stadium, West Block, T2487302, F2488290. *Tourism Centre*, 3/2 BBD Bagh (E), T2488271, F2485168. Closed 1330-1415. *ITDC*, 46C, JL Nehru Rd, T2420901. *Arunachal Pradesh*, 4B Chowringhee Place, T2486500. *Assam*, 8 Russell St, T2498332. *Himachal Pradesh*, 25 Camac St, T2476847. *Jammu* and *Kashmir*, 12 JL Nehru Rd, T2485791. *Meghalaya*, 9 Russell St, T290819.

Darjeeling and North Bengal

6

Darjeeling and North Bengal

276 Darjeeling and North Bengal

276 Darjeeling

284 Darjeeling treks

286 Kalimpong

289 Siliguri

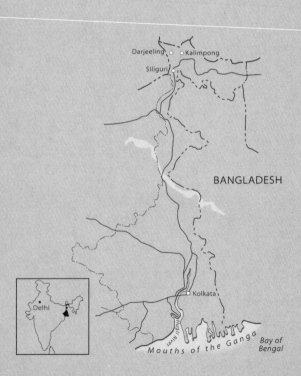

The northern foothills of West Bengal's Himalaya are one of the great tea growing regions of the world. They can still be reached by the romantic steam-pulled 'toy train' now a World Heritage Site. Darjeeling, one of the picturesque hill stations imprinted with images of the Colonial inheritance is overlooked by the everlasting snows of the great Kanchendzonga Range.

★ Darjeeling

দার্জিলিং

and North Bengal

Population: 73,000
Altitude: 2,134 m
Phone code: 0354
Colour map 3, grid B1

For tens of thousands of visitors from the steamy summer heat of the plains Darjeeling (Darjiling) has been the place to get away from it all. It is the principal escape from Kolkata. The idyllic setting, the exhilarating air outside town and stunning views of the Kangchendzonga range when there are gaps in the clouds attract trekkers too. Built on a crescent-shaped ridge Darjeeling is surrounded by hills which are thickly covered with coniferous forests and terraced tea gardens. Between June and September the monsoons bring heavy downpours, sometimes causing landslides, but the air clears after mid-September. Winter evenings are cold enough to demand log fires and warm clothing.

Ins & outs **Getting there** Bagdogra, near Siliguri, is Darjeeling's nearest airport where jeeps and share-taxis tout for business since buses only run from Siliguri (see below). Trains connect New Jalpaiguri/Siliguri with Kolkata and other major cities. The 'toy train' runs from Siliguri/NJP in season but it is very slow. Most people reach Darjeeling by bus or share-taxi and arrive at the Bazar Bus stand in the lower town, though some taxis go to 'Clubside' on the Mall, which is more convenient for most accommodation. Buses from Gangtok arrive near the GPO. Roads can get washed away during the monsoons and may remain in poor condition even in Oct. **Getting around** Darjeeling's roads slope quite gently so it is easy to walk around the town; the air quality is poor in the lower town due to diesel exhaust fumes. For sights away from the centre you need to hire a taxi. Clubside is the most convenient rank, but bargain, especially out of season.

History Darjeeling (officially spelt Darjiling, but rarely used) means 'region of the *dorje* – thunderbolt'. The surrounding area once belonged to Sikkim, although parts were annexed from time to time by the Bhutanese and Nepalese. The East India Company returned the territory's sovereignty to the Rajas of Sikkim, which led to the British obtaining permission to gain the site of the hill-station called *Darjeeling* in 1835, in return for an annual payment. It was practically uninhabited and thickly forested but soon grew into a popular health resort after a road and several houses were built and tea-growing was introduced. The Bengal Government escaped from the Kolkata heat to take up its official summer residence here. The upper reaches were originally occupied by the Europeans, who built houses with commanding views. Down the hillside on terraces sprawled the humbler huts and bazars of the Indian town.

The town The railway station is in the lower part of town on Hill Cart Rd, with the taxi and bus stands. The lower and upper roads are linked by a series of connecting roads and steep steps. The Chowrasta is a focal point with the busy Nehru Road and The Mall leading off it. The Shrubbery (Government House) is at the north end on Birch Hill with St Andrew's Church at the highest point. Be prepared for seasonal water shortages and frequent and persistent power cuts. After dark, since street lights are rare, a torch is essential.

Observatory Hill, sacred to **Siva**, is pleasant for walks though the views of the mountains are obscured by tall trees. The pedestrianized Mall to the east of the hill offers good views near the Chowrasta. Beware of the monkeys; they bite.

Aloobari Monastery on Tenzing Norgay Rd is open to visitors. Tibetan and Sikkimese handicrafts made by the monks are for sale.

The **Tibetan Refugee Self-help Centre** with its temple, school, and hospital is on Gandhi Road, T52346 (closed Sunday). After the Chinese invasion, thousands of Tibetan refugees settled in Darjeeling (many having accompanied the Dalai Lama) and the rehabilitation centre was set up in 1959 to enable them to continue to practise their skills and provide a sales outlet. You can watch them at work (carpet weaving, spinning, dyeing, woodwork, etc) during the season, when it is well worth a visit (closes for lunch, and disappointing off-season). The shop sells carpets (orders accepted), textiles, curios or jewellery, though not cheap to buy.

Hayden Hall, 42 Laden La Rd, T53166, a Christian charity, runs social, medical and crafts based programmes (contact hayden@cal.vsnl.net.in). **Volunteers** (teachers, medics, care workers) able to spend at least 6 months are welcome at both but be prepared for very basic conditions in remote areas for some projects.

Tea gardens The garden closest to Darjeeling is the Happy Valley Tea Estate (2 km walk from the Market) using the 'orthodox' method (see box: mainly May-October). ■ *Visitors 0800- 1200, 1300-1630 (best in the morning); closed Sun, Mon.*

Natural History Museum, off Mall Road, has a large collection of fauna of the region. Visit recommended. ■ *1000-1600, Wed afternoons; closed Thu, Rs 2.*
Himalayan Mountaineering Institute and Everest Museum. The institute was previously headed by the late Tenzing Norgay who shared the first climb of Everest in 1953. It traces the history of attempted climbs from 1857 and displays old mountaineering equipment including that used on that historic Tenzing-Hillary climb. Recommended. ■ *0900-1300, 1400-1600, closed Tue in winter. Rs 6 (includes Zoo), still camera, Rs 10, video Rs 20. T52438. Entrance is through the zoo on Jawahar Rd West.*

Ava Art Gallery has exceptional embroidered portraits. ■ *Ghoom, T52469. 0800-1200, 1230-1800.*

Lloyds Botanical Gardens near the market was laid out in 1878 on land given by Mr W Lloyd, owner of the Lloyd's Bank. It has a modest collection of Himalayan and Alpine flora including banks of azaleas and rhododendrons, magnolias, orchids, a hothouse and a herbarium. ■ *0600-1700, closed Sun and bank holidays.* Victoria Falls which is only impressive in the monsoons provides added interest to a three-hour nature trail. The zoo next to Mountaineering Institute (combined ticket Rs 6).

Climate: Darjeeling
Best time to visit: Apr-Jun & Oct-Nov

Darjeeling & North Bengal

High-altitude wildlife includes Himalayan black bear, Siberian tiger, red pandas, yaks and llama. There are large enclosures over a section of the hillside though at feeding time and wet weather they retreat into their small cement enclosures giving the impression that they are restricted to their cells. The zoo has a reasonably successful snow leopard breeding programme. The Captive Breeding Centre has a separate entrance. ■ *1000-1600*. Visit the shrubbery behind Raj Bhawan on Birch Hill for spectacular views of Kangchendzonga.

Darjeeling

Darjeeling & North Bengal

N
Not to scale

■ **Sleeping**
1 Alice Villa
2 Aliment & Triveni
3 Andy's
4 Bellevue, Tourist office,
  Indian Airlines & South
  Indian Café
5 Broadway
6 Central
7 Dekeling & Dekeva's
  Restaurant
8 Ivanhoe

9 Lewis Jubilee Complex
10 Mahakal Palace
11 Maple Tourist Lodge
12 Mayflower
13 New Elgin
14 Pagoda
15 Prestige
16 Shangrila & Chinese
   Restaurant
17 Sinclairs
18 Tourist Lodge
19 Tower View

20 Valentino & Chinese
   Restaurant
21 Windamere

● **Eating**
1 Amigos
2 Glenary's
3 Hasty-Tasty
4 Himalaya & Nathmull's
5 Keventer's
6 New Dish & Lhasoo
7 Park

Tea

An ancient Chinese legend suggests that 'tay', tea, originated in India, although tea was known to have been grown in China around 2700 BC. It is a species of Camellia, Camellia thea. After 1833, when its monopoly on importing tea from China was abolished, the East India Company made attempts to grow tea in Assam using wild 'chai' plants found growing there and later introduced it in Darjiling and in the Nilgiri hills in the South. Today India is the largest producer of tea in the world. Assam grows over half and Darjiling about a quarter of the nation's output. Once drunk only by the tribal people it has now become India's national drink.

The old 'orthodox' method of tea processing produces the aromatic lighter coloured liquor of the Golden Flowery Orange Pekoe in its most superior grade. The fresh leaves are dried by fans on 'withering troughs' to reduce the moisture content and then rolled and pressed to express the juices which coat the leaves. These are left to ferment in a controlled humid environment in order to produce the desired aroma. Finally the leaves are dried by passing them through a heated drying chamber and then graded – the unbroken being the best quality, down to the 'fannings' and 'dust'. The more common 'crushing, tearing, curling' (CTC) method produces tea which gives a much darker liquor.

Most of Darjiling's tea is sold through auction houses, the largest centre being in Kolkata. Tea tasting and blending are skills which have developed over a long period of time and are highly prized. The industry provides vital employment in the hill areas and is an assured foreign exchange earner.

Excursions

Ghoom Monastery (8 km, *altitude:* 2,550 m) The important Yiga-Choling Gompa, a Yellow-hat Buddhist Monastery (built in 1875) 8 km from town, houses famous Buddhist scriptures. You can visit Ghoom on the steam 'Toy Train' (April-June, October- November).

Batasia Loop, 5 km away on the way to Ghoom which allows the narrow-gauge rail to do a figure of eight loop, has a war memorial with a pleasant small park with good mountain views (Rs 3). See 'Toy Train' under Siliguri. A few spruced up carriages do a 'tourists only' steam train ride from Darjeeling to Batasia Loop and back with photo stops at Ghoom and Batasia daily at 1000. Fare Rs 200 but limited to 40 persons so go early to book a place.

Chunnu Falls, 10 km down a steep switchback road, has turned an impressive waterfall into an artificial concrete park with flower beds, metal stairways and viewing platforms. Limited refreshments are served on a pleasant terrace.

The disused **Lebong Race Course** (8 km), once possibly the smallest and highest in the world and still pleasant for a walk, was started as a parade ground in 1885.

Tiger Hill (11km, *altitude:* 2,590 m) It is worth rising as early as 0400 to make the one hour journey for a breathtaking view (weather permitting) of the sunrise on Kangchendzonga. Mount Everest (8,846 m), 225 km away, is visible on a clear day. A WBTDC *Tourist Lodge* has dorm beds (Rs 100); '*VIP Room*' serves coffee. ■ *Getting there: jeeps from Darjeeling, Rs 400. You may wish to walk back from Tiger Hill (about two hours) or visit Ghoom on the way back.* **Senchal Lake**, close to Tiger Hill, supplies Darjeeling with water and makes a good picnic spot.

Trekking

Darjeeling offers many excellent trekking options (see page 284). Contact a local trek agent or DGHC, T54214.

Tours

DGHC, from Tourist Office (minimum eight). **Tour 1**: Tiger Hill, Senchal

Lake, Ghoom Monastery, Batasia Loop. 0400-0730. Rs 60. **Tour 2**: Local sightseeing. Ava Gallery, Manjusha Emporium, Dhirdham Temple, Himala- yan Mountaineering Institute, Zoo, Ropeway, Lebong Racecourse, Tibetan Refugee Self-help Centre. 0930-1230, 1330-1630. Rs 60. **Tour 3**: Mirik. 0800-1730. Rs 95.

Essentials

Sleeping

Most are within 1 km from the station

Several include all meals in season (mid-Mar to Jun, mid-Sep to Nov) & offer discounts off-season. Some charge extra for Christmas & New Year

AL-A *Mayfair* The Mall, opposite Raj Bhavan gate, T56376, F52674, superb location, among terrace gardens, 21 rooms (5 attractive wooden attics), 11 cottages on hillside below Mall, furnishings showing signs of wear, good Tiffany's restaurant. **A** *Windamere*, Observatory Hill, T54041, F54043, 27 spacious rooms (no phone or TV), dated bathrooms (limited hot water), enviable position with good views (when clear), sun terraces, charming, plenty of character, a 'Raj' experience – memorabilia, coal fires ("fill room with smoke"), 'hotties' in bed, pre-war piano favourites to accompany 'tea', $110 includes disappointing meals. **A** *New Elgin*, 32 HD Lama Rd, T54114, F54267, 25 rooms in character rambling bungalow, top floor rooms in annexe refurbished (shut windows against monkeys!), good food, pleasant terrace, some adverse reports on facilities, billing and cleanliness, overpriced. Recommended.

B *Sinclairs*, 18/1 Gandhi Rd, T56431, F54355, 54 rooms (central heating), restaurant, bar. **B** *Chancellor*, 5 SM Das Rd (awaiting a buyer). **B** *Darjeeling Gymkhana Resort*, The Mall, T54391, F54390, 12 modern rooms, Indian vegetarian restaurant, club on doorstep, wooded location. **B-C** *Central*, Robertson Rd, T54480, F56050, 52 rooms, refurbishing. **B-C** *Mahakal Palace*, Coochbehar Rd, T52026, 22 rooms some in 4-bed bungalows, heated, terrace restaurant. **C** *Dekeling Resort at Hawk's Nest*, 2 AJC Bose Rd (15 min walk from centre), T53092, F53298, dekeling@dte.vsnl.net.in, 4 spacious suites with fire-places in restored old wooden Raj retreat, charming Tibetan hospitality, superb isolated position with mountain views. **C** *Valentino*, 6 Rockville Rd, T2228, 17 clean rooms with mountain views, central heating, Chinese restaurant recommended, bar; WBTDC **C** *Tourist Lodge*, Bhanu Sarani, behind Gymkhana Club, T54411, 15 rooms (smaller, cheaper), breakfast and evening meal incl, superb views and warm. **C-D** *Bellevue*, Chowrasta, T54075, F54330, www.darjeelinghotels.com 43 simple rooms (Rs 80 fire-wood), bit shabby (musty in the monsoons), some large (eg Room 35), 'Old Bellvue' above the newer section is in a pleasant garden with some bright, airy rooms, limited snacks, convenient location, good K'dzonga view from roof at sunrise; **C-D** *Dekeling* 51 Gandhi Rd (the Mall), T54159, F53289, dekeling@dte.vsnl.net.in, 11 rooms with bath on upper floors, 4 attic (Rs 400-600) good *Dekeva's* restaurant, charming family; **C-D** *Ivanhoe*, 4 Franklyn Prestage Rd (opposite St Andrew's), T56082, 7 large rooms with modern bath (hot water, good showers), some with fires (1st Flr better), **B** suites, restaurant, pleasant, character house with atmosphere, quiet.

Some budget hotels offer 3/4 bedded rooms; most have limited menu in restaurants

D *Alice Villa*, 41 HD Lama Rd near DGHC Tourist Office, Chowrasta, T54181, 21 large clean rooms, cosy bungalow. Recommended; WBTDC **D** *Maple Tourist Lodge*, Old Kutchery Rd, T54413, 10 rooms, breakfast and meal incl. **D** *Shangrila*, 5 Nehru Rd, near Chowrasta, T54149, 10 rooms, some with good views, good restaurant, exchange. **E** *Andy's*, 102 Zakir Hussain Rd, 5 mins from Chowrasta past pony sheds, T53125, 10 very clean, airy rooms, some with Indian WC (Rs 250), upper floors with small hot shower (Rs 300), birdseye views from rooftop, kitchenette, storage for trekkers, friendly Gurung family, recommended; **E** *Prestige*, Laden La Rd (up steps, above GPO), T53199, rooms with bath, hot water (Rs 300), no heating so sunny side recommended (others can be damp), some with good views, clean, friendly, good but busy and very noisy, popular with Indian tourists; **E-F** *Pagoda*, 1 Upper Beechwood Rd, very friendly, clean but basic rooms, some with bath (limited bucket hot water), central yet quite peaceful, good value. **F** *Broadway*, 3 Coochbehar Rd, 29 rooms, good location with roof-top views; **F** *Lewis Jubilee Complex* (DGHC), Dr SK Pal Rd, T56395, 30 rooms (Rs 100-150), 6-bed dorm (Rs 30), plus meal Rs 50; **F** *Youth Hostel* (WB), Dr Zakir Hussain Rd, T52290, mainly dorm (Rs 25) being renovated, superb position, no restaurant, trekking info, out of town but popular. Other guest houses on Dr Zakir Hussain Rd on the way up to the *Hostel*, incl **F** *Tower View* 8/1, beyond TV Tower, pleasant rooms, dorm, homely, knowledgeable owner. Recommended; **F** *Aliment* at 84, 100 m below *Hostel*, small, quite clean, bright rooms, hot shower (Rs 150), cheap food, packed with travellers, good atmosphere, 'library', fairly quiet, highly recommended; **F** *Triveni* at 85, well kept rooms, home-cooked meals.

Expensive *New Elgin*. Charming dining room with character, good meals, very pleasant service.

Eating
Hotels with restaurants will usually serve non-residents. Several have bars

Mid-range *Dekeva's*, 52 Gandhi Rd. International. Charming, cosy, local meals recommended (Rs 200), also fast food. *Glenary's*, Nehru Rd, tea-room with excellent confectionery (Rs 15+), friendly, first class breakfast, Kalimpong cheese and wholemeal bread sold; refurbished licensed restaurant upstairs serves very good food, pleasant atmosphere. **New Dish** JP Sharma Rd (below Lhasoo). Chinese. Adventurous menu, excellent chicken entrées, friendly staff. Recommended. *Park*, opposite State Bank of India. Chinese. Clean, pleasant atmosphere, good food. *Valentino*. Chinese recommended, also Continental.

Cheap *Amigos*. good Chinese. *Asian*, behind Nehru Rd. Excellent Bengali dishes. *Chopstix*, near Rly station. *Shangrila*, Nehru Rd. Chinese, Tibetan, Nepalese. In a garden. *Gol Ghar*, Main Bazar. Indian. Excellent meat dishes with *chapatis*, *naan* and *rotis*. *Lhasoo*, JP Sharma Rd. Tibetan. Friendly, good value. *South Indian Café*, Chowrasta. Indian. Very good vegetarian meals.

Cafés *Hasty Tasty*, Laden La Rd. Very good Indian fast food, not the cheapest but worth it. *Himalaya*, Laden La Rd. Good, cheap breakfasts. *Keventer's*, deteriorated. *Lunar*, Gandhi Rd, does snacks.

The old *Gymkhana Club* has 3 good **snooker** tables (Rs 20 per hour), **badminton**, **squash**, **tennis** and **roller skating**. Temporary membership Rs 30 per day, staff excellent. *Darjeeling Club*, Nehru Rd, T54348, the old Planters' Club, a relic of the Raj, membership (Rs 50 per day), allows use of pleasant colonial restaurant (Rs 200 buffet), bar, **billiards**, a bit run down, but log fires, warm and friendly. **Riding**: Pony rides are popular on the Mall starting at Chowrasta; also possible to do a scenic half-day ride to Ghoom – agree price, in writing! **River rafting**: on the Tista, 2-day all-inclusive tented trips covering 25-65 km, Rs 450-1200, contact DGHC Tourism.

Sports

Buddha Jayanti in **Apr-May** celebrates the birth of the Buddha in the monasteries.

Festivals

Handicrafts The local handicrafts sold widely including Buddhist *tankhas* which are hand painted scrolls surrounded by Chinese brocade, good wood carving, carpets, handwoven cloth, jewellery, copper, brass and white metal religious curios such as prayer wheels, bowls and statues. The Chowrasta shops are closed on Sun and Chowk Bazar on Thu. *Tibetan Refugee Self-Help Centre*, Gandhi Rd (see Sights); *Hayden Hall*, 42 Laden La Rd, colourful woollen goods made by local women's co-op; *Gram Shilpa*, for *khadi* cotton and silk, well-stocked and very helpful. Curios from Chowrasta, *H Mullick* (a cut above the rest), *Eastern Arts*. Also, on Nehru Rd (*Nepal Curios*), Laden La Rd (*Dorjee*).

Shopping
The markets are very colourful & worth visiting

  Books *Oxford Bookshop*, Chowrasta, good stock especially local interest, amiable staff, recommended.

Darjeeling & North Bengal

Photography *Das Studios* on Nehru Rd, also stationery, postcards, sells interesting black-and-white prints from Raj days; order from album (1-2 days).

Tea *Nathmull's*, Laden La Rd (above GPO), nathmulls@goldentipstea.com, an institution, vast selection (Rs 90-3,000 a kg), avoid fancy packs, knowledgeable owner; totally reliable, easy to carry, an ideal gift (Delhi, 11 Kaka Nagar Market opp Delhi Golf Club, T462242).

Tour operators *Clubside Tours & Travels*, T16 JP Sharma Rd, T54646, F54123, hotel, tours/treks, good jeep hire, air tickets. *Juniper Tours*, behind police island, New Car Park, Laden La Rd, T52095, F53549, also *Indian Airlines*, *Jet Airways* agent; *Pineridge Travels*, Chowrasta, T53912, also *Trek-Mate*. **Trekking agents** *Himalayan Adventures*, Das Studios, Nehru Rd, T54090, dastrek@aussie mail.com.au *Himalayan Travels*, at *Sinclairs*, Gandhi Rd, T54544, long established; *Himalayan Nature Foundation*, opposite Dirdham Temple, T52237, experienced trekking agent, for Singalila, Sikkim etc. *Tushita Treks*, 9/1 Pamu Bldg, TN Rd, T53120.

Transport **Local Bus operators**: *N Bengal STC*, T3133; *Gurkha PAKU*, Chowk Bazar Bus Stand, T53487; *Darjeeling Siliguri Syndicate*, Motor Stand; *Singamari Syndicate*, Main Taxi Stand, T52820; *Sikkim SNT agent*, T52101. **Taxi**: private taxis charge approximately Rs 7 for Nehru Rd to Top Station; taxi stand, Robertson Rd/Laden La Rd. The **Ropeway Cable Car**: starts from North Point, 3 km fom Chowk Bazar (share taxi Rs 5) connects Top Station with Takver in Singla Valley on the Little Rangit River, pleasant tea garden area. In season, 0930-1600 (15 mins each way) Rs 45 return.

Long distance Air: Nearest airport, **Bagdogra** (90 km), see page 290. Transfer by car or coach is 2-3½ hrs. Taxis charge approximately Rs 120 when carrying 7; the W Bengal Tourism Coach costs Rs 60. *Indian Airlines*, *Belle Vue Hotel*, Chowrasta, T52355. Weekdays 1000-1700, Sun 1000-1300. Tourist Information counter.

NH31 connects Darjeeling with other parts of India **Road**: For tours: *Clubside Tours*, JP Sharma Rd, T54646; *Darjeeling Transport Corp*, 30 Laden La Rd, T52074. Maruti vans, jeeps, Land Rovers and a few Sumos are available. Prices vary according to the season so negotiate rates. Share **taxi** to **Siliguri**, Rs 80 (3 hrs). **Jeep** (for 5) Kalimpong or Bagdogra, Rs 900; **Siliguri** Rs 600; **Gangtok**, Rs 1,500. **Bus** Fast services between Kolkata and Siliguri with connections to Darjeeling (see Siliguri). North Bengal STC, Darjeeling, T35133. **Darjeeling to/from Siliguri and Bagdogra**: During the 'season', W Bengal STC bus (Rs 40) from Bazar Bus Stand, or more comfortable Tourist Bus (min 6 passengers), leaving from *Tourist Lodge* and the traffic island near Keventers (3-3½ hrs) – tickets from tourist office, *Bellvue Hotel*. One visitor felt "for thrills and spills, no fairground attraction can rival the narrow hairpinned, switchback road that climbs the Himalayan foothills to Darjeeling". **Gangtok**: SNT bus from near post office. *Darjeeling Motor Service*, Laden La Rd, T52101. **Kalimpong**: Jeeps and buses from the Bazar Motor stand: direct Jeep (2 hrs) and DGHC minibus; buses are infrequent, slower and not much cheaper. In winter, Kalimpong Motor Syndicate, small office tucked away under the bazar, Rs 50/60.

Nepal: Land Rovers between 0600 and 0900 for journey to the border (Panitanki-Kakarbhitta). Private buses have connections from Siliguri (see above), through ticket (Rs 450). Alternatively, Pashupati Fatak on the border (Mirik Rd) has buses to Kathmandu (enquire locally first).

Train: Siliguri, which is 80 km away, and **New Jalpaiguri Junc** (broad gauge), are the nearest stations to Darjeeling (see Siliguri below). The narrow gauge **'Toy Train'** does additional 'Joy Rides': dep 1000, through Batasia Loop and stops at Ghoom; returns 1230.

Directory **Banks** (Limited hrs) *Bank of Baroda*, Robertson Rd, cash against Visa/Mastercard; *Grindlays* for Amex (£/$, 1130-1330), Rs 100 commission; *State Bank of India*, Laden La Rd, cashes Thomas Cook

The Darjeeling Himalayan Railway – a mini miracle

For many people the somewhat erratic narrow gauge Toy Train between New Jalpaiguri and Darjeeling, with its 0.6 m (2 ft) gauge track and hauled by sparkling tank engines, is a rewarding experience. The brainchild of an East Bengal railway agent Franklyn Prestage, the train promised to open access to the hills from the sweltering humidity of the Kolkata plains in the summer. Following the line of an earlier steam tramway, the name was changed to the Darjeeling Himalayan Railway Company in 1881. It is a stunning achievement, winding its way up the hillside, often with brilliant views over the plains. It usually takes 11 or 12 hours to travel the 82 km with gradients of up to one in 19, despite the scheduled time of seven to eight hours (Rs 250). At Ghoom, it reaches 2,438 m and then descends 305 m to Darjeeling. Now a World Heritage Site, the railway is likely to continue to run as a steam 'tourist' railway.

TC's, Amex ($ only), very slow. **Communications** Post: GPO, Laden La Rd. **Telegraph office:** Gandhi Rd. **Medical services** Planters' Hospital, Nehru Rd, T54327. Sadar Hospital, T54218. Mariam Nursing Home, below Gymkhana Club, T54328, has been recommended for its medical facilities. Tibetan Men Tse Khang, 26 HD Lama Rd (Mon-Fri, 0900-1200, 1400-1600). **Chemists:** Frank Ross, Nehru Rd, Puri, Nehru Rd, above Keventer's. **Tourist offices** W Bengal, 'Belle Vue', 1st Flr, 1 Nehru Rd, T54050. 0930-1730, off-season 1000-1630, very helpful officer. Also at Rly station, and at New Car Park, Laden La Rd. **Darjeeling, Gorkha Hill Council (DGHC)**, Silver Fir (below Windamere), The Mall, T/F54214. **Sikkim**, T25277. **Useful addresses** Foreigners' Registration Office: Laden La Rd, T54260; for **Sikkim permits:** go to District Magistrate, Lebong Cart Rd (north of centre), then get form stamped at FRO, and return to DM; takes about 2 hrs.

Short excursions from Darjeeling

Mirik, with its forests of *Cryptomeria japonica*, orange orchards, tea gardens and cardamom plantations, is an attractive resort. **Sumendu Lake** with its 3.5 km cobbled promenade, offers boating (Rs 40). You can visit the carpet weaving centre at Krishannagar or trek to Kurseong and Sandakphu.

Mirik
49 km from Darjeeling
Altitude: 1,730 m

Sleeping D *Jagjeet*, T43206, good rooms, restaurant, bar; **E-F** *Tourist Lodge & Cottages* (DGHC), T43237, modern rooms (Rs 350), dorm (Rs 30), pleasant cottages above lake (Rs 750), good restaurant. At **Dudhia** (on Siliguri road): *Gakul Wayside Inn*, Rs 450.

Transport Road: Access from Bagdogra airport (55 km), Darjeeling (50 km) and Siliguri (52 km). To/from Darjeeling: buses, 0630 to 1500; Jeep, 1200, 1330.

The small, peaceful hill station ('Place of the White Orchid'), surrounded by tea gardens, has some popular boarding schools. You can visit the Makaibari Tea Estate (4 km, closed Monday) and the Forest Museum on Dow Hill.
  At Tung nearby, the St Alphonsus Social and Agricultural Centre, run by a Canadian Jesuit is working with the local community through education, housing, agricultural, forestry and marketing projects. They welcome **volunteers**, contact SASAC, Tung, Darjeeling, West Bengal, T42059.

Kurseong
Phone code: 03554
Altitude: 1,458 m

Sleeping D *Tourist Lodge* (WBTDC), Hill Cart Rd, T44409, 16 rooms, restaurant, bar, Tourist Centre, good views; **E** *Amarjeet*, 12 Hill Cart Rd, T44678, 14 rooms, restaurant.

Transport Train: The 'Toy Train' stops here; passenger service to Darjiling most of the year. **Road**: 51 km from Siliguri, off the main Darjeeling road, or via Pankhabari. Buses and taxis from Siliguri, 3 hrs, Darjeeling, 2 hrs.

Darjeeling & North Bengal

Darjeeling treks

Walks lead in gentle stages along safe roads and through wooded hills up to altitudes of 3,660 m. The best trekking season is in April-May when the magnolias and rhododendrons are in full bloom, or October-November. In the spring there may be the occasional shower. In the autumn the air is dry and the visibility excellent.

You can do a short trek to **Tiger Hill** about 5 km away (see Darjeeling above) but if there is more time, the agents in Darjeeling can organize four to seven day programmes. The favourite early morning destination for sunrise views of Kangchendzonga. Subhas Ghising, leader of the Gorkha National Liberation Front, started bulldozing the top of the hill for an airport before the Government of West Bengal ordered a stop. For trek agents, see Darjeeling above.

The *Tourist Bureau* in Darjeeling will provide detailed information, plan the trek and book your accommodation and also obtain necessary equipment (sleeping bag, wind-jacket etc) and arrange a Sherpa guide. **NB** Trekking gear can be hired from the *Youth Hostel* where there is a very useful book of helpful suggestions from other trekkers.

Himalayan Mountaineering Institute (see under Museums above) runs some courses for trekkers (about Rs 250 for Indians, Rs 1,200 for foreigners).

Sandakphu Most trekkers and visitors either walk or drive by jeep to Sandakphu, a small settlement located at 3,636 m on the Singalila Ridge. A good viewing point 100 m above Sandakphu offers fantastic views, including the famous northern face of Everest (8,846 m), Kangchendzonga (8,598 m), Chomolhari, the highest peak in Bhutan, and numerous peaks like Pandim that lie in Sikkim. Everest is 140 km from Sandakphu as the crow flies.

The entire area is a birdwatcher's paradise with over 600 species including orioles, minivets, flycatchers, finches, sunbirds, thrushes, piculets, falconets and Hoodson's Imperial pigeons. The mixed rhododendron, oak and conifer forests of the area are particularly well-preserved.

Phalut, 22 km from Sandakphu, along an undulating, partly jeepable track, Phalut is at the junction of Nepal, Sikkim and West Bengal. It offers even closer views of Kangchendzonga. It is best to avoid trekking here in May-June and mid-September to 25 October when large numbers of college trekking teams from West Bengal can descend on the area. March and November are highly recommended for clear mountain views.

Singalila Trek The 160 km Singalila trek starts from the small border town of **Manebhanjang** 26 km from Darjeeling. The journey to and from Darjeeling can be done by bus or you can hire a Land Rover or jeep and be driven there early in the morning. There is a frontier check post at **Sukiapokhri**, 7 km short of Manebhanjang, where you need to enter your passport details in the register. **NB** If you have not arranged for transport to meet you at a particular point then it is entirely possible to travel back to Darjeeling from every roadhead by public bus with services at least once daily, often three to four times daily.

Sleeping *Trekkers' Huts*, mostly with 15-25 beds and costing Rs 25-50/bed have been built or refurbished in Tonglu, Sandakphu, Phalut, Gorkhey, Molle, Rammam, Rimbick and Siri Khola. Although usually available, it is wise to book in advance from the Deputy Commissioner, Improvement Fund Trust, Darjeeling, during May/June and October when these trails can be very busy. Any trek agent in Darjeeling will arrange these bookings for a small fee. Private lodges like the *Sherpa Lodge* in Rimbick and Rammam and other trailside lodges in Meghma, Jaubari and Kalpokhri, are usually friendly, flexible and provide a reasonable but basic accommodation.

Day 1 To Tonglu 1 km beyond Manebhanjang town you reach a rough stone paved track leading sharply up to the left. Tonglu (3,030 m) is 11 km from this point if you follow the jeep track, slightly less if you take the frequent but very steep short cuts. **Sleeping** Tonglu *Trekkers' Hut* has 24 beds and a fine view of the Kangchendzonga range. There are tea shops at **Chitre** and **Meghma**. *Hotel Indica*, Meghma, is a simple Tibetan home (homemade cheese hanging from ceiling) but unfortunately dirty.

Day 2 To Jaubari and Gairibans A level walk along the ridge takes you past the long 'mani' wall to the Nepalese village of Jaubari where the trail turns sharply to the right back into Indian territory and down to the village of Gairibans in a forest clearing. No visa necessary. **Sleeping** At Jaubari, the **F** *Teacher's Lodge* is excellent value, including meals. There is a large *Trekkers' Hut* at Gairibans with about 20 beds.

Day 3 To Sandakphu It is 14 km uphill to Sandakphu, with a lunch break in Kalpokhri about midway. The last 3 km from Bhikebhanjang (tea shop) to Sandakphu are particularly steep but the views from the Singalila Ridge make it all worthwhile. Another viewpoint is 100 m above Sandakphu (see above). **Sleeping** Three *Trekkers' Huts* each with its own dining area, toilets and cookhouse – caretakers can arrange simple meals on extra payment.

Darjeeling treks

Darjeeling & North Bengal

Although Gorkhey, Phalut, Rammam & Rimbick lie just S of the border with Sikkim, entering Sikkim is not permitted on this route

To do a **circular walk** continue 21 km along the Singalila ridge to **Phalut** (3,600 m) where there is a *Trekkers' Hut*. Alternatively you can retrace your steps 4 km back towards **Bhikebhanjang** and then take a 16 km long trail through fine forests of the Singalila National Park down to **Rimbick** from where there is a daily bus to Darjeeling. From Phalut continue northeast for 7 km down to the *Trekkers' Hut* at **Gorkhey** where you can stay the night, or walk 3 km to the village of **Samanden**, 'hidden' in a hanging valley and a further 6 km to **Rammam**. Sleeping *Sherpa Lodge*, in a garden, recommended for friendly service (bus tickets and seats reserved) and good food. Alternatively, the *Trekkers' Hut* is about 1 km before Rammam village. From Rammam it is a two hour walk down to the attractive *Trekkers' Hut* at Siri Khola and a further two hours to Rimbick. This entire area is particularly rich in birdlife.

An alternative quieter trail links Sabarkum (7 km before Phalut on the main Sandakphu-Phalut trail) with Rammam with a possible overnight halting place at the **Molley** *Trekkers' Hut*. Good *dahl bhat* and *rakshi/tongba:* share the kitchen fire with the family. Sherpas eat in a shack 200 m uphill from the *Youth Hostel*.

In winter the lower altitude trails that link Rimbick with Jhepi (18 km) can be very attractive for birdwatchers. Ask in Darjeeling for alternative trekking routes as there is an extensive network of varied trails that link the hillside towns and villages.

Those with five days to spare can return by the **Rammam-Rimbick-Jhepi-Bijanbari** route (153 km). From Rammam you can cross by a suspension bridge over the Siri Khola River and follow the path up the valley. The path, a little obscure in places, leads to Dentam in Sikkim (**NB** Entry into Sikkim is not permitted). This less well-trodden valley has rich birdlife (particularly kingfishers), and excellent views of undisturbed forest. From **Bijanbari** (762 m) it is possible to return to Darjeeling, 36 km away, in a Jeep or climb a further 2 km to Pulbazar and then return to Darjeeling 16 km away. Those wishing to only go to Rimbick may return to Manebhanjang via Palmajua and Batasi (180 km), which takes one day.

★ Kalimpong কালিম্পং

Phone code: 03552
Colour map 3, grid B1
Population: 41,000
Altitude: 1,250 m

Set in beautiful wooded mountain scenery, Kalimpong, a remote hill station, has been a meeting point of the once 'three Closed Lands' on the trade route to Tibet, Bhutan and Nepal. It has a relaxed and unhurried air about it. Away from the crowded and rather scruffy centre near the Motor Stand with the sports ground to one side, the town becomes more spaced out as mountain roads wind up and down the hillsides leading up to the monasteries, mission schools and orchid nurseries nearby. The name is said by some to be derived from pong (stronghold) of kalon (king's minister), or from Kalibong, a plant fibre.

Ins & outs   **Getting there** Bagdogra is the nearest airport and New Jalpaiguri the nearest railhead. Buses and shared taxis from there arrive at the bazar Motor Stand in about 3 hrs. From Darjeeling, the 51 km journey (2½ hrs) is through beautiful scenery. The road winds down through the Lopchu former Peshok tea estates and then descends to 250 m at Tista where it crosses the river on a 'new' concrete bridge. 'Lovers' Meet' and 'View Point' give superb views of the Rangit and Tista rivers. **Getting around** The centre is compact enough to be seen comfortably on foot. The surroundings are ideal for walking though some may prefer transport to visit nearby sights. **Climate** Best season is Mar-Jun, Sep-Feb. The gentle climate has warm summers (around 30°C) and cool winters (down to 7°C).

The traditional **market** at the 10th Mile has great atmosphere. The *haat* here every Wednesday and Saturday draws colourful villagers who come to sell fruit, unfamiliar vegetables, traditional medicines, woollen cloth, yarn and much more. It is remarkably clean and laid back, a delight to explore and find unusual merchandise – curly young fern tops, bamboo shoots, dried mushrooms, fragrant spices, musk, *chaang* paraphernalia, large chunks of brown soap, and tiny chickens in baskets alongside gaudy posters.

Sights

Nurseries Kalimpong excels in producing orchids, amaryllis, roses, cacti, dahlias and gladioli. *Ganesh Mani Pradhan*, 12th Mile, *Universal*, 8th Mile, 3 km along Tista Road, *Shanti Kunj*, BL Dikshit Road, *Himalayan*, East Main Road, are among many. The *Takdah Orchid Centre* (44 km) sells 110 varieties. Some visitors are disappointed.

Monasteries The oldest, the **Thongsa Gompa** Bhutanese monastery, 10th Mile (1692) has been renovated. Further north, the Tibetan monastery

Kalimpong

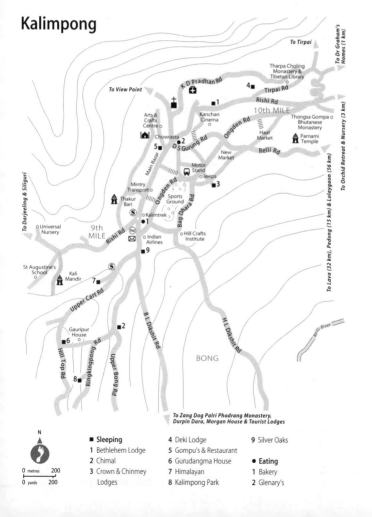

To Tirpai

To Dr Graham's Homes (1 km)

Tharpa Choling Monastery & Tibetan Library

K D Pradhan Rd

To View Point

4

Tirpai Rd

Rishi Rd

1

10th MILE

Kanchan Cinema

Onyden Rd

Thongsa Gompa o Bhutanese Monastery

To Orchid Retreat & Nursery (3 km)

Arts & Crafts Centre

Chowrasta

2

5

D S Gurung Rd

Haat Market

Parnami Temple

Main Bazar

New Market

Relli Rd

Motor Stand

Jeeps

Mintry Transport

Onyden Rd

3

Thakur Bari

Sports Ground

Bag Dhara Rd

To Darjeeling & Siliguri

Universal Nursery

9th MILE

Rishi Rd

Kalimtrek

Pol

Indian Airlines

9

Hill Crafts Institute

To Lava (32 km), Pedong (15 km) & Lolaygaon (56 km)

To Orchid Retreat & Nursery

St Augustine's School

Kali Mandir

7

Upper Cart Rd

Gauripur House

6

2

B L Dikshit Rd

H L Dikshit Rd

Relli River

Hill Top Rd

Ringkingpong Rd

Upper Bong Rd

8

BONG

To Zang Dog Palri Phodrang Monastery, Durpin Dara, Morgan House & Tourist Lodges

N

0 metres 200
0 yards 200

■ **Sleeping**
1 Bethlehem Lodge
2 Chimal
3 Crown & Chinmey Lodges
4 Deki Lodge
5 Gompu's & Restaurant
6 Gurudangma House
7 Himalayan
8 Kalimpong Park
9 Silver Oaks

● **Eating**
1 Bakery
2 Glenary's

(Yellow Hat) at Tirpai, the **Tharpa Choling** (1922) has a library of Tibetan manuscripts and *thangkas*, see page 236. The **Pedong** Bhutanese monastery (1837) near the old Bhutanese Damsang Fort at Algara (15 km) holds ceremonial dances every February. At Durpin Dara, the highest point in Kalimpong with superb views, stands the **Ringkinpong** monastery of Zang Dog Palri Phodrang. Unique outside Tibet, it retains its special lamaistic order with a school of Tibetan Medicine and is particularly interesting when prayers are being chanted.

Dr Graham's Homes, 3 km, was started by the missionary Dr John Anderson Graham in 1900 when he admitted six needy children. Now there are 1,200 pupils, many of whom live on an extensive site on Deolo hill. Volunteers able to spend at least 6 months should write in advance.

Walks There are pleasant hikes through Tista Rd and rice fields to **Chitray Falls**, 9 km, a three hour walk to **Bhalu Khop** and a 1½ hours' downhill walk from the Motor Stand to the Relli River.

Treks You can trek from **Lava** (32 km; monastery and weekly market on Tuesday), or **Lolaygaon** (56 km) which has spectacular views of Kangchendzonga, or picnic on the river beaches at Tista Bazar and Kalijhora.

Lepcha Museum, Bag Dhara, has an ethnology collection.

Essentials

Sleeping
Hotels open all year may offer discounts from Nov-Mar; some do not accept credit cards

B *Silver Oaks*, Main Rd, T55296, F55368, 25 rooms, some with good views, good restaurant (own fruit and vegetables), pleasant garden; **B** *Orchid Retreat*, Ganesh Villa (longish walk from town), T/F55389, thakro@cal2.vsnl.net.in, in interesting Orchid Nursery, 6 rooms in traditional thatched cottages (built with local materials), hot water (no TV or phone), home-cooked meals (Rs 100-150), lovely terrace garden with special palm collection, personal attention, peaceful. Highly recommended. **B-C** *Gurudangma House*, Hill Top Rd, T55204, F55290, rooms in house and cottage with meals, Alpine tents, gardens, personal service (will collect from motor stand). **B** *Himalayan* (Heritage Hotel), Upper Cart Rd (10 min walk town centre), T55248, F55122, 20 rooms, 8 spacious suites in newer imaginatively designed 'cottages', rest in stone-built characterful family home of the MacDonalds (rooms better upstairs), lovely verandah, mountain views, attractive gardens, set menu meals at set times, helpful management. Recommended – good value off-season; WBTDC **B-C** *Morgan House*, Singamari, Durpin Dara Hill, T55384, 3 km centre, 7 rooms with bath (good views from upstairs), restaurant, bar, beautiful location, gardens, characterful. **C** *Kalimpong Park*, Ringkingpong Rd, T55304, F55982, 19 simply furnished, good-sized, airy rooms, **B** suites (some in older 2-storeyed house), good restaurant, bar, exchange, garden, pleasant peaceful location, knowledgeable owner. WB Tourism lodges are clean and simple, breakfast and dinner usually included. **D** *Crown Lodge*, Bus Stand, T55846, 21 clean well-maintained rooms with bath, hot water (from Rs 250) (free morning tea!), generator, very friendly and helpful, pleasant, recommended; **E** *Bethlehem Lodge*, Rishi Rd (5 min walk from Motor Stand), T55185, decent rooms with bath, newish and quite clean. **E** *Deki Lodge*, Tirpai Rd, uphill from Motor Stand, T55095, clean, basic rooms, good meals, very friendly Tibetan family, good value; **F** *Chinmoy Lodge*, near Bus Stand. Newish, good value. **E-F** *Gompu's*, off Main Rd, T55818, clean rooms (from Rs 150), good restaurant, but some questionable reports.

At Singamari **C** *Tashiding Tourist Lodge*, T55929, 6 large rooms; **D** *Hill Top Tourist Complex*, T55654, off Ringkingpong Rd, 2 km from centre, 10 rooms; annexed **F** *Youth Hotel*. **D-E** *Chimal*, Ringkingpong Rd, 1 km from Bus Stand, T55776, 10 clean, sparse rooms (cement floor) with bath, some with hot water (Rs 250-500), restaurant, pleasant location, terrace with views. *Aashiana*, KD Pradhan Rd, T56717. Finds visitors **D-E** rooms in comfortable homes, simple apartments or humble huts (Rs 200-800) and also organizes visits to local events.

Bakeries sell good bread and cakes including *Glenary's*, opposite the Arts Centre. *Gompu's*, rear of hotel, is informal with good views, friendly, very good food, incl Chinese. *Maharaja* does good South Indian. *Fast Food Restaurant*, Main Rd, opposite Main Bazar, does very good Indian snacks.

Eating
Most shut at 2000

Handicrafts: *Arts & Crafts Centre*, near Motor Stand, embroidered clothes, fire-screens; *Soni Emporium*, near Motor Stand, Mani Link Rd, specializes in Himalayan handicrafts. **Paper**: Gangjong, Puritam Rd (near Sports ground), an interesting hand-made paper factory, worth visiting. **Tailors**: *Naseem's* in the market, for good salwar kameez; *Lotus*, Main Rd, for cloth and tailoring.

Shopping
Tibetan & Nepalese handicrafts & woven fabrics are particularly good

Most arrange car/jeep hire. Treks are usually not available off-season. *Kalimpong Tours & Travels*, T55545; *Kalimtrek*, Main Market, Himalayan Stores, T55448, F55290, organizes treks, arranges paying-guest accommodation; Mintry Transport, Main Rd, T55741.

Tour operators

Air Nearest airport is at Bagdogra; a new airport is being built which will allow flights to Paro, Kathmandu and Dhaka, 80 km, 3½ hrs by car, Rs 700 (see Siliguri); also taxi seat or bus Rs 75. *Indian Airlines* information, T55741. **Train** The nearest railhead is New Jalpaiguri/Siliguri station, 67 km. Tickets from **Rly Out Agency**, Kalimpong Motor Stand. **Road Bus**: State and private buses use the Motor Stand. Several to **Siliguri**, 3 hrs; **Darjeeling**, 3½ hrs; **Gangtok**: 3½ hrs (very scenic), Rs 37. N Bengal STC sells tickets, Motor Stand, T55719, SNT, Bus Stand, T55319. **Kolkata**: fast 'Rocket' buses. **Darjeeling**: DGHC **minibus** (contact *Kalimpong Tours & Travels*). **Jeep**: Faster; every 30 mins, 2-3 hrs, Rs 600; ask for pick-up point in Darjeeling for return trip.

Transport
Kalimpong is off the NH31A to Gangtok. Land Rovers or taxis to Siliguri & Bagdogra, last dep 1500

Banks Banks don't change money; *Emporium*, Mani Link Rd, accepts Visa and Mastercard. **Useful addresses** There is a **hospital** and a **post office** near the police station.

Directory

Siliguri শিলিগুড়ি

Surrounded by tea plantations, Siliguri is a largely unattractrive transport junction with a vast truck park to the north and a busy main road lined with shops. The narrow-gauge steam 'Toy Train' to Darjeeling starts from here during the tourist season. Siliguri has little of interest in itself, but is a base of travel into the hills and to the Jaldapara National Park. "Nothing to do other than shop, change or withdraw money."

Phone code: 0353
Colour map 3, grid B1
Population: 227,000
Altitude: 125 m

Getting there The airport is at Bagdogra 14 km away where share-taxis and jeeps tout aggressively for business. **New Jalpaiguri** (NJP), 5 km away, is the broad-gauge railway junction for Kolkata. Most long distance buses operate from the **Central Bus Terminus** (CBT) on Hill Cart Road. **Getting around** The town stretches along the length of the main Hill Cart Road, with buses, and auto-rickshaw and taxi stands. The area around Siliguri station and the Bus Terminus with budget hotels nearby, is easy to cover on foot.

Ins & outs

Essentials

B *Cindrella*, Sevoke Rd, 3rd mile (out of town), T547136, F531173, www.cindrellahotels.com 50 comfortable rooms, some a/c, competent vegetarian restaurant, pool, internet, car hire, pick-up from airport, efficient, best in Siliguri. **B** *Sinclairs*, Mallaguri (Airport Rd), T522674, F522743,

Sleeping
Hill Cart Rd is officially Tenzing Norgay Rd

Darjeeling & North Bengal

pressman_india@hotmail.com 54 comfortable rooms, good restaurants, pool, attentive service. **C-D** *Embassy*, Sevoke More (near Hill Cart Rd), T435251, comfortable rooms with bath, restaurant. WBTDC **C-D** *Mainak* (WBTDC), Hill Cart Rd (near rly station), T432830, F432859, 38 comfortable rooms, 14 a/c (rooms vary), well-kept gardens, very good restaurant and bar. Recommended (can book *Madarihat Lodge*, Jaldapara, see page 292). **D** *Chancellor*, Sevoke More, T432360, 7 clean rooms with bath (hot water), restaurant, pleasant management. Recommended. **D-E** *Ranjit*, Hill Cart Rd, T431680, 60 clean but variable rooms, few a/c, good restaurant, bar; **D-E** *Vinayak*, Hill Cart Rd, T431130, 29 clean rooms, some a/c, good restaurant.

WBTDC has: **E** *Tourist Lodge*, Hill Cart Rd (near rly station), T431028, 10 rooms with bath, dorm, and **F** *Youth Hostel*, Kangchendzonga Stadium, 130 beds. **E** *Mount View*, Hill Cart Rd, opposite Junc Station, T425919, very pleasant rooms (Rs 250), clean, good restaurant (wide choice), recommended; **E** *Tourist Services Agency*, a quiet street opposite Central Bus Terminus, T430872, some newer rooms upstairs, relaxed and popular; **E-F** *Baidyanath*, Hill Cart Rd, near NJP station, T426761, 14 clean rooms and toilets, 2 dorms, good food in airy restaurant. **F** *Railway Retiring Rooms*, at Siliguri Junc, and New Jalpaiguri, 4 rooms and 6 dorm beds in each, vegetarian snacks.

Eating In hotels: *Hill Mount View*, *Mainak*, *Sinclairs* (very good Chinese). *Miami*, Hill Cart Rd, 1 km from NJP station.

Shopping On Hill Cart Rd: *Bidhan* and *Hongkong Markets*. *AK Choudhary's* cane work, Mongaldeep Building.

Tours Mirik via Sukna, Rs 60; Dooars, Jalpeswar, Jaldapara via Phuntsholing, Rs 400-500 (weekends); by taxi, Jaldapara, overnight at *Madarihat* or *Holong Lodge*, Rs 120-135.

Transport **Air** Nearest airport, **Bagdogra** with tourist information counter and little else; security checks can be rigorous. Daily flights to **Kolkata**, Delhi via Guwahati. *Indian Airlines*, *Mainak Tourist Lodge*, T431495, airport, T450666; *Jet Airways*, Vinayak Bldg, Hill Cart Rd, T435876, airport, T430589, daily. **Helicopter** daily in fine weather to Sikkim (see page 302). Transfer: STC buses to Darjeeling and Gangtok. Taxis (for sharing) to Darjeeling (Rs 700), Gangtok (Rs 1,200), Kalimpong and Siliguri (Rs 150).

Road Siliguri is on NH31; Darjeeling (80 km), Gangtok (114 km) and Kalimpong (54 km) and served by State buses from

Siliguri

To Darjeeling

MALLAGURI
PRADHAN NAGAR
Siliguri Junction Station
Mahananda Bridge
Taxi Stand
Jet Airways
SEVOKE MORE
Hong Kong Market
Bidhan Market
Central Reservation Office
Kangchendzonga Stadium
Church Rd
Sevoke Rd
Bidhan Rd
Hospital Rd
Burdwan Rd
Tenzing Norgay Rd (Hill Cart Rd)
To Badgogra Airport & Kolkata
By-Pass Rd
To Cindrella, Kalimpong (NH 31)
NJP Station
To Kolkata

N

0 metres 800
0 yards 800

■ **Sleeping**
1 Baidyanath & Miami Restaurant
2 Chancellor & Embassy
3 Hill Mount View
4 Mainak Tourist Lodge & Indian Airlines
5 Ranjit
6 Sinclairs
7 Tourist Lodge
8 Tourist Services Agency
9 Vinayak & Moulik Internet
10 Youth Hostel

🚌 **Transport**
1 Dooars Bus Stand
2 SNT Bus Station & Sikkim Tourist Office
3 Tenzing Norgay Central Bus Terminus

Darjeeling & North Bengal

WB, Bihar, Sikkim and Bhutan. **Taxi**: opposite *Air View Hotel*, Hill Cart Rd and on Sevoke Rd, and rly stations to connect with most trains. To **Darjeeling**, share taxi (Rs 100) for 5-7 passengers, 3-3½ hrs. **NB** Try to arrive in Siliguri or New Jalpaiguri in daylight (before 1900). **Bus**: **Tenzing Norgay Terminus** (CBT) next to the Junc Rly Station; **SNT Bus Station**, is across the Hill Cart Rd. Buses to N Bengal go from the **Dooars Bus Stand** at the junction of Sevoke and Bidhan Rds. The overnight North Bengal STC's 'Rocket' bus service between **Kolkata and Siliguri** dep 2100 from Hill Cart Rd, 12 hrs, Rs 160, a/c Rs 330. Reserve seats in Kolkata, T281854 or in Burdwan Rd, Siliguri, T20531. They can be very full and noisy. **Darjeeling** State buses (4 hrs, Rs 50) from CBT and Sevoke Rd, or more comfortable Tourist Bus (for minimum 6), Rs 80. **Kalimpong** 2-3 hrs. N Bengal STC, Sevoke Rd, T20531. **Madarihat** (for Jaldapara) leave from bus station on Hill Cart Rd. **Gangtok** SNT buses, 5 hrs; reserve near Mahananda Bridge, Hill Cart Rd, T21496. Deluxe private buses from CBT, Junction Station (separate ticket window), Rs 75.

Bhutan: *Bhutan Transport*, Hill Cart Rd, T43227 (0900-1130, 1330-1630). To **Phuntsholing**: few buses daily, Rs 100, 3-4 hrs.

Nepal: to **Kathmandu** buses (or more conveniently taxi or Land Rover), to Panitanki on the border (35 km, 1 hrs); transfer to Kakarbhitta by cycle-rickshaw. **Kakarbhitta**, the Nepalese border town has only basic accommodation. **Visa** US$1 per day (15-60 days) and 1 photo. **Banks** do not change Rs 500 notes. Buses dep at 0400, 0500 to arrive at Kathmandu (or Pokhra) via W Nepal Highway (595 km), same evening (15-16 hrs); the journey can be very tiring. Tickets from *Tourist Services Agency*, Pradhan Nagar, Siliguri, T26547; Siliguri to Kakarbhitta (Rs 120); Kakarbhitta to Kathmandu/Pokhra (Nep Rs 320); also through tickets. From Kakarbhitta it is also possible to **fly** (seasonal) from Bhadrapur (34 km, with free transfer to airstrip) to Kathmandu (1 hr) by RNAC or Everest Air (Nep Rs 1400); agent *Sharma Travels*. Alternatively, get a taxi to Biratnagar in Nepal (150 km) and fly from there to Kathmandu (US$99). Footprint's *Nepal Handbook* is highly recommended.

Train Siliguri Junc (narrow gaurge, T20017) and **New Jalpaiguri** ('NJP' broad gauge, T21190), 5 km away, both with tourist information. There are buses, cycle-rickshaws (Rs 25), trains and taxis (Rs 40) between the two. NJP has good connections to other important centres in India. **NB** For long distance rail journeys from NJP, first buy tickets at Siliguri (Computerized Reservations, Bidhan Rd near Stadium), T23333, 1000-1300, 1330-1700 (for 1st class tickets, avoid queue; go to Chief Reservations Officer at side of building), then to NJP station for train. Porters demand Rs 50 for 2 cases. **Darjeeling**: from **Kolkata** to NJP by train, then bus or narrow-gauge '**Toy Train**' from NJP station (see page 283), 0715, 0900, 8 hrs (also stops at Siliguri Junc); return from Darjeeling 0825, 1000 during the tourist season. Services are often disrupted by landslides during the rains, though the upper section from Kurseong (accessible by bus/jeep) continues to run; check beforehand. Take special care of luggage; thefts reported. **NB** The Darjeeling Himalayan Railway (DHR) has been upgraded to a 'World Heritage Site'! Plans have been prepared by British consultants for the DHR to operate as a 'tourist railway', run by a company owned by Indian Railways. Check if running. From NJP to **Kolkata (S)**: *Darjeeling Mail, 3144* (AC/CC&AC/II), 1845, 14 hrs. **Kolkata (H)**: *Kamrup Exp, 5660* (AC/II), 1645, 13½ hrs; *Kanchenjunga Exp, 5658* (AC/II), 0800, 12 hrs. Darjeeling Rly Station: Reservations: T2555. Enquiries: 1000-1200, 1300-1600. **New Delhi**: *NE Exp, 5621*, 1725, 27 hrs; *Rajdhani Exp* (Mon, Wed, Thur, Fri), 2423, 1240, 21 hrs.

Banks Banks on Hill Cart and Sevoke Rds; office below *Delhi Hotel*, opposite CBT, Hill Cart Rd, fast, efficient, good rate, 1000-1400. **Communications** Internet: *Moulik*, behind *Vinayak*, Hill Cart Rd, T432312, Rs 190 per hr. **Medical services** Chemists: on College Rd. Hospital: T430150; *North Bengal Clinic*, T420441. Recommended. **Tourist offices** *Bhutan*, near rly station. *Sikkim*, Hill Cart Rd; *W Bengal*, 1st Flr, Hill Cart Rd, T21632; also at *Mainak*, NJP Station and airport. **Travel**

Directory

Darjeeling & North Bengal

agent *Help Tourism* (Assoc of Conservation & Tourism), 143 Hill Cart Rd (1st Flr), T535893, F433683, helptour@shivanet.com. Recommended for eastern Himalaya.

The river Torsa flows through this sanctuary. The riverine forests of sal, khair, sheeshu harbour the one-horned rhino, elephants, wild boar, bison, deer, leopard, gaur and the occasional tiger. It covers an area of 116 sq km and is situated close to Phuntsoling in Bhutan. Trained elephants are available to take visitors around. The best time to visit is from November to April when forest cover is thinner. ■ *Getting there: 160 km from Bagdogra airport, 224 km from Darjeeling.*

Sleeping Simple and inexpensive, at **Hollong**: **E** *Forest Lodge*, built of timber on stilts deep inside the sanctuary, 6 km from Madarihat, 7 rooms (all meals), the lodge is very popular and is en route to Phuntsholing in Bhutan, book well in advance through Tourist Bureau, Siliguri or DFO, Kolkata, T222774. At **Madarihat**: **F** *Travellers' Haven Tourist Lodge*, on park fringe, T62230, 8 rooms and restaurant (1 meal obligatory). At **Baradabri**: **F** *Youth Hostel and Lodge*, 4 km from Hasimara rly station, 18 km from Madarihat, 3 rooms, 14 beds in 4 dorm, meagre catering, reserve through DFO, Jalpaiguri, T838, Coochbehar, T247, Tourism Centre, Jalpaiguri, T183 or Kolkata, T2488271, F2485168. At **Hasimara**: **F** *Nilpara Forest Bungalow*, 2 rooms, very basic, caretaker will prepare a simple meal if requested but take all provisions.

Transport Air: *Indian Airlines* has daily flights from Kolkata to Bagdogra (½ hr) and also from Guwahati and Delhi. From airport, bus to Siliguri; then 4 hrs scenic drive through tea gardens to Jaldapara (155 km). There is an airfield at Hasimara. **Road Bus**: Express buses from Kolkata to Madarihat or Siliguri to Park (128 km). Forest Dept transport to Hollong inside the sanctuary. **Train**: Hasimara Station (4 km from park) has trains from Siliguri Junction.

Sikkim

7

Sikkim

296 Background

299 Gangtok
303 Rumtek Monastery

304 East Sikkim
304 Chhangu Lake

304 West Sikkim
305 Pemayangtse

308 North Sikkim

309 Trekking in Sikkim

309 Kangchendzonga National Park

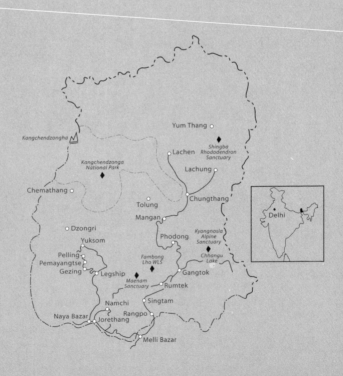

Kangchendzonga, the third highest mountain in the world, dominates the skyline of eastern Sikkim. Renowned for its rich flora and fauna as for its ethnically varied population, Sikkim's original inhabitants, the Lepchas, call the region Nye-mae-el ('Paradise'). To the later Bhutias it is Beymul Denjong ('The Hidden Valley of Rice'). The name Sikkim itself is commonly attributed to the Tsong word Su-khim meaning New or Happy House.

With 660 species of orchids, some found at altitudes as high as 3,000 m, Sikkim is an orchid-lovers' paradise. Tourism is still in its infancy, with the monasteries of Rumtek and Pemayangtse just two of the fascinating centres of Buddhism in the state which are attracting growing numbers of visitors. Sikkim is beginning to attract ramblers and trekkers too.

Sikkim

Background

The land
Population: 420,000
Area: 7,298 sq km

Sikkim nestles between the peaks of the eastern Himalaya, stretching only 112 km from south to north and 64 km from east to west. Flat land is a rarity and the state encompasses the upper valley of the Tista River, a tributary of the Brahmaputra while the watershed forms the borders with Tibet and Nepal. In the east the Chumbi valley lies between Sikkim and Bhutan, a tongue of Tibetan land that gives Sikkim its strategic and political sensitivity.

The Sikkimese believe Kangchendzonga (8,586 m, *Kanchenjunga*), the 'Five Treasures of the Great Snows', to be the repository of minerals, grains, salt, weapons and holy scriptures. On its west is the massive 31-km long Zemu glacier. Various explorers and mountaineers have claimed to have seen **yeti** or their prints in the vicinity of the mountain and its glacier, and in common with other regions of the Himalaya and Karakoram the 'abominable snowman' has its place in folklore.

Climate In the lower valleys Sikkim's climate is sub-tropical. Above 1,000 m, it is temperate, while the tops of the higher mountains are permanently under snow. Sikkim is one of the wettest regions of the Himalaya, most rain falling between June and September.

Flora and fauna Plant and animal life reflect differences in altitude, aspect and rainfall. In the lowest parts there is wet sal (*Shorea robusta*) forest with 660 species of orchids. This gives way to tropical evergreen mountain and rain forests (tree ferns, epiphytes, bamboos, oak, beech, chestnut, giant magnolia, rhododendron) and conifers up to the treeline at 3,600 to 4,200 m. The alpine forests have beautiful primulas, gentians, blue poppies, wild strawberry, raspberry and rhubarb. The animal and bird life is correspondingly rich, with 81 species of mammals, including wild asses and yaks in the north, and bears, lesser (red) pandas, silver foxes and leopards in the tropical forests. The 600 bird species include pheasants, teal, partridges, cuckoos, babblers and thrushes.

History From the 13th century Tibetans immigrated into Sikkim, including the Namgyal clan in the 15th century, who gradually won political control. In 1642 Phuntsog Namgyal (1604-70) became the **Chogyal** (king). He presided over a social system based on Tibetan Lamaistic Buddhism, and divided the land into 12 *Dzongs* (fortified districts).

In the 18th century Sikkim was much reduced in size, losing land to Nepal, Bhutan and the British. When the Gurkhas of Nepal launched a campaign into Tibet and were defeated by the Chinese in 1791-2, Sikkim won back its northern territories. The narrow Chumbi valley that separates Sikkim from Bhutan remained with Tibet.

When the British defeated Nepal in 1815, the southern part of the country was given back to Sikkim. However, in the next conflict with Nepal, Darjeeling was handed over to the British in return for their assistance. In 1848 the Terai region at the foot of the mountains was annexed by the British.

Nepalis migrated into Sikkim from the beginning of the 19th century, eventually becoming more numerous than the local inhabitants. This led to internal conflict which subsequently also involved the British and the Tibetans. When the British refused to stop the influx of Nepalis, the *Gyalpos* (Kings) enlisted Tibetan help. The British won the ensuing battles and declared Sikkim a Protectorate in 1890. The state was controlled by a British Political Officer who effectively stripped the *Gyalpos* of executive power. It was many years before the Sikkimese regained control.

People Three tribes – the Naong, Chang and Monday are believed to have inhabited Sikkim in prehistoric times.

The **Lepchas**, who call themselves Rongpas and claim to be the original inhabitants of Sikkim, may have come from Tibet well before the eighth century and brought Lamaistic Buddhism, which is still practised. They are now regarded as the indigenous peoples. They are deeply religious, peaceloving and shy but cheerful. Most have accepted Mahayana Buddhism, while retaining the pre-Buddhist Bon practices. The government has reserved the **Dzongu** area in North and Central Sikkim for Lepchas, now making up less than 10% of the population. For a long time, the Lepchas' main contact with the outside world was the market-place at Mangan, where they bartered oranges and cardamom. Their alphabet was only devised in the 18th century by the king.

The **Magar**, a minority group, are renowned as warriors and were involved in the coronation of Phuntsog Namgyal, the first Chogyal of Sikkim in 1642.

The **Bhotias** (meaning 'of Bhot/Tibet') or Bhutias entered Sikkim in the 13th century from Kham in Tibet, led by a prince of the later Namgyal Dynasty. Many adapted to sedentary farming from pastoral nomadism and displaced the Lepchas. Some, however, retained their older lifestyle, and combined animal husbandry with trading over the Trans-Himalayan passes: Nathula (4,392 m), Jelepla (4,388 m), Donkiala (5,520 m) and Kongrala (4,809 m). Over the years the Bhotia have come into increased contact with the Lepcha and intermarried with them. Nearly every Bhotia family has one member who becomes a monk. Traditionally, the priesthood was regarded as the intellectual as well as spiritual élite. Monasteries remain the repositories of Bhotia culture and festivals there are the principle social events. However, those who have visited Ladakh or Zanskar may find them architecturally and artistically a little disappointing. The Bhotias are famous for their weaving, especially hand-woven rugs from Lachen, and are also skilled wood carvers.

The **Newars** entered Sikkim in large numbers from Nepal in the 19th century. Skilled in metal and wood work, they were granted the right by the Chogyal to mine copper and mint the Sikkimese coinage. Other Nepali groups followed. With high altitude farming skills, they settled new lands and built houses directly on the ground unlike the Lepcha custom of building on stilts. The Newars were followed by the Chettris and other Nepali clans who introduced Hinduism which became more popular as their numbers swelled.

Religion In Sikkim, as in Nepal, Hinduism and Buddhism have interacted and amalgamated so Himalayan Hinduism includes a pantheon of Buddhist *bodhisattvas* as well as Hindu deities. The animist tradition also retains a belief in evil spirits.

Buddhist **prayer flags** flutter in the breeze everywhere. The different types (wind, luck, victory etc) are printed with texts and symbols on coloured pieces of cloth and are tied to bamboo poles or trees. **Prayer wheels** carrying inscriptions (which should be turned clockwise) may vary in size from small hand-held ones to vast drums which are installed by a monastery or stupa. Whitewashed masonry **chortens** (**stupas**) are not always reliquaries, but usually commemorate the Buddha or Bodhisattva; the structure symbolizing the elements (earth, water, fire, air, ether). The eight **lucky signs** appear as – parasol, pot or vase, conch shell, banner, two fishes, lotus, knot of eternity and the wheel of Law (Dharma Chakra). Bowls of **water** (Thing Duen Tsar) are offered in prayer from left to right during Buddhist worship. The gift of water from one who is free from greed and meanness is offered to quench thirsty spirits and to wash the feet, and represents flower (or welcome), incense, lamp, perfume and food.

Culture
Each ethnic group has an impressive repertoire of folk songs & dances

Sikkim

👉 *Permits*

Free permits are issued to foreigners to enter Sikkim for up to 15 days (renewable twice). These allow visits to Gangtok, Rumtek, Phodong, Mangan, Gezing, Pemayangtse, Namchi, Pakyong, Rabangla and Soreng. Apply to an Indian mission abroad when applying for an Indian visa (enclosing two extra photos), or at any FRO (Foreigners' Registration Office) or the Sikkim Tourism Office in New Delhi, Kolkata or Siliguri. Rangpo on the border can issue a two-day permit extendable in Gangtok.

Certain areas in north and west Sikkim (Chumthang, Yumthang, Lachen, Chhangu, Dzongri) have been opened to groups of 4 to 20 trekkers and for mountain biking and water sports. The group permits can be arranged by a local travel agent; apply with a passport and photo.

To get your permit extended at the Foreigners' Registration Office at Gangtok, first visit the Magistrate's Office at the Secretariat on the ridge overlooking town to get a "No Objection" endorsement.

Festivals Since the 22 major festivals are dictated by the agricultural cycle and the Hindu-Buddhist calendar, it is best to check dates with the Tourist office.

February *Losar* Tibetan New Year – preceded by Lama dances in Rumtek. *Bumche* at Tashiding.

June *Saga Dawn* A Buddhist festival with huge religious processions round. *Rumtek chaams* Dance festival in commemoration of the eight manifestations of Guru Padmasambhava, who established Buddhism in Tibet.

August/September *Pang Lhabsol* commemorates the consecration of Kangchendzonga as Sikkim's guardian deity; the Lepchas believe that the mountain is their birth place. The masked warrior dance is especially spectacular – Kangchendzonga appears in a red mask, her commander in a black one, while warriors wear traditional armour of helmets, swords and shields. Special celebrations are held in Pemayangtse.

September/October *Dasain*, one of the most important Nepali festivals, coincides with *Dasara* in North India (see page 50). On the first day barley seeds are planted in prayer rooms, invocations are made to Durga, and on the eighth day buffalo and goats are ritually sacrificed. *Diwali* (the Festival of Lights) follows *Dasain*.

December *Kagyat Dances* performed by monks (especially at Enchey), accompanied by religious music and chanting, enact themes from Buddhist mythology and end with the burning of effigies made of flour, wood and paper. This symbolizes the exorcism of evil spirits and the ushering in of prosperity for the coming year. *Losoog* (*Namsoong* for Lepchas at Gangtok) is the Sikkimese New Year, also called *Sonam Losar*. Farmers celebrate their harvest and beginning of their new cropping calendar.

Modern Sikkim **Government** In 1950, Sikkim became a Protectorate of India under a special treaty. In 1973 demands for accession to India by the local population consisting mainly of Nepalis grew, and Sikkim was formally made an associate state. The Gyalpos lost their power as a result of the new democratic constitution and Sikkim became the 22nd state in the Union in 1975. Although there is no separatist movement, India's takeover and the abolition of the monarchy, supported by many of those of Nepali origin, is still resented by many Sikkimese who don't really regard themselves as 'Indians'. The state enjoys some special tax and other privileges, in part because of its highly sensitive geopolitical location on the disputed border with China.

★ Gangtok

Gangtok or 'High Hill', the capital, sits on a ridge overlooking the Ranipul River. The setting is spectacular with fine views of the Kangchendzonga range but the town appears to have lost some of its quaint charm with the mushrooming of concrete buildings along the national highway and the main road. The crowded New Market (Naya Bazar) on Mahatma Gandhi Marg and the colourful Lall Bazar are where all the town's commercial activity is concentrated. Away from the bustle, there are many serene areas and quiet back alleys which remain virtually untouched.

Phone code: 03592
Colour map 3 grid B1
Population: 25,000
Altitude: 1,547 m

Most visitors arrive by the very attractive road from North Bengal (NH31A) which is motorable throughout the year except in very wet weather (mid-June to September), when there may be landslips. The old Teesta suspension bridge was taken down (pillars and wires can still be seen) and a new bridge was built further down in 1996. Permits and passports are checked at Rangpo where short 2-day permits (extendable in Gangtok) are available.

Getting there There are tentative plans to have an airport near Gangtok in 2 yrs. SNT buses terminate at the Paljor Stadium Road stand while private buses stop short of the main bazar. Ask to be dropped near the Tourist Office which has some hotels and restaurants within easy reach. If you hire a jeep to Gangtok ask to be taken to your hotel since the taxi/jeep stand is 2 km short of the centre. **Getting around** The busy hub around MG Marg is about a 20 min' walk from end to end. Away from the bazars, the town is very pleasant for walking around. For venturing further you will need to hire a jeep or taxi.

Ins & outs
Clothing: summer: light woollens & cotton, winter: heavy woollens

Suggested tour You can stay a few days in Gangtok, making day trips to Rumtek and Phodong then move to Gezing or Pelling. From there you can walk up to Pemayangtse and perhaps visit Khechopari Lake before continuing to Kalimpong or Darjeeling in West Bengal. Numerous hair-pin bends make road journeys extremely slow so expect to cover 30 to 40 km per hour. Conditions deteriorate considerably during the monsoon and can sometimes make travel impossible.

Sikkim

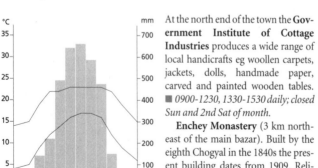

Climate: Gangtok
Best time to visit: Mar-May, Oct-Nov

At the north end of the town the **Government Institute of Cottage Industries** produces a wide range of local handicrafts eg woollen carpets, jackets, dolls, handmade paper, carved and painted wooden tables. ■ *0900-1230, 1330-1530 daily; closed Sun and 2nd Sat of month.*

    Enchey Monastery (3 km northeast of the main bazar). Built by the eighth Chogyal in the 1840s the present building dates from 1909. Religious dances are held in August and December; see Festivals above.

    The **Palace of the Chogyal** is only open once a year in the last week of December for the *Pang Lhabsol*

Sights
MG Marg is Mahatma Gandhi Marg; PS Rd is Paljor Stadium Rd

festival. Below this is the **Tsuklakhang** or Royal Chapel, standing on a high ridge where coronations and royal marriages took place. This is the major place of worship and has a large and impressive collection of scriptures. The interior is lavishly decorated with woodcarving and murals and houses a number of Buddha images. Visitors are welcome during Tibetan New Year but may not be permitted at other times; photography prohibited.

Moving south along the road you pass the **Secretariat** complex on your left. Beyond this is the **Deer Park**, loosely modelled on the famous one at Sarnath with a statue of the Buddha.

To the south, the important **Do-drul Chorten** with a golden top, contains relics and a complete set of holy texts. The surrounding 108 prayer wheels should be turned clockwise only. Nearby is a monastery for young lamas with large statues of the Buddha and Guru Padmasambhava.

The unique **Research Institute of Tibetology** on a hilltop was established in 1958 to promote research on Tibet and Mahayana Buddhism. ■ *1000-1600 daily except Sun*. The library maintains a large and important Buddhist collection with many fine *thangkas*, icons and art treasures on display.

For orchid lovers the small Flowershow near Whitehall has a good display, Rs 5, from mid-March. The **Deorali Orchid Sanctuary**, south of town, has 200 species.

There are pleasant **walks** around Gangtok. **Tashi Viewpoint** via Enchey Monastery is 9 km. Go early to watch the sun rise over the Kangchendzonga range. **Hanuman Tok**, a hill with a small temple (8 km), is another viewpoint.

Tours **Gangtok** From Tourist Information Centre. **Morning Tour** – Govt Institute of Cottage Industries, Deer Park, Chorten, Research Institute of Tibetology, Orchid Sanctuary and Enchey Monastery. In season daily 0930-1230. Rs 45. **Afternoon Tour** – Orchidarium and Rumtek Monastery, 1400/1430-1700. Rs 55.

Outside Gangtok Phodong Tour Rs 70 (more expensive by car). **West Sikkim** (minimum 16) Friday at 1030 returning Sunday 1600 (2 nights), Rs 600. **Treks in West Sikkim**. Private Tour companies offer similar tours and treks.

Sleeping **A** *Norkhill*, above Paljor Stadium,
Heating essential in winter; dogs bark at night, take ear plugs. Expect discounts in Jul, Aug, Dec & Jan
T23186, F23187. 30 clean rooms in old palace, meals included, spacious public rooms, good views and gardens, exchange, curio shop, once excellent but standards slipping. **A-B** *Netuk House*
■ *on maps, pages 301 & 300. Price codes: see inside front cover*
(Heritage Hotel), Tibet Rd (follow road up hill and ask), T22374, F24802, netuk@sikkim.org 8 comfortable clean rooms with modern shower in an extension to a traditional family home, excellent Sikkimese meals, bar, quiet location, mountain views, friendly, excellent service. Highly recommended (reservations: also Darjeeling T0354-54041, F54043); also excellent new hotel in Pelling.
Related map Gantok, page 301
B *Tashi Delek*, MG Marg, T22991, F22362, tashi delek@sikkim.org. 60

Gangtok centre

■ **Sleeping**
1 Chumbi Residency
2 Green
3 Jopuno & Mist Tree Mountain
4 Lhakpa
5 Mayur
6 Modern Central
7 Netuk House
8 Sonam Delek
9 Sunny Guest House
10 Tibet

ordinary rooms and **A** suites (better on upper floors), excellent restaurant, bar, exchange, airlines counter, terrace garden with enthralling views, friendly service, owner has great stories to tell of Sikkim's past. Pricey but recommended. **B-C** *Tibet* (Dalai Lama Trust), PS Rd, T22523, F26223, 30 rooms. Good views from rooms at rear, popular restaurant (see below), bar, exchange, good Tibetan books and crafts for sale, very pleasant, peaceful and charming, good value. Recommended.

C *Chumbi Residency*, Tibet Rd, T26618, F22707, chumbires@sikkim.org Tall modern hotel, 25 good rooms on 2nd-4th floors (no lift), **B** suites, coffee shop (Indian, Chinese), young dynamic manager. **C-D** *Denzong Inn*, near Lall Bazar, T22692, F22362. 24 rooms, good suites, restaurant, terrace. Recommended. **D** *Golden Nest*, below Assembly Building, T27008. New, clean, well furnished, 'superior' rooms (Rs 750) very comfortable, restaurant (limited menu, beer), good service. **C-D** *Mandaar Tourist Lodge* (WB Tourism), TNHS Rd, T24314. 15 rooms, restaurant. **D** *Jopuno* PS Rd, T23502, F22707 (at Institute of Hotel Management). 12 rooms (4 **C** deluxe), good restaurant and service, eager young staff. **D** *Mayur* (Sikkim Tourism), PS Rd, T22825. 27 rooms with bath (rooms vary), good restaurant, bar. **D** *Mist Tree Mountain*, PS Rd, Pradhan Towers, T23827, F26339. Newish, good value rooms (Rs 400-500) 7-bed dorm (Rs 100), restaurant. **D** *Orchid*, NH31A, T23151. 21 rooms, some with bath, front rooms better, restaurant (good Chinese) and bar, clean, good value. **D** *Superview Himalchuli*, Zero Point, T22714, F34643. Rooms with hot water (some **E** 4-bed), dorm (Rs 75), roof terrace restaurant with mountain views, bar, quiet, elevated position.

D-E *Green*, MG Marg, T/F23354, greenhotel@gokulnet.com 45 rooms, some with bath but no views (Rs 250-475), good restaurant (Indian. Chinese). **D-E** *Sonam Delek*, Tibet Rd, T22566, 20 rooms with bath best for views, restaurant, terrace garden. **D-E** *Siniolchu Lodge* (Sikkim Tourism), above town, near Enchey Monastery, T22074. 24 rooms on 3 floors up a hillside, some with bath and heating, good views, restaurant, bar, tours. **E** *Lhakpa*, Tibet Rd, T23002. 3 clean rooms in traditional house, some with bath, cheaper dorm, restaurant (very good Chinese), bar, roof terrace with views, good value. Recommended. **E** *Sunny Guest House*, next to Private Bus Stand, T22179. Some rooms with bath (from Rs 250) in pleasant hotel, super K'dzonga views from top floor. **E-F** *Modern Central*, Tibet Rd, T23417. Clean rooms with toilets, some with bath, hot showers, reasonable restaurant, good value jeep tours (eg

Some budget hotels charge extra for heaters

Sikkim

Gangtok

To Tashi View Point (9 km), Lachen & Phodong

Saibaba Mandir

TV Tower

Government Institute of Cottage Industries

Himalayan Nursery

Zero Point

Council House

Enchey Monastery

Helipad

Tashi Namgyal Academy

N Sikkim Highway

Hanuman Mandir

SNT & Booking Office

Paljor Stadium Rd

Catholic Centre

Paljor Stadium

To Natu La

CNI Church

White Hall

Bhanu Path

The Ridge

Private Bus Stand

Tibet Rd

Taxis ii

Taxis iii

Palace of the Chogyal

Foreigners' Reg Office

Supermarket

Tsuklakhang (Royal Chapel)

Taxis i

M G Marg

Karl Rd

Secretariat

Lall Bazar

Deer Park

NH31A

Naya Bazar

Government Press

Research Institute of Tibetology

Deorali Orchid Sanctuary

Do-drul Chorten

To Orchidarium, Rongpu, Rumtek & Darjeeling

■ Sleeping
1 Denzong Inn
2 Mandaar Tourist Lodge
3 Norkhill
4 Orchid
5 Siniolchu Lodge
6 Superview Himalchuli
7 Tashi Delek

N

Not to scale

*Related map
A Gantok centre,
page 300*

Chhangu $12 with permit, Yuksom US$50 per day), very friendly and helpful owner, backpackers' choice. Highly recommended. **F** *Primula Lodge*, Church Rd, T23599. Clean, basic with shared bath. Recommended.

Eating

● *on maps, pages 301 & 300*

Lightly spiced Sikkimese meat & vegetable dishes are usually eaten with noodles or rice. 'Churpi' is a local yak milk curd cheese. For the special 'Chimney Soup' order a day ahead

In hotels Expensive: *Snow Lion*, *Hotel Tibet*, T22523. Very good Sikkimese and Tibetan. Momos are "out of this world" but some poor reports on service, "flat beer, noisy and crowded". *Netuk House*, T22374. Excellent Sikkimese (order ahead). Unusual delicately flavoured authentic home cooking, charming service, try the chhang. *Blue Poppy*, *Tashi Delek*. International. Good meals from Rs 300 (Sikkimese recommended, order in advance). **Mid-range**: *Mayur* hotel. Good Tandoori.

Outside hotels Mid-range: *Tibet* below High Court, MG Rd (also Kazi Rd). Café menu. **Cheap**: *Blue Sheep*, Tourist Office Building. Indian, Continental, Sikkimese at lunchtime, fast food on ground floor. Traditional, very clean, bar. *China Pilot*, Star Cinema Building, MG Rd, for very good-value Chinese. *House of Bamboo*, MG Rd. Indian vegetarian, *Porkey's*, Supermarket, MG Rd. Fast food. Sausages etc, young crowd.

Bars

Bars in most restaurants serve local spirits distilled at Rangpo – brandy, rum, whiskey and liqueurs. *Chhang* is the unofficial national drink. A wooden bamboo mug (*thungba*) is filled with fermented millet through which boiled water is allowed to percolate; the drink is sipped through a bamboo straw. You can enjoy this mildly intoxicating pleasant drink for over an hour simply by adding hot water.

Sports

For trekking contact tourist office or tour companies

Sport Mountaineering: Himalayan Mountaineering Institute based in Yuksom offers climbing courses in stunning surroundings. **River rafting**: on rivers Tista (from Dikchu or Singtam, 1 hr drive from Gangtok) and Rangit (from **Melli Bazar**, 4 km from Teesta Bridge, which has a *Wayside Inn* for refreshments, or **Rishi**) arranged by Tourism Dept and private travel agents eg *Tashila*, 1 day US$45, 2-day US$70, some Grade 2-3 rapids. A 2-hr ride en route to Pemayangtse is ideal for the beginner; wonderful scenery.

Shopping

Books *Good Books*, MG Marg, below Gandhi statue, small but interesting. **Handicrafts**: Traditional crafts include carpets, *thangkas*, traditional jewellery, shirts, boots and fur caps and wood carving. *Handcrafts Centre*, Zero Point, Mon-Sat 0930-1230, 1300-1530 where you can watch artisans; *Charitrust Handicrafts*, *Tibet Hotel* modest collection, good quality and prices; also books on Tibet. *Rural Development Agency*, MG Marg and Naya Bazar. The **markets** are interesting; **Lall Bazar** (*Haat* on Sun, closed Thu) sells some unusual local fruit and vegetables and yak's milk cheese fresh and dried (skewered on string).

Tour operators

Brothers, Sarda Building MG Marg, T24454, F24635, good rafting, monastery visits, hikes. *Sikkim Tours*, PO Box 155, GPO, Church Rd, T22188, F27191, sikkimtours@sikkim.org For treks and birdwatching. *Potala*, PS Rd (opposite *Hotel Tibet*), T24434, F22707. Good vehicles, treks,rafting. *Tashila*, NH31A opposite petrol pump, T22206, F22155. Arranges coach tours and river rafting. *Yak & Yeti*, NH31A, Zero Point, T/F24643, yakyeti@mailcity.com For adventure tours.

Transport

Taxis charge exhorbitant rates to ferry passengers arriving at the taxi stand; from there it is a stiff 2 km climb to the centre

Air Nearest airport is **Bagdogra** (124 km); see page 282, under Siliguri. *Indian Airlines*, Tibet Rd, T23099. 1000-1300, 1400-1600; *Jet Airways*, MG Marg. To Gangtok: shared taxi, 4½-5 hrs, Rs 250 each, or *Snow-Lion* mini-bus; or get an SNT bus to Siliguri where bus/taxi to Gangtok is available. A daily government 4-seater **helicopter** runs between Bagdogra and Gangtok; unreliable since heavy cloud or rain prevents flights – but is an excellent option (Rs 1,500 each way, 10 kg luggage) with mesmerizing views. Tickets from Bagdogra airport counter or through a Gangtok travel agent.

Road Bus: SNT (Sikkim Nationalized Transport) Bus Stand, NH31A, T22016, 0900-1300, 1400-1600. Private buses from West Point Taxi Stand, NH31A, T22858. Some only operate in the high season. Buy tickets 24 hrs in advance; hotels can help. Long distance journeys about Rs 60. To **Rumtek** 1600 (1500 holidays) 1 hr; **Namchi**, which has a Govt 80-bed *Youth Hostel*, 0800, 1500 (4½ hrs); **Namok, Phodong, Chungthang, Mangan** 0800, 1300 (return 1500); **Gezing**, 0700, 1300 (5 hrs); **Jorethang (then Pelling)**, 0800. For North Bengal: **Bagdogra** (about 5 hrs); **Darjeeling**, 94 km, between 0700-1330; from Darjeeling 0730-1400 (6-7 hrs); to **Kalimpong**, 75 km, 0830-1930 (4-4½ hrs), from Kalimpong 0700-1315; to **NJP/Siliguri** (115 km), 0700-1415 (4½-5 hrs); from Siliguri 0630-1300, 5 hrs. To **Kolkata** 1300; from Kolkata 1700; a/c bus Rs 280. **Taxis**/**jeeps** (for sharing): Stands (i) Lall Bazar (East Sikkim), (ii) Private Bus Stand (for North Bengal) and (iii) Children's Park (West Sikkim). Fixed rate charts within Gangtok, but negotiable for sightseeing. Rs 1,200 per day for travel outside Sikkim, Rs 1,000 within Sikkim; plus night halt Rs 200. **Chhangu**, Rs 400 return; **Rumtek**, shared, from 1030, Rs 25; **Yoksum**, Rs 800.

Train Nearest railway stations are at **Siliguri/New Jalpaiguri** Computerized Bookings, SNT Compound, for tickets (no tourist quota), 0800-1400.

Banks Open 1000-1400, Sat 1000-1200 (exchange rate usually verified at 1100). *State Bank of India*, MG Marg. *State Bank of Sikkim*, Tibet Rd. Good rate. **Communications** Post: GPO, Stadium Rd and PO in Gangtok Bazar. **Internet:** at the Secretariat, modern pentiums in a quiet, pleasant room; Rs 40 per hr (connections can be slow); printing expensive; *Green Hotel* on request. **Medical services** On Stadium Rd: *STNM Hospital* opposite *Hotel Mayur*, T22059 and *Unique Chemists*. **Tourist offices** *Sikkim*, MG Marg, Gangtok Bazar, T22064. Open in season Mon-Sat, 0900-1900, off season 1000-1600. Apply for permits here. *Dept of Tourism*, T23425. **Useful addresses** Ambulance: T102, 22059. Fire: T101, 22001. Police: T100, 22033. Foreigners' Regional Registration Office: Tibet Rd, Mon-Fri, 0900-1300. | **Directory**

South from Gangtok

Sikkim

Saramsa Gardens The gardens, 14 km south of Gangtok, contain over 500 indigenous species in what is more like a botanical garden with large orchidariums. *Best season*: March-early May (visitors may be disappointed at other times). The road to Saramsa forks east off the NH31a a few kilometres south of **Tadong** which has a couple of places with rooms and refreshments including the fairly modern *Tashi Tadong* and the *Daragaon*.

Further south, near the West Bengal border, Rangpo has a small bazar. Entry Permits are issued and checked here. **Sleeping** Sikkim Tourism **E** *Tourist Lodge*, T03592-40818, seven rooms (Rs 330) and a simple restaurant and basic toilets, where you can stop for a snack and drink. | **Rangpo**

Standing in one of the attractive lower valleys southwest of Gangtok with fluttering prayer flags, the monastery is the headquarters of the Kagyu ('Black Hat') order of Tibetan Lamaistic Buddhism. The 16th Gyalwa Karmapa (died 1981) fled Tibet after the Chinese invasion, bringing with them whatever statues, *thangkas* and scriptures they could carry. At the invitation of the Chogyal they settled in Rumtek. The new monastery was built in the 1960s in the traditional style as a faithful copy of the Kagyu headquarters in Chhofuk, Tibet, with typical monastic paintings and intricate woodwork. The **Dharma Chakra Centre** with the unique **golden reliquary** of the 16th Gyalwa is here. | ★ **Rumtek Monastery**
Phone code: 03592
Colour map 3, grid B1
Altitude: 1,550 m
24 km SW of Gangtok

Visitors are dropped at the gate at the bottom of a gentle uphill path; passports may be checked. A 20-minute walk past local houses and a couple of typical curio shops leads to the monastery. Outside, you may see pairs of monks chanting prayers in their quarters or catch some younger ones playing football in the field! The main hall is very impressive but lacks the atmosphere of Pemayangtse. Visitors are welcome at Rumtek but are requested not to disturb the monks during prayers (usually 0400, 1800). Upstairs, in the adjacent building you can watch the wood-block printing of texts on handmade paper. The peace is broken when hordes of tourists arrive.

Sleeping **B** *Shambhala Mountain Resort*, T52240, F530020, parekh.house@gems. net.in In a large estate, 500 m before the monastery, 31 cottages in traditional tribal styles spread around grounds, or comfortable rooms in main building, most with good views from balconies, vegetarian restaurant (wide choice), bar, exchange, pick-up from Siliguri arranged. **C** *Martam Village Resort*, Gangkha, Upper Martam, 5 km from the monastery. 11 thatched cottages built in traditional style with large picture windows overlooking the valley, good meals, pleasant, contact Gangtok T23314, F24391. Recommended. **D-E** *Jharna*, T22714. Some rooms with hot water, restaurant, bar. **E** *Sungay*, lower end of village. Basic but clean, friendly and helpful. **F** *Sangay*, near monastery gate. The older guesthouse, fairly clean shared toilet, friendly.

Festivals **Feb** Special colourful *Losar* dances are held 2 days before the Tibetan New Year (check date). Arrive 3 days earlier to see rehearsals without masks pujas and ceremonies are held during this period. **Jun** The important Rumtek *chaam* is performed on the 10th day of the 5th month of the Tibetan calendar; masked dancers present 8 manifestations of the Guru Rimpoche. Tours in Jul-Aug from Gangtok.

Transport **Bus**: daily dep from Gangtok about 1600 (1 hr) along a steep narrow road, return dep about 0800. **Taxi**: from Gangtok, Rs 200 (return about Rs 350). **Shared Jeep**: Rs 25 each; until 1400 (in season, 1700). **Rumtek** to **Pemayangtse**, 4 hrs.

East Sikkim

Chhangu Lake (Tsomgo)
36 km from Gangtok
Altitude: 3,774 m

The lake is on the Nathu La Highway, the old trade route to Lhasa which until 1962 saw regular mule trains leave and return to Gangtok. The precipitous road passes through the Kyongnosla Sanctuary and leads to the holy lake which is completely frozen in winter, up to mid-May. It is best to visit March to May, September to mid-December. There are excellent views of Kangchendzonga from the nearby ridge and superb sunsets. On the way there is the **Shiv Gufa**, a few minutes' walk from the road. You have to enter the tiny cave on your hands and knees to see a small Siva image and several tridents embedded in the soft floor. The drive there is scenic but the lake area is overcrowded and spoilt by snack kiosks and loud Hindi music. Disappointing. ■ *Getting there: Organized tour or by jeep through travel agents (permit needed). Allow 6 hrs for the return trip, Rs 400 for jeep.*

Kyongnosla Alpine Sanctuary
Altitude: 3,200 m- 4,100 m

Background The sanctuary, 31 km from Gangtok, extends from the '15th Mile' check post to the ridges bordering Rongchu and Chhangu Lake. Among the junipers and silver firs the sanctuary harbours some rare ground orchids and rhododendrons and numerous medicinal plants including the *Panax pseudo-ginseng*. The best season is from April to August, October to November. Apply for permit (Rs 5) to Chief Wildlife Warden, Sikkim Forest Dept, Deorali, Sikkim 737102.

Wildlife The Himalayan marmot has been reintroduced here. Other mammals include goral, serow, red panda, Himalayan black bear, Tibetan fox and yellow-throated martens and very colourful pheasants.

Trekking Two easy treks lead to the Shiv Gufa (1 km away) and Kheding (4 km) while longer and more difficult ones to Simulakha, Namnang Lakha and Nakcho are very scenic. Trekkers with permits for Chhangu may return from Nakcho via the lake.

Sleeping Basic, raised **F** *Log Huts*, with two rooms in each at Kyongnosla and Lamnang Lakha.

West Sikkim

Gezing (Gyalshing) is at the crossroads of bus routes and has a busy market with food stalls and shops selling provisions. **Sleeping** Most are above the main square including: **D-E** *Atri*, rooms with bath (hot water). **E-F** *Kanchendzonga*, T50755. Simple rooms, shared toilets. **F** *Bamboo House*, basic rooms, poor toilets, local food. ■ *Getting there: An early bus or jeep from Gangtok allows you to see Tashiding, then stop overnight at Gezing or Pelling.* Buses can be crowded, especially during *Pujas* and *Diwali*; get ticket on bus if ticket counter is busy. SNT buses to Gangtok (0800, 1300), 5-5½ hrs, Rs 50 (or go via Pelling and Jorethang); Yuksom via Tashiding (1300), 4 hrs; Siliguri (0630, 1300), 5 hrs. Shared **jeep** to Darjeeling, Rs 60.

Gezing
105 km W of Gangtok

A full day trip by car from Gangtok, along a very scenic road, Pemayangste (Perfect Sublime Lotus) was built during the reign of the third Chogyal Chador Namgyal in 1705. It is about 7 km from Gezing, above the main road to Pelling.

The awe-inspiring **monastery**, Sikkim's second oldest, is near the start of the Dzongri trek. The walls and ceiling of the large *Dukhang* (prayer hall) have numerous *thangkas* and wall paintings, and there is an exceptional collection of religious artworks including an exquisite wooden sculpture on the top floor depicting the heavenly palace of Guru Rimpoche – the *Santhokpalri*, which was believed to have been revealed in a dream.

The old stone and wood buildings to the side are the monks' quarters. According to tradition the monks have been recruited from the leading families in Sikkim as this is the headquarters of the Nyingmapa sect. Annual *chaam* dances are held at the end of February; and in September. ■ *0700-1600; Rs 10; good guided tours, 0700-1000 and 1400-1600 (if closed, ask for key). No photography inside. Norma Lama, in charge of the monastery plans to restore the roof and murals.*Take an early morning walk to the rear of the monastery to see a breathtaking sunrise in perfect peace.

The **Denjong Padma Choeling Academy** (DPCA) here, set up to educate needy children has several ancillary projects (crafts, weaving, dairy) and welcomes volunteers who can at the same time learn about Buddhism and local culture. The Meditation Centre, T50656, offers courses and can accommodate visitors for a small charge (and volunteers, free) at the new hostel (see below). It can be a very rewarding experience.

★ Pemayangste
Phone code: 03593
112 km W of Gangtok,
72 km from Darjeeling
Altitude: 2,085 m
Colour map 3, grid B1

For many, the monastery is the highlight of their visit to Sikkim – it has a certain aura about it

Sikkim

Rabdanste The ruined palace of the 17th- to 18th-century capital of Sikkim is along the Gezing-bound track from the monastery, 3 km from Pelling. ■ *Getting there: from the main road, turn left just before the white sign "Gezing 6 km", cross the archery field and turn right behind the hill. Follow the narrow rocky track for 500 m to reach the palace.*

Sleeping Sikkim Tourism's **D** *Mount Pandim* (15 minute walk, below monastery), T50756. 25 large rooms with bath (barely OK), some with beautiful views, Indian and Chinese meals (non-residents order in advance), very slow service (get there early for breakfast), peaceful but run down, reservations, Tourist Office, Gangtok. **F** *DPCA Hostel*, half-way to Pelling, 9 decent dorms, geysers and vegetarian meals. Govt **F** *Trekkers' Hut* has 4 5-bed dorms.

Transport From Gezing: bus to monastery, 1000-1430, Rs 15; shared jeep, Rs 60.

Pelling
Phone code: 03593
2 km from the monastery & 9 km by road from Gezing

Pelling sits on a ridge with good views of the mountains. The small town has three areas linked by a winding road: Upper and Middle with views and hotels, and Lower Pelling with banks and other services. Upper Pelling is expanding rapidly with new hotels springing up to accommodate honeymooners from Kolkata.

You can visit the **Sanga Choelling Monastery** (circa 1697), possibly the oldest in Sikkim, which has some colourful mural paintings. The hilltop monastery is about 3 km along a fairly steep track through thick woods (about 30 minutes). The area is excellent for **walking**.

Power & water cuts can last 4 hrs or more & dogs are prone to bark through the night!

Sleeping With over 30 places to choose from, the following are recommended: **C-D** *Touristo*, nice rooms (Rs 600-1,200). **D** *Norbu Gang*, Main Rd, T50566. Rooms with bath (Rs 550-700), better views from those away from road, restaurant. Superb views from terrace. **D** *Sikkim Tourist Centre*, Upper Pelling, near Jeep Stand, T50855 (Siliguri, T/F433683). Simple rooms, some with views (Rs 500-700), cheaper on roadside, rooftop restaurant (cooking excellent but service fazed by large numbers), tours. **D-E** *Haven*, Khechopari Rd, Middle Pelling. Clean doubles with running hot water (Rs 350-450). **E** *Garuda*, Upper Pelling, near bus stop, T50614. Rooms in basic lodge with bath, hot water (from Rs 200, heaters Rs 35), dorm, restaurant (breakfast on roof-top with mountain views), helpful staff, backpackers'/trekkers' favourite (interesting tips and info). **E** *Parodxong*, Middle Pelling. Friendly. **F** *Sisters Family Guest House*, near *Garuda*, T50569. Simple clean rooms, shared bath (from Rs 150).

Eating *Alpine*, Khechopari Road (below Garuda). Chinese, Kashmiri especially good. Wooden cottage, painted yellow, run by friendly Ladakhi lady. Don't miss the local *chhang* brewed in the area. You can sample it at *Mount Pandim Hotel* or in a local home.

Tour operators *Help Tourism*, Sikkim Tourist Centre, T50855, (Kolkata T033-4550917), affiliated to WB Govt, good information and tours. *Simvo Tours*, Hotel Sonam, T50696, good tours.

Transport Bus: to Gezing: bus or walk along steep downhill track, 1 hr. To Khechopari Lake: last bus dep 1400, or you can walk 5 hrs (part very steep; last 3 hrs follows road). Buses and share-**jeeps** to Yuksom, Damthang, Gangtok (4 hrs). **Siliguri**: SNT bus 0700; tickets sold at provision store next to Hotel Pelling where it starts and stops uphill at *Garuda* at the **jeep stand**.

Directory Bank *State Bank of India*, exchange rates unavailable daily so unable to help! **Tourist offices** *Sikkim*, Upper Pelling, near *Garuda*, T50855. Helpful.

Khechopari Lake
26 km from Gangtok

A three-day gentle **trek** to this 'wishing' lake, Yuksom and back to Pelling is possible without a permit. A road west off the Pelling-Yuksom road leads to this tranquil lake where the clear waters reflect the surrounding densely wooded slopes of the hills with a monastery above – Lepchas believe that birds remove any leaf that floats down. Prayer flags flutter around the lake and it is particularly moving when leaflamps are floated with special prayers at dusk. The sanctity of the lake may be attributed to its shape in the form of a foot (symbolizing the Buddha's footprint) which can be seen from the surrounding hills.

Sikkim

Sleeping F *Pilgrims' Lodge*, on edge of the lake, renovated, transformed, cleaner (Rs 140), enterprising Mr Tenang provides Sikkimese porridge and millet bread, short hikes (circular) that bring guests back to the lodge for another night's stay! A small shop sells food. Families also offer to take in guests.

Transport From **Pelling**: Jeep share, 1½ hrs; **Tashiding** (3 options): (i) 0700 bus to Gezing, then jeep. (ii) Bus to Yuksom 1500 (reported irregular) from 'junction', 10 km from lake; overnight in Yuksom, then bus at 0700 (or jeep) to Tashiding, 1 hr. (iii) Hitching a lift on the Pelling to Tashiding jeep which passes the 'junction' at about 1400; try sitting on top of jeep to enjoy the beautiful scenery!

The gold topped **monastery**, 40 km from Gezing, was built by the half-sister of **Tashiding** Chador Namgyal in 1716. It stands on a conical hill between the Rathong and Rangit rivers on a spot consecrated by Guru Rimpoche. The gompa has been refurbished and all the frescos repainted. The most sacred *chorten* in Sikkim is here so even the sight of Tashiding is thought to bring blessing. You will see numerous stones with high-class carvings of *mantras* around the monastery. Pilgrims attend the *Bumchu* festival in February/March to drink water from the sacred pot which has never run dry for over 300 years. Below the monastery is the small Tshchu Phur cave where Guru Rinpoche meditated; follow the trail on the left of the entrance to Tashiding until you see a small house opposite and the painting on the rocks. Carry a torch if you plan to crawl into the cave.

Sleeping and eating F *Laxmi*, cheap rooms OK. Common bath very smelly. F *Siniolchu*, 5 clean rooms (3 on upper floor are big and beautiful). Dorm beds, shared bath, hot water, meals, friendly. F *Trekkers' Hut*.

Transport From Yuksom or Gezing: **bus** or **jeep** via Legship; or climb 6 km (2 hrs). From Pemayangtse: a day's **walk**.

Yuksom, 42 km north from Pelling by jeepable road, is where the first Chogyal **Yuksom** was crowned in 1641. The wooden altar and stone throne above the Kathok *Phone code: 03695* lake are below the Norbu Gang chorten in a beautifully peaceful pine forest. The simple **Hermit's retreat** at **Dhubdi** (circa 1700) is up on a hill (45 minutes' walk).

Sleeping and eating C-D *Tashigang* Main Road, T50587/70205 (Siliguri T0353-433683). 21 good rooms (from Rs 650), own vegetable garden, tennis, very welcoming. Also simple lodges near the bus stop. F *Trekkers' Hut*, camping allowed. Local meals available in the village.

Transport Bus: to Gezing and Tashiding, 0700. **Shared jeep:** to **Pelling** Rs 60 each, **Gangtok** Rs 100 each; sightseeing Rs 800; guide Rs 110.

North Sikkim

Phodong
Colour map 3, grid B1

The renovated early 18th-century monastery is 1 km above the north Sikkim Highway, about 2 km before Phodong village. It is a pleasant walk up to the little-visited gompa where friendly monks show you around; the track is jeepable. A further hike of 2 km takes you to the **Labrang** monastery of the Nyingmapa sect. Below the track nearby is the ruined palace of **Tumlong** which was the capital of Sikkim for most of the 19th century.

Sleeping F *Yak and Yeti* is friendly, quiet, clean and good value. Some rooms with toilet, hot water in buckets, meals. Recommended.

Transport From Gangtok: **bus** to start of jeep track, 0800 (2 hrs), Rs 35; return bus, 1500. **Jeeps** travel up to Labrang.

Route

The road north which is in a very poor condition and can lead to long delays passes **Lachung** where there is a very basic *Forest Bungalow* with four rooms (no bedding) and the **E** *Alpine Resort* with two rooms and a dorm. Some 6 km further, **E** *Yekchey Tourist Lodge*, is better. A few kilometres along the highway is a private cottage which takes guests.

Shingba Forest Reserve

The road to Yumthang enters the Shingba Forest Reserve which is lined with rhododendrons which harbour civets and blood pheasants. The Rhododendron Sanctuary has 24 of the 40 species found in Sikkim and has attractive ground cover of aconites, gentians, poppies, saxifrages, potentillas and primulas.

Yumthang
Colour map 3, grid B1
135 km N of Gangtok
Altitude: 3,700 m

The attractive high valley of Yumthang is surrounded by mountains. The alpine meadow near the tree-line is a seasonal grazing ground for yaks. A few minutes' walk from the main road beyond a log bridge over the river Lachung are some sulphur hot springs. There is also a *Log House* with two rooms (no electricity); contact Forest Dept. Permit needed. Yumesamdung above Yumthang is now accessible. ■ *Getting there: jeep hire from Gangtok or Tour organized by a travel agent.*

Trekking in Sikkim

Trekking is in its infancy and many of the routes are through areas that seldom see foreigners. Consequently, facilities are poorly developed though the paths are usually clear. You do not need previous experience since most treks are between 2,000-3,800 m. An added attraction is that dzos (cross between a cow and a yak) will carry your gear instead of porters. The trekking routes also pass through villages which will give an insight into the tribal people's lifestyle.

Best time to visit: Mar-late May, Oct-early Dec

A guide to Sikkim, Darjeeling area and Bhutan by **Rajesh Verma**, 1995, for a brief introduction to the state and descriptions of treks in the area, with trekking profiles. The U 502 sheets for Sikkim are NG 45-3 and NG 45-4. PP Karan published a map at the scale of 1:150,000 in 1969. Price US$3, available from the Program Director of Geography, George Mason University, Fairfax, VA 22030, USA. Sikkim Himalaya (Swiss Alpine Club) – Huber 1:50,000. Very detailed, £16.

Further reading & maps

Foreigners must be in a group of four at least before applying for a permit to trek (agents can assist but may charge). A Sikkim Police Liaison Officer will usually accompany the group which should be organized by an approved agent. Lachung and Yumthang valleys in North Sikkim (five days) and Chhangu in East Sikkim (one day) are now open to foreigners. **Trekking agents** are listed under Gangtok (above) and Darjeeling (see page 282). Tourist Information Centre, Gangtok has tents for Rs 20 per night. Yuksom can arrange guides, Rs 100, cook/porter Rs 60-75 and yak/pony Rs 110-150; book trekkers' huts (Rs 50 per head).

Permits

Rabongla (2,155 m, 24 km before Legship from Gangtok) has *Hotel Maenam* with simple, clean rooms, and excellent food. The trek from there through the sanctuary to Maenam peak (3,260 m) which dominates the town, takes about three hours. The sanctuary harbours red panda, civet, blood pheasant and black eagle and is most beautiful when the magnolia and rhododendron are in bloom in April-May. Bhaledunga, another 30-minute hike along the ridge, on the steep cliff edge above the Teesta, juts out in the shape of a cock's head.

Maenam Sanctuary

Kangchendzonga National Park

The park offers **trekking** routes through picturesque terraced fields of barley, past fruit orchards to lush green forests of pines, oak, chestnut, rhododendrons, giant magnolias, then to high passes crossing fast mountain streams and rugged terrain.

Colour map 3, grid B1

Animals in the park include Himalayan brown bear, black bear, the endangered musk deer, flying squirrel, Tibetan antelope, wild asses and Himalayan wild goats. The red panda found between 3,000-4,000 m lives mostly on tree-tops. There are about 600 species of birds.

The Kangchendzonga trek now falls wholly within the newly designated Kangchendzonga National Park. The park office in **Yuksom**, about 100 m below the trekkers' huts, housed in a shiny new building has interesting exhibits – stuffed birds, posters about the local wildlife and a couple of locally found musk deer in an enclosure in the wooded yard. Helpful staff. Park **entry fee** (for trekkers) Rs 150. Tourists are also required to pay for all accompanying porters, yak men, pack animals and local support crew that adds approximately another Rs 100 to the entry fee.

A local non-governmental organization has done a great deal to **clean up** the camp sites on the Kangchendzonga trail which were increasingly becoming filthy and polluted with the larger numbers of trekkers going in. Toilets have been rebuilt and waste is now carefully channelled away from streams. Garbage is disposed of by burying in large pits, and seminars and discussions are held regularly amongst the village folk of Yuksom and Tsokha to educate them on more sustainable methods of forest exploitation. The example set has been very encouraging and it is hoped that this programme transplanted to other trekking areas.

Fambong Lho Wildlife Reserve The reserve, a little beyond Rumtek, is 25 km from Gangtok across the Ranipool Valley. There are serene junglewalks in the hills, leading to waterfalls, mountain views, jungles with orchids, birds and wildlife (marten, fox, red panda, boar – even wolf and sloth bear). You are free to go on your own (though this is not advisable on some stretches) and can climb or walk for anything from one to six days. The entry fee is Rs 5 and there are log huts at Golitar and Tumin, Rs 50.

Gangtok – Pemayangtse – Yuksom – Dzongri

See also Darjeeling Treks, page 284

It is possible to trek from **Pemayangtse** (eight to 15 days) or **Naya Bazar** (seven to eight days). From Darjeeling, a shorter trek goes to Singla and Pemayangtse.

The route is from Gangtok to Pemayangtse via Rumtek, then on to Yuksom, Bakhim and Dzongri (described briefly below). Although it is not a long trek there are excellent views throughout as you travel up the Ratong Chu River to the amphitheatre of peaks at the head of the valley. These include Kokthang

Sikkim treks

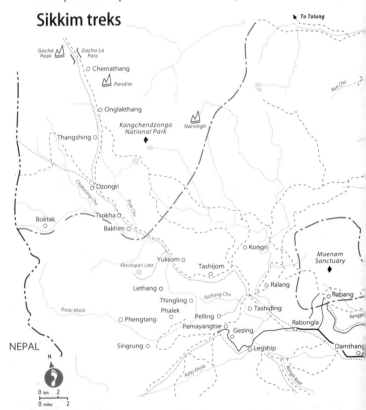

(6,150 m), Ratong (6,683 m), Kabru Dome (6,604 m), Forked Peak (6,116 m) and the pyramid of Pandim (6,720 m) past which the trail runs.

From Pemayangtse the route passes through terraced fields of rice, barley and corn. After crossing the Rimbi Khola River on a narrow suspension bridge, the road gradually rises to Yuksom.

Sleeping Govt **E** *Trekkers' Huts* with rooms and dorm for overnight stops are fairly clean, although the toilets are basic. Bring sleeping bags; meals are cooked by a caretaker. The huts are in picturesque locations at **Pemayangtse, Yuksom, Tsokha** and **Dzongri**.

Yuksom (28 km from Pemayangtse, two hours' drive) is the base for a trek to the Gocha La. This eight to nine day trek includes some magnificent scenery around Kangchendzonga.

Yuksom – Thangshing – Gocha La

Day 1 Yuksom to Tsokha An eight- hour climb to the growing village of Tsokha, settled by Lepcha yak herders and Tibetan refugees. The first half of the climb passes through dense semi-tropical forests and across the Prek Chu on a suspension bridge. A steep climb of six hours leads first to **Bakhim** (2,740 m) which has a tea stall and a *Forest Bungalow*. There are good views back down the trail. The track then goes on through silver fir and cypress to Tsokha (2,950 m), the last village on the trek. *Trekkers' hut, camping ground* and good private *lodge*.

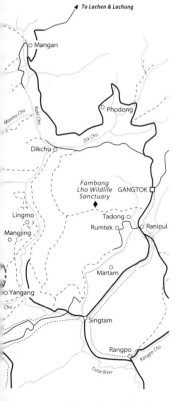

Day 2 Tsokha to Dzongri Mixed temperate forests gradually give way to rhododendron. **Phodang** is less than three hours up the track. Pandim, Narsingh and Joponu peaks are clearly visible, and a further one hour climb takes the track above the rhododendron to a ridge. A gentle descent leads to Dzongri (4,030 m, 8 km from Bakhim), where nomadic yak herders stay in huts. There is a *trekkers' hut* and *camping ground*. Dzongri attracts occasional pilgrims to its *chortens* containing Buddhist relics. From the exposed and wind-swept hillsides nearby you can get a good panoramic view of the surrounding mountains and see a spectacular sunrise or sunset on Kangchendzonga.

May be taken as a rest day to acclimatize

Day 3 Dzongri to Thangshing A trail through dwarf rhododendron and juniper climbs the ridge for 5 km. Pandim is immediately ahead. A steep drop descends to the Prek Chu again, crossed by a bridge, followed by a gentle climb to Thangshing (3,900 m). The southern ridge of Kangchendzonga is ahead. There is a *Trekkers' hut* and *camping ground*.

Sikkim

Day 4 Thangshing to Samity Lake The track leads through juniper scrub to a steeper section up a lateral moraine, followed by the drop down to the glacial – and holy – Samity Lake. The surrounding moraines give superb views of Kangchendzonga and other major peaks. You can camp here at 4,250 m or stay at a *Trekkers' hut* with two rooms and a kitchen.

Day 5 To Chemathang & Gocha La and return The climb up to Chemathang (4,800 m) and Gocha La (4,900 m) gives views up to the sheer face of the eastern wall of Kangchendzonga itself. Tibetans collect sprigs of the scrub juniper growing in abundance here to use in religious rites. It is a vigorous walk to reach the pass, but almost equally impressive views can be gained from nearby slopes. Much of the walk is on the rough moraine.

Day 6 Samity Lake to Thangshing Return to Thangshing. This is only a two-hour walk, so it is possible to take it gently and make a diversion to the yak grazing grounds of Lam Pokhari Lake (3,900 m) above Thangshing. You may see some rare high altitude birds and blue sheep.

Day 7 Thangshing to Tsokha The return route can be made by a lower track, avoiding Dzongri. Dense rhododendron forests flank the right bank of the Prek Chu, rich in birdlife. The day ends in Tsokha village.

NB See page 309 for detailed trekking advice. **Leeches** can be a special problem in the wet season, below 2,000 m.

Sikkim

Assam, Meghalaya & Arunachal Pradesh

8

Assam, Meghalaya &
Arunachal Pradesh

316 Assam
317 Guwahati
323 Kaziranga National Park
325 Manas National Park
326 Tezpur
327 Jorhat
329 Sibsagar

332 Meghalaya
333 Shillong
337 Cherrapunji

339 Arunachal Pradesh
339 Itanagar - Naharlagun
341 Tawang Monastery

The Northeast is a true frontier region. It has over 2,000 km of border with Bhutan, China, Myanmar (Burma) and Bangladesh and is connected to the rest of India by a narrow 20 km wide corridor of land. One of the most ethnically and linguistically diverse regions in Asia, each of the states has its distinct culture and tradition.

Deep forests cover the sparsely populated foothills of the Himalaya which comprise Arunachal Pradesh, only recently opened to visitors. To its south, Assam, which occupies the lush lowlands of the Brahmaputra Valley is the most densely populated and largest of the states. Meghalaya's beautiful hills have the dubious distinction of being the wettest region in the world.

A Permit is needed to enter Arunachal Pradesh.

Assam

The lush valley of the Brahmaputra, one of the world's great rivers, provides the setting for Assam's culturally rich and diverse communities. Although it is tea which has given the state a world name, the fertile river valley has been the home to generations of rice farmers, and tribal populations continue to have a significant presence in parts of the state.

The land

Population: 24 mn
Area: 78,438 sq km

Assam stretches nearly 800 km from east to west, the length of the narrow floor of the Brahmaputra Valley. The Himalaya to the north and the Shillong Plateau to the south can be clearly seen. The state is dominated by the Brahmaputra, one of the great rivers of the world, which has a fertile alluvial plain for growing rice and is also famous for tea. Earthquakes are common, that in 1950 being estimated as the fifth biggest earthquake ever recorded.

Climate Avoid the monsoon! Assam is in one of the wettest monsoon belts in the world. Even the central Brahmaputra valley, protected by the rainshadow of the Shillong Plateau, has over 1,600 mm of annual rainfall. The rest of the Assam Valley has up to 3,200 mm a year, mostly concentrated between May and September. Although summer temperatures are high, from December to March it can be cold, especially at night.

History The Ahoms, a Shan ruling tribe, arrived in the area in the early 13th century, deposed the ruler and established the kingdom of 'Assam' with its capital in Sibsagar. They later intermixed with Aryan stock and also with existing indigenous peoples (Morans, Chutiyas) and most converted to Hinduism. The Mughals made several attempts to invade without success, but the Burmese finally invaded Assam at the end of the 18th century and held it almost continuously until it was ceded to the East India Company in 1826. The British administered it in name until 1947 though many areas were beyond their effective control.

People The ethnic origin of the Assamese varies from Mongoloid tribes to those of directly Indian stock, but the predominant language is Assamese, similar to Bengali. There has been a steady flow of Muslim settlers from Bengal since the late 19th century. Nearly 90% of the people continue to live in rural areas.

Modern Assam The Assam Valley is in a strategically sensitive corridor for India, lying close to the Chinese frontier. Its sensitivity has been increased by the tension between local Assamese and immigrant groups. The then Prime Minister Rajiv Gandhi achieved an Accord in 1985 with the AASU (All Assam Students Union). The Assam Gana Parishad (AGP), the opposition party, emerged as a result of the struggles. The Congress Government negotiated accords with various tribal groups for greater autonomy at the district level to counter the rise of secessionist movements but the Bodo Liberation Front continues to operate from bases along the Bhutan-Assam border. In early 2000 there were still sporadic terrorist attacks, including a bomb attack in February which killed the Minister for Forests and Public Works, though foreign tourists have never been targets. The May 1996 elections saw Congress support diminished and the AGP returning to power under the Chief Minister Prafulla Mohanta. The chief issue

Visiting the Northeast

The Northeast has been a politically sensitive region since Independence. Insurgency in places continues to surface making travel in some areas unsafe. Arunachal Pradesh, most of Assam, Meghalaya and Mizoram are largely free of problems. Nevertheless, advice on travel to these and the other states should be taken locally.

Permits Visitors to Assam, Meghalaya and Tripura do not need permits but may need to register on arrival and departure. **Foreigners** visiting Arunachal Pradesh,

Nagaland, Manipur and Mizoram may obtain Restricted Area Permits from the Ministry of Home Affairs, Foreigners Division, Lok Nayak Bhavan, Khan Market, New Delhi 110003. Send two photos and allow up to six weeks. **Indians** require Inner Line Permits from the Ministry of Home Affairs. Groups of four should travel together to get a permit; the State Tourist Offices can usually help.

Check the political situation and rules as they are subject to change.

has been the inability of the state's economy to provide jobs for the growing population. A strong anti-immigrant and secessionist protest movement remains close to the surface, focusing on migrants from Bangladesh. The Government has been claiming major success in agricultural production, rice output having boomed in the late 1990s. However, the resulting fall in rice prices has also caused trouble for the government, caught between the conflicting interests of its urban and rural populations.

The state government has designated several wildlife sanctuaries as national parks which attract higher entry fees from foreigners (Rs 175), only a part of which goes towards wildlife and habitat preservation. **Wildlife**

★ Guwahati

Despite its commanding position on the south bank of the mighty Brahmaputra, it is easy to forget that Guwahati is a riverside town, the waterside having little impact on peoples' lives. The main entrance point for visitors to the Northeastern states, the city retains a relaxed and friendly atmosphere. Paltan Bazar, where most visitors arrive, is very busy and crowded. North of the railway it is much quieter and has a rural feel.

Phone code: 0361
Colour map 4, grid B2
Population: 578,000
Altitude: 55 m

Getting there Borjhar airport (23 km) has flights to Kolkata, Delhi, Bagdogra and airports throughout the Northeast. It has occasional coaches, shared taxis and auto-rickshaws for transfer to town. The railway station is in the central Paltan Bazar, while most State and private buses arrive immediately to its south. **Getting around** It is easy to walk around the two main commercial areas of Paltan and Pan (pronounced *Paan*) Bazars which have most of the hotels and restaurants. Always carry a torch when walking at night since large holes in pavements in places lead straight down into sewer channels. Red minibuses or 'canters' are cheap and very efficient around the city (conductors call out the stops), whereas auto-rickshaws need hard bargaining. Political incidents in the city are rare so military presence usually remains discreet and low-key.

Ins & outs
Clothing: Summer – cottons, winter – woollens

Guwahati, on the site of the ancient capital of a succession of local chieftains, was once known as *Pragjyotishpur* ('the city of astrology'). The **Navagrah** (nine planets) **Temple** on a hill here was the ancient centre of astronomy and **History**

Assam, Meghalaya & Arunachal Pradesh

👉 *Plantation labour*

Tea was first discovered growing in Assam in 1823 by Robert Bruce, although it was his younger brother Charles Alexander who pioneered the establishment of the first tea plantations. Today Assam produces most of India's tea. Old colonial tea planters' bungalows surrounded by neat rows of emerald green tea bushes dominate the landscape, particularly in Upper Assam. After an early experiment using imported Chinese labourers ended in near mutiny, the British began the mass recruitment of

Adivasis from the Choto Nagpur plateau, Andhra Pradesh and Orissa. They have now been assimilated into Assamese society. One of the largest groups of organized labour in India today, they enjoy benefits undreamed of by other workers including free health care, education and subsidized food. The lifestyle of the plantation, hardly changed since the days of the Raj, has been tarnished lately by the rise of insurgency, with tea companies being targeted for extortion and kidnapping.

astrology. It was also a centre of learning and a place of Hindu pilgrimage. In the seventh century, Hiuen Tsang described its beautiful mountains, forests and wildlife. Today it is the business capital while **Dispur**, the 'Capital Area', is just to the south.

Sights The **Janardhan Temple** (10th century) in the heart of the city, was rebuilt in the 17th century. The Buddha image here uniquely blends Hindu and Buddhist features. The **Umananda** (Siva) **Temple**, on Peacock Island in the Brahmaputra, can be reached by ferry. An Ahom king built the temple in 1594, believing Uma, Siva's consort, had stayed there. Ask the priests about the few rare golden langurs here.

Kamakhya Temple (8 km southwest) Believed to be an old Khasi sacrificial site on Nilachal Hill, it has been a centre for Tantric Hinduism and Sakti worship. Rebuilt in 1665 after the 10th-century temple was destroyed by a Brahmin convert to Islam, it typifies Assamese temple architecture with its distinctive beehive-shape *sikhara* (spire), the nymph motifs and the long turtleback hall. The dark sanctum contains the creative part of the goddess which is said to have fallen here and pilgrims enter to touch the wet *yoni* of Kamakhya (Sakti). Western visitors may be allowed into the sanctum but should be prepared for the charged atmosphere and to walk barefoot on a floor sprinkled with the sacrificial blood of a goat. ■ *0830-1300, 1500-1600 (Sun 0830-1200).* Ask for Hemen Sarma, a knowledgeable resident Brahmin, on entering the complex. Further up the hill is a smaller temple and a Viewpoint with panoramic views of the Brahmaputra. See Festivals below. ■ *Getting there: a bus from MG Road (towards Adabari Bus Stand) can drop you near Kamakhya. Take a 'canter' from AT Road to the temple or walk up the steep and slippery rocky path at the back of the hill.*

Basistha Ashram (12 km) Believed to be sage Basistha's (Vasistha) hermitage, it is a scenic spot with three mountain streams nearby.

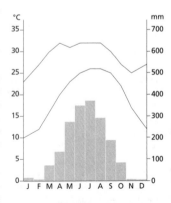

Climate: Guwahati

North Guwahati, a sleepy town across Saraighat Bridge, which can also be reached by any ferry from the ghat. The **Digheswari Temple** is worth a visit. Take a rickshaw from the other bank or an auto-rickshaw or shared four-wheeler (Bikram).

Bordua, 15 km north of Nagaon, with a museum, is where the Vaishnavite reformer **Shri Sankardeva** was born in 1449. He was a great scholar, poet and musician (see also Majuli below).

Assam Forest Museum has collections of timber, cane and ivory work, tusks **Museums** and horns. ■ *1000-1600 weekdays, 1000- 1330 Sat; guided tours.* **Assam State Museum**, which is being improved, covers epigraphy, sculpture, natural history et cetera; sections on village life, crafts and ethnography are particularly interesting. A small museum, well lit, thoughtfully displayed with notes in English and informative on neighbouring cultures. Leaflet available. Photography with permission. ■ *1000-1615 (Nov-Mar), 1000-1700 (Apr-Oct), closed Mon and 2nd, 4th Sat. Rs 2.* **Commercial Museum**, Guwahati University, has collections of art and craft, commercial products, minerals and rocks, coins, et cetera. ■ *1230-1830, Mon-Sat, closed Sun and University holidays. No photography.*

Guwahati

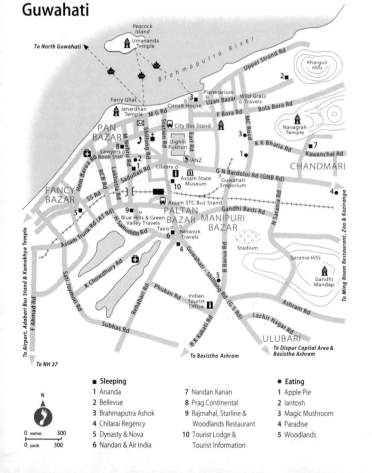

Assam, Meghalaya & Arunachal Pradesh

■ Sleeping		● Eating
1 Ananda	7 Nandan Kanan	1 Apple Pie
2 Bellevue	8 Prag Continental	2 Iantosh
3 Brahmaputra Ashok	9 Rajmahal, Starline &	3 Magic Mushroom
4 Chilarai Regency	Woodlands Restaurant	4 Paradise
5 Dynasty & Nova	10 Tourist Lodge &	5 Woodlands
6 Nandan & Air India	Tourist Information	

Zoo & Botanical Gardens Largely an open-enclosure zoo with landscaped gardens, it has swamp tapirs, rhinos, tigers, lions, panthers and rich birdlife; several species from Northeast India which are not often seen elsewhere. Restaurants and souvenir shops. ■ *Oct-Mar 0800-1600, Apr-Sep 0700-1630. Closed Fri. Entry Rs 5, Cameras: still camera Rs 5, telephoto lens Rs 25, video Rs 250. Auto-rickshaw from town Rs 40. Alternatively take a local bus along GNB Road to the flyover (Rs 2), climb steps up to the flyover; take a southbound bus to the zoo (Rs 2). A few direct buses go all the way.*

Tours **Assam Tourism**, *Tourist Lodge*, Station Rd, T547102. **City**: Basistha Ashram, Zoo, Museum, Kamakhya Temple, Govt Sales Emporium. 0900-1500. Rs 75. Tuesday, Sunday (minimum 10). **River Cruises**, from near Janardhan Temple, winter 1500, 1600; summer 1600, 1700, one hour, Rs 40. **Kaziranga**: November-April, dep 0900, arr 1600, return 1600 on following day, Rs 530, foreigners Rs 1,120 (inclusive) allows only from 1500 to 1000 (on next day) in the park. Separate morning buses, dep 0700, 5½ hrs. **Shillong**: dep 0700, Rs 175 (tiring, since the windy hill roads take 3½ hrs each way). **Bhalukpong** and **Orchid Centre**, Tipi (Permit needed), 2-day, Sunday, Rs 520. *Wild Grass* tours (see below) may be more reliable.

Essentials

Sleeping
Staff often have little English
You may need to complete 4 copies of the hotel registration slip and then register with the police (fairly quick). Most hotels outside Guwahati require photocopies of passport identification and the visa page.

B *Brahmaputra Ashok* (ITDC), MG Rd, T541064, F540870. 50 rooms (on riverside best), good restaurant, no pool. **B** *Dynasty*, SS Rd, T510496, F522112. 68 comfortable rooms, good restaurants. **B-C** *Nandan*, GS Rd, opposite IA, T540855, F542634, nandan@gw1.vsnl.net.in 55 rooms, some a/c, expensive suites, restaurants, *Upavan* fot snacks, bar. Recommended. **B-C** *Rajmahal*, Paltan Bazar (near bus stand), T522478, F521559. 80 rooms (cheaper, good value), excellent restaurant, all services, pool in summer (non-residents Rs 75, 45 minutes), modern. **C** *Bellevue*, MG Rd, on river front opposite Raj Bhawan, T540847. 45 rooms, restaurant (Continental recommended), elevated woodland setting, quiet. **C** *Prag Continental*, M Nehru Rd, Pan Bazar, T543785, F524554, 62 rooms, some a/c, terrace restaurants, *Continental Café*. Most medium priced hotels have some a/c rooms and tend to serve Indian meals only: **D** *Nova*, SS Rd, T523464. Clean rooms (some **C** a/c) in 4-storey block (extra bed Rs 100/150), reasonable restaurant (Indian, Chinese) but slow service (room service quicker), pleasant, friendly and helpful. **D** *Chilarai Regency*, HP Brahmachari Rd, Paltan Bazar, T541530, F547917. 44 large rooms (some a/c), bar, exchange.

Some budget hotels at Sadullah & M Nehru Rd crossing; those in Paltan Bazar are often full by the afternoon
D-E *Starline*, Md Shah Rd, Paltan Bazar, T542450. 74 clean rooms (Rs 300-500), 12 a/c with hot water 24 hrs (Rs 550), Indian/Chinese restaurant, polite and helpful staff. **E** *Nandan Kanan*, Navagraha Rd (next to temple). 7 rooms with bath (Rs 350-400) in new hotel, restaurant, garden with great views, beautiful hilltop location. **E-F** *Ananda*, M Nehru Rd, T544832. Small dark rooms but pleasant, vegetarian dining hall. **F** *Tourist Lodge* (Assam Tourism), opposite rly station, T544475. 21 fairly clean simple rooms with nets, toilets and balcony, canteen, staff speak little English but are friendly, tourist information, good value. **F** *Railway Retiring Rooms*, rooms (some a/c), small dorm, book at Enquiry Counter.

Eating Assamese *thalis* including rice, fish and vegetable curry, often cooked with mustard. You might try vegetarian *Kharoli*, *Omita Khar* (papaya cooked with burnt 'bark' of the banana plant). **Expensive**: Only larger hotels serve Continental food and have bars.

Specially recommended: *Bellevue* for Continental. *Dynasty* for Chinese. *Raj Mahal*. **Mid range**: *Ming Room*, Rajgarh Rd, near Chandmari Flyover. Very good Chinese. **Cheap**: *Jantosh*. Assamese. Takeaway and ice cream, clean. *Apple Pie*, MC Rd. Pastries, shakes and ice creams. *Magic Mushroom*, MC Rd. International. Clean, good quality, varied menu (Rs 25-50), trendy blue psychedelic décor, very friendly and helpful owner. Recommended. *Paradise*, GNB Rd, Chandmari, T546904. Assamese. Serves "perfect *thalis*" (Rs 55), very clean and friendly, closes 1530-1800 (cycle rickshaw from station, Rs 10). Recommended. *Station restaurant*, does good omelettes (Rs 7). *Woodlands*, AT Rd (older branch on GS Rd). Indian vegetarian. Clean, a/c, specializes in lunch and dinner *thalis* (Rs 40).

Guwahati Planetarium, Uzan Bazar, daily 1700 English show (good equipment), Rs 10. Recommended. **Sport Swimming**: *Assam Swimming Club*, Ambari and Pool in Nehru Stadium. **Paddle boats**: on the Long Pond (Digholi Pukhuri near the Museum Bus Stop). Spend a pleasant hour with a cup of coffee from the canteen. **Entertainment**

Magh Bihu in Jan and *Rongali Bihu* in mid-**Apr**, the week-long festivities are celebrated with singing and dancing. **Jun**: *Ambubachi* marks the end of Mother Earth's menstrual cycle with a fair at Kamakhya Temple. In **Sep** the *Manasa Festival* there honours the Snake goddess. You can watch devotees dancing and entering into trances from galleries on the hillside. *Assam Tea Festival* is celebrated on **26-28 Dec** with events in various places. **Festivals**

Muga, pat and *endi* silks, hats, bamboo and cane baskets, flutes, drums and pipes are typical of the area. Guide prices: silk per metre: *muga* Rs 400+ (saris Rs 4,000+), *pat* Rs 250 (saris Rs 2,00+), *endi* Rs 150-300. *Pat mikhala* and *shador*, Rs 1,500, *endi* shawls Rs 300+, You need to bargain in Pan Bazar and Fancy Bazar. **Shopping**

    Assam Co-op Silk House, HB Rd, Pan Bazar, for pure silk items; *Khadi Gramudyog*, near *Guwahati Emporium*. *Assam* at Ambari, sells silks, bamboo, wood, brass and ceramics. *Manipur*, Paltan Bazar; *Purbashree*, GNB Rd, has traditional crafts; *Tantuja*, Ulubari, has Bengal handloom. **Books** in Pan Bazar: *Lawyers Book Stall*, one of the region's oldest and largest; *Modern Book Depot*, best collection on the region at rear.

Hemanta Doley, Sankardeva Udyan, Machkhowa, T 512121, for river trips; *Network Travels*, GS Rd, T522007, F522105. Imaginative tours, *Indian Airlines* agent, efficient and reliable. *Rhino*, M Nehru Rd, T540061. For visiting game reserves and Shillong. *Wild Grass*, Barua Bhavan, 107 MC Rd, Uzan Bazar, T546827, F630465, wildgrss@gw1.dot.net.in Very helpful, knowledgeable, efficient. Highly recommended for good value wildlife, tribal tours and Arunachal (can get a permit in 5 days), free travel advice on phone (Nov-Apr). See also, bus operators. **Tour operators**

Local Auto-rickshaw: Paltan Bazar to Fancy Bazar Rs 20, Fancy Bazar to Navagraha Temple Rs 25). **Bus**: (see below). Red **minibus** 'canters' or 'Omni taxis' cover main roads, Rs 3-5. These are prone to accidents. **Taxi**: sightseeing Rs 100 per hr (excluding petrol); *Guwahati Taxis*, Paltan Bazar, near Police Station; *Green Valley*, Silpukhuri, T545289, cars/jeeps Rs 700 per day plus overnight Rs 150. **Ferry**: to North Guwahati from MG Rd Ferry Ghat. Others to **Peacock Island**: Rs 6 each way. 0700-1700. **Transport**
1,151 km from Kolkata, Well connected by road to all major centres of the NE region ; at the junction of NH31, 37 & 40

Long distance Air: Information T84235. Transport to town: *Indian Airlines* and *Rhino Travels* coaches connect with Kolkata flights, Rs 40, 1 hr. Taxi Rs 300, share taxi Rs 100, 45 mins. Auto-rickshaw, Rs 150. *Indian Airlines*, Ganeshguri, near Dispur, T564420, airport, T84375; 0900-1600. **Kolkata**, 2 daily; some weekly to **Agartala, Delhi, Imphal, Lilabari**. *Jet Airways*, Silpukhri, GNB Rd, T522402: to **Bagdogra, Kolkata, Delhi, Imphal**; *Sahara*, GS Rd, T547808: to **Delhi, Dibrugarh**. **Helicopter**:

Meghalaya Transport Corp to **Shillong**, Mon-Sat (am and pm), Rs 1,000, and on to **Tura**; tickets at airport.

Between midnight & 0500 buses are not allowed to enter the city, but taxis are

Road Bus: Private coaches (and taxis) operate from Paltan Bazar, with waiting rooms, left-luggage, snack bars. Operators: *Assam Valley*, T546133, *Blue Hills*, T547911, *Green Valley*, T544636, and others have buses to all the Hill States. **Assam STC Stand**, Paltan Bazar, T547941. Left-luggage, Rs 3 per day. Reservations 0630-1230, 1330-1700. Meghalaya STC, T547668. Buses to: **Aizawl** (11 hrs); **Imphal** (579 km); **Itanagar** (11 hrs); **Jorhat via Kohora (for Kaziranga)**, Rs 86 (6 hrs); **Kaziranga and Upper Assam**: bus for Tinsukia and Digboi (0700 a/c; 0730), halt at *Wild Grass Resorts* after 4 hrs. **Kohima** 2000, 2015, 2030 (13 hrs); **Shillong** (103 km) hourly, 0600-1700, Rs 40 (3½ hrs); **Silchar** 1730; **Siliguri**; **Tezpur** every 30 mins (3½ hrs). **City Bus Stand**, Station Rd (north end): to **Hajo**, Rs 6 (1¼ hr). **Adabari Bus Stand**, AT Rd (4 km west of centre) reached by 'canters' from MG Rd, has buses to Hajo (Rs 7), Orang and Nalbari etc. **Taxi**: from Paltan Bazar: Shillong Rs 625 (5 sharing, Rs 125 each, they fill up quickly when trains arrive).

Train Station has snack bars, chemists, tourist information, left-luggage (trunks and suitcases only), on showing ticket. Enquiries: T540330. Reservations: 100 m north of the station on Station Rd, T541799, 0800-1330, 1400-2000; Foreign Tourists, Counter 3, where great patience is needed! In Jun 2000 the Railways Board announced the opening of the new line from Guwahati along the south bank of the Brahmaputra to Jogighopa, which should cut delays and speed up journey times when fully operational by the end of 2000. Timetables on the new line were not finalised at the time of going to press in mid-2000. To **Kolkata (H)**: *Kanchenjunga Exp 5658* (AC/II), 2200, 22½ hrs. *Kamrup Exp 5660* (AC/II), 0700, 23¾ hrs. *Saraighat Exp 3026* Mon, Thu, 18 hrs. To **Delhi (D)**: *Rajdhani Exp 2423*, Mon, Thu, Fri, 0600, 28 hrs. *Northeast Exp 5621*, 0830, 35¾ hrs. To **Dibrugarh** *Rajdhani Exp 2423*, Sat. Via Dimapur: *Brahmaputra Mail 4056*, 1430, 16 hrs.

Directory **Airlines** *Air India*, GS Rd, T561881, *BA*, Pelican Travels, *Hotel Brahmaputra Ashok*, T545149. **Banks** *United Bank of India*, HB Rd, Pan Bazar. TC exchange, min Rs 50 commission. *State Bank of India*, Pan Bazar and *Grindlays Bank*, Dighali Pukhari, GNB/Earl Rds, Mon-Fri 1000-1500, Sat 1000-1230. TC Commission 1% or Rs 100, but quick and efficient. **Communications** Post: GPO (entrance on Shillong Rd) with Speed Post (7 days). Counter 1 for evaluation and 14 for stamps, then basement for franking. CTO: in Pan Bazar. **Couriers**: on GS Rd. **Internet**: *Sangita Communications*, Anuradha Cinema Complex, GNB Rd, 0830-2000, Rs 120 per hr. **Photocopying**: north of Shillong Rd. **Medical services** Christian Hospital, Chatribari, T540193. *Good Health*, GS Rd, T566911. *Medical College*, Bhangagarh, T561477. With 24-hr chemists outside. *MM Choudhury Hospital*, Pan Bazar, T543998. **Tourist offices** *Assam*, Station Rd, T542748, F547102. Counters at airport and Rly station. *Arunachal Pradesh*, RC Barua Rd, Bhaskar Nagar, T562859, F566720. *India*, BK Kakati Rd, Ulubari, T547407. Mon-Fri 0930-1730, Sat 1000-1300, airport counter, helpful for planning trips to other parts of India. *Manipur*, Rajgarh Rd, T540707. *Meghalaya*, Ulubari, GS Rd, T527276. 1000-1700 except Sun. *Tripura*, GS Rd, Ulubari, T528761. **Useful numbers** Ambulance T561477, **Fire** T540222, **Police** T100.

Excursions **Hajo** A friendly and peaceful town, 34 km across the river, which produces bell-metal work, is sacred to three religions. The **Hayagriba Madhab** Hindu temple is said to contain a Buddhist relic; some believe this is where the Buddha attained Nirvana. Its hilltop location is more spectacular than the temple itself. The 'main' street behind the tank stocked with fish leads to an old Ganesh temple after 2 km; a friendly priest might allow you in. Hajo is also sacred to Muslims since the **Poa Mecca mosque** built by Pir Ghiasuddin Aulia is supposed to have 'quarter' (*pao*) of the sanctity of Mecca. ■ *Getting there: buses from Adabari Bus Stand, Rs 12, 1 hr. The last return bus departs Hajo around 1600 but may be very crowded, forcing you to travel on the roof.*

Sualkuchi The small village on the north bank of the Brahmaputra is famous for silk production from non mulberry leaf-fed worms hence its unique natural colour. Every household is involved with weaving of *muga*, *endi* or *pat* silk; prices are 30% cheaper than in Guwahati. There are also brass-workers here. ■ *Getting there: ferry service from Guwahati; also buses to/from Hajo, 20 mins.*

Pabitora A small wildlife sanctuary a two-hour drive from Guwahati (60 km), on the border of Nagaon and Kamrup districts, has rhinos.

Madan Kamdev, 45 km north of Guwahati, has been called Assam's Khajuraho. The temples which may date from the 11th-12th century, possibly reconstructed in the 18th, are believed to be Shaivite and associated with tantric practices . The site spread across several low hills have begun to be excavated and the ruins of the 24 or so temples show erotic sculptures comparable to those at Khajuraho. More are expected to be found in the adjacent swamp Jalpeswar and other mounds nearby. The principle shrine to Uma-Mahesvara (Siva-Parvati) at Madan Kamdev (Kama is the Hindu God of Love) is still in use. The site museum has a collection of local finds. A Tourist Lodge is scheduled to open. *Getting there* Buses from Guwahati go to Baihata on NH31 (5 km from the site); rickshaws run to the temples.

★ Kaziranga National Park

Kaziranga Reserve Forest was declared a game sanctuary in 1916 to save the Indian greater one-horned rhino and became a national park in 1974. In a beautiful setting on the banks of the Brahmaputra, and with the Karbi Anglong Hills to the south, the 430 sq km park combines elephant grass mixed with thorny rattan cane, areas of semi-evergreen forest and shallow swamps.

Phone code: 031776
Colour map 4, grid B3
Altitude: 65 m

Guwahati is 215 km from Kohora, the entry point to Kaziranga, a World Heritage Site, on the NH37. See page 324 for further details. **Climate**: Summer maximum 35°C, minimum 18°C; Winter maximum 24°C, minimum 7°C. Annual rainfall 2,300 mm, heavy in summer. Best season: Mid-Nov to end-Apr (Dec, Jan best for birds); closed mid Apr-mid Oct during monsoons. Clothing: cottons; a warm jacket for sudden cool weather.(early elephant ride and jeep after dusk, even in summer).

Ins & outs

The **rhino** population is about 1,200 here (1,500 in the country) but you can still easily see them in the marshes and grasslands. Poachers still kill the animal for its horn for its use in Chinese and Tibetan medicine – a single horn (1 kg) can fetch a very high price. The catastrophic floods in September 1998 led to

Wildlife

Kaziranga National Park

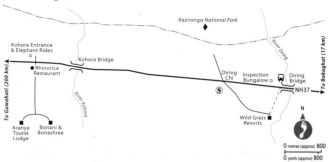

Assam, Meghalaya & Arunachal Pradesh

drowning of at least 35 rhinos but the park has limped back to normalcy. Money raised through donations are being used to rebuild jeep tracks and viewing towers. The park also has over 1,000 wild buffalo, sambar, swamp deer (over 500), hog deer, wild pig, hoolock gibbon, elephants (about 1,000) pythons and tiger (80 in 1997), the only predator of the docile rhino. There is a rich variety of shallow-water fowl including egrets, pond herons, river terns, black-necked stork, fishing eagles and adjutant storks, pelicans and the rare Bengal florican. There are otters and dolphins in the river.

Viewing

Keep receipts as fees are valid for several trips during 1 day

Entry into the park is by own vehicle, hired jeep or trained elephants. Whereas elephants cover less ground than motor vehicles, they can get a lot closer to the wildlife, particularly rhinos and buffalo. They carry four and a seat may be booked through the Forest Range Officer, the night before the visit. **Elephant rides**, 0530-0630 or 0630-0730, Rs 525 foreigners (Indians Rs 120), plus jeep transfer between town and elephant pick-up, Rs 120.

The Dept of Tourism, Kaziranga and private agents hire out **jeeps** for 5-6 people. Govt: Rs 400 for three hours; private: Rs 550 for 50 km or 2½ hours; *Wild Grass Resorts* charge Rs 10 per km, for example Eastern Range, Rs 700. **NB** A car or jeep must be accompanied by a Forest Dept guide (free), who can give directions as well as spot wildlife. Cars and jeeps pay a road toll, Rs 150.

There are three road routes for visiting the park. **The Kaziranga Range** – Kohora, Daflang, Foliomari; the **Western Range** – Baguri, Monabeel, Bimoli, Kanchanjuri; and the **Eastern Range** – Agortoli, Sohola, Rangamatia, where you may see a lot of wildlife but at a distance.

■ *Park roads open 0800-1100, 1400-1630. Entry for foreigners, Rs 175. Cameras (for each trip during any day): still Rs 175, telephoto lens Rs 210, video Rs 525 (professional Rs 7,000). 25% discount on fees after 3 consecutive days.*

Tours **Assam Tourism** offers a two-day tour (see under Guwahati). Tour operators may be more reliable.

Essentials

Sleeping **C** *Wild Grass Resorts*, lovely location, 1.5 km from NH37, 5.5 km from Kohora (ask for Kaziranga IB Bus Stop, 400 m north of resort), T62437, (Guwahati T0361-546827, F630465). 19 rooms (Rs 850), wood floors, cane furniture, deluxe camping (4 new tents, common bath, Rs 250), very good buffet lunch (Rs 50/65), pool, excellent service, spotless, relaxing, beautiful walks through forests and tea plantations, tours, pick up from Guwahati for groups. Highly recommended. Assam Tourism's **D** *Aranya Tourist Lodge*, 1 km south of Kohora, T62409. 24 rooms with bath and balcony, some a/c, simple garden, restaurant and bar (slow service), very friendly (Rs 450; off-season Rs 350). Recommended. Nearby **D-E** *Bonani*, T62423. 5 a/c rooms (Rs 350). **F** *Bonashree*, still cheaper, 9 rooms (Rs 175), a large verandah, pleasant garden, but often full. *Dormitory*, linen optional, 5 or 12-bed (Rs 15), no cupboards,. Reservations: Deputy Director, Tourism, Kaziranga, T62444. Also *Dhansri* and *Green Reed*, off the main road, between the 2.

Transport **Air** Nearest airport is at Jorhat (88 km). See page 321. Check if foreign tourists must use Guwahati airport (see page 317). **Road** Best to ask *Wild Grass*, if they have a vehicle going from Guwahati, or confirm timings of private buses. **ASTC** buses between Guwahati and Jorhat via **Kohora** stopping at **Nagaon** (30 mins, where you can stop overnight); departs 0900, 1000, 1100, 1230, Rs 77, 5-6 hrs. **Private**: *Green Valley* (office behind bus station) coaches dep Guwahati for Tinsukia and Digboi, 0700 (non a/c, Rs 85), 0730 (a/c, Rs 125); lunch stop at *Wild Grass Resorts*, after 4 hrs. To **Guwahati**: a/c

The riddle of the Brahmaputra

According to Hindu scriptures the Brahmaputra River – the son of Brahma – rises in a sacred pool known as the Brahmakund in the eastern part of Arunachal Pradesh. In fact it rises in Tibet where it is known as the Tsangpo, and flows in an easterly direction before suddenly turning south, plunging through the Himalayan range in a series of spectacular rapids before continuing westwards towards the Bay of Bengal.

The source of the river was one of the great riddles of modern geography. Although by the end of the last century it was generally assumed that the Tsangpo and the Brahmaputra were the same, European explorers were unable to follow the course of the river to Tibet because of hostile tribes, difficult terrain and China's isolationist policies. Instead, the British recruited Indians, disguised them as traders and sent them on missions of exploration. The pundits as they were known, provided valuable intelligence on Russian and Chinese designs in Central Asia at the height of the 'Great Game'. In 1884, one of the pundits, Kintup, returned to India claiming he had seen the Tsangpo as a great waterfall. The prospect of discovering a cataract rivalling the Niagara Falls excited many geographers, but in 1924 Frank Kingdom Ward, the botanist and explorer, penetrated the last 70 km stretch of the Tsangpo Gorge to prove conclusively that there was no great waterfall along the river.

bus from Dibrugarh stops at resort for lunch; leaves at 1330. *Kaziranga Forest Lodge* has 10 seats reserved on the Express coach between Golaghat and Guwahati. Assam Tourism bus, dep 0930 from *Bonashree Lodge*, arr Guwahati 1600, Rs 75 (lunch Rs 30). **NB** It is a very bumpy ride; best to get a seat near the front. From **Shillong** get a Jorhat bus and switch at **Jorabat** for Kaziranga. **Train** Furkating (75 km) has the nearest station with trains from Guwahati; buses via Golaghat.

Useful services **Post office** near the Tourist Lodge and at the park. The Wildlife Society has a **library** of books and magazines and may show wildlife films to groups. Range Officer, T62428. Divisional Forest Officer, Bokakhat, T68007. *Kaziranga Safari*, T037376-325468, F325782, can book accommodation. | **Directory**

Panbari Forest Reserve, 12 km from Kaziranga, has hoolock gibbons and a good variety of birdlife. Contact the Forest Officer, Guwahati for permission. | **Panbari**

★ Manas National Park

A World Heritage Site, and one of India's most beautiful sanctuaries, Manas lies in the Himalayan foothills, southeast of the river Manas, on the Assam-Bhutan border. Over half the area is covered with tall grass and scattered patches of woodland with simul, khoir, udal, sida, bohera and kanchan trees. This changes to dense semi-evergreen forest in the upper reaches and even to conifer on hills towards Bhutan. | Phone code: 03666
Colour map 4, grid B1
Altitude: 70 m

Entry permit It is essential to enter via Barpeta Road by car or taxi. Permits are issued by the Field Director, Manas Project Tiger, Barpeta Road, T03666-32289 (home, T32288), after he obtains confirmation of a police escort to accompany you. Pick up provisions. Use the Bansbari gate with a Forest Range Office (20 km, 30 mins) to get to Mathanguri in the park proper, (20 km, 30 mins). Do book a car/taxi for the return journey. If you travel during dawn (0500) and before sunset (0400) you may see some wildlife. **Climate**: Summer maximum 35°C, minimum 18°C; Winter maximum 24°C, minimum 7°C. Annual rainfall: 4,100 mm. Season: Nov-Mar. Clothing: heavy | **Ins & outs**
Travel is not permitted after sunset

Assam, Meghalaya & Arunachal Pradesh

pullover/jacket for evenings, sun hat, canvas shoes for wading through slippery streams essential (and several changes of clothing!).

Background The Manas, with a buffer zone 2,800 sq km (including two other far flung sanctuaries), and a core area of 391 sq km, was demarcated in 1977/8 when the preservation programme 'Project Tiger' was launched. At the last count there were over 80 tigers. UNESCO has released funds to help the national park recover from the damage caused by Bodo rebels. **NB** Political troubles can lead to sudden closure of the park so get local advice before you plan to visit; contact *Wild Grass Tours*, Guwahati, T0361-546827, F630465.

Wildlife The forests are home to most of the larger animals found in Kaziranga, most common being wild buffalo, swamp deer, hog deer, sambar and elephant. Some 22 of the animal and bird species are on the endangered list of the IUCN including the rare capped and golden langur which can be seen among the flowering trees, mostly on the Bhutan side. There are also pigmy hog, hispid hare, slow lorris, clouded leopard, rhino and tiger. The sanctuary is rich in birdlife (over 400 species), and attracts migratory flocks of redstarts, forktails, mergansers and ruddy shelduck. Otters are frequently seen in the Manas River.

Viewing Occasionally boats (for 2-8) are for hire from the Forest Beat Officer, Mathanguri. To see the animals from close range, an elephant ride is best. These start from Mathanguri (one hour, 0900-1200, 1400-1700, Rs 525 for foreigners). Charges for entry and camera are similar to Kaziranga (see above).

Essentials

Sleeping **F** *Mathanguri Forest Lodge*, built on hill overlooking Manas River is in a poor state but has the advantage of being within the park. Forest Dept's *Forest Lodge*, and *Bhutan Tourist Lodge*, Mathanguri are very simple but clean and well maintained, cook available but bring provisions (from Barpeta Rd), camping possible, book well in advance. Prefabricated *Rest House* provides linen but no electricity, open Nov-Apr. Contact Field Director, Manas Tiger Reserve, PO Barpeta Rd, T2153. If you arrive late at **Barpeta Road** you will need to spend the night there: **E** *Doli*, 200 m from station, 18 rooms with fan, net, bath (Rs 300), abundant food, helpful staff. Recommended. The town has *medical facilities*, *Tourist Information Office* (T2149), *banks* and *Post Office*.

Transport **Train** Nearest station at Barpeta Road (40 km) with trains to **Guwahati** and **Kolkata**. **Road** **Bus**: on good fair weather road between Guwahati and Barpeta Road but no buses beyond; taxis charge, Rs 450-600 per journey.

Tezpur

Phone code: 03712
Colour map 4, grid B2

Once known as Sonitpur, the "city of blood", Tezpur is a on the north bank of the Brahmaputra 180 km northeast of Guwahati. A focus of ancient myths, the town has lost some of its colonial flavour. Tezpur is the site of Assam's first tea plantations. Its ancient origins can be seen at Da Parbatia, west of town, which has the entrance gate of an early Gupta style temple, while a large stone inscription commemorates the Ahom general Kalia Bhomorahe near the river bridge. The pleasant Cole Park (Chitralekha Udyan), with a lake, remains a relaxing oasis amongst the modern day bustle. It is open 0800-1930, Rs 5.

Sleeping **D** *Luit*, Ranu Singh Rd, 100m bus stand, T22083, F21220. 38 rooms, some a/c (Rs 650 plus **& eating** 30% tax), best in new wing, restaurant, bar, travel. **E** *Basanth* Main Rd, T30831. Good clean well maintained rooms (Rs 250). **F** *Tourist Lodge* (Assam Tourism), opposite Chitralekha Park, T21016. 6 large rooms with bath (Rs 170) and dorm (Rs 30), very quiet and peaceful, tourist Information. Basic small guest houses include *Central Lodge*, T21117.

Air: Saloni airport is to the north: **Indian Airlines**, T20083, T20353. Flies to/from Kolkata   **Transport**
via Imphal. **Road**: Frequent **buses** to/from **Guwahati**; **Kaziranga** until 1400, Rs 20. Daily
to **Itanagar** (4 hrs); **Tawang** (12 hrs). **Taxi**: to **Orang**/Nameri, Rs 500 plus petrol.

Tourist office T21016. Forest Office, West Assam Wildlife Div, T20854, for angling at Bhoreli.   **Directory**

Nameri National Park The 210 sq km park on the Arunachal border with   **Around Tezpur**
evergreens, bamboo and some open grassland is on the river **Jia Bhoreli**,
about 40 km north of Tezpur. The best time to visit is from October to April. It
is home to about 20 endangered white-winged wood ducks among 300 bird
species. There are tigers and elephants (29 and 225 counted in 1997), Indian
bison, barking and hog deer. Viewing is on elephant back as there are no roads.
You can walk/trek within the park with a forest guide/guard. Entry/camera
fees are similar to Kaziranga (see above).

An **Eco camp** at Potasali organizes white-water rafting and mahseer fishing
on the Bhoreli. The *Assam Anglers' Association* (T02712-20004), rip.magdel@
axcess-net.in) operate a strict 'catch-record-release' system to conserve the
golden Mahseer. Rafting, for fishing or nature watching, for two people on
rubber rafts, Rs 650 per day, Rs 300 transport to/from raft.

Bhalukpong, 20 km west of Nameri, just beyond the Arunachal Pradesh
border, en route to Tawang, has a hot spring an orchid garden and good fishing. You can camp (own tent) on the picturesque bank of the river Jia Bhoreli
(see page 341).

Sleeping and eating C-D *Eco Camp*, T03712-24246. Six Swiss cottage tents
with thatched cover, some with bath (Rs 650-800), 6-bed dorm (Rs 105), wash
block, meals. Contact Wild Grass Tours, T0361-546827. **F** *Forest Lodge*, contact Range Officer. *Eco Eats* has some tribal dishes. ■ *Getting there: Taxi
to/from Tezpur, 1 hr, Rs 200-250. Bus: from Balipura, change for Bhalukpong.*

Often called a miniature Kaziranga, the 76 sq km park, 66 km northwest of Tezpur,   **Orang**
has similar flora and fauna, though viewing is not as rewarding. This is compen-   **National**
sated by its peaceful and intimate atmosphere, especially if staying inside the park.   **Park**
Sleeping F *Bungalows*, two at park entrance, two 1.5 km inside the park, over-   *Colour map 4, grid B2*
looking river. Each with two double rooms (Rs 175 per room), bring own provi-
sions, cook/guide will prepare your food. Reservations, Div Forest Officer, Mangal
Doi, T03713-22065. ■ *Getting there: A car is best from Tezpur (2 hrs), then from
Orang to the park (15 km bumpy, dust track) and for within the park.*

Jorhat

Jorhat is one of Assam's major tea centres (*Tea festival* in November) and is   *Colour map 4, grid B4*
convenient for visiting Majuli island to the north.   *Phone code: 0376*

D-E *Paradise*, Solicitor's Rd (off AT Rd), T321521, F323512. 31 rooms, 9 a/c, restaurant,   **Sleeping**
bar, exchange. **F** *Tourist Lodge* (Assam Tourism), MG Rd, T321579. Decent large rooms
(Rs 175), Tourist information, very helpful and friendly. Other **F** hotels are along Gar-Ali.

Mid-range *Belle Amies Food & Fun Junction*, Gar-Ali. Indian/Chinese. Colour-coded   **Eating**
menu to indicate hotness! **Cheap** *Canteen* at State Bus Stand, does good *roti*

Assam, Meghalaya & Arunachal Pradesh

i breakfasts (toilets). *Rajhans*, AT Rd. Indian snacks. *Woodlands*, BG Rd (between MG Rd and Gar Ali). Indian. Good *thalis*. Internet.

Transport **Air** Jorhat has the main airport for the far Northeast 7 km from town with airlines coach or autos for transfer. *Indian Airlines*, T320011, Airport, T320970, to **Kolkata** via **Dimapur**; *Jet Airways*, T325652: **Kolkata**, Wed, Fri. **Train** The station (3 km southeast of bus stand) has no toilets). To **Guwahati**: *Intercity Exp 5606*, 2130, 8½ hrs, via Lumding with narrow gauge to **Haflong**: 0715, 1½ hrs (beautiful route but tourists are discouraged; Haflong Tourist Lodge is now occupied by military). **Road** **Bus**: ASTC Stand on AT Rd has a good canteen. Private buses leave from outside ASTC: to Guwahati, 0600-0730 and 2000-2130, 7 hrs, Rs 115; Sibsagar (55 km); Dibrugarh (131 km). Ticket booths are nearby.

Directory **Services** *State Bank of India*, AT Rd. Exchanges TCs (show proof of purchase). **Internet** *Sigma*, AT Rd (near Gar-Ali), Rs 150 per hour. **Tourist office** Station Rd.

Around Jorhat **Majuli Island** is possibly the largest river island in the world, though con-
Phone code: 03775 stantly changing and now reduced to around 700 sq km. The flooding of the
Foreigners must register Brahmaputra River means that that at times Majuli is reduced to a cluster of
on arrival and departure islands, some as small as a hut top. Roads keep shifting but villagers adapt to
at the nearest police rerouting by building cost effective bamboo bridges. Cut off from the main-
station land to the south about 400 years ago, it is served by ferries from Jorhat and North Lakhimpur, but it can still be accessed from the north by road during summer. Majuli is also a bird-watchers paradise.

At the forefront of Assamese Vaishnava culture, the island is an important centre for arts, crafts and science. Work is in progress to declare it a World

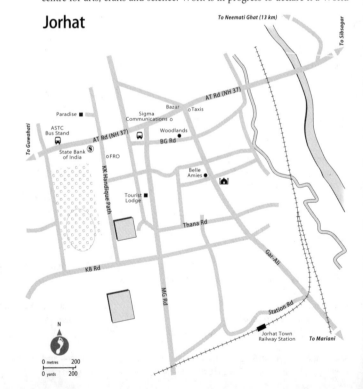

Jorhat

Heritage Site. The satras (monasteries) here, inspired by the 15th-century saint Sankardeva and his disciple Madhavdeva are worth visiting. They are essentially small self-contained, self-sufficient villages where Vishnu is worshipped through regular performances of dance-dramas at the temples.

Some satras can be visited on foot in and around **Kamalabari** and **Garmur** but for others a rickshaw (or taxi) is handy. **Auniati**, a few kilometres west of Kamalabari, has an Angami tribal museum with old manuscripts, utensils, jewellery and handicrafts. **Bengenatti**, east of Uttar Kamalabari, is a centre for performing arts and tribal dance forms. Others worth visiting are at Nauten Kamalabari and Dekhinpat.

Sleeping and eating *Circuit House* (Rs 100), contact SDO, Majuli, T74424, ahead but often booked. At Garmur, the main town, *Woodlands*, 8 rooms, reservations T74439. At Kamalabari: *Uttar Kamalabari Satra*, very basic, bring own bedding and leave a donation, usually booked through *Wild Grass* but you may try to reserve on T73392, ask to call Dulal Saikia (the head priest) to the phone, then ring back after 10 mins. At Nauten Kamalabari (8 km from Garmur), *Guest House*, spartan, no hot water (Rs 30). Food is available at simple eating houses. Carry drinking water.

Transport Buses from Jorhat (at junction of MG and AT Roads) to Neemati (13 km north); allow 1 hr. Government ferry from Neemati, 1000, 1600, return 1330 (confirm timings); crossing time varies seasonally as boats have to circumnavigate sand bars. Buses run from the ghat to Kamalabari (about 5 km) and Garmur (8.5 km). You can also arrange private boats at the jetty for transporting a car.

The sanctuary at **Bhalowguri** (16 km) was designated in 1998. Contact Forest Range Officer at Mariani. Bus from the top of MG Road, Jorhat, go via **Mariani** (18 km southeast).

Hollong Park Gibbon Sanctuary

Sibsagar

District headquarters of the largest tea and oil producing area in the Northeast, Sibsagar was the Ahom capital for two centuries, preceded by Gargaon and Rangpur. There are several royal tanks. Daupadi (the Ahom King's wife) built the huge tank here in 1734. On the east bank there is birdwatching tower and a library. The tower of the Siva Dol on its bank is one of the tallest Siva temples in India. *Sivaratri* is celebrated in March.

Phone code: 03772
Colour map 4, grid B4

The **Joysagar** at **Rangpur**, 5 km away, and the three temples on its bank date from 1697. **Talatal Ghar** (6 km), the seven-storeyed palace with three underground floors, was built between 1696-1714. Two underground tunnels are said to have connected the palace with the Dikhow River, at the 16th century Ahom capital at Gargaon, 15 km away. The East India Company is held responsible for their disappearance! ■ *Getting there: local bus from BG Road Bali Ghat, Rs 5, 20 minutes; then cycle-rickshaw Rs 10.*

Excursions

Charaideo (28 km east) became the first capital in 1253 of the Ahom kings, who ruled for 600 years, while their last capital was Jorhat before the British took over power. Vast hemispherical, royal burial mounds, *maidams* have been found here. These are earth covered funeral chambers where the embalmed bodies of the king were laid to rest with attendants who were sometimes buried alive in a custom discontinued in the 18th century.

E *Siddhartha*, BG Rd, T223276, F20430. 29 rooms, restaurant, bar, modern. **Sleeping**
E-F *Brahmaputra*, BG Rd, T22000. 48 rooms, restaurant, helpful, clean.

Assam, Meghalaya & Arunachal Pradesh

Recommended. Assam Tourism **F** *Tourist Lodge*, near Siva Dol, T22394. 6 rooms (often full), very helpful Tourist Office.

Transport Nearest airport: Jorhat (60 km). Nearest railway station: Simaluguri (20 km). Regular buses to Guwahati, Kaziranga, Simaluguri.

Directory *Trishuli Travels*, Hospital Rd near State Bus Stand. *GPO* near Siva Dol.

Digboi
Phone code: 03751

The oil fields of upper Assam were first exploited in 1879, the first wells came on stream here in 1892 and a refinery opened in 1900. Although Digboi's own resources are drying up, the region has considerable potential though the industry has been severely disrupted by political troubles. To visit, contact OIL, T3451. The surrounding forest is also a haven for birdlife. You may visit at your own risk with permission of OIL. There is an 18-hole golf course and a British Second World War cemetery nearby. **Sleeping** For those wishing to visit Arunachal for Miao, Deban Valley, Namdapha Forest Reserve, where facilities are limited. **C-D** *Guest House*, Indian Oil Corporation (IOC), 22 large, spacious rooms with hot water (Rs 900, Rs 650 single), TV, excellent location overlooking forest. Reservations, Mr SR Koneru, Chief Admin Manager, T64715, F64470.

Dibrugarh
Phone code: 0373
Colour map 4, grid B4

Much of the old town of Dibrugarh was destroyed during the 1950 earthquake. The new town on the Brahmaputra is surrounded by tea estates.

Sleeping D *Natraj*, H Singhania Rd, Main Bazar, T31375, 500 m from rly. 27 rooms, some a/c (Rs 400-610), restaurant, bar, visits to tea gardens. **D-E** *East End*, New Market, T220098, F22300. 30 rooms, some a/c (Rs 250-600) restaurant (Indian, Chinese). **D-E** *Goswami*, few doors from *Mona Lisa*, T21250. 12 rooms, some a/c (Rs 350-650) pricey, dining hall, Green Valley Tours office and bus pick-up. **D-E** *Mona Lisa*, Mancotta Rd, Chowkidinghee, T21416. 19 rooms, some very large, best in new wing (Rs 300-450; a/c Rs 650-750), good restaurant, bar. **F** *Paying guest* accommodation in an Assamese home, Rs 150-200 including breakfast, contact Binoy Dowerah (son Rajan, a *Wild Grass* guide) T22289. Travel information. Recommended.

Eating Mid-range *Mona Lisa* and *Garden Treat*, below flyover. Both recommended.

Transport Air The airport is 16 km from town. **Indian Airlines**, T20114, Airport, T82525, to **Kolkata**, Mon, Wed, Fri, Sun. **Sahara**, T31216. Delhi via **Guwahati**, Tue, Thu, Sat, Sun. **Train** To Guwahati: *BP Mail*, *4055*, 1930; New Delhi Link *Rajdhani Exp*, *2423* Thu (AC/II), 1530 (from New Delhi,Sun, 1700); *Kamrup Exp*, *5660* (AC/II), 1330, 16½ hrs, continues to NJP and Kolkata (H). Local *BG Pass* to Ledo (via Tinsukia), 0700, 1600 (not Sat). **Road Bus**: Private stand on AT Rd. *Green Valley* bus to Guwahati (Rs 175), Kaziranga (Rs 130) pick up from Goswami Guest House at 0715.

Tinsukia
Phone code: 0374

Tinsukia, a major transport junction in the Northeast, is convenient for visiting the nearby Dibru-Saikhowa National Park and the small Borajan Reserve Forest.

Sleeping and eating In **D-E** *Highway*, AT Rd, T336383, F335455, 500 m from New Tinsukia station. 20 rooms, some a/c, veg restaurant, modern. Recommended. *Jyoti*, Rangagora Rd, T333245, F332608. 20 rather grubby rooms, some a/c (Rs 275-500), hot water, restaurant. **F** *President* Station Rd, T20789. 32 rooms, vegetarian restaurant, TV, basic, noisy. *New Leaf* at *Hotel Highway*. Cheap vegetarian restaurant. Best in town. *Cakes & Bakes*, opposite Hotel Jyoti. Burgers, pizzas and excellent cakes, good value.

Transport Train: The 2 stations are 3 km apart: **Junction** (being run down, has **F** *Retiring Rooms* and very basic vegetarian refreshments. **New Tinsukia** has most of the long distance trains. **Buses** ASTC stand on AT Rd; private buses from top end of Rangagora Rd. To Jorhat Rs 75.

Directory Communications *Sygma Systems*, near Railway Overbridge, AT Rd. **Travel agent** *Classic Travels* AT Rd, T786125. A **Wildlife** Information Centre is planned on Rangagora Rd.

Borajan Reserve Forest, 5 km away, is a small (4.5 sq km) patch of forest which is home to five species of primate (Hoolock gibbon, capped langur, slow loris, stump tailed macaque and common macaque) but are not easy to spot. Best to visit by car (see Mr Eunush Ali below). | **Around Tinsukia**

A national park since March 1999, on the southern flood plain of the Brahmaputra near Tinsukia, this is largely a semi-wet evergreen forest. Best: November-March. Temperature range: 6°C-36°C. Average annual rainfall: 2,300-3,600 mm. | **Dibru-Saikhowa National Park**

Approach Entry points: **Guijan** on the southern boundary and **Dhola** (near Saikhowa Ghat) at the northern edge, both accessible by bus from Tinsukia. From Guijan, a boat across the river takes you to the Range Office at the park entrance. If you cross from Dhola, the Range Office is 5 km into the park at Narbarmora; it is better to notify your arrival beforehand. See Kaziranga above for usual park fees.

Wildlife The 340 sq km core area within a large bio-sphere reserve is a refuge for some endangered species (tiger, leopard, leopard cat, clouded leopard, elephant et cetera). The rich birdlife includes the very rare white-winged wood duck.

Sleeping The Forest Department has one double bedded room at Guijan, carry provisions. Contact DFO, Rangagora Rd, Tinsukia, T331472 (T333082 home).

Information The retired DFO, Mr Eunush Ali, knowledgeable about wildlife and the Northeast, assists tourists, T333079.

Margherita, on the Margherita is on Dihing River at the foot of the Patkoi Range, and was named by Italian railway engineers in the late 19th century after the Queen of Italy. The town is surrounded by tea estates and is the Northeast headquarters of Coal India Ltd. The last of the steam railway engines in Assam, is still operating. | **Margherita** *Colour map 4, grid B5*

The small coal mining town of Ledo, 6 km northwest of Margherita, was the headquarters of Northern Combat Area Command during the Second World War and is the start of the 470 km Stilwell Road. | **Ledo** *Colour map 4, grid B5*

Named after Gen Joseph Stilwell, the road was the most ambitious and costliest engineering project of the war (US$137,000,000 at the time). Once a two lane, all-weather bitumen highway linking Ledo with Myitkyina in North Burma through the Pangso Pass and with Kunming in China (1,029 miles) it is now closed beyond Nampong in Arunachal Pradesh. A sign, 6 km west of Ledo, commemorates the Road to Mandalay but there is little else that remains of the massive Allied presence here.

In the remote southeastern corner of Assam, the area around the Barak Valley, accessible from Silchar, offers trekking opportunities virtually unknown to the foreigner. A hilltop Siva temple with wonderful views is only a four-hour trek from the foothills. Contact Mr SR Ray, Explorer Club, Shyama Prasad Road, Shillongpatty, T32691. | **Silchar** *Phone code: 03842* *Colour map 4, grid C3*

Transport Air *Indian Airlines*, T20072, flies to Kolkata.

Assam, Meghalaya & Arunachal Pradesh

Meghalaya

Entry permits, see page 317
Population: 2.4 mn
Area: 22,500 sq km

Meghalaya, the 'abode of the clouds', with its pine clad hills, beautiful lakes, high waterfalls, and huge caverns, has been called 'the Scotland of the East' because of the similarity of climate, terrain and scenery. The wettest region in the world, between May and September the rain comes down like waterfalls as the warm monsoon air is forced up over the hills. Home to the Garo, Khasi and Jaintia tribes, the hill state retains an untouched feel. There are traditional Khasi villages near Shillong with views into Bangladesh.

The land Much of the plateau is made up of the same ancient granites as are found in peninsular India; its south facing slope, overlooking Bangladesh, is very steep. The hills rise to heights just under 2,000 m which makes it pleasantly cool but it is also one of the wettest places on the earth (Mawsynram has received more than 20 m of rainfall in one year). Much is still densely forested. Shillong is the only important town; 80% of the people live in villages. Compact and isolated, Meghalaya's rolling plateau lies in a severe **earthquake** belt. The entire town of Shillong was destroyed in an earthquake in 1897.

History The Khasi, Jaintia and Garo tribes each had their own small kingdoms until the 19th century when the British annexed them. The Garos, originally from Tibet, were animists. The Khasis are believed to be Austro-Asiatic. Jaintias are Mongolian and similar to the Shans of Burma. They believed in the universal presence of god and so built no temples. The dead were commemorated by erecting **monoliths** and groups of these can be seen in Khasi villages in central Meghalaya between Shillong and Cherrapunji. In the 19th century many Jaintias were converted to Christianity by missionaries, although they continued many of their old traditions.

People Meghalaya is divided into three distinct areas, the Garo, Khasi and Jaintia Hills, each with its own language, culture and particular customs. All three tribes are matrilineal, passing down wealth and property through the female line, with the youngest daughter taking the responsibility of caring for the parents. Most young people here learn English at school and are very welcoming and friendly.

Festivals **Shillong April**: *Shad Suk Mynsiem*, two-day folk-dance festival of thanksgiving; **June-July**: *Behdeinkhlam*, Khasi *Shed Nongkrem* dance festival at **Smit**; **October-November**: five-day *Nongkrem Dances* for harvest and *Autumn Festival*; **November**: *Wangala* Garo '100 Drums festival' at **Asanangre** near Tura during harvest, and *Laho* dances at **Jowai**.

Government The hill-state was created on 21 January 1972. Since 1980 the Congress Party has dominated Lok Sabha elections, but it has never won more than 25 of the 60 State Assembly seats. The Hill Peoples Union, though a minority, has claimed the largest number of seats, but once again the Congress won both Lok Sabha seats in the 1998 elections. The present Chief Minister, EK Mawlong, has been campaiging for greater foreign and domestic private investment in the state to relieve the chronic unemployment and reduce the threat of militant opposition.

★ Shillong

Shillong, among pine clad hills and lakes, retains a measure of its colonial past especially around the Ward Lake. Unattractive newer buildings have encroached open spaces and an air of decay has set in.

Phone code: 0364
Colour map 4, grid C2
Population: 222,000
Altitude: 1,496 m

Getting there Helicopters take just 25 mins to fly in from Guwahati. However, most people travel in to the central Police Bazar by bus. **Getting around** Shillong is quite spread out though the centre is fairly compact. The steep hills make rickshaws unsuitable but it is easy to find taxis and the city buses are relatively cheap and efficient. Due to simmering ethnic tension it is unsafe to walk around in unfamiliar parts of town after dark, although it is all right to travel by car. **Climate** Summer maximum 23°C, minimum 15°C; Winter maximum 16°C, minimum 4°C; Annual rainfall 2,030mm, mostly Jun-Sep. Best season Oct-May. Clothing: Rainwear essential. Summer: cottons, light woollens. Winter: woollens.

Ins & outs

The horse-shoe shaped **Ward Lake** set in a landscaped botanical garden and popular for boating is near Raj Bhavan, a two-minute walk from Police Bazar. The **Botanical Garden** is behind it. ■ *0900-1700.* The **Butterfly Museum** with a large collection is in a private house between Police Bazar and Wahingdoh, where butterflies are bred for conservation and sale. ■ *1000-1600.* The **golf course**, amidst pines is ideal for an early morning walk. *Tee & Putt* provides good freshly brewed coffee. **Bara Bazar** is well worth a visit to see authentic local colour. It attracts tribal people, mainly women, who come to buy and sell produce – vegetables, spices, pots, baskets, chickens and even bows and arrows. Small stalls sell real Khasi food. Just over a kilometre away is **Lady Hydari Park**, designed like a Japanese garden where you will see the pine native to the area – *Pinus khasiana*. It is well laid out with its **Forest Museum** and Mini Zoo. ■ *0830-1630; Rs 2; cameras: still Rs 10. Video/movie Rs 1,000.* The nearby **Crinoline Waterfalls** has a swimming pool surrounded by orchids, potted bonsais and a rock pool with reeds and water lilies. At Lumparing, Laban, the Buddhist **Lamasery** near the Assam Club is interesting but be prepared for a steep climb.

Sights

Shillong Peak (10 km, 1,960 m) Three kilometres from the Cherrapunji road, Shillong Peak commands spectacular views, **Laitkor Peak** on the same

Meghalaya

ridge, 3 km from the Shillong-Jowai Road is under Air Force control; visitors have to report at the barrier. Buses drop you at the appropriate junction. **Elephant Falls** (12 km), off the Cherrapunji road, is a scenic spot with two high falls. You can walk down to the lowest pool and get a good view, though the falls themselves are less impressive between November and May. The attractive **Umiam Lake** (Barapani), 16 km, offers fishing and boating. **D** *Orchid Lake Resort*, T64258, 18 rooms (Rs 575).

Museums **State Museum**, Lachumiere, has ethnographic and archaeological objects. ■ *1000-1600, Mon-Sat, except 2nd and 4th Sat and holidays. Guides, occasional films. No photography.* **Rhino Memorial Museum**, Hospital Road, in a striking building, has a good tribal collection with a bizarre mix of military paraphernalia! **Tribal Research Institute**, Mawlai, has indigenous exhibits of the tribal people. ■ *1000-1600, Mon-Sat.* **Zonal Anthropological Museum**, Lachumiere, T3459. ■ *1000-1630, Mon-Sat, except second Sat.*

Tours **Meghalaya Tourism**, T226220, departs from MTDC, Jail Road: **Local sightseeing** (a few minutes at most sights, 2½ hours at Umiam Lake). 0830-1530. Rs 75. **Cherrapunji**, **Nohkalikai Falls**, **Mawsmai cave** (torch essential!) and **Falls**: 0800-1600 (15-20 minutes at each place). Rs 95. Recommended.

Excursions **Mawsynram** (55 km) The **Mawjymbuin Cave** has water dripping from a breast-shaped stone onto what looks like a Siva lingam. The rainfall record has beaten that of Cherrapunji, with over 20 m in one year. ■ *Getting there: from Shillong bus at 1400, 3 hrs, Rs 15.* **Jakrem** (64 km) has hot springs. ■ *Getting there: bus at 1400, 3 hrs, Rs 14.*

Shillong

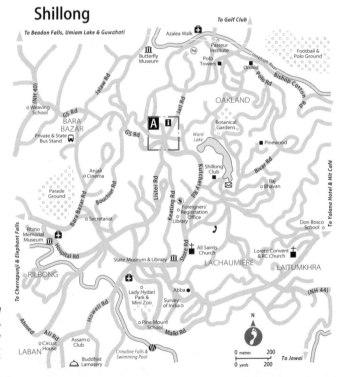

Related map A Shillong centre, page 336

The Archery Stakes

The Archery Stakes, unique to Shillong, take place every day except Sunday. Members of different clubs shoot 1,500 arrows at a cylindrical bamboo target for four minutes. The punters count the number that stick and anyone who has guessed the last two digits of the number of arrows that stick is rewarded with an 80:1 win. A second shoot takes place an hour later when the odds are 6:1 but if you correctly forecast both results the odds are as high as 4,500:1. Naturally, the bookies are the best-dressed men in town!

Start times of the event vary so ask locally in the morning, and to find the exact field, go to the Polo Ground and mime! There are bookies' shops all over town and elsewhere in the state; bets are even placed as far off as Kolkata and Mumbai! The Stakes were legalized only in 1983 when the state government realized that it could raise a hefty 40% tax on the daily money spinner. The central government is planning to ban state government lotteries.

Essentials

B-C *Polo Towers*, Polo Grounds, Oakland Rd, T222341, F220090. 50 well-appointed rooms, exchange (cash), excellent packages (meals, sightseeing etc) on advance booking, modern and efficient. **C** *Centre Point*, GS Rd, Police Bazar, T225239, F225239. 24 comfortable modern rooms with views, good restaurant (Indian, Chinese). **C** *Pinewood* (Meghalaya Tourism), near Raj Bhavan, T223116, F224176. 40 old-fashioned rooms (all crying out for a coat of paint), a Raj relic, best in nostalgic old bungalow, spacious grounds, good restaurants, bar, exchange (cash), golf. **C-D** *Alpine Continental*, Thana-Quinton Rd, T220991, F220996, alpineshillong@hotmail.com 41 comfortable rooms and suites, hot water (0730-1030), Rs 690-825, reasonable restaurant, small cosy bar, exchange (cash, TCs'), proud of its terrace garden, prompt room service, friendly and helpful, good discounts off-season. **D** *Shillong Club*, Kutchery Rd, T226938. 18 rooms (Rs 450-650), 'colonial' club, Indian restaurant, bar, tennis, billiards.

E *Orchid* (Meghalaya Tourism), Polo Rd, T224933, F224176. 34 rooms getting run-down (from Rs 250), best on top floor, restaurant, bar. **E** *Yalana*, Main Rd, Laitumkrah (near Don Bosco), T211240. 17 rooms (Rs 225-325) in new comfortable hotel, restaurant, good room service, very friendly. Recommended. **F** *Youth Hostel*, opposite Tel Exchange, T221246. Rooms and dorm (Rs 30). In *Police Bazar*: **E** *Embassy*, Market Complex, AC Lane, T223164, F223290. 20 rooms, 24 hr hot water (Rs 260-400), TV, restaurant (poor service). **E** *Monsoon*, GS Rd, T223316, F221840. 25 rooms with bath, hot water (Rs 250-400), Indian meals. **E** *Pine Borough*, T220698. 20 rooms with bath (Rs 330), restaurant, bar. **F** *Baba Tourist Lodge*, GS Rd, T211285. 27 rooms, restaurant, basic, friendly, clean.

You can try a local pork dish, *dohkhleh* (minced brains with onion and spices) with *jadoh* (rice flavoured with turmeric or pig's blood!) and *saag* (greens) with spicy *tung tap* (hot chutney made with dried fish) at small restaurants in Bara Bazar and a stall behind *Centre Point*. For variety try hotels *Centre Point* or *Pinewood*. **Mid-range**: *Abba* Malki Point and GS Rd. Delicious Chinese, closed Sun. *Ambrosia*, Red Hill Rd. Continental. Fast food and pastry shop. *Eecee* near Bus Stand, Police Bazar. Western. Good restaurant and delicious cakes, and *Bakery* opposite, with pizzas and fast food. Both recommended. **Cheap**: *Hits*, by Nazareth Hospital, Laitumkhra. International. Excellent for breakfast and lunch, delicious chocolate cake, run by four friendly sisters (who also offer cheap rooms to women travellers).

Sleeping
■ *on map, pages 334 & 336*

GS Rd is now U Tirot Sing Rd; Jail Rd is Pa Togan Sangma Rd; Jowai Rd is Rev Nichols Roy Rd; Kutchery Road is Mahatma Gandhi (MG) Road. Despite the change, old names continue to be used

Eating

Assam, Meghalaya & Arunachal Pradesh

New World, GS Rd. Good Chinese. *Regal*, Police Bazar. Serves South Indian. Hotel *Yalana* is recommended for Indian/Chinese. Better **bars** at *Pinewood*, *Polo Towers* and *Shillong Club* for more atmosphere. *Kiad* the local rice wine, is popular in roadside bars.

Entertainment **Golf**: 19-hole course at the Golf Club; clubs for hire; the wettest, and also one of the most beautiful 'natural' courses in the world. **Swimming**: Club near Crinoline Waterfalls, 0600-1630 (ladies 1100-1200, 1400-1500). **Watersports**: Umiam Lake (16 km) for water-skiing, boating and fishing.

Shopping You can get handwoven shawls, canework, Khasi jewellery, handicrafts, orange flower honey. The Khasi women's costume (*jainsem*) can be worn as a Western dress. Emporia: on Jail Rd, Police Bazar: *Meghalaya Handicrafts*, *Purbashree*, *Khadi Gramodyog* and *Manipur Emporium*. *Assam Govt Sales Emporium*, GS Rd. *Assam Co-op Silk House*, Bara Bazar. In Bara Bazar, tribal women sell attractive Khasi silver, gold and amber jewellery. **Books** *Modern Book Depot*, Police Bazar near *Monsoon*. One opposite is bigger and better! **Photography** *Jai Studio* Keating Rd. For films, photo-postcards.

Tour operators *Blue Hill Travels*, Police Bazar. Very helpful. *Cultural Pursuits*, Mawlai, Nongpdeng, T229016, F227282. Organize 'eco-adventure' tours of Assam, Meghalaya, and promise an unusual adventure. *Jais*, YMCA, IGP Point, T222777, F224654. *Meghalaya Adventures*, Hotel Centre Point T225210 (office T224465). Offers cave tours. Visitors may contact *Patricia Mukkim* a local teacher-cum-journalist, T230593, patria@technologist.com She is well informed about local culture, history etc.

Transport **Local** Metered, yellow-top **taxis** cruise the town picking up passengers to share rides. Flag one down and hop in if he is going your way; short hops, eg Police Bazar to Laitumkhrah, Rs 5. MTDC taxis at *Pinewood Ashok* or the Tourist Office. Sightseeing, Rs 1,200 (8 hrs, 100 km).

Air Helicopter: Meghalaya Transport Corporation, T223200. Flies from Guwahati (Mon-Sat) and Tura. Tickets from MTC Bus Stand, Jail Rd. Transport to **Guwahati airport** (127 km): taxi, Rs 850 (4 hrs), nearly double for dep after 1100, or hourly bus, Rs 40. **Road Bus**: Meghalaya STC, T223200. Bus stand on Jail Rd. To Guwahati, frequent, 0600-1700, 3½ hrs, Rs 35-45 (no reservations); Rs 30; Silchar, 2100, 11½ hrs, Rs 90-150. Also from stand near Anjali Cinema, Bara Bazar to towns in Meghalaya. Private bus companies have offices/booths around Police Bazar for long-distance connections in the Northeast, eg *Blue Hill*. Tourist **Taxi** Association, Police Bazar, share taxi to Guwahati, Rs 125, 3 hrs. **Train**: Guwahati (103 km) the nearest railhead. Tickets from MTC Bus Stand, T223200. 0600-1100, 1300-1600.

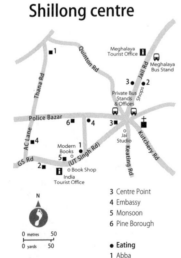

Shillong centre

3 Centre Point
4 Embassy
5 Monsoon
6 Pine Borough

● **Eating**
1 Abba
2 Bakery
3 Eecee
4 Jadoh Stall

■ **Sleeping**
1 Alpine Continental
2 Baba Tourist Lodge

Related map
Shillong, page 334

Assam, Meghalaya & Arunachal Pradesh

Airlines *Jet Airways*, Rap's Mansion, Kutchery Rd. *Sheba Travels*, Police Bazar, T227222. Indian Airlines agent, and airport coach. **Banks** *State Bank of India*, Kutchery Rd, 1st Floor. Mon-Fri 1130-1400. *Indian Overseas Bank*, GS Rd (Police Bazar end). Both change currency and TCs. **Communications** GPO: GS Rd, Police Bazar. **Internet:** *Patria*, Nohgrimbah Rd, near Police Station, Laitumkrah, T223532. Rs 150 per hr. **Medical services** *Civil Hospital*, GS Rd, T226381. *Nazareth Hospital*, Laitumukhrah, T224052. *Woodland Nursing Home*, Dhankheti Police Point. *G Das Hospital* (women and children), near Polo Bazar. **Ambulance**, T224100. **Chemists** in Police Bazar. **Tourist offices** *India*, GS Rd, Police Bazar, T225632. 1000-1700, free Shillong map. *Meghalaya*, opposite Meghalaya Bus Stand, Jail Rd, T226220. *Directorate of Tourism*, Nokrek Building, 3rd Meghalaya Secretariat, Lower Lachaumiere, T226054, tourism@meghalaya.ren.nic.in 0700-1800. Very helpful. MTDC, *Orchid Hotel*, T224933, F224176, mtdc@meghalaya.ren.nic.in 1030-1630. **Useful addresses** *Foreigners' Registration Office*, Lachumiere near State Museum. *Under Secretary Home* (passports), T224201, ext 2308. Can grant visa extensions.

Directory

Around Shillong

The old administrative headquarters of the Khasis, picturesque Cherrapunji is a pleasant, quiet town spread out along a ridge with gravestones dotting the surrounding hillocks. Best time to visit for spectacular views is October-January, the drier months. The heat and humidity can be oppressive much of the year. By March it is hazy most days and the odd torrential shower is not unusual. It once held the record as the wettest place on earth with a rainfall record of 23,000 mm, but nearby Mawsynram has surpassed this. On average it still gets 11,500 mm annually.

Cherrapunji
Phone code: 03637
Colour map 4, grid C2
Area: 56 sq km
Altitude: 1,300 m

The colourful weekly **Ka Iewbah Sohrarim market** is held every eight days. The local orange flower honey is sold from a house (clearly signed) just below Cherra Bazar (about 100 m on the road; avoid plastic bottles). Surprisingly, a variety of banana here actually contains seeds.

Excursions Nohkalikai Falls, reputedly the world's fourth highest, is 5 km away, near Sohrarim. A vendor sells good orange flower honey. *Montana Tourism*, Cherra Bazar, arranges group tours (US$10). Limestone **caves** nearby include Krem Mawmluh (4,503 m) with a five river passage and Krem Phyllut (1,003 m) at **Mawsmai**, with a large fossil passage and two stream ways. Mawsmai also has high waterfalls in the wet season. The UFO-like *Orchid Restaurant*, opposite the falls, serves good food.

Sleeping and eating Only an **F** PWD *Guest House*, contact Sub-Divisional Officer, T22236, or Deputy Commissioner, East Khasi Hills, Shillong. Cherra Bazar has a few basic eateries.

Transport Local Taxi: from Cherra Bazar for Nohkalikai Falls, Krem Mawmluh and a view over the plains of Bangladesh (on a clear day), Rs 250-300 with bargaining; also share taxis to both. *Meghalaya Tourism*, Shillong, runs **tours** which visits several sights nearby. **Long distance Bus:** from Shillong, to Cherrapunji, Rs 13, ½ hr; Mawmluh, Rs 18, 2 hrs.

The place has caught the peoples' imagination as possibly claiming the distinction of being the second largest river island in Asia (after Majuli). For the intrepid only, since it may involve a 15 km hike uphill from **Nongstoin** (two to three hours by bus, west of Shillong), though some estimate the approach to be a 1½ hour walk!

Nongkhrum

Sixty five kilometres southeast of Shillong, Nartiang was the summer capital of the Jaintia Kings. Behind the village, a field contains giant monoliths, some 8 m high. It is a serene, surreal site. The Durga temple was originally 500 years ago

Nartiang

Assam, Meghalaya & Arunachal Pradesh

but the new orange structure has nothing to recommend it. *Getting there:* it is 8 km off the NH44 towards Jowai and takes 2½ hours. A taxi is essential. Ask for a driver who speaks the language.

Jowai Jowai, 64 km southeast of Shillong on NH44, is the headquarters of the **Jaintia Hills**, circled by the Myntdu River. The market, full of tribal women, is particularly colourful. ■ *Getting there: From Shillong: cars take 2½ hrs, buses a little longer.*

Excursions Krem Sweep (Syndai), 40 km further south, Syndai has many caves used by ancient warriors as hide-outs including 'Krem Sweep' which has a vast chamber. India's longest (6,381 m) and deepest (106.8 m) Eocene Age cave with several cataracts and waterfalls is Krem **Um-Lawan**, 60 km southeast of Jowai near **Lumshnong**.

Tura The headquarters of the **West Garo Hills** District, **Tura** sits at the foot of the
Phone code: 03651 jungle clad 1,457 m Nokrek Peak. It is a spread-out town with a slow pace of
Colour map 4, grid C1 life. Tura Bazar is dominated by the new supermarket, a three-storey
220 km SW of Guwahati red-and-white, mini shopping mall and underground car park. The small fruit
Altitude: 657 m and vegetable market in the basement is well organized. A Museum-cum-Cultural Complex is planned 200 m west of Orchid Lodge. Weekly tribal markets are held in surrounding villages.

Nokrek Peak can be reached by a 5 km trek, but involves rock climbing, so is best not attempted alone. **Nokrek National Park** is 55 km away. Ask the tourist office for a guide. ■ *Jeeps from Tura Bazar: Rs 1,150-1,500 for the round trip (daily rate).* **Naphak Lake**, 112 km, near the Simsang River is good for fishing and bird watching.

Sleeping and eating E *Orchid Lodge* (MTDC), New Tura (4 km from Tura Bazar), city bus to Dakopgre stops outside (Rs 3), or auto-rickshaw (Rs 40; Rs 60 at night.), T22568. 7 rooms (Rs 300), dorm (Rs 56), TV (variable reception despite a giant satellite dish), dining hall meals at set times, Tourist Office (tours of Siju, Balpakram). Basic **F** *Lodges* in Tura Bazar. **Cheap**: Simple places in Tura Bazar include *Santi Hotel*, Rikman Shopping Point. Popular for *thali* lunches.

Transport Helicopter services to/from Shillong and Guwahati. **Local bus**: To **Baghmara** 106 km (for Siju, none direct), 1300, 4-5 hrs, along the Bangladesh border, Rs 36. Buy a ticket a day ahead from the booth near the MTC Bus Stand, Tura Bazar; to avoid a rugby scrum, ask your hotel to buy your ticket for a small fee. Private buses to Guwahati (8 hrs, Rs 100), Shillong (12 hrs, night bus arrives at 0400, Rs 250) Siliguri from Tura Bazar. Booking offices are easy to find.

Siju Southeast of Tura just below the town, with others nearby, is one of India's
Colour map 4, grid C1 longest caves (4.8 km) with a fine river passage. Groups of at least four are needed for going caving so look out on noticeboards. It is more enjoyable and cheaper to travel this way.

Balpakram National Park, between Baghmara and Siju, is 167 km from Tura. The small park on the Meghalaya-Bangladesh border is noted for its wide variety of animals including red panda, wild elephants and tigers. The spectacular Balpakram plateau surrounded by steep cliffs is sacred to both Garos and Khasis.

Sleeping *Tourist Lodge* (MTDC), Siju, take own provisions, chowkidar will cook for you. Another at Baghmara.

Transport Bus: Baghmara, 45 km, 1½ hrs; from there to Tura, leaves at 0900.

Arunachal Pradesh

This is Northeast India's largest and remotest state. The Tawang Monastery, Population: 1.2 mn
birthplace of the sixth Dalai Lama and home to countless Buddhist treasures, is a Area: 84,000 sq km
major attraction, along with the state's rich tribal heritage and its wonderful vari-
ety of orchids.

On the Northeast frontier of India, Arunachal Pradesh stretches from the foot- **The land**
hills of the eastern Himalayas to their peaks. The Brahmaputra, known here as
the Siang River, enters the state from China and flows through a deeply cut valley. Stretching from the snow capped mountains of the Himalaya to the steamy
plains of the Brahmaputra valley, there is an extraordinary range of forests
from the Alpine to the subtropical – from rhododendrons to orchids, reeds
and bamboo. It is an orchid lover's paradise with over 550 species identified.
The wildlife includes elephants, clouded leopard, snow leopard, tiger, sloth
bear, Himalayan black bear, red panda and musk deer. The Namdapha
National Park is near Miao.

The entire region had remained isolated since 1873 when the British stopped **History**
free movement. After 1947 Arunachal became part of the North East Frontier
Agency (NEFA). Its strategic significance was demonstrated by the Chinese
invasion in 1962, and the Indian government subsequently broke up the
Agency giving statehood to all the territories surrounding Assam. Having long
borders with China and Myanmar, Arunachal is a truly Frontier state. The
state was opened to tourists in 1995 with the first foreigners being given permission to trek only as recently as 1998.

The Arunachali **people** are the state's greatest attraction. In the capital **Culture**
Itanagar you may even see Nishi warriors wearing their hornbill caps, carrying
bearskin bags and their knives in monkey-skin scabbards.
   A great diversity of the tribal people speak over 60 different dialects. Most
have an oral tradition of recording their historic and cultural past by memoriz-
ing verses handed down through generations. Some Buddhist tribes have,
however, maintained written records, largely recording their religious history.

★ Itanagar – Naharlagun

Itanagar, the capital and Naharlagun, 10 km away, together provide the capital's Phone code: 0360
administrative offices. Itanagar, sited between two hills, has the Governor's Resi- Colour map 4, grid B3
dence on one and a new Buddhist temple on the other, with shops, bazar, tradi- Population: 17,300
tional huts and more recent earthquake-proof wooden-framed buildings in Altitude: 750 m
between. The capital has been identified as Mayapur, the 11th century capital of
the Jiti Dynasty.

Getting there Visitors arriving at Lilabari or North Lakhimpur in Assam take 2 hrs by **Ins & outs**
bus (or a little less by taxi) to Itanagar, calling at Naharalagun Bus Station before
climbing up along a scenic road to the new capital. There are regular buses from

Assam, Meghalaya & Arunachal Pradesh

Permission to enter

Permits may be given by the Resident Commissioner, Govt of Arunachal Pradesh, Nyaya Marg, Delhi, T3013956 or Liaison Officer, Roxi Cinema, JL Nehru Road, Kolkata, or Arunachal State Government (ask Wild Grass, Guwahati). Foreigners must book a group tour through an approved Indian travel agent.

Independent travel is not encouraged. Itanagar, Ziro, Along, Pasighat, Miao, Namdapha, Tipi and Bhalukpong are open to tourists. The daily tariff requirement is US$150 ($50 to the state government and $100 to cover the costs of the travel agent). See page 317.

Guwahati and Shillong. **Getting around** Frequent buses run between Itanagar and Naharalagun from 0600-2000. Cycle-rickshaws are only available in Naharlagun. **Climate**: Rainfall: 2,660 mm. Best season: Oct-Mar.

Sights The yellow-roofed **Buddhist Temple** stands in well-kept gardens on a hilltop with good views. The **Gyaker Sinyi** (Ganga Sekhi Lake), 6 km, is reached by a rough road through forests of bamboo and tree ferns. On reaching the foot of the hill, walk across a bamboo bridge, up steps cut on the hillside to reach a ridge overlooking the forest lake. The brick fort (14th-15th century) is believed to have been built by King Ramachandra. In Naharlagun, the **Polo Park** is on top of a ridge with interesting botanical specimens including the cane thicket, which looks like palm, as well as a small zoo.

Museum **Jawaharlal Nehru Museum** Good coverage of tribal people – collection of art, wood carvings, musical instruments and religious objects. First floor has archaeological finds from Malinthan, Itafort, Noksaparbat and others, textiles, ornaments and weapons. ■ *Daily, except Mon.* There are district museums in Along, Bomdila, Pasighat, Tezu and Ziro holding collections of art and crafts. ■ *1000-1700. Photography is prohibited.*

Essentials

Sleeping & eating Reserve at least a month in advance. **In Itanagar B** *Donyi-Polo Ashok*, Sector C, T212626, F212611. 20 rooms, 2 a/c suites, restaurant. **D** *Arun Subansiri*, T212806. 30 rooms, restaurant. **E** *Bomdila*, T212664. **In Naharlagun E** *Hornbill*, T44419. 14 rooms, some deluxe. **F** *Lakshmi*, 19 rooms (1st Flr better). **F** *Youth Hostel*, 60 beds.

Shopping The cotton textiles are colourful and are beautifully patterned. You can also get wooden masks and figures, cane belts and caps. *Handicrafts Centres* have shawls, *thangkas*, handloom, wood carvings, cane and bamboo work and carpets; you can watch tribal craftsmen trimming, cutting and weaving cane.

Tour operators *Arunachal Travels*, Itanagar, agents for *Indian Airlines*. *Blue Hills*, Naharlagun.

Transport **Local Taxi**: Rs 350 plus fuel per day. Naharlagun/Itanagar Rs 150 plus fuel; Rs 20 (shared taxi). **Long distance Air**: Nearest airport is **Lilabari** in Assam, 57 km from Naharlagun, 67 km from Itanagar which has twice weekly flights from Guwahati. Transfer by bus. *Indian Airlines*; T22760. From Kolkata access is best through **Dibrugarh** (1½ hrs) by *Indian Airlines*, Mon, Wed, Fri, Sun. **Road Bus**: APST from Naharlagun Bus Station. **Guwahati**, 381 km, 8 hrs, Rs 80-100; **Shillong**, 481 km, Rs 110. **Ziro**, 6 hrs, **North Lakhimpur**; **Bomdila**, Mon, Thu, 12 hrs. *Blue Hills* overnight coach to Guwahati, 11½ hrs. Enquiries: T4221. **Train**: The nearest convenient railhead is North Lakhimpur in Assam, 50 km from Naharlagun and 60 km from Itanagar; Harmoti station is 23 km from Naharlagun. **Rly Out Agency** at Naharlagun bus station, T4209. Nearest railheads for the bigger towns: **Along**: Silapathar; **Tezu**: Tinsukia; **Namdapha**: Margherita.

Tourist office *India*, Sector 'C', Naharlagun, T4328. *Arunachal Pradesh*, Naharlagun. **Useful services** There are **banks** and **post offices** at Itanagar and Naharlagun. **Hospitals:** Itanagar, Naharlagun.

Directory

Bomdila and Tawang

To reach **Tawang** from Tezpur in Assam (the nearest airport), the road north crosses the border at **Bhalukpong** and continues towards Bomdila passing through low wooded slopes for about 60 km. On the bank of the Bhoreli River in the upper plains is **Tipi** (190 m), with the Orchid Research Centre and a glasshouse with 500 species of orchids. From there the road rises sharply to reach Bomdila. The journey, all the way, is spectacular, passing waterfalls, terraced paddy fields, alpine forests and mountain streams.

Route

Bomdila has marvellous views of the snowcapped mountains. It has a craft centre, apple orchards and Buddhist *gompas*. **Sleeping** in the **Upper Town** **C** *Siphiyang Phong*, opposite play ground, T22373. Decent rooms with hot showers. **E** *Tourist Lodge*, T22049. 8 rooms, hot showers. Nearby **E-F** *La* among a few new hotels. **Tour companies and travel agents** *Himalayan Holidays*, T22356, F22118, good information and treks in the region.

Bomdila
Phone code: 03782
Colour map 4, grid B2
Altitude: 2,530 m

Transport Buses from main bus stand, Lower Town, **Tezpur** and **Tarung**, 8 hrs. Private buses from Himalayan Holidays to **Tezpur**, 7 hrs.

For the next 180 km the route passes through the pretty Dirang Valley shrouded in pine woods, then climbs to the **Sela Pass** at 4,215 m which presents a far starker view. The successor to Lama Guru Rimpoche has been found in a village here. Stop a while here, along one of the highest motorable roads in the world. **Jaswantpur**, 4 km from the pass, has the *samadhi* to the brave Jawan (soldier) Jaswant Singh which commemorates how he, his fiancee and her friend valiantly held up the advancing Chinese army in 1971 for three days before laying down their lives. Drivers along this road (many of them ex-army personnel) stop to pay their respects at the poignant memorial. You see a high-altitude lake and the trout hatchery at Nuranang just below the pass before reaching Tawang.

Route

★ Tawang Monastery

Set in breathtakingly beautiful scenery at over 3,000 m, the monastery, one of the largest in India, is the birthplace of the sixth Dalai Lama. The second oldest Buddhist monastery in the world (after Lhasa), it houses over 500 *lamas* belonging to the Gelugpa (Reformed) Sect of Mahayana Buddhist monks. Buddhism arrived in the area with Padmasambhava in the eighth century but the local Monpas were converted to the Tantric Buddhist cult only after the establishment of the monastery here in the 17th century. During renovations, the main building was completely rebuilt. Treasures include a 5.5-metre high Buddha, numerous sculptures, *thangkas* and priceless manuscripts. Tawang also has the only Lady Lamasery (Buddhist Monastery for nuns) in Asia. The three-day annual festival is usually in early January. Prayers are held every

Phone code: 03794
Colour map 4, grid B1

Assam, Meghalaya & Arunachal Pradesh

morning and afternoon. A craft centre produces woollen carpets. **Sleeping D-E** *Tourist Lodge*, T22359. Twenty well furnished but poorly maintained rooms (Rs 200-700), contact Deputy Commissioner, T22221 (reservations T22222). Private lodges include: **D-E** *Paradise*, Old Bazar, T22063, 22307. Pleasant, clean, spacious rooms with bath, some deluxe (Rs 250-500), small dining room serving simple freshly cooked meals. The manager, Pushpa Wong Chu, also arranges jeep hire and takes guided tours. ■ *Getting there: regular buses from Bomdila. Cars take nearly 2 days from Guwahati (400 km) through rough terrain. Foreigners are advised to travel in a small group in a hired vehicle; from Tezpur, allow 12 hours. Check feasibility locally and don't travel after dark since visibility on the narrow mountain roads can be very poor at night.*

Excursions **The Lake District** Just above Tawang, beyond the monastery, is an exceptionally beautiful area with about 30 high altitude lakes. After a fork and an army outpost, the road continues towards **Klemta**, just a few kilometres from the Indian border. There are a few scattered monasteries and a shrine to all faiths at the spot where Guru Nanak rested as he trekked into Tibet, 500 years ago. ■ *Getting there: Hire a jeep and guide, carry snacks and drinks, and be prepared for steep, treacherous mountain roads but it is worth it for the breathtaking mountain scenery.* **Ptso**, 25 km from Tawang, has a small cabin by a lake.

Central Arunachal **Malinithan** Old granite images of Hindu deities were found in **Malinithan** in the foothills of West Siang District, while in Dibang Valley the ruins of **Bismaknagar Palace** date from the 12th century. Direct buses from Itanagar (185 km) and North Lakhimpur (109 km) to Malinithan. **Sleeping F** *Inspection Bungalow*, 4 rooms; contact Asst Comm, Likabali, West Siang.

Ziro

Phone code: 037892
Colour map 4, grid B3
150 km N of Itanagar
Altitude: 1,475 m

Ziro lies in a very picturesque level valley of the Apatani plateau, surrounded by pine-covered mountains. The **Apatani tribals** who live in small, densely populated villages, have evolved a sophisticated system of irrigated paddy cultivation. **Sleeping F** *Inspection Bungalow* and *Circuit House*, T30, 8 rooms. Reservations Dy Comm, Lower Subansiri Dist. ■ *Getting there: daily buses from Itanagar and Lilabari (100 km).*

Eastern Arunachal **Parasuram Kund** The lake via Eastern Arunachal, attracts thousands of pilgrims at Makar Sankranti (mid-January) who come to the Fair and take a holy bath. **Sleeping** Spartan Government *Tourist Lodge*; contact Dy Commissioner, Tezu, well in advance.

Namdapha National Park The national park (200-4,500 m) is unique as it is home to four particular members of the cat family (tiger, leopard, snow-leopard and clouded leopard). Best season is from October to April. **Sleeping** In *Forest Bungalow*. ■ *Getting there: Dibrugarh (140 km) has the nearest airport. State buses from there go to Miao, the entry point, via Margherita (64 km), the nearest railhead where you can also hire taxis.*

Background

9

Background

345 History

345 Settlement and early history

353 Modern India

353 Politics and institutions

356 Economy

358 Religion

358 Hinduism

372 Islam

373 Buddhism

376 Sikhism

377 Culture

377 Language

378 Literature

380 Architecture

382 Music and dance

384 Land and environment

384 Geography

385 Climate

386 Vegetation

389 Wildlife

History

Settlement and early history

The settlement history of the Indian Himalaya reflects a range of influences. Migrants from Mongolia and Central Asia to the north gave a distinctive ethnic character to many of the Himalayan peoples, and South east Asian tribal groups had a strong influence on ethnic character in the east. Yet the dominant influences have largely been from the Indian plains to the south, notably in the spread of the major religions practised in the mountain regions.

The first village communities in South Asia grew up on the arid western fringes of the Indus Plains 10,000 years ago. Over the following generations successive waves of settlers – sometimes bringing goods for trade, sometimes armies to conquer territory and sometimes nothing more than domesticated animals and families in search of land and peace – moved across the Indus and into India. They left an indelible mark on the landscape and culture of all the countries of modern South Asia.

The first settlers

A site at Mehrgarh, where the Indus Plains meet the dry Baluchistan Hills in modern Pakistan, has revealed evidence of agricultural settlement as early as 8500 BC. By 3500 BC agriculture had spread throughout the Indus Plains and in the thousand years following there were independent settled villages well to the east of the Indus.

At its height the Indus Valley civilization covered as great an area as Egypt or Mesopotamia. However, the culture that developed was distinctively South Asian. The language is still untranslated.

India from 2000 BC to the Mauryas

In about 2000 BC Moenjo Daro, widely presumed to be the capital of the Indus Valley Civilization, became deserted and within the next 250 years the entire civilization disintegrated. Whatever the causes, some features of Indus Valley culture were carried on by succeeding generations.

From 1500 BC northern India entered the Vedic period. Aryan settlers moved southeast towards the Ganga valley. Classes of rulers *(rajas)* and priests *(brahmins)* began to emerge. Grouped into tribes, conflict was common. In one battle of this period a confederacy of tribes known as the Bharatas defeated another grouping of 10 tribes. They gave their name to the region to the east of the Indus which is the official name for India today – Bharat.

The centre of population and of culture shifted east from the banks of the Indus to the land between the rivers Yamuna and Ganga. This region became the heart of emerging Aryan culture, which, from 1500 BC onwards, laid the literary and religious foundations of what ultimately became Hinduism, spreading to embrace the whole of India.

The first fruit of this development was the Rig Veda, the first of four Vedas, composed, collected and passed on orally by Brahmin priests from 1300 BC to about

The Vedas

1000 BC. In the later Vedic period, from about 1000 BC to 600 BC, the Sama, Yajur and Artha Vedas show that the Indo-Aryans developed a clear sense of the Ganga-Yamuna *doab* as 'their' territory. Modern Delhi lies just to the west of this region, central both to the development of history and myth in South Asia. Later texts extended the core region from the Himalaya to the Vindhyans and to the Bay of Bengal in the east. Beyond lay the land of mixed peoples and then of barbarians, outside the pale of Aryan society. From the earliest Vedic writings it is clear that the Himalaya were increasingly well known, and seen to play a vital role in the character and well-being of people living on the plains. The high peaks were regarded as the homes of the gods, the greatest known mountain, meru, was regarded as the pivot of the universe, and the Ganges was worshipped as the ultimate source of fertility and prosperity.

From the sixth to the third centuries BC the region from the foothills of the Himalaya across the Ganga plains to the edge of the Peninsula was governed under a variety of kingdoms or Mahajanapadhas – 'great states'. Trade gave rise to the birth of towns in the Ganga plains themselves, and a trade route was established that ran from Taxila (20 km from modern Islamabad in Pakistan) to Rajgir 1,500 km away in what is now Bihar. It was into these kingdoms of the Himalayan foothills that the Buddha was born.

The Mauryas

Alexander the Great Small communities of Greek origin settled in the Punjab and Northwest Frontier following Alexander's invasion of 326 BC. Although his stay was brief, the Hellenistic influence in Northwest India gave rise to a distinct style of Greco-Indian art termed Gandhara which persisted until the fifth century AD and influenced the later Guptas. Descendents of Alexander's soldiers can still be traced in some northwestern Himalayan villages.

Within a year of the retreat of Alexander the Great from the Indus, **Chandragupta Maurya** established the first indigenous empire to exercise control over much of the subcontinent.

The centre of political power had shifted steadily east into wetter, more densely forested but also more fertile regions.

Asoka The greatest of the Mauryan emperors, Asoka took power in 272 BC. He inherited a full blown empire, but extended it further by defeating the Kalingans in modern Orissa, before turning his back on war and preaching the virtues of Buddhist pacifism. Asoka's empire stretched from Afghanistan to Assam and from the Himalaya to Mysore. The state maintained itself by raising revenue from taxation – on everything, from agriculture, to gambling and prostitution. He decreed that 'no waste land should be occupied and not a tree cut down' without permission, not out of a modern 'green' concern for protecting the forests, but because all were potential sources of revenue for the state.

Asoka (described on the edicts as 'the Beloved of the Gods, of Gracious Countenance') left a series of inscriptions on pillars and rocks across the subcontinent. One of the most accessible for modern visitors is now in the Indraprastha fort in Delhi, where Feroz Shah Tughluq had it taken in the 14th century.

Through the edicts Asoka urged all people to follow the code of **dhamma** or dharma which encouraged toleration, non-violence, respect for priests and those in authority and for human dignity.

A period of fragmentation: 185 BC to 300 AD

Beyond the Mauryan Empire other kingdoms had survived in South India. Internal trade also flourished and Indian traders carried goods to China and Southeast Asia.

Asoka had given patronage to Buddhist religious orders but it was the development of strong trading and merchant guilds that extended patronage beyond individual royal households.

Some of the most important features of modern Hinduism date from the period of Chandra Gupta (AD 319) and his successors. The sacrifices of Vedic worship were given up in favour of personal devotional worship, known as bhakti. Tantrism, both in its Buddhist and Hindu forms, with its emphasis on the female life force and worship of the Mother Goddess, developed. The focus of worship was increasingly towards a personalized and monotheistic deity, represented in the form of either Siva or Vishnu. The myths of Vishnu's incarnations also arose at this period.

The **Brahmins**, the priestly caste who were in the key position to mediate change, refocused earlier literature to give shape to the emerging religious philosophy. In their hands the Mahabharata and the Ramayana were transformed from secular epics to religious stories. The excellence of contemporary sculpture both reflected and contributed to an increase in image worship and the growing role of temples as centres of devotion.

Eventually the Gupta Empire crumbled in the face of repeated attacks from the northwest, this time by the Huns. By the end of the sixth century Punjab and Kashmir had been prised from Gupta control and the last great Hindu empire to embrace the whole of North India and part of the Peninsula was at an end.

Regional kingdoms and cultures

The collapse of Gupta power in the north opened the way for successive smaller kingdoms to assert themselves. In doing so the main outlines of the modern regional geography of South Asia began to take clear shape. The Gangetic plains were constantly fought over by rival groups, none of whom were able to establish unchallenged authority. Regional kingdoms developed, often around comparatively small natural regions.

The spread of Islamic power

From about 1000 AD the external attacks which inflicted most damage on Rajput wealth and power came increasingly from the Arabs and Turks. Mahmud of Ghazni raided the Punjab virtually every year between 1000 and 1026, attracted both by the agricultural surpluses and the wealth of India's temples. By launching annual raids during the harvest season, Mahmud financed his struggles in Central Asia and his attacks on the profitable trade conducted along the Silk road between China and the Mediterranean.

The Delhi Sultanate

Muslim political power was heralded by the raids of Mu'izzu'd Din from 1192 onwards inflicting crushing defeats on Hindu opponents from Gwalior to Benaras. The foundations were then laid for the first extended period of Muslim power, which came under the Delhi sultans.

A succession of dynasties followed, drawing on refugees from Genghis Khan's raids. In 1290 the first dynasty was succeeded by the Khaljis, which in turn gave way to the Tughluqs in 1320. The Delhi sultans were open to local influences and employed Hindus in their administration. In the mid-14th century their capital, Delhi, was one of the leading cities of the contemporary world but in 1398 their control came to an abrupt end with the arrival of the Mongol Timur.

Timur's limp caused him to be called Timur-i-leng (Timur the Lame, known to the west as Tamburlaine).

After Timur, it took nearly 50 years for the Delhi Kingdom to become more than a

Background

local headquarters. Even then the revival was slow and fitful. The last Tughluqs were succeeded by an undistinguished line of Sayyids, who later called themselves sultans and Lodi kings (1451-1526) and moved their capital to Agra.

The forces of the Delhi Sultanate were in disarray, while all over North India Hindus had lost power. Many were forced into the Himalaya, where they formed 'Pahari'(Hill) kingdoms, for example in Garhwal, Chamba and Kangra.

The Delhi Sultanate never achieved the dominating power of earlier empires or of its successor, the Mughal Empire. It exercised political control through crushing military raids and the exaction of tribute from defeated kings, but there was no real attempt to impose central administration. Power depended on maintaining vital lines of communication and trade routes, keeping fortified strongholds and making regional alliances.

The Mughal Empire

Within 150 years of taking power in Delhi the Delhi sultans had lost control of both Bengal and Kashmir. These came under the rule of independent Muslim sultans until nearly the end of the 16th century, when the Mughals brought them firmly back under central authority.

In North India it is the impact of the Mughal rule that is most strikingly evident today. The descendants of conquerors, with the blood of both Tamburlaine (Timur) and Genghis Khan in their veins, they came to dominate Indian politics from Babur's victory near Delhi in 1526 to Aurangzeb's death in 1707. Their legacy was not only some of the most magnificent architecture in the world, but a profound impact on the culture, society and future politics of South Asia.

Babur Founder of the Mughal Dynasty, Babur was born in Russian Turkestan on 15 February 1483, the fifth direct descendant on the male side of Timur and 13th on the female side from Genghis Khan. He established the Mughal Empire in 1526 but when he died 4 years later, the Empire was still far from secured. Yet he had not only laid the foundations of political and military power but had also begun to establish courtly traditions of poetry, literature and art which became the hallmark of subsequent Mughal rulers.

Within two generations the Mughals had become fully at home in their Indian environment and brought some radical changes. Babur was charismatic. He ruled by keeping the loyalty of his military chiefs, giving them control of large areas of territory. However, his son Humayun was forced to flee Delhi, only returning to power a year before his death.

Akbar Akbar, who was to be the greatest of India's emperors was only 13 when he took the throne in 1556. The next 44 years were one of the most remarkable periods of South Asian history, paralleled by the Elizabethan period in England, where Queen Elizabeth I ruled from 1558 to 1603. Although Akbar inherited the throne, it was he who really created the empire.

It was Akbar who created the administrative structure employed by successive Mughal emperors to sustain their power. Revenue was raised using detailed surveying methods. Rents were fixed according to the quality of the soil in a move which was carried through into British revenue raising systems.

Akbar deliberately widened his power base by incorporating Rajput princes into the administrative structure and giving them extensive rights in the revenue from land.

Akbar was a patron not just of art but of an extraordinary range of literature. His library contained books on 'biography, theology, comparative religion, science, mathematics, history, astrology, medicine, zoology and anthropology'.

Artistic treasures abound from Akbar's court – paintings, jewellery, weapons – often bringing together material and skills from across the known world. Examples can be seen not just in India, but at major museums in Europe and the United States. Akbar's intellectual interests were extraordinarily catholic. He met the Portuguese Jesuits in 1572 and welcomed them to his court in Fatehpur Sikri, along with Buddhists, Hindus and Zoroastrians, every year between 1575 and 1582.

Akbar's eclecticism had a purpose, for he was trying to build a focus of loyalty beyond that of caste, social group, region or religion. Like Roman emperors before him, he deliberately cultivated a new religion in which the emperor himself attained divinity, hoping thereby to give the empire a legitimacy which would last. While his religion disappeared with his death, the legitimacy of the Mughals survived another 200 years, long after their real power had almost disappeared.

Akbar died of a stomach illness in 1605. He was succeeded by his son, Prince Salim, **Jahangir** who inherited the throne as Emperor Jahangir ('*world seizer*'). He added little to the territory of the empire, but he did consolidate the Mughals' hold on the Himalayan foothills. More interested in art and literature than in territorial gains, Jehangir found particular pleasure in the Vale of Kashmir, bringing it firmly within his power and helping to transform the cultural geography of the Jhelum Valley.

By 1622 Jahangir's Persian wife Nur Jahan effectively controlled the empire but despite her power she was unable to prevent accession of her least favoured son, Prince Khurram, to the throne in 1628. He took the title of Shah Jahan (*Ruler of the World*) and in the following 30 years his reign represented the height of Mughal power.

The Mughal Empire was under attack in the Deccan and the northwest when Shah **Shah Jahan** Jahan became Emperor. He tried to re-establish and extend Mughal authority in both regions by a combination of military campaigns and skilled diplomacy.

But he too commissioned art, literature and, above all, architectural monuments, on an unparalleled scale. The Taj Mahal may be the most famous of these, but a succession of brilliant achievements can be attributed to his reign. From miniature paintings and manuscripts, which had been central features of Mughal artistic development from Babur onwards, to massive fortifications such as the Red Fort in Delhi, Shah Jahan added to the already great body of outstanding Mughal art, architecture and town building.

The need to expand the area under Mughal control was felt even more strongly by **Aurangzeb** Aurangzeb ('*The jewel in the throne*'), than by his predecessors. When he seized power at the age of 40, he needed all his political and military skills to hold on to an unwieldy empire that was in permanent danger of collapse from its own size.

The rise of British power

The Himalaya were among the last regions to be affected by the advent of British power. The British were unique among the foreign rulers of India in coming by sea rather than through the northwest and in coming first for trade rather than for military conquest. The ports that they established – Madras (now Chennai), Bombay (Mumbai) and Calcutta (Kolkata) – became completely new centres of political, economic and social activity. Before them Indian empires had controlled their territories from the land. The British dictated the emerging shape of the economy by controlling sea-borne trade. From the middle of the 19th century railways transformed the economic and political structure of South Asia and it was those three centres of British political control, along with the late addition of Delhi, which became the focos of economic development and political change.

The decline of Muslim power

The extension of East India Company power in the Mughal periphery of India's south and east took place against a background of weakening Mughal power at the centre in Delhi and on the Peninsula. Some of the Muslim kingdoms of the Deccan refused to pay the tribute to the Mughal Empire that had been forced on them after defeats in 1656. This refusal and their alliance with the rising power of Sivaji and his Marathas, had led Aurangzeb to attack the Shi'i-ruled states of Bijapur (1686) and Golconda (1687), in an attempt to reimpose Mughal supremacy.

The decay of the Mughal Empire has been likened to 'a magnificent flower slowly wilting and occasionally dropping a petal, its brilliance fading, its stalk bending ever lower'. Nine emperors succeeded Aurangzeb between his death and the exile of the last Mughal ruler in 1858. It was no accident that it was in that year that the British ended the rule of its East India Company and decreed India to be its Indian empire.

The East India Company's push for power

Alliances In the century and a half that followed the death of Aurangzeb, the British East India Company extended its economic and political influence into the heart of India and on towards the Himalaya. As the Mughal Empire lost its power India fell into many smaller states, including Himalayan kingdoms, some of which had enjoyed a degree of autonomy from Mughal power. The Company undertook to protect the rulers of several of these states from external attack by stationing British troops in their territory. In exchange for this service the rulers paid subsidies to the Company which often crippled the local ruler. The British extended their territory through the 18th century as successive regional powers were annexed and brought under direct Company rule.

The impact of this policy was felt directly in the Himalaya. In Garhwal, for example, where the Gurkhas had overrun the small Hindu led kingdom in 1803, the British expelled the Gurkhas, taking the eastern part as directly ruled British Garhwal and returning the Tehri Garhwal to the former Raja. The most important strategic events, however, took place in peninsular India the Marathas, the central Indian confederacy which had also threatened the Mughals, were not defeated until the war of 1816-18, a defeat which had to wait until Napoleon was defeated in Europe and the British could turn their wholehearted attention once again to the Indian scene. Even then the defeat owed as much to internal faction fighting as to the power of the British-led army. Only the northwest of the subcontinent remained beyond British control until well into the 19th century.

In 1818 India's economy was in ruins and its political structures destroyed. Irrigation works and road systems had fallen into decay and gangs terrorized the countryside. The peace and stability of the Mughal period had long since passed. Between 1818 and 1857 there was a succession of local and uncoordinated revolts in different parts of India. Some were bought off, some put down by military force.

A period of reforms

While existing political systems were collapsing, the first half of the 19th century was also a period of radical social change in the territories governed by the East India Company. In 1828 **Lord William Bentinck** banned the burning of widows on the funeral pyres of their husbands (**sati**) and then moved to suppress **thuggee** (the ritual murder and robbery carried out in the name of the goddess Kali). But his most far reaching change was to introduce education in English, promising funds to impart "to the native population the knowledge of English literature and science through the medium of the English language". Out of this concern were born new educational institutions such as the

Calcutta Medical College. From the late 1830s massive new engineering projects began to be taken up. Control of the foothills of the western Himalaya, especially where the Ganga entered the plains, allowed the British to begin a century of canal building, diverting major rivers to irrigate huge tracts of agricultural land on the plains. The canals were followed by the railways. After linking the colonial cities these apread across India. Lines went north from Lolkata to the tea gradens of North Bengal and Assam, bringing the eastern Himalaya with far easier range. In the Western Himalaya lines climbed into the foothills at Shimla and Kangra.

The innovations stimulated change and change contributed to the growing unease with the British presence.

The Rebellion

Out of the growing discontent and widespread economic difficulties came the Rebellion or 'Mutiny' of 1857 (now widely known as the First War of Independence). Appalling scenes of butchery and reprisals marked the struggle, which was only put down by troops from outside.

The Period of Empire

The 1857 rebellion marked the end not only of the Mughal Empire but also of the East India Company, for the British Government in London took overall control in 1858. Yet within 30 years a movement for self-government had begun and there were the first signs of a demand among the new western educated élite that political rights be awarded to match the sense of Indian national identity.

The movement for independence went through a series of steps. The creation of the Indian National Congress in 1885 was the first all-India political institution and was to become the key vehicle of demands for independence. However, the educated Muslim élite of what is now Uttar Pradesh saw a threat to Muslim rights, power and identity in the emergence of democratic institutions which gave Hindus, with their built-in natural majority, significant advantages.

The Indian National Congress

The educated Muslim community of North India remained deeply suspicious of the Congress, making up less than 8 of those attending its conferences between 1900-1920. Muslims from UP created the All-India Muslim League in 1906. The nature of the future Independent India was still far from clear, however. The British conceded the principle of self-government in 1918, but however radical the reforms would have seemed 5 years earlier they already fell far short of heightened Indian expectations.

The Muslim League

Into a tense atmosphere Mohandas Karamchand Gandhi returned to India in 1915 after 20 years practising as a lawyer in South Africa. On his return the Bengali Nobel Laureate poet, Rabindranath Tagore, had dubbed him 'Mahatma' – Great Soul. The name became his. He arrived as the government of India was being given new powers by the British parliament to try political cases without a jury and to give provincial governments the right to imprison politicians without trial. In opposition to this legislation Gandhi proposed to call a *hartal*, when all activity would cease for a day, a form of protest still in widespread use. Such protests took place across India, often accompanied by riots.

Mahatma Gandhi

On 13 April 1919 a huge gathering took place in the enclosed space of Jallianwala Bagh in Amritsar. It had been prohibited by the government and General Dyer ordered troops to fire on the people without warning, killing 379 and injuring at least a further 1,200. It marked the turning point in relations with Britain and the rise of Gandhi to the key position of leadership in the struggle for complete independence.

Background

The thrust for Independence Through the 1920s Gandhi developed concepts and political programmes that were to become the hallmark of India's Independence struggle. Rejecting the 1919 reforms Gandhi preached the doctrine of *swaraj*, or self rule, developing an idea he first published in a leaflet in 1909. He saw swaraj not just as political independence from a foreign ruler but, in Judith Brown's words, as made up of three elements: "It was a state of being that had to be created from the roots upwards, by the regeneration of individuals and their realization of their true spiritual being ... unity among all religions; the eradication of Untouchability; and the practice of *swadeshi*." Swadeshi was not simply dependence on Indian products rather than foreign imports, but a deliberate move to a simple life style, hence his emphasis on hand spinning as a daily routine.

Ultimately political Independence was to be achieved not by violent rebellion but by *satyagraha* – a "truth force" which implied a willingness to suffer through non-violent resistance to injustice. This gave birth to Gandhi's advocacy of "non-cooperation" as a key political weapon and brought together Gandhi's commitment to matching political goals and moral means. Although the political achievements of Gandhi's programme continues to be strongly debated the struggles of the 1920s established his position as a key figure in the Independence movement.

In 1930 the Congress declared that 26 January would be Independence day – still celebrated as Republic Day in India today. The Leader of the Muslim League, Mohammad Iqbal, took the opportunity of his address to the League in the same year to suggest the formation of a Muslim state within an Indian Federation. Also in 1930 a Muslim student in Cambridge, **Chaudhuri Rahmat Ali**, coined a name for the new Muslim state – **PAKISTAN**. The letters were to stand 'P' for Punjab, 'A' for Afghania, 'K' for Kashmir, 'S' for Sind with the suffix '*stan*', Persian for country. The idea still had little real shape however and waited on developments of the late 1930s and 1940s to bear fruit.

By the end of second world war the positions of the Muslim League, now under the leadership of **Mohammad Ali Jinnah** and the Congress led by Jawaharlal Nehru, were irreconcilable. While major questions of the definition of separate territories for a Muslim and non-Muslim state remained to be answered, it was clear to General Wavell, the British Viceroy through the last years of the War, that there was no alternative but to accept that independence would have to be given on the basis of separate states.

Independence and Partition

One of the main difficulties for the Muslims was that they made up only a fifth of the total population. Although there were regions both in the northwest and the east where they formed the majority, Muslims were also scattered throughout India. It was therefore impossible to define a simple territorial division which would provide a state to match Jinnah's claim of a '*two-nation theory*'. On 20 February 1947, the British Labour Government announced its decision to replace Lord Wavell as Viceroy with Lord Mountbatten, who was to oversee the transfer of power to new independent governments. It set a deadline of June 1948 for British withdrawal. The announcement of a firm date made the Indian politicians even less willing to compromise and the resulting division satisfied no one.

When Independence arrived – on 15 August for India and the 14 August for Pakistan, because Indian astrologers deemed the 15th to be the most auspicious moment – many questions remained unanswered. Several key Princely States had still not decided firmly to which country they would accede. Kashmir was the most important of these, with results that have lasted to the present day.

Modern India

India, with over1 billion people in 2001, is the second most populated country in the world after China. That population size reflects the long history of human occupation and the fact that an astonishingly high proportion of India's land is relatively fertile. Sixty percent of India's surface area is cultivated today, compared with about 10 in China and 20 in the United States. The Himalayan regions are mong the least densely populated of the entire country. Himachal Pradesh, for example, has a population of on 5 million in an area of over 50,000 square kilometres.

Although the birth rate has fallen steadily over the last 50 years, initially death rates fell faster and the rate of population increase has continued to be above 2% – or 18 million – a year. Today nearly 30% of the population lives in towns, and cities have grown dramatically. In 1971, 109 million people lived in towns and cities. The figure was estimated to have grown to over 300 million in 2001.

Politics and institutions

When India became Independent on 15 August 1947 it faced three immediate crises. Partition left it with a bitter struggle between Muslims on one side and Hindus and Sikhs on the other which threatened to tear the new country into pieces at birth. An estimated 13 million people migrated between the two new countries of India and Pakistan and perhaps 1 million were killed in the slaughter that accompanied the migration. Almost immediately it plunged into an inconclusive 15 month war with Pakistan over Kashmir. Finally it had the task of developing a constitution which would allow the often conflicting interest groups which made up Indian society to cement their allegiance to the new State.

In the years since independence, striking political achievements have been made. With the 2 year exception of 1975-77, when Mrs Gandhi imposed a state of emergency in which all political activity was banned, India has sustained a democratic system in the face of tremendous pressures. The General Elections of March 1998, which involved an electorate of over 400 million, were the country's twelfth. Their results produced a minority government which only survived fifteen months, resulting in the thirteenth general election in September 1999.

The constitution

Establishing itself as a sovereign democratic republic, the Indian parliament accepted Nehru's advocacy of a secular constitution. The President is formally vested with all executive powers exercised under the authority of the Prime Minister.

Effective power under the constitution lies with the Prime Minister and Cabinet, following the British model. In practice there have been long periods when the Prime Minister has been completely dominant. In principle parliament chooses the Prime Minister. The Parliament has a lower house (the *Lok Sabha*, or 'house of the people') and an upper house (the *Rajya Sabha* – Council of States). The former is made up of directly elected representatives from the 543 parliamentary constituencies (plus two nominated members from the Anglo-Indian community), the latter of a mixture of members elected by an electoral college and of nominated members. Constitutional amendments require a two-thirds majority in both houses.

India's federal constitution devolves certain powers to elected state assemblies.

Background

Each state has a Governor who acts as its official head. Many states also have two chambers, the upper generally called the Rajya Sabha and the lower (often called the Vidhan Sabha) being of directly elected representatives. In practice many of the state assemblies have had a totally different political complexion from that of the Lok Sabha. Regional parties have played a far more prominent role, though in many states central government has effectively dictated both the leadership and policy of state assemblies.

States & Union Territories Union territories are administered by the President "acting to such an extent as he thinks fit". In practice Union territories have varying forms of self-government. Pondicherry has a legislative Assembly and Council of Ministers. The 69th Amendment to the Constitution in 1991 provided for a legislative assembly and council of Ministers for Delhi. The Assemblies of Union Territories have more restricted powers of legislation than full states.

Secularism One of the key features of India's constitution is its secular principle. This is not based on the absence of religious belief, but on the commitment to guarantee freedom of religious belief and practice to all groups in Indian society. Some see the commitment to a secular constitution as under increasing challenge, especially from the Hindu nationalism of the Bharatiya Janata Party, the BJP. The BJP persuaded a number of minor regional parties to join it in government after the 1998 elections, appearing to move away from its narrowly defined conception of a Hindu state. As it approaches the 1999 elections the BJP is torn between the narrowly defined Hindu beliefs of its core support and the electoral demands of an enormously varied population. However, it appears to have gained support from the military confrontation with Pakistan in June/July 1999.

The judiciary India's Supreme Court has similar but somewhat weaker powers to those of the United States. The judiciary has remained effectively independent of the government except under the Emergency between 1975-77.

The civil service India continued to use the small but highly professional administrative service inherited from the British period. Renamed the Indian Administrative Service (IAS), it continues to exercise remarkable influence across the country. The administration of many aspects of central and regional government is in the hands of this élite body, who act largely by the constitutional rules which bind them as servants of the state. Many Indians accept the continuing efficiency and high calibre of the top ranking officers in the administration while believing that the bureaucratic system as a whole has been overtaken by widespread corruption.

The police India's police service is divided into a series of groups, numbering nearly 1 million. While the top ranks of the Indian Police Service are comparable to the IAS, lower levels are extremely poorly trained and very low paid. In addition to the domestic police force there are special groups: the Border Security Force, Central Reserve Police and others. They may be armed with modern weapons and are called in for special duties.

The armed forces Unlike its immediate neighbours India has never had military rule. It has approximately 1 million men in the army – one of the largest armed forces in the world. Although they have remained out of politics the armed services have been used increasingly frequently to put down civil unrest especially in Kashmir, where there are currently around 400,000 troops.

The Congress Party For over forty years Indian national politics was dominated by the Congress Party. Its strength in the Lok Sabha often overstated the volume of its support in the country,

The Indian flag

In 1921, the All Indian Congress considered a red and green flag to represent the two dominant religious groups (Hindu and Muslim); Gandhi suggested white be added to represent the other communities, as well as the charka (spinning wheel) symbolizing the Swadeshi movement, now centred in the party flag.

In 1931, the Indian National Congress adopted the tricolor as the national flag. This was intended to have no communal significance. The deep saffron denoted 'Courage and Sacrifice', the white 'Truth and Peace' and dark green 'Faith and Chivalry'. On the white stripe, the Dharma chakra represented the Buddhist Wheel of Law from Asoka's Lion capital at Sarnath.

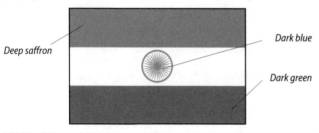

Deep saffron

Dark blue

Dark green

however and state governments have frequently been formed by parties – and interests – only weakly represented at the centre.

The Congress won overall majorities in seven of the ten general elections held before the 1996 election, although in no election did the Congress obtain more than 50% of the popular vote. It was defeated only in 1977 and in 1989 when the Opposition parties united against it. In the latter election it still gained the largest number of seats, though not enough to form a government on its own and it was unable to find allies.

The Congress had built its broad based support partly by championing the causes of the poor, the backward castes and the minorities. It regained power in mid-1991 in the wake of Rajiv Gandhi's death and under Narasimha Rao's leadership it succeeded in governing for its full 5-year term, introducing the most radical economic reform programme since Independence. In 1998 its popular support completely disappeared in some regions and fell below 30 nationally. It appeared to enjoy an upsurge in state elections in 1999 and forced the resignation of the BJP Government in mid-1999. However, in the elections of September-October 1999 Sonia Gandhi, Rajiv Gandhi's Itlaian born widow, failed to achieve the much vaunted revivial in the Party's fortunes.

Political activity outside the Congress can seem bewilderingly complex. There are no genuinely national parties. The only alternative governments to the Congress have been formed by coalitions of regional and ideologically based parties. Parties of the left – Communist and Socialist – have never broken out of their narrow regional bases. The **Communist Party of India** split into two factions in 1964, with the Communist Party of India Marxist **(CPM)** ultimately taking power in West Bengal and Kerala. In the 1960s the **Swatantra Party** (a liberal party) made some ground nationally, opposing the economic centralization and state control supported by the Congress.

At the right of the political spectrum, the **Jan Sangh** was seen as a party of right wing Hindu nationalism with a concentrated but significant base in parts of the north, especially among higher castes and merchant communities. The most organized political force outside the Congress, the Jan Sangh merged with the

The Non-Congress Parties

Background

Janata Party for the elections of 1977. After the collapse of that government it re-formed itself as the **Bharatiya Janata Party** (BJP). In 1990-91 it developed a powerful campaign focusing on reviving Hindu identity against the minorities. The elections of 1991 showed it to be the most powerful single challenger to the Congress in North India. In the decade that followed it became the most important national alternative to the Congress across northern India and established a series of footholds and alliances in the South.

A wide spectrum of parties exercises power across the states of the Indian Himalaya. From Kashmir, where the political situation continues to be shaped by the state of emergency, it is impossible to predict what form of government would emerge if a peaceful resolution to the conflict were to be achieved. In Himachal and Uttaranchal the BJP holds a slight majority over the Congress, while in the Eastern Himalaya the parties contesting for power range from the Communist Party of India Marxist, the CPI(M), to the Congress, and the Gorkhaland Peoples Party.

Recent developments In September 1998, national elections saw the BJP return as the largest single party at the head of a broad coalition, the National Democratic Alliance (NDA) under the Prime Ministerhip of Atal Behari Vajpayee. It has withstood subsequent regional difficulties, and seems set to remain in power for its full term.

Economy

Agriculture Although agriculture now accounts for less than 30% of India's GDP, it remains the most important single economic activity. More than half India's people depend directly on agriculture and its success has a crucial effect on the remainder of the economy.

Agriculture in the Indian Himalaya is remarkably varied, reflecting the widely different conditions of climate, soil and relief. Cereal farming dominates the valleys and lower terraces. Rice, the most important single foodgrain in India, is common in the warmer wetter valleys.

Other crops – barley, sorghum and the millets – are also grown extensively. However, in the eastern Himalaya and small parts of the west tea is the most important single crop. The high value teas of Darjeeling are among the finest in the world.

Between independence and the late 1960s most of the increase in India's agricultural output came from extending the cultivated area. About 60% of the total area of India is now cultivated. In the last 20 years increasingly intensive use of land through greater irrigation and use of fertilizer, pesticides and high yielding varieties of seeds (HYVs) has allowed growth to continue. The area under irrigation has risen to over 35% in 2001, while fertilizer use has increased 25 times since 1961. Indian agriculture is dominated by small holdings. Only 20% of the land is farmed in units of more than 10 ha (compared with 31% 20 years ago), while nearly 60% of farms are less than one hectare. While the "Green Revolution" – the package of practices designed to increase farm output – has had its opponents, it has now transformed the agricultural productivity of many regions of India, allowing a population twice the size of that thirty years ago to be fed without recourse to imports or aid. Much of this has been achieved as the result of seed breeding and agricultural research in India's own agricultural research institutions.

Resources & industry Unlike peninsular India, which has extensive resources of iron ore, coal, bauxite and some other minerals, the Himalaya have few accessible mineral resources. Overall Indian reserves of coal at likely rates of use are estimated at well over 100 years (at least 30 billion tonnes, plus 6 billion tonnes of coking coal). Medium and high grade iron ore reserves (5 billion tonnes) will last over 200 years at present extraction rates.

Oil, coal and gas provide the energy for just over half India's 100 million kw electric generation capacity, 20 million kw being hydro and 2 million mw nuclear.

Power generation By 2001 India's power production had grown to over 450 billion kwh, but demand has risen so fast that many states continue to have power blackouts or 'loadshedding'. Firewood is estimated to provide nearly 30% of the total energy requirement, agricultural waste 9% and cow dung 7%, a universal fuel in some poorer areas, The Indian Himalaya have provided major sources of Hydro-Electricity from the Bhakra-Nangal dam in the western Himalaya, built as part of the Indus Waters Treaty arrangements agreed between India and Pakistan in 1960. However, the future of large dams in the Himalaya is extremely uncertain, as the long-running dispute over the Tehri dam in Uttaranchal demonstrates.

In the early 1950s India embarked on a programme of planned industrial development. Borrowing planning concepts from the Soviet Union, the government tried to stimulate development through massive investment in the public sector, imposing a system of tight controls on foreign ownership of capital in India and playing a highly interventionist role in all aspects of economic policy. The private sector was allowed to continue to operate in agriculture and in a wide range of 'non-essential' industrial sectors. **India's Five Year Plans**

Although significant achievements were made in the first two Five Year Plans (1951-56, 1956-61), the Third Five Year Plan failed catastrophically. Agriculture was particularly hard hit by three poor monsoons. After a period of dependence on foreign aid at the end of the 1960s, the economy started moving forward again. The 'Green Revolution' enabled Indian agriculture to increase production faster than demand and through the 1980s it was producing surplus foodgrains, enabling it to build up reserves.

Industrial development continued to lag behind expectations, however. Although India returned to the programme of Five Year Plans (in 2000 it was nearing the end of the Ninth Plan), central control has been progressively loosened.. Defence spending has been cut from 3.8% to about 3% of GNP though the Government reversed this trend in August 1999. In 2000 the economy had re-established growth with single figure inflation. Foreign exchange reserves were at an all time high in mid-2000 and inward investment also registered significant increases.

India today has a far more diversified industrial base than seemed imaginable at Independence. It produces goods, from aeroplanes and rockets to watches and computers. The influence of India's manufacturing industry reaches every village. The most striking modern development is in the IT sector. According to the London Financial Times since the early 1990s India has become one of the world's leading centres for software development. With an expected 5 million Indians on the net by 2001, India is rapidly transforming itself into a computer based society. Yet despite the economic successes, many in India claim that the weaknesses remain profound. Perhaps half of the population continues to live in absolute poverty and despite surplus grain production many still lack an adequate diet. Poverty is still pronounced in many Himalayan villages, and the lack of job opportunities has contributed to a steady flow of young people, especially men, to the cities of the plains. **Achievements & problems**

While India's industrial economy is producing a range of modern products, many are still uncompetitive on world markets. Furthermore, critics within India increasingly argue that goods are made in factories that often fail to observe basic safety and health rules and that emit enormous pollution into the environment. On top of that, the industrial expansion barely seems to have touched the problems of unemployment. Employment in India's organized industry has risen from 12 million in 1961 to over 28 million in 2000, yet during the same period the number of registered unemployed rose from 1.6 million to over 36 million.

Background

Religion

It is impossible to write briefly about religion in India without greatly oversimplifying. Over 80% of Indians are Hindu, but there are significant minorities. Muslims number about 120 million and there are over 20 million Christians, 18 million Sikhs, 6 million Buddhists and a number of other religious groups. Each community is represented in the Indian Himalaya. One of the most persistent features of Indian religious and social life is the caste system. This has undergone substantial changes since Independence, especially in towns and cities, but most people in India are still clearly identified as a member of a particular caste group. The Government has introduced measures to help the backward, or 'scheduled' castes, though in recent years this has produced a major political backlash.

Hinduism

It has always been easier to define Hinduism by what it is not than by what it is. Indeed, the name 'Hindu' was given by foreigners to the peoples of the subcontinent who did not profess the other major faiths, such as Muslims or Christians. The beliefs and practices of modern Hinduism began to take shape in the centuries on either side of the birth of Christ. But while some aspects of modern Hinduism can be traced back more than 2,000 years before that, other features are recent. Hinduism has undergone major changes both in belief and practice, originating from outside as well as from within. As early as the sixth century BC the Buddhists and Jains had tried to reform the religion of Vedism (or Brahmanism) which had been dominant in some parts of South Asia for 500 years.

Key ideas

A number of ideas run like a thread through Hinduism. According to the great Indian philosopher and former President of India, S Radhakrishnan, religion for the Hindu "is not an idea but a power, not an intellectual proposition but a life conviction. Religion is consciousness of ultimate reality, not a theory about God".

Some Hindu scholars and philosophers talk of Hinduism as one religious and cultural tradition, in which the enormous variety of belief and practice can ultimately be interpreted as interwoven in a common view of the world. Yet there is no Hindu organization, like a church, with the authority to define belief or establish official practice. There are spiritual leaders and philosophers who are widely revered and there is an enormous range of literature that is treated as sacred. Not all Hindu groups believe in a single supreme God. In view of these characteristics, many authorities argue that it is misleading to think of Hinduism as a religion at all.

Be that as it may, the evidence of the living importance of Hinduism is visible across India. Hindu philosophy and practice has also touched many of those who belong to other religious traditions, particularly in terms of social institutions such as caste.

Darshan One of Hinduism's recurring themes is 'vision', 'sight' or 'view' – **darshan**. Applied to the different philosophical systems themselves, such as *yoga* or *vedanta*, 'darshan' is also used to describe the sight of the deity that worshippers hope to gain when they visit a temple or shrine hoping for the sight of a 'guru' (teacher). Equally it may apply to the religious insight gained through meditation or prayer.

Background

Many Hindus also accept that there are four major human goals; material prosperity (*artha*), the satisfaction of desires (*kama*) and performing the duties laid down according to your position in life (*dharma*). Beyond those is the goal of achieving liberation from the endless cycle of rebirths into which everyone is locked (*moksha*). It is to the search for liberation that the major schools of Indian philosophy have devoted most attention. Together with dharma, it is basic to Hindu thought.

The four human goals

The Mahabharata lists 10 embodiments of **dharma**: good name, truth, self-control, cleanness of mind and body, simplicity, endurance, resoluteness of character, giving and sharing, austerities and continence. In *dharmic* thinking these are inseparable from five patterns of behaviour: non-violence, an attitude of equality, peace and tranquillity, lack of aggression and cruelty and absence of envy. Dharma, an essentially secular concept, represents the order inherent in human life.

The idea of *karma*, 'the effect of former actions', is central to achieving liberation. As C Rajagopalachari put it: "Every act has its appointed effect, whether the act be thought, word or deed. The cause holds the effect, so to say, in its womb. If we reflect deeply and objectively, the entire world will be found to obey unalterable laws. That is the doctrine of karma".

Karma

The belief in the transmigration of souls (*samsara*) in a never-ending cycle of rebirth has been Hinduism's most distinctive and important contribution to Indian culture. The earliest reference to the belief is found in one of the Upanishads, around the seventh century BC, at about the same time as the doctrine of karma made its first appearance. By the late Upanishads it was universally accepted and in Buddhism and Jainism it is never questioned.

Rebirth

AL Basham pointed out that belief in transmigration must have encouraged a further distinctive doctrine, that of non-violence or non-injury – *ahimsa*. The belief in rebirth meant that all living things and creatures of the spirit – people, devils, gods, animals, even worms – possessed the same essential soul. One inscription threatens that anyone who interferes with the rights of Brahmins to land given to them by the king will 'suffer rebirth for 80,000 years as a worm in dung'. Belief in the cycle of rebirth was essential to give such a threat any weight!

Ahimsa

Schools of philosophy

It is common now to talk of six major schools of Hindu philosophy. *Nyaya, Vaisheshika, Sankhya, Yoga, Purvamimansa* and *Vedanta*.

Yoga, can be traced back to at least the third century AD. It seeks a synthesis of the spirit, the soul and the flesh and is concerned with systems of meditation and self denial that lead to the realization of the Divine within oneself and can ultimately release one from the cycle of rebirth.

Yoga

These are literally the final parts of the Vedic literature, the Upanishads. The basic texts also include the Brahmasutra of Badrayana, written about the first century AD and the most important of all, the Bhagavad-Gita, which is a part of the epic the Mahabharata. There are many interpretations of these basic texts. Three are given here.

Vedanta

Advaita Vedanta holds that there is no division between the cosmic force or principle, *Brahman* and the individual Self, *atman* (also referred to as 'soul'). The fact that we appear to see different and separate individuals is simply a result of ignorance. This is termed *maya* (illusion), but Vedanta philosophy does not suggest

The four stages of life

Popular Hindu belief holds that an ideal life has four stages: that of the student, the householder, the forest dweller and the wandering dependent or beggar (sannyasi). These stages represent the phases through which an individual learns of life's goals and of the means of achieving them.

One of the most striking sights today is that of the saffron clad sannyasi *(sadhu) seeking gifts of food and money to support*

himself in the final stage of his life. There may have been sadhus even before the Aryans arrived. Today, most of these have given up material possessions, carrying only a strip of cloth, a danda *(staff), a crutch to support the chin during* achal *(meditation), prayer beads, a fan to ward off evil spirits, a water pot, a drinking vessel, which may be a human skull and a begging bowl. You may well see one, almost naked, covered only in ashes, on a city street.*

that the world in which we live is an illusion. *Jnana* (knowledge) is held as the key to understanding the full and real unity of Self and Brahman. **Shankaracharya** , born at Kalady in modern Kerala, in the seventh century AD, is the best known Advaitin Hindu philosopher. He argued that there was no individual Self or soul separate from the creative force of the universe, or Brahman and that it was impossible to achieve liberation (*moksha*), through meditation and devotional worship, which he saw as signs of remaining on a lower level and of being unprepared for true liberation.

Vishishtadvaita The 12th-century philosopher, **Ramanuja**, repudiated such ideas. He transformed the idea of God from an impersonal force to a personal God and viewed both the Self and the World as real but only as part of the whole. In contrast to Shankaracharya's view, Ramanuja saw *bhakti* (devotion) as of central importance to achieving liberation and service to the Lord as the highest goal of life.

Dvaita Vedanta The 14th-century philosopher Madhva believed that Brahman, the Self and the World are completely distinct. Worship of God is a key means of achieving liberation.

Worship

As S Radhakrishnan puts it, for millions of Hindus: "It does not matter what conception of God we adopt so long as we keep up a perpetual search after truth".

Puja For most Hindus today worship ('performing puja') is an integral part of their faith. The great majority of Hindu homes will have a shrine to one of the gods of the Hindu pantheon. Individuals and families will often visit shrines or temples and on special occasions will travel long distances to particularly holy places such as Haridwar, Gangotri, Amarnath and many others. Such sites may have temples dedicated to a major deity but may also have numerous other shrines in the vicinity dedicated to other favourite gods.

Acts of devotion are often aimed at the granting of favours and the meeting of urgent needs for this life – good health, finding a suitable wife or husband, the birth of a son, prosperity and good fortune. In this respect the popular devotion of simple pilgrims of all faiths in South Asia is remarkably similar when they visit shrines, whether Hindu, Buddhist or Jain temples, the tombs of Muslim saints or even churches.

Puja involves making an offering to God and *darshan* (having a view of the deity). Hindu worship is generally, though not always, an act performed by individuals. Thus Hindu temples may be little more than a shrine on a river bank or in the

Karma – an eye to the future

According to the doctrine of karma, every person, animal or god has a being or 'self' which has existed without beginning. Every action, except those that are done without any consideration of the results, leaves an indelible mark on that 'self', carried forward into the next life.

The overall character of the imprint on each person's 'self' determines three features of the next life: the nature of his next birth (animal, human or god), the kind of family he will be born into if human and the length of the next life. Finally, it controls the good or bad experiences that the self will experience. However, it does not imply a fatalistic belief that the nature of action in this life is unimportant. Rather, it suggests that the path followed by the individual in the present life is vital to the nature of its next life and ultimately to the chance of gaining release from this world.

middle of the street, tended by a priest and visited at special times when a darshan of the resident God can be obtained. When it has been consecrated, the **image**, if exactly made, becomes the channel for the godhead to work. According to KM Sen "in popular Hinduism, God is worshipped in different forms" showing "a particular attachment to a particular figure in Hindu mythology". Images are, Françoise Bernier quotes "something before the eyes that fixes the mind".

Holy places

Certain rivers and towns are particularly sacred to Hindus. The Himalaya give rise to the holy rivers Ganga and Yamuna, and cradle the holy town of Haridwar and the holy abode of Badrinath.

Rituals & festivals

The temple rituals often follow through the cycle of day and night, as well as yearly lifecycles. The priests may wake the deity from sleep, bathe, clothe and feed it. Worshippers will be invited to share in this process by bringing offerings of clothes and food. Gifts of money will usually be made and in some temples there is a charge levied for taking up positions in front of the deity in order to obtain a darshan at the appropriate times.

Every temple has its special festivals. At festival times you can see villagers walking in small groups, brightly dressed and often high spirited, sometimes as far as 80-100 km.

Hindu Deities

Today three Gods are widely seen as all-powerful: Brahma, Vishnu and Siva. Their functions and character are not readily separated. While Brahma is regarded as the ultimate source of creation, Siva also has a creative role alongside his function as destroyer. Vishnu in contrast is seen as the preserver or protector of the universe. Vishnu and Siva are widely represented (where Brahma is not) and have come to be seen as the most powerful and important. Their followers are referred to as Vaishnavite and Shaivites respectively and numerically they form the two largest sects in India.

Brahma

Popularly Brahma is interpreted as the Creator in a trinity, alongside Vishnu as Preserver and Siva as Destroyer. In the literal sense the name Brahma is the masculine and personalized form of the neuter word Brahman.

In the early Vedic writing, *Brahman* represented the universal and impersonal principle which governed the Universe. Gradually, as Vedic philosophy moved towards a monotheistic interpretation of the universe and its origins, this impersonal power was increasingly personalized. In the Upanishads, Brahman was

Background

Many in One

One of the reasons why Hindu faith is often confusing to the outsider is that as a whole it has many elements which appear mutually self-contradictory but which are tolerated or reconciled by Hindus as different facets of the ultimate Truth. Such tolerance is particularly evident in the attitude of Hindus to the nature of divinity. C Rajagopalachari writes that a distinction that marks Hinduism sharply from the monotheistic faiths is that "the philosophy of Hinduism has taught and trained the Hindu devotee to see and worship the Supreme Being in all the idols that are worshipped, with a clarity of understanding and an intensity of vision that would surprise the people of other faiths. The Divine Mind governing the Universe, be it as Mother or Father, has infinite aspects and the devotee approaches him or her, or both, in any of the many aspects as he may be led to do according to the mood and the psychological need of the hour."

seen as a universal and elemental creative spirit. Brahma, described in early myths as having been born from a golden egg and then to have created the Earth, assumed the identity of the earlier Vedic deity Prajapati and became identified as the creator.

Some of the early Brahma myths were later taken over by the Vishnu cult. For example in one story Brahma was believed to have rescued the earth from a flood by taking the form of a fish or a tortoise and in another he became a boar, raising the Earth above the flood waters on his tusk. All these images were later associated with Vishnu.

By the fourth and fifth centuries AD, the height of the classical period of Hinduism, Brahma was seen as one of the trinity of Gods – *Trimurti* – in which Vishnu, Siva and Brahma represented three forms of the unmanifested supreme being. It is from Brahma that Hindu cosmology takes its structure. The basic cycle through which the whole cosmos passes is described as one day in the life of Brahma – the *kalpa*. It equals 4,320 million years, with an equally long night. One year of Brahma's life – a cosmic year – lasts 360 days and nights. The universe is expected to last for 100 years of Brahma's life, who is currently believed to be 51 years old.

By the sixth century AD Brahma worship had effectively ceased (before the great period of temple building), which accounts for the fact that there are remarkably few temples dedicated to Brahma. Nonetheless images of Brahma are found in most temples. Characteristically he is shown with four faces, a fifth having been destroyed by the fire from Siva's third eye. In his four arms he usually holds a copy of the Vedas, a sceptre and a water jug or a bow. He is accompanied by the goose, symbolizing knowledge.

Sarasvati Seen by some Hindus as the 'active power' of Brahma, popularly thought of as his consort, Sarasvati has survived into the modern Hindu world as a far more important figure than Brahma himself. In popular worship Sarasvati represents the goddess of education and learning, worshipped in schools and colleges with gifts of fruit, flowers and incense. She represents 'the word' itself, which began to be deified as part of the process of the writing of the Vedas, which ascribed magical power to words.

Normally white coloured, riding on a swan and carrying a book, she is often shown playing a vina. She may have many arms and heads, representing her role as patron of all the sciences and arts.

Vishnu Vishnu is seen as the God with the human face. From the second century a new and passionate devotional worship of Vishnu's incarnation as Krishna developed in the

How Sarasvati turned Brahma's head

Masson-Oursel recounts one myth that explains how Brahma came to have five heads. "Brahma first formed woman from his own immaculate substance and she was known as Sarasvati, Savitri, Gayatri or Brahmani. When he saw this lovely girl emerge from his own body Brahma fell in love with her. Sarasvati moved to his right to avoid his gaze, but a head immediately sprang up from the god. And when Sarasvati turned to the left and then behind him, two new heads emerged. She darted towards heaven and a fifth head was formed. Brahma then said to his daughter, 'Let us beget all kinds of living things, men, Suras and Asuras'. Hearing these words Sarasvati returned to earth, Brahma wedded her and they retired to a secret place where they remained together for a hundred (divine) years".

South. By 1,000 AD Vaishnavism had spread across South India and it became closely associated with the devotional form of Hinduism preached by **Ramanuja**, whose followers spread the worship of Vishnu and his 10 successive incarnations in animal and human form. For Vaishnavites, God took these different forms in order to save the world from impending disaster. AL Basham has summarized the 10 incarnations (see Table).

Rama and **Krishna** By far the most influential incarnations of Vishnu are those in which he was believed to take recognizable human form, especially as Rama (twice) and Krishna. As the Prince of Ayodhya, history and myth blend, for Rama was probably a chief who lived in the eighth or seventh century BC.

Although Rama is now seen as an earlier incarnation of Vishnu than Krishna, he came to be regarded as divine very late, probably after the Muslim invasions of the 12th century AD. The story has become part of the cultures of Southeast Asia.

Rama (or Ram – pronounced to rhyme with *calm*) is a powerful figure in contemporary India. His supposed birthplace at Ayodhya became the focus of fierce disputes between Hindus and Muslims in the early 1990's.

Krishna is worshipped extremely widely as perhaps the most human of the gods. His advice on the battlefield of the Mahabharata is one of the major sources of guidance for the rules of daily living for many Hindus today.

Lakshmi Commonly represented as Vishnu's wife, Lakshmi is widely worshipped as the goddess of wealth. Earlier representations of Vishnu's consorts portrayed her as Sridevi, often shown in statues on Vishnu's right, while Bhudevi, also known as Prithvi, who represented the earth, was on his left. Lakshmi is popularly shown in her own right as standing on a lotus flower, although eight forms of Lakshmi are recognized.

Hanuman The Ramayana tells how Hanuman, Rama's faithful servant, went across India and finally into the demon Ravana's forest home of Lanka at the head of his monkey army in search of the abducted Sita. He used his powers to jump the sea channel separating India from Sri Lanka and managed after a series of heroic and magical feats to find and rescue his master's wife. Whatever form he is shown in, he remains almost instantly recognizable.

Professor Wendy Doniger O'Flaherty argues that "Siva is in many ways the most uniquely Indian god of them all". She argues that the key to the myths through which his character is understood, lies in the explicit ambiguity of Siva as the great ascetic and at the same time as the erotic force of the universe.

Siva

Background

Hindu Deities

Deity	Association	Relationship
Brahma	Creator	One of Trinity
Sarasvati	Education and culture, "the word"	
vina, lotus, plam leaves, rosary	Hamsa	
Siva	Creator/destroyer	One of Trinity
Bhairava	Fierce aspect of Siva	
Parvati	Benevolent aspect of	Consort of Siva,
(Uma)	female divine power	mother of Ganesh
Kali	The energy that destroys	Consort of Siva
Durga	In fighting attitude	Consort of Siva
Ganesh/	God of good beginnings,	Son of Siva
Ganapati	clearer of obstacles	
Skanda	God of War/ bringer of disease	Son of Siva and
(Karttikkeya, Murugan, Subrahmanya)		Ganga
Vishnu	Preserver	One of Trinity
Prithvi/	Goddess of Earth	Wife of Vishnu
Bhudevi		
Lakshmi	Goddess of Wealth	Wife of Vishnu
Agni	God of Fire	
Indra	Rain, lightning and thunder	
Ravana	King of the demons	

Ardhanarisvara, the male/female form of Siva

Vishnu, Preserver of the Universe

Krishna, eighth incarnation of Vishnu

Durga, Mother-goddess, destroyer of demons

Attributes	Vehicle
4 heads, 4 arms, upper left holds water pot and rosary or sacrificial spoon, sacred thread across left shoulder	Hamsa (goose/swan)
Wife of Brahma	Two or more arms,
Linga; Rudra, matted hair, 3 eyes, drum, fire, deer, trident; Nataraja, Lord of the Dance	Bull - Nandi
Trident, sword, noose, naked, snakes, garland of skulls, dishevelled hair, carrying destructive weapons	Dog
2 arms when shown with Siva, 4 when on her own, blue lily in right hand, left hand hangs down	Lion
Trident, noose, human skulls, sword, shield, black colour	Lion
4 arms, conch, disc, bow, arrow, bell, sword, shield	Lion or tiger
Goad, noose, broken tusk, fruits	Rat/ mouse/ shrew
6 heads, 12 arms, spear, arrow, sword, discus, noose cock, bow, shield, conch and plough	Peacock
4 arms, high crown, discus and conch in upper arms, club and sword (or lotus) in lower, right hand in abhaya gesture, left holds pomegranate, left leg on treasure pot	Garuda - mythical eagle
Seated or standing on red lotus, 4 hands, lotuses, vessel and fruit	Lotus
Sacred thread, axe, wood, bellows, torch, sacrificial spoon	2-headed ram
Bow, thunderbolt, lances	
10 heads, 20 arms, bow and arrow	

Siva as Nataraj

Ganesh, bringer of prosperity

Parvati, wife of Siva

Kali, the "black" Mother-goddess

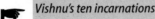

Vishnu's ten incarnations

Name	Form	Story
1 Matsya	Fish	Vishnu took the form of a fish to rescue Manu (the first man), his family and the Vedas from a flood.
2 Kurma	Tortoise	Vishnu became a tortoise to rescue all the treasures lost in the flood, including the divine nectar (Amrita) with which the gods preserved their youth. The gods put Mount Kailasa on the tortoise's back and when he reached the bottom of the ocean they twisted the divine snake round the mountain. They then churned the ocean with the mountain by pulling the snake
3 Varaha	Boar	Vishnu appeared again to raise the earth from the ocean's floor where it had been thrown by a demon, Hiranyaksa. The story probably developed from a non-Aryan cult of a sacred pig.
4 Narasimha	Half-man, half lion	Having persuaded Brahma to promise that he could not be killed either by day or night, by god, man or beast, the demon Hiranyakasipu then terrorized everybody. When the gods pleaded for help, Vishnu appeared at sunset, when it was neither day nor night, in the form of a half man and half lion and killed the demon.
5 Vamana	A dwarf	Bali, a demon, achieved supernatural power by asceticism. To protect the world Vishnu appeared before him in the form of a dwarf and asked him a favour. Bali granted Vishnu as much land as he could cover in three strides. Vishnu then became a giant, covering the earth in three strides. He left only hell to the demon.
6 Parasurama	Rama with the axe	Vishnu was incarnated as the son of a Brahmin, Jamadagni as Parasurama and killed the wicked king for robbing his father. The king's sons then killed Jamadagni and in revenge Parasurama destroyed all male kshatriyas, 21 times in succession.
7 Rama	The Prince of Ayodhya	As told in the Ramayana, Vishnu came in the form of Rama to rescue the world from the dark demon, Ravana. His wife Sita is the model of patient faithfulness while Hanuman, is the monkey-faced god and Rama's helper.
8 Krishna	Charioteer of Arjuma Many forms	Krishna meets almost every human need, from the mischievous child, the playful boy, the amorous youth to the Divine.
9 The Buddha		Probably incorporated into the Hindu pantheon in order to discredit the Buddhists, dominant in some parts of India until the 6th century AD. An early Hindu interpretation suggests that Vishnu took incarnation as Buddha to show compassion for animals and to end sacrifice.
10 Kalki	Riding on a horse	Vishnu's arrival will accompany the final destruction of this present age, Kaliyuga, judging the wicked and rewarding the good.

Siva is interpreted as both creator and destroyer, the power through whom the universe evolves. He lives on Mount Kailasa with his wife **Parvati** (also known as **Uma**, **Sati**, **Kali** and **Durga**) and two sons, the elephant-headed Ganesh and the 6-headed Karttikeya, known in South India as Subrahmanya. To many contemporary Hindus they form a model of sorts for family life. In sculptural representations Siva is normally accompanied by his 'vehicle', the bull (nandi).

Siva is also represented in Shaivite temples throughout India by the linga, literally meaning 'sign' or 'mark', but referring in this context to the sign of gender or phallus and yoni. On the one hand a symbol of energy, fertility and potency, as Siva's symbol it also represents the yogic power of sexual abstinence and penance. The linga has become the most important symbol of the cult of Siva. O'Flaherty suggests that the worship of the linga of Siva can be traced back to the pre-Vedic societies of the Indus Valley civilization (c2000 BC), but that it first appears in Hindu iconography in the second century BC.

From that time a wide variety of myths appeared to explain the origin of linga worship. The myths surrounding the 12 **jyotirlinga** (linga of light) found at centres like Ujjain go back to the second century BC and were developed in order to explain and justify linga worship.

Siva's alternative names Although Siva is not seen as having a series of rebirths, like Vishnu, he none the less appears in very many forms representing different aspects of his varied powers. Some of the more common are:

Mahadeva The representation of Siva as the god of supreme power, which came relatively late into Hindu thought, shown as the linga in combination with the *yoni*, or female genitalia.

Rudra Siva's early prototype, who may date back to the Indus Valley Civilization.

Virabhadra Siva created Virabhadra to avenge himself on his wife Sati's father, Daksha, who had insulted Siva by not inviting him to a special sacrifice. Sati attended the ceremony against Siva's wishes and when she heard her father grossly abusing Siva she committed suicide by jumping into the sacrificial fire. This act gave rise to the term *sati* (*suttee*, a word which simply means a good or virtuous woman). Recorded in the *Vedas*, the self immolation of a woman on her husband's funeral pyre probably did not become accepted practice until the early centuries BC. Even then it was mainly restricted to those of the kshatriya caste.

Nataraja, the Lord of the Cosmic Dance

Nandi Siva's vehicle, the bull, is one of the most widespread of sacred symbols of the ancient world and may represent a link with Rudra, who was sometimes represented as a bull in pre-Hindu India. Strength and virility are key attributes and pilgrims to Siva temples will often touch the Nandi's testicles on their way into the shrine.

Ganesh is one of Hinduism's most popular gods. He is seen as the great clearer of obstacles. Shown at gateways and on door lintels with his elephant head and pot belly, his image is revered across India. Meetings, functions and special family gatherings will often start with prayers to Ganesh and any new venture, from the opening of a building to inaugurating a company, will not be deemed complete without a Ganesh puja.

Ganesh

Shakti is a female divinity often worshipped in the form of Siva's wife Durga or Kali. As Durga she agreed to do battle with Mahish, an *asura* (demon) who threatened to dethrone the gods. As Kali ('black') the mother goddess takes on her most fearsome form and character. Fighting with the chief of the demons, she was forced to use every weapon in her armoury, but every drop of blood that she drew became 1,000 new giants. The only way she could win was by drinking the blood of all her enemies. Having succeeded she was so elated that her dance of triumph threatened the earth. She even threw her husband Siva to the ground and trampled over him, until she realized to her shame what she had done. She is always shown with a sword in one hand, the severed head of the giant in another, two corpses for earrings and a necklace of human skulls.

Shakti, The Mother Goddess

The worship of female goddesses developed into the widely practised form of devotional worship called Tantrism. Goddesses such as Kali became the focus of worship which often involved practices that flew in the face of wider Hindu moral

Worship of Siva's linga

Worship of Siva's linga – the phallic symbol of fertility, power and creativeness – is universal across India. Its origins lie in the creation myths of the Hindu trinity and in the struggle for supremacy between the different Hindu sects. Saivite myths illustrate the supreme power of Siva and the variety of ways in which Brahma and Vishnu were compelled to acknowledge his supreme power.

One such story tells how Siva, Vishnu and Brahma emerged from the ocean, whereupon Vishnu and Brahma begged him to perform creation. Siva agreed – but then to their consternation disappeared for 1,000 celestial years. They became so worried by the lack of creation that Vishnu told Brahma to create, so he produced everything that could lead to happiness. However, no sooner had Brahma filled the universe with beings than Siva reappeared. Incensed by the usurping of his power by Brahma, Siva decided to destroy everything with a flame from his

mouth so that he could create afresh.

As the fire threatened to consume everything Brahma acknowledged Siva's total power and pleaded with him to spare the creation that Brahma had brought forth. "But what shall I do with all my excess power?" "Send it to the sun", replied Brahma, "for as you are the lord of the sun we may all live together in the sun's energy."

Siva agreed, but said to Brahma "What use is this linga if I cannot use it to create?" So he broke off his linga and threw it to the ground. The linga broke through the earth and went right into the sky. Vishnu looked for the end of it below and Brahma for the top, but neither could find the end. Then a voice from the sky said "If the linga of the god with braided hair is worshipped, it will grant all desires that are longed for in the heart." When Brahma and Vishnu heard this, they and all the divinities worshipped the linga with devotion."

and legal codes. Animal and even human sacrifices and ritual sexual intercourse were part of Tantric belief and practice, the evidence for which may still be seen in the art and sculpture of some major temples. Tantric practice affected both Hinduism and Buddhism from the eighth century AD.

Skanda The God of War, Skanda became known as the son of Siva and Parvati. One legend suggests that he was conceived by the Goddess Ganga from Siva's seed.

Gods of the warrior caste Modern Hinduism has brought into its pantheon over many generations gods who were worshipped by the earlier pre-Hindu Aryan civilizations. The most important is **Indra**, often shown as the god of rain, thunder and lightning. To the early Vedic writers the clouds of the southwest monsoon were seen as hostile, determined to keep their precious treasure of water to themselves and only releasing it when forced to by a greater power.

Mitra and **Varuna** have the power both of gods and demons..

Agni, the god of fire, is a god whose origins lie with the priestly caste rather than with the kshatriyas, or warriors. Riding on a ram, wearing a sacred thread, he is often shown with flames leaping from his mouth for he is the god of ritual fire.

Surya, the god of the sun, fittingly of overpowering splendour is often described as being dark red, sitting on a red lotus or riding a chariot pulled by the seven horses of the dawn (representing the days of the week).

Devas & Asuras In Hindu popular mythology the world is also populated by innumerable gods and demons, with a somewhat uncertain dividing line between them. Both have great power and moral character and there are frequent conflicts and battles between them.

Auspicious signs

Some of Hinduism's sacred symbols are thought to have originated in the Aryan religion of the Vedic period.

Om The Primordial sound of the universe, 'Om' (or more correctly the three-in-one 'Aum') is the Supreme syllable. It is the opening and sometimes closing, chant for Hindu prayers. Some attribute the three constituents to the Hindu triad of Brahmka, Vishnu and Siva. It is believed to be the cosmic sound of Creation which encompasses all states from wakefulness to deep sleep and though it is the essence of all sound, it is outside our hearing.

Svastika Representing the Sun and it's energy, the svastika usually appears on doors or walls of temples, in red, the colour associated with good fortune and luck. The term derived from the Sanskrit 'svasti' is repeated in Hindu chants. The arms of the symbol point in the cardinal directionswhich may reflect the ancient practice of lighting fire sticks in the four directions. When the svastika appears to rotate clockwise it symbolizes positive creative energy of the sun; the anti-clockwise svastika, symbolizing the autumn/winter sun, is considered unlucky.

Six-pointed star The intersecting triangles in the 'Star of David' symbol represents Spirit and Matter held in balnce. A central dot signifies a particle of Divinity. Incorporated as a decorative element in some Muslim buildings such as Humayun's Tomb in Delhi.

Lotus The 'padma' or 'kamal' flower with it's many petals appears not only in art and architecture but also in association with gods and godesses. Some deities are seen holding one, others are portrayed seated or standing on the flower, or as with Padmanabha it appears from Vishnu's navel. The lotus represents purity, peace and beauty, a symbol also shared by Buddhists and Jains and as in nature stands away and above the impure, murky water from which it emerges. In architecture, the lotus motif occurs frequently and often represented in the base and capitals of columns.

| Om | Svastika | Six-pointed star | Lotus |

Hindu Society

Dharma is seen as the most important of the objectives of individual and social life. But what were the obligations imposed by dharma? Hindu law givers, such as those who compiled the code of Manu (AD 100-300), laid down rules of family conduct and social obligations related to the institutions of caste and jati which were beginning to take shape at the same time.

Although the word caste was given by the Portuguese in the 15th century AD, the main feature of the system emerged at the end of the Vedic period. Two terms – varna and jati – are used in India itself and have come to be used interchangeably and confusingly with the word caste.

Caste

Varna, which literally means colour, had a fourfold division. By 600 BC this had become a standard means of classifying the population. The fair-skinned Aryans distinguished themselves from the darker skinned earlier inhabitants. The priestly varna, the Brahmins, were seen as coming from the mouth of Brahma; the Kshatriyas were warriors, coming from Brahma's arms; the Vaishyas, a trading community, came

The sacred thread

The highest three varnas were classified as "twice born" and could wear the sacred thread symbolizing their status. The age at which the initiation ceremony (upanayana) for the upper caste child was carried out, varied according to class – 8 for a Brahmin, 11 for a Kshatriya and 12 for a Vaishya.

The boy, dressed like an ascetic and holding a staff in his hand, would have the sacred thread (yajnopavita) placed over his right shoulder and under his left arm. A cord of three threads, each of nine twisted strands,

it was made of cotton for Brahmans, hemp for Kshatriyas or wool for Vaishyas. It was – and is – regarded as a great sin to remove it.

The Brahmin who officiated would whisper a verse from the Rig Veda in the boy's ear, the Gayatri mantra. Addressed to the old solar god Savitr, the holiest of holy passages, the Gayatri can only be spoken by the three higher classes. AL Basham translated it as: "Let us think on the lovely splendour of the god Savitr, that he may inspire our minds".

from Brahma's thighs and the Sudras, classified as agriculturalists, from his feet. Relegated beyond the pale of civilized Hindu society were the untouchables or outcastes, who were left with the jobs which were regarded as impure, usually associated with dealing with the dead (human or animal) or with excrement.

Jati Many Brahmins and Rajputs are conscious of their varna status, but the great majority of Indians do not put themselves into one of the four varna categories, but into a jati group. There are thousands of different jatis across the country. While individuals found it impossible to change caste or to move up the social scale, groups would sometimes try to gain recognition as higher caste by adopting practices of the Brahmins such as becoming vegetarians. Many used to be identified with particular activities and occupations used to be hereditary. Caste membership is decided simply by birth. Although you can be evicted from your caste by your fellow members, usually for disobedience to caste rules such as over marriage, you cannot join another caste and technically you become an outcaste.

The Dalits Gandhi spearheaded his campaign for independence from British colonial rule with a powerful campaign to abolish the disabilities imposed by the caste system. Coining the term *Harijan* (meaning 'person of God'), which he gave to all former outcastes, Gandhi demanded that discrimination on the grounds of caste be outlawed. Lists – or 'schedules' – of backward castes were drawn up during the early part of this century in order to provide positive help to such groups. The term itself has now been widely rejected by many former outcastes as paternalistic and as implying an adherence to Hindu beliefs which some explicitly reject and today many argue passionately for the use of the secular term 'dalits' – the 'oppressed'.

Affirmative action Since 1947 the Indian government has extended its positive discrimination (a form of affirmative action) to scheduled castes and scheduled tribes, particularly through reserving up to 30% of jobs in government-run institutions and in further education, leading to professional qualifications for these groups and members of the scheduled castes are now found in important positions throughout the economy. Furthermore, most of the obvious forms of social discrimination, particularly rules which prohibit eating or drinking with members of lower castes, or from plates and cups that have been touched by them, have disappeared. Yet caste remains an extremely important aspect of India's social structures.

Marriage, which is still generally arranged by members of all religious communities, continues to be dictated almost entirely by caste and clan rules. Even in cities, where traditional means of arranging marriages have often broken down and where many people resort to advertising for marriage partners in the columns of the Sunday newspapers, caste is frequently stated as a requirement. Marriage is generally seen as an alliance between two families. Great efforts are made to match caste, social status and economic position, although the rules which govern eligibility vary from region to region. In some groups marriage between even first cousins is common, while among others marriage between any branch of the same clan is strictly prohibited.

Caste also remains an explosive political issue. Attempts to improve the social and economic position of harijans and what are termed 'other backward castes' (OBCs) continues to cause sometimes violent conflict.

Hindu reform movements

Hinduism today is a more self-conscious religious and political force than it was even at Independence in 1947. Reform movements of modern Hinduism can be traced back at least to the early years of the 19th century. These movements were unique in Hinduism's history in putting the importance of political ideas on the same level as strictly religious thinking and in interrelating them.

In the 19th-century English education and European literature and modern scientific thought, alongside the religious ideas of Christian missionaries, all became powerful influences on the newly emerging western educated Hindu opinion. That opinion was challenged to re-examine inherited Hindu beliefs and practice.

Some reform movements have had regional importance. Two of these originated, like the **Brahmo Samaj**, in Bengal. The **Ramakrishna Mission** was named after a temple priest in the Kali temple in Calcutta, Ramakrishna (1834-1886), who was a great mystic, preaching the basic doctrine that 'all religions are true'. He believed that the best religion for any individual was that into which he or she was born. One of his followers, **Vivekenanda**, became the founder of the Ramakrishna Mission.

While for its secular life India follows the Gregorian calendar, for Hindus, much of **The Hindu** religious and personal life follows the Hindu calendar (see also Festivals). This is based **calendar** on the lunar cycle of 29 days, but the clever bit comes in the way it is synchronized with the 365 day Gregorian solar calendar of the west by the addition of an 'extra month' (*adhik maas*), every 2½-3 years.

Hindus follow two distinct eras. The *Vikrama Samvat* which began in 57 BC (and is followed in Goa), and the *Salivahan Saka* which dates from 78 AD and has been the official Indian calendar since 1957. The *Saka* new year starts on 22 March and has the same length as the Gregorian calendar. In North India it is celebrated in the second month of *Vaisakh*.

The year itself is divided into two, the first six solar months being when the sun 'moves' north, known as the *Makar Sankranti* (which is marked by special festivals), and the second half when it moves south, the *Karka Sankranti*. The first begins in January and the second in June. The 29 day lunar month with its 'dark' (*Krishna*) and 'bright' (*Shukla*) halves based on the new (*Amavasya*) and full moons (*Purnima*), are named after the 12 constellations, and total a 354 day year. The day itself is divided into eight *praharas* of three hours each and the year into six seasons: *Vasant* (spring), *Grishha* (summer), *Varsha* (rains), *Sharat* (early autumn), *Hemanta* (late autumn), *Shishir* (winter).

Background

				Hindu &
Chaitra	March-April	*Ashwin*	September-October	**Hindu &**
Vaishakh	April-May	*Kartik*	October-November	**corresponding**
Jyeshtha	May-June	*Margashirsha*	November-December	**Gregorian**
Aashadh	June-July	*Poush*	December-January	**calendar**
Shravan	July-August	*Magh*	January-February	**months**
Bhadra	August-September	*Phalgun*	February-March	

Islam

Islam is a highly visible presence in India today. Even after partition in 1947 over 40 million Muslims remained in India and today there are around 120 million. It is the most recent of imported religions. Islamic contact with India was first made around 636 AD and then by the navies of the Arab Mohammad al Qasim in 710-712 AD.

The victory of the Turkish ruler of Ghazni over the Rajputs in AD 1192 established a 500 year period of Muslim power in India. By AD 1200 the Turkish sultans had annexed Bihar in the east, in the process wiping out the last traces of Buddhism with the massacre of a Buddhist monastic order.

The contact between the courts of the new rulers and the indigenous Hindu populations produced innovative developments in art and architecture, language and literature. Hindus and Hindu culture were profoundly affected by the spread and exercise of Muslim political power, but Islam too underwent major modifications in response to the new social and religious context in which the Muslim rulers found themselves.

Muslim beliefs The beliefs of Islam (which means 'submission to God') could apparently scarcely be more different from those of Hinduism. Islam, often described as having "five pillars" of faith (see box) has a fundamental creed; 'There is no God but God; and Mohammad is the Prophet of God' (*La Illaha illa 'Ilah Mohammad Rasulu 'Ilah*). One book, the Qur'an, is the supreme authority on Islamic teaching and faith. Islam preaches the belief in bodily resurrection after death and in the reality of heaven and hell.

Islam has no priesthood. The authority of Imams derives from social custom and from their authority to interpret the scriptures, rather than from a defined status within the Islamic community. Islam also prohibits any distinction on the basis of race or colour and most Muslims believe it is wrong to represent the human figure. It is often thought, inaccurately, that this ban stems from the Qur'an itself. In fact it probably has its origins in the belief of Mohammad that images were likely to be turned into idols.

Muslim Sects During the first century after Mohammad's death Islam split in to two sects which were divided on political and religious grounds, the Shi'is and Sunni's. The religious basis for the division lay in the interpretation of verses in the Qur'an and of traditional sayings of Mohammad, the Hadis. Both sects venerate the Qur'an but have different *Hadis*. They also have different views as to Mohammad's successor.

The **Sunnis** – always the majority in South Asia – believe that Mohammad did not appoint a successor and that Abu Bak'r, Omar and Othman were the first three caliphs (or vice-regents) after Mohammad's death. Ali, whom the Sunni's count as the fourth caliph, is regarded as the first legitimate caliph by the Shi'is, who consider Abu Bak'r and Omar to be usurpers. While the Sunni's believe in the principle of election of caliphs, Shi'is believe that although Mohammad is the last prophet there is a continuing need for intermediaries between God and man. Such intermediaries are termed Imams and they base both their law and religious practice on the teaching of the Imams.

The two major divisions are marked by further sub-divisions.

From the Mughal emperors, who enjoyed an unparalleled degree of political power, down to the poorest peasant farmers of Bengal, Muslims in India have found different ways of adjusting to their Hindu environment. Some have reacted by accepting or even incorporating features of Hindu belief and practice in their own. Akbar, the most eclectic of Mughal emperors, went as far as banning activities like cow slaughter which were offensive to Hindus and celebrated Hindu festivals in court.

The five pillars of Islam

In addition to the belief that there is one God and that Mohammed is his prophet, there are four further obligatory requirements imposed on Muslims. Daily prayers are prescribed at daybreak, noon, afternoon, sunset and nightfall. Muslims must give alms to the poor. They must observe a strict fast during the month of Ramadan. They must not eat or drink between sunrise and sunset. Lastly, they should attempt the pilgrimage to the Ka'aba in Mecca, known as the Hajj. Those who have done so are entitled to the prefix Hajji before their name.

Islamic rules differ from Hindu practice in several other aspects of daily life. Muslims are strictly forbidden to drink alcohol (though some suggest that this prohibition is restricted to the use of fermented grape juice, that is wine, it is commonly accepted to apply to all alcohol). Eating pork, or any meat from an animal not killed by draining its blood while alive, is also prohibited. Meat prepared in the appropriate way is called Halal. Finally, usury (charging interest on loans) and games of chance are forbidden.

The Islamic Calendar

The calendar begins on 16 July 622 AD, the date of the Prophet's migration from Mecca to Medina, the Hijra, hence AH (Anno Hejirae). *Murray's Handbook for travellers in India* gave a wonderfully precise method of calculating the current date in the Christian year from the AH date: "To correlate the Hijra year with the Christian year, express the former in years and decimals of a year, multiply by .970225, add 621.54 and the total will correspond exactly with the Christian year".

The Muslim year is divided into 12 lunar months, totalling 354 or 355 days, hence Islamic festivals usually move 11 days earlier each year according to the solar (Gregorian) calendar. The first month of the year is *Moharram,* followed by *Safar, Rabi-ul-Awwal, Rabi-ul-Sani, Jumada-ul-Awwal, Jumada-ul-Sani, Rajab, Shaban, Ramadan, Shawwal, Ziquad* and *Zilhaj.*

Buddhism

India was the home of Buddhism, which had its roots in the early Hinduism, or Brahmanism, of its time. Today it is practised only on the margins of the subcontinent, from Ladakh, Nepal and Bhutan in the north to Sri Lanka in the south. Most are very recent converts, the last adherents of the early schools of Buddhism having been killed or converted by the Muslim invaders of the 13th century.

The 1951 Census of India recorded only 181,000 Buddhists. However, in October 1956 Dr BR Ambedkar, a Hindu leader of the outcaste community and writer of the Indian Constitution, embraced Buddhism and was joined by 200,000 other outcastes. The movement has continued, particularly in Western India and there are now approximately 7 million Buddhists. However, India's Buddhist significance is now mainly as the home for the extraordinarily beautiful artistic and architectural remnants of what was for several centuries the region's dominant religion.

India has sites of great significance for Buddhists around the world. Some say that the Buddha himself spoke of the four places his followers should visit. **Lumbini**, the Buddha's birthplace, is in the Nepali foothills, near the present border with India. **Bodh Gaya**, where he attained what Buddhists term his 'supreme enlightenment', is about 80 km south of the modern Indian city of Patna; the deer park at **Sarnath**, where he preached his first sermon and set in motion the Wheel of the Law, is just outside Varanasi; and **Kushinagara**, where he died at the age of 80, is 50 km east of

Gorakhpur. There were four other sacred places of pilgrimage – **Rajgir**, where he tamed a wild elephant; **Vaishali**, where a monkey offered him honey; **Sravasti**, associated with his great miracle; and **Sankasya**, where he descended from heaven. The eight significant events associated with the holy places are repeatedly represented in Buddhist art.

In addition there are remarkable monuments, sculptures and works of art, from Gandhara in modern Pakistan to Sanchi and Ajanta in central India, where it is still possible to see the vivid evidence of the flowering of Buddhist culture in South Asia. In Sri Lanka, Bhutan and Nepal the traditions remain alive.

The Buddha's Life

Siddharta Gautama, who came to be given the title of the Buddha – the Enlightened One – was born a prince into the warrior caste in about 563 BC. He was married at the age of 16 and his wife had a son. When he reached the age of 29 he left home and wandered as a beggar and ascetic. After about 6 years he spent some time in Bodh Gaya. Sitting under the Bo tree, meditating, he was tempted by the demon Mara, with all the desires of the world. Resisting these temptations, he received enlightenment. These scenes are common motifs of Buddhist art.

The next landmark was the preaching of his first sermon on 'The Foundation of Righteousness' in the deer park near Benaras. By the time he died the Buddha had established a small band of monks and nuns known as the *Sangha* and had followers across North India. His body was cremated and the ashes, regarded as precious relics, were divided among the peoples to whom he had preached. Some have been discovered as far west as Peshawar, in Pakistan and at Piprawa, close to his birthplace.

After the Buddha's death

From the Buddha's death, or *parinirvana*, to the destruction of Nalanda (the last Buddhist stronghold in India) in 1197 AD, Buddhism in India went through three phases. These are often referred to as Hinayana, Mahayana and Vajrayana, though they were not mutually exclusive, being followed simultaneously in different regions.

Hinayana

The Hinayana or Lesser Way insists on a monastic way of life as the only path to the personal goal of *nirvana* (see box page 375) achieved through an austere life. Divided into many schools, the only surviving Hinayana tradition is the **Theravada**, Buddhism, which was taken to Sri Lanka by the Emperor Asoka's son Mahinda, where it became the state religion.

Mahayana

In contrast to the Hinayana schools, the followers of the Mahayana school (the Greater Way) believed in the possibility of salvation for all. They practised a far more devotional form of meditation and new figures came to play a prominent part in their beliefs and their worship – the **Bodhisattvas**, saints who were predestined to reach the state of enlightenment through thousands of rebirths. They aspired to Buddhahood, however, not for their own sake but for the sake of all living things. The Buddha is believed to have passed through numerous existences in preparation for his final mission. Mahayana Buddhism became dominant over most of South

The Buddha in Bhumisparsha-mudra calling the earth to witness

The Buddha's Four Noble Truths

The Buddha preached Four Noble Truths: that life is painful; that suffering is caused by ignorance and desire; that beyond the suffering of life there is a state which cannot be described but which he termed nirvana; and that nirvana can be reached by following an eightfold path.

The concept of nirvana is often understood in the west in an entirely negative sense – that of 'non-being'. The word has the rough meaning of 'blow out' or 'extinguish', meaning to blow out the fires of greed, lust and desire. In a more positive sense it has been described by one Buddhist scholar as "the state of absolute illumination, supreme bliss, infinite love and compassion, unshakeable serenity and unrestricted spiritual freedom". The essential elements of the eightfold path are the perfection of wisdom, morality and meditation.

Asia and its influence is evidenced in Buddhist art from Gandhara in north Pakistan to Ajanta in Central India.

Vajrayana

A new branch of Buddhism, Vajrayana, or the Vehicle of the Thunderbold, appeared which began to lay stress on secret magical rituals and cults of female divinities in order to gain supernatural powers. The Buddha and the bodhisattvas were attributed female counterparts or 'Taras' who became vehicles of salvation. The new 'Diamond Way' adopted the practice of magic, yoga and meditation as in Hinduism. It became associated with secret ceremonies, chanting of mystical 'mantras' and taking part in orgiastic rituals in the cause of spiritual gain in order to help others. The ideal of the Vajrayana Buddhist was to be 'so fully in harmony with the cosmos as to be able to manipulate the cosmic forces within and outside himself'. It had developed in the north of India by the seventh century AD, matching the parallel growth of Hindu Tantrism and was adopted by the Tibetans as the correct vehicle for attaining salvation. The magical power associated with Vajrayana requires instruction from a teacher or Lama, hence the Tibetan form is sometimes referred to as 'Lamaistic'.

Buddhist beliefs

Buddhism is based on the Buddha's own preaching. However, when he died none of those teachings had been written down. He developed his beliefs in reaction to the Brahmanism of his time, rejecting several of the doctrines of Vedic religion which were widely held in his lifetime: the Vedic gods, scriptures and priesthood and all social distinctions based on caste. However, he did accept the belief in the cyclical nature of life and that the nature of an individual's existence is determined by a natural process of reward and punishment for deeds in previous lives – the Hindu doctrine of karma (see page 359). In the Buddha's view, though, there is no eternal soul. He denied the identification of the Self with the everchanging Mind-Body (here, some see parallels in the Advaita Vedanta philosophy of Self-*Brahman* in Hinduism). In Buddhism, *Anatta* (no-Self), overcame the egoistical Self, given to attachment and selfishness.

Following the Buddha's death a succession of councils was called to try and reach agreement on doctrine. The first three were held within 140 years of the Buddha's death, the fourth being held at Pataliputra (modern Patna) during the reign of the Emperor Asoka (272-232 BC), who had recently been converted to Buddhism. Under his reign Buddhism spread throughout South Asia and opened the routes through Northwest India for Buddhism to travel into China, where it had become a force by the first century AD.

Background

Buddhism's The decline of Buddhism in India probably stemmed as much from the growing
decline similarity in the practice of Hinduism and Buddhism as from direct attacks.
Mahayana Buddhism, with its reverence for Bodhisattvas and its devotional
character, was more and more difficult to distinguish from the revivalist Hinduism
characteristic of several parts of North India from the seventh to the 12th centuries
AD. The Muslim conquest dealt the final death blow, being accompanied by the
large scale slaughter of monks and the destruction of monasteries. Without their
institutional support Buddhism faded away.

Sikhism

Guru Nanak, the founder of the religion was born just west of Lahore and grew up
in what is now the Pakistani town of Sultanpur. His followers, the Sikhs, (derived from
the Sanskrit word for 'disciples') form perhaps one of India's most recognizable
groups. Beards and turbans give them a very distinctive presence and although they
represent less than 2 of the population they are both politically and economically
significant.

Sikh beliefs The first Guru, accepted the ideas of *samsara* – the cycle of rebirths – and *karma*
(see page 359) from Hinduism. However, Sikhism is unequivocal in its belief in the
oneness of God, rejecting idolatry and any worship of objects or images. Guru Nanak
believed that God is One, formless, eternal and beyond description.

Guru Nanak also fiercely opposed discrimination on the grounds of caste. He saw
God as present everywhere, visible to anyone who cared to look and as essentially
full of grace and compassion.

Some of Guru Nanak's teachings are close to the ideas of the Benaras mystic
Kabir, who, in common with the Muslim mystic sufis, believed in mystical union
with God. He transformed the Hindu concept of *maya* into the belief that the values
commonly held by the world were an illusion.

Guru Nanak preached that salvation depended on accepting the nature of God. If
man recognized the true harmony of the divine order (*hookam*) and brought
himself into line with that harmony he would be saved. Rejecting the prevailing
Hindu belief that such harmony could be achieved by ascetic practices, he
emphasized three actions; meditating on and repeating God's name (*naam*), 'giving',
or charity (*daan*) and bathing (*isnaan*).

Many of the features now associated with Sikhism can be attributed to **Guru
Gobind Singh**, who on 15 April 1699, started the new brotherhood called the
Khalsa (meaning 'the pure', from the Persian word *khales*), an inner core of the
faithful, accepted by baptism (*amrit*). The 'five ks' date from this period: *kesh* (uncut
hair), the most important, followed by *kangha* (comb, usually of wood), *kirpan*
(dagger or short sword), *kara* (steel bangle) and *kachh* (similar to 'boxer' shorts). The
dagger and the shorts reflect military influence.

The Khalsa also explicitly forbade the seclusion of women, one of the common
practices of Islam. It was only under the warrior king Ranjit Singh (1799-1838) that
the idea of the Guru's presence in meetings of the Sikh community (the *Panth*) gave
way to the now universally held belief in the total authority of the **Guru Granth**, the
recorded words of the Guru in the scripture.

The Golden Temple in Amritsar, built at the end of the 16th century, is the holiest
site of Sikhism.

Culture

Language

The graffiti written on the walls of any Indian city bear witness to the number of major languages spoken across the country, many with their own distinct scripts. In all the states of North and West India an Indo-Aryan language – the easternmost group of the Indo-European family – is predominant. Sir William Jones, the great 19th-century scholar, discovered the close links between Sanskrit (the basis of nearly all North Indian languages) German and Greek. He showed that they all must have originated in the common heartland of Central Asia, being carried west, south and east by the nomadic tribes who shaped so much of the subsequen t history of both Europe and Asia.

As the pastoralists from Central Asia moved into South Asia from 2000 BC onwards, the Indo-Aryan languages they spoke were gradually modified. **Sanskrit** developed from this process, emerging as the dominant classical language of India by the sixth century BC, when it was classified in the grammar of **Panini**. It remained the language of the educated until about AD 1000, though it had ceased to be in common use several centuries earlier. The Muslims brought Persian into South Asia as the language of the rulers, where it became the language of the numerically tin y but politically powerful élite.

Sanskrit

The most striking example of Muslim influence on the earlier Indo-European languages is that of the two most important languages of India and Pakistan, Hindi and Urdu respectively. Most of the other modern North Indian languages were not written until the 16th century or after. Hindi developed into the language of the heartland of Hindu culture, stretching from Punjab to Bihar and from the foothills of the Himalaya to the marchlands of central India.

Hindi & Urdu

At the east end of the Ganga plains Hindi gives way to Bengali (Bangla), the language today of over 50 million people in India. Linguistically it is close to Assamese.

Bengali

Scripts

It is impossible to spend even a short time in India or the other countries of South Asia without coming across several of the different scripts that are used. The earliest ancestor of scripts in use today was **Brahmi**, in which Asoka's famous inscriptions were written in the third century BC. Written from left to right, a separate symbol represented each different sound.

For about a thousand years the major script of northern India has been the Nagari or Devanagari, which means literally the script of the 'city of the gods'. Hindi, Nepali and Marathi join Sanskrit in their use of Devanagari. The Muslim rulers developed a right to left script based on Persian and Arabic.

Devanagari

Many of the Indian alphabets have their own notation for numerals. This is not without irony, for what in the western world are called 'Arabic' numerals are in fact

Numerals

Background

of Indian origin. In some parts of South Asia local numerical symbols are still in use, but by and large you will find that the Arabic number symbols familiar in Europe and the West are common.

The role of English

English now plays an important role across India. It is widely spoken in towns and cities and even in quite remote villages it is usually not difficult to find someone who speaks at least a little English. Other European languages are almost completely unknown. The accent in which English is spoken is often affected strongly by the mother tongue of the speaker and there have been changes in common grammar which sometimes make it sound unusual. Many of these changes have become standard Indian English usage, as valid as any other varieties of English used around the world.

Literature

The Vedas Sanskrit was the first all-India language. Its literature has had a fundamental influence on the religious, social and political life of the entire region. Its earliest books, the four Vedas, were memorized and recited. The Rig Veda, a collection of 1,028 hymns probably did not reach its final form until about the sixth century BC, but the earliest may go back as far as 1300 BC.

Not all the verses are directly religious, but its main function was to provide orders of worship for priests responsible for the sacrifices which were central to the religion of the Indo-Aryans. Two later texts, the Yajurveda and the Samaveda, served the same purpose. A fourth, the Atharvaveda, is largely a collection of magic spells.

The Brahmanas Central to the Vedic literature was a belief in the importance of sacrifice. At some time after 1000 BC a second category of Vedic literature, the Brahmanas, began to take shape. Story telling developed as a means to interpret the significance of sacrifice. The most famous and the most important of these were the Upanishads, probably written at some time between the seventh and fifth centuries BC.

The Mahabharata The Brahmanas gave their name to the religion emerging between the eighth and sixth centuries BC, Brahmanism, the ancestor of Hinduism. Two of it's texts remain the best known and most widely revered epic compositions in South Asia, the Mahabharata and the Ramayana.

Dating the Mahabharata

Tradition puts the date of the great battle described in the Mahabharata at precisely 3102 BC, the start of the present era, and names the author of the poem as a sage, Vyasa. Evidence suggests however that the battle was fought around 800 BC, at **Kurukshetra. It was another 400 years before priests began to write the stories down, a process which was not complete until 400 AD. The original version was about 3,000 stanzas long, but it now contains over 100,000 – eight times as long as Homer's Iliad and the Odyssey put together.**

Good & evil The battle was seen as a war of the forces of good and evil, the **Pandavas** being interpreted as gods and the **Kauravas** as devils. The arguments were elaborated and expanded until about the fourth century AD by which time, as Shackle says, "Brahmanism had absorbed and set its own mark on the religious ideas of the epic and Hinduism had come into being". A comparatively late addition to the

The story of Rama

Under Brahmin influence, **Rama** was transformed from the human prince of the early versions into the divine figure of the final story. Rama, the 'jewel of the solar kings', became deified as an incarnation of Vishnu. The story tells how Rama was banished from his father's kingdom. In a journey that took him as far as Sri Lanka, accompanied by his wife Sita and helper and friend Hanuman (the monkey-faced God depicted in many Indian temples, shrines and posters), Rama finally fought the king **Ravana**, again changed in late versions into a demon. Rama's rescue of Sita was interpreted as the Aryan triumph over the barbarians. The epic is widely seen as South Asia's first literary poem and is known and recited in all Hindu communities.

Ravana, demon king of Lanka

Mahabharata, the Bhagavad-Gita is the most widely read and revered text among Hindus in South Asia today.

The Ramayana

Valmiki is thought of in India as the author of the second great Indian epic, the Ramayana. Like the Mahabharata, it underwent several stages of development before it reached its final version of 48,000 lines.

Sanskrit Literature

Sanskrit was always the language of the court and the élite. Other languages replaced it in common speech by the third century BC, but it remained in restricted use for over 1,000 years after that period. The remarkable Sanskrit grammar of Panini helped to establish grammar as one of the six disciplines essential to understanding the Vedas properly and to conducting Vedic rituals. The other five were phonetics, etymology, meter, ritual practice and astronomy. Sanskrit literature continued to be written in the courts until the Muslims replaced it with Persian, long after it had ceased to be a language of spoken communication. One India's greatest poets, **Kalidasa**, contributed to the development of Sanskrit as the language of learning and the arts.

Vatsyana's Kamasutra not only explores the diversity of physical love but sheds light on social customs. In architecture the Nagara and Dravida styles were first developed. The Brahmins also produced theses on philosophy and on the structure of society, but these had the negative effect of contributing to the extreme rigidity of the caste system which became apparent from this period onwards.

Literally 'stories of ancient times', the Puranas are about Brahma, Vishnu and Siva. Although some of the stories may relate to real events that occurred as early as 1500 BC, they were not compiled until the fifth century AD. Margaret and James Stutley record the belief that "during the destruction of the world at the end of the age, Hayagriva is said to have saved the Puranas. A summary of the original work is now preserved in Heaven!"

The Colonial Period

As the British extended their political power so the role of English grew. There is now a very wide Indian literature accessible in English, which has thus become the latest of the languages to be used across the whole of South Asia.

In the 19th century English became a vehicle for developing nationalist ideals. However, notably in the work of **Rabindranath Tagore**, it became a medium for religious and philosophical prose and for a developing poetry. Tagore himself won the Nobel Prize for Literature in 1913 for his translation into English of his own work, Gitanjali. Leading South Asian philosophers and thinkers of the 20th century have written major works in English, including not only MK Gandhi and Jawaharlal Nehru, the two leading figures in India's Independence movement, but S Radhakrishnan, Aurobindo Ghose and Sarojini Naidu, who all added to the depth of Indian literature in English.

Some suggestions for reading are listed in Essentials (see page 58). In addition, several South Asian regional languages have their own long traditions of both religious and secular literature which are discussed in the relevant sections of this Handbook.

Architecture

Over the 4,000 years since the Indus Valley civilization flourished, art and architecture have developed with a remarkable continuity through successive regional and religious influences and styles.

The Buddhist art and architecture of the third century BC left few remains, but the stylistic influence on early Hindu architecture was profound. From the sixth century AD the first Hindu religious buildings to have survived into the modern period were constructed in south and East India.

Coming into India as vanquishing hordes, the early Muslims destroyed much that was in their path. Temples that had been encrusted with jewels were left bare and mosques were built out of the stones of destroyed temples. Yet the flowering of Islamic architecture which followed was not simply a transplant from another country or region, but grew out of India's own traditions. That continuity reflected many forces, not least the use made by the great Mughal emperors of local skilled craftsmen and builders at every stage of their work.

Painting, sculpture, inlay work, all blended skills from a variety of sources and craftsmen – even occasionally from Europe. What emerged was another stepping stone in a tradition of Indian architecture, which wove the threads of Hindu tradition into new forms. The Taj Mahal was the ultimate product of this extraordinary process. Yet regional styles developed their own special feature and the main thrust of Hindu and Muslim religious buildings remains fundamentally different.

Hindu Temple Buildings

The principles of religious building were laid down by priests in the *Sastras*. Every aspect of Hindu, Jain and Buddhist religious building is identified with conceptions of the structure of the universe. This applies as much to the process of building – the timing of which must be undertaken at astrologically propitious times – as to the formal layout of the buildings. The cardinal directions of north, south, east and west are the basic fix on which buildings are planned. George Michell suggests that in addition to the cardinal directions, number is also critical to the design of the religious building. The key to the ultimate scale of the building is derived from the measurements of the sanctuary at its heart.

Indian temples were nearly always built according to philosophical understandings of the universe. This cosmology, of an infinite number of universes, isolated from each other in space, proceeds by imagining various possibilities as to its nature. Its centre is seen as dominated by **Mt Meru** which keeps earth and heaven apart. The concept of *separation* is crucial to Hindu thought and social practice. Continents, rivers and oceans occupy concentric rings around the mountain, while the stars encircle the mountain in another plane. Humans live on the continent of **Jambudvipa**, characterized by the rose apple tree (*jambu*).

Mandalas The Sastras show plans of this continent, organized in concentric rings and entered at the cardinal points. This type of diagram was known as a **mandala**. Such a geometric scheme could be subdivided into almost limitless small compartments, each of which could be designated as having special properties or be devoted to a particular deity. The centre of the mandala would be the seat of the major god. Mandalas provided the ground rules for the building of stupas and temples across India and gave the key to the symbolic meaning attached to every aspect of religious buildings.

The focal point of the temple, its sanctuary, was the home of the presiding deity, the 'womb-chamber' (*garbhagriha*). A series of doorways, in large temples leading through a succession of buildings, allowed the worshipper to move towards the final encounter with the deity to obtain *darshan* – a sight of the god. Both Buddhist and Hindu worship encourage the worshipper to walk clockwise around the shrine, performing *pradakshina*.

Temple design

The elevations are symbolic representations of the home of the gods. Mountain peaks such as Kailasa are common names for the most prominent of the towers. The tallest of these towers rises above the *garbagriha* itself, symbolizing the meeting of earth and heaven in the person of the enshrined deity. In contrast to the extraordinary profusion of colour and life on the outside, the interior is dark and cramped but here it is believed, lies the true centre of divine power.

Buddhist and Hindu architecture probably began with wooden building, for the rock carving and cave excavated temples show clear evidence of copying styles which must have been developed first in wooden buildings. The third to second century BC caves of the Buddhists were followed in the seventh and eighth centuries AD by free standing but rock-cut temples. They were subsequently replaced by temples built entirely out of assembled material, usually stone.

Temple development

Muslim religious architecture

Although the Muslims adapted many Hindu features, they also brought totally new forms. Their most outstanding contribution, dominating the architecture of many North Indian cities, are the mosques and tomb complexes (*dargah*). The use of brickwork was widespread and they brought with them from Persia the principle of constructing the true arch. Muslim architects succeeded in producing a variety of domed structures, often incorporating distinctively Hindu features such as the surmounting finial. By the end of the great period of Muslim building in 1707, the Muslims had added magnificent forts and palaces to their religious structures, a statement of power as well as of aesthetic taste.

European buildings

Nearly two centuries of architectural stagnation and decline followed the demise of Mughal power. Not until the end of the Victorian period, when British imperial ambitions were at their height, did the British colonial impact on public rather than

Background

The big screen

The hugely popular Hindi film industry comes mainly out of the tradition of larger-than-life productions with familiar story lines performed as escapist entertainment for the community. The stars lead fantasy lives as they enjoy cult status with a following of millions. It is not surprising that should they choose to turn their hand to politics, they find instant support in an unquestioning, adoring electorate. The experience of a Bollywood film is not to be missed - at least once in your life. Television has made a visit to a cinema redundant though it's always easy to find one in any sizeable town; the gaudy posters dominate every street scene. Be prepared for a long sitting with a standard story line, set characters and lots of action as the typical multi-million rupee blockbusters attempt to provide something to please everybody. Marathon melodramas consist of slapstick comedy contrasted with tear-jerking tragedy, a liberal sprinkling of moralizing with a tortuous disentangling of the knots tied by the heroes, heroines, villains and their extended families. The usual ingredients are the same: shrill Hindi "film music", unoriginal songs mouthed to the voice of playback artistes, hip-jerking dancing by suggestively clad figures which lack all subtlety when it comes to sexual innuendo, honeymooning couples before a backdrop of snowy mountains, car chases and violent disasters - these will keep you enthralled for hours. On a serious note, there are ample examples of truly brilliant works by world-class Indian film makers (Satyajit Ray, Rithwik Ghatak, Shyam Benegal, Aparna Roy to name a few) but they are not usually box office successes or made for popular consumption so they have to be sought out.

domestic architecture begin to be felt. At the end of the 19th century wanted to recapture and enhance a tradition for which they had great respect. They have left a series of buildings, both in formerly British ruled territory and in the Princely States, which illustrate this concern through the development of what became known as the Indo-Saracenic style.

The British hill stations in the Himalayan foothills were developed to provide a comfortable escape from the plains for several months. Houses for the ruling classes in Shimla, Nainital, Mussoorie, Darjeeling and Shillong sometimes incorporated features harking back incongruously to the gothic and half-timbered buildings of 'home'. These were often complemented with impressive town halls, churches, club houses, libraries and band stands.

Music and dance

Music Indian music can trace its origins to the metrical hymns and chants of the Vedas, in which the production of sound according to strict rules was understood to be vital to the continuing order of the Universe. Through more than 3,000 years of development and a range of regional schools, India's musical tradition has been handed on almost entirely by ear. The chants of the **Rig Veda** developed into songs in the **Sama Veda** and music found expression in every sphere of life, reflecting the cycle of seasons and the rhythm of work.

Over the centuries the original three notes, which were sung strictly in descending order, were extended to five and then seven and developed to allow freedom to move up and down the scale. The scale increased to 12 with the addition of flats and sharps and finally to 22 with the further subdivision of semitones. Books of musical rules go back at least as far as the third century AD. Classical music was totally intertwined with dance and drama, an interweaving reflected in the term *sangita*.

At some point after the Muslim influence made itself felt in the north, north and South Indian styles diverged, to become Carnatic (Karnatak) music in the south and Hindustani music in the north. However, they still share important common features: *svara* (pitch), *raga* (the melodic structure) and *tala* or *talam* (metre).

The essential structure of a melody is known as a **raga** which usually has five to seven notes and can have as many as nine (or even 12 in mixed ragas). The music is improvised by the performer within certain governing rules and although theoretically thousands of ragas are possible, only around a hundred are commonly performed. Ragas have become associated with particular moods and specific times of the day.

Land and environment

Geography

India falls into three major geological regions. The north is enclosed by the great arc of the Himalaya. Along their southern flank lie the alluvial plains of the Ganga and to the south again is the Peninsula.

The origins of India's landscapes

Only 100 million years ago the Indian Peninsula was still attached to the great land mass of what geologists call 'Pangaea' alongside South Africa, Australia and Antarctica. Then as the great plates on which the earth's southern continents stood broke up, the Indian Plate started its dramatic shift northwards, eventually colliding with the Asian plate. As the Indian Plate continues to get pushed under the Tibetan Plateau so the Himalaya continue to rise.

The Himalaya The Himalaya dominate the northern borders of India, stretching 2,500 km from northwest to southeast. They are unparalleled anywhere in the world. Of the 94 mountains in Asia above 7,300 m, all but two are in the Himalaya. Nowhere else in the world are there mountains as high.

The Himalaya proper, stretching from the Pamirs in Pakistan to the easternmost bend of the Brahmaputra in Assam, can be divided into three broad zones. On the southern flank are the Shiwaliks, or Outer Ranges. To their immediate north run the parallel Middle Ranges of Pir Panjal and Dhauladhar and to the north again is the third zone, the Inner Himalaya, which has the highest peaks, many of them in Nepal.

The central core of the Himalayan ranges did not begin to rise until about 35 million years ago. The latest mountain building period, responsible for the Shiwaliks, began less than 5 million years ago and is still continuing, raising some of the high peaks by as much as 5 mm a year. Such movement comes at a price and the boundary between the plains and the Himalayan ranges is a zone of continuing violent earthquakes and massive erosion.

Himalayan profile

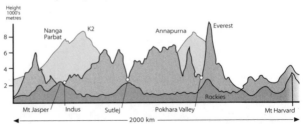

As the Himalaya began their dramatic uplift the trough which formed to the south of the newly emerging mountains was steadily filled with the debris washed down from the hills, creating the Indo-Gangetic plains. Today the alluvium reaches depths of over 5,000 m in places.

The Gangetic Plains

The silts washed down from the Himalaya have made it possible for intensive rice cultivation to be practised continuously for hundreds of years, though they cause problems for modern irrigation development. Dams in the Himalayan region are being rapidly filled by silt, over 33 million tonnes being deposited behind the Bhakra Dam on the Sutlej River alone.

Climate

Himalayan climates vary dramatically in relation to height above sea level and position relative to the main rain bearing winds of the monsoon.

The term monsoon refers to the wind reversal which replaces the dry northeasterlies, characteristic of winter and spring, with the very warm and wet southwesterlies of the summer. The arrival of the monsoon is as variable as is the amount of rain which it brings. What makes the Indian monsoon quite exceptional

The monsoon

Monsoon is an Arabic word meaning 'season'

Rainfall

Mean annual maximum precipitation (mm)

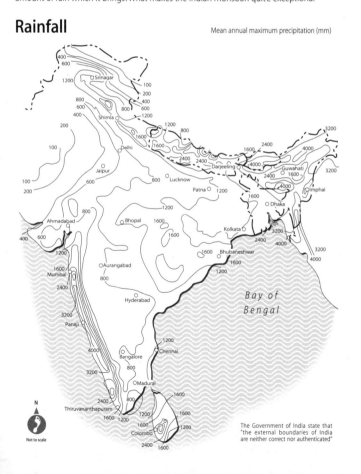

The Government of India state that "the external boundaries of India are neither correct nor authenticated"

Not to scale

Background

is not its regularity but the depth of moist air which passes over the subcontinent. Over India the highly unstable moist air flow is over 6,000 m thick compared with only 2,000 m over Japan, giving rise to the bursts of torrential rain which mark out the wet season.

Winter & spring Winters throughout the Himalaya are generally dry. High pressure builds up over Central Asia and cold north-easterly winds cross the Indian Himalaya, warming as they travel south. At high altitude winter is bitterly cold, and snow commonly comes down to below 2000 metres, but there are often wonderfully clear skies and beautful views across the high peaks. As the snows recede into April and May the hill stations warm up in daytime and the higher passes gradually clear. In the east however, heavy showers become increasingly common through April on wards..

Summer From April onwards much of India becomes almost unbearably hot. Temperatures of over 50°C on the plains are not unknown. It is a time of year to get up to the hills. At the end of May the upper air westerly jet stream, which controls the atmospheric system over the Indo-Gangetic plains through the winter, suddenly breaks down. It re-forms to the north of Tibet, thus allowing very moist southwesterlies to sweep across South India and the Bay of Bengal. They then double back northwestwards, bringing tremendously heavy rain first to the eastern Himalaya then gradually spreading northwestwards.

The wet season The monsoon season, which lasts from between 3 and 5 months depending on
Travel can be seriously the region - the Shillong plateau has received as much as 26 m in one year! If you
disrupted during the are travelling in the wetter parts of the Himalaya during the monsoon you need
monsoon season. Be to be prepared for extended periods of torrential rain and major disruption to
prepared for delays travel.

Vegetation

India's tropical location and its position astride the wet monsoonal winds ensured that 16 different forest types were represented in India.

Mountain At between 1,000-2,000 m in the eastern hill ranges of India wet hill forest includes
forests & evergreen oaks and chestnuts. Further west in the foothills of the Himalaya are belts
grassland of subtropical pine at roughly the same altitudes. Deodars (*Cedrus deodarus*) form large stands and moist temperate forest, with pines, cedars, firs and spruce, is dominant, giving many of the valleys a beautifully fresh, alpine feel.

Between 3,000-4,000 m alpine forest predominates. Rhododendron are often mixed with other forest types. Birch, juniper, poplars and pine are widespread.

There are several varieties of coarse grassland along the southern edge of the Terai and alpine grasses are important for grazing above altitudes of 2,000 m. A totally distinctive grassland is the bamboo (*Dendo calamus*) region of the eastern Himalaya.

Trees

Flowering trees Many Indian trees are planted along roadsides to provide shade and they often also produce beautiful flowers. The **Silk Cotton Tree** (*Bombax ceiba*), up to 25 m in height, is one of the most dramatic. The pale greyish bark of this buttressed tree usually bears conical spines. It has wide spreading branches and keeps its leaves for most of the year. The flowers, which appear when the tree is leafless, are cup-shaped, with curling, rather fleshy red petals up to 12 cm long while the fruit produce the fine, silky cotton which gives it its name.

Other common trees with red or orange flowers include the Dhak (also called the 'Flame of the forest' or *Palas*), the Gulmohur, the Indian coral tree and the Tulip tree. The smallish (6 m) deciduous **Dhak** (*Butea monosperma*), has light grey bark and a gnarled, twisted trunk and thick, leathery leaves. The large, bright orange and sweet pea-shaped flowers appear on leafless branches. The 8-9 m high umbrella-shaped **Gulmohur** (*Delonix regia*), a native of Madagascar, is grown as a shade tree in towns. The fiery coloured flowers make a magnificent display after the tree has shed its feathery leaves. The scarlet flowers of the **Indian Coral Tree** (*Erythrina indica*) also appear when its branches with thorny bark are leafless. The tall **Tulip Tree** (*Spathodea campanulata*) (not to be confused with the North American one) has a straight, darkish brown, slender trunk. It is usually evergreen except in the drier parts of India. The scarlet bell-shaped, tulip-like, flowers grow in profusion at the ends of the branches from November to March.

The familiar apple, plum, apricot and cherry grow in the cool upland areas of India. In the warmer plains tropical fruits flourish. The large, spreading **Mango** (*Mangifera indica*) bears the delicious, distinctively shaped fruit that comes in hundreds of varieties. The evergreen **Jackfruit** (*Artocarpus heterophyllus*) has dark green leatery leaves. The huge fruit (up to 90 cm long and 40 cm thick), growing from a short stem directly off the trunk and branches, has a rough, almost prickly, skin and is almost sickly sweet. The **Banana** plant (*Musa*), actually a gigantic herb (up to 5 m high) arising from an underground stem, has very large leaves which grow directly off the trunk. Each large purplish flower produces bunches of up to 100 bananas. The **Papaya** (*Carica papaya*) grows to about 4 m with the large hand-shaped leaves clustered near the top. Only the female tree bears the fruit, which hang down close to the trunk just below the leaves.

Fruit trees

Of all Indian trees the **Banyan** (*Ficus benghalensis*) is probably the best known. It is planted by temples, in villages and along roads. The seeds often germinate in the cracks of old walls, the growing roots splitting the wall apart. If it grows in the bark of another tree, it sends down roots towards the ground. As it grows, more roots appear from the branches, until the original host tree is surrounded by a 'cage' which eventually strangles it. The famous one in Kolkata's Botanical Gardens is more than 400 m in circumference.

Other trees

Related to the banyan, the **Pipal** or **Peepul** (*Ficus religiosa*), also cracks open walls and strangles other trees with its roots. With a smooth grey bark, it too is commonly found near temples and shrines. You can distinguish it from the banyan by the absence of aerial roots and its large, heart shaped leaf with a point tapering into a pronounced 'tail'. It bears abundant 'figs' of a purplish tinge which are about 1 cm across.

Acacia trees with their feathery leaves are fairly common in the drier parts of India. The best known is the **Babul** (*Acacia arabica*) with a rough, dark bark. The leaves have long silvery white thorns at the base and consist of many leaflets while the flowers grow in golden balls about 1 cm across.

The **Eucalyptus** or **Gum Tree** (*Eucalyptus grandis*), introduced from Australia in the 19th century, is now widespread and is planted near villages to provide both shade and firewood. There are various forms but all may be readily recognized by their height, their characteristic long, thin leaves which have a pleasant fresh smell and the colourful peeling bark.

Bamboo (*Bambusa*) strictly speaking is a grass which can vary in size from small ornamental clumps to the enormous wild plant whose stems are so strong and thick that they are used for construction and for scaffolding and as pipes in rural irrigation schemes.

Flowering plants

Common in the Himalaya is the beautiful flowering shrub or tree, which can be as tall as 12 m, the **Rhododendron** which is indigenous to this region. In the wild the commonest colour of the flowers is crimson, but other colours, such as pale purple occur too. From March to May the flowers are very noticeable on the hill sides. Another common wild flowering shrub is **Lantana**. This is a fairly small untidy looking bush with rough, toothed oval leaves, which grow in pairs on the square and prickly stem. The flowers grow together in a flattened head, the ones near the middle being usually yellowish, while those at the rim are pink, pale purple or orange. The fruit is a shiny black berry.

Many other flowering plants are cultivated in parks, gardens and roadside verges. The attractive **Frangipani** (*Plumeria acutifolia*) has a rather crooked trunk and stubby branches, which if broken give out a white milky juice which can be irritating to the skin. The big, leathery leaves taper to a point at each end and have noticeable parallel veins. The sweetly scented waxy flowers are white, pale yellow or pink. The **Bougainvillea** grows as a dense bush or climber with small oval leaves and rather long thorns. The brightly coloured part (which can be pinkish-purple, crimson, orange, yellow et cetera) which appears like a flower is not formed of petals, which are quite small and undistinguished, but by large papery bracts.

The unusual shape of the **Hibiscus**. The trumpet shaped flower as much as 7 or 8 cm across, has a very long 'tongue' growing out from the centre and varies in colour from scarlet to yellow or white. The leaves are somewhat oval or heart shaped with jagged edges. In municipal flowerbeds the commonest planted flower is probably the **Canna Lily**. It has large leaves which are either green or bronzed and lots of large bright red or yellow flowers. The plant can be more than 1 m high.

Crops

Of India's enormous variety, the single most widespread crop is **rice** (commonly *Orysa indica*). This forms the most important staple in South and East India, though other cereals and some root crops are also important elsewhere. The rice plant grows in flooded fields called *paddies* and virtually all planting or harvesting is done by hand. Millets are favoured in drier areas inland, while wheat is the most important crop in the northwest.

There are many different sorts of millet, but the ones most often seen are finger millet, pearl millet (bajra) and sorghum (jowar). **Finger millet**, commonly known as ragi (*Eleusine corocana*), is so-called because the ear has several spikes which radiate out, a bit like the fingers of a hand. Usually less than 1 m high, it is grown extensively in the south. Both **pearl millet** (*Pennisetum typhoideum*, and **sorghum** (*Sorghum vulgare*) look superficially similar to the more familiar maize though each can be easily distinguished when the seed heads appear. Pearl millet, has a tall single spike which gives it its other name of bulrush millet. The sorghum bears an open ear at the top of the plant.

To some people India is the home of **tea** (*Camellia sinensis*) which is a very important cash crop. It is grown on a commercial scale in tea gardens in areas of high rainfall, often in highland regions. Over 90% comes from Assam and West Bengal in the Northeast. Left to itself tea grows into a tree 10 m tall. In the tea gardens it is pruned to waist height for the convenience of the tea pluckers and forms flat topped bushes, with shiny bright green oval leaves.

Sugar cane (*Saccharum*) is another commercially important crop. This looks like a large grass which stands up to 3 m tall. The crude brown sugar is sold as jaggery and has a flavour of molasses.

Wildlife

The Himalayan range which stands as a high barrier to wind and rain causes a distinct variation in climate on its northern and southern aspects which is also responsible for the distinctive character of the flora and fauna found along this long range. Altitude too plays its part in providing a rich diversity of habitat for plant and wildlife, from the steamy foothills to the peaks in permanent freeze.

Three distinct zones can be noted in this belt: the Forest, the Western and the Transition Zone.

The Forest Zone The lower slopes of the Himalayan foothills are areas of dense tropical forest where bamboos, sal and silk-cotton can be found which harbour tiger, elephants, gaur, sambar and barking deer. On the higher slopes (1,500-2000 m) the vegetation changes to oaks, magnolia, birches and laurels, with the appearance of pines and firs, rhododendrons in the cooler temperate forests at elevations up to 3,500 m and alpines. The Western Himalaya are colder and drier than the east and this affects both the flora and the fauna. The vegetation in the Eastern Himalaya ranges from Tropical evergreen forest through sub-tropical grassland and forest to temperate and alpine up to 5,500 m with tree ferns, orchids, primula, firs, pines and a range of fauna from goat-antelopes such as the goral and serow to the red panda and musk deer.

The **Western Himalayan Zone** covers the stretch from Western Ladakh across to Kashmir where you will find Ibex and Hangul (Kashmir stag).

Around 28° N is a remarkable **Transition Zone** above the tree-line where Oriental species give way to species endemic to the vast region covered by ice during the last great Ice Age, the Palaearctic, of which the high altitude Himalayan region is a relict. This distinct divide is particularly marked in the Eastern Himalaya. South of the line, civets, fruit bats, mogooses appear whereas to the north are found marmots, bharal and musk deer. The high plateau of Eastern Ladakh with its bare mountains and icy desert climate, harbours the Kiang (Tibetan wild ass), yak, Woolly hare and bharal (blue sheep).

Conservation

Alarmed by the rapid loss of wildlife habitat the Indian Government established the first conservation measures in 1972, followed by the setting up of national parks and reserves. Some 25,000 sq km were set aside in 1973 for Project Tiger. Now tigers are reported to be increasing steadily in several of the game reserves. The same is true of other, less well known species. Their natural habitat has been destroyed both by people and by domesticated animals (there are some 250 million cattle and 50 million sheep and goats). Many of the animals found in the Himalaya are killed as trophy or for their meat or wool. Recently, there have been worrying discoveries of large numbers of tiger skins and bones for sale.

There are now nearly 70 national parks and 330 sanctuaries in addition to programmes of afforestation and coastline preservation. Most parks and sanctuaries are open from October-March; but Corbett and Rajaji in Uttar Pradesh are open from mid-June to mid-November.

The animals

The **tiger** (*Panthera tigris*), which prefers to live in fairly dense cover, is most likely to be glimpsed as it lies in long grass or in dappled shadow. The **leopard** or **panther** as it is often called in India (*Panthera pardus*), is far more numerous than the tiger, but is even more elusive. The all black form is not uncommon in areas of higher

The cats

Background

Project Tiger

At one time the tiger roamed freely throughout the sub-continent and at the beginning of this century the estimated population was 40,000 animals. Gradually, due mainly to increased pressure on its habitat by human encroachment and resulting destruction of the habitat, the numbers of this beautiful animal dwindled to fewer than 2,000 in 1972. This was the low point and alarmed at the approaching extinction of the tiger, concerned individuals with the backing of the Government and the World Wildlife Fund, set up Project Tiger in 1973. Initially 9 parks were set up to protect the tiger and this was expanded over the years. However, despite encouraging signs in the first decade the latest tiger census suggests that there are still fewer than 2,500.

rainfall such as Northeast India, though the typical form is seen more often. The pride of the Himalaya, is the elusive **Snow Leopard** (*Panthera uncia*) with its handsome speckled, grey coat and long bushy tail. It inhabits scrub and forest near the snow line, descending to alpine areas at times and can survive at a wide range of altitude. A number is still found in Ladakh and in the Pin Valley, Spiti. It preys on large ungulates, small mammals and large birds.

The lynx (*Felis lynx* isabellinus) with its black-tipped ears and short tail survives mainly on smaller animals (eg hares) and birds. It also has a coat which attracts high prices.

Civets include the white whiskered **Himalayan palm civet** (*Paguma larvata*) which are found on trees on the lower slopes, surviving on fruits, small rodents and birds.

Elephant & rhino   The **Indian elephant** (*Elephas maximus*) has been domesticated for centuries and today it is still used as a beast of burden. In the wild it inhabits hilly country with forest and bamboo, where it lives in herds which can number as many as 50 or more individuals. They are adaptable animals and can live in all sorts of forest, except those in the dry areas. Wild elephants are mainly confined to reserves, but occasionally move out into cultivation, where they cause great damage. The **great Indian one-horned rhinoceros** (*Rhinoceros unicornis*) has folds of skin which look like rivet covered armour plating. It stands at up to 170 cm at the shoulder.

Deer, antelope, oxen & their relatives   Once widespread, these animals are now largely confined to the reserves. The male deer (stags) carry antlers which are branched, each 'spike' on the antler being called a tine. Antelopes and oxen, on the other hand, have horns which are not branched.

Deer   **Deer**   There are several deer species in India, mainly confined to very restricted ranges. Three species are quite common. The largest and one of the most widespread, is the magnificent **sambar** (*Cervus unicolor*) which can be up to 150 cm at the shoulder. It has a noticeably shaggy coat, which varies in colour from brown with a yellowish or grey tinge through to dark, almost black, in the older stags. The sambar is often found on wooded hillsides and lives in groups of up to 10 or so, though solitary individuals are also seen. **Hangul** (barasingha) Deer (*Cervus elephus hanglu*), with 12 point antlers, are seen in the Dachigam National Park in Kashmir. Now endangered, they used to be numerous in the valleys of northern Kashmir, and from Kishtwar to Chamba and would migrate to higher slopes in the summer. They return to Dachigam in September in the rutting season.

The much smaller **chital** or **spotted deer** (*Axis axis*), only about 90 cm tall, are seen in herds of 20 or so, in grassy areas. The bright rufous coat spotted with white is unmistakable; the stags carry antlers with three tines.

The **Musk deer** (*Moschus moschiferus*) found at over 4,000 m is unique for its musk

Background

Elephants – a future in the wild?

Elephants are both the most striking of the mammals and the most economically important. The Indian elephant (Elephas maximas), smaller than the African, is the world's second largest land mammal. Unlike the African elephant, the male rarely reaches a height of over 3 metres; it also has smaller ears. Other distinguishing features include the high domed forehead, the rounded shape of the back and the smooth trunk with a single 'finger' at the end. Also the female is often tuskless or bears small ones called tushes and even the male is sometimes tuskless (makhnas). The Indian elephant has 5 nails on its front feet and 4 on the back (compared to the African's 4 and 3 respectively). There are approximately 6,500 elephants living in the wild in

northern West Bengal, Assam and Bhutan. There are a further 2,000 in Central India and 6,000 in the three South Indian states of Kerala, Tamil Nadu and Karnataka. There are plans for a new elephant reserve on the borders of Bhutan and India.

The loss of habitat has made wild elephants an increasing danger to humans and about 300 people are killed every year by wild elephants, mainly in the North-east. The tribal people have developed skilled techniques for capturing and training wild elephants, which have been domesticated in India for about 5,000 years. They need a lot of feeding – about 18 hours a day. Working elephants are fed on a special diet, by hand straight at the mouth and they eat between 100 and 300 kgs per day.

gland which is coveted for its strong scent. This long-legged deer/antelope has a coat of coarse greyish brown hair which turns dark in winter and tends to feed early and late in the day. They do not have horns but the male develops two small tusks.

Antelope These animals live in open grasslands, never too far from water. The beautiful **blackbuck** or **Indian antelope** (*Antilope cervicapra*), up to 80 cm at the shoulder, may be seen in Jaldapara in North Bengal. The distinctive colouring and the long spiral horns make the stag easy to identify. The coat is chocolate brown above, very sharply demarcated from the white of the underparts. The females do not usually bear horns and like the young, have yellowish brown coats. The **Tibetan antelope** or Chiru, with long, straightish horns and the prized fine underwool which is collected to produce the highly valued *shahtush* is being protected.

The very graceful **chinkara** or **Indian gazelle** (*Gazella gazella*) is only 65 cm at the shoulder. The light russet colour of the body has a distinct line along the side where the paler underparts start. Both sexes carry slightly S-shaped horns. Chinkara live in small groups in rather broken hilly countryside.

Oxen The wild **yak** (*Bos grunniens*), found on bleak Himalayan hillsides, the largest of the Himalayan animals, has a shaggy, blackish brown coat and large horns; the domesticated animals are often piebald and the horns much smaller.

The **Indian bison** or **gaur** (*Bos gaurus*) can be up to 200 cm at the shoulder with a heavy muscular ridge across it. Both sexes carry curved horns. The young gaur is a light sandy colour, which darkens with age, the old bulls being nearly black with pale sandy coloured 'socks' and a pale forehead. Basically hill animals, they live in forests and bamboo clumps and emerge from the trees to graze and are present in the eastern Himalaya.

The **bharal** or **blue sheep** (*Pseudois nayaur*) are found grazing on the open slopes around 4,000 m and among low scrub. About 90 cm at the shoulder, it has a grey-blue body and the adult male has smooth cylindrical horns that curve

Sheep & goats

Background

Two peas in a pod

Antelope and deer are often confused, but they are two quite distinct groups of animals and are easy to tell apart. Deer have solid, branched antlers which are made of bone, have a blood supply and are grown and shed each year. Antelope on the other hand carry horns which are not shed, but grow a bit every year leaving ring marks on the horn. They are hollow and are made of modified skin, rather like nails and claws. Both deer and antelope are found in India, though antelopes are far more common in Africa.

backwards over the neck. The **ibex** (*Capra ibex*), the high altitude goat with magnificent curved horns (the male is bearded) which move in groups of 30 or 40. They inhabit alpine grasslands but can also negotiate steep slopes. The **Himalayan tahr** (*Hemitragus jemlahicus*), a wild goat with a shaggy coarse coat (the male has impressive long hairs over its shoulder), short horns and long legs, remains in the cover of steep forested slopes, between 2,500 to 4,500 m. The **markhor** (*Capra falconeri cashmirensis*) is distinguished by their flat spiralled horns and the thick coat which changes from a rusty grey in winter to a shorter reddish brown in the summer. The male has a prominent mane of long hair. They can be found in the Western Himalaya between 600 -3,500 m, in alpine pastures as well among birch and conifer trees and on steep, rocky slopes. The **goral** (*Nemorhaedus goral*) is a goat-antelope with short curved horns. Sure-footed, they are found in grassland and scrub between 1,800 and 3,000 m as well as steep rocky slopes. Some can be spotted near Corbett.

Bears   The **brown bear** (*Ursus arctos*), found in the Western Himalaya in sub-alpine and alpine areas, is omnivorous and will eat anything from small rodents to domestic sheep and goats as well as supplement its diet with fruit and grain. The **Himalayan black bear** (*Selenarctos thibentanus*) which migrates from its summer territory near the snowline down to the dense forests of the foothills (1,500 m) in the winter tends to be more nocturnal and is also an omnivore.

The **sloth bear** (*Melursus ursinus*), about 75 cm at the shoulder, lives in broken forest, but may be seen on a lead accompanying a street entertainer who makes it 'dance' to music as a part of an act. They have a long snout, a pendulous lower lip and a shaggy black coat with a yellowish V-shaped mark on the chest.

Primates   The **common langur** (*Presbytis entellus*), 75 cm, is a long-tailed monkey with a distinctive black face, hands and feet. Usually a forest dweller, it is found almost throughout India. The **rhesus macaque** (*Macaca mulatta*), 60 cm, is more solid looking with shorter limbs and a shorter tail. It can be distinguished by the orange-red fur on its rump and flanks.

Others   The rare **Kyang** (*Equus hemionus kiang*), the wild ass, is found in large herds at elevations of over 4,500 m near Pangong Lake in eastern Ladakh. The fawn body has a distinctive dark stripe along the back. The dark mane is short and erect. The **wild boar** (*Sus scrofa*) has mainly black body and a pig-like head; the hairs thicken down the spine to form a sort of mane. A mature male stands 90 cm at the shoulder and, unlike the female, bears tusks. The young are striped. Quite widespread, they often cause great destruction among crops.

One of the most important scavengers of the countryside, the **striped hyena** (*Hyena hyena*) found in open scrub in the low Himalaya, usually comes out at night. It is about 90 cm at the shoulder with a large head with a noticeable crest of hairs along its sloping back.

The **jackal** (*Canis aureus*), a lone scavenger in towns and villages, looks like a cross between a dog and a fox and varies in colour from shades of brown through to black. The bushy tail has a dark tip.

The **common giant flying squirrel** are common in the larger forests of India, except in the northeast (*Petaurista petaurista*). The body can be 45 cm long and the tail another 50 cm. They glide from tree to tree using a membrane stretching from front leg to back leg which acts like a parachute.

Palm squirrels are very common. The **five-striped** (*Funambulus pennanti*) and the **three-striped palm squirrel** (*Funambulus palmarum*), are both about the same size (30 cm long, about half of which is tail). The five-striped is usually seen in towns. The **Himalayan marmot** (*Marmota bobak*), found above 4,000 m, hibernate in winter in their burrows in the ground.

The two bats most commonly seen in towns differ enormously in size. The larger so-called **flying fox** (*Pteropus giganteus*) has a wing span of 120 cm. These fruit-eating bats, found throughout, except in the driest areas, roost in large noisy colonies where they look like folded umbrellas hanging from the trees. In the evening they can be seen leaving the roost with slow measured wing beats. The much smaller **Indian pipistrelle** (*Pipistrellus coromandra*), with a wing span of about 15 cm, is an insect eater. It comes into the house at dusk, roosting under eaves and has a fast, erratic flight.

The **common mongoose** (*Herpestes edwardsi*) lives in scrub and open jungle. It kills snakes, but will also take rats, mice and chicken. Tawny coloured with a grey grizzled tinge, it is about 90 cm in length, of which half is pale-tipped tail.

Birds

In the Western Himalaya, Corbett provides good opportunities to see a large number of species though most hill stations make a good base. It is best to visit the area before the monsoon sets in in mid-June to see breeding colonies, and again at the end of the monsoon in November to see migrants. In the East Himalaya. visit Darjeeling (and Tiger Hill nearby) and Sikkim when the rhododendron are out in April and early May, and after the monsoon, when the skies clear from late October to December. Species vary mainly from Central Asian Palaeartctic to Oriental.

Some birds perform a useful function scavenging and clearing refuse. One of the most widespread is the brown **pariah kite** (*Milvus migrans*, 65 cm).

Town & village birds

The **house crow** (*Corvus splendens*, 45 cm) on the other hand is a very smart looking bird with a grey body and black tail, wings, face and throat. It occurs in almost every town and village in India. The **jungle crow** (*Corvus macrorhynchos*, 50 cm) originally a bird of the countryside has started to move into populated areas and in the hill stations tends to replace the house crow. Unlike the house crow it is a glossy black all over and has a much deeper, hoarser caw.

The **feral pigeon**, or **blue rock dove** (*Columba livia*, 32 cm), found throughout the world, is generally a slaty grey in colour. It invariably has two dark bars on the wing and a white rump. The **little brown dove** (*Streptopelia senegalensis*, 25 cm) is bluey grey and brown above, with a pink head and underparts and a speckled pattern on the neck. The **collared dove** (*Streptopelia decaocto*, 30 cm) with a distinct half collar on the back of its neck, is common, especially in the drier parts of India.

Bulbuls are common in gardens and parks. The **red-vented bulbul** (*Pycnonotus cafer*, 20 cm), a mainly brown bird, can be identified by the slight crest and a bright red patch under the tail. The **house sparrow** (*Passer domesticus*, 15 cm) can be seen in towns throughout the mainland. The ubiquitous **common myna** (*Acridotheres tristis*, 22 cm), feeds on lawns, especially after rain or watering. Look for the white

Background

under the tail and the bare yellow skin around the eye, yellow bill and legs and in flight the large white wing patch.

A less common, but more striking bird also seen feeding in open spaces, is the **hoopoe** (*Upupa epops*, 30 cm), easily identified by its sandy plumage with black and white stripes and long thin curved bill. The marvellous fan-shaped crest is sometimes raised. Finally there is a member of the cuckoo family which is heard more often than seen. The **koel** (*Eudynamys scolopacea*, 42 cm), is commonly heard during the hot weather – kuoo-kuoo-kuoo, the double note starts off low and flute-like, rises in pitch and intensity, then suddenly stops, only to start all over again. The male is all black with a greenish bill and a red eye; the female streaked and barred.

The **rose-ringed parakeet** (*Psittacula krameri*, 40 cm) is found throughout India up to about 1,500 m while the **pied myna** (*Sturnus contra*, 23 cm) is restricted to northern and central India. The rose-ringed parakeet often forms huge flocks, an impressive sight coming in to roost. The long tail is noticeable both in flight and when the bird is perched. They can be very destructive to crops, but are attractive birds which are frequently kept as pets. The pied myna, with its smart black and white plumage is conspicuous, usually in small flocks in grazing land or cultivation. It feeds on the ground and on village rubbish dumps. The all black **drongo** (*Dicrurus adsimilis*, 30 cm) is almost invariably seen perched on telegraph wires or bare branches. Its distinctively forked tail makes it easy to identify.

Weaver birds are a family of mainly yellow birds, all remarkable for the intricate nests they build. The most widespread is the **baya weaver** (*Ploceus philippinus*, 15cm) which nest in large colonies, often near villages. The male in the breeding season combines a black face and throat with a contrasting yellow top of the head and the yellow breast band. In the non-breeding season both sexes are brownish sparrow-like birds.

Hill birds Land above about 1,500 m supports a distinct range of species, although some birds, such as the ubiquitous **common myna**, are found in the highlands as well as in the lower lying terrain.

The highland equivalent of the red-vented bulbul is the **white-cheeked bulbul** (*Pycnonotus leucogenys*, 20 cm) which is found in gardens and woodland in the Himalaya up to about 2,500 m and as far south as Bombay. It has white underparts with a yellow patch under the tail. The black head and white cheek patches are distinctive. The crest varies in length and is most prominent in birds found in Kashmir, where it is very common in gardens. The **red-whiskered bulbul** (*Pycnonotus jocosus*, 20 cm) is widespread in the Himalaya and the hills of South India up to about 2,500 m. Its pronounced pointed crest, which is sometimes so long that it flops forward towards the bill, white underparts and red and white 'whiskers' serve to distinguish it. It has a red patch under the tail.

In the summer the delightful **verditer flycatcher** (*Muscicapa thalassina*, 15 cm) is a common breeding bird in the Himalaya up to about 3,000 m. It is tame and confiding, often builds its nest on verandahs and is seen perching on telegraph wires. In winter it is much more widely distributed throughout the country. It is an active little bird which flicks its tail up and down in a characteristic manner. The male is all bright blue green with somewhat darker wings and a black patch in front of the eyes. The female is similar, but duller.

Another species associated with man is the **white wagtail** (*Motacilla alba*, 21 cm), very common in the Himalayan summer up to about 3,000 m. It is always found near water, by streams and lakes, on floating vegetation and among the house boats in Kashmir. Its black and white plumage and constantly wagging tail make it easy to identify.

Yet another species common in Kashmir and in other Himalayan hill stations is the **red-billed blue magpie** (*Urocissa erythrorhyncha*, 65 cm). With a long tail and striking blue plumage, contrasting with its black head, it is usually seen in small flocks as it flies from tree to tree. This is not so much a garden bird, but prefers tea gardens, open woodland and cultivation.

Jungle fowl and pheasants   The highlands of India, especially the Himalaya, are the home of the ancestors of domestic hens and also of numerous beautiful pheasants. These are mainly forest dwellers and are not easy to see as they tend to be shy and wary of man.

The red faced **Kaleej** (*Lophura leucomelanura*) or black fowl. The male has a long shiny black arched tail while the female is rich brown. They are found across the length of the Himalaya, in the dense undergrowth of all types of forest, decending to lower altitudes in winter.

The **Blood pheasant** is found in the Eastern Himalaya (Sikkim, North Bengal, Arunachal) and are seen between about 3,500-4,500 m, in thick ground cover among pine, rhododendron and bamboo. The male is brightly coloured - grey and green with a red throat and splashes of crimson on the breast and tail (hence its name). The female is rufous brown with a grey crest and nape. Both have a red patch around the eye.

The brilliant green and blue **Himalayan Monal** (*Lophophorus Impejanus*) is found near the tree line where there is thick cover, mainly in Himachal . The female is a duller brown bird.

The endangered **Western Tragopan** (*Tragopan melanocephalus*) or Horned Pheasant is found in parts of Himachal (around Manali and Great Himalayan National Park) and Kashmir. The male is highly coloured - bright red, with white spots and a blue neck; the horns come into their own in courtship display. The female is duller, being grey with black and white spots. **Snow Partridges** may be seen in alpine meadows above the tree line in the Western Himalaya.

Last but not least, mention must be made of India's national bird, the magnificent and well-known **Peafowl** (*Pavo cristatus*, male 210 cm, female 100 cm), which is more commonly known as the peacock. Semi-domesticated birds are commonly seen and heard around towns and villages, especially in the northwest of India. In the wild it favours hilly jungles and dense scrub.

Raptors seen between 2000 and 5000 m include the massive Golden Eagle (*Aquila chrysaetos*), a metre from beak to tail, which usually appear in pairs. It is very dark brown with a rufous hindcrown and hindneck. Lämmergeier (*Gypaetus barbatus*) or the Bearded Vulture (so called because of its black chin feathers), is seen at lower altitudes. It is smaller, with a cream, feathery head and neck, dark grey upper parts and is pale underneath.

Reptiles and amphibians

India is famous for its reptiles, especially its snakes which feature in many stories and legends. In reality, snakes keep out of the way of people. One of the most common is the **Indian rock python** (*Python molurus*) a 'constrictor' which kills it's prey by suffocation. Usually about 4 m in length, they can be much longer.

The other large snakes favoured by street entertainers are cobras. The various species all have a hood which is spread when the snake draws itself up to strike. They are all highly venomous and the snake charmers prudently de-fang them to render them harmless. The best known is probably the **spectacled cobra** (*Naja naja*), which has a mark like a pair of spectacles on the back of its hood. The largest venomous snake in the world is the **king cobra** (*Ophiophagus hannah*) which is 5 m in length. It is usually brown, but can vary from cream to black and lacks the spectacle marks of the other. In their natural state cobras are generally inhabitants of forest regions.

Equally venomous, but much smaller, the **common krait** (*Bungarus caeruleus*) is

• •

☞ *Room at the park...*

Booking accommodation in national parks can be very frustrating for independent travellers. In many parks it is essential to book in advance. Offices outside may tell you that it is fully-booked, even when outgoing tourists say that the accommodation is empty. This is because cancellation information is not relayed to all offices.

The only way in is patient, friendly persistence, asking for just one day inside. This can then be extended once in. Be prepared for a lot of frustration, especially in Ramnagar (Corbett National Park). Where possible go to the park itself and book. You may prefer to try a specialist travel agent in one of the main towns in the region.

• •

just over 1 m in length. The slender, shiny, blue-black snake has thin white bands which can sometimes be almost indiscernible. They are found all over the country except in the northeast where the canniballistic **banded krait** with bold yellowish and black bands have virtually eradicated them.

Footnotes

10

Footnotes

399 Glossary

405 Useful words and phrases

407 Useful Ladakhi words and phrases

408 Eating out

411 Index

417 Advertiser index

418 Shorts

419 Map index

426 Coloured maps

Glossary

Words in *italics* are common elements of words, often making up part of a place name

A

aarti   (arati) Hindu worship with lamps

abacus   square or rectangular table resting on top of a pillar

acanthus   thick-leaved plant, common decoration on pillars, esp Greek

acharya   religious teacher

Adi Granth   Guru Granth Sahib, holy book of the Sikhs

Adinatha   first of the 24 Tirthankaras, distinguished by his bull mount

agarbathi   incense

Agni   Vedic fire divinity, intermediary between gods and men; guardian of the Southeast

ahimsa   non-harming, non-violence

alinda   verandah

ambulatory   processional path

amla/amalaka   circular ribbed pattern (based on a gourd) at the top of a temple tower

amrita   ambrosia; drink of immortality

ananda   joy

Ananda   the Buddha's chief disciple

Ananta   a huge snake on whose coils Vishnu rests

anda   literally 'egg', spherical part of the stupa

Andhaka   demon killed by Siva

anna   (ana) one sixteenth of a rupee (still occasionally referred to)

Annapurna   Goddess of abundance; one aspect of Devi

antarala   vestibule, chamber in front of shrine or cella

antechamber   chamber in front of the sanctuary

apsara   celestial nymph

apse   semi-circular plan, as in apse of a church

arabesque   ornamental decoration with intertwining lines

architrave   horizontal beam across posts or gateways

ardha mandapam   chamber in front of main hall of temple

Ardhanarisvara   Siva represented as half-male and half-female

Arjuna   hero of the Mahabharata, to whom Krishna delivered the Bhagavad Gita

arrack   alcoholic spirit fermented from potatoes or grain

Aruna   charioteer of Surya, the Sun God; Red

Aryans   literally 'noble' (Sanskrit); prehistoric peoples who settled in Persia and North India

asana   a seat or throne (Buddha's) pose

ashram   hermitage or retreat

Ashta Matrikas   The eight mother goddesses who attended on Siva or Skanda

astanah   threshold

atman   philosophical concept of universal soul or spirit

atrium   court open to the sky in the centre In modern architecture, enclosed in glass

Avalokiteshwara   Lord who looks down; Bodhisattva, the Compassionate

avatara   'descent'; incarnation of a divinity

ayah   nursemaid, especially for children

B

baba   old man

babu   clerk

bada   cubical portion of a temple up to the roof or spire

badgir   rooftop structure to channel cool breeze into the house (mainly North and West India)

badlands   eroded landscape

bagh   garden

bahadur   title, meaning 'the brave'

baksheesh   tip 'bribe'

baluster   (balustrade) a small column supporting a handrail

bandh   a strike

bandhani   tie dyeing

banian   vest

baradari   literally 'twelve pillared', a pavilion with columns

barrel-vault   semi-cylindrical shaped roof or ceiling

bas-relief   carving of low projection

basement   lower part of walls, usually with decorated mouldings

batter   slope of a wall, especially in a fort

bazar   market

bedi   (vedi) altar/platform for reading holy texts

begum   Muslim princess/woman's courtesy title

belvedere   summer house; small room on a house roof

bhabar   coarse alluvium at foot of Himalayas

Bhadrakali   Tantric goddess and consort of Bhairav

Bhagavad-Gita   Song of the Lord; section of the Mahabharata

Bhagiratha   the king who prayed to Ganga to descend to earth

bhai   brother *

Bhairava   Siva, the Fearful

bhakti   adoration of a deity

bhang   Indian hemp

bharal   Himalayan blue sheep

Bharata   half-brother of Rama

bhavan   building or house

bhikku   Buddhist monk

Bhima   Pandava hero of the Mahabharata, famous for his strength

bhisti   a water-carrier

bhogamandapa   the refectory hall of a temple

bhumi   literally earth; a horizontal moulding of a sikhara

bidi   (beedi) leaf 'cigarette'

bigha   measure of land – normally about one-third of an acre

Bodhisattva   Enlightened One who has renounced Nirvana

Brahma   Universal self-existing power; Creator in the Hindu Triad.

Brahmachari   religious student, accepting rigorous discipline (eg chastity)

Brahman   (Brahmin) highest Hindu (and Jain) caste of priests

Brahmanism   ancient Indian religion, precursor of modern Hinduism

Buddha   The Enlightened One; founder of Buddhism

bund   an embankment

bundh   (literally closed) a strike

burj   tower or bastion

burqa   (burkha) over-dress worn by Muslim women observing purdah

bustee   slum

C

cantonment   planned military or civil area in town

capital   upper part of a column

caryatid   sculptured human female figure

used as a support for columns

cave temple   rock-cut shrine or monastery

cenotaph   commemorative monument, usually an open domed pavilion

chaam   Himalayan Buddhist masked dance

chadar   sheet worn as clothing

chai   tea

chaitya   large arched opening in the façade of a hall or Buddhist temple

chajja   overhanging cornice or eaves

chakra   sacred Buddhist wheel of the law; also Vishnu's discus

Chandra   Moon; a planetary deity

chang   barley/rice beer

chapatti   unleavened Indian bread cooked on a griddle

chaprassi   messenger or orderly usually wearing a badge

char   sand-bank or island in a river

char bagh   formal Mughal garden, divided into quarters

charan   foot print

charka   spinning wheel

charpai   'four legs' – wooden frame string bed

chatt(r)a   ceremonial umbrella on stupa (Buddhist)

chauki   recessed space between pillars; entrance

chaukidar   (chowkidar) night-watchman; guard

chauth   25% tax raised for revenue by Marathas

cheri   outcaste settlement; slum (Tamil Nadu)

chhang   strong mountain beer of fermented barley maize rye or millet or rice

chhatri   umbrella shaped dome or pavilion

chhetri   (kshatriya) Hindu warrior caste

chogyal   heavenly king (Sikkim)

choli   blouse

chorten   Himalayan Buddhist relic shrine or memorial stupa

chowk   (chauk) a block; open place in a city where the market is held

chunam   lime plaster or stucco made from burnt seashells

circumambulation   clockwise movement around a shrine

clerestory   upper section of the walls of a building which allows light in

cloister   passage usually around an open square

corbel   horizontal block supporting a vertical structure or covering an opening

cornice   horizontal band at the top of a wall

crenellated   having battlements

crewel work   chain stitching

crore   10 million

cupola   small dome

curvilinear   gently curving shape, generally of a tower

cusp, cusped   projecting point between

small sections of an arch

D

daal   lentils, pulses

dacoit   bandit

dado   part of a pedestal between its base and cornice

dahi   yoghurt

dais   raised platform

dak bungalow   rest house for officials

dak   post

dakini   sorceress

Dakshineshvara   Lord of the South; name of Siva

dan   gift

dandi   wooden 'seat' carried by bearers

darbar   (durbar) a royal gathering

dargah   a Muslim tomb complex

darshan   (darshana) viewing of a deity

darwaza   gateway, door

Dasara   (dassara/dussehra/dassehra) 10 day festival (Sep-Oct)

Dasaratha   King of Ayodhya and father of Rama

Dattatraya   syncretistic deity; an incarnation of Vishnu, a teacher of Siva, or a cousin of the Buddha

daulat khana   treasury

dentil   small block used as part of a cornice

deodar   Himalayan cedar; from *deva-daru*, the 'wood of the gods'

deval   memorial pavilion built to mark royal funeral pyre

devala   temple or shrine (Buddhist or Hindu)

devasthanam   temple trust

Devi   Goddess; later, the Supreme Goddess

dhaba   roadside restaurant (mainly North India) truck drivers' stop

dhansak   Parsi dish made with lentils

dharamshala   (dharamsala) pilgrims' rest-house

dharma   moral and religious duty

dharmachakra   wheel of 'moral' law (Buddhist)

dhobi   washerman

dhol   drums

dholi   (dhooli) swinging chair on a pole, carried by bearers

dhoti   loose loincloth worn by Indian men

dhyana   meditation

dikpala   guardian of one of the cardinal directions mostly appearing in a group of eight

dikshitar   person who makes oblations or offerings

distributary   river that flows away from main channel

divan (diwan)   smoking-room; also a chief minister

Diwali   festival of lights (Oct-Nov)

diwan   chief financial minister

doab   interfluve, land between two rivers

dokra   tribal name for lost wax metal

casting (cire perdu)

double dome   composed of an inner and outer shell of masonry

Draupadi   wife-in-common of the five Pandava brothers in the Mahabharata

dry masonry   stones laid without mortar

duar   (dwar) door, gateway

dun   valley

dupatta   long scarf worn by Punjabi women

Durga   principal goddess of the Shakti cult

durrie   (dhurrie) thick handloom rug

durwan   watchman

dvarpala   doorkeeper

dvipa   lamp-column, generally of stone or brass-covered wood

E

eave   overhang that shelters a porch or verandah

ek   the number 1, a symbol of unity

ekka   one horse carriage

epigraph   carved inscription

F

faience   coloured tilework, earthenware or porcelain

fakir   Muslim religious mendicant

fan-light   fan-shaped window over door

fenestration   with windows or openings

filigree   ornamental work or delicate tracery

finial   emblem at the summit of a stupa, tower, dome, or at the end of a parapet

firman   edict or grant issued by a sovereign

foliation   ornamental design derived from foliage

frieze   horizontal band of figures or decorative designs

G

gable   end of an angled roof

gadba   woollen blanket (Kashmir)

gaddi   throne

gadi/gari   car, cart, train

gali   (galli) lane; an alley

gana   child figures in art

Gandharva   semi-divine flying figure; celestial musician

Ganesh   (Ganapati) elephant-headed son of Siva and Parvati

Ganga   goddess personifying the Ganga river

ganj   market

ganja   Indian hemp

gaon   village

garbhagriha   literally 'womb-chamber'; a temple sanctuary

garh   fort

Garuda   Mythical eagle, half-human Vishnu's vehicle

Gauri 'Fair One'; Parvati

Gaurishankara Siva with Parvati

ghagra (ghongra) long flared skirt

ghanta bell

ghat hill range, hill road; landing place; steps on the river bank

ghazal Urdu lyric poetry/love songs, often erotic

ghee clarified butter for cooking

gherao industrial action, surrounding home or office of politician or industrial manager

giri hill

Gita Govinda Jayadeva's poem of the Krishnalila

godown warehouse

gompa Tibetan Buddhist monastery

goncha loose woollen robe, tied at waist with wide coloured band (Ladakh)

Gopala (Govinda) cowherd; a name of Krishna

Gopis cowherd girls; milk maids who played with Krishna

Gorakhnath historically, an 11th-century yogi who founded a Saivite cult; an incarnation of Siva

gosain monk or devotee (Hindi)

gram chick pea, pulse

gram village; gramadan, gift of village

gumbaz (gumbad) dome

gumpha monastery, cave temple

gur gur salted butter tea (Ladakh)

gur palm sugar

guru teacher; spiritual leader, Sikh religious leader

gurudwara (literally 'entrance to the house of God'); Sikh religious complex

H

Haj (Hajj) annual Muslim pilgrimage to Mecca

hakim judge; a physician (usually Muslim)

halwa a special sweet meat

hammam Turkish bath

Hanuman Monkey devotee of Rama; bringer of success to armies

Hara (Hara Siddhi) Siva

harem women's quarters (Muslim), from 'haram', Arabic for 'forbidden by law'

Hari Vishnu Harihara, Vishnu- Siva as a single divinity

Hariti goddess of prosperity and patroness of children, consort of Kubera

hartal general strike

Hasan the murdered eldest son of Ali, commemorated at Muharram

hat (haat) market

hathi pol elephant gate

hathi (hati) elephant

hauz tank or reservoir

havildar army sergeant

Hidimba Devi Durga worshipped at Manali

hindola swing

hippogryph fabulous griffin-like creature with body of a horse

Hiranyakashipu Demon king killed by Narasimha

Holi spring festival (Feb-Mar)

hookah 'hubble bubble' or smoking vase

howdah seat on elephant's back, sometimes canopied

Hussain the second murdered son of Ali, commemorated at Muharram

huzra a Muslim tomb chamber

hypostyle hall with pillars

I

lat pillar, column

icon statue or image of worship

Id principal Muslim festivals

Idgah open space for the Id prayers

ikat 'resist-dyed' woven fabric

imam Muslim religious leader

imambara tomb of a Shiite Muslim holy man; focus of Muharram procession

Indra King of the gods; God of rain; guardian of the East

Ishana Guardian of the North East

Ishvara Lord; Siva

iwan main arch in mosque

J

jadu magic

Jagadambi literally Mother of the World; Parvati

jagati railed parapet

jaggery brown sugar, made from palm sap

jahaz ship: building in form of ship

jali literally 'net'; any lattice or perforated pattern

jamb vertical side slab of doorway

Jambudvipa Continent of the Rose-Apple Tree; the earth

Jami masjid (Jama, Jumma) Friday mosque, for congregational worship

Jamuna Hindu goddess who rides a tortoise; river

Janaka Father of Sita

jangha broad band of sculpture on the outside of the temple wall

jarokha balcony

jataka stories accounts of the previous lives of the Buddha

jawab literally 'answer,' a building which duplicates another to provide symmetry

jawan army recruit, soldier

jaya stambha victory tower

jheel (jhil) lake; a marsh; a swamp

jhilmil projecting canopy over a window or door opening

-ji (jee) honorific suffix added to names out of reverence and/or politeness; also abbreviated 'yes' (Hindi/Urdu)

jihad striving in the way of god; holy war by Muslims against non-believers

Jina literally 'victor'; spiritual conqueror or Tirthankara, after whom Jainism is named

Jogini mystical goddess

Jyotirlinga luminous energy of Siva manifested at 12 holy places, miraculously formed lingams

K

kacheri (kutchery) a court; an office for public business

kadal wooden bridge (Kashmir)

Kailasa mountain home of Siva

kalasha pot-like finial of a tower

Kali literally 'black'; terrifying form of the goddess Durga, wearing a necklace of skulls/heads

Kalki future incarnation of Vishnu on horseback

kameez women's shirt

kangri snow mountain (Ladakh)

kankar limestone pieces, used for road making

kapok the silk cotton tree

karma impurity resulting from past misdeeds

Kartikkeya (Kartik) Son of Siva, God of war

kashi-work special kind of glazed tiling, probably derived from Kashan in Persia

kati-roll Muslim snack of meat rolled in a 'paratha' bread

keep tower of a fort, stronghold

keystone central wedge-shaped block in a masonry arch

khadi woven cotton cloth made from home-spun cotton (or silk) yarn

khal creek; a canal

khana suffix for room/office/place; also food or meal

khanqah Muslim (Sufi) hospice

kharif monsoon season crop

kheda enclosure in which wild elephants are caught; elephant depot

khet field

khondalite crudely grained basalt

khukri traditional curved Gurkha weapon

kirti-stambha 'pillar of fame,' free standing pillar in front of temple

kohl antimony, used as eye shadow

kos minars Mughal 'mile' stones

kot (kota/kottai/kotte) fort

kothi house

kotla citadel

Krishna Eighth incarnation of Vishnu

Kubera Chief yaksha; keeper of the treasures of the earth, Guardian of the North

kumar a young man

Kumari Virgin; Durga

kumbha a vase-like motif, pot

Kumbhayog auspicious time for bathing to wash away sins

kumhar (kumar) potter

kund lake, well or pool

kurta Punjabi shirt

kushok head lama

kutcha (cutcha/kacha) raw; crude; unpaved; built with sun-dried bricks

L

la Himalayan mountain pass
lakh 100,000
Lakshmana younger brother of Rama
Lakshmi Goddess of wealth and good fortune, consort of Vishnu
lama Buddhist priest in Tibet
lassi iced yoghurt drink
lath monolithic pillar
lathi bamboo stick with metal bindings, used by police
lingam (linga) Siva as the phallic emblem
lintel horizontal beam over doorway
liwan cloisters of a mosque
Lokeshwar 'Lord of the World', Avalokiteshwara to Buddhists and form of Siva to Hindus
lunette semicircular window opening
lungi wrapped-around loin cloth, normally checked

M

madrassa Islamic theological school or college
maha great
Mahabharata Sanskrit epic about the battle between the Pandavas and Kauravas
Mahabodhi Great Enlightenment of Buddha
Mahadeva literally 'Great Lord'; Siva
mahal palace, grand building
mahalla (mohulla) division of a town; a quarter; a ward
mahant head of a monastery
maharaja great king
maharani great queen
maharishi (Maharshi) literally 'great teacher'
Mahavira literally 'Great Hero'; last of the 24 Tirthankaras, founder of Jainism
Mahayana The Greater Vehicle; form of Buddhism practised in East Asia, Tibet and Nepal
Mahesha (Maheshvara) Great Lord; Siva
Mahisha Buffalo demon killed by Durga
mahout elephant driver/keeper
mahseer large freshwater fish found especially in Himalayan rivers
maidan large open grassy area in a town
Maitreya the future Buddha
makara crocodile-shaped mythical creature symbolizing the river Ganga
makhan butter
mali gardener
Manasa Snake goddess; Sakti
manastambha free-standing pillar in front of temple
mandala geometric diagram symbolizing the structure of the Universe
mandapa columned hall preceding the temple sanctuary
mandi market
mandir temple

mani (mani wall) stones with sacred inscriptions at Buddhist sites
mantra chant for meditation by Hindus and Buddhists
maqbara chamber of a Muslim tomb
Mara Tempter, who sent his daughters (and soldiers) to disturb the Buddha's meditation
marg wide roadway
masjid literally 'place of prostration'; mosque
mata mother
math Hindu or Jain monastery
maulana scholar (Muslim)
maulvi religious teacher (Muslim)
maund measure of weight about 20 kilos
mausoleum large tomb building
maya illusion
medallion circle or part-circle framing a figure or decorative motif
meena enamel work
mela festival or fair, usually Hindu
memsahib married European woman, term used mainly before Independence
Meru mountain supporting the heavens
mihrab niche in the western wall of a mosque
mimbar pulpit in mosque
Minakshi literally 'fish-eyed'; Parvati
minar (minaret) slender tower of a mosque
mitthai Indian sweets
mithuna couple in sexual embrace
mofussil the country as distinct from the town
Mohammad 'the praised'; The Prophet; founder of Islam
moksha salvation, enlightenment; literally 'release'
momos Tibetan stuffed pastas dumplings
monolith single block of stone shaped into a pillar
muballigh second prayer leader
mudra symbolic hand gesture
muezzin mosque official who calls the faithful to prayer
Muharram period of mourning in remembrance of Hasan and Hussain, two murdered sons of Ali
mukha mandapa, hall for shrine
mullah religious teacher (Muslim)
mural wall decoration
musalla prayer mat
muta limited duration marriage (Leh)
muthi measure equal to 'a handful'

N

nadi river
Naga (nagi/nagini) Snake deity; associated with fertility and protection
nagara city, sometimes capital
nakkar khana (naggar or naubat khana) drum house; arched structure or gateway for musicians
nal staircase
nal mandapa porch over a staircase

nallah (nullah) ditch, channel
namaaz Muslim prayers, worship
namaste common Hindu greeting (with joined palms) translated as: 'I salute all divine qualities in you'
namda rug
Nandi a bull, Siva's vehicle and a symbol of fertility
nara durg large fort built on a flat plain
Narayana Vishnu as the creator of life
nata mandapa (nat-mandir; nritya sala) dancing hall in a temple
Nataraja Siva, Lord of the cosmic dance
nath literally 'place' eg Amarnath
natya the art of dance
nautch display by dancing girls
navagraha nine planets, represented usually on the lintel or architrave of the front door of a temple
navaranga central hall of temple
navaratri literally '9 nights'; name of the Dasara festival
nawab prince, wealthy Muslim, sometimes used as a title
niche wall recess containing a sculpted image or emblem, mostly framed by a pair of pilasters
nirvana enlightenment; literally 'extinguished'
niwas small palace
nritya pure dance

O

obelisk tapering and usually monolithic stone shaft
ogee form of moulding or arch comprising a double curved line made up of a concave and convex part
oriel projecting window

P

pada foot or base
padma lotus flower, Padmasana, lotus seat; posture of meditating figures
pagoda tall structure in several stories
pahar hill
paisa (poisa) one hundredth of a rupee
palanquin covered litter for one, carried on poles
pali language of Buddhist scriptures
pan leaf of the betel vine; sliced areca nut, lime and other ingredients wrapped in leaf for chewing
panchayat a 'council of five'; a government system of elected councils
pandal marquee made of bamboo and cloth
pandas temple priests
pandit teacher or wise man; a Sanskrit scholar
pankah (punkha) fan, formerly pulled by a cord
parapet wall extending above the roof
pargana sub-division of a district usually

comprising many villages; a fiscal unit

Parinirvana the Buddha's state prior to nirvana, shown usually as a reclining figure

parishads political division of group of villages

parterre level space in a garden occupied by flowerbeds

Parvati daughter of the Mountain; Siva's consort

pashmina fine wool from a mountain goat

Pashupati literally Lord of the Beasts; Siva

patan town or city (Sanskrit)

patel village headman

patina green film that covers materials exposed to the air

pau measure for vegetables and fruit equal to 250 grams

pediment mouldings, often in a triangular formation above an opening or niche

peon servant, messenger (from Portuguese *peao*)

perak black hat, studded with turquoise and lapis lazuli (Ladakh)

peristyle range of columns surrounding a court or temple

Persian wheel well irrigation system using bucket lift

pice (old form) 1/100th of a rupee

pida (pitha) basement

pietra dura inlaid mosaic of hard, semi-precious stones

pilaster ornamental small column, with capital and bracket

pinjra lattice work

pipal Ficus religiosa, the Bodhi tree

pir Muslim holy man

pitha base, pedestal

pithasthana place of pilgrimage

podium stone bench; low pedestal wall

porch covered entrance to a shrine or hall, generally open and with columns

portico space enclosed between columns

pradakshina patha processional passage

pralaya the end of the world

prasadam consecrated temple food

prayag confluence considered sacred by Hindus

puja ritual offerings to the gods; worship (Hindu)

pujari worshipper; one who performs puja (Hindu)

pukka literally 'ripe' or 'finished'; reliable; solidly built

punya merit earned through actions and religious devotion (Buddhist)

Puranas literally 'the old' Sanskrit sacred poems

purdah seclusion of Muslim women from public view (literally curtains)

Q

qabr Muslim grave

qibla direction for Muslim prayer

qila fort

Quran holy Muslim scriptures

qutb axis or pivot

R

rabi winter/spring season crop

Radha Krishna's favourite consort

raj rule or government

raja king, ruler (variations include rao, rawal)

rajbari palaces of a small kingdom

Rajput dynasties of western and central India

Rakshakas Earth spirits

Rama Seventh incarnation of Vishnu

Ramayana Sanskrit epic – the story of Rama

Ramazan (Ramadan) Muslim month of fasting

rani queen

rath chariot or temple car

Ravana Demon king of Lanka; kidnapper of Sita

rawal head priest

reredos screen behind an altar

ri mountain (Ladakh)

rickshaw 3-wheeled bicycle-powered (or 2-wheeled hand-powered) vehicle

Rig (Rg) Veda oldest and most sacred of the Vedas

Rimpoche blessed incarnation; abbot of a Tibetan Buddhist monastery

rishi 'seer'; inspired poet, philosopher

rumal handkerchief, specially painted in Chamba (Himachal Pradesh)

rupee unit of currency in India

S

sabha columned hall (sabha mandapa, assembly hall)

sabzi vegetables, vegetable curry

sadhu ascetic; religious mendicant, holy man

sagar lake; reservoir

sahib title of address, like 'sir'

Saiva (Shaiva) the cult of Siva

sal a hall

sal hardwood tree of the lower slopes of Himalayan foothills

salaam literally 'peace'; greeting (Muslim)

salwar (shalwar) loose trousers (Punjab)

samadh(i) literally concentrated thought, meditation; a funerary memorial

samsara transmigration of the soul

samudra large tank or inland sea

sangam junction of rivers

sangarama monastery

sangha ascetic order founded by Buddha

sankha (shankha) the conch shell (symbolically held by Vishnu); the shell bangle worn by Bengali women

sanyasi wandering ascetic; final stage in the ideal life of a man

sarai caravansarai, halting place

saranghi small four-stringed viola shaped

from a single piece of wood

Saraswati wife of Brahma and goddess of knowledge

sarkar the government; the state; a writer; an accountant

sarod Indian stringed musical instrument

sarvodaya uplift, improvement of all

sati (suttee) a virtuous woman; act of self-immolation on a husband's funeral pyre

Sati wife of Siva who destroyed herself by fire

satyagraha 'truth force'; passive resistance

sayid title (Muslim)

schist grey or green finely grained stone

seer (ser) weight (about 1 kg)

sepoy (sepai) Indian soldier, private

serow a wild Himalayan antelope

seth merchant, businessman

seva voluntary service

shahtush very fine wool from the Tibetan antelope

Shakti Energy; female divinity often associated with Siva

shala barrel-vaulted roof

shalagrama stone containing fossils worshipped as a form of Vishnu

shaman doctor/priest, using magic, exorcist

shamiana cloth canopy

Shankara Siva

sharia corpus of Muslim theological law

shastras ancient texts defining temple architecture

shastri religious title (Hindu)

shehnai (shahnai) Indian wind instrument like an oboe

sherwani knee-length coat for men

Shesha (Sesha) serpent who supports Vishnu

shikar hunting

shikara boat (Kashmir)

shisham a valuable building timber

sikhara (shikhara) curved temple tower or spire

shloka (sloka) Sanskrit sacred verse

singh (sinha) lion; Rajput caste name adopted by Sikhs

sinha stambha lion pillar

sirdar a guide who leads trekking groups

Sita Rama's wife, heroine of the Ramayana epic

sitar classical stringed musical instrument with a gourd for soundbox

Siva (Shiva) The Destroyer in the Hindu triad of Gods

Sivaratri literally 'Siva's night'; a festival (Feb-Mar)

Skanda the Hindu god of war; Kartikkeya

soma sacred drink mentioned in the Vedas

spandrel triangular space between the curve of an arch and the square enclosing it

squinch arch across an interior angle

sri (shri) honorific title, often used for 'Mr';

404

repeated as sign of great respect

sridhara pillar with octagonal shaft and square base

stalactite system of vaulting, remotely resembling stalactite formations in a cave

stambha free-standing column or pillar, often for a lamp or figure

steatite finely grained grey mineral

stele upright, inscribed slab used as a gravestone

sthan place (suffix)

stucco plasterwork

stupa hemispheric Buddhist funerary mound

stylobate base on which a colonnade is placed

sudra lowest of the Hindu castes

sufi Muslim mystic; sufism, Muslim mystic worship

sultan Muslim prince (sultana, wife of sultan)

Surya Sun; Sun God

svami (swami) holy man; a suffix for temple deities

svastika (swastika) auspicious Hindu/ Buddhist cross-like sign

swadeshi home made goods

swaraj home rule

swatantra freedom

syce groom, attendant who follows a horseman

tabla a pair of drums

tahr wild goat

tahsildar revenue collector

taikhana underground apartments

takht throne

talao (*tal*, talar) water tank

taluk administrative subdivision of a district

tamasha spectacle; festive celebration

tandava (dance) of Siva

tank lake dug for irrigation; a masonry-lined temple pool with stepped sides

tapas (tapasya) ascetic meditative self-denial

Tara literally 'star'; a goddess

tar-chok prayer flag (Ladakh)

tatties cane or grass screens used for shade

tehsil subdivision of a district (North India)

tempera distemper; method of mural painting by means of a 'body', such as white pigment

tempo three-wheeler vehicle

terai narrow strip of land along Himalayan foothills

terracotta burnt clay used as building material

thali Indian vegetarian 'plate' meal

thana a police jurisdiction; police station

thangka (thankha) cloth (often silk) painted with a Tibetan Mahayana deity

tiffin snack, light meal

tika (tilak) vermilion powder, auspicious mark on the forehead; often decorative

tikka tender pieces of meat, marinated and barbecued

tillana abstract dance

tirtha ford, bathing place, holy spot (Sanskrit)

Tirthankara literally 'ford-maker'; title given to 24 religious 'teachers', worshipped by Jains

tonga two-wheeled horse carriage

topi (topee) pith helmet

torana gateway; two posts with an architrave

tribhanga triple-bended pose for standing figures

Trimurti the Hindu Triad, Brahma, Vishnu and Siva

tripolia triple gateway

trisul the trident chief symbol of the god Siva

triveni triple-braided

tsampa ground, roasted barley, eaten dry or mixed with milk, tea or water (Himalayan)

tsemo peak (Ladakh)

tso lake (Ladakh)

tulsi sacred basil plant

tympanum triangular space within cornices

Uma Siva's consort in one of her many forms

untouchable 'outcastes', with whom contact of any kind was believed by high caste Hindus to be defiling

Upanishads ancient Sanskrit philosophical texts, part of the Vedas

usta painted camel leather goods

ustad master

uttarayana northwards

vahana 'vehicle' of the deity

vaisya the 'middle-class' caste of merchants and farmers

Valmiki sage, author of the Ramayana epic

Vamana dwarf incarnation of Vishnu

vana grove, forest

Varaha boar incarnation of Vishnu

varam village (Tamil)

varna 'colour'; social division of Hindus into Brahmin, Kshatriya, Vaishya and Sudra

varnam South Indian musical etude, conforming to a raga

Varuna Guardian of the West, accompanied by Makara (see above)

Vayu Wind god; Guardian of the North-West

Veda (Vedic) oldest known Hindu religious texts

vedi (bedi) altar, also a wall or screen

verandah enlarged porch in front of a hall

vihara Buddhist or Jain monastery with cells around a courtyard

vilas house or pleasure palace

vimana towered sanctuary containing the cell in which the deity is enshrined

vina plucked stringed instrument, relative of sitar

Vishnu a principal Hindu deity; the Preserver (and Creator)

vyala (yali) leogryph, mythical lion-like sculpture

-wallah suffix often used with a occupational name, eg rickshaw-wallah

wazir chief minister of a raja (from Turkish 'vizier')

wazwan ceremonial meal (Kashmir)

yagya (yajna) major ceremonial sacrifice

Yaksha (Yakshi) a demi-god, associated with nature

yali see vyala

Yama God of death, judge of the living

yantra magical diagram used in meditation; instrument

yatra pilgrimage

Yellow Hat Gelugpa Sect of Tibetan Buddhism – monks wear yellow headdress

yeti mythical Himalayan animal often referred to as 'the abominable snowman'

yoga school of philosophy stressing mental and physical disciplines; yogi

yoni a hole symbolising female sexuality; vagina

yul village

yura water channel (Ladakh)

zamindar a landlord granted income under the Mughals

zari silver and gold thread used in weaving or embroidery

zenana segregated women's apartments

zilla (zillah) district

Useful Hindi words and phrases

Pronounce
ā as in ah　　*ī as in bee*
ō as in oh　　*u as in oo in book*
nasalized vowels are shown as aṇ uṇ etc
These marks to help with pronunciation
do not appear in the main text

Useful words and phrases

Hello, good morning, goodbye
namaste
Thank you/ no thank you
dhanyavād or shukriyā / nahīṇ'shukriyā
Excuse me, sorry
māf kījiye
Yes/ no
jī hāṇ / jī nahīṇ
never mind/ that's all right
koi bāt nahīṇ
What is your name?
āpkā nām kyā hai?
My name is ....
merā nām .... hai
Pardon?
phir batāiye
How are you?
kyā hāl hai?
I am well, thanks, and you?
maiṇ thīk hūṇ, aur āp?
Not very well
maiñ thīk nahīṇ hūṇ
Where is the ....?
.........kahāṇ hai?
Who is ....?
.... kaun hai?
What is this?
yeh kyā hai?

Shopping

How much is this?
iskā kyā dām hai?
How much does that make?
Kitnā huā?
That makes (20) rupees
(bīs) rupaye
That is very expensive!
bahut mahangā hai!
Make it a bit cheaper!
thorā kam kījiye!

The hotel

What is the room charge?
kirāyā kitnā hai?

Please show the room
kamrā dikhāiye
Is there an airconditioned room?
kyā a/c kamrā hai?
Is there <u>hot water</u>?
<u>garam pānī</u> hai?
... a bathroom/ fan/ mosquito net
....bathroom/ pankhā/ machhar dānī
Is there a large room?
barā kamrā hai?
It's not clean
sāf nahīṇ hai
Please clean it
sāf karwā dījiye
Are there clean sheets/ blanket?
sāf chādareṇ/kambal haiṇ?
This is OK
yah thīk hai
Bill please
bill dījiye

Travel

Where's the <u>railway station</u>?
<u>railway station</u> kahāṇ hai?
How much is the ticket to <u>Shimla</u>?
<u>Shimla</u> kā ticket kitne ka hai?
When does the <u>Shimla</u> bus leave?
<u>Shimla</u> bus kab jāegī?
How much?
kitnā?
left/right
bāieṇ/dāhinā
go straight on
sīdhā chaliye
nearby
nazdīk
Is it near the <u>station</u>?
<u>station</u> ke pās hai?
Please wait here
yahāṇ thahariye
Please come at <u>8</u>
<u>āth bajai</u> ānā
Quickly
jaldi
stop
rukiye

Restaurants

Please show the menu
menu dikhāiye
No <u>chillis</u> please
<u>mirch</u> nahīṇ dālnā
....<u>sugar/ milk/ ice</u>
<u>chīnī/ doodh/ baraf</u>....

A bottle of water please
  ek botal pāni dījiye
...do not open it
  ......kholnā nahīṇ
sweet/ savoury
  mīthā/ namkīn
spoon, fork, knife
  chamach, kānṭā, chhurī

Time and days
right now abhī
morning suba
afternoon dopahar
evening shām
night rāt
today āj
tomorrow/ yesterday kal/ kal
day din
week haftā
month mahīnā
year sāl

Sunday ravivār
Monday somvār
Tuesday mangalvār
Wednesday budhvār
Thursday vīrvār
Friday shukravār
Saturday shanivār

Numbers
1 ek
2 dō
3 tīn
4 chār
5 pānch
6 chhai
7 sāt
8 āth
9 nau
10 das
11 gyāra
12 bārāh
13 terāh
14 chaudāh
15 pandrāh
16 solāh
17 satrāh
18 athārāh
19 unnīs
20 bīs
100/ 200 sau/ do sau
1000/ 2000 hazār/do hazār
100,000 lākh

Basic vocabulary (see also eating out)
airport, bank, bathroom, bus, doctor,
embassy, ferry, hotel, hospital, juice,
police, restaurant, station, stamp, taxi,
ticket, train (these are used locally
though often pronounced differently
eg daktar, haspatāl)

and aur
big barā
café/ food stall dhābā/ hotel
chemist dawāi kī dukān
clean sāf
closed band
cold thandā
day din
dirty gandā
English angrezi
excellent bahut achhā
food/ to eat khānā
hot (spicy) jhāl, masāledār
hot (temp) garam
luggage samān
medicine dawāi
newspaper akhbār
of course, sure zaroor
open khulā
police station thānā
road rāstā
room kamrā
shop dukan
sick (ill) bīmār
silk reshmī/ silk
small chhotā
that woh
this yeh
town shahar
water pānī
what kyā
when kab
where kahāṇ/ kidhar
which/who kaun
why kiuṇ
with ke sāthh

Fruit (phal)
apple seb
banana kelā
coconut nāriyal
green coconut dāb
lemon nimbu
lychee lichi
mango āmb
orange santrā
pineapple anānās

Useful Ladakhi words and phrases

		Numbers	
Hello, good morning, goodbye	*ju-lay*	1	*chik*
Thank you	*thuk-shey*	2	*nyiss*
Yes/no	*o/mā*	3	*sum*
This is OK	*digches ī nokt?*	4	*zhi*
I	*nga*	5	*nga*
you	*nyerang*	6	*tuk*
What is your name?	*nyerang ni minge*	7	*dun*
	chi in-lay?	8	*gyat*
What is it?	*chi in-lay?*	9	*gu*
How much is it?	*tsam in-lay?*	10	*chu*
It is expensive!	*ma rinchan rak!*	11	*chuk-chik*
Please take	*namches*	12	*chuk-nyiss*
hotel	*hotel/donkhang*	13	*chub-sum*
Where is the hotel/gompa?		14	*chub-zhi*
	hotel/gompa karwayot?	15	*cho-nga*
room	*nang*	16	*chu-ruk*
		17	*chub-dun*
Travel		18	*chub-gyat*
horse	*sta*	19	*churgu*
left	*yoma*	20	*nischu*
right	*yospa*	100	*gya*
straight	*ka-tang*	1000	*stong-chik*
slow	*kulea*		
fast	*gyogspa*		
Take me to the hotel	*nya hotel*		
	khyrazat		

Time and day
now *daksa*
later *stingne*
morning *ngatok*
evening *pitok*
night *tsanisan*
today *dring*
tomorrow *tō-ray*
day *zhak*
week *dunzhak*

Food and drink
barley flour (roasted) *ngampha*
   (*tsampa*)
bread *tagi*
dumplings (stuffed) *momo*
food *karji*
meat *sha*
milk *ōmā*
rice *das*
soup *thukpa*
sugar *kara*
tea *chā*
water (drinking *tung chu*

Eating out

Pronounce
ā as in ah   *ī* as in bee
ō as in oh   *u* as oo in book
nasalized vowels are shown as *an un* etc
Note These marks to help with
pronunciation do not appear in the
main text.

Eating out is normally cheap and safe but
menus can be dauntingly long and full of
unfamiliar names. North Indian dishes
are nearly universal.

Basic food vocabulary (Hindi)
gosht, mās   meat, usually mutton
  (sheep)
jhinga   prawns
macchli   fish
murgh   chicken
panīr   drained curds (cubes or pieces)
sabzī   vegetables

Vegetables
āloo   potato
baingan   aubergine
band gōbi   cabbage
bhindi   okra, ladies' fingers
gājar   carrots
khumbhi   mushroom
matar   peas
piāz   onion
phool gōbi   cauliflower
sāg   spinach

Pulses (beans and lentils)
masoor dāl   pink, round split lentils
moong dāl   popular in North India
chanā dāl   chick pea
rājmā   red kidney beans
Urhad dāl   small black beans

Spices and herbs
adrak (ādā)   ginger
dāl chini   cinnamon
dhaniya   coriander
elaichi   cardamom
garam masālā   aromatic mixture of
  'hot' spices, whole or ground
  (cardamom, cinnamon, cloves, cumin,
  black peppercorn etc)
haldi   turmeric
imli   tamarind
jīra (zeera)   cumin
kari pattā   'curry' leaf
kalonji   onion seed

laung   clove
mirch   chilli
pudina   mint
sarson (rai)   mustard
saunf   fennel
tej patta   bay leaf
tīl   sesame
zāfrān/kesar   saffron

Cooking mediums
tel   oil
ghī   clarified butter
makkhan   butter

Methods of preparation
Many items on restaurant menus are
named according to well-known
methods of preparation, roughly
equivalent to terms such as 'Provençal'
or 'sauté'.
bhoona   in a thick, fairly spicy sauce
chops   minced meat, fish or
  vegetables, covered with mashed
  potato, crumbed and fried
cutlet   minced meat, fish, vegetables
  formed into flat rounds or ovals,
  crumbed and fried (eg prawn cutlet,
  flattened king prawn)
do piaza   with onions (added twice
  during cooking)
dumphuk   steam baked
jhāl frāzi   spicy, hot sauce with
  tomatoes and chillies
Kashmiri   cooked with mild spices,
  ground almonds and yoghurt, often
  with fruit
kebab   skewered (or minced and
  shaped) meat or fish; a dry spicy dish
  cooked on a fire
kīma   minced meat (usually 'mutton')
kofta   minced meat or vegetable balls
korma   in fairly mild rich sauce using
  cream /yoghurt
masālā   marinated in spices (fairly hot)
Madras   hot
makhani   in butter rich sauce
Mughlai   rich North Indian style
Nargisi   dish using boiled eggs
navratan curry   ('9 jewels') colourful
  mixed vegetables and fruit in mild
  sauce
Peshwari   rich with dried fruit and nuts
  (Northwest Indian)

tandoori   baked in a tandoor (special clay oven) or one imitating it

tikka   marinated meat pieces, baked quite dry

vindaloo   hot and sour Goan meat dish using vinegar

Ordering a meal

A **thāli** for which you might pay Rs 15 (in small dhabas) to Rs 50, is usually the cheapest way of eating; the menu is fixed but refills are normally offered. You will be expected to eat with your fingers although a spoon is usually available. When ordering from a menu, you might like to try some 'bread' and/or rice, a vegetable and/or meat curry, bhāji, dāl, raita and pāpad. It is perfectly acceptable to order as little as some bread or rice and a vegetable dish or dāl. Sweets are an extra. Gulāb jāmun, rashmalāi and kulfi are popular.

Some typical dishes

Regional dishes are described in their appropriate sections.

aloo gosht   potato and mutton stew (North India)

aloo gobi   dry potato and cauliflower with cumin

aloo, matar, kumbhi   potato, peas, mushrooms in a dryish mildly spicy sauce

bhindi bhaji   lady's fingers fried with onions and mild spices

boti kebab   marinated pieces of meat, skewered and cooked over a fire

dāl makhani   lentils cooked with butter

dum aloo   potato curry with a spicy yoghurt, tomato and onion sauce

kīma mattar   mince meat with peas

matar panīr   curd cheese cubes with peas and spices (and often tomatoes)

murgh massāllam   chicken in rich creamy marinade of yoghurt, spices and herbs with nuts

Nargisi kofta   boiled eggs covered in minced lamb, cooked in a thick sauce

rogan josh   rich, mutton/ beef pieces in creamy, red sauce

sāg gosht   mutton and spinach

sāg panīr (pālak panīr)   Drained curd sautéd with chopped spinach in mild spices

Rice

bhāt/sādā chāwal   plain boiled rice

biriyāni   partially cooked rice layered over meat and baked with saffron

khichari   rice and lentils cooked with turmeric and other spices

pulao/ pilau   fried (and then boiled) rice cooked with spices (cloves, cardamom, cinnamon) with dried fruit, nuts or vegetables. Sometimes cooked with meat, like a biriyāni

Roti – breads

chapāti (phoolka, roti)   thin, plain, wholemeal unleavened bread cooked on a tawa (griddle), usually made from āta (wheat flour). Makkai-ki-roti is with maize flour. Soft, thicker version of poori, made with white flour

nān   oven baked (traditionally in a tandoor) white flour leavened bread often large and triangular; sometimes stuffed with almonds and dried fruit

parāthā   fried bread layered with ghī (sometimes cooked with egg or stuffed with potatoes)

poori   thin deep-fried, puffed rounds of flour

Accompaniments

achār   pickles (usually spicy and preserved in oil)

chutnī   often fruit or tomato, freshly prepared, sweet and mildly spiced

dahī   plain yoghurt

namak   salt

papad, pappadom   deep fried, pulse flour wafer rounds

raita   yoghurt with shredded cucumber, pinapple or other fruit, or bundi (tiny batter balls)

Sweets

These are often made with reduced/ thickened milk, drained curd cheese or powdered lentils and nuts. They are sometimes covered with a flimsy sheet of decorative, edible silver leaf

barfi   fudge-like rectangles/diamonds

khīr   thickened milk rice/vermicelli pudding

gājar halwa   dry sweet made with thickened milk, carrots and spice

gulāb jāmun   dark fried spongy balls, soaked in syrup

halwa   rich sweet made from cereal, fruit, vegetable, nuts and sugar

kulfi   cone-shaped Indian ice cream
with pistachhios/almonds, uneven in
texture

jalebi   spirals of fried batter soaked in
syrup

laddoo   lentil based batter 'grains'
shaped into orange rounds

rasgulla (roshgulla) balls of curd in
clear syrup

rasmalāi   spongy curd rounds, soaked
in sweetened cream and garnished
with pistachio nuts

sandesh   dry sweet made of curd
cheese

Snacks

bhāji, pakora   vegetable fritters
(onions, potatoes, cauliflower,
aubergine etc) deep-fried in batter

chāt   sweet and sour cubed fruit and
vegetables flavoured with tamarind
paste and chillis

chanā choor, chioora ('Bombay mix')
lentil and flattened rice snacks mixed
with nuts and dried fruit

kachori   fried pastry rounds stuffed
with spiced lentil/ peas/ potato filling

namkīn   savoury pastry bits

samosā   cooked vegetable or meat
wrapped in pastry circle into 'triangles'
and deep fried

Drinks

chai   tea boiled with milk and sugar

doodh   milk

kāfi   ground fresh coffee boiled with
milk and sugar

lassi   cool drink made with yoghurt
and water, salted or sweetened

nimboo pāni   refreshing drink made
with fresh lime and water, chilled
bottled water, added salt or sugar
syrup - avoid ice

pāni   water

Index

A

Abub Sahar, P&H 171
acacia 387
access from Delhi 76
accommodation, hotels
  31
Agni 117, 368
Agoda, Utt 121
Ahoms 316
AIDS 65
air conditioning 32
air ticket agents 23, 52
air travel 22
airport transfer 25
Ajit Singh 209
Akbar 348
Akhnoor, J&K 231
Alchi, J&K 234, 251, 257
alcohol 47
Alexander, the Great 346
Ali, Chaudhuri Rahmat
  352
Almora, Utt 133
alpine forests 296
altitude sickness 64
Ambedkar, Dr BR 373
amphibians 395
Anchar, Lak 224
Andretta, HP 206
antelope 391
antelope, blackbuck 391
antelope, Indian 391
antelope, Tibetan 391
art and architecture,
  reading list 68
Arunachal Pradesh 339
Asaf Khan 227
Asoka 346
Assam 316
Atholi, HP 216
Attargo, HP 169
Auli, Utt 116
Auniati, As 329
Aurangzeb 349
Aut, HP 173, 174
auto rickshaws 38
Automobile Assoc 37

B

babul tree 387
Babur 348
Badrinath, Utt 110, 117
Bagdogra, WB 290
Bageshwar, Utt 122, 137
Baghmara, Meg 338

Baha'i Temple, Delhi 82
Baha'u'llah 82
Bahrmaur, HP 214
Baijnath, HP 205
Baijnath, Utt 136
Bajaura Temple, HP 177
Bakhim, Sik 311
Bakr-Id 51
Balpakram National Park,
  Npk, Meg 338
Baltis 236
bamboo 387
banana 387
Banderpunch, Mnt 111
Banganga, J&K 233
Banjar, HP 174, 213
banyan tree 387
Baragarh Peak, Mnt 180
Barai, Riv 260
Barak Valley, As 331
Baralacha La, Pas 196, 215
Barog, HP 159
Barpeta Road, As 326
Barseri, HP 164
Basgo, J&K 234, 250
Bashleo, Pas 213
Baspa Valley, HP 164,
  216
Bassi, HP 205
Batal, HP 170
baya weaver 394
bear, brown 392
bear, Himalayan black
  392
bear, sloth 392
bears 309, 392
Beas, Riv 171
Bema, J&K 254
Benapol 24
Bengali, Teach Yourself
  68
Bengenatti, As 329
Bentinck, Lord William
  350
Berinag, Utt 137
Bhabha Valley, HP 163,
  217
Bhagirath, King 112
Bhakra Dam, HP 171
bhakti 347
Bhalowguri 329
Bhalukpong, Aru 327
Bhalukpong, As, Npk
  327
bharal 391
Bharari, Utt 122

Bharatiya Janata Party
  (BJP) 354, 356
Bharmaur, HP 214
Bhim Tal 132
bhoj patra 166
Bhojbasa, Utt 112, 120
Bhoreli River, As 327
Bhotias 116, 297
Bhowali, Utt 133
Bhudevi 363
Bhutan, border and
  transport 291
Bhutan-India border 24
Bhutias, Bhotias 297
Biama, J&K 254
big cats 389
Bijanbari, WB 286
Bijli Mahadev, HP 177
Bijrani, Utt 142
Bilaspur HP 171
Binsar, Utt 135
bird watching 52
Birds 393
birds, reading list 69
bison, Indian 391
Black Hole, Calcutta 265
blackbuck 391
blue sheep 391
boar, wild 392
Bodhisattvas 374
Bollywood 382
Bomdila, Aru 341
booklist, Ladakh 238,
  248
books on India 67
border crossings 23, 24
Bordua, Ass 319
Bose, Rash Behari 195
Bose, SC 209
bougainvillea 388
Brahma 361
Brahmanism 358
Brahmaputra, Riv, As
  316, 325
Brahmaur, HP 214
Brahmpukar, HP 171
Brandy Nala, J&K 196
Buddha, The 374
Buddhism 375
Buddhist symbols 297
Buddhist, holy sites 374
Bugdiar, Utt 127
bulbul, red-vented 393
bulbul, red-whiskered
  394
bulbul, white-cheeked
  394

Burne-Jones 265
Burphu, Utt 127
buses 36
Byasi, Utt 113

C

Calcutta (WB) 264
calendar, Hindu 49, 371
calendar, Indian 49
camping 34
canna lily 388
car hire 36
car travel 36
cashmere 225
caste 369
cattle fair, Kullu 177
cave paintings, Utt 135
caves, Meg 338
Central Delhi 77
Chail, HP 158
Chaini, HP 174
Chakki, HP 209
Chamathang, J&K 253
Chamba, HP 211
Chamoli, Utt 115
Chandra, Riv 170
Chandrabhaga, Riv 193
Chandragupta Maurya
  346
Chandrakhani, Pas 219
Chandratal, Lak 215
Chands, The 133
chang 237
changing money 21
Changpas 236
Charaideo, As 329
Charcha, Pas 260
charities 29
Charnock, J 264
Chatta Chowk 83
Chaubatia, Utt 143
Chaukori, Utt 137
checklist, health 59
checklist, trekkers' 58
cheer pheasant 158
Chemathang, Sik 312
Cherrapunji, Meg 337
Chhalal, HP 179
chhang 302
Chhangu, Sik 304
Chharabra, HP 157, 213
Chhatru, HP 170
Chhota Dhara, HP 170
children, health 60

children, travelling with 27
Chillung, J&K 257
chinar tree 227
chinkara 391
Chirbasa, Utt 120
chital 390
Chitre, WB 285
Choglamsar, J&K 248
Chogyal 296
Chokhapani, HP 217
chorten 297
Chowringhee, Calcutta 265
Christmas 50
Chumchar, J&K 257
Church of St John in the Wilderness 129
cinema 51, 382
civet, palm 390
climate 385
clothes 30
clothing 19
cobra, king 395
cobra, spectacled 395
common langur 392
common mongoose 393
common myna 393
communications 44
Communist Party, Marxist 355
conduct 27
confidence tricksters 30
Congress, Indian National 351
Constitution 353
copper ware 134
Corbett National Park, Nk, Utt 138
Corbett, Jim 139, 142
courtesy 27
Craft Museum, Delhi 83
Craignano, HP 157
credit cards 21
cricket 52
crocodile 139
crops 388
crow, house 393
crow, jungle 393
cuisine 46
currency 20
currency transfer 21
Curzon Trail 125
Curzon, Lord 213
cycling 38

D

Dah, J&K 254
Daksa 104
Dal, Lak, Srinagar 224
Dalai Lama 199
Dalhousie 209
Dalits 370
Danes Folly, HP 157
Dankar 169

Daoras 171
Daranghati Sanctuary, Nk, HP 162
Darcha, HP 191, 196
Dards 236
Darjeeling Himalaya Railway 283
Darjeeling, WB 276
Darla Ghat, HP 171
Darma Valley Trek 127
darshan 358
Dasara 50
Debal, Utt 124
deer 390
deer, musk 390
deer, spotted 390
Dehra Dun and Uttaranchal 96
Dehra Dun, Utt 96
Delhi 76
Deo Tibba, Mnt 219
Deoprayag, Utt 113
Departure Tax, India 25
Deskit, J&K 257
Dhak tree 387
Dhakuri, Utt 123
Dhakwani, Utt 126
Dhanchho, HP 215
Dhangarhi, Utt 140
Dhanolti, UP 100
Dharamshala, HP..198
dharamshalas 34
Dharchula, Utt 128
dharma 346
Dhaula Dhar, Mnt 148
Dhauladhar, Mnt 201
Dhikala, Utt 140
Dhubdi, Sik 307
Dibrugarh, As 330
Dibru-Saikhowa National Park, As, npk 331
Digboi, As 330
Dikhuli, see Dhikala, Utt 140
diplomatic representations 71
discounted air fares 22
Dispur, As 318
Diwal (Divali) 50
Diwan-i-Am 83
Doditial, Utt 121
dol, Hinduism 361
Donkiala, Pas, Sik 297
dove, blue rock 393
dove, collared 393
dove, little brown 393
Dr Graham's Homes, Kalimpong 288
drinks 47
driving 36
Drokhpa, J&K 253, 254
Droks 236
drongo 394
drugs 30
Drukpas 258
Dudhia, WB 283
Durga 177

Duryodhana 122
Dwali, Utt 123
Dwarahat, Utt 143
Dwarka 111
dzo 309
Dzongri, Sik 311
Dzongu, Sik 297

E

earthquake 162, 332
earthquake, As 316
East India Company 350
elephant rides, Corbett 139
elephant, Indian 390
elephants 391
Elgin, Lord 198
email 44
embassies 71
Enchey Monastery, Gangtok 299
Entry permits, Northeast Hills 317
equipment, trekkers' 58
eucalyptus 387
Everest, Mnt 284
exchange 21

F

Fagu, HP 158
Fambong Lho Wildlife Reserve, Sik 310
fax 45
festivals 49
film 51
finger millet 388
Fishing 52
flycatcher, verditer 394
flying fox bat 393
food 46
fossils 170, 218
frangipani 388

G

Gaddis 211
Gaggal, HP 208
Gairal, Utt 142
Gairibans, WB 285
Gandeswar, Utt 135
Gandha, Pas 256
Gandhi, Indira 79
Gandhi, MK 136, 351
Ganesh 367
Ganesh Chaturthi 50
Ganga, Goddess 112
Ganga, River, source of 120
Ganghar, Utt 127
Gangnani, Utt 112
Gangori, Utt 121
Gangotri, Utt 110, 112
Gangtok, Sik 299
Garampani, Utt 133

Garhwal, Utt 110
Garmur, As 329
Garo Hills, Meg 338
Garos 332
Garur, Utt 136
Gauchar, Utt 115
Gaumukh, Utt 112, 120
gaur 391
Gaurikund waterfall 112
Gaurikund, Utt 114
gazelle, Indian 391
Gelugpa 248, 250, 258, 259
Gete, HP 218
getting there 22
Gezing, Sik 305
Ghanahatti, HP 171
Ghangharia, Utt 117
Ghat, Utt 126
Ghayaghi 174
Ghiyas'ud-Din Tughluq Tughluq, Ghiyas'ud-Din 82
Ghoom 283
Ghoom, WB 279
Ghungri, see Kungri, HP 169
gibbons 329
goats 391
Gocha La 311
Gondhla, HP 193
Gongmaru, Pas 256
goral 392
Gorkhey, WB 286
Govind Sagar, Lak 171
Govindghat, Utt 117
Gramphoo, HP 170, 192
Granville, W 265
Great Himalayan National Park, Npk, HP 175
Gulab Singh of Jammu 224
Gular-dogi, Utt 113
Gulmohur tree 387
Guptakashi, Utt 113
gur gur 237
Gurkhas 94, 111, 206
Guru Ghantal, HP 195
Guru Granth 376
Guwahati, As 317
Gwaldam, Utt 123
Gyalshing, Sik 305

H

Hadimba 184
Hadsar 215
Hajo, As 322
Hamta Pas 215
hangul 390
Hankar, J&K 256
Hanuman 363, 379
Hanuman Chatti, Utt 122
Haridwar, Utt..103
Harijans 370

Har-ki-Dun, Utt 122
Hathi Parbat, Mnt 118
Hauz Khas, Delhi 81
Hazrat Nizamuddin,
   Delhi 81
Hazratbal, J&K 228
health 57, 59
Hemis, J&K 249
Hemis, Npk, J&K 256
Hemkund, Utt 117
hibiscus 388
Hikim, HP 170
Himachal Pradesh
   145-220
Himalaya 384
Himalayan Environment
   Trust Code 55
Himalayan tahr 392
Hinayana Buddhism 374
Hindi, teach yourself 68
Hindu deities 361
Hindu holy sites 361
Hindu, holy abodes 111
Hinduism 358
history, reading list 68
hitchhiking 39
Holi 49
Holidays and festivals 49
Hollong Park Gibbon
   Sanctuary, As 329
hoopoe 394
hotel categories 33
hotels, India 31
house sparrow 393
houseboats, J&K 229
Humayun 79
Humayun's Tomb, Delhi
   81
hyena, striped 392

I

ibex 392
ibex, Siberian 169
Id-ul-Fitr 51
Id-ul-Zuha 51
Iltutmish Tomb 82
Independence 352
Independence Day 50
India Gate 77
Indian coral tree 387
Indian National Army
   195
Indian Tourist Offices
   overseas 18
Indra 368
Indrail Pass 40
Indus, Riv 234, 255
Inner Line Permits 160
innoculations 60
insect pests 32
Iravati, Riv 211
Islam 372, 374
Itanagar - Naharlgun,
   Aru 339
Itransport to India
   travel 22

J

Jabli, HP 158
jackal 393
jackfruit 387
Jacob, Sir SS 151
Jagatsukh, HP 182
Jageswar, Utt 135
Jahangir 209, 224, 349
Jahlma, HP 193
Jai Singh II, Maharaja 79
Jaintia Hills, Meg 338
Jaintias 332
Jakrem, Meg 334
Jallianwala Bagh 351
Jalori Pass 174, 213
Jalori Pass, HP 174
Jama Masjid, Delhi 83
Jambudvipa 381
Jamlu 218
Jammu and Kashmir
   State 221
Jammu City, J&K 230
Jangi, HP 167
Janki Chatti, Utt 111
Janmashtami 50
Jantar Mantar, Delhi 79
Jari, HP 179, 219
Jaswantpur, Aru 341
jati 370
Jaubari 285
Jawalamukhi, HP..208
Jelepla, Pas, Sik 297
Jeolikote, Utt 133
Jeori, HP 162
Jespa, HP 196
Jhakhri, HP 161
Jhelum, Riv 229
Jhepi, WB 286
Jia Bhoreli 327
Jibhi, HP 174
Jinchan Valley 256
Jiuri, HP 162
Jogindernagar, HP 205
Jones, Sir W 265
Jorhat, As 327
Joshimath, Utt 116, 126
Jowai, Meg 338
juniper 235
jyoitirlinga, Utt 114, 135
jyotirlinga, HP 205
jyotirlingas 367

K

Kabir 376
Kafnoo, HP 163, 217
Kagyu Buddhists 199
Kah, HP 167
Kailash, Mt 137
Kakarbhiita, Nepal 291
Kalachakra Temple, HP
   165
Kaladhungi, Utt 142
Kalatope, HP 209
kaleej 395
Kali 367
Kalidasa 379
Kalimpong, WB 286
Kalka, HP 158, 166
kalpa, Hindu cosmic
   time 362
Kalyani, Utt 121
Kamalabari, As 329
Kang, Pas 216
Kangchendzonga
   National Park, Sik 309
Kangchendzonga, Mnt,
   Sik 296
Kangra, HP..207
Kangra School, painting
   207
Kangra Valley 206
Kankhal, UP 104
Kanol, Utt 125
Kaphini, Glc, Utt 123
Karchham, HP 163
Kargil, J&K 234
karma 359
Karmapa Lama 199
Karnaprayag, Utt 115
Karsha, J&K 259
Karttikeya 136, 366
Karu, J&K 257
Karzog, J&K 253
Kasauli, HP 159
Kashmiri language 225
Kasol 179
Kasol, HP 219
Katarmal, Utt 134
Kathgodam, Utt 128
Katoch, Sansar Chand II
   206
Katra, J&K 233
Katrain, HP..180
Katyurs 136
Kaza, HP 170, 218
Kaziranga, Npk, As 323
Kedarnath, Utt..110, 113
Kedarnath Musk Deer
   Sanctuary, Nk, Utt 115
Kedartal, Utt 121
Keylong, HP..194
Khabo, HP 167
Khajjiar, HP 210
khalsa 376
Khalsi, J&K 234
Khaltse, J&K 234, 254
Khardong Monastery
   195
Khardung La, Pas, HP
   254
Kharsali, Utt 112
Khasis 332
Khati, Utt 123
Khechopari Lake, Sik
   306
Khinanauli, Utt 142
Khirganga, HP 179, 219
Khoksar, HP 192
Khurna, Riv 260
Ki, HP 170
Kibber, HP 170, 218
Kilar, HP 216
Kilbury, Utt 132
Kinnaur, HP 163, 216
Kinner Kailash, Mts, HP
   165
Kipling, Lockwood 150
kite, pariah 393
Klemta, Aru 342
koel 394
Kongrala, Pas, Sik 297
Konke, Pas 256
Kothi, HP 166
krait, banded 396
krait, common 395
Krem Sweep (Syndai),
   Meg 338
Kufri, HP..157
Kullu (Kulu, HP)..176
Kullu Valley, treks 218
Kumbh Mela 105
Kungri, HP 169
Kunzum La, Pas 170,
   218
Kurseong, WB 283
Kusumpti, HP 156
kyang 392
Kyd, Col 265
Kyongnosla Alpine
   Sanctuary, Sik 304

L

Labrang, Sik 308
Lachalung La, Pas 196
Lachung, Sik 308
Ladakh, J&K 235
Lahul 215
Lahul (Lahaul, HP)..191
Lahul trekking 215
Lake District, Aru 342
Lakshmi 363
Lalkuan, UP 132
Lalung Gompa, HP 169
Landour, UP 99
language 377
lantana 388
Larji Gorge, HP 174
Ledo, As 331
leeches 57, 312
Leh, J&K 238
Leh, HP 190
Lekir, J&K 251
Lekir (Likir), J&K 234
leopard 389
Lepchas 297
Lilam, Utt 126
linga 366
Lingti Valley 170
liquor permits 19
literature, Indian,
   reading list 69
Lohajung, Pas 124
Loharkhet, Utt 123
Lokpal, Utt 117
Longstaff, T 127
Losar 170

Luhri, HP 160
Lumshnong, Meg 338
Lutyens, Sir E 77

M

Madan Kamdev 323
Madhva 360
Maenam Sanctuary, Sik 309
Magar 297
mage, Hinduism 361
magpie, red-billed blue 394
Mahabharata 378
Mahadeva 367
Maharishi Mahesh Yogi 107
Mahasivaratri 49
Mahayana 374
Mahayana Buddhism 300
Mahish, Mahishasura 367
Mahmud of Ghazni 347
Malana 218
Malana Valley, HP 219
malaria 63
Malinithan, Aru 342
Mana, Utt 118
Manali, HP..182
Manali to Leh 191
Manas, Npk, As 325
mandala, Hindu architecture 381
Mandalay, Road to 331
Mandi
  Sahor, HP..172
Manebhanjang, WB 284
mango 387
Manikaran, HP 179
Manimahesh, Lak 214
Mansar, Lak 231
Mansarovar, Utt 137
maps for trekkers 58
maps, India 70
maps, trekking 59
Margherita, As 331
Mariani, As 329
Markha, J&K 256
markhor 392
marmot 393
marriage, arranged 370
Mashobra, HP 157
Masrur, HP..208
matrilineal 332
Mawmluh, Meg 337
Mawsmai, Meg 337
Mawsynram, Meg 334
McLeodganj, HP 198
meditation 52
meditation,
  Dharamshala 199, 204
meditation, Rishikesh 108
Meghalaya 332
Meghma, WB 285

Melli, Sik 302
Memorial Ghats, Delhi 79
Meru, Mnt 121
Miao-Namdapha, Npk, Aru 342
Mihrbahri 227
Mikkim, HP 169
Milam Glacier trek 126
Milam Glacier, Utt 127, 137
Minamarg, J&K 234
mineral resources, India 356
minjar 212
Mirik, WB 283
Mitra 368
Miyar Nullah, HP 216
Molley 286
monal, Himalayan 395
money 20
money transfer 21
Mons 236
monsoon 385
Morang, HP 167
mosquito protection 32
Mother Goddess 367
motorbike tours 52
motorcycling 38
Mountain railway,
  Kangra 208
mountain rly, Darjeeling 283, 291
mountain rly, Kangra 207
mountain rly, Shimla 155
mountain sickness
  advice, Leh 247
mountaineering 58
mountaineering,
  booklist 58
Mountbatten, Lord 352
Mudh, HP 217, 219
Mughals 224, 348
Muharram 51
Mu'izzu'd Din 347
Mulbekh, J&K 234
Munsiari, Utt 126, 137
mural paintings, HP 167
Museums
  Craft 83
  National, Delhi 83
  Swatantra Sangrama
  Sangrahalaya 83
music 382
Muslim architecture,
  Delhi 81
Muslim League 351
Mussoorie, Utt..99
Mutiny, The 351
myna, pied 394

N

Naddi Gaon, HP 200
Naggar, HP..180

Nagin, Lak 224
Naina (Cheena) Peak, Utt 129
Nainital, Utt 128
Nakli La, Pas 196
Nalagarh, HP 159
Naldera 158
Naldera, HP 213
Namdapha National
  Park, Aru 342
Nameri National Park,
  As, Npk 327
Namgyals 236, 296
Namik, Glc 137
Namika, Pas 234
Namlung, Pas 256
Nanda Devi trek 126
Nanda Devi, Mnt 122, 136
Nanda Kund, Utt 127
Nandanvan, Mnt 121
Nandaprayag, Utt 115
Nandi 367
Naphak Lake, Meg 338
Narkanda, HP 160, 213
narrow gauge railway,
  Kangra 208
narrow gauge railway,
  Shimla 155
narrow gauge railway,
  Kangra 207
Nartiang, Meg 337
Nataraja 367
Nathpa, HP 161
Nathula, Pas, Sik 297
National Museum, Delhi 83
National Parks
  Rajaji 110
Naukuchiyatal, Utt 132
Navaratri 50
Neelkanth, Utt 117
Nehru Kund, HP 186
Nehru Museum, Delhi 83
Nepal, transport to 291
Ner Chowk 171
New Delhi
  sights 77
New Jalpaiguri, WB 289
New Year's Day 49
Newars 297
newspapers, India 45
Nimaling, J&K 256
Nimmu, J&K 250
Nirath, HP 160
Nizamuddin, Delhi 81
Nohkaklikai Falls, Meg 337
Nokrek National Park,
  Meg 338
Nolji, UP 99
non-cooperation 352
Nongkhrum, Meg 337
Nongstoin, Meg 337
North-eastern Hill States 313

Nowgaon, Utt 122
Nubra Valley, J&K 254
Nubra Valley, J&K 253
Nur Jahan 228
Nurpur, HP 209
Nyingmapa 305
Nyoma, J&K 253

O

Ochterlony, D 265
ogla, HP 164
Old Delhi 82
Orang, As, Npk 327
orchids, Aru 341
orchids, Sik 303
orchids, WB 287
overland to India 23
oxen 391

P

Pabitora, As 323
Pachhu Valley Utt 127
Padmasanbhava 172
Pahari 94
Pakistan 352
Palampur, HP..205
palas 387
Pampore 229
Panamik, J&K 254, 257
Panch Kedars, Utt 114
Panch Prayags 115
Panchuli, Glc 137
Panchuli, Mnt 137
Pandavas 114
Pandoh, HP 174
Pang, J&K 191, 196
Pangi valley, Val 216
Pangi, HP 166
Pangong Tso, Lak 235
Pangong-Tso (Lake) 254
Pangot, Utt 133
Panini 379
Panitanki, WB 291
panther 389
papaya 387
papier mâché 226
parakeet, rose-ringed 394
Parasuram Kund, Lak,
  Aru 342
Parbati, see Parvati, HP
parcel post 44
Parliament House, Delhi 77
Partition 352
partridges, snow 395
Parvati 136, 366
Parvati Valley, HP 179, 219
Parwanoo, HP..158
pashmina 225
Pattan Valley 193
peacock 395
peafowl 395

pearl millet 388
Pelling, Sik 306
Pemayangste, Sik 305, 310
Pensi La, Pass 259
Peon, HP 173
permits for trekkers 57
Phalut, WB 284
pheasant, blood 395
Phodong, Sik 308, 311
photography 59
Phugtal monastery 260
Phurkiya, Utt 123
Phyang, J&K 234, 250
pigeon, feral 393
pilgrimage 115
Pin Valley National Park, HP 169
Pin Valley, HP 169, 217, 219
pipal 387
pipistrelle, Indian 393
Pir Panjal, Mnt 148, 224
Pithorgarh, Utt 137
police 30
population 353
poste restante 44
Prashar, HP 173
prayer flag, Buddhist 297
prayer wheel, Buddhist 297
pre-paid taxis, airport 25
primates 392
Prini, HP 186
Printiki, Pas 256
Project Tiger, As 139, 326
Project Tiger, Corbett 140
Ptso, Aru 342
Puga, J&K 253
Puh, HP 167
Puja 360
Pulga, HP 179, 180
pundits 325
Purana Qila (Old Fort) 79
Purni, J&K 260

Q

Qutb Minar, Delhi 82

R

Rabongla, Sik 309
radio 46
Radio frequencies 46
radio, India 45
rafting, Ladakh 245
rafting, near Rishikesh 108
rafting, Sikkim 302
raga 383
Raghunathj, Kullu 172

Rail Museum, Delhi 83
railway, steam, see steam engine 331
Raison, HP 180
Raj Ghat, Delhi 79
Rajagopalachari, C 110
Rajaji National Park 110
Rajasthan Canal project 171
Rajputs 224
Rakcham, HP 164
Rakh, HP 215
Raksha bandhan 50
Ralam, Glc, Utt 137
Ralam, Utt 127
Rama 230, 363, 379
Ramadan 51, 373
Ramakrishna 371
Ramanuja 360, 363
Ramayana 379
Ramganga, Riv, Utt 138
Ramgarh Fort 159
Ramgarh, Utt 133
Ramlila 50
Rammam, WB 286
Ramnagar, Utt 140
Ramni Pass, Utt 126
Rampur Bushahr, HP 160
Rampur, HP 213
Rangpo, Sik 303
Rangpur, As 329
Ranikhet, Utt..143
Ransi, Utt 114
raptors 395
Rashtrapati Bhavan, Delhi 77
Rauslikhal, UP 100
Ravi, Riv 171, 213
reading list 67
rebirth 359
Recong Peo, HP 165
Red Fort: Delhi 82
religion 28
religion, reading list 69
religious sites, visiting 28
Reptiles 395
restricted areas, India 19
retiring rooms 33
Rewalsar, Lak, HP 173
rhesus macaque 392
rhinoceros 323
rhinoceros, great Indian one-horned 390
rhododendron 388
rhododendrons, Sik 308
rice 388
Rilkote, Utt 127
Rimbick, WB 284
Ripchar, Val, J&K 256
Rishikesh, Utt..106
river running 51
Rizong, J&K 234
rock python, Indian 395
Roerich, Nicholas 181
Rohtang, Pas 192

Rongpas 297
Roopkund, Utt 123
Roorkee, Utt 98
Ruding, HP 193
Rudra 367
Rudranath, Utt 115
Rudraprayag, Utt 113
Rudugaira Valley, Utt 121
rumal embroidery 211
Rumtek Monastery, Sik 303
Rupshu, J&K 253

S

Sach, Pas 216
Sadhu 360
safety, India 30
saffron 164, 229
Saharanpur, Utt..99
Sahor Mandi, HP..172
Samanden, WB 286
sambar 390
samsara 359
Samtanling, J&K 257
Sandakphu, Mnt, WB 284
Sangam 169
Sangam, HP 217
Sangla, HP..164
Sankardeva, Sri 319
Sankri, Utt 122
sapphire 216
Sarahan, HP..162
Saramsa Gardens, Sik 303
Sarapduli, Utt 142
Sarasvati 362
Sarchu, HP 191, 196
Saspul, J&K 234
sati 350, 367
Satopanth, Lak, Utt 118
scripts 377
seasons 49, 371
Secretariats, Delhi 77
sects, Hinduism 361
security 29
security on trains 30
security, air lines 23
Sela Pass 341
Senchal, Lak, WB 279
sending money 21
Seraj, HP 213
Sereuil Lake, HP 175
Sethan, HP 185
Shah Jahan 228, 349
shahtush 225
Shakti worship 367
Shalaghat, HP 171
Shankaracharya 117, 360
Shansa, HP 193
sheep 391
shellfish 61
Sher Shah, Suri 79

Shergol, J&K 234
Shey, J&K 248
Shi'a 237
Shi'a Muslims 372
Shichling, HP 169
Shillakong, Val 256
Shillong Peak, Mnt, Meg 333
Shillong, Meg 333
Shimla (Simla, HP)..150
Shingba, Sik 308
Shingo La, Pas, J&K 215, 260
Shingo, Riv, J&K 260
Shivling, Mnt, Utt 121
Shiwaliks, Mnt 224
Shogdu, J&K 256
Shoja, HP 174
Shrikhand Mahadev, Mnt, HP 162
Shyok Valley, J&K 257
Siang River, Arunachal Pr 339
Sibsagar, As 329
Siju, Meg 338
Sikhism 376
Sikkim 293-312
Sikkim, eco-tourism, Sik 309
Silchar, As 331
Siliguri, WB 289
silk cotton tree 386
Singalila Trek, treks, WB 284
Singh, Sobha 206
Singla La, Pas, J&K 259
Siraj-ud-Daula 264
Siri, Delhi 81
Sissu, HP 193
Sita 379
Siva 112, 205, 363
Siva, alternative names 367
Sivaratri 49
Skanda 368
skiing, HP 157
skiing, Utt 116
Smythe, Frank 118
snakes 395
snow leopard 390
Sobala, Utt 128
soft drinks 47
Solan, HP..158
Solang, HP 185
Someswar, Utt 136
Sonamarg, J&K 234
Sonparayag, Utt 114
sorghum 388
South New Delhi 81
Spiti 167, 218
Spiti trekking 215
Spiti, HP 163
Spituk, J&K 255
Spituk, J&K 234, 250, 255
sport 51

squirrel, five-striped palm 393
squirrel, giant flying 393
squirrel, three-striped palm 393
Sridevi 363
Srinagar, Utt..113
Srinagar J&K 227
Stakna, J&K 249
Stapski, Pas 256
steam engine, As 331
Stilwell Rd, As 331
Stok, J&K 248
stop-overs 22
Stops along the Kangra Valley Railway 205
stupa 297
Sualkuchi, As 323
Subrahmanya 366
sugar cane 388
Sujanpur Tira, HP 207
Sukiapokari, WB 284
Sultan, Utt 142
Sumdahchenmo, J&K 257
Sumdo, HP 167, 218
Sumdu, Utt 127
Sumkhetar, HP 172
Sundar Dhunga, Glc, Utt 123
Sundernagar, HP 171
Sunni Muslims 372
Surinsar, Lak 231
Surya 368
Sutlej, Riv, HP 171
Sutoi, Utt 125
suttee 367
swadeshi 352
swaraj 352
Swatantra Party 355
Swatantra Sangrama Sangrahalaya Museum 83

T

Tabo, HP 167, 218
Tadong, Sik 303
Taglang La, Pas 197
Tagore, Rabindranath 209, 380
tahr, Himalayan 392
Takthak, J&K 257
Tandi, HP 193
Tangyar, J&K 257
tantra 347
Tapovan, Utt 121, 126
Tapri, HP 163
Tashiding, Sik 307
Tashigang, HP 170
Tattapani, HP 158
Tawang Monastery, Aru 341
taxis 25, 37
Tayul Monastery, HP 195
tea 279, 388

Teh, HP 196
Tehri, UP 111
television, India 45
temple architecture, Muslim 381
temple, Hindu architecture 380
Teresa, Mother 267
Tezpur, As 326
thali 46
Thangi, HP 216
Thangshing, Sik 311
Theog, HP 158
Theravada 374
Thikse, J&K 248
Thirot, HP 193
thuggee 350
Tibetology 300
tiger 110, 326, 389
Tiger 139
tigers 138
Tiggur, J&K 257
Timur (Tamburlaine) 103, 347
Tinsukia, As 330
Tipi, Aru 341
Tipi, As 320
tipping 29
Tirthan Sanctuary, HP 175
Tirthan Valley, HP 174
toilets 32
Tonglu, WB 285
tour operators 15
Tourist Offices overseas, Indian 18
touts 43
Toy Train, Darjeeling 283, 291
tragopan, western 395
train travel 39
Trans Himalaya, Mnt, J&K 224
travel by air 34
travel by road 35
travel tips, air 35
travel tips, bus 36
travel tips, car 37
Travel Tips, motorcycle 39
travel tips, rail 42
travel, air 22
travellers' cheques 20
Trees
  gum 387
  jackfruit 387
trees, reading list 69
trekking 53
trekking agents 54
trekking areas
  Darjeeling 279-286
  Garwhal & Kumaon 120-123
  Himachal 213-219
  Ladakh 255
  Sikkim 309-312
  Zanskar 259

trekking, booklist 58
tribal peoples, Arunachal Pr 339
tribal peoples, Himalaya 148
tribal peoples, Meghalaya 334
tribal peoples, Sikkim 297
Trilokinath, HP 193, 213
Triund, HP 201
tsampa (ngamphe) 237, 259
Tsangpo, Riv 325
Tsokar, J&K 253
Tsokha, Sik 311
Tsomgo, Sik 304
Tso-Moriri Lake, J&K 253
Tughluq, Firoz Shah 81
Tugluqabad, Delhi 82
tulip tree 387
Tung, WB 283
Tungnath, Utt 114
Tura, Meg 338

U

Udaipur, HP 194
Udeypur, HP 194, 213, 216
Uma 366
Umiam, Lak, Meg 334
Una, HP 171
Upat, Utt 143
Upper Mulling, HP 217
Uttarkashi, Utt 112, 121

V

vaccinations 60
Vaishno Devi, J&K 233
Vajrayana 236, 375
Vale of Kashmir, J&K 224
Valley of Flowers, Utt 117
Valley of the Gods 176
varna 369
Varuna 368
Vasant Panchami 49
Vashisht (Vashistha), HP 184
Vasuki Tal, Utt 114
Vasuki, Mnt, Utt 121
Vedanta 359
Vedas 345, 378
vegetation 386
Victoria Memorial, Calcutta 267
Virabhadra 367
Vishnu 103
Vishnuprayag, Utt 116
Vivekenanda, Swami 134
voluntary work, Darjeeling 277

voluntary work, Dharamshala 200
voluntary work, Kalimpong 288
voluntary work, Kurseong 283
voluntary work, Ladakh 242
voulntary work, Sikkim 305
Vyasa 118

W

wagtail, white 394
Wakha Gorge, J&K 234
Wangtu, HP 163
water 62
water supply 32
water, drinking 47
Wavell, Lord 352
weather 45
White water rafting 51
white-water rafting, Ladakh 245
Wildflower Hall site 157
wildlife, reading list 69
Wildlife, Sikkim 296
willows 193
women travellers 30
work permits 19
World Biosphere Reserve, Utt 122
World Heritage Site, Kaziranga 323
World Heritage Site, Manas 325
worship, Hindu 360

Y

yak 238, 391
Yama 111
Yamunotri, Utt 110
Yamuna, Riv (Jumna) 111
yoga 52
Yoga 359
yoga, Rishikesh 108
yoni 366
youth hostels 34
Yuksom, Sik 307, 311
Yumthang, Sik 308

Z

Zangla, J&K 259
Zanskar, J&K 258
Zanskar, Riv, J&K 259
Zanskaris 258
Zemu, Glc, Sik 296
Zingzingbar, HP 196
Ziro, Aru 342
Zoffany, J 265
Zoji, La Pas, J&K 234

Advertisers

Colour section
Ibex Expeditions, India
Pettitts

34 Encounter Overland, UK
16 Exodus Travels, UK
22 Gateway to India, UK
16 Paradise Holidays, India
16 Royal Expeditions Pvt Ltd, India
17 Snow Lion Expeditions, USA
17 Trans Indus, UK
22 USIT Campus, UK

Shorts

180	A Russian in the Kullu Valley
369	Auspicious signs
246	Be ecology conscious
46	Best short-wave frequencies
242	Conversation to construction
283	Darjeeling Himalaya Railway - a mini miracle
172	Dasara in Kullu
391	Elephants - a future in the wild?
21	Exchange rates
228	Exercise caution
199	Fight over the flight of the living Buddha
26	First impressions
182	Freedom walking
14	Himalaya climate
55	Himalayan environment trust code of practice
364	Hindu Deities
33	Hotel categories
363	How Sarasvati turned Brahma's head
160	Human sacrifice in the Himalaya
18	India Tourist Offices Overseas
35	Indian Airlines: approximate economy fares on popular routes
361	Karma - an eye to the future
57	Leeches
362	Many in One
20	Money matters
126	Nanda Devi on apricot brandy, Conquering
39	On the road on a motorbike
192	Only for the determined
340	Permission to enter
115	Pilgrimage: purification and piety
318	Plantation labour
239	Prepare for a different lifestyle in Leh
390	Project Tiger
50	Purnima (Full Moon)
41	Rajdhani train timetable
396	Room at the park...
237	Running hot and cold
298	Sikkim permits
279	Tea
382	The big screen
375	The Buddha's Four Noble Truths
45	The email explosion
373	The five pillars of Islam
360	The four stages of life
36	The hazards of road travel
355	The Indian flag
207	The little-known 'mountain' railway
229	The most expensive spice in the world
325	The riddle of the Brahmaputra
370	The sacred thread
151	The seasonal move of government
379	The story of Rama
166	The stuff to record the epics
218	The valley of the Gods
139	Tiger, tiger, burning bright ...
245	To fly or not to fly
25	Touching down
43	Train touts
392	Two peas in a pod
244	Unlucky in Leh
366	Vishnu's ten incarnations
317	Visiting the Northeast
225	Warning
62	Water purification
368	Worship of Siva's linga

Maps

252	Alchi Choskor
140	Corbett National Park
210	Dalhousie
278	Darjeeling
285	Darjeeling treks
97	Dehra Dun
	Delhi
85	Connaught Place
78	New Delhi
80	Old Delhi
86	Paharganj
200	Dharamshala
301	Gangtok
300	Gangtok centre
120	Garhwal & Kumaon treks
319	Guwahati
103	Haridwar
104	Haridwar centre
384	Himalayan profile
385	India rainfall
40	Indian Himalayan railways
231	Jammu
328	Jorhat
287	Kalimpong
323	Kaziranga National Park
195	Keylong
165	Kinnaur & Spiti
	Kolkata
266	Kolkata
268	Kolkata, around Sudder Street
270	Kolkata, Park Street
178	Kullu
214	Kullu Valley treks
255	Ladakh & Zanskar treks
12	Ladakh - Little Tibet
243	Leh centre
241	Leh orientation
183	Manali
185	Manali centre
192	Manali to Leh
202	McLeodganj
333	Meghalaya
100	Mussoorie
99	Mussoorie centre
130	Nainital
134	Nainital-Almora area
124	Nanda Devi area treks
13	North Bengal and Sikkim
161	Rampur Bushahr
106	Rishikesh
334	Shillong
336	Shillong centre
152	Shimla
154	Shimla Mall & the Ridge
157	Shimla, around
310	Sikkim treks
290	Siliguri
228	Srinagar
11	The Foothills
13	The Northeastern Hills
11	The Old Hindustan - Tibet Road
12	The Valley of the Gods

Footnotes

Temperature conversion tables

°C	°F	°C	°F
1	34	26	79
2	36	27	81
3	38	28	82
4	39	29	84
5	41	30	86
6	43	31	88
7	45	32	90
8	46	33	92
9	48	34	93
10	50	35	95
11	52	36	97
12	54	37	99
13	56	38	100
14	57	39	102
15	59	40	104
16	61	41	106
17	63	42	108
18	64	43	109
19	66	44	111
20	68	45	113
21	70	46	115
22	72	47	117
23	74	48	118
24	75	49	120
25	77	50	122

Will you help us?

We try as hard as we can to make each Footprint Handbook as up-to-date and accurate as possible but, of course, things always change. Many people write to us - with corrections, new information, or simply comments.

If you want to let us know about an experience or adventure - hair-raising or mundane, good or bad, exciting or boring or simply something rather special - we would be delighted to hear from you. Please give us as precise information as possible, quoting the edition number (you'll find it on the front cover) and page number of the Handbook you are using.

Your help will be greatly appreciated, especially by other travellers. In return we will send you details about our special guidebook offer.

email Footprint at:
HIM1_online@footprintbooks.com

or write to:
Elizabeth Taylor
Footprint Handbooks
6 Riverside Court
Lower Bristol Road
Bath BA2 3DZ
UK

Map 1

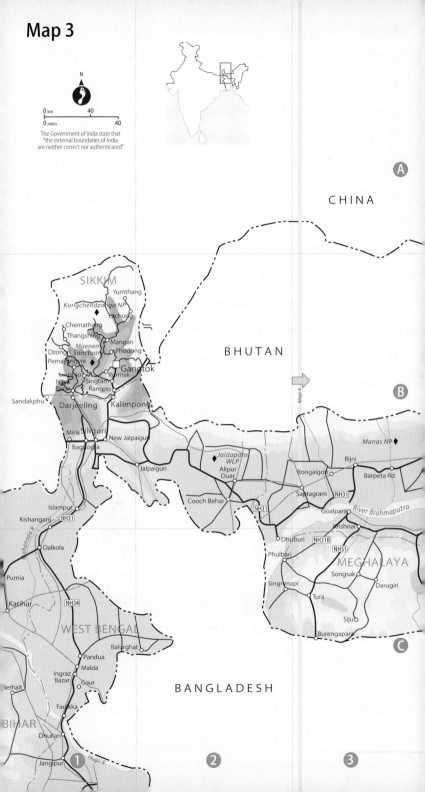

Map 4

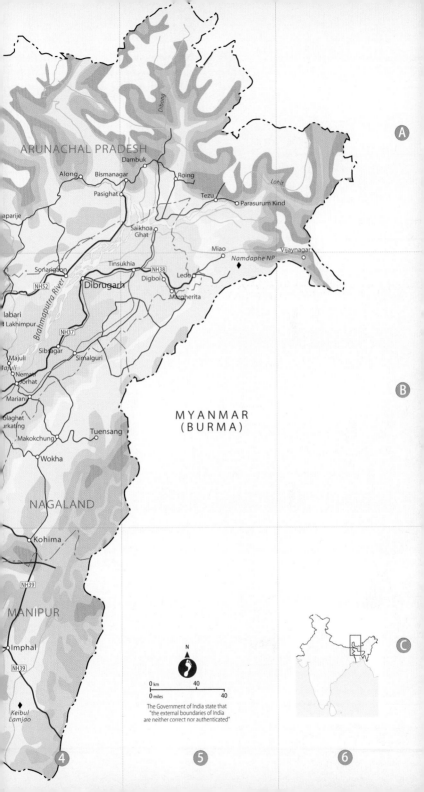

"If 'the essence of real travel' is what you have been secretly yearning for all these years, then Footprint are the guides for you."
Under 26

"Who should pack them – people who want to escape the crowd."
The Observer

"Footprint Handbooks, the best of the best."
Le Monde, Paris

"The guides for intelligent, independently-minded souls of any age or budget."
Indie Traveller

"Intelligently written, amazingly accurate and bang up-to-date. Footprint has combined nearly 80 years' experience with a stunning new format to bring us guidebooks that leave the competition standing."
John Pilkington, writer and broadcaster

Acknowledgements

We record our warmest thanks to a number of people who helped us to update this new edition. We are particularly grateful to our researchers for their painstaking efforts and their wholehearted commitment to the Handbook.

We are particularly indebted to Jaideep Mukerji, Vancouver for his expert advice on the Indian Himalaya.

We have a host of other travellers to thank for their generous help in amending, updating and correcting information and sharing their experiences or ideas for improvement in the hope that fellow travellers will benefit. Our warmest thanks to all who wrote to us during the year.

A special mention goes to Bill Aitken, Mussoorie, India. Cyrus Dadachanji, Mumbai, India. Devangshu Datta, Kolkata, India. Ian Large, Antwerp, Brussels. Steve Scott, Blackpool, UK. Simon Watson Taylor, London, UK.

Irfan Ahmed, New Delhi, India; Paul Andrews, England; Jose Augustine, Thiruvananthapuram, India; Manju Barua, Guwahati, India; Klaus Behrendt, Stuttgart, Germany; Anne-Marie Berg, Lund, Sweden; Claire Bonham-Carter, London, England; Regine Bossert; Boy en Marielle; Andy Brody; Steven Cassidy, London; Lee Choonho, Korea; Deirdre Coffey; Russell Cohen; JeanClaude Colla, Lugano, Switzerland; Catherine Comte; Luca Crocco, Mjur, Oxford, UK; Sudarshan Das, Balasore, India; Colonel PS Davis, Papplewick, England; Dr Richard Davis, Newcastle/Tyne, England; Fred H DeVinney, Oakland, Ca, USA; Wilfred Dierick, Netherlands; Remco Dubbeldam, Rotterdam, Holland; Steve Edgerton, De Haan, Belgium; Offer Eshel, Israel; Dr Puran Ganeriwala, Stafford, England; Dirk Geeroms, Belgium; Jim Giles, London, England; Claudia Glaeser, Switzerland; Dr Travers Grant, Rusper, England; Dr and Mrs Robin Harrod; John Heap, Harrogate, England; Cathy Hillman, Epsom, England; Alasdair Hind, Edinburgh, Scotland; Gordon Hoehne, Braunschweig, Germany; Jos Holzer, Nijmegen, The Netherlands; Barry Hughes, Edinburgh, Scotland; Penny and Geoffrey Hughes, Baginton, England; David Hunt, Lewes, England; Bijo Jacob, Thiruvananthapuram, India; Aditya Jalan, Patna, India; John J Jones; Maike Juta, Düsseldorf, Germany; Jessica Kaekkeboom, Enschede, The Netherlands; Seth Kasten; Dr. Ditza Kempler, Tel Aviv, Israel; Anton Keulaars, Tamil Nadu; Johann Kokoschinegg, Graz, Austria; Armin Kowarsch, Ternitz, Austria; Arun Kundu Faridabad, Haryana, India; Christian Kuendig, Maennedorf, Switzerland; Bernard Lazarevitch, France; Catherine Lewis; Rupert Lory, Sydney, Australia; Roy McKenzie, South Africa; Sarah McKibber, NY, USA; Valentina Maffei, Rome, Italy; Arabind Menon, Trivandrum, India; Katrin Mueller, Germany; Arthur Murray; Bernice Nikijuluw; Keith Oberg; Hazel Orchard, Hove, England; Valerie Parkinson; Donella Perkins; Jesper Pettersen, Oslo, Norway; Eric Pezet; GE Quinan, Harrow-on-the-Hill, England; Hannah Satz, Jerusalem, Israel; Caroline Schmutz, Switzerland; Steve Scott, Blackpool, England; Nanneke Seegers, Netherlands; Michael and Diana Seymour, Grantham, England; Darren Shepherd, Tenbury Well, England; Dr Cornelius Sigglekow; Wayne Smits; PN Sripada, Hospet, India; Dinah Swayne, London, England; Amy Taylor, Healdsburg, CA, USA; Tom K Tolk, Düsseldorf, Germany; Emerick W Toth, Bandon, Republic of Ireland; Rosanne Trottier; Tim Tucker; BL Underwood, Colchester; Ana Maria Uribe; Jan Vergauwe; Sandra Vick, Edinburgh, Scotland; Andrew Whitehead, London, England; Will Wyatt; Peter Yore, Kells, Ireland.

Robert and Roma Bradnock

Robert went to India overland in 1966, as a research student at Cambridge, to spend a year in South India and travel widely across the country. That journey was the first of many visits, living and working throughout the sub-continent. Since joining the School of Oriental and African Studies in 1968, where he is now head of the Department of Geography, he has carried out and supervised research covering the whole region. As an international authority he comments on South Asian current affairs across the world and lectures extensively in Britain and Europe.

A Bengali by birth, Roma was brought up in Kolkata (Calcutta), where, after graduating, she worked as a librarian. Her travels across the sub-continent had started early but to widen her horizons she went to Europe, and England subsequently became her home. Her work with Footprint started with the South Asian Handbook 1992 while her daughters were growing up. In addition to the India Handbook she and her husband now write the Footprint Sri Lanka and Goa Handbooks and the soon to be published handbooks on Rajasthan and Gujarat, Indian Himalaya and South India. They return to the sub-continent each year to research and seek out yet unexplored corners.